The Palgrave Handbook of Fulfillment, Wellness, and Personal Growth at Work

Joan Marques
Editor

The Palgrave Handbook of Fulfillment, Wellness, and Personal Growth at Work

Editor
Joan Marques
School of Business
Woodbury University
Burbank, CA, USA

ISBN 978-3-031-35493-9   ISBN 978-3-031-35494-6 (eBook)
https://doi.org/10.1007/978-3-031-35494-6

© The Editor(s) (if applicable) and The Author(s), under exclusive licence to Springer Nature Switzerland AG 2023

This work is subject to copyright. All rights are solely and exclusively licensed by the Publisher, whether the whole or part of the material is concerned, specifically the rights of translation, reprinting, reuse of illustrations, recitation, broadcasting, reproduction on microfilms or in any other physical way, and transmission or information storage and retrieval, electronic adaptation, computer software, or by similar or dissimilar methodology now known or hereafter developed. The use of general descriptive names, registered names, trademarks, service marks, etc. in this publication does not imply, even in the absence of a specific statement, that such names are exempt from the relevant protective laws and regulations and therefore free for general use.
The publisher, the authors, and the editors are safe to assume that the advice and information in this book are believed to be true and accurate at the date of publication. Neither the publisher nor the authors or the editors give a warranty, expressed or implied, with respect to the material contained herein or for any errors or omissions that may have been made. The publisher remains neutral with regard to jurisdictional claims in published maps and institutional affiliations.

Cover illustration: paci77/Getty images

This Palgrave Macmillan imprint is published by the registered company Springer Nature Switzerland AG
The registered company address is: Gewerbestrasse 11, 6330 Cham, Switzerland

Preface

With the world of work going through changes at a magnitude very few of us had envisioned, it is not surprising that aspects of fulfillment, wellness, and growth are gaining even more prominence on our radar than ever before. The awareness that has emerged through the COVID-19 pandemic has transformed many viewpoints on what work should look and feel like. A team of 52 globally dispersed scholars took on the challenging task to conduct research, engage in reflections, and write down their findings and perspectives on the critical context of fulfillment, wellness, and growth.

The work of these scholars is captured in this handbook and divided in three sections.

Part I highlights the context of fulfillment.

In Chapter 1, Douglas J. Cremer shines a historical light on the way our perspective on work has shifted. He underscores that, over time, we have begun to experience work less as a process resulting in a series of accomplishments and more as a cycle of repetitive, partial, and unending tasks, whether on the assembly line or in the office cubicle. Cremer stresses that understanding how and why we got to this place in our experience of work is essential to grasping what can be done to reveal a sense of fulfillment in our personal and working lives.

In Chapter 2, Debra J. Dean focuses on soft skills as a conscious choice to greater collaboration at work. She observes that leaders and followers alike are noticing a lack of softs skills in the workplace causing problems with human interaction. She comments that, while this phenomenon has been a growing problem for decades, it is more obvious post-COVID-19 than it was before the announcement of the pandemic. She subsequently explores issues leading up to this phenomenon and practical approaches for improving soft skills consciously for better collaboration at work.

In Chapter 3, Preethi Misha and Marius van Dijke take a deep dive into the aspect of meaning at work. They assert that, with more individuals pursuing meaning at work, more organizations have begun to recognize the importance of fostering work that can be personally significant and meaningful to organizations members. Filling a perceived gap in the investigation around the implications of the absence or the drive to find meaning at work, Misha and Van Dijke provide an overview of the meaning at work literature and shed light on the implications of three dimensions of meaning at work: the presence, absence, and quest for meaning at work.

In Chapter 4, Orneita Burton and Seonhee Jeong focus on spiritual guidance in the personal efficacy of work. Describing work as a divine gift that sustains life, defines purpose, and creates a wholesome balance of our time and space, resources and energies, they define work as the center of creating economic value for a shared community while adding personal meaning to our existence. They share the opinion that, to find ourselves in our work, the efficacy of servant leadership and spiritual guidance is needed as contributing factor to fulfill both personal and community needs, as derived from a service-oriented lifestyle. As such, these authors attempt to create a positive association between work, vocation or career choice, purpose, and calling, adding spiritual guidance to personal efficacy and ownership of work.

In Chapter 5, Letizia Milanesi, Silvia Biraghi, and Rossella C. Gambetti analyze fulfillment from a consumer's angle, examining thrifting practices as an act of eudaimonia. They bring into perspective the advent of apps and technologies, which are making it continuously easier to, for instance, resell and buy old clothes or items, thus bringing thrifting practices more intensely and openly into the ethical and sustainable circuit of consumption. These authors subsequently explore and elaborate how thrifting can represent a realm where consumers pursue the attainment of an eudaimonic state and a flourishing virtuous life.

In Chapter 6, Sheldene Simola examines the role of dignity in workplace well-being from a relational cultural stance. She explores the nature and meaning of dignity within the relational cultural theory (RCT) with the aim to identify RCT-related skills in support of employee dignity and well-being. Building upon RCT, dignity is conceptualized as "mutuality of mattering." Simola discusses two interrelated and overarching RCT-related skills in support of employee dignity and well-being.

In Chapter 7, Albena Pergelova, Jeremy Zwiegelaar, and Shelley Beck consider the promise and limits of self-employment as a path to fulfillment and well-being at work. They alert us that, while there is a general positive association between self-employment and well-being, for specific groups of self-employed/entrepreneurs (e.g., women entrepreneurs, immigrant entrepreneurs, etc.) the relationship between being independent and achieving fulfillment, personal growth and wellness through their work can be complex and multifaceted. As a result, these authors view both the promise and the limits of self-employment as a path to well-being for the self-employed with a particular focus on women entrepreneurs and immigrant entrepreneurs.

In Chapter 8, shepherding engineering leadership, Ankit Agarwal advocates a combined approach to leading and creating employee engagement. After first describing the different realms of a shepherd and an engineer, Agarwal proposes combining these two practitioner approaches to minimize employee disengagement and maximize employee satisfaction. Shepherds don't want their flock to reduce in number because of a wolf (or wolves) among their sheep. In the same way, engineers want to stay current with the systems they design. Together, both mindsets could ensure employees understand why leaders do what they do and, from a leader's perspective, emphasize the practices necessary to help employees succeed. By introducing the "Shepherding Engineering Leadership (SEL)", Agarwal proposes a leading mindset; the nurturing attribute of leading employees (shepherding); and actionizing developing systems that promote employee development and their idea implementation (engineering).

Part II highlights the context of Wellness.

In Chapter 9, Duysal Askun invites us to gravitate from Organizational Oneness to Organizational Wellness. Explaining how humans are systems inside the organizational systems, she invites us to think about them as whole systems, and consider them as active agents playing critical roles inside the organizations. This will enable us to think of the role of consciousness at all levels: individual, work-unit/team-level, and organizational. For organizations to provide a healthy space for employee health and well-being, culture seems to be prominent. The relationship between personal-organizational wellness thus depends on many factors at different levels in terms of both structure and process.

In Chapter 10, Jeannel E. King explores the possibilities of creative-spiritual agency (CSA) as a pathway for individuals to find meaning in their work, particularly in the context of the COVID-19 pandemic. King introduces CSA as a new cross-disciplinary construct for organizational change research and discusses its potential to help individuals find meaning in their work. The author thereby explores the theoretical and definitional underpinnings of CSA, provides examples of CSA in action, and makes suggestions for cultivating and applying CSA at work.

In Chapter 11, Aikaterini Grimani and George Gotsis elaborate on inclusive leadership as a construct invested with a strong potential to promote humane and collaborative organizations. The study they present aims to provide a framework of assessing the role of leader inclusiveness in informing collaborative healthcare work environments in times in which the intrinsic worthiness of the human person is highly at stake. They thereby emphasize practices that mitigate social disadvantage, alleviate human suffering, and make patients feel that they are appreciated and valued in a state of vulnerability.

In Chapter 12, Jody A. Worley focuses on empathy as a wellness driver in the workplace, describing it is an ability-based, interactional relationship building process, in addition to being an affective-based emotional concept. Worley reviews current literature to explore how empathy may function as a multiplier for wellness, and underscores that empathy facilitates social interaction in many ways that are linked to positive health outcomes.

In Chapter 13, Edyta Janus and Agnieszka Smrokowska-Reichmann dive deeper in another aspect that is at the forefront of our professional performance these days: remote work. They describe some of the paradoxes tied to remote work, such as the fact that it is easy to arrive at the workplace, but more difficult to leave, and the fact that during remote work, interpersonal contacts are established faster and easier, but can also be more limited and superficial than in a traditional workplace. Their evaluation aims to prepare us that, in post-industrial societies, increasingly immersed in virtual reality, the importance and scope of remote work will grow.

In Chapter 14, Simona Leonelli and Emanuele Primavera emphasize the importance of individual resilience related to work tasks complexity and unpredictability. Focusing on the healthcare environment, they investigate how nurses' individual resilience affects their perceived stress levels, analyzing how the characteristics of the work tasks can improve or worsen the above relationship. The authors' study among Italian nurses shows that increasing levels of individual resilience reduce stress perceptions, but this beneficial effect decreases when work tasks become more complex and unpredictable.

In Chapter 15, Gerben Wortelboer and Martijn Pieter Van der Steen zoom in on the well-being of precarious workers. They explain that the identity construction of workers has come under pressure because work has become increasingly precarious, due to less secure, short-term, and more flexible employment arrangements. As a consequence, worker identity itself has become more unstable, as organizations provide fewer cultural resources for workers' identity development. Building on an inductive qualitative study of approximately 34,000 items of the Internet forum Reddit, these authors examine precarious workers' processes of identity construction through online discourses of quiet quitting. This examination emphasizes workers' resilience in coping with their precariousness through online identity workspaces and demonstrates that workers can develop these online identity workspaces in spontaneous and self-organized ways to construct meaningful identities and, in the process, detach from the workplace as an important site for identity construction.

In Chapter 16, Nidhi Kaushal discusses significant measures of Ancient Indian Ethos toward wellness and growth in the workplace. Kaushal's study provides an introduction to the wisdom, expertise, standards, belief-system, and functioning of ancient India because its diversity includes the inclusion and influence of many cultures, and their significance gets reflected through the activities of its entrepreneurs and organizational people. It analyzes the indigenous ethos, techniques of managing change and adversity, psychology of innovation and implementation, and workplace dynamics to provide a new prospect of learning to the modern managers and leaders of the present era. It also highlights the significance of several approaches required for the fulfillment, wellness, and growth of the employees at work.

In Chapter 17, Nazha Gali and Susanna L. M. Chui cover the concepts of well-being and how it relates to research on entrepreneurship and entrepreneurial pursuit. The concept of psychological well-being plays a vital role in scholarly work and policy debates. An entrepreneurial pursuit can be a source of satisfaction and personal fulfillment and can push the entrepreneur in achieving their goals and persisting with their entrepreneurial endeavors under conditions of uncertainty. The authors emphasize the importance of investigating well-being as a crucial outcome in entrepreneurship research. They draw upon the important role of well-being as being a driver for entrepreneurial pursuits (whether the antecedent to entrepreneurial pursuit is the lack of well-being or on the contrary positive affect).

In Chapter 18, Jesus Juyumaya contributes to delivering insights to motivate Latin American employees in the twenty-first century. Juyumaya suggests that Latin American employees have particular reasons to seek transformational leadership behaviors, which help them feel more engaged at work and help increase their task performance. Examining the moderating role of Latin American cultural practices in the relationship between digital work characteristics and work design, this author proposes potential solutions based on cultural practices. These solutions can moderate the challenging relationship between twenty-first-century digital job characteristics and their positive/adverse effects on work design in Latin America.

In Chapter 19, Ariana Chang and Ying-Tzu Lin discuss the interesting topic of finding dignity in "dirty work" in order for its constituents to construct a positive identity. Chang and Ying-Tzu's study examines the dynamics of workplace dignity in the dirty work context of sex work in Taiwan. Sex workers endure multiple stigmas and discrimination compared to those in other dirty work occupations. Stigmatization has been linked to negative consequences, including poorer work satisfaction, higher stress and burnout, and poor mental and physical health. They explore how dignity is constructed by dirty workers. Their findings suggest that there is a quintessential need for tailored assistance to address the interconnected dimensions of stigma encountered by dirty workers.

In Chapter 20, Roman Terekhin and Maria Feddeck provide a theoretical framework of how the employee-centered culture of the future should look. They argue that it will be based on four pillars: Compassion, Community, Cooperation, and Continuous Development (4Cs). Terekhin and Feddeck also underscore the potential of peer coaching groups as an accessible, low-cost, practical attribute for future-facing organizations and explain how key elements of peer coaching groups can foster the 4Cs culture of the future.

In Chapter 21, Wanda Krause makes an appeal for leading individual and collective well-being for planetary health. This author argues that leaders neglecting individual and collective well-being and work-life balance, including their own health and well-being, will result in greater disengagement, dissatisfaction, and wellness. Krause discusses how critical it is to take a broader stance to recognize the individual and collective well-being to support planetary health, and provides recommendations for how to work with the trends and specifically describes the essential qualities and practices executive and senior leaders need to be able to support resilient, adaptable, engaged, and healthy individuals and collectives for planetary health.

In Chapter 22, Amy Tong Zhao enlightens us about employee boundary management practices and challenges. She stresses that online social networks (OSNs), such as Facebook, Twitter, and WeChat, are widespread in both personal and business settings, which has profoundly shifted employees' professional/personal boundary management practices. Tong Zhao first introduces the conceptualizations of boundary management and blurring boundary, discussing current topics and issues with great concerns by practitioners and researchers such as roles transition between work and personal lives, and the self-presentation motivation. The author then reviews the key antecedents and outcomes of boundary management, discusses the difficulties in dealing with blurring boundaries, and provides an overview of the boundary management measurement, significance, and future research directions.

In Chapter 23, Peter Mutuku Lewa and Susan K. Lewa discuss strategic changes toward engagement, wellness, and growth. They thereby present key ideas of the theory of strategic change, wellness, and growth, and how strategic change can be implemented toward engagement, inclusion, wellness, and growth. The authors wrote this chapter with reference to experts' opinion, published works, articles, reports, extant literature, and empirical literature review.

Part III highlights the context of Personal Growth.

In Chapter 24, Joan Marques presents conscious practices toward personal and collective growth. Acknowledging the deep effects of the COVID-19 pandemic on the way we work today the author lists several ways in which matters have changed, including remote work, the speed of change, the lack of stability, the mega exposure to information due to the Internet, and the increased diversity, which may represent challenges if not managed well. The author then discusses three conscious practices available toward personal and collective growth, including Vipassana (insight) meditation, attraction of a mentor to serve as a source of reflection, and the internal application of a mind shift to expand perspectives on experiences.

In Chapter 25, Isabel Ong and Chia-Yu Kou set out to understand the way in which individuals build and maintain their resilience when facing a volatile work environment. These authors found that the inhibitor for individuals to reframe their situation is related to being unable to rest. Increased working hours and a lack of work-life boundaries inhibit individuals' pathways to resilience. The study findings highlight that both direct managers and senior managers play an important role in shaping individuals' meaning-making processes, and their narratives could encourage subordinates to demonstrate optimism around the challenge. Ong and Kou-Barrett also suggest organizations to consider interventions such as instituting long and short breaks, and mindfulness training to mitigate the negative impact from lack of rest.

In Chapter 26, Ginger Grant suggests us to revision the way we work. Grant considers it crucial that organizations "revision" the way they lead, work, adapt to change, and collaborate creatively in ways that leverage and grow available talent, moving from innovation control to a more dynamic, design-driven innovation delivery. In this new world of work, characterized by new ways of organizing and working, new leadership styles, new benchmarks, and caring work cultures are also required. Grant stresses that a leadership growth mindset is essential to balance the elements of strategy, process, and culture essential for long-term success in a complex environment.

In Chapter 27, Charlie Wall-Andrews and Reima Shekeir explain that the recent pandemic provided an opportunity for many individuals to reflect and consider pursuing happiness by changing careers or following their dreams through new venture creation. The authors state that people may start a business out of opportunity or necessity, but more research is needed to explore how people can find happiness in pursuing entrepreneurial activities. Wall-Andrews and Shekeir then conceptualize how entrepreneurs can achieve personal growth and happiness by working with passion, and conclude by outlining the opportunities and challenges faced by entrepreneurs.

In Chapter 28, Mateo Cruz, Yaromil Fong-Olivares, Wiley C. Davi, and María Jose Taveras Soriano address the role of social justice in diversity, equity, and inclusion (DEI) work with executive learners. They underscore that few Executive Education programs in the US train leaders from a social justice perspective. As a result, leaders remain ill-equipped to address social justice within or outside their organizations. The authors therefore discuss the case for adding social justice to DEI training for executives. They thereby showcase one DEI training program that centers social justice in its design and content.

In Chapter 29, Cara W. Jacocks and R.G. Bell remind us that members of the disabled workforce are extremely large in number, with approximately 1 in 4 US citizens having at least one identifiable disability. Unfortunately, disabled workers are not represented in similar proportions in the US labor force specifically. Jacocks and Bell describe the disabled workforce in the US, barriers that prevent disabled workers from attaining meaningful, gainful employment in the US, and the benefits of hiring members of the disabled workforce (for both disabled and nondisabled employees). They also identify opportunities to overcome systemic barriers that prevent disabled workers from entering the US workforce and data that demonstrates which US states provide the most overall assistance for workers with disabilities, including promoting independence and productivity.

In Chapter 30, Nidhi Kaushal invites us to consider servant leadership as an inextricable technique and persuasive criterion for emerging leaders. She presents the eminence of women, who are naturally and intrinsically empowered as servant leaders due to their feminist attributes of compassion and sense of sacrifice, and identifies the significance of folk wisdom to comprehend this leadership style. Kaushal further explicates the significance of conscientiousness, humility, and dignity of the leader through selfless service and exhibits servant leadership as an exemplary persuasive criterion for employees to develop a human perspective toward others.

In Chapter 31, Kurt April explores the intricate relationship between leader growth and development, and authenticity, offering insights into some key enablers and stumbling blocks of authenticity. In discussing the enablers and stumbling blocks, various developmental approaches that facilitate the cultivation of authentic leadership are identified, including transformative learning and unlearning, reflective and contemplative practices, the role of feedback, as well as the need for therapy and coaching. Ultimately, April finds, authenticity is about the enactment of important beliefs, values, principles, and identities of leaders, since they affect relationships with subordinates, colleagues, and the broader stakeholder community.

In Chapter 32, Anil K. Maheshwari, Deeppa Ravindran, Mohan Gurubatham, and Nupur Maheshwari examine the similarities and differences between flow and higher states of consciousness. Using an empirical study, these authors report that there may be a reduction of barriers to flow through higher states of consciousness. They thereby discuss the possibility of experiencing flow more often in a VUCA world through being established in higher states of consciousness.

In Chapter 33, Victor Senaji Anyanje and Thomas Anyanje Senaji review the need for organizations to deploy strategies and implement actions that are consistent with their mission and vision. They explore the notion of conscious business performance: what it is, how it can be engendered, and the pitfalls to guard against.

On behalf of all the authors who contributed their time, expertise, and research efforts to this timely handbook, we wish each reader an insightful experience and all the best in finding fulfillment, wellness, and growth on their professional path.

May All Beings Be Happy.

Burbank, USA   Joan Marques

Gratitude

Expressing gratitude can be a tricky thing
Because it has so many dimensions
And the message may differ from one to another
Depending on underlying intentions

We've come this far and hope to proceed
Toward a promising future—as a team
The perspectives are not always rosy: agreed
Sometimes resembling a nightmare rather than a dream

But wherever the path takes us from here
And even if we don't always see eye to eye
I hope—no, I trust—that we wish each other well
And be the wind under each other's wings as we fly

I'm not one for fine words most of the time
In fact, I don't even like to talk
But I wanted to express my appreciation today
To each of you, through this educational walk

We've weathered tough times
And they're definitely not over or through
But we're here now—and we're still going strong
So, I want to simply end with a heartfelt: Thank You!

—Joan Marques

Contents

Part I Fulfillment

1 How We View Work: A Historical Perspective 3
   Douglas J. Cremer

2 Soft Skills as a Conscious Choice to Greater Collaboration at Work 19
   Debra J. Dean

3 Meaning at Work: Dimensions, Implications and Recommendations 33
   Preethi Misha and Marius van Dijke

4 Spiritual Guidance in the Personal Efficacy of Work 59
   Orneita Burton and Seonhee Jeong

5 An Analysis of Consumers' Thrifting Practices as an Act of Eudaimonia 79
   Letizia Milanesi, Silvia Biraghi, and Rossella C. Gambetti

6 The Role of Dignity in Workplace Well-Being: A Relational Cultural Perspective 97
   Sheldene Simola

7 The Promise and Limits of Self-Employment as a Path to Fulfillment and Well-Being at Work 113
   Albena Pergelova, Jeremy Zwiegelaar, and Shelley Beck

8 Shepherding Engineering Leadership: A Combined Approach to Leading and Creating Employee Engagement 141
   Ankit Agarwal

Part II Wellness

9 From Organizational Oneness to Organizational Wellness: The Role of Individuals, Teams, and Organizations from a Whole Systems Framework 161
Duysal Askun

10 Inside Job: Exploring Meaningful Work Through Creative-Spiritual Agency 183
Jeannel E. King

11 Embracing Inclusive Leadership for Collaborative Healthcare Work Environments: Fostering Wellness in Ambivalent Situations 209
Aikaterini Grimani and George Gotsis

12 Empathy as a Wellness Driver in the Workplace 231
Jody A. Worley

13 Making a Workplace a Happy One: Benefits and Risks of Remote Work in a Socio-Philosophical Perspective 251
Edyta Janus and Agnieszka Smrokowska-Reichmann

14 Coping with Stress: The Importance of Individual Resilience and Work Tasks Complexity and Unpredictability 267
Simona Leonelli and Emanuele Primavera

15 Precarious Workers' Wellbeing: Identity Development Through Online Discourses of Quiet Quitting 281
Gerben Wortelboer and Martijn Pieter Van der Steen

16 Significant Measures of Ancient Indian Ethos Towards Wellness and Growth in the Workplace 303
Nidhi Kaushal

17 Entrepreneurship: An Auspicious Context for Examining Its Connection to Wellbeing 323
Nazha Gali and Susanna L. M. Chui

18 Motivating Latin American Employees in the Twenty-first Century 339
Jesus Juyumaya

19 Embracing Stigma? Finding Workplace Dignity in Dirty Work 355
Ariana Chang and Ying-Tzu Lin

20	Why Workplace Peer Coaching Groups Are Vital for the Corporate Culture of the Future Roman Terekhin and Maria Feddeck	371
21	Leading Individual and Collective Well-being for Planetary Health Wanda Krause	387
22	Employee Boundary Management Practices and Challenges Amy Tong Zhao	401
23	Strategic Changes Toward Engagement, Wellness, and Growth Peter Mutuku Lewa and Susan K. Lewa	425

Part III Personal Growth

24	Conscious Practices Toward Personal and Collective Growth Joan Marques	447
25	Individual Resilience in a Volatile Work Environment Isabel Ong and Chia-Yu Kou	461
26	ReVisioning the Way We Work: Organizational Creative Capacity and Expanded Cultures of Care Ginger Grant	483
27	Conceptualizing Passion as an Entrepreneurial Pathway Charlie Wall-Andrews and Reima Shakeir	497
28	Adding the "J" for Justice: How Executive Education Can Center Social Justice in Diversity, Equity, Inclusion (DEI) Training for Corporate Leaders Mateo Cruz, Yaromil Fong-Olivares, Wiley C. Davi, and María Jose Taveras	523
29	Workforce Members with Disabilities: An Underutilized Talent Pool for Mutual Growth Cara W. Jacocks and R.G. Bell	543
30	Servant Leadership: An Inextricable Technique and Persuasive Criterion for Emerging Leaders Nidhi Kaushal	565
31	Leader Growth and Development: Authenticity Enablers and Stumbling Blocks Kurt April	589

32	**Reducing the Barriers to Flow Experience Through Development of Consciousness** Anil K. Maheshwari, Deeppa Ravindran, Mohan Gurubatham, and Nupur Maheshwari	607
33	**Conscious Business Performance in a Global Village** Victor Senaji Anyanje and Thomas Anyanje Senaji	625

Index   637

Editor and Contributors

About the Editor

Joan Marques has reinvented herself from a successful media and social entrepreneur in Suriname, South America, to an innovative "edupreneur" (educational entrepreneur) in California, US. Her entrepreneurial career spans over four decades and includes the creation and successful management of companies in Public Relations and Advertising, Import and Export, Real Estate, Media Productions, and a Non-Profit, focused on women's advancement. In the US, she has been a co-founder of the *Business Renaissance Institute* and the *Academy of Spirituality and Professional Excellence* (ASPEX).

Based on her impressive career and ongoing influence, she was awarded the highest state decoration of her home country, Suriname: *Commander (Commandeur) in the Honorary Order of the Yellow Star*, in 2015. That same year, she was also awarded the *Dr. Nelle Becker-Slaton Pathfinder Award* from the Association of Pan-African Doctoral Scholars in Los Angeles, for her exemplary and groundbreaking professional performance. In 2019, she was awarded the *Kankantrie Life Time Achievement Award* for her accomplishments in Education from the Suriname American Network Inc. in Miami, FL. In 2016, she was granted the *Faculty Scholarly-Creative Award* as well as the *Faculty*

Ambassador Award, both awarded by Woodbury University's Faculty Association.

She holds a Ph.D. in Social Sciences (focus: *Buddhist Psychology in Management*) from Tilburg University's Oldendorff Graduate School and an Ed.D. in Organizational Leadership (focus: *Workplace Spirituality*) from Pepperdine University's Graduate School of Education and Psychology. She also holds an M.B.A. from Woodbury University and a B.Sc. in Business Economics from MOC, Suriname. Additionally, she has completed post-doctoral work at Tulane University's Freeman School of Business.

She is a frequent speaker and presenter at academic and professional venues. In 2016, she gave a TEDx-Talk at College of the Canyons in California, titled "*An Ancient Path Towards a Better Future*", in which she analyzed the Noble Eightfold Path, one of the foundational Buddhist practices, within the realm of contemporary business performance. In recent years, she has conducted presentations and workshops on multiple forums, such as at the Management, Spirituality and Religion research colloquia at the Academy of Management Annual Meetings in 2018 and 2019 on *Phenomenology as a Qualitative Research Method*; a keynote address titled "*Ethical Leadership: How Morals Influence Your Communication*" at the Center for Communication and Public Relations, in Paramaribo, Suriname, and an interactive workshop with thought leaders and development coaches at the Knowledge and Expertise Center Suriname, titled "*On Leadership, Ethics and Social Responsibility*". Since 2019, she also represented her home country Suriname on the annual CALIFEST literary festival in Los Angeles, where she conducted workshops on successful writing and publishing. In 2016, she presented at the Kravis Leadership Institute at Claremont McKenna College, on female leadership during the annual *Women and Leadership Alliance* (WLA) conference, resulting in the collective work, "Women's Leadership Journeys: Stories, Research and Novel Perspectives" (Routledge, 2019) in which she contributed the chapter, "*Courage: Mapping* the *Leadership Journey*". She further conducts regular presentations at the Academy of Management and at business venues in Los Angeles as well as for professional audiences in Miami and Suriname.

Her research interests pertain to Awakened Leadership, Buddhist Psychology in Management, and Workplace Spirituality. Her works have been widely published and cited in both academic and popular venues. She has written more than 150 scholarly articles, which were published in prestigious scholarly journals such as *The Journal of Business Ethics, Business and Society, International Journal of Organizational Analysis, Leadership & Organization Development Journal, The International Journal of Management Education, Journal of Communication Management, Journal of Management Development, Organization Development Journal,* and *Human Resource Development Quarterly*. She has (co)authored and (co)edited more than 35 books, among which, *Innovative Leadership in Times of Compelling Changes* (Springer, 2022); *Leading with Diversity, Equity and Inclusion* (Springer, 2022, with Satinder Dhiman); *Exploring Gender at Work: Multiple Perspectives* (Palgrave, 2021); *Leading with Awareness* (Routledge, 2021); *New Horizons in Positive Leadership and Change* (Springer, 2020), and *Social Entrepreneurship and Corporate Social Responsibility* (Springer, 2020). *The Routledge Companion to Inclusive Leadership* (2020), *Lead with Heart in Mind* (Springer, 2019), *The Routledge Companion to Management and Workplace Spirituality, Engaged Leadership: Transforming through Future-Oriented Design* (with Satinder Dhiman—Springer, 2018); *Ethical Leadership, Progress with a Moral Compass* (Routledge, 2017); *Leadership, Finding Balance Between Acceptance and Ambition* (Routledge, 2016); *Leadership Today: Practices for Personal and Professional Performance* (with Satinder Dhiman—Springer, 2016); *Business and Buddhism* (Routledge, 2015); and *Leadership and Mindful Behavior: Action, Wakefulness, and Business* (Palgrave Macmillan, 2014).

She currently serves as Dean at Woodbury University's School of Business, in Burbank, California. She is also a Full Professor of Management and teaches business courses related to leadership, ethics, creativity, social entrepreneurship, and organizational behavior in graduate and undergraduate programs.

She is a member of the executive committee of the *Management, Spirituality and Religion* interest group of the Academy of Management, the world's largest organization for management scholars, where she serves on the leadership track.

Contributors

Ankit Agarwal Lecturer in Management and Program Director Bachelor of Business (Management), Adelaide Business School, University of Adelaide, Adelaide, SA, Australia

Victor Senaji Anyanje The East African University, Nairobi, Kenya

Kurt April University of Cape Town, Cape Town, South Africa

Duysal Askun Jones School of Business, Rice University, Houston, TX, USA

Shelley Beck Oxford Brookes Business School, Oxford Brookes University, Oxford, UK

R.G. Bell Satish and Yasmin Gupta College of Business, The University of Dallas, Irving, TX, USA

Silvia Biraghi LABCOM, Università Cattolica del Sacro Cuore, Milan, Italy

Orneita Burton Department of Management Sciences and Information Systems, College of Business Administration, Abilene Christian University, Abilene, TX, USA

Ariana Chang Bachelor's Program in Interdisciplinary Studies, Fu Jen Catholic University, New Taipei, Taiwan

Susanna L. M. Chui Department of Management Hang Shin Link, School of Business, The Hang Seng University of Hong Kong (HSU), Siu Lek Yuen, Hong Kong

Douglas J. Cremer History and Interdisciplinary Studies, College of Liberal Arts and Sciences, Woodbury University, Burbank, CA, USA

Mateo Cruz Bentley University, Waltham, MA, USA

Wiley C. Davi Bentley University, Waltham, MA, USA

Debra J. Dean Department of Business and Leadership, Regent University, Virginia Beach, VA, USA

Marius van Dijke Rotterdam School of Management, Erasmus University, Rotterdam, The Netherlands

Maria Feddeck Weatherhead School of Business, Case Western Reserve University, Cleveland, Ohio, US

Yaromil Fong-Olivares Bentley University, Waltham, MA, USA

Nazha Gali Strategy and Entrepreneurship Department, Odette School of Business, University of Windsor, Windsor, ON, Canada

Rossella C. Gambetti LABCOM, Università Cattolica del Sacro Cuore, Milan, Italy

George Gotsis Department of History and Philosophy of Science, National and Kapodistrian University of Athens, Athens, Greece

Ginger Grant Humber College, Toronto, ON, Canada

Aikaterini Grimani Warwick Business School, University of Warwick, Coventry, UK

Mohan Gurubatham Department of Psychology, HELP University, Kuala Lumpur, Malaysia

Cara W. Jacocks Satish and Yasmin Gupta College of Business, The University of Dallas, Irving, TX, USA

Edyta Janus Department of Occupational Therapy, Institute od Applied Sciences, University of Physical Education in Krakow, Kraków, Poland

Seonhee Jeong Department of Business, Wittenberg University, Springfield, OH, USA

Jesus Juyumaya Escuela de Ingeniería Comercial, Facultad de Economía y Negocios, Universidad Santo Tomás, Santiago, Chile

Nidhi Kaushal Leadership Practitioner/Researcher, Yamunanagar, India

Jeannel E. King Saybrook University, Pasadena, CA, USA

Chia-Yu Kou Cranfield School of Management, Cranfield University, Cranfield, UK

Wanda Krause Royal Roads University, MA Global Leadership Program, School of Leadership Studies, Victoria, BC, Canada

Simona Leonelli Department of Economics and Management "M. Fanno", University of Padova, Padova, Italy

Peter Mutuku Lewa University of Kwazulu Natal, Durban, South Africa

Susan K. Lewa Jomo Kenyatta University of Agriculture and Technology, Nairobi, Kenya

Ying-Tzu Lin Department of Business Administration, Fu Jen Catholic University, New Taipei, Taiwan

Anil K. Maheshwari Maharishi International University, Fairfield, IA, USA

Nupur Maheshwari Fairfield, IA, USA

Joan Marques School of Business, Woodbury University, Burbank, CA, USA

Letizia Milanesi LABCOM, Università Cattolica del Sacro Cuore, Milan, Italy

Preethi Misha Nottingham Business School, Nottingham Trent University, Nottingham, UK

Isabel Ong Willis Towers Watson, London, UK

Albena Pergelova Department of International Business, Marketing, Strategy and Law, School of Business, MacEwan University, Edmonton, AB, Canada

Emanuele Primavera "Spirito Santo" Hospital, Pescara, Italy

Deeppa Ravindran Kuala Lumpur, Malaysia

Thomas Anyanje Senaji The East African University, Nairobi, Kenya

Reima Shakeir Leonard N. Stern School of Business, New York University, New York, NY, USA

Sheldene Simola School of Business, Trent University, Peterborough, ON, Canada

Agnieszka Smrokowska-Reichmann Department of Occupational Therapy, Institute od Applied Sciences, University of Physical Education in Krakow, Kraków, Poland

María Jose Taveras Bentley University, Waltham, MA, USA

Roman Terekhin Weatherhead School of Business, Case Western Reserve University, Cleveland, Ohio, US

Martijn Pieter Van der Steen Faculty of Economics and Business, University of Groningen, Groningen, Netherlands

Charlie Wall-Andrews The Creative School, Toronto Metropolitan University, Toronto, ON, Canada

Jody A. Worley University of Oklahoma, Norman, OK, USA

Gerben Wortelboer Faculty of Economics and Business, University of Groningen, Groningen, Netherlands

Amy Tong Zhao Department of Organization & Strategic Management, Guanghua School of Management, Peking University, Beijing, China

Jeremy Zwiegelaar Oxford Brookes Business School, Oxford Brookes University, Oxford, UK

List of Figures

Fig. 9.1	Consciousness gap in an interpersonal arena (Adopted from Askun, 2020)	168
Fig. 10.1	Adaptation of Rosso et al.'s (2010) Four Pathways to Meaningful Work	187
Fig. 10.2	Adaptation of Lips-Wiersma and Morris' (2009, 2018) Holistic Development Framework, or Map of Meaningful Work	189
Fig. 10.3	A creative synthesis of Rosso et al.'s (2010) Four Pathways Model and Lips-Wiersma and Morris' (2009, 2018) Map of Meaningful Work. Contributions from Rosso et al.'s (2010) model are represented in black, while contributions from Lips-Wiersma and Morris' (2009) model are represented in red tones	190
Fig. 10.4	An emerging framework for creative-spiritual agency and meaningful work. In this figure, the yin-yang symbol represents the interconnected nature of creativity and spirituality	199
Fig. 15.1	Data structure	288
Fig. 18.1	A work design model in a context of digital work characteristics and cultural practices in Latin America	350
Fig. 19.1	Collective reframing in sex work	366
Fig. 20.1	Effect of PCGs on corporate culture	381
Fig. 24.1	Conscious practices toward personal and collective growth	457
Fig. 26.1	Complexity vs understanding	488
Fig. 26.2	VUCA vs BANI (Adapted from infographic by Stephan Grabmeier)	489
Fig. 27.1	Current framework used by Global Entrepreneurship Monitor	509
Fig. 27.2	Proposed conceptual framework that includes passion as a motivator	509

Fig. 28.1	The Schwarz model of mutual learning (*Source* Schwarz, R. M. (2016). *The Skilled Facilitator: A Comprehensive Resource for Consultants, Facilitators, Coaches, and Trainers*. John Wiley & Sons, Incorporated)	530
Fig. 28.2	The "Race and…" intersectionality approach to social justice	534
Fig. 32.1	V-theory: A 2-step model of transcendence	612
Fig. 32.2	Comparing the flow model and consciousness/TM models	614

LIST OF TABLES

Table 2.1	Touloumakos list of soft skills	21
Table 5.1	The data set	88
Table 6.1	Types of resistance reflected within four responses to indignity involving humiliation	105
Table 7.1	Advancing research on self-employment and well-being: a summary of future research opportunities	129
Table 12.1	Comparison of topics on empathy in the workplace	241
Table 12.2	Empathy self-report questionnaires	244
Table 14.1	Full sample characteristics	273
Table 14.2	Descriptive statistics and correlations for study variables	273
Table 14.3	Regression Analysis results differentiating by COVID-19 and non-COVID-19 wards	274
Table 15.1	Summary of data scraped from Reddit	286
Table 18.1	GLOBE 2020 definitions of cultural practices dimensions	347
Table 18.2	Possible effects of digital work characteristics and cultural practices in Latin America on work design and potential solutions	349
Table 25.1	Developing proactive resilience	464
Table 25.2	Data structure	467
Table 26.1	Shifting from a fixed mindset to a growth mindset	487
Table 26.2	Old vs new way of work in uncertainty	492
Table 26.3	Aligning employee and leadership perspectives on culture	493
Table 32.1	States of consciousness	611
Table 32.2	Similarities between flow and higher states of consciousness	615
Table 32.3	Differences between flow and higher states of consciousness	616
Table 32.4	Fundamentals of progress related to flow experience and higher states of consciousness	617
Table 32.5	Flow dimensions coded for all interviews (8 TMers and 8 non-TMers)	618

PART I

Fulfillment

CHAPTER 1

How We View Work: A Historical Perspective

Douglas J. Cremer

INTRODUCTION

Simply put, from the beginning of human existence, the expenditure of effort has been required to obtain the energy necessary to sustain life. For thousands of years, human beings lived lives as foragers, as hunters and gatherers, killing other animals for meat and collecting fruits, vegetables, and grains from the surrounding environment. We made clothing, shelter, tools, and weapons from available materials, such as stone, bone, antlers, hides, grasses, and wood. We developed language, culture, and social organization to create the collaboration that made our hunting, gathering, and making easier and provided meaning for our existence. In many ways, our lives still revolve around these three kinds of activities, although they have become increasingly complex and interrelated. We still need to provide food and care for ourselves and our families (however we constitute family these days). We still need to acquire (if not make our own) clothing, shelter, tools, and sometimes even weapons, even if only for self-defense and hunting. We still need to collaborate with others in meaningful ways to share these efforts, speak with each other, and organize

---

D. J. Cremer (✉)
History and Interdisciplinary Studies, College of Liberal Arts and Sciences, Woodbury University, Burbank, CA, USA
e-mail: Douglas.Cremer@woodbury.edu

© The Author(s), under exclusive license to Springer Nature Switzerland AG 2023
J. Marques (ed.), *The Palgrave Handbook of Fulfillment, Wellness, and Personal Growth at Work*,
https://doi.org/10.1007/978-3-031-35494-6_1

ourselves in social, political, and cultural ways. Despite our increased technological, scientific, cultural, social, and political accomplishments, and the multiple divisions of effort and organization we have created, these basics still hold.

Starting about 12,000 years ago, independently in several places around the globe, human beings began to shift from nomadic hunter-gatherer lives to settled domesticated lives. Animals were tamed, cereal grains cultivated, and people themselves settled into larger communities to protect the animals and crops they were now using for food and other resources. The very word "domesticated" literally means to belong to a home, and a home requires something being in a fixed location. With domestication came increased security of food and material resources, increased population size, and complex social organizations. It also became possible to divide the different kinds of effort required for survival and growth among different individuals in a more specialized manner. Nomadic forager groups (as we can observe in the limited number of such societies that still survive) tend to divide basic tasks by sex, with females doing most of the gathering and males doing most of the hunting, but this division is not absolute. Children and elderly members of the community assisted in gathering, as well as cleaning and maintaining their temporary living sites. Settled domesticated groups, with many more requirements for survival and growth, can divide and assign tasks in a more complex arrangement, and something like our current social and class structure began to emerge.

Take, for example, the tasks regularly done around the home, an extension of the effort females, older children, and the elderly had done in caring for younger children and gathering foods around a forager's temporary nomadic location. Childcare, food collection and preparation, cleaning and mending, all the regular, cyclical efforts to maintain the family and household were done not only by females, older children, and the elderly, but also by adult males who were assigned to domestic service in more well-to-do households. Servants, slaves, and temporarily hired help could be female or male, young or old, and all were dedicated to the tasks around the maintenance of the domestic household and family. The nature of this effort was of necessity repetitive, embedded in the cycle of waking and sleeping, gathering and preparing, consuming and cleaning. It would also include the less regular but still repetitive effort of reproduction of human beings themselves: sexual relations, pregnancy, birth, education and training, tending the ill and injured, and eventually dealing with death and burial. Included in this domestic labor is the labor of farming and animal husbandry, activities tied to the annual growth cycle of crops and the longer life cycle of livestock. The annual cycle of preparing the ground, planting the seed, tending the land, and harvesting the produce, the longer cycle of breeding, feeding, protecting, and harvesting the products of animal life, these efforts by their nature require a constant labor of care, tending, repair, and renewal. All this effort we generally understand as labor, taking a cue from what we call the birthing process itself. It is inescapable, regular, repetitive, often risky, painful, and difficult, and absolutely essential to our existence.

Similarly, in nomadic hunter-gatherer societies, females and males of a variety of ages were occupied with the making of various tools and implements necessary for survival. Animal bones were used to make sewing needles, while hides were treated to serve as clothing and shelter. Flint cores and other stones were chipped and flaked to make knives, axes, and similar cutting instruments. Branches and wood were used to make frames for shelters, bows for arrows, and shafts for spears. These activities were extended in settled domestic societies to include stone working for shelters, temples, and statues, wood and metal working for tools, weapons, furnishings, and artistic decorations, underground and surface mining for mineral resources, and the building of shops and storehouses for the collection, trading, and selling of various goods and supplies. What distinguishes this effort from the domestic labor described above is that most of it is productive (rather than reproductive), linear (rather than repetitive), and aimed at creating specific objects and structures that have a certain durability and strength so that they may serve their purposes for a long period of time. In making these things, a plan or design is required, and a definite beginning, middle, and end of the process can be seen. This kind of effort we generally understand as work, as signified by the double meaning of the word, both as the process of production (artists work at their craft) and as the object produced (the actual works of art). It is directional, creative, productive, not particularly associated with risk, pain, and suffering and often aimed at making our existence easier and more enjoyable.

As foraging hunter-gatherer societies shifted toward settled domesticated ones, the two forms often existed side by side, within given societies and between them. Some societies created mixed structures, with some people being settled and others continuing a nomadic existence, with members often moving between the two forms of life. Other societies, some settled, some nomadic, existed alongside one another, often in conflict as settled societies claimed land that had been used for hunting and gathering, and nomadic hunter-gatherers raided settled societies for food and resources. The resulting expansion of settled domesticated societies and the reduction of nomadic hunter-gatherer societies, at least in the eyes of the former, created a status differential, where inhabitants of settled societies saw themselves as superior to the nomadic peoples, elevating the kinds of work done only in emerging towns and cities (crafts and manufacture) as superior to the repetitive labor done by hunter-gatherers.

The result of the combination of these processes was a basic class structure seen across almost all settled domesticated societies. The toil of domestic labor was reserved for adult females, as well as children, servants, and slaves of either sex. Due to its repetitive and never-ending nature, such labor was seen as less desirable and of lower status. This included agricultural labor as well, where the cyclical effort of farming as well as the intense labor and risks involved linked it to domestic labor and thus lower status. In contrast, the effort put into artisanal or marketplace work was undertaken mainly by males, along with a few females, and because of its planned, directive, and often creative nature was seen as more desirable and of higher status. Status differentials thus became increasingly complex, with inhabitants of urban centers, whatever their actual roles and occupations, feeling superior to inhabitants of rural villages and agricultural farms, who in turn saw themselves as superior to the remaining nomadic peoples. Within urban centers, there was also increased status differentiation by the kind of labor or work one did as well as by the amount of wealth acquired. Eventually, some males were able to free themselves from either labor or work, leaving it to females, servants, or slaves to accomplish and establishing themselves at the top of the status and class hierarchy.

Although simplified and subject to various qualifications (as all generalizations are), this division of effort and status in settled domesticated societies has generally held from the beginning of agricultural societies about 12,000 years ago through the beginning of the modern industrial era about 250 years ago. As these societies grew and developed, they became even more and more specialized, creating ruling classes, warrior classes (often one and the same), and religious classes, usually dominated by males, whose activities were shaped by governing, protecting, controlling, and disciplining the populations under their authority. Neither truly labor nor work, in the above senses, the efforts of these groups are more properly seen as political and organizational, their energy expended in planning and leadership. What became the elites of these societies, who through power and wealth were exempted from both reproductive labor and productive work, were able to engage in the political and organizational activities reserved for them. Their status as elites meant freedom from these other, lower, forms of effort, so that those whose lives were spent in domestic labor and artisanal work were seen as both of a lower status and as not really free. Moreover, they saw themselves, and only themselves, as engaged in meaningful and fulfilling efforts. This distinction between the free, high-status leaders whose responsibilities and associations created meaning for their lives, and the unfree, low-status laborers and workers, whose tasks and efforts were not seen by these elites as meaningful, is an important factor in our understanding to this day of what we mean by labor and work, meaning and fulfillment.

Labor and Work

Although we often use the terms labor and work interchangeably these days, they have a history that marks them as rather different things practically and linguistically. The modern English word "labor" stems from French and Latin, while "work" comes from Old English and Old Saxon, with connections to Dutch and German. Labor here generally signifies exertion, effort, toil, suffering, pain, hardship, and fatigue. Work then includes a different range of actions: acting, doing, manufacturing, producing, using, and remunerating.

Work can at times be laborious, and labor can sometimes produce work, but generally these have been understood as distinct terms, each carrying markers of rank and status as well as describing the kinds of. Effort and energy employed. Their connections to the division of effort described above can be seen in their etymological roots. The clear distinction is that labor is repetitive and difficult, often requiring suffering and pain, while work is linear and creative, requiring planning and focus.

Looking at other languages outside of English helps see this distinction even more clearly. In French, the equivalent word for labor is "travail," derived from the Vulgar Latin "tripaliare," to torture, probably from the Latin "tripalis," an instrument of torture and execution similar to a crucifix, although made of an "X" attached to a straight post. "Travail," much like the English "labor," is understood as toil, painful, arduous, even torturous effort, and the word itself has been taken with this meaning into Modern English as well. Modern French has also taken this word as equivalent to the modern English word "work" in a similar way, exhibiting the blurring of these terms that will be discussed below. In modern German, "Werk" as a noun, as in its English cognate, signifies an artifact created through "wirken" as a verb. In contrast, the noun "Arbeit" has its roots in older German meaning toil, labor, hardship, and distress. That it is also used to describe male and female workers ("Arbeiter" and "Arbeiterin") also shows how modern uses have made work and labor synonymous, despite their different origins and meanings. How is it that labor and work, originally different terms for different forms of effort performed by different social classes, came to be synonymous with each other? More importantly, how did the idea of "work," the creative production of artifacts, tools, even works of art, become associated with the suffering, pain, and even torture of "labor?".

In pre-modern societies, the distinction between labor and work was clearer than it is today, although it certainly was not absolute. There were some aspects of domestic labor that had to be done at the workshop, the place where things were produced. Floors had to be swept, materials replenished and restocked, and tools mended and repaired. Servants and apprentices supplied this labor, and the latter were also trained in the work of the journeymen and artisans, with the idea that the apprentices would one day join the rank of workmen (this was a primarily male occupational world). Even in shops and markets, males and females (husbands and wives, brothers and sisters, for example) would more often work alongside each other, laboring to maintain the family business and working with the materials and customers of the shop. These were closely related activities, often performed by any and all members of the family, regardless of sex. Conversely, although much of the effort expended in the household was laborious, the production of small artifacts or implements for local trade or sale was often part of the domestic economic activity. There was never a clean division of labor and work, and they often overlapped, but the essential division between low-status domestic labor and higher-status artisanal and commercial work was clear and obvious to all.

The industrial revolution of the eighteenth century made this all much more complicated and in both directions. Labor penetrated the workshop more and more, and work penetrated the household more and more. Early industrialization revolved around textile production, especially the production of cotton cloth and clothing for retail sale. Initially, merchants brought raw cotton to homes in the countryside, where women often cleaned, separated, spun, and weaved this into cloth, which was then picked up by the cotton merchants in exchange for piece rate payment. This was initially done as a supplement to all of the domestic labor these women did, but as demand grew, it could become the full-time work of some in the household while others shared the domestic labor that was still required. Productive work, with a clear beginning, middle, and end, and aimed at creating objects for the marketplace, becomes more and more common within the world of domestic labor. Despite its productive nature, the process of getting the raw cotton and producing the cotton cloth also became a repetitive, cyclical process, detached from the production of the final finished product, actual cotton clothing. That work was done by other women, seamstresses to whom the cloth was provided who then dyed, cut, and stitched the cloth into articles of clothing. Sometimes one might find all these operations in one household, but most often they were done in separate places, with the cotton merchant serving as the transporting agent between them. This was the beginning of what we now call the division of labor in the production process, laborers whose work is only a part of the overall process of making and creating, separated from both the initial and end products of their efforts. It is the beginning of the blurring the distinction between labor and work, both in actual experience and in our language about them.

The creation of modern factories continued this process of blurring the distinction between labor and work. The work of cotton production was gathered into common buildings (the word "factory" originally designated a warehouse, a large, enclosed space; only after industrialization did the term come to signify a place of mechanized production), both to reduce transportation costs and to apply new technologies in production that could not be done in separate households. Making the machines required for textile production became its own productive process, also done in factories, with iron and coal as the raw materials on which this transformation was based. Within these factories, workers were given specific tasks to perform as part of the production process, detached from artisanal processes where one could see a product being created from start to finish. Instead, workers repetitively performed singular tasks, attaching a part, pushing a lever, or placing an object, etc. Work in industrial spaces became more and more like domestic labor: repetitive, arduous, and dangerous, and thus also of lower status than other forms of urban work.

The transformations of industrialization were many, complex, and wide-ranging. Populations, which began rapidly growing at the same time, moved from rural to urban spaces, seeking both work and the freedom and enjoyment of urban life. Steam power, machine tools, canals and railways, slums and tenements, child labor and union strikes, suburb creation and industrial pollution, all of the charms and challenges of an increasingly urban, industrial society that we recognize in the modern world came into being. With this transformation, the older worlds of labor and work melted into one another, traditions rooted in location and religion were tested and changed, and new forms of power and authority created. Elites were increasingly freed from labor as servant and slave classes grew, and their efforts at leadership and organization intensified. Yet even the activity of elites was touched by this blurring of labor and work. In managing change, processing information, marshaling resources, and dealing with the increased number of workers under their authority, their efforts became more and more like labor, a repetitive cycle of paperwork, orders, and decisions, what we see as the world of management these days.

All levels of society, which before these transformations had seen their status distinctions and responsibilities so clearly laid out before them, now saw the collapse of these distinctions in terms of their day-to-day activities and efforts. All work threatened to become laborious in different ways, with no one who could see, as in pre-modern times, the entire production process as a work of their own hands, even with the assistance of others, from beginning to end. Work among the lower levels of the status hierarchy became even more dangerous and deadly, more toil and travail than it had been before, and even among the higher levels, the risks of entrepreneurial activity in a capitalist society, risk, and danger became more profound, with the specter of bankruptcy and poverty always on the horizon. Those in the middle, shopkeepers, farmers, artisans, what we would today refer to as small business holders, came under tremendous pressure from competition and the vagaries of the business cycle. It is little wonder that we have been left with an inability to distinguish between work and labor in our language and in the ways that we experience the world of our activity and exertion of effort.

The technological and communicative revolutions of the twentieth century have if anything intensified this collapse of labor into work and work into labor. Aside from those engaged in agricultural and industrial labor, and the shift in population from the former to the latter is increasing across the globe, the increase in the size of the service sector of the economy, people engaged in offering assistance, support, entertainment, and information to others, has also changed the world of work and labor. On the one hand, there is repetitive labor in service provision, the need for cleaning, maintenance, childcare, food provision, and other forms of domestic toil conducted for others in homes or in workplaces. On the other hand, there is creative work in planning, developing, and executing more complex tools and designs, including computer programming and technical analysis, financial transactions and organizational structures, communication networks and transportation flows. Even in an individual day, office work, with its spreadsheets, organizational charts, paperwork processing, and seemingly endless meetings, from workers in cubicles (or in online video forums) to executives in suites, is very often a combination of repetitive labor and creative work, and more often than not more of the former than the latter.

This picture of labor and work is simplified and subject to various qualifications (as all generalizations are), but it captures in some way the profound transformations of the past 250 years as well as the rapidly transformative era of the last 50 years. There has been a breakdown of traditional caste and class distinctions, especially the ones that limited an individual's life choices to a narrow realm determined by one's family ancestry and lineage. Class and status tenacity across generations still exists in many ways, but depending upon one's location on the planet, it may be much more malleable than before. There has been an increase in the freedom to choose occupations, life partners, place of residence, and family size, among many other aspects of modern life. This collapse of rigid distinctions between different forms of life, which we have experienced as an increase of freedom, if not opportunities for a meaningful life, has been accompanied by the blurring of the lines between labor and work, so much so that what we perceive of as work is, more often than not, whatever our occupation, also toil, trouble, redundancy, risk, and, in short, labor. In the process, whatever meaning, satisfaction, fulfillment, or even joy we may have found in the changing circumstances of our lives and our work has also appeared to recede from our grasp, leaving us confused and making us wonder if we ever really had a grasp on what was happening to us to begin with.

Fulfillment and Meaning

For most of human history, people have engaged in labor and work because of necessity or compulsion. Fulfillment and meaning, let alone choice and freedom, had little room in agricultural subsistence economies where living through each season was a challenge for those with little property to cultivate, let alone for the numerous servants and slaves who had little choice in the matter, or for the women confined to household obligations, including childbearing and childrearing. The quest for what the Greek philosopher Aristotle referred to as eudaemonia, literally a "good spirit" or better translated as happiness, living well, or human flourishing, was reserved for male elites who were by their social position freed from both labor and work and thus able to pursue meaningful activity with others, whether through political, cultural, intellectual, or artistic life. Meaning and purpose were to be found in these activities, in a life of virtue, a combination of personal character and morally good actions. Human flourishing was seen as the fulfillment of human potential, the full exercise of our talents and abilities, and the realization of ambitions that were great and magnanimous. Fulfillment, as in the completion of a full project, a life project, if you will, and one done meaningfully, that is, with great significance and importance, was only possible for those freed from the burdens of labor and work. It was neither a feeling nor an emotion; it was not derived from labor or work. In fact, those that had to spend their time in labor or work would not have the time or freedom to pursue living well, and for them, it would not even be considered a life goal. In the ancient world, only by achieving wealth and freedom, and thus independence from toil or economic effort, could one even conceive of living well, of being happy or fulfilled.

For those whose lives were spent in labor or work, what one could achieve at best was a sense of satisfaction or accomplishment. Both terms arise in the fifteenth century in English, derived from Old French and Latin. The first, satisfaction, comes from the act of penance, the fulfillment of a penitent act, and the sense of having done enough to discharge an obligation. At the end of a day of intense labor, having completed one's tasks, prepared meals and cleaned the home, gathered the crops or bedded the animals, and escaped injury or worse, one could at best feel a sense that the day's toil had been satisfied. The second, accomplishment, signified the completion of a thing or a task, the ability to look backward upon finishing a project. Certainly, this would be a familiar feeling to someone who had conceived, planned, gathered, and executed a work with a clear beginning, middle, and end. Much in the same way we have blurred the line between labor and work, we can also see how a feeling of either satisfaction or accomplishment can follow from what we colloquially call "a job well done." Neither, however, would be confused with the greater sense of fulfillment or meaning in our lives. Perhaps they are a precondition, in that one would hardly be able to be fulfilled without sense of satisfaction or accomplishment, but they are not the same thing. Labor that is satisfactorily accomplished, or work that is accomplished satisfactorily, still has to be done again the next day, and the limited sense of fulfillment this may grant is as fleeting as dawn of the following day.

Even after the industrial and technological revolutions, this concept of what constitutes fulfillment and meaning in life has had tremendous staying power. As more people have gained relative wealth and freedom in their lives through the power of the industrial and democratic revolutions of the late eighteenth and early nineteenth centuries, aspiring to more than satisfaction and accomplishment and striving toward fulfillment and meaning has seemed increasingly possible. What had been possible only for the wealthy male elites of the past was apparently now within reach of more and more men and even some women in the modern era. The growth of a new upper class of property holders and highly compensated business owners and managers opened the possibility of a fulfilled and meaningful life for many. The conflict that arose within this expanded sense of opportunity and possibility was that in order to accumulate the wealth that was a prerequisite for freedom and thus a prerequisite for fulfillment, one still had to work. The new elites of the modern era were not men whose wealth was derived from large landed agricultural wealth worked by slaves and managed by overseers, nor were they men who could become detached from the day-to-day operation of their factories and businesses where laborers and employees generated their wealth for them in the form of surplus profit. In order to acquire wealth and freedom, they had to expend tremendous effort in their acquisition and stay on top of the process in order to secure them. Even the new industrial and management elites could not escape the necessity of work and labor, and thus began the process of turning this effort into a virtue itself, where hard work and laborious toil in the name of wealth accumulation and the freedom it promised (but very often never realized) became the signifiers of a fulfilled and meaningful life.

So just as the worlds of labor and work have increasingly blurred together, our ideas of satisfaction, accomplishment, fulfillment, and meaning have blended together in our minds. Except for the relatively small class of rentiers, of individuals who truly live off only their property and investments as managed by others on their behalf, most everyone is engaged in labor or work of some kind, from those in the primary sector of agriculture, mining, and other extractive industries, to those in the secondary sector of industrial production where raw materials are turned into finished tools, machinery, and other products, to this in the tertiary sector of service industries and financial markets. All these groups are increasingly part of liberal democratic political orders where individual rights and freedom are the bedrock of a constitutional order. Unlike the ancient and classical worlds, everyone is working, and everyone is free, at least as a desired and ideal aspiration for those who are unemployed or unfree. The older distinction between the unfree laboring majority, who can never experience fulfillment of meaning in life, and the free independent minority, for whom fulfillment and meaning are possible, has also collapsed, leaving us in a very confused and often frustrating position. Work, even laborious, risky, tedious effort, is seen as an essential and inescapable component of life, a source of virtuous behavior and choices, and thus is no longer seen as a barrier to fulfillment and meaning. At the same time, the idea of freedom, and the ability to seek a life of fulfillment and meaning, has been increasingly attached to the idea of universal human rights and detached from the necessity of wealth, at least in the abstract. The result of this process is that having a meaningful and fulfilled life is an aspiration, if not expectation, that is more and more common.

Yet as we have learned over the years, these aspirations and expectations are very often not met, and while we desire fulfillment and meaning in our lives, our lives are more and more centered around our laborious work, and we find ourselves unable to achieve that feeling of satisfaction and accomplishment, let alone meaning and fulfillment. We do not desire a return to older ways where human flourishing was restricted to a few, who achieved fulfillment and meaning at the expense of the great majority who were denied any opportunity of human happiness. There are those who advocate an "ownership society" where more and more people acquire income-generating property and assets as the solution to this dilemma, yet we also do not desire simply learning to live with the current imbalanced situation where so many see no way available to live a fulfilled and meaningful life because they are overwhelmed with the combination of the repetitive, laborious, and often dangerous work they do for income and the repetitive, laborious, and often tedious work they do in caring for their families and homes. For those exhausted and stressed from the combination and blurring of work life and home life, from the inability of find that elusive "work-life balance" that others advocate, the advice to seek fulfillment and meaning outside of work, in family, community, religion, or charity, rings hollow and unachievable. All these alternatives in effect advocate an escape from labor and work, either through wealth generation or through alternate actions apart from the workplace and the home.

We thus live in a world where finding fulfillment and meaning in the blended and blurred experience of domestic labor and workplace employment is difficult at best, and escape from the burdens of domestic labor and workplace employment appears to be both a distant dream and, even if achieved, dependent upon others remaining behind to endure the toil and risk so we can be free. Despite the contradictions, we are forced to look for fulfillment and meaning within the common experience of labor and work that we experience. Our sense of satisfaction and accomplishment, old sentiments that are still fleetingly accessible in both domestic and employed efforts, may be a place to start. They are still available even in the repetitive, laborious world of our domestic lives and even occasionally in the tedious, redundant world of our work lives. They are, however, and always have been, slender reeds on which to construct a deeply felt sense of fulfillment and meaning in our lives as a whole. Our relationships and partnerships in our homes and workplaces, interactions that have always been there as a source of comfort and support, are also fragile structures solely to rely upon in building a fulfilled and meaningful life. Work relationships, for all the efforts of some employers to create a familial atmosphere, are easily broken with frequent restructurings, occupational mobility, competition for position and compensation, and the regular hiring and firing cycle of business life. Even our domestic relationships are caught up in responsibilities for care, conflicting personalities, generational tensions, and the burdens of caring for the young and the elderly. All the doors that appear open to us to find or create a fulfilled and meaningful life seem to quickly shut themselves, whether we look beyond or within the total world of domestic labor and employed work. What then are we to do?

Work and Fulfillment

In all of the above, labor and work have been conceived of as means to other ends: domestic labor to the reproduction and maintenance of life itself and artisanal work to the production and maintenance of the tools and implements life requires. Even in their modern blurred condition, laborious work is still mostly thought of as a means to other ends: survival, income, security, social advancement, wealth, etc. In both cases, we have often sought fulfillment and meaning in activity outside of labor and work in the world of community activity, thus seeing the labor and work as only the means to obtain fulfillment and meaning somewhere else. We have seen, however, that these distinctions are no longer relevant to the way we actually live our lives. The transformations of the industrial, technological, and democratic revolutions have exploded the limits of labor, work, and social activity to involve all of life. We live in an inseparable world where all three are intertwined and inextricably part of each other.

At one time, Max Weber famously argued that in modernity one does not work to live, rather one lives to work, to achieve, to make a mark on the world. This has led many of us to focus on our work lives as the source of fulfillment and meaning. We invest in education, training, skill development, career development, relationship building, resume expansion, and all the other techniques of self-improvement related to our occupational advancement, seeking therein the meaning that apparently has escaped us. We strive to build a work life that will fill our lives with achievement, success, and meaning, and yet find ourselves chasing these goals, continually frustrated by how they always seem to ever be out of our reach. Because of this frustration and failure, we have now come to realize that the distinction between work and life that this shift depends upon has all but disappeared. We see this most notably in the world of the new knowledge worker, who carries the means and materials of her work around with her all time in her cell phone and laptop computer. We see it in the changing 24-hour shifts of care workers, the end of the weekend (let alone the Sabbath or Sunday) as a meaningful shared time without work or labor (no matter the day, the domestic toil of cooking, cleaning, and caring has always had to be done), and the pressure to be constantly at work in some way all of the time, either in answering the constant stream of email, in taking care of our health, in serving others in our community, or in some other activity focused on self-improvement such as education or career development. Just as the distinction between labor and work has vanished, so too has the difference between work and life. It is all the same stream of effort and anxiety, toil and creativity, means and ends.

The conditions of contemporary life thus require a new approach, one that no longer views our decisions as caught between either work or life, but as activity that embraces both work and life as part of the total experience of living. We are no longer in an either/or situation, of having to choose between work or life, toil or meaning, but one of both/and, of finding a way to live meaningfully with our work. The ancient distinctions between domestic labor, public work, and community activity, where meaning and fulfillment are only for the few and only in the final arena of communal action, have melted away. So, too, have the distinctions between means and ends, between those things that serve as our tools and paths toward a life of fulfillment and meaning. Immanuel Kant had famously argued that we should not treat people merely as means, as devices that only serve us and our needs, but as ends, as individuals with their own motives, desires, and goals. The reality is that people will always be in some sense our means to meet our needs. We need each other for comfort and companionship, for intimacy and affection, for collaborative effort, and for economic support. Kant had proposed substituting ends for means, making a choice for either one or the other. Our blurred reality requires us to embrace both means and ends, to see each other in mutuality as ways to achieve what we desire, and thus ourselves as ways for others to achieve their desires, as well as to see each other as autonomous, independent, fully human beings who are ends in and of themselves. Similarly, we need to see the intersection of labor, work, and social activity as all part of our common human existence and to see all of it as a potential source of fulfillment and meaning.

To see work as laborious and risky repetition, as creative and directional effort, and as social and communal action, is also to see labor as an unending series of chores and cares for others, as creative and adaptive responses to changing situations and needs, and as effort undertaken with and for others in our communities and society. Taken together, as two sides of the same blurringly spinning coin, labor and work can be sources of fulfillment and meaning. To see meaningful activity as the source of fulfillment means to gather all the slender reeds of satisfaction and accomplishment, relationships and partnerships, means and ends, into one collective bundle of lived experience and strive to seek fulfillment in the combination of all aspects of our lives. How we do this will be as creative and individual as is each one of us. Finding, discovering, or creating a sense of fulfillment and meaning will require a reorientation toward the reality of our blurred existence, a refusal to believe we need to constantly choose between either work or fulfillment in life, and a recognition that everything from the simplest, repetitive task to the most inspiring, creative project, to the more difficult, collaborative efforts we undertake, can provide fulfillment for, and reveal meaning to, us.

Perhaps the trick is not in seeking fulfillment, not in striving to find meaning in what we do, but in waiting for what fulfills us to reveal itself in the whirl of activity that surrounds us and spins us along with it. If we are attentive to our labor, present to our work, and committed to our activity with others, if we see all three as interconnected and interrelated, as essential and inescapable, we will refuse the feeling that we have to choose either one or the other and embrace both and all of them together. Perhaps then the meaning of our lives will reveal itself, and the sense of fulfillment comes to us, not as another labor to endure or work to create or activity to add, but as the connections between them all that find themselves drawn together and held in a dynamic tension in our own particular and individual lives. There is a reason that the literature on wellness at work, which is more than sixty years old, has often centered on holistic and comprehensive approaches to well-being, including meditation, exercise, diet, stress relief, and recreation focused on the combination of mind, body, and spirit. It has intuited this need to center and focus ourselves in order to be able to see what may be revealed to us. Yet even these solutions, often undertaken as self-help projects of a different sort, fail to satisfy our need for meaning and fulfillment. They often fall short, appearing at best as partial answers, just as living to work and throwing ourselves into our labors and achievements has been. Only approaches that embrace the totality of our lives as we actually live and experience them, in the whirl of toil and effort, in the struggle to maintain our relationships and our sense of self, have the potential to show us the fulfillment and meaning that already exists and is accessible to us, if only we pay enough attention and allow it to reveal itself to us.

If this all sounds a lot like the practice of meditation and mindfulness, it is probably not coincidental that the turn toward learning how to pay close attention to the present moment and see how it is intertwined with the past and the future comes at a time of increasingly rapid change, transgressive boundary shifting, and instability in our given roles and functions in work and in life. There is an intuition at work here that sees the blurring and blending we have described above and seeks to address the challenges of these particular times, not through a new course of action, but by a distancing from activity, work, and labor, in order to gain a new perspective on it all. There is more here, however, than just meditation and mindfulness. It is not a choice between active engagement and effort to find meaning or passive receptivity and awareness that lets fulfillment reveal itself. It is both our immersion in the world of action, of laboring and working to care for others and ourselves, to construct things and make plans to ease our current lives and improve our futures, and our ability to reflect and absorb all that we experience and learn through our doing of these many things in the world, through our caring and constructing, that meaning and fulfillment can be found.

Conclusion

From the beginning of human existence, we have had to labor and work, expend our energy and toil away at our tasks, in order not only to survive, but also to thrive. For many centuries, certainly since the beginnings of settled agricultural societies that gradually replaced the nomadic forager lives our ancestors lived, this effort has been distributed between different classes of people, some enslaved, subjugated, and oppressed into the most menial and laborious kinds of effort, others freed to some extent to craft devices and furnishings to ease our lives, and still fewer others who were freed from this labor and this work to seek fulfillment and meaning in concert with other free men of wealth. In this span of human history, it has been only a short time since all these distinctions began to breakdown and blur together in the wake of the tremendous democratic, industrial, and technological revolutions of our time. The result has been the dissolution of the boundary between labor and work and the experience of either as tedious, repetitive, seemingly unending, and often dangerous and risky effort. The traditional paths toward fulfillment and meaning, through upward mobility and freedom from laborious work, have been closed off by these same changes, just as the challenge to find fulfillment and meaning has been extended to all of humanity.

We have learned in this time that various strategies to meet this challenge have failed. We have tried working to live, living to work, giving up on being able to find fulfillment, insisting on creating a work-life balance, seeking more wealth and power, creating a broad ownership class, settling for whatever we can get, building a better resume, and escaping into our inner and private lives, all without finding fulfillment and meaning. What all these strategies have in common is that they fail to recognize and accept the reality of our contemporary situation, where labor has become work, work has become labor, and all our human activities for ourselves and with others have been consumed in the vortex of constant striving and effort, where the borders of work and life have dissolved and the boundaries of our responsibilities and ambitions are no longer visible. They have also failed to recognize that the solutions we seek have to be universal and democratic, available to all, not just the privileged few, leaving none behind, including all those who labor at the tasks with the lowest status and with unrecognized importance. Whatever new approaches to finding fulfillment and meaning in this world of seemingly unending, laborious work and activity we shall find, they will have to look realistically at the totality of our lived existence, with all its competing and conflicting demands, and all our aspirations for wellness, healing, and wholeness.

References

Arendt, H. (1998). *The human condition*. University of Chicago Press. (2nd edition. Original work published 1958).

Aristotle. (2014). *The nicomachean ethics*. (C. D. C. Reeves, Trans.) Hackett Publishing Company. (Original work published ca. 335–322 BCE).

Barker, G. (2009). *The agricultural revolution in prehistory: Why did foragers become farmers?* Oxford University Press.

Barnhart, R. K. (1995). *The barnhart concise dictionary of etymology: The origins of american english words*. Harper Collins.

Bauman, Z. (2000). *Liquid modernity*. Polity Press.

Bellwood, P. (2004). *First farmers: The origins of agricultural societies*. Blackwell.

Berman, M. (1982) *All that is solid melts into air: The experience of modernity*. Verso Books.

Diamond, J. (1997). *Guns, germs and steel: A short history of everybody for the last 13,000 years*. Norton.

Hahn, T. N. (2007). *For a future to be possible: Buddhist ethics for everyday life*. Parallax Press.

Hobsbawm, E. (1998). *Industry and empire: From 1750 to the present day*. The New Press. (Rev. edition. Original work published 1968).

Kant, I. (2018). *Groundwork of the metaphysics of morals*. (Allan W. Wood, Trans.) Yale University Press. (Original work published 1785).

Landes, D. S. (2003). *The unbound prometheus: Technological change and industrial development in western europe from 1750 to the present*. Cambridge University Press. (2nd edition. Original work published 1969).

Piketty, T. (2014). *Capital in the twenty-first century*. (Arthur Goldhammer, Trans.) Harvard University Press.

Stearns, P. N. (2018). *The industrial revolution in world history.* Routledge. (4th edition. Original work published 2013).

Weber, M. (2011). *The protestant ethic and the spirit of capitalism.* (Stephen Kalberg, Trans.) Oxford University Press. (Rev. edition. Original work published 1920).

CHAPTER 2

Soft Skills as a Conscious Choice to Greater Collaboration at Work

Debra J. Dean

INTRODUCTION

Many schools and employee development classes teach the basics of management and leadership. One area that is sorely missed has been soft skills. This gap has never been more evident than in recent years and continues to be a growing problem as employees are returning to work after the announcement of the COVID-19 pandemic. This chapter will explore the possible reasons why soft skills have emerged as such a gap, empirical evidence as to why it is vitally important for a person to understand and comprehend the topic of soft skills, and practical next steps for mastering these skills. Master of Business Administration (MBA) programs typically teach accounting, economics, ethics, finance, and a slew of management courses for one to master managing marketing, operations, organizations, people, projects, and supply chains. In these courses, the lack of soft skills permeates the program leaving colleges and universities churning out people who can do the work from a task perspective, but not necessarily people who can work alongside other people in a productive and positive manner.

D. J. Dean (✉)
Department of Business and Leadership,
Regent University, Virginia Beach, VA, USA
e-mail: drdebra@drdebradean.com

© The Author(s), under exclusive license to Springer Nature Switzerland AG 2023
J. Marques (ed.), *The Palgrave Handbook of Fulfillment, Wellness, and Personal Growth at Work*,
https://doi.org/10.1007/978-3-031-35494-6_2

Soft Skills

Shek et al. (2017) explained that hard skills have been referred to as the academic or technical skills one needs for work. Soft skills, on the other hand, are referred to as transferable skills "related to the qualities of an individual"; such skills are also known as "generic skills, skills of employability, or people skills" (Shek et al., p. 337). Touloumakos (2020) adds phrases such as social skills and interactional skills to the list. From an employer perspective, Shek et al. found that 77% of employers considered soft skills and hard skills equally important, and 16% of employers weighted soft skills as more important than hard skills.

Defining soft skills requires attention to the way a person interacts with themselves, another person, or a group of people. For some, the idea of spending time on soft skills equates to a waste of time. While working on my dissertation in 2016 and 2017, I spent time training and coaching employees on servant and spiritual leadership dimensions of agapao love, altruism, empowerment, faith/hope, humility, inner life, meaningful work, serving, trust, vision, and building a sense of community. I remember employees and students that refused to attend my meetings or challenged me on the idea that one should do their work because they are getting paid for it. Specifically, there were three out of more than 100 that challenged me on this topic and the relevance of such skills to a for-profit, corporate society.

One student argued that younger generations were weak and in need of pampering to get in touch with their feelings. This was my first major indication that working with different generations in the same organization, let alone the same team, could bring about problems managers and leaders may be unprepared to handle. For example, in a hypothetical situation, Ben and Dave work together on a team. Ben is an employee with active military experience and has a history of hardships. He grew up in an abusive home and left for the Army to escape the abuse in hopes of a better life. While in the Army, he fought on the front lines in Vietnam and returned to a country that spat on him, called him names, and left him feeling alone, abandoned, and unwanted. He was a hard worker but essentially had to learn how to manage those emotions in a way that would permit him to move forward and forge ahead. His current corporate job was easy compared to the first 30 years of his life. At work, he mostly kept to himself and did his job.

Dave is an employee that works in the same department as Ben. Dave spent much of his life on a rigorous schedule pre-planned by his parents to keep him involved in sports and extracurricular activities. Dave is outgoing and spends time chatting with his co-workers about sports and various topics from the activities he enjoys outside of work.

Ben and Dave are both top performers in the department. The two of them seem to work well together at the surface, but in monthly 1-on-1 meetings with their supervisor, Dave is more vocal about his feelings than Ben, whereas Ben is more concerned with tasks on his to-do list and meeting deadlines.

Both employees know how to do their job, but as time goes on, they have a hard time interacting with one another in a respectful and productive way. This hypothetical situation is a classic example of how two people need soft skills to work together better.

Touloumakos (2020) explained that part of the problem with soft skills is with the definition itself stating that "the term soft skills has often become so stretched that their limits have become, in turn, vague" (p. 4). Succi and Canovi (2020) defined soft skills as follows:

> Soft skills represent a dynamic combination of cognitive and meta-cognitive skills, interpersonal, intellectual and practical skills. Soft skills help people to adapt and behave positively so that they can deal effectively with the challenges of their professional and everyday life. (p. 1835)

According to Touloumakos (2020), the phrase "soft skills" comprises the opportunity for the inclusion of a variety of attitudes, attributes, predispositions, qualities, traits, values, and volitions. Touloumakos list of soft skills, noted as not an exhaustive list, is shown in Table 2.1.

Perhaps many of these skills were overlooked in leadership theories of the past because there were unwritten rules that most people adhered to in their everyday life. The first of those rules is the Golden Rule, drawn from Matthew 7:12 stating, "Therefore, whatever you want men to do to you, do also to them, for this is the Law and the Prophets." In generations past, more time was spent on training a child to interact with others. As more American women went to work in the 1960s and 1970s, there were fewer family members raising

Table 2.1 Touloumakos list of soft skills

Ability to plan and achieve goals	Critical judgment	Interpersonal Savvy	Professionalism
Adaptability	Decision Making	Leadership Skills	Responsibility
Aesthetics	Diversity	Learning to Learn Other Skills	Self-Awareness
Analytical Thinking	Effective and Productive Interpersonal Interactions	Lookism	Social Skills
Articulation	Effectiveness	Managing Oneself	Team Skills
Cognitive Ability or Processes	Emotional Intelligence	Managing Skills	Thinking Skills
Communication Skills	Emotional Labor	Manipulation of Knowledge	Trustworthiness
Conflict Resolution	Flexibility	Negotiation	Uncertainty
Coping Skills	Good Attitude	Persuasion Skills	Willingness to Learn
Courtesy	Hardworking	Problem Solving	Work Ethic
Creativity/Innovation	Integrity	Professional Appearance	Working Under Pressure

children. Instead, children were sent to daycares, before and after school programs, or left alone and unsupervised at home. The term latchkey emerged for generation X children as they were the first generation in U.S. history to miss out on parenting during their most formative years. From that point forward, each generation has seen exponential growth in the number of children placed in childcare centers designed to take care of the child while the parent is away at work. The lack of parental influence has appeared as a colossal gap in child development as they struggle with knowing how to process tough times, how to get along with friends, how to respect other people and their property, how to tolerate and embrace differences, how to resolve conflict, and how to respond to a difficult day. This is monumental in explaining how the workforce has ended up where it is today with such a huge gap to fill relating to soft skills.

During a 2020 presentation on the topic of workplace spirituality, I had a conversation with a young woman who said she was taught to argue her point in all situations. She had not considered the option of listening to opposing viewpoints and having an open mind. Instead, she was fully engaged and ready to rumble or riot at all times. This conversation opened my mind to the reality that somewhere, somehow, the Golden Rule train fell off the tracks. This also helped to explain that if a generation or two of children had been taught this way of life, there was no wonder how protests get so out of hand as freeway riots and highway revolts seemingly emerged overnight in 2020 and 2021. This conversation also opens the door to consider an intentional agenda that is underway teaching people of all ages to disrespect their parents, disobey authority, and retaliate when they do not get their way.

The phrase "Karen" refers to a person being angry, entitled, and obnoxious while making a scene in public. At a basketball game in 2022, I sat to watch my 13-year-old play ball. In the audience was a person verbally abusing the referees, coaches, and players. She was lashing out loudly that her team was losing, and it was not fair. Instead of being nice, the visual display made many in the crowd feel uncomfortable and even move their seat to get further away from her. The game was stopped and a general announcement was made for everyone to take their seats (although only one person was acting out) and for no one to talk to the players, coaches, or referees. "Karen" continued to behave inappropriately but was not reprimanded directly.

Soft skills may be viewed as ancillary skills necessary for one to do their job; however, they are emerging as vitally important for a person to do the job well. Heckman and Kautz (2012) reinforced that soft skills predict and produce success in life. Millar et al. (2018) referred to soft skills as attitudes concerning emotion, empathy, and emotional intelligence. Soft skills were referred to as conscientiousness, grit, openness to experience, personality traits, and self-control in a study by Anderoni et al. (2020). Kikon and Karlsson (2020) focused on care as a soft skill in their study where training centers taught soft skills to help students become more employable. Trainers assisted students in learning how to pick up on facial expressions, adjust body language, and discussed make-up colors for sobriety and grace. Students were expected to walk, talk, dress, and apply communication skills that were pleasant and professional. Zainal-Abidin et al. (2019) explained that soft skills are intangible, non-technical, and personality specific. They include survival skills such as communication, critical thinking, decision-making, emotional intelligence, ethics, honesty, independence, integrity, interpersonal, leadership, listening, negotiation, problem-solving, reasoning, resilience, self-motivation, stress and time management, and teamwork (Zainal-Abidin et al., 2019).

Role of Technology

Experts have reported the increase in technology use as a reason why interpersonal and effective social skills are decreasing. In a study by Pew Research (2020), 71% of the participants reported cell phone use hurting one's ability to learn effective social skills and develop healthy relationships. The rise of screen time for children and adults is noticeably causing concerns and accusations of parents putting an iPad or cell phone in front of a child to entertain them instead of using the time to parent. Although experts such as the American Academy of Paediatrics recommend no more than 2-hours per day of screen-time, the amount of time spent with a cell phone, iPad, computer, laptop, or television increases each year. Technology addiction is a major problem as reports show 400 million people globally are addicted to the Internet, 50% of American teenagers are addicted to their smartphones, and Americans between the ages of 8 and 28 spend about 44.5 hours per week in front of a screen (Galov, 2022). Additionally, U.S. teens are spending more than seven hours in front of a screen each day. The result of increased screen time correlates with aggressive behavior, anxiety, arguments between child and siblings and/or child and parents, bad attitude, poor posture, bullying, carpal tunnel syndrome, compromised immunity, depression, eating problems, eye strain, headaches, inability to interact with people in a healthy and productive way, failure to understand one's own emotions, limited social skills, lower grades, lower intellect, obesity, pornography exposure, increased radiation contact, sleep problems, increased levels of stress, tech-neck, violence, and witnessing activity that misaligns with one's family values. Additionally, the increased use of technology exposes viewers to video challenges such as the outlet challenge, ice cream challenge, shell-on challenge, and the MOMO challenge, all encouraging people to participate in rude and risky behavior. In prior years, such videos would not be allowed as family-friendly content. With more time spent with technology, there is less time spent with people reinforcing socially acceptable behavior.

Role of the Family

Zainal-Abidin et al. (2019) reported the life story of a young adult who developed soft skills to thrive in life despite vulnerable beginnings. The skills were fostered by his parents and soft skill development commenced before entering school. Abidin et al. recognized the role of the family in developing the soft skills with their son and stated that establishing these skills as early as possible is critical for lasting effects. Abidin reinforced the need for families to develop, nurture, and reinforce such skills.

Prior to the latchkey kid era in the 1960s and 1970s, the majority of U.S. children were reared in the home, families attended church, home life included at least one daily sit-down home-cooked meal at the dinner table, and grandparents were close by. This family dynamic enabled constant reinforcement of family values. Today, few families eat a meal together. Fishel (2020) explained that in the past 30–40 years, there are fewer families eating together. She explained that "only about 30% of families regularly eat dinner together, despite family mealtime being hugely beneficial for kids" (para. 2). There appear to be differences in family mealtime based on socioeconomic demographics and ethnicity. Fishel noted that low-income families spend less time eating together than those with more household income. Trofholz et al. (2018) conducted a study on family meals with African Americans, Native Americans, Latinos, Hmongs, Soalis, and White families. Trofholz et al. (2018) found that all groups reported the importance of family meals and the opportunity to use the time to learn from parents and/or grandparents as meals were prepared and consumed together at a dinner table, "not scattered around the house" (p. 167). Non-white participants spoke more of learning to cook from their other family members, and learning to behave during mealtime was important.

In previous generations, proper behavior was reinforced with television shows, music, movies, newspapers, and other media outlets. There were organizations developed to allow or prohibit certain forms of media. The first film to receive a copyright was created by Thomas Edison in 1894. It was called *The Edison Kinetoscopic Record of a Sneeze* (also known as *Fred Ott's Sneeze*). Edison sponsored the second film directed by William Dickson titled, *Carmencita*. This film showed a female Spanish dancer twirling. It was not allowed to be shown in some places because when she twirled, her legs and underpants could be seen. The first documentary and feature film was the *Corbett-Fitzsimmons Fight* of 1897. It was filmed on 11,000 feet of film in Carson City, Nevada. The 111-minute film was shown in ten cities across the United States. Seven of those states deemed the film illegal and imposed fines for showing the film. In 1907, Chicago hosted 115 nickelodeons, also known as 5-cent movie theaters which resulted in the establishment of an official censorship party where the Chief of Police had the power to issue (or not issue) permits for movies that met his standard. In 1909, the Mayor of New

York shut down 660 theaters because the films were considered "reprehensible." This led to the creation of the National Board of Censorship. In 1915, the United States Supreme Court ruled in the case of Mutual Film Corporation vs. Ohio Industrial Commission. Chief Justice Edward White explained, "the exhibition of moving pictures is a business, pure and simple, originated and conducted for profit like other spectacles, and not to be regarded as part of the press of the country or as organs of public opinion within the meaning of freedom of speech and publication." This gave permission for an organization or a person to say a movie is allowed or not allowed based on some type of standard. In 1922, the creation of the Motion Picture Producers and Distributors of America (MPPDA) led to employing William Hays who made lists of things filmmakers should not do or should be careful with. His lists included men and women in bed together, methods of smuggling, ridicule of clergy, and trafficking of illegal drugs. These efforts led to the Hays Code, formally known as the Motion Picture Production Code of 1930. This work gained leverage once the MPPDA collaborated with the National Legion of Decency. Originally known as the National Legion of Decency, the film rating system was started in 1934 by the Catholic Church. Their goal was to identify objectionable content in motion pictures. In 1965, the organization was renamed the National Catholic Office for Motion Pictures. Their ratings started as C for condemned, B for partly objectionable, and evolved to O for morally offensive. In 1980, the organization closed up shop after providing ratings for 16,251 feature films. Since the 1980s, the exposure to content that would typically be deemed as morally repulsive, indecent, or reprehensible has been on the rise. Instead of a formal organization overseeing the decency of media from a national perspective, this is now left to be governed in the home on an individual basis. However, with the increase in technology use and decrease in parental involvement, children have grown up, literally, "left to their own devices."

In previous generations, there were newspaper columns such as Ask Ann Landers and Dear Abby. Ask Ann Landers was created in 1943 by Ruth Crowley and handed over to Esther Pauline "Eppie" Lederer in 1955. This American advice column ran for 56 years and was featured in 1200 newspapers, having more than 90 million readers. Lederer's daughter, Margo Howard, relaunched the column on June 4, 2019, at www.AnnLanders.com. Howard explained that common sense is not all as common in the twenty-first century as it was when her mother wrote the column. Dear Abby was Lederer's twin sister. They were born in 1918 as Pauline and Eppie Friedman in Sioux City, Iowa. It is expected that 65 million subscribers of the Chicago Tribune and the New York Daily News Syndicate read Dear Abby each day. An excerpt from The Desert Sun, Palm Springs, California, June 6, 1970, article from Dear Abby is shown below:

> DEAR ABBY: I notice that on occasion you have reprinted articles on request, which I think is fine, especially those which uphold morality in young people. However, I urge you to reprint the 10 Commandments for the 20th Century Husband. With so much infidelity going on and the divorce rate skyrocketing, it is needed now more than ever.
> Thank you,
>
> Grateful Sailor

> DEAR GRATEFUL, With pleasure. Ten Commandments for the 20th Century Husband:
> 1. Thou shall put thy wife before thy mother, thy father, thy daughter, and they son, for she is thy lifelong companion.
> 2. Abuse not thy body either with excessive food, tobacco, or drink, that thy days may be many and healthful in the presence of thy loved one.
> 3. Permit neither thy business nor thy hobby to make of thee a stranger to thy children, for the precious gift a man giveth his family is his time.
> 4. Forget not the virtue of cleanliness
> 5. Make not thy wife a beggar, but share willingly with her thy worldly goods.
> 6. Forget not to say, "I love you." For even though thy love be constant, thy wife doth yearn to hear the words.
> 7. Remember that the approval of thy wife is worth more than the admiring glances of a hundred strangers. Cleave unto her and forsake all others.
> 8. Keep thy home in good repair, for out of it cometh the joys of thy old age.
> 9. Forgive with grace. For who among us does not need to be forgiven?
> 10. Honor the Lord thy God all the days of thy life, and thy children will rise up and call thee blessed.
>
> Truly Yours,
>
> ABIGAIL VAN BUREN

Succi and Canovi (2020) conducted a study on soft skills and noted the lack of soft/transferable skills has been a controversial debate for more than three decades between higher education institutions and employer groups. About six decades ago, the women's liberation movement was in full motion with more mothers leaving their families to go to work. Nearly five decades points back to a time where latchkey kids were learning to live on their own or children were being placed in daycare centers for the first time. Four decades points to a time where the National Catholic Office for Motion Pictures closed their doors and the captain abandoned the media monitoring ship. It has been more than three decades since the internet permeated the majority of homes and businesses in the United States, and nearly two decades since the invention of the iPhone. The iPad was created just over one decade ago. This timeline lays out the path of where the train derailed, the ship was abandoned, and the innocent American child was left to their own devices. This is the timeline that lays out some of how we got to a place in time where employees struggle with basic soft skills of communication, problem-solving, ethics, flexibility/adaptability, interpersonal skills, emotional intelligence, ability to work in a team, critical and innovative thinking, creativity, self-confidence, coping with uncertainty, willingness to accept, and responsibility.

Role of the Church

Throughout the history of the United States, the church has been a mostly stable establishment for teaching soft skills. However, as with the rise in technology and the decrease in family time, church attendance has also played a role in the rising need for soft skill training. Gallup reports that 70% of U.S. adults attended church in 1999, and in 2020, before the pandemic, only 47% attended church. Despite the expectation that church attendance will reinforce the values taught in the home, fewer people are committed to attending church now than in the past. The trend of declining church attendance shows a steady decline since the start of the twenty-first century (Jones, 2021).

Butler (2021) conducted a study on African American millennials. She found that participants did not attend church for various reasons including the opportunity to do church in different ways (at home watching TV, reading the Bible, etc.); the notion of not wanting to force their children to go to church; overall disinterest in the church because they do not like dressing up, they find it boring, or they want to have fun; church trauma from a previous experience; or lack of purpose where pastors are only talking about prosperity and not preaching doctrinal truth about sin, hell, and Christian living. Another theme that emerged was family religious values. This theme is more specific to the concept of soft skills as participants commented on honesty, integrity, and the act of not offending others, and one participant noted that her father quotes scripture for everything. Butler (2021) explained that church values were consistent with participants "trying to be a good person and practicing values of morality" (p. 144).

Attending church is vitally important for a leader or follower seeking to acquire soft skills. Thompson (2021) wrote about soft skills found in scripture. Using 1 Timothy 3:1–7 as a guide, one can see that leaders should be trustworthy and noble. Being above reproach infers having impeccable character. Being sober-minded demands a person to have a clear head and not be easily influenced. Having self-control includes one's temper in person, in writing (even on social media), and everywhere. Being respectable involves the clothes one wears, the actions one does, and overall living a life worthy of respect. Being hospitable is the act of inviting people into your home, into your car, and into your life. Below is the full text from 1 Timothy 3:1–7. This pericope is often used specifically for leaders in the church; however, there is nothing wrong with using it as a standard for leaders in the workplace, in the home, or in the community.

> Here is a trustworthy saying: Whoever aspires to be an overseer desires a noble task. Now the overseer is to be above reproach, faithful to his wife, temperate, self-controlled, respectable, hospitable, able to teach, not given to drunkenness, not violent but gentle, not quarrelsome, not a lover of money. He must manage his own family well and see that his children obey him, and he must do so in a manner worthy of full respect. (If anyone does not know how to manage his own family, how can he take care of God's church?) He must not be a recent convert, or he may become conceited and fall under the same judgment as the devil. He must also have a good reputation with outsiders, so that he will not fall into disgrace and into the devil's trap.

Recently, I met with a manager at a well-known Christian organization. Prior to our meeting, his car did not start. Upon arrival, he commented how his car battery needed a jumpstart and there was a lady walking in the parking lot of his workplace. He commented about how she worked for a Christian organization yet did not help him when he deliberately asked if he could use her car to jump his battery. It is important to realize that Christians are not perfect people; most will humbly admit they are sinners trying to live a better life. So, expecting a church or Christian workplace to be full of perfect people is unrealistic. There are no perfect people. Being hospitable is the act of going out of one's way to help another person. Being gentle, according to Thompson (2021), infers the leader is not a bully. Not being a lover of money incites the act of pride or greed found in the Seven Deadly Sins, the Seven Sins God Hates (Proverbs 6:16–19), and the Ten Commandments (Exodus 20, Deuteronomy 5). Leaders should also manage their households competently and keep their children under control. This is a business practice seen over and over as leaders are expected to take care of their family first before exerting energy on their work or extracurricular activities. The story of J. Robert Ouimet is a great example of a business leader who made a mess of his home life (2013, p. 8). He owned and operated a frozen food conglomerate in Canada as a successful businessman, yet he turned to alcohol and neglected his wife and children. Searching for answers, he made many pilgrimages to Calcutta to visit Mother Teresa. Through prayer and her guidance, he radically changed the way he lived. She told him to first take care of his wife. That was his top priority. Secondly, he was to take care of his children. Thirdly, he was to tend to the needs of his 400 employees.

Winston (2018) exegetically studied the Beatitudes (Matthew 5:3–12, Luke 6:20–23). His quest was to document virtues that organizations could use for evaluating employees, employee development, and seeking new employees. The Beatitudes in Matthew 5 read,

> Blessed are the poor in spirit, for theirs is the kingdom of heaven.
> Blessed are those who mourn, for they will be comforted.
> Blessed are the meek, for they will inherit the earth.
> Blessed are those who hunger and thirst for righteousness, for they will be filled.
> Blessed are the merciful, for they will be shown mercy.
> Blessed are the pure in heart, for they will see God.
> Blessed are the peacemakers, for they will be called children of God.
> Blessed are those who are persecuted because of righteousness, for theirs is the kingdom of heaven.
> Blessed are you when people insult you, persecute you and falsely say all kinds of evil against you because of me.
> Rejoice and be glad, because great is your reward in heaven, for in the same way they persecuted the prophets who were before you.

At first, it may be difficult to understand how these Beatitudes relate to organizational soft skills, but Winston breaks them down in an easy-to-understand way. For example, blessed are the poor in spirit refers to being teachable and humble. Winston (2018) explained that blessed are those who mourn refers to a person mourning death or, in more general terms, a person being sad. Winston and Tucker (2011) wrote that this virtue shows a concern for others somewhere between the vices of disregarding and controlling. Blessed are the meek refers to a person being gentle and maintaining self-control. When an employee hungers and thirsts for righteousness, they are laying "the foundation for customer service, treatment of employees, and service to the community" (Winston, 2018, p. 16). Blessed are the merciful refers to justice, grace, and mercy. In the workplace, these soft skills require patience as the manager seeks first to understand the situation and then apply a disciplinary action fairly. Blessed are the pure in heart relates to the mission of the work itself and the calling or purpose of the employee in doing the work. Winston explained, "if the work is not a calling then don't do it and if the work is a calling then shout it from the mountain tops and tell the world the important purpose it has" (p. 26). Kilroy (2008) developed an instrument to measure seven leadership behaviors using the Beatitudes. This instrument could be used with employee development curriculum.

The Fruit of the Spirit (Galatians 5, 22–23) is another great resource for leaders and followers to enhance their soft skills. The fruits are love, joy, peace, patience, kindness, goodness, faithfulness, gentleness, and self-control. In a 2018 study using the Fruit of the Spirit Scale (Bocarnea et al., 2018), I found that each of the nine fruits were related to employee engagement, job satisfaction, organizational commitment, and organizational spirituality. Love predicted employee engagement; love, peace, and faithfulness predicted job satisfaction; love, joy, peace, and gentleness predicted organizational commitment; and joy, patience, and self-control predicted organizational spirituality

(Dean, 2019). Practically, love can be shown in many ways in the workplace. Talking to employees, being real and authentic, genuinely caring for others, knowing employee names and the names of people they care for, inquiring about life outside of work, and sending cards to acknowledge important events like birthdays are all ways to show love. Joy can be shown as leaders and followers celebrate accomplishments, work anniversaries, attained goals, birthdays, and success. Peace can be demonstrated by building trust, establishing respect, constructing support, and cultivating collaboration. Patience is shown with time: be slow to anger, take time to talk about more than work, slow down to make sure others understand before forging ahead, and participate in long-term planning. Faithfulness refers to sticking to the task, showing up, and following through. Gentleness is shown with true humility, communication, and trust. Self-control is a focus on virtuous values requiring organization, planning, structure, and proactive use of time.

Conclusion

In conclusion, this chapter focused on the history of how soft skills have emerged as a monumental gap to fill in the twenty-first century and practical ways to accomplish this daunting, yet urgent task. This chapter explored issues leading up to this phenomenon and practical approaches for improving soft skills consciously for better collaboration at work. This chapter presented two instruments to measure soft skills from the perspective of the Beatitudes and the Fruit of the Spirit. Several lists of soft skills were provided to offer direction for training and development departments, along with high schools, colleges, and universities with the act of customizing curricula to fill the soft skill gap. Urgency is placed on the value of more time with family and more time in church to help develop soft skills, while less time should be spent on technology and media found to be morally repulsive, indecent, or reprehensible. The attention to soft skills has emerged as a national crisis as more people are taking to the streets and are publicly displaying cruel and unusual behavior as a means of social interaction. This is the time for families, schools, and workplaces to put the train back on the track and man the ship once again in an effort to repair the moral fabric of America through the promotion of soft skills.

References

Andreoni, J., Di Girolamo, A., List, J. A., Mackevicius, C., & Samek, A. (2020; 2019). Risk preferences of children and adolescents in relation to gender, cognitive skills, soft skills, and executive functions. *Journal of Economic Behavior & Organization, 179*, 729–742. https://doi.org/10.1016/j.jebo.2019.05.002

Bocarnea, M. C., Henson, J. D., Huizing, R. L., Mahan, M. L., & Winston, B. E. (2018). *Evaluating employee performance through christian virtues*. Palgrave Macmillan.

Butler, J. D. (2021). *African american millennials' experience with church attendance apathy and family religious values* (Order No. 28769703). Available from ProQuest Dissertations & Theses Global; ProQuest One Academic. (2587865474).

Conger, J. A., & Kanungo, R. N. (1987). Toward a behavioral theory of charismatic leadership in organizational settings. *The Academy of Management Review, 12*(4), 637–647. https://doi.org/10.2307/258069

Dean, D. (2019). Integration of Christian values in the workplace. *The Journal of Biblical Perspectives in Leadership, 9*(1). Retrieved April 23, 2022, from https://www.regent.edu/acad/global/publications/jbpl/vol9no1/Vol9Iss1_JBPL_Full_Issue.pdf

Fishel, A. (2020). *Harvard edcast: The benefit of family mealtime.* Harvard Graduate School of Education. Retrieved April 18, 2022, from https://www.gse.harvard.edu/news/20/04/harvard-edcast-benefit-family-mealtime#:~:text=Family%20therapist%20Anne%20Fishel%20says,being%20hugely%20beneficial%20for%20kids.

Galov, N. (2022). *20 eye-twitching tech addiction facts for 2022.* WebTribunal. Retrieved April 23, 2022, from https://webtribunal.net/blog/tech-addiction-facts/#gref

Heckman, J. J., & Kautz, T. (2012). Hard evidence on soft skills. *Labour Economics, 19*(4), 451–464. https://doi.org/10.1016/j.labeco.2012.05.014

Jones, J. M. (2021, November 20). *U.S. church membership falls below majority for first time.* Gallup.com. Retrieved April 18, 2022, from https://news.gallup.com/poll/341963/church-membership-falls-below-majority-first-time.aspx#:~:text=WASHINGTON%2C%20D.C.%20%2D%2D%20Americans'%20membership,2018%20and%2070%25%20in%201999.

Kikon, D., & Karlsson, B. G. (2020). Light skin and soft skills: Training indigenous migrants for the hospitality sector in india. *Ethnos, 85*(2), 258–275. https://doi.org/10.1080/00141844.2018.1543717

Kilroy, J. J. (2008). Development of seven leadership behavior scales based upon the seven leadership values inspired by the beatitudes. ProQuest. UMI: AAT 3340922.

Millar, A., Devaney, J., & Butler, M. (2018; 2019). Emotional intelligence: Challenging the perceptions and efficacy of 'Soft skills' in policing incidents of domestic abuse involving children. *Journal of Family Violence, 34*(6), 577–588. https://doi.org/10.1007/s10896-018-0018-9

Ouimet, J. R. (2013). *Everything has been loaned to you: The biography of a Transformational Ceo.* St. Pauls.

Pew Research Center. (2020). *Parenting approaches and concerns related to digital devices.* Retrieved April 30, 2022, from https://www.pewresearch.org/internet/2020/07/28/parenting-approaches-and-concerns-related-to-digital-devices/

Shek, D. T. L., Leung, J. T. Y., & Merrick, J. (2017). Paradigm shift in youth development: Development of "soft skills" in adolescents. *International Journal on Disability and Human Development, 16*(4), 337–338. https://dx.doi.org.ezproxy.regent.edu//https://doi.org/10.1515/ijdhd-2017-7001

Succi, C., & Canovi, M. (2020). Soft skills to enhance graduate employability: Comparing students and employers' perceptions. *Studies in Higher Education (Dorchester-on-Thames), 45*(9), 1834–1847. https://doi.org/10.1080/03075079.2019.1585420

Thompson, C. (2021, January 2). *Why 'soft skills' are a biblical requirement.* Lifeway Research. Retrieved April 18, 2022, from https://research.lifeway.com/2020/01/28/why-soft-skills-are-a-biblical-requirement/

Touloumakos, A. K. (2020). Expanded yet restricted: A mini review of the soft skills literature. *Frontiers in Psychology, 11*, 2207–2207. https://doi.org/10.3389/fpsyg.2020.02207

Trofholz, A. C., Thao, M. S., Donley, M., Smith, M., Isaac, H., & Berge, J. M. (2018; 2017). Family meals then and now: A qualitative investigation of intergenerational transmission of family meal practices in a racially/ethnically diverse and immigrant population. *Appetite, 121,* 163–172. https://doi.org/10.1016/j.appet.2017.11.084

Van Buren, A. (1970, June 6). *Dear Abby.* Palm Springs and Coachella Valley News. Retrieved April 23, 2022, from https://www.desertsun.com/

Winston, B. E. (2018). The virtues from the beatitudes. *Biblical principles of hiring and developing employees* (pp. 1–41). Springer International Publishing. https://doi.org/10.1007/978-3-319-70527-9_1

Winston, B., & Tucker, P. (2011). The beatitudes as leadership virtues. *The Journal of Virtues & Leadership, 2*(1). Regent University, School of Business & Leadership, Virginia Beach, VA 23464. Retrieved April 18, 2022, from https://www.regent.edu/acad/global/publications/jvl/vol1_iss1/home.htm?q=&s

Zainal-Abidin, Y., Awang-Hashim, R., & Nordin, H. (2019). Amir's life story: Resilience and other soft skills development to thrive, despite vulnerable beginnings. *The Qualitative Report, 24*(12), 2934–2953. https://ezproxy.regent.edu/login?url=https://www.proquest.com/scholarly-journals/amirs-life-story-resilience-other-soft-skills/docview/2331238850/se-2

Meaning at Work: Dimensions, Implications and Recommendations

Preethi Misha and Marius van Dijke

INTRODUCTION

He who has a why in his life can live with almost any how
                                                                Nietzsche

Victor Frankl's (1985) Man's Search for Meaning brings to fore the cardinal issue of the psychological significance of meaning in life (Kasler et al., 2012). Rooted in existential psychology (Isik & Uzbe, 2015), research on meaning in life has served as a central point of interest for understanding human behavior (Emmons, 2003). Previous research has defined meaning in life as individuals' global evaluation of the significance of their life (Martela & Steger, 2016). Steger et al. (2006) define meaning in life as "the sense made of, and significance felt regarding, the nature of one's being and existence" (p. 81). Studies in positive psychology concur meaning in life as an element of happiness and life satisfaction (Park et al., 2009). In this chapter, we extend this literature on meaning in life to understand the phenomena of meaning at the workplace. Given that work serves as an increasingly prominent domain of life

---

P. Misha (✉)
Nottingham Business School, Nottingham Trent University, Nottingham, UK
e-mail: preethi.misha@ntu.ac.uk

M. van Dijke
Rotterdam School of Management, Erasmus University, Rotterdam, The Netherlands

© The Author(s), under exclusive license to Springer Nature Switzerland AG 2023
J. Marques (ed.), *The Palgrave Handbook of Fulfillment, Wellness, and Personal Growth at Work*,
https://doi.org/10.1007/978-3-031-35494-6_3

(Hoffmann-Burdzińska & Rutkowska, 2015; Rapaport et al., 1998), it stands to reason that people will pursue the experience that their work is meaningful and significant. However, literature on the meaning at work has largely looked at how organizations can make work more engaging and interesting to its employees, and consequently, the benefits of perceived meaning at the workplace. Despite the large stream of research that focuses on how organizations can provide meaning to workers, studies also acknowledge that the extent to which organization members actually experience meaning at work can vary. In line with these studies, we provide a review of the dimensions of meaning at work that is the presence, the absence and the search for meaning at work. We also unpack the implications of these dimensions and provide recommendations for workers, leaders and organizations to support organization members' meaning at work.

Meaning at work is understood as organizational members' subjective perceptions that their work has purpose, significance, and impacts others in a positive way (Pratt & Ashforth, 2003; Steger et al., 2012). Scholarship on understanding the nature, determinants and processes of meaning at work continues to flourish as employees expect their work to meet not only economic needs but also social and psychological needs (Rosso et al., 2010). Multiple examples can be brought to bear on the pressing need for research on meaning at work in organizational contexts. For instance, a survey by BetterUp (2018) found that, on average, employees indicated to be willing to give up to a quarter of their total future lifetime earnings in exchange for meaningful work. The survey also suggested that work organizations that address their members' search for meaning unlock a plethora of benefits such as increased employee commitment, productivity and engagement. In line with these findings, organizational scholars have demonstrated large correlations between perceiving one's work as meaningful with a number of outcomes such as higher engagement (May et al., 2004), organizational identification (Pratt et al., 2006) and empowerment (Spreitzer, 1995). Further, the Job Characteristics Theory (Hackman & Oldham, 1976) finds perceiving one's work to be meaningful to be a key dimension that positively impacts work performance, job satisfaction and employee well-being. Despite these advancements in research that investigates the positive consequences of finding meaning at work, research that explores the implications of the contrary, that is, the absence of meaning or the quest of meaning at work, is comparatively limited. In the upcoming sections, we provide conceptualizations of meaning at work, followed by a review of the dimensions of meaning at work, and conclude with recommendations for not only organizations but also to individuals to enhance their experiences of meaning at work.

Literature Review

Meaning, Meaning in Life, and Meaning at Work

Baumeister (1991, p. 15) defined meaning as a "mental representation of possible relationships among things, events, and relationships. Thus, meaning connects things". Meaning thus refers to what something signifies and pertains to the cognitive process of meaning-making whereby people interpret, analyze and understand their experiences (Allan et al., 2019). Meaning in life, understood as "the ontological significance of life from the point of view of the experiencing individual" (Crumbaugh & Maholick, 1964, p. 201), is often considered as a positive variable which can be deemed as a sign of wellbeing (Ryff, 1989), as an enabler of adaptive coping (Park & Folkman, 1997) and even as an indicator of therapeutic growth (Crumbaugh & Maholick, 1964; Frankl, 1965). Baumeister (1991) explains that a more semantic understanding takes the form of "What does my life mean?" and used the concept of meaning in life to denote the lasting effects that help in building self-worth in a person's life.

Meaning at the workplace is defined as the subjective experience that one's work has purpose, significance, allows for personal growth and contributes to the greater good (Steger et al., 2012). The meaning at work literature identifies two important sources from which meaning can be derived at the workplace—what I do, and with whom I do it (Fox, 1980; Guevara & Ord, 1996; Hall et al., 2013; Morin, 2008; Ros et al., 1999). The "what I do" aspect concerns itself with the employee finding meaning in or relating to their job tasks, while the "with whom I do" denotes that employees derive meaning through relationships and interactions with leaders, colleagues, families and stakeholders (Pratt & Ashforth, 2003; Hall et al., 2013). Supporting this assertion, the interpersonal sensemaking model (Wrzesniewski et al., 2003) proposes that in their quest for meaning at work, organizational members typically look up to significant others such as co-workers and leaders who through a variety of ways such as communicating the organizational vision (van Knippenberg, 2020) or via job-crafting opportunities (Ghadi et al., 2015) can provide followers with a sense that their work activities and contributions matter and are meaningful (e.g., Kotter, 1999; Podolny et al., 2005; Raelin, 2003; Selznick, 1957). Experiencing meaning in one's work intimately ties to understanding "who am I" thereby relating directly to developing identity at work (Johns, 2010).

Meaning in Life Versus Meaning at Work

Although Baumeister's inquiry primarily revolved around meaning in life, scholars have argued that Baumeister's theorizations also analogously apply to investigating the phenomena of meaning at the workplace (Dik et al., 2013; Hall et al., 2013; Steger et al., 2006). The authors elucidate that given individuals spend most of their waking hours at the workplace, work contexts can be seen as a major determinant of an individual's identity (Dik et al., 2013; Hall et al., 2013; Steger et al., 2006). Further, Hall et al. (2013) analyzed empirical data from the '5C' global study of careers that comprised of qualitative analysis across eleven countries. The study found three universal factors representing career success, namely job satisfaction, career success and the job itself. The authors link these findings with Baumeister's principles of meaning by suggesting that a) job satisfaction directly contributes to achieving meaning at work and can be based on the attainment of job-related goals, b) achievement lends itself to perceptions of meaning and self-worth especially when achievement can lead to a particular position in the social hierarchy and c) when the work itself is designed to have social impact and significance, it can lead to increased sense of efficacy and self-worth. Thus, branching out from the idea that meaning at work is an individual's interpretation of what work means to him or her (Wrzesniewski et al., 2003), Hall and colleagues (2013) suggest that meaning at the workplace unfolds when employees find their work to be personally significant, worthwhile, purposeful and valuable, a conceptualization that has received consensus in the literature.

Meaning at the workplace is understood as the subjective experience that one's work has purpose, significance, allows for personal growth and contributes to the greater good (Steger et al., 2012). Conceptually, meaning at work is considered a sub-domain of "meaning" that acts as a potential source of meaning in life (Allan et al., 2015; Emmons, 2003). Based on this, Hall et al. (2013) argue that the meaning a person achieves in his or her life would be somewhat correlated to the meaning achieved at work. Several studies evidence the relationship between meaning in life and meaning at work. When asked to indicate the sources of their life meaning, common responses included relationships, work, religion and service (Baum & Stewart, 1990; Ebersole & Devogler, 1981; Emmons, 2003). Fegg et al. (2007) conducted a nationwide meaning in life study in Germany and the results of their empirical research supported the assertion that participants consistently report work as a major source of meaning. Allan et al. (2015) observe that few studies have examined both meaning in life and at work in the same study; however, Duffy et al. (2013) found a correlation of 0.49 between the two variables in working professionals. A multitude of studies have also exemplified how well-being in life can affect meaning at the workplace. For instance, Bonebright, Clay and Ankemann (2000)'s study demonstrates how workaholism and work-life conflict negatively correlate with meaning in life whereas work enjoyment is positively correlated with meaning in life. The authors also note that adolescents who report purposeful career goals also report higher meaning in life. Thus, work forms a significant part of people's lives (Hall, 2008); therefore, work has certain elements that are in common with the other facets of life, thereby contributing to a person's entire identity (Hall et al., 2013). In summary, there is some reason for researchers to believe that experiencing meaning at work translates into greater meaning in life, and it is essential to embrace this dichotomy where it is not possible to view a person's work as distinct from one's life.

The Presence, Absence and the Drive to Find Meaning at Work: Implications on Well-Being

Steger et al. (2012) note that perceptions of meaning can be operationalized by two contrapositions, namely a "presence of meaning" or a "search for meaning". Other scholars point toward an additional dimension, that of experiencing the lack or an absence of meaning (see Bailey & Madden, 2016; Lips-Wiersma & Morris, 2009). In comparison with the presence of meaning at work, the implications of experiencing a lack of meaning at work (Bailey & Madden, 2016) and searching for meaning at work (Steger et al., 2012) have received lesser research attention. While some researchers believe that searching for meaning is a very basic and fundamental aspect of human life that pushes individuals to pursue their central human endeavor (e.g., Frankl, 1963), other researchers conceptualize the search for meaning as a warning sign that meaning has been lost (Baumeister, 1991) and interchangeably use the search for meaning with the absence of meaning. Critics argue that the search for meaning although stems from a perceived lack of meaning in life is always marked by drive and orientation toward finding meaning in life. In contrast to the absence of meaning, studies prove that the search for meaning can be an adaptive indicator (Davis et al., 1998; King et al., 2016; Mascaro & Rosen, 2005). Despite the widely accepted notion that the search for meaning can be regarded as simply the absence of meaning (Klinger, 1998), Steger et al., (2008a, 2008b) reviewed factor-analytic and multitrait-multimethod matrix (MTMM) evidence that indicates they should be differentiated. In the current chapter, we build on the aforementioned views and differentiate the two constructs.

Presence of Meaning at Work

Research in the area of positive psychology considers the presence of meaning as an element of happiness and satisfaction (Park et al., 2009; Petersen & Seligman, 2004). Building on Steger et al. (2012), the presence of meaning at work can be understood as the experience where one perceives their work to have purpose, significance, allowing for personal growth and contributing to the greater good. Experiencing a presence of meaning is strongly associated with well-being and thriving (Scollon & King, 2004), is associated with positive aspects such as happiness and well-being (Cohen & Cairns, 2012), and has been suggested to positively influence self-worth (Baumeister, 1991), lower depression, higher positive affect and greater life satisfaction (King et al., 2016; Steger et al., 2006). Perceptions of a strong presence of meaning at work relates to organization members seeing their work to be worthy, characterized by coherence, direction as well as experiencing a good sense of belonging

(Schnell, 2009), a personal sense of uplifting directedness (Rodríguez-Carvajal et al., 2019), less dependency upon leaders to provide meaning at work (Lopez et al., 2015), happiness and well-being (Janicke-Bowles et al., 2019; Myers, 2013), positive self-image (Torrey & Duffy, 2012) and higher levels of psychological well-being (Arnold et al., 2007; Khumalo et al., 2014).

Related studies have found that a correlation between the presence of sense of belonging to be a significant indicator of the presence of meaning at work (e.g. Noble-Carr et al., 2014). Vos (2018) adds that being socially connected, belonging to a specific community and confirming to the group's tradition is an important experience of feeling meaningful. Steger and Dik (2009) add that those with a high presence of meaning at work are often much more engaged and enthusiastic at work and display more citizenship behaviors owing to their commitment to the organization. A related example can be seen in a meaning in life survey where individuals who scored higher on the presence (versus search) for meaning in their life indicated that they spend more time helping those in need and spending as well as more time with children. These participants also identified more strongly with being a giver than a taker (Baumeister et al., 2013). Extending this example to the workplace, Grant (2007) states that employees who achieve high meaning at work want their efforts to make the organization a better place. A high presence of meaning at work is often accompanied by feelings of connections with work members and have demonstrated higher levels of interpersonal and organizational citizenship (Johnson & Chang, 2006).

Absence of Meaning at Work

The absence of meaning often takes the form of a situation referred to as anomie—where a lack of connection exists between one's personal worldviews and the organization's values (Tsahuridu, 2006). Understood as a 'sense of social malintegration' (Cohen, 1993, p. 344), the absence of meaning at work has said to lead to disengagement (Atkouf, 1994; May et al., 2004) and is primarily characterized by feelings of boredom (Ojica, 2022), powerlessness, low intrinsic fulfillment and self-estrangement (Sarros et al., 2002; Stein et al., 2019). Lepisto and Pratt (2017) add that the absence of meaning at work comprises perceptions of 'being used for purposes other than one's own' (p. 105) and can take form of perceptions that one's work is pointless, and feelings of isolation and a lack of supportive relationships (Bailey & Madden, 2016), work alienation or feeling of uncertainty about one's work (Stein et al., 2019). Sarros et al. (2002) further add that lacking meaning at work can also take the form the inability to match one's personal contributions at the workplace to the organizational vision and a larger purpose in general.

Early scholarship that tacitly explored the absence of meaning at work took the form of remedying the ensuing negative effects instead of exploring the nature and dimensions of the phenomena itself. These studies included recommendations of making work enjoyable and engaging with the understanding that meaning at work stems solely from the work domain. As research in the area of meaning at work grew, a number of researchers acknowledged that work design or work itself formed one of the three dimensions of meaning at work, with the individual and relationships with others comprising two additional dimensions of meaning at work. This is why Beadle (2017, 2019) takes into consideration theories of motivation and suggests that irrespective of how well a firm designs a job, experiences of meaning at work will always vary. Beadle (2017) further argues that jobs designed in line with the job characteristics model that are said to enhance meaning at work have not always succeeded, and attributes this problem to the fact that the design of jobs has the needs of the firm in mind, whereas perception of meaning at work stems at an individual level, that is, from first understanding what is important to ourselves. Similarly, Rosso et al. (2010) postulate that the way people experience their work and hence the variations in peoples' perceptions of meaning at work is highly driven by their underlying values, beliefs and motivations.

The foundational work on the negative effects of perceptions of the lack of meaning at work on employee well-being can be seen in the works of Lucas and Kornhauser (1966) and Seeman (1967). As discussed earlier, early studies responding to these negative effects, however, turned their attention toward recommendations to make work that is interesting and creative and interesting, thereby benefiting their well-being (Savvides & Stavrou, 2020). The authors note that it was only with the introduction of the job characteristics theory (Hackman & Oldham, 1976) and the self-determination theory (Ryan & Deci, 2001) that research began to address intrinsically meaningful work by acknowledging factors beyond the work domain such as the self and the role of significant others (e.g., peers and leaders) that determine the extent of meaning at work.

Search for Meaning at Work

According to Steger et al. (2008a), the construct of search for meaning is a complex one, both conceptually and empirically. The search for meaning is understood as the process of striving for one's understanding concerning "the meaning, significance, and purpose" of his or her life (Steger et al., 2008a, 2008b, p. 43). The search for meaning in life involves identity formulation and therefore ranks among the most significant evolving issues for individuals (Ho et al., 2010; Kiang & Fuligni, 2010). In adolescents, the search for meaning is also an important protective factor in school-to-work transitions (Fry, 1998; To & Sung, 2017). Isik and Uzbe (2015, p. 588) define the search for meaning as "people's will to build or foster significance, meaning, and purpose". Victor Frankl's 'man's search for meaning' (1985) exemplifies that a search for meaning is the primary motivation in one's life and not a secondary justification of visceral drives.

Dik et al. (2013) shed light by explaining how meaning at work is for most people a central part of their identity, which can be reflected when they are asked what do you do, the response to which is often defined by work, i.e., I am ___. The authors add that for some, work can also be a barometer for testing their self-worth. In 2009, Kelly Services, a leading recruitment firm, surveyed approximately 100,000 workers across Europe, North America and the Asia Pacific region and asked, "Would you take a lesser role or lower wage if you felt that your work contributed to something more important or more meaningful to you or your organization?", to which 51% of the respondents answered positively. A decade later, the results from their 2019 survey reveal that 77% of committed workforce (in comparison with the overall workforce) indicated meaning at the workplace correlated with higher levels of commitment. Positive psychology studies associate the search for meaning with anxiety and strain (Steger et al., 2008a).

Research suggests that individuals may actively seek life meaning when their needs are unfulfilled (e.g., Baumeister, 1991; Klinger, 1998), thus suggesting that the search for meaning is linked with undesirable emotions (e.g., frustration, Schultze & Miller, 2004) such as anxiety and strain (Steger et al., 2008a, 2008b). Related studies show that the search for meaning in life can be associated with numerous negative outcomes. For example, analyses of 154 undergraduate students from a US university revealed that the search for meaning correlates with depression, neuroticism and several negative emotions (Steger et al., 2006). Researchers (e.g., Kiang & Fuligni, 2010; Li et al., 2021) add that the process of searching for meaning entails uncertainty and stress. Empirical studies have also shown that the search for meaning relates to increased dependence on other individuals and anxiety (Lopez et al., 2015), less life satisfaction (Park et al., 2010), greater anxiety, rumination, depression (Adams, 2000; Steger et al., 2006, 2008a) and suicidal ideations (Kleiman & Beaver, 2013). A limitation, however, is all of the aforementioned empirical studies examined searching for meaning in life and not at work.

Research acknowledging employees' desire to find meaning in their work is increasingly receiving impetus. For instance, the relationship between searching for meaning in life and subjective well-being is debated in the literature. There are currently two opposing views regarding their association. On the one hand, the meaning-making model (Park, 2013) assumes that individuals who encounter negative life events may search for meaning which serves as a resilience factor that moderates the negative effect of adverse events on subjective well-being. Some scholars also assume that searching for meaning encourages people to overcome challenges, seek new opportunities and that it fuels their desire to understand and organize experiences, leading to increased adjustment, especially when people experience negative events (Frankl, 1963; Vohs et al., 2019). Other scholars have argued that the search for meaning only occurs in individuals whose needs have been frustrated and should thus be seen as an indicator of psychological dysfunction (Baumeister, 1991; Klinger, 1998). To reconcile these opposing views, some have proposed that searching helps people who have experienced distress to cope with stressful and adverse situations, but that searching for meaning may be harmful for those not facing frustrated situations as it may represent a loss of life goals (Damásio & Koller, 2015). Maddi (1967) adds that when those searching for meaning are unable to do so, they experience what is called an existential vacuum, which when confronted by stressful situations can lead to cognitive behaviors such as devaluing personal goals, disengagement from activity and dull and depressive state of mind. Proulx (2013) goes to the extent of asserting that human beings are the only animals with the power to forego survival (via suicide) if their meaning impulses remain unsatisfied.

In contrast to the aforementioned review, an important point to note is that related studies also show that the relationship between the search for meaning and diminished well-being can actually differ across countries and cultures. For instance, the search for meaning was found to have a positive (rather than negative) relationship with mental health in some collectivist cultures (e.g., Datu, 2015). Related studies further demonstrate this inconsistency where participants' search for meaning was negatively related to the presence of meaning between US participants, but was found to be positively related to the presence of meaning between Japanese individuals. Such an inconsistency indicates that the concept of search for meaning can evoke distinctive interpretations in different cultures and may also moderate cultural effects on what exactly constitutes as meaning (Steger et al., 2008b).

Discussion

When children are asked of their potential future occupations, they pronounce them in terms of what they will be (artists, doctors, firemen, etc.), something that exceeds merely what they will do for a living (Ariely et al., 2008). Such thinking holds true across all age groups—for instance, "What do you do?" has become as common a part and parcel of an introduction as the archaic "How do you do?". There is an increased awareness that work is more than promotions, pay rises and sustenance (Dik et al., 2013). The fusion of work with meaning, purpose-driven lives and pursuing beyond-the-self goals are hallmarks of meaning at the workplace (Dik et al., 2013). Research suggests that a number of purpose driven and meaningful elements such as respecting and valuing employees (Byrne, Pitts, Chiaburu & Steiner, 2011), providing autonomy (Dik et al., 2013) and clarity around how each employees' attributes uniquely add value at the workplace (Dik et al., 2009). Meaning at the workplace is also socially constructed with employees striving to create collective identity, one that is complemented by individual goals aligned with organizational goals, plus work tasks that can feed a broader purpose (van Knippenberg, 2020). This is why the upcoming section not only includes recommendations derived from the work design literature, but also focuses on three other elements, namely the self, others and purpose-driven work.

'Self' and Meaning

Hedonia and Eudaimonia. Many of us have asked ourselves: What makes my job worthwhile? Is my job meaningful? Huta (2015) contends that the responses we develop to these questions shape our priorities, goals, values and choices. In conceptions of the ideal job as characterized by a sense of purpose and meaning, the two perspectives that have figured most prominently in the literature are the hedonic view and the eudaimonic view (Ryan & Deci, 2001). Hedonia is broadly understood as man's pursual of happiness, life satisfaction and reducing negative effects (Russo-Netzer, 2018; Ryan et al., 2008). On the other hand, eudaimonia supports the notion that well-being is achieved when individuals live in accordance with their authentic selves, characterized by self-actualization, meaning in life, purpose, individual growth (Ryff et al., 2004; Waterman, 1993) and commitment toward shared goals and values at the group level (Massimini & Delle Fave, 2000; Russo-Netzer, 2018). Russo-Netzer (2018) observes that while hedonia addresses more immediate and fundamental needs, eudaimonia can be seen as a sort of a higher pleasure, one that enables individuals to develop their potential and address virtues, values and vision at both individual and collective levels. Therefore, it can be understood that hedonia is generally related to personal satisfaction and eudaimonia is associated with both personal satisfaction and outlooks on life that go beyond self-interest (Peterson et al., 2005). Huta and Ryan (2010) note that although empirically and theoretically distinct, both hedonia and eudaimonia are considered to have complementary functions. Russo-Netzer (2018) adds that a combination of both eudaimonic and hedonic pursuits is linked to optimal functioning, as reflected in more complete and comprehensive well-being and mental health than results from either pursuit on its own. Russo-Netzer (2018) and Huta and Ryan (2010) note that hedonia and eudemonia in combination guide individuals' orientations as well as motives for actions, experiences, behaviors or activities. Despite the two perspectives being discussed for over 2,000 years by philosophers, including ancient Greek philosophers Aristotle and Aristippus, and more recently by psychologists and psychiatrists such as Maslow, Jung and Freud, it is time to consider more systematically how these concepts might be applied in practice.

Huta (2015) conducted a systematic review on hedonia and eudemonia and unpacked the implications at the workplace. The author recommends one way of addressing hedonic and eudemonic concerns is by being guided by big questions: How does this bigger picture operate? What is its purpose? What matters in this bigger context? Huta (2015) adds that searching answers to contribution to the bigger picture is a central task of adulthood and helps restore meaning at an individual level. Eudemonic theories of well-being which focus on an individual's psychological strengths and personal growth advocate that a search for meaning is important and finding meaning results in maximizing one's potentials and work performance (see Deci & Ryan, 2008; Maslow, 1971). More recently, Thorsteinsen and Vittersø (2018) conducted an empirical study and found that the eudaimonic part of well-being is vital to ignite and sustain goal pursuit processes and in contrast, hedonic part of well-being is more related to the outcome phase—a combination of which keeps employees driven and content.

Understanding One's Work Orientation

Work orientation is defined as employees' beliefs about the role of work in their life and is largely reflected in their feelings about work, behaviors at the workplace, and the types of goals they strive to meet through working (Wrzesniewski, 1999). In simple, work orientations are internalized evaluations that employees conduct about what makes their particular work worth doing (Pratt et al., 2013). Out of the many theories that explain work orientation (e.g., extrinsic vs intrinsic), the dominant model in the literature is the tripartite model of work orientation comprising of job, career and calling. The management literature describes those with job orientation as individuals that seek out jobs that provide financial security where work provides meaning as long as it provides the resources that are required for activities outside of work. Despite this understanding of "work to live" attitude, Bellah (1985) suggested that individuals with a job orientation value hard work and individual discipline. In a similar vein, those with a career orientation derive meaning at the workplace through records of achievement, promotion, perceived career success and status (Baumeister, 1991). The final aspect of the model, calling as an orientation, subsumes the employee into a community of practice whose activity is characterized by meaning and value in itself rather than profits or work outputs; a calling therefore links the individual not just to the fellow workers, but also to the larger community (Bellah, 1985). Work calling tends to involve two main orientations or elements, namely a serving orientation that involves helping others because of moral duty (Bunderson & Thompson, 2009) and a craftsmanship orientation that involves fulfillment from the work itself (Pratt et al., 2013). Understanding one's orientation in relation to job, career or calling can clarify ambiguity in relation to what one seeks, and such clarity can thereby help channel efforts toward achieving meaning at the workplace.

Dual Reflexivity

Bangali and Guichard (2012) suggest that one way in which employees can achieve meaning at work is through dual reflexivity. Dual reflexivity is described as a mode of relating the self (as a future subject) to the self (as a present object) by taking the perspective of a certain state of perfection or of a certain ideal that the person wants to achieve (Erikson, 1959; Lacan, 1977). The advantage of this form of reflexivity is that it leads the employee to define and implement behaviors that aim at achieving this notion of ideal state by moving intentionally from the presently experienced situation to the desired future situation. An example for this can be seen in athletes—it is because the young high-level athletes daydreamt about themselves on an Olympic podium that they made the efforts required to get there (Pouyaud et al., 2017). This notion is also supported by Foucault (1982) who endorses individuals to constitute themselves as objects to themselves, from the standpoint of a certain ideal they wish to achieve. If implemented in practitioner trainings, individuals would typically define and subsequently implement experiences or behaviors to achieve a certain state in connection with their standards of this ideal. Empirical research supports this idea and proposes that this ideal generally corresponds to a certain expected identity formation related to either a certain end state or a particular character's image with whom they identify (Pouyaud & colleagues, 2017). This emerging mode of relating to oneself and to one's present and potential experiences entails an identification with the internalized image and establishes a summation of a certain self.

'Others' and Meaning

Leaders as Meaning-Givers. In its essence, the most fundamental element of leadership entails creating a vision for the organization and articulating this vision to give a sense of meaning and purpose to organizational members (Lloyd & Trapp, 1999; Raelin, 2003, 2006; Selznick, 1957; van Knippenberg, 2020). The provision of meaning as a core function of leadership is thus common theme in leadership theorizations (Eisenbeiß & Boerner, 2013; Fruhen et al., 2022; Sosik, 2000). As early as 1989, Conger described leaders as "meaning-makers" referring to leaders giving expression to what members of the group undertake to accomplish in their work together (Raelin, 2006; Ulrich, 2011). Despite the general theoretical recognition that leaders function as the primary sources of followers' meaning at work (Conger, 1989; Gioia & Chittipeddi, 1991; Selznick, 1957, van Knippenberg, 2020), empirical explorations around the extent to which followers experience or in contrast, lack or search for meaning at work remain overdue. Substantiating leaders' roles in providing contextual cues, van Knippenberg (2020) explains how the core role of leadership in organizations is mobilizing and motivating people for the pursuit of the organization's purpose. Aligning individuals' purpose with organizations' purpose infers strong value connotations in the sense that it intertwines how meaningful and value-based the contributions of organizational members are (van Knippenberg, 2020). The author adds that purpose and associated meaning answer the questions why one does the job, and why this is valuable, important and worth doing (Lepisto & Pratt, 2017; van Knippenberg, 2020). A sense of meaning at the workplace, one that has positive value, is a strongly motivational state. A presence of meaning versus the absence or search for meaning is important because activities that are subjectively meaningful are associated with intrinsic motivation, persistence and a drive to perform well (Shamir, 1990; Spreitzer, 1995; van Knippenberg, 2020). A majority of empirical accounts, however, have overwhelmingly focused on leader effectiveness and the resultant follower behavioral outcomes in relation to job performance such as creativity, engagement and motivation (Bass, 1990). In this vein, van Knippenberg (2020) argues that Selznick's (1957) early propositions on leaders being the primary drivers of creating purpose and meaning at work received negligible follow-up.

Another leadership element that has received support in enhancing meaning at work relates to empowerment which is defined as the motivational concept of self-efficacy (Conger & Kanungo, 1998; Spreitzer, 1995). Reviews (Spreitzer, 2008) and meta-analyses (Seibert et al., 2011; Dulebohn et al., 2012) summarize how leaders can provide followers with high or low degrees of empowerment which can affect followers' perceptions of meaning at the workplace. A high-quality leader-member exchange (LMX) relationship entails that followers receive greater attention, feelings of empowerment and also access to information from their leaders which helps followers better understand the meaning and impact of their work (Hill et al., 2014). Related to this, there is evidence to suggest that supervisors are more likely to empower those employees with whom they believe to have a higher-quality leader-member exchange relationship thereby allowing them greater influence in decision making (Hill et al., 2014; Scandura et al., 1986) and delegating valuable or esteemed work that is deemed to be meaningful to them more frequently (Schriesheim et al., 1998). Thomas and Velthouse (1990) conducted an extensive review of the empowerment literature and concluded that the multifaceted construct of empowerment entailed increased intrinsic task motivation. The authors explain that empowerment manifested as a combination of four cognitions mediating an individual's orientation to his or her work role: meaning at work, self-determination, competence and impact. Although this understanding has traditionally transpired as elements of transformational leadership (Bass, 1996) by empowering followers through idealized influence and inspirational motivation toward the organizational purpose, when it comes to leadership, the literature on meaning at work has tapped extensively into cues, interactions and sense of belongingness, and could benefit from examining empowerment more closely.

The 'Job' and Meaning

Job Design. Scholars assert that the design of employees' jobs can determine the extent to which employees find their job to be worthy and meaningful (Hackman & Oldham, 1980). Job design is understood as specifying the methods or contents of any job in such a manner that various requirements of the job holder can be effectively satisfied (Buchanan, 1979). In a comprehensive test of the Job Characteristics Model, Johns et al. (1992) found that meaning at work was a predominantly robust mediator of the association between all core job characteristics and work outcomes, a finding that was subsequently confirmed in a meta-analysis by Humphrey et al. (2007). Given the potent affective and motivational properties of meaning at the workplace (Johns, 2010), it follows that leaders and organization members should play a key role in the design of jobs. However, Johns (2010) argues that aspects of job design are often overlooked, and that organizational members are often left to extract meaning from contextual cues rather than the intended design of the job.

Another implication for organizational members pertains to job crafting which complements the above-mentioned point on achieving meaning in work. Job crafting is described as the process involving self-initiated change behaviors that employees partake in with the goal of aligning their jobs with their own preferences and passions (Wrzesniewski & Dutton, 2001). Job crafting is one of the critical tools used by employees to make their jobs more meaningful and typically involves three categories of personal characteristics that employees use to craft their jobs (Berg et al., 2013). The first characteristic involves crafting their job in alignment with their motives (e.g., passions, enjoyment), the second with their strengths (e.g., public speaking or problem solving) and third with their passion (e.g., learning a language or technology). Berg et al. (2013) note that workplace job-crafting strategies can be enhanced if employees irrespective of their position in the formal hierarchy adopt a mindset that values proactivity. The authors add that making sizeable shifts to one's job may not be practically realistic; therefore, a job-crafting mindset can help focus on small wins, a mindset that can help improve meaning at the workplace that when sustained over time can help make the incremental changes grow into larger significant changes.

Meaning at Work as Serving Others

> Many regard the emptiness at the heart of pluralism as a flaw. Its consequences among individuals are looked upon as illnesses: anomie, alienation, loneliness, despair, loss of meaning etc. … at the spiritual core there is an empty shrine.
>
> (Novak, 1982, pp. 52–53)

Turnbull (2001) argues that it is the quest for meaning which has made concepts such as empowerment, self-managed teams and other work-based participation philosophies rather attractive 'tools' in contemporary organizations. The author further contends that organizations today have made these initiatives so easy to introduce to the workforce, and are marketed internally under the guise of the dogma of becoming "world class" organizations and thereby seeming to fulfill the essential functions of providing a sense of identity, meaning, serving society and purpose to those whose identity is in question. Comprehensive studies by Lips-Wiersma and Morris (2009) underline the importance of becoming and expressing self, creating unity with others and serving others. Similarly, meaning at the workplace is understood to be achieved while working together with others and when the work consists of an element of serving others (Frémeaux & Pavageau, 2020; Vos, 2018). According to this argument, the establishment of meaning at the workplace involves employees' personal growth, moral development, group acceptance, creating an impact upon others and the ability to stay true to oneself (Voss, 2007; Frémeaux & Pavageau, 2020). A large part of experiencing meaning at work involves unity with others in relation to sharing values, belonging to a group, working together and the ability to see a connection between work and a transcendent cause that meets the needs of humanity (Frémeaux & Pavageau, 2020; Lips-Wiersma & Morris, 2009, p. 501). Where the nature of work may not involve elements of serving others, organizations can increasingly engage in a range of philanthropical activities involving their employees in community service or provide incentives for sustainable activities.

Keeping Up with Protean Careers

A final recommendation we propose is one that explains how meaning can be achieved at the workplace by building on theories of career construction. Career construction theory explains the interpersonal and interpretive processes through which employees assign meaning and direction on their professional behaviors (Savickas, 2011). The theory views work as social construction and contends that meaningful work is a necessity to the society (Hartung & Taber, 2013), thereby aligning with neoclassical perspectives on career calling (see Hall & Chandler, 2005; Bunderson & Thompson, 2009). Savickas (2011) and Hartung and Taber (2013) note that while neoclassical approaches view external sources that contribute to a career calling (e.g., destiny or divine calling), the theory of career construction deduces calling as an inner sense of direction and purpose. In this regard, Hall et al. (2018) add the importance of acknowledging the protean career attitudes. Individuals with protean career attitudes are determined upon using their own values (versus organizational values) to guide their career and are rather independent in managing their professional behavior (Briscoe et al., 2006). An individual who does not embrace protean attitudes will be more likely to rely on external standards, as opposed to internally developed ones, and be more likely to seek external direction in workplace attitudes. Hall et al. (2018) add that protean individuals generally work well if the organization allows them to find their own meaning at work; however, such individuals can also be difficult to manage if they find no meaning or identity at the workplace. For organizations, it is imperative to discuss the extent to which organization members are aligned with their career calling or have a sense of purpose or direction at work. In that, organizations need to especially distinguish between protean and non-protean orientations. However, the implications of searching for meaning at work can make protean individuals frustrated and confused, and easily swayed toward directions that offer them the sense of meaning they seek. In a report on protean career strategies, Falcão (2015) states that the new mantra is to seek jobs where one can find meaning or even fun. As such, there is no doubt that an individual's career is a central part of an individual's identity, search for meaning, personal growth, status, social network, financial security and ultimately survival and happiness. And yet few career strategies seem to deliver on these goals (Falcão, 2015). As such, it can be concluded that an improvement in an individual's career can have a great positive personal impact, restore a sense of meaning and purpose, and an improvement in several individuals' careers may have an even larger positive societal impact.

Conclusion

This chapter aimed to provide an overview of the dimensions of experiencing meaning at work. Organization members differ greatly in the extent to which they experience meaning at work. Where some perceive a strong presence of meaning in their work, other can experience either a lack of meaning or a drive to find meaning at work. The psychological literature on meaning at work describes the different ways in which individuals can reinforce the meaning they give to their work, and these descriptions converge on the idea of finding meaning through the nature of the work itself, having meaningful relationships with others and engaging in work that benefits the society. Despite this knowledge, lacking or the quest to finding meaning can be strenuous and complex and involve not only the individual but peers, leaders and the work infrastructure. To this, we conclude with recommendation from three perspectives with the aim of not only long-term experiences of meaning at work, but also "short-wins" that can aid individual well-being.

References

Adams, M. (2000). *Better happy than rich?: Canadians, money, and the meaning of life*. Penguin Books.

Aktouf, O. (1994). The management of excellence: Deified executives and depersonalized employees. In *Search of meaning* (pp. 124–150).

Allan, B. A., Batz-Barbarich, C., Sterling, H. M., & Tay, L. (2019). Outcomes of meaningful work: A meta-analysis. *Journal of Management Studies, 56*(3), 500–528. https://doi.org/10.1111/joms.12406

Allan, B. A., Duffy, R. D., & Douglass, R. (2015). Meaning in life and work: A developmental perspective. *The Journal of Positive Psychology, 10*(4), 323–331. https://doi.org/10.1080/17439760.2014.950180

Ariely, D., Kamenica, E., & Prelec, D. (2008). Man's search for meaning: The case of Legos. *Journal of Economic Behavior & Organization, 67*(3–4), 671–677.

Arnold, K. A., Turner, N., Barling, J., Kelloway, E. K., & McKee, M. C. (2007). Transformational leadership and psychological well-being: The mediating role of meaningful work. *Journal of Occupational Health Psychology, 12*(3), 193. https://doi.org/10.1037/1076-8998.12.3.193

Bailey, C., & Madden, A. (2016). *What makes work meaningful—or meaningless*. MIT Sloan management review.

Bangali, M., & Guichard, J. (2012). The role of dialogic processes in designing career expectations. *Journal of Vocational Behavior, 81*(2), 183–190. https://doi.org/10.1016/j.jvb.2012.06.006

Bass, B. M. (1985). *Leadership and performance beyond expectations*. Collier Macmillan.

Bass, B. M. (1990). From transactional to transformational leadership: Learning to share the vision. *Organizational Dynamics, 18*(3), 19–31. https://doi.org/10.1016/0090-2616(90)90061-S

Bass, B. M. (1996). *A new paradigm for leadership: An inquiry into transformational leadership*.

Baum, S. K., & Stewart, R. B., Jr. (1990). Sources of meaning through the lifespan. *Psychological Reports, 67*(1), 3–14. https://doi.org/10.2466/pr0.1990.67.1.3

Baumeister, R. F. (1991). *Meanings of life*. Guilford Press.

Baumeister, R. F., Vohs, K. D., Aaker, J. L., & Garbinsky, E. N. (2013). Some key differences between a happy life and a meaningful life. *The Journal of Positive Psychology, 8*(6), 505–516. https://doi.org/10.1080/17439760.2013.830764

Beadle, R. (2017). Virtue and the case for meaningful work. In *Handbook of virtue ethics in business and management* (pp. 835–843). https://doi.org/10.1007/978-94-007-6510-8_40

Beadle, R. (2019). Work, meaning, and virtue. In *The Oxford handbook of meaningful work* (pp. 73–87).

Bellah, R. N. (1985). Creating a new framework for new realities: Social science as public philosophy. *Change: The Magazine of Higher Learning, 17*(2), 35–39.

Berg, J. M., Dutton, J. E., & Wrzesniewski, A. (2013). Job crafting and meaningful work. In B. J. Dik, Z. S. Byrne, & M. F. Steger (Eds.), *Purpose and meaning in the workplace* (pp. 81–104). American Psychological Association.

BetterUp. (2018). *Workers value meaning at work; new research from BetterUp shows just how much They're willing to pay for it*. https://www.betterup.com/press/workers-value-meaning-at-work-new-research-from-betterup-shows-just-how-much-theyre-willing-to-pay-for-it

Bonebright, C. A., Clay, D. L., & Ankenmann, R. D. (2000). The relationship of workaholism with work–life conflict, life satisfaction, and purpose in life. *Journal of Counseling Psychology, 47*(4), 469. https://doi.org/10.1037/0022-0167.47.4.469

Brassai, L., Piko, B. F., & Steger, M. F. (2011). Meaning in life: Is it a protective factor for adolescents' psychological health? *International Journal of Behavioral Medicine, 18*(1), 44–51. https://doi.org/10.1007/s12529-010-9089-6

Briscoe, J. P., Hall, D. T., & DeMuth, R. L. F. (2006). Protean and boundaryless careers: An empirical exploration. *Journal of Vocational Behavior, 69*(1), 30–47. https://doi.org/10.1016/j.jvb.2005.09.003

Buchanan, D. (1979). *The development of job design. Theories and techniques*. Saxon House, Aldershot.

Bunderson, J. S., & Thompson, J. A. (2009). The call of the wild: Zookeepers, callings, and the double-edged sword of deeply meaningful work. *Administrative Science Quarterly, 54*(1), 32–57. https://doi.org/10.2189/asqu.2009.54.1.32

Byrne, Z., Pitts, V., Chiaburu, D., & Steiner, Z. (2011). Managerial trustworthiness and social exchange with the organization. *Journal of Managerial Psychology, 26*(2). https://doi.org/10.1108/02683941111102155

Cohen, D. V. (1993). Creating and maintaining ethical work climates: Anomie in the workplace and implications for managing change. *Business Ethics Quarterly*, 343–358. https://doi.org/10.2307/3857283

Cohen, K., & Cairns, D. (2012). Is searching for meaning in life associated with reduced subjective well-being? Confirmation and possible moderators. *Journal of Happiness Studies*, *13*(2), 313–331. https://doi.org/10.1007/s10902-011-9265-7

Conger, J. A. (1989). *The charismatic leader: Behind the mystique of exceptional leadership*. Jossey-Bass.

Conger, J. A., & Kanungo, R. N. (1998). *Charismatic leadership in organizations*. Sage.

Crumbaugh, J. C., & Maholick, L. T. (1964). An experimental study in existentialism: The psychometric approach to Frankl's concept of noogenic neurosis. *Journal of Clinical Psychology*, *20*(2), 200–207. https://doi.org/10.1002/1097-4679(196404)20:2%3c200::AID-JCLP2270200203%3e3.0.CO;2-U

Damásio, B. F., & Koller, S. H. (2015). Complex experiences of meaning in life: Individual differences among sociodemographic variables, sources of meaning and psychological functioning. *Social Indicators Research*, *123*, 161–181. https://doi.org/10.1007/s11205-014-0726-3

Datu, J. A. D. (2015). Validating the revised self-construal scale in the Philippines. *Current Psychology*, *34*, 626–633. https://doi.org/10.1007/s12144-014-9275-9

Davis, C. G., Nolen-Hoeksema, S., & Larson, J. (1998). Making sense of loss and benefiting from the experience: Two construals of meaning. *Journal of Personality and Social Psychology*, *75*(2), 561. https://doi.org/10.1037/0022-3514.75.2.561

Deci, E. L., & Ryan, R. M. (2008). Self-determination theory: A macrotheory of human motivation, development, and health. *Canadian Psychology/psychologie Canadienne*, *49*(3), 182. https://doi.org/10.1037/a0012801

Dik, B. J., Byrne, Z. S., & Steger, M. F. (2013). *Purpose and meaning in the workplace*. American Psychological Association.https://doi.org/10.1037/14183-000

Dik, B. J., Duffy, R. D., & Eldridge, B. M. (2009). Calling and vocation in career counseling: Recommendations for promoting meaningful work. *Professional Psychology: Research and Practice*, *40*(6), 625. https://doi.org/10.1037/a0015547

Duffy, R. D., Allan, B. A., Autin, K. L., & Bott, E. M. (2013). Calling and life satisfaction: It's not about having it, it's about living it. *Journal of Counseling Psychology*, *60*(1), 42. https://doi.org/10.1037/a0030635

Dulebohn, J. H., Bommer, W. H., Liden, R. C., Brouer, R. L., & Ferris, G. R. (2012). A meta-analysis of antecedents and consequences of leader-member exchange: Integrating the past with an eye toward the future. *Journal of Management*, *38*(6), 1715–1759. https://doi.org/10.1177/0149206311415280

Ebersole, P., & Devogler, K. L. (1981). Meaning in life: Category self-ratings. *The Journal of Psychology*, *107*(2), 289–293. https://doi.org/10.1080/00223980.1981.9915236

Eisenbeiß, S. A., & Boerner, S. (2013). A double-edged sword: Transformational leadership and individual creativity. *British Journal of Management*, *24*(1), 54–68. https://doi.org/10.1111/j.1467-8551.2011.00786.x

Emmons, R. A. (2003). Personal goals, life meaning, and virtue: Wellsprings of a positive life. In C. L. M. Keyes & J. Haidt (Eds.), *Flourishing: Positive psychology and the life well-lived* (pp. 105–128). American Psychological Association. https://doi.org/10.1037/10594-005

Erikson, E. H. (1959). *Identity and the life cycle: Selected papers*. W.W. Norton.

Falcão, H. (2015). Protean career strategies. *Asian Management Insights*, *2*(2), 60–65.

Fegg, M. J., Kramer, M., Bausewein, C., & Borasio, G. D. (2007). Meaning in life in the federal republic of Germany: Results of a representative survey with the schedule for meaning in life evaluation (SMiLE). *Health and Quality of Life Outcomes, 5*(1), 59. https://doi.org/10.1186/1477-7525-5-59

Foucault, M. (1982). The subject and power. *Critical Inquiry, 8*(4), 777–795.

Fox, R. C. (1980). The social meaning of death. *Annals of the American Academy of Political and Social Science, 447*, 1–146.

Frankl, V. E. (1965). The concept of man in logotherapy. *Journal of Existentialism, 6*(21), 53–58.

Frankl, V. E. (1963). *Man's search for meaning: An introduction to logotherapy*. Pocket

Frankl, V. E. (1985). *Man's search for meaning*. Simon and Schuster.

Frémeaux, S., & Pavageau, B. (2020). Meaningful leadership: How can leaders contribute to meaningful work? *Journal of Management Inquiry*. https://doi.org/10.1177/1056492619897126

Fruhen, L. S., Andrei, D. M., & Griffin, M. A. (2022). Leaders as motivators and meaning makers: How perceived leader behaviors and leader safety commitment attributions shape employees' safety behaviors. *Safety Science, 152*, 105775. https://doi.org/10.1016/j.ssci.2022.105775

Fry, P. S. (1998). *The development of personal meaning and wisdom in adolescence: A reexamination of moderating and consolidating factors and influences*. Lawrence Erlbaum Associates Publishers.

Ghadi, M. Y., Fernando, M., & Caputi, P. (2015). Describing work as meaningful: Towards a conceptual clarification. *Journal of Organizational Effectiveness: People and Performance, 2*(3), 1–38. https://doi.org/10.1108/JOEPP-11-2014-0064

Gioia, D. A., & Chittipeddi, K. (1991). Sensemaking and sensegiving in strategic change initiation. *Strategic Management Journal, 12*(6), 433–448.

Grant, A. M. (2007). Relational job design and the motivation to make a prosocial difference. *Academy of Management Review, 32*(2), 393–417. https://doi.org/10.5465/amr.2007.24351328

Guevara, K., & Ord, J. (1996). The search for meaning in a changing work context. *Futures, 28*(8), 709–722.

Hackman, J. R., & Oldham, G. R. (1976). Motivation through the design of work: Test of a theory. *Organizational Behavior and Human Performance, 16*(2), 250–279. https://doi.org/10.1016/0030-5073(76)90016-7

Hackman, J. R. (1980). Work redesign and motivation. *Professional Psychology, 11*(3), 445. https://doi.org/10.1037/0735-7028.11.3.445

Hall, D. T. (2008). Reflections on calling and careers in community psychology. *Journal of Prevention & Intervention in the Community, 35*(1), 107–112. https://doi.org/10.1300/J005v35n01_09

Hall, D. T., & Chandler, D. E. (2005). Psychological success: When the career is a calling. *Journal of Organizational Behavior: The International Journal of Industrial, Occupational and Organizational Psychology and Behavior, 26*(2), 155–176. https://doi.org/10.1002/job.301

Hall, D. T., Feldman, E., & Kim, N. (2013). Meaningful work and the protean career. In B. J. Dik, Z. S. Byrne, & M. F. Steger (Eds.), *Purpose and meaning in the workplace* (pp. 57–78). American Psychological Association. https://doi.org/10.1037/14183-004

Hall, D. T., Yip, J., & Doiron, K. (2018). Protean careers at work: Self-direction and values orientation in psychological success. *Annual Review of Organizational Psychology and Organizational Behavior, 5*, 29–156. https://doi.org/10.1146/annurev-orgpsych-032117-104631

Hartung, P. J., & Taber, B. J. (2013). Career construction: Heeding the call of the heart. In B. J. Dik, Z. S. Byrne, & M. F. Steger (Eds.), *Purpose and meaning in the workplace* (pp. 17–36). American Psychological Association. https://doi.org/10.1037/14183-002

Hill, N. S., Kang, J. H., & Seo, M. (2014). The interactive effect of leader–member exchange and electronic communication on employee psychological empowerment and work outcomes. *The Leadership Quarterly, 25*(4), 772–783. https://doi.org/10.1016/j.leaqua.2014.04.006

Ho, M. Y., Cheung, F. M., & Cheung, S. F. (2010). The role of meaning in life and optimism in promoting well-being. *Personality and Individual Differences, 48*(5), 658–663. https://doi.org/10.1016/j.paid.2010.01.008

Hoffmann-Burdzińska, K., & Rutkowska, M. (2015). Work life balance as a factor influencing well-being. *Journal of Positive Management, 6*(4), 87–101. https://doi.org/10.12775/JPM.2015.024

Humphrey, S. E., Nahrgang, J. D., & Morgeson, F. P. (2007). Integrating motivational, social, and contextual work design features: A meta-analytic summary and theoretical extension of the work design literature. *Journal of Applied Psychology, 92*(5), 1332. https://doi.org/10.1037/0021-9010.92.5.1332

Huta, V. (2015). The complementary roles of Eudaimonia and Hedonia and how they can be pursued in practice. In *Positive psychology in practice: Promoting human flourishing in work, health, education, and everyday life* (pp. 159–182). https://doi.org/10.1002/9781118996874.ch10

Huta, V., & Ryan, R. M. (2010). Pursuing pleasure or virtue: The differential and overlapping well-being benefits of hedonic and eudaimonic motives. *Journal of Happiness Studies, 11*(6), 735–762. https://doi.org/10.1007/s10902-009-9171-4

Isik, S., & Uzbe, N. (2015). Personality traits and positive/negative affects: An analysis of meaning in life among adults. *Educational Sciences: Theory & Practice, 15*(3). https://doi.org/10.12738/estp.2015.3.2436

Janicke-Bowles, S. H., Rieger, D., & Connor, W. (2019). Finding meaning at work: The role of inspiring and funny YouTube videos on work-related well-being. *Journal of Happiness Studies, 20*, 619–640. https://doi.org/10.1007/s10902-018-9959-1

Johns, G. (2010). Some unintended consequences of job design. *Journal of Organizational Behavior, 31*(2/3), 361–369. https://doi.org/10.1002/job.669

Johns, G., Xie, J. L., & Fang, Y. (1992). Mediating and moderating effects in job design. *Journal of Management, 18*(4), 657–676. https://doi.org/10.1177/014920639201800404

Johnson, R. E., & Chang, C. (2006). "I" is to continuance as "we" is to affective: The relevance of the self-concept for organizational commitment. *Journal of Organizational Behavior: The International Journal of Industrial, Occupational and Organizational Psychology and Behavior, 27*(5), 549–570.

Kasler, J., Izenberg, P., Elias, M. J., & White, G. (2012). Meaning in life, hope, and priorities for the future. In *Student Attitudes* (pp. 29–50).

Khumalo, I. P., Wissing, M. P., & Schutte, L. (2014). Presence of meaning and search for meaning as mediators between spirituality and psychological well-being in a South African sample. *Journal of Psychology in Africa, 24*(1), 61–72. https://doi.org/10.1080/14330237.2014.904095

Kiang, L., & Fuligni, A. J. (2010). Meaning in life as a mediator of ethnic identity and adjustment among adolescents from Latin, Asian, and European American backgrounds. *Journal of Youth and Adolescence, 39*, 1253–1264. https://doi.org/10.1007/s10964-009-9475-z

King, L. A., Heintzelman, S. J., & Ward, S. J. (2016). Beyond the search for meaning: A contemporary science of the experience of meaning in life. *Current Directions in Psychological Science, 25*(4), 211–216. https://doi.org/10.1177/09637214166563

Kleiman, E. M., & Beaver, J. K. (2013). A meaningful life is worth living: Meaning in life as a suicide resiliency factor. *Psychiatry Research, 210*(3), 934–939. https://doi.org/10.1016/j.psychres.2013.08.002

Klinger, E. (1998). *The search for meaning in evolutionary perspective and its clinical implications.* Lawrence Erlbaum Associates Publishers.

Kotter, J. P. (1999). *John P. Kotter on what leaders really do.* Harvard Business Press.

Lacan, J. (1977). *The mirror stage. Écrits: A selection.* Tavistock. Inglaterra.

Lepisto, D. A., & Pratt, M. G. (2017). Meaningful work as realization and justification: Toward a dual conceptualization. *Organizational Psychology Review, 7*(2), 99–121. https://doi.org/10.1177/2041386616630039

Li, J., Dou, K., & Liang, Y. (2021). The relationship between presence of meaning, search for meaning, and subjective well-being: A three-level meta-analysis based on the meaning in life questionnaire. *Journal of Happiness Studies, 22*(1), 467–489. https://doi.org/10.1007/s10902-020-00230-y

Lips-Wiersma, M., & Morris, L. (2009). Discriminating between 'meaningful work' and the 'management of meaning.' *Journal of Business Ethics, 88*(3), 491–511. https://doi.org/10.1007/s10551-009-0118-9

Lloyd, B., & Trapp, R. (1999). Bosses or leaders? *Leadership & Organization Development Journal, 20*(6), 332–336.

Lopez, F. G., Ramos, K., Nisenbaum, M., Thind, N., & Ortiz-Rodriguez, T. (2015). Predicting the presence and search for life meaning: Test of an attachment theory-driven model. *Journal of Happiness Studies, 16*(1), 103–116. https://doi.org/10.1007/s10902-013-9498-8

Lucas, Y., & Kornhauser, A. (1966). Mental health of the industrial worker. A Detroit study. *Revue française de sociologie, 7*(4), 552. https://doi.org/10.2307/3319718

Maddi, S. R. (1967). The existential neurosis. *Journal of Abnormal Psychology, 72*(4), 311. https://doi.org/10.1037/h0020103

Martela, F., & Steger, M. F. (2016). The three meanings of meaning in life: Distinguishing coherence, purpose, and significance. *The Journal of Positive Psychology, 11*(5), 531–545.

Mascaro, N., & Rosen, D. H. (2005). Existential meaning's role in the enhancement of hope and prevention of depressive symptoms. *Journal of Personality, 73*(4), 985–1014. https://doi.org/10.1111/j.1467-6494.2005.00336.x

Maslow, A. H. (1971). *The farther reaches of human nature.* Penguin Press.

Massimini, F., & Delle Fave, A. (2000). Individual development in a bio-cultural perspective. *American Psychologist, 55*(1), 24. https://doi.org/10.1037/0003-066X.55.1.24

May, D. R., Gilson, R. L., & Harter, L. M. (2004). The psychological conditions of meaningfulness, safety and availability and the engagement of the human spirit at work. *Journal of Occupational and Organizational Psychology, 77*(1), 11–37. https://doi.org/10.1348/096317904322915892

Morin, E. M. (2008). *The meaning of work, mental health and organizational commitment.* Institut de recherche en santé et en sécurité du travail du Québec.

Myers, G. D. (2013). Foreword. In J. Dik Bryan, S. Byrne Zinta & F. Steger Michael (Eds.), *Purpose and meaning in the workplace* (1st ed., pp. xi–xv). American Psychological Association.

Noble-Carr, D., Barker, J., McArthur, M., & Woodman, E. (2014). Improving practice: The importance of connections in establishing positive identity and meaning in the lives of vulnerable young people. *Children and Youth Services Review, 47*, 389–396. https://doi.org/10.1016/j.childyouth.2014.10.017

Novak, M. (1982). *The spirit of capitalism*. Madison Books.

Ojica, A. S. (2022). Relationship between meaningful work and cyberloafing: The mediating role of boredom at work. *Studia Doctoralia. Psychology and Educational Science, 13*(2), 133–138. https://doi.org/10.47040/sdpsych.v13i2.150

Park, C. L. (2013). The meaning making model: A framework for understanding meaning, spirituality, and stress-related growth in health psychology. *European Health Psychologist, 15*(2), 40–47.

Park, C. L., & Folkman, S. (1997). Meaning in the context of stress and coping. *Review of General Psychology, 1*(2), 115–144. https://doi.org/10.1037/1089-2680.1.2.115

Park, N., Park, M., & Peterson, C. (2010). When is the search for meaning related to life satisfaction? *Applied Psychology: Health and Well-Being, 2*(1), 1–13. https://doi.org/10.1111/j.1758-0854.2009.01024.x

Park, N., Peterson, C., & Ruch, W. (2009). Orientations to happiness and life satisfaction in twenty-seven nations. *The Journal of Positive Psychology, 4*(4), 273–279. https://doi.org/10.1080/17439760902933690

Petersen, C., & Seligman, M. (2004). *Character strengths and virtues: A handbook and classification*. American Psychological Association and Oxford University Press.

Podolny, J. M., Khurana, R., & Hill-Popper, M. (2005). Academy of management review. *Academy of Management Review, 26*(3), 565–567. https://doi.org/10.1016/S0191-3085(04)26001-4

Pouyaud, J., Cohen-Scali, V., Robinet, M., & Sintes, L. (2017). Life and career design dialogues and resilience. *Psychology of career adaptability, employability and resilience* (pp. 49–64). Springer. https://doi.org/10.1007/978-3-319-66954-0_4

Pratt, M. G., & Ashforth, B. E. (2003). Fostering meaningfulness in working and at work. *Positive Organizational Scholarship: Foundations of a New Discipline, 309*, 327.

Pratt, M. G., Pradies, C., & Lepisto, D. A. (2013). Doing well, doing good, and doing with: Organizational practices for effectively cultivating meaningful work. In *Purpose and meaning in the workplace* (pp. 173–196).

Pratt, M. G., Rockmann, K. W., & Kaufmann, J. B. (2006). Constructing professional identity: The role of work and identity learning cycles in the customization of identity among medical residents. *Academy of Management Journal, 49*(2), 235–262. https://doi.org/10.5465/amj.2006.20786060

Peterson, C., Park, N., & Seligman, M. E. (2005). Orientations to happiness and life satisfaction: The full life versus the empty life. *Journal of Happiness Studies, 6*, 25–41. https://doi.org/10.1007/s10902-004-1278-z

Proulx, T. (2013). Beyond mortality and the self: Meaning Makes a Comeback. In K. D. Markman, T. Proulx & M. J. Lindberg (Eds.), *The psychology of meaning* (p. 71).

Raelin, J. A. (2003). *Creating leaderful organizations: How to bring out leadership in everyone* Berrett-Koehler Publishers.

Raelin, J. A. (2006). Finding meaning in the organization. *Sloan Management Review, 47*(3), 64–68.

Rapaport, R., Bailyn, L., Kolb, D., & Fletcher, J. K. (1998). *Relinking life and work: Toward a better future*. Pegasus Communications.

Rodríguez-Carvajal, R., Herrero, M., van Dierendonck, D., de Rivas, S., & Moreno-Jiménez, B. (2019). Servant leadership and goal attainment through meaningful life and vitality: A diary study. *Journal of Happiness Studies, 20*(2), 499–521. https://doi.org/10.1007/s10902-017-9954-y

Ros, M., Schwartz, S. H., & Surkiss, S. (1999). Basic individual values, work values, and the meaning of work. *Applied Psychology, 48*(1), 49–71. https://doi.org/10.1111/j.1464-0597.1999.tb00048.x

Rosso, B. D., Dekas, K. H., & Wrzesniewski, A. (2010). On the meaning of work: A theoretical integration and review. *Research in Organizational Behavior, 30*, 91–127. https://doi.org/10.1016/j.riob.2010.09.001

Russo-Netzer, P. (2018). "This is what real spirituality is all about": A phenomenological exploration of the experience of spirituality outside institutional religion. *Psychology of Religion and Spirituality*. https://doi.org/10.1037/rel0000169

Ryan, R. M., & Deci, E. L. (2001). On happiness and human potentials: A review of research on hedonic and eudaimonic well-being. *Annual Review of Psychology, 52*(1), 141–166. https://doi.org/10.1146/annurev.psych.52.1.141

Ryan, R. M., Patrick, H., Deci, E. L., & Williams, G. C. (2008). Facilitating health behaviour change and its maintenance: Interventions based on self-determination theory. *The European Health Psychologist, 10*(1), 2–5.

Ryff, C. D. (1989). Happiness is everything, or is it? Explorations on the meaning of psychological well-being. *Journal of Personality and Social Psychology, 57*(6), 1069. https://doi.org/10.1037/0022-3514.57.6.1069

Ryff, C. D., Singer, B. H., Dienberg Love, G. (2004). Positive health: Connecting well–being with biology. *Philosophical Transactions of the Royal Society of London. Series B: Biological Sciences, 359*(1449), 1383–1394. https://doi.org/10.1159/000353263

Sarros, J. C., Tanewski, G. A., Winter, R. P., Santora, J. C., & Densten, I. L. (2002). Work alienation and organizational leadership. *British Journal of Management, 13*(4), 285–304. https://doi.org/10.1111/1467-8551.00247

Savickas, M. L. (2011). Constructing careers: Actor, agent, and author. *Journal of Employment Counseling, 48*(4), 179–181. https://doi.org/10.1002/j.2161-1920.2011.tb01109.x

Savvides, E., & Stavrou, E. (2020). Purpose, meaning, and wellbeing at work. In *The Palgrave handbook of workplace well-being* (pp. 1–27). https://doi.org/10.1007/978-3-030-02470-3_36-2

Scandura, T. A., Graen, G. B., & Novak, M. A. (1986). When managers decide not to decide autocratically: An investigation of leader–member exchange and decision influence. *Journal of Applied Psychology, 71*(4), 579. https://doi.org/10.1037/0021-9010.71.4.579

Schnell, T. (2009). The sources of meaning and meaning in life questionnaire (SoMe): Relations to demographics and well-being. *The Journal of Positive Psychology, 4*(6), 483–499. https://doi.org/10.1080/17439760903271074

Schriesheim, C. A., Neider, L. L., & Scandura, T. A. (1998). Delegation and leader-member exchange: Main effects, moderators, and measurement issues. *Academy of Management Journal, 41*(3), 298–318. https://doi.org/10.2307/256909

Schultze, G., & Miller, C. (2004). The search for meaning and career development. *Career Development International*.

Scollon, C. N., & King, L.A., 2004. Is the good life the easy life? *Social Indicators Research, 68*, 127–162. https://doi.org/10.1023/B:SOCI.0000025590.44950.d1

Seeman, M. (1967). On the personal consequences of alienation in work. *American Sociological Review*, 273–285. https://doi.org/10.2307/2091817

Seibert, S. E., Wang, G., & Courtright, S. H. (2011). Antecedents and consequences of psychological and team empowerment in organizations: A meta-analytic review. *Journal of Applied Psychology, 96*(5), 981. https://doi.org/10.1037/a0022676

Selznick, P. (1957). No title. *Law and the Structures of Social Action*. https://doi.org/10.2307/2390698

Shamir, B. (1990). Calculations, values, and identities: The sources of collectivistic work motivation. *Human Relations, 43*(4), 313–332. https://doi.org/10.1177/001872679004300400

Sosik, J. J. (2000). The role of personal meaning in charismatic leadership. *Journal of Leadership Studies, 7*(2), 60–74. https://doi.org/10.1177/107179190000700206

Spreitzer, G. M. (1995). Psychological empowerment in the workplace: Dimensions, measurement, and validation. *Academy of Management Journal, 38*(5), 1442–1465. https://doi.org/10.2307/256865

Spreitzer, G. M. (2008). Taking stock: A review of more than twenty years of research on empowerment at work. *Handbook of Organizational Behavior, 1*, 54–72.

Steger, M. F., & Dik, B. J. (2009). If one is looking for meaning in life, does it help to find meaning in work? *Applied Psychology: Health and Well-Being, 1*(3), 303–320. https://doi.org/10.1111/j.1758-0854.2009.01018.x

Steger, M. F., Dik, B. J., & Duffy, R. D. (2012). Measuring meaningful work: The work and meaning inventory (WAMI). *Journal of Career Assessment, 20*(3), 322–337. https://doi.org/10.1177/1069072711436160

Steger, M. F., Frazier, P., Oishi, S., & Kaler, M. (2006). The meaning in life questionnaire: Assessing the presence of and search for meaning in life. *Journal of Counseling Psychology, 53*(1), 80. https://doi.org/10.1037/0022-0167.53.1.80

Steger, M. F., Kashdan, T. B., Sullivan, B. A., & Lorentz, D. (2008a). Understanding the search for meaning in life: Personality, cognitive style, and the dynamic between seeking and experiencing meaning. *Journal of Personality, 76*(2), 199–228. https://doi.org/10.1111/j.1467-6494.2007.00484.x

Steger, M. F., Kawabata, Y., Shimai, S., & Otake, K. (2008b). The meaningful life in japan and the United States: Levels and correlates of meaning in life. *Journal of Research in Personality, 42*(3), 660–678. https://doi.org/10.1016/j.jrp.2007.09.003

Stein, M., Wagner, E. L., Tierney, P., Newell, S., & Galliers, R. D. (2019). Datification and the pursuit of meaningfulness in work. *Journal of Management Studies, 56*(3), 685–717. https://doi.org/10.1111/joms.12409

Thomas, K. W., & Velthouse, B. A. (1990). Cognitive elements of empowerment: An "interpretive" model of intrinsic task motivation. *Academy of Management Review, 15*(4), 666–681. https://doi.org/10.2307/258687

Thorsteinsen, K., & Vittersø, J. (2018). Striving for wellbeing: The different roles of hedonia and eudaimonia in goal pursuit and goal achievement. *International Journal of Wellbeing, 8*(2). https://doi.org/10.5502/ijw.v8i2.733

To, S., & Sung, W. (2017). Presence of meaning, sources of meaning, and subjective well-being in emerging adulthood: A sample of Hong Kong community college

students. *Emerging Adulthood, 5*(1), 69–74. https://doi.org/10.1177/2167696816649804
Torrey, C. L., & Duffy, R. D. (2012). Calling and well-being among adults: Differential relations by employment status. *Journal of Career Assessment, 20*(4), 415–425. https://doi.org/10.1177/1069072712448894
Tsahuridu, E. (2006). Anomie and ethics at work. *Journal of Business Ethics, 69*, 163–174. https://doi.org/10.1007/s10551-006-9074-9
Turnbull, S. (2001). Corporate ideology–meanings and contradictions for middle managers. *British Journal of Management, 12*(3), 231–242. https://doi.org/10.1111/1467-8551.00196
Ulrich, D. (2011). Leaders who make meaning meaningful. *Human Resource Management International Digest, 19*(2).
van Knippenberg, D. (2020). Meaning-based leadership. *Organizational Psychology Review, 10*(1), 6–28. https://doi.org/10.1177/2041386619897618
Vohs, K. D., Aaker, J. L., & Catapano, R. (2019). It's not going to be that fun: Negative experiences can add meaning to life. *Current Opinion in Psychology, 26*, 11–14. https://doi.org/10.1016/j.copsyc.2018.04.014
Vos, J. (2018). *Meaning in life: An evidence-based practice handbook for practitioners.*
Voss, C. A. (2007). Learning from the first operations management textbook. *Journal of Operations Management, 25*(2), 239–247. https://doi.org/10.1016/j.jom.2006.05.013
Waterman, A. S. (1993). Two conceptions of happiness: Contrasts of personal expressiveness (eudaimonia) and hedonic enjoyment. *Journal of Personality and Social Psychology, 64*(4), 678. https://doi.org/10.1037/0022-3514.64.4.678
Wrzesniewski, A. E. (1999). *Jobs, careers, and callings: Work orientation and job transitions.*
Wrzesniewski, A., & Dutton, J. E. (2001). Crafting a job: Revisioning employees as active crafters of their work. *Academy of Management Review, 26*(2), 179–201. https://doi.org/10.5465/amr.2001.4378011
Wrzesniewski, A., Dutton, J. E., & Debebe, G. (2003). Interpersonal sensemaking and the meaning of work. *Research in Organizational Behavior, 25*, 93–135. https://doi.org/10.1016/S0191-3085(03)25003-6

CHAPTER 4

Spiritual Guidance in the Personal Efficacy of Work

Orneita Burton and Seonhee Jeong

INTRODUCTION

The meaning and purpose of work have been studied extensively within knowledge communities, either from a theoretical perspective (Ashmos & Duchon, 2000; Steger et al., 2012) or through literature on spirituality as a source of meaning in work (Greenhaus, 2003; Murray & Workman, 2015; Taylor & McKenzie, 2009). As employees, people seek to find deeper connections between their work and their personal values and beliefs, minimizing the focus on work as just a paycheck or for job security. With a broad domain of scholarly literature to draw from in defining work, a multi-faceted meaning and purpose can be derived, depending on the specific area of interest.

The general view of work is to engage in service to self, another person or entity for monetary or other means of compensation, where wages are paid based on the work provided. Under this definition, work is a tradeoff of resources based on an exchange of value between parties.

When this definition is viewed as our sole reason for work, it is no wonder we are depressed, disenchanted, unfulfilled and even borderline dismissive when it comes to work. This pessimistic view is inevitable despite the degree of

---

O. Burton (✉)
Department of Management Sciences and Information Systems, College of Business Administration, Abilene Christian University, Abilene, TX, USA
e-mail: oxb00a@acu.edu

S. Jeong
Department of Business, Wittenberg University, Springfield, OH, USA

© The Author(s), under exclusive license to Springer Nature Switzerland AG 2023
J. Marques (ed.), *The Palgrave Handbook of Fulfillment, Wellness, and Personal Growth at Work*,
https://doi.org/10.1007/978-3-031-35494-6_4

material gains derived from work. We are thus defeated before we begin each day. Fortunately, with the recent COVID-19 pandemic, people were given time to reconsider this definition and search for a deeper meaning of work beyond the source of economic provision.

To better understand the purpose of work, the concept of work must be considered in its various forms. From a religious perspective, work is often defined by the need to take care of an environment that is part of the natural design in creation. Therefore, what we do in community is particularly connected to our personal giftedness. Gifted individuals possess unique skills and abilities that allow them to identify and address community needs in sustainable ways. It is therefore important to focus on the proper utilization of our personal skills to address community needs. Smith and Vargo (2019) provide insights into the importance of personal giftedness in business and offer recommendations for organizations to harness these skills in their operations.

We also need to consider the idea of personal efficacy through work compared to general employment. Through personal efficacy, we fulfill our true purpose and calling in using our God-given giftedness to meet higher-order needs versus simply having a job to satisfy physical goals. Maslow's hierarchy of needs suggests this relationship (Maslow, 1943), which includes psychological and spiritual dimensions above satisfying the basics of physical provision. Maslow proposed five levels of human needs that are arranged in a hierarchical order, with basic physiological needs (i.e., food, water and shelter) at the bottom, safety, belongingness and esteem in the middle, and the need for self-actualization at the top. Maslow argued that people have a hierarchy of needs that must be met in order to reach their full potential which emerges after basic physical and psychological needs are met.

Maslow's theory suggests that human motivation is driven by the desire to meet various needs, and that individuals are motivated to seek higher levels of the hierarchy once their lower-level needs are met. Although the very notion of a hierarchy of needs has been subject to criticism and debate, Maslow's hierarchy remains a prominent and influential theory to inform the need for gratification beyond working to achieve financial means.

Personal efficacy is a vital factor in job performance and satisfaction (Judge et al., 2007). This study found that individuals who feel their work aligns with their personal giftedness experience greater job satisfaction and are more likely to remain with their employer. In contrast, those who view employment as merely a means of satisfying physical wants and needs are less likely to feel fulfilled in their work. This outcome was confirmed and coined as the "Great Resignation" with the willingness of employees to quit their jobs in search of better ones during the pandemic (Mearian, 2023).

Considering these areas of focus, we share reflections on work that transcend our limited understanding of the multiple ways we are provided for in a created world and thus realize the greater purpose of work beyond a transactional exchange. The following sections address the discussion areas covered in this work to reveal the true meaning and purpose of work as viewed through a spiritual lens:

- Creation and the Burden of Work
- Purpose of Work
- Work as a Calling
- A Purpose and a Calling
- Work as a Service—Our Purpose at Work
- An Entrepreneurial Mindset
- God at Work

We conclude with a summary of perspectives from each topic area.

Creation and the Burden of Work

The first known reference to work is found at the beginning of the Creation, mentioned in the book of Genesis, from the Bible:

> The Lord God took the man and put him in the Garden of Eden to work it and take care of it. (NIV, 2011, Genesis 2:15)

From this reference, there is an understanding, from the beginning, that mankind's purpose is to work and take care of creation. The text says God planted a garden and put people in it as a place to enjoy (NIV, 2011, Genesis 2:8–14). The environment is described as one filled with trees that were pleasing to the eye and good for food. A river watered the garden that flowed from Eden and separated into four headwaters: Pishon, which traveled through land rich in gold and jewels; Gihon, which watered the lands of Cush; Tigris, which ran through the east of Asshur; and the Euphrates, which exists by this name even today. The details as given indicate purpose and design in Creation.

However, initially, there is no indication of work as an unpleasant job or unendurable labor. God placed Adam in the garden to "take care of it," indicating purposed work for Adam in caring for Creation. In fact, in the next chapter, the Fall of Man is recorded after Adam and his wife Eve disobeyed God. After the Fall, God cursed the ground, making it difficult to work and tend to yield produce. The passage says,

> By the sweat of your brow you will eat your food until you return to the ground. (NIV, 2011, Genesis 3:19)

Prior to the fall, food was readily available without work required from Adam. However, after the Fall, mankind would have to work for his bread and livelihood.

The indication in referencing these passages is that, today, it is sometimes believed that work is to be intentionally burdensome and overbearing, conducted without joy or hope for gain beyond satisfying daily hunger. However, this interpretation is not consistent with other Scriptures that explain the forgiving nature of God as our Father in a fallen world:

> Come unto me, all ye that labor and are heavy laden, and I will give you rest. Take my yoke upon you, and learn of me; for I am meek and lowly in heart: and ye shall find rest unto your souls. For my yoke is easy, and my burden is light. (KJV, 1987, Matthew 11:28–30)

> Blessed are all who fear the Lord, who walk in obedience to him. You will eat the fruit of your labor; blessings and prosperity will be yours. Your wife will be like a fruitful vine within your house; your children will be like olive shoots around your table. Yes, this will be the blessing for the man who fears the Lord. (NIV, 2011, Psalm 128:1–4)

Our work may become sacrificial when personal commitments require that we place work before more pleasurable pursuits. Our work may be difficult, as some work requires heavy labor, and, in many cases, more work is required for more gain. However, all work has a spiritual purpose: to draw us to seek and respect God's ways, to follow His guidance in provision.

How we work matters in the seriousness and determination with which we pursue a better outcome. What work we do does matter in leading us to God. In Biblical wisdom, Jesus is the ultimate example of how our priorities and the work we do matter to God. When we make seeking the divine nature our priority, we engage intentionally in our work. As a result, our vocational choices align with His will, and our preferences take a back seat to a sovereign plan:

> You then, my son, be strong in the grace that is in Christ Jesus. And the things you have heard me say in the presence of many witnesses entrust to reliable people who will also be qualified to teach others. Join with me in suffering, like a good soldier of Christ Jesus. No one serving as a soldier gets entangled in civilian affairs, but rather tries to please his commanding officer. Similarly, anyone who competes as an athlete does not receive the victor's crown except by competing according to the rules. The hardworking farmer should be the first to receive a share of the crops. Reflect on what I am saying, for the Lord will give you insight into all this. (NIV, 2011, 2 Timothy 2:1–7)

Purpose of Work

As with Adam, the purpose of work is to take care of our environment, whether family, employer, in our service to others and in our own businesses. What we do in community is also defined by our personal giftedness; therefore, we have a need to focus on the utilization of our personal skills to address community needs.

Greenhaus (2003) views work as a spiritual endeavor when people pursue it with a sense of purpose. Spirituality can inform people's perspective on work so they can pursue work as a source of meaning and fulfillment in their career (Murray & Workman, 2015). For example, Taylor and McKenzie (2009) studied 386 healthcare professionals who completed a survey that assessed their perceptions of work, spirituality and organizational values. The results found that employees who perceived their work as meaningful reported higher levels of spirituality and greater alignment between their personal values and those of the organization. Moreover, employees who felt supported by their organization and felt that their work contributed to a greater good reported higher levels of spirituality and job satisfaction (Duchon & Plowman, 2005; Karakas, 2010; Lips-Wiersma & Morris, 2009).

Individuals who see work as vocation and a form of calling should pursue work that aligns with their inner values and aspirations. For example, the Buddha taught that work can be a means of achieving enlightenment and that one's occupation should be chosen with care and intention (Maupin, 2007; Scherer, 2019). In Buddhism, the concept of right livelihood is an essential part of the Eightfold Path, which is the foundation of Buddhist practice (Hasegawa, 2017; Wallace, 2001). Right livelihood refers to engaging in work that is ethical, beneficial to oneself and others, and in line with one's values and principles. It emphasizes the importance of work as a means of personal growth, self-expression and service to others.

Organizations that choose employees who align their personal values with corporate values provide opportunities and work that strengthens and develops their employee's spiritual awareness. At the same time, value-driven leaders who prioritize the well-being of their employees and stakeholders create an organizational culture that supports employees' personal and spiritual growth (Blanchard & O'Connor, 2019; Fry & Nisiewicz, 2013).

Greenhaus (2003) examines the various ways in which spirituality can be leveraged to create a more meaningful and fulfilling work experience, such as through organizational values and practices that align with an individual's beliefs and values. An organization that values honesty, integrity and ethical behavior, for example, may create a more spiritually fulfilling work environment for individuals who prioritize these values in their personal lives. An organization might implement policies that support work-life balance or provide opportunities for employees to engage in volunteer work or community service. These practices can help individuals feel that their work is meaningful and aligned with their values.

Work as a Calling

The definition of calling is believed to be fundamentally rooted in religious and spiritual domains as a transcendent summons (Dik & Duffy, 2009; Dik et al., 2012). Unfortunately, contemporary trends for research on calling in management and organizational literature often exclude religious and spiritual orientations (Wrzesniewski, 2012; Wrzesniewski et al., 1997), and thus do not consider calling a reliable management construct. As such, concepts associated with calling are used loosely and often interchangeably with vocation, career and job, and dismiss the complementary spiritual goals of service and personal transformation (Cho, 2021; Oswalt, 2000).

In the past two decades, research on work as a calling has grown exponentially in management scholarship (Schabram et al., 2022). Although the term of calling is traditionally attributed to religion and ministry to follow God's will (Hardy, 1990), contemporary research on calling is currently found in both religious and secular settings (Bunderson & Thompson, 2009; Placher, 2005). Two standards of widely adopted definitions of calling exist in management literature: one from Wrzesniewski (in Wrzesniewski et al., 1997) and another from Dik and Duffy (2009).

Research by Wrzesniewski and colleagues (1997) operationalized calling distinct from job and career within the domain of organizational literature. Those who see work as calling find meaning and tasks imbued with personal, social or moral significance (Wrzesniewski, 2012). In this perspective, calling renders work inseparable from one's identity, i.e., the question of who we are. Employees who view work as a job perceive transactional values of economic and financial security in their tasks. Career emphasizes progress over one's advancement and achievements in terms of social standing, prestige, competency and power.

On the other hand, Dik and Duffy (2009) conceptualized calling as a guiding force toward purposeful work with altruistic intentions. Additionally, Dik et al. (2012) empirically tested the definitions of calling as different from vocation. According to Dik and Duffy (2009, p. 427), calling contains three components, defined as (a) a transcendent summons, experienced as originating beyond the self, (b) to approach a particular life role in a manner oriented toward demonstrating or deriving a sense of purpose or meaningfulness, and (c) holds other-oriented values and goals as primary sources of motivation. The definition of vocation only includes two later components of calling without the first transcendent summons.

In following the definition of calling given by Dik and Duffy (2009), the majority of calling literature in management does not address true calling as a guiding force, but merely vocation. Because of this limitation, our understanding of calling lacks an essential and original complement when associated with spirituality.

We believe that the full insight of spirituality in calling can enrich our responses to these and related questions:

First, what is the nature of calling when it is not associated with work or is not relegated to a profession or occupation (e.g., non-profit work, volunteer work and work after retirement)? When we find ourselves "being purposeful" in volunteering, helping families, friends and neighbors, and serving the common good, can we define such acts as calling? At the same time, is calling tied to works considered "successful" only in a physical sense? What about traditional service work such as janitorial services, factory or construction work, homemakers and others that are not always considered "career" work? What is the (alternative) research framework or definition of calling that adequately captures the nature of service or the temporal nature of meaningful events or activities? How do we measure calling aside from its closely related constructs of vocation, career and job?

Most empirical studies on calling over-represent unique populations and extreme contexts due to the fact that the meaning of work among service-oriented activities is highly salient (Eisenhardt, 1989). Much of the research around calling has largely been studied within contexts of professions or service-oriented work such as pastors, doctors, firefighters, educators, musicians and CEOs (Haney et al., 2015). Although people working in any occupation can view their work as a calling (Wrzesniewski et al., 1997), empirical studies tend to highlight specific domains of work (Thompson & Christensen, 2018) given that caregiving professionals are more likely to experience a calling in their careers (Bloom et al., 2021). Even when a variety of business occupations are considered, a study found higher calling scores in musicians and artists than those identified in business and management (Dobrow & Tosti-Kharas, 2011).

However, another general application of calling is absent when used outside its spiritual base. John says in 12:26, ESV: "If anyone serves me, he must follow me; and where I am, there will my servant be also." In this view, "ministry," as taken from the Greek word diakoneo, means "to serve." In the tenets of Christian teaching, every believer is called to serve, following Jesus in our service to others. However, the message as presented is that we are called to a certain way of living—i.e., the way of authentic service, in what we do and how we live—compared to a certain vocation. In this perspective, we are called, not to a vocation, but to a way of life. In Christian thought, Jesus was the servant of all. In fact, He was the epitome of servant leadership—the Servant King. Christ shares in the Gospels the importance of serving, and we are called to follow Him as He serves others.

Second, how does a sense of calling emerge? What is the process of experiencing a calling? How do we discern calling as a transcendent summons compared to a call for spiritual transformation?

This question directly addresses the critical component of spirituality in calling defined by Dik and Duffy (2009). Collectively, calling research assumes that there is a process of events that occur in calling: first, there "exists" a calling; next, an individual "hears" the call; and lastly, when the person heeds the call, the response becomes a predictor of career and general life outcomes (Dobrow, 2013). Numerous studies (Austin & Ecker, 2015; Conklin, 2012; Coulson et al., 2012; Duffy et al., 2012; Hernandez et al., 2010) identified a series of attributes for events that assist in the process of realizing or discerning one's calling: the support of others, personal struggles or adversity, exposure to a calling domain (e.g., doctor exposed to health care), societal effect, change in self and personal reflection. However, the role of spiritual discernment and transformation in this process through a direct or indirect relationship with a divine or guiding force is rarely considered or discussed. Oswalt (2000) suggests that a holy life is the unifying theme of the Bible, as we are called to "be" vs called to "do." In this way, spiritual transformation is a significant component of the intended outcome in a call to service.

Third, how do we explore the possible "dark side" of a calling that hinders individual progress yet creates prosperity for those who render service? For example, missional activity has been known to establish conditions that exploit people to create income for the called, or requires people to work for low wages to compete with a non-profit business activity (Lupton, 2011; Miller, 2016); where a calling results in people working under unfavorable conditions or work that does not require the use of their God-given creative talents; when a calling results in eliminating the entrepreneurial pursuits of local businesses when charitable organizations flood markets with free goods; where seeking, having or living by a calling may lead to negative life situations for other people?

The very concept of spiritual calling implies that one's work is missional, i.e., intended to benefit the greater community and society (Cho, 2021; Dik & Duffy, 2009). Dominant research on calling suggests positive dual benefits when life goals align with a calling. Likewise, a higher sense of calling is more likely to result in increased life and job satisfaction, better health and less absence from work (Hall et al., 2012; Wrzesniewski et al., 1997), a more meaningful life and work experience (Duffy & Sedlacek, 2007; Duffy et al, 2012), higher organizational commitment and work engagement (Duffy et al., 2011; Hirschi, 2012) and service-oriented outcomes. Prosocial results of calling are also reported such as lower conflict at work and working in harmony (Dik et al., 2009, 2012; Hall et al., 2012; Steger et al., 2010).

People who believe they have answered their calling are more likely to have positive feelings and greater satisfaction at work (Hall et al., 2012). Alternatively, an unanswered perceived calling linked to their current job is associated with negative life satisfaction and well-being (Berg et al., 2010; Marsh et al., 2020). As calling is positively related to a willingness to sacrifice and being diligent toward organizational duty (Bunderson & Thompson, 2009), it is quite plausible that calling can also engender higher work-related stress with longer work hours or with less compensation. A decision to endure stress and deal with conflict at the workplace to honor one's perception of calling (Oates et al., 2008; Treadgold, 1999) might justify and even reinforce decisions to endure toxic environments and higher levels of stress and conflict.

A Purpose and a Calling

Purpose and calling are often considered under the same definition in association with work. Freeney (2021) suggests that purpose falls under a general responsibility, whereas calling is associated with specialization or a specific role. Viewed another way, purpose is the destination, and how to get there is through our calling. In this sense, our calling includes the use of our unique talents, abilities and spiritual gifts.

However, another perspective is to see purpose as a vocation, defined by our gifts (the what), and calling as how we prepare for and conduct the work or vocation we choose. We are called to a way of life, a way to live and not necessarily what we do. As young adults, we are often concerned that we choose the "right" vocation or career. Such concern is understandable considering the complexity of the world we live in today. However, what we do in calling is not as important as learning how to live in practicing our vocation.

To identify a vocation that is guided, not by our choice, but by spiritual guidance, Bricker (2020) suggests five ways to determine a career path:

1. ***Discern Your Spiritual Gifts***
   It is easier to determine God's will for your career when you know what your spiritual gifts are. In this way, you will be better prepared to know how to serve God in your career.

   The Holy Spirit gifts all believers with at least one spiritual gift. Biblical references define spiritual gifts to include serving, teaching, giving, encouragement, discernment, leadership, mercy, words of wisdom, words of knowledge, healing, faith and the gift of helps (NIV, 2011, Romans 12:6–8; 1 Corinthians 12:4–11; 1 Corinthians 12:28). God also gave us natural gifts. For some, this may be painting, others writing poetry or playing a musical instrument. Others might navigate mathematics, chemistry and engineering fields with ease and personal enjoyment.

   When we have discerned our spiritual gifts, we can determine which career God is more likely to lead us into because He has blessed us with the spiritual gifts to do the job successfully.

2. ***Seek spiritual guidance through prayer.*** Talking with God in prayer is the best way to determine God's will for our career. If we don't have a relationship with God, this is the best way to initiate a relationship by asking for His guidance and thus begin a divine relationship as a source of strength and assurance that will guide us throughout our lives. With spiritual guidance, we can talk through different career options with God. Bricker (2020) says we can *"...pour out your heart to Him and tell Him how you want to serve Him in whatever career we choose."*

   If we communicate with God conversationally in prayer, we find peace knowing that He is trustworthy in His time, in every place. Therefore, the vocation we choose does not determine our fate. Our responsibility is how we conduct our lives in faithful response to the opportunity to serve. If we make a dedicated effort to pray consistently, there is no wrong choice in vocation. Paul tells us to pray continually, without ceasing (NIV, 2011, 1 Thessalonians 5:16–18). God cares about how our career aligns with His plans and purpose. However, this is something that God works out. He wants us to bring our concerns, worries and desires about

our future career to Him. Therefore, ask God to direct you to the career He wants for you as part of His provision for all people.
3. ***Seek spiritual guidance through reading divinely inspired Scriptures.*** Reading God's Word is essential to hear from a divine source rather than another less reliable source. This is important not only for career decisions but also in other areas of our lives. To be comfortable with our decisions, regular confirmation is reassuring and can offset feelings of doubt and uncertainty as we wait for an option to materialize. Because God speaks to us through His Word, it is critical that we read the Bible to hear from Him and discern His will.
4. ***Consult Trusted Counsel***. Consulting trusted second person spiritual guidance is a practical way to determine God's will for our career choices. Talking with others who have a relationship with us and who also have a close spiritual relationship with the divine can help us better determine where God is leading us. Parents, advisors, teachers, ministers and mentors who have a true spiritual relationship can help point us in the right direction for a career of service.

    Trusted second person spiritual relationships in your life should know you well enough to help talk through different options for your career. Establishing trusted spiritual relationships can also help synthesize a career search after consulting God in prayer. These trustworthy friends or family members could be a great source for networking and encouragement as you wait patiently to see a clear path ahead.
5. ***Practice Patience***

    Being patient is necessary to confirm God's will for our career path. "*When we are job searching, it is easy to become impatient with the process of resumes, applications, and waiting to hear back from potential employers*" (Bricker, 2020). Although waiting can be difficult, asking God to help us wait patiently will strengthen our faith and provide encouragement as He shapes the time and circumstances around our career. It is important to remember that God has a plan that includes us as He provides for many needs according to His purpose.
6. ***Practice Trust***

    Doubting casts a shadow on any plan. Even before an outcome is decided, the tendency to wait in doubt weakens the spirit and opens the door for hasty decisions and poor career choices. There is always the temptation to doubt God's faithfulness because doubt deteriorates our relationship with the Divine, which is the intent of dark forces that challenge God's authority. The defense against doubt is to decide to trust in God, no matter the outcome. Sometimes God will close the door on a career (or even a relationship) that, through our wisdom, we thought we wanted. The option may make financial sense or appear to be aligned with our dream job (or relationship). However, if we are not chosen for a position, trust that God knows best and is still working in our best interest. Serving God is the path and end goal of every decision. Even if we do not obtain our dream choices, we can serve God in whatever path He opens. Prioritizing God's plan for our life will ensure that whatever career, whatever the path, we will find fulfillment and perfect provision.

> And we know that in all things God works for the good of those who love him, who have been called according to his purpose. (NIV, 2011, Romans 8:28)

In making personal vocational choices without consulting God, the outcome can be a wrong focus or misguided view on the purpose of life. In any vocational choice, our priority is to grow to live like God in Christ as our example. Being in a relationship with Christ means we live like him, not merely in what we choose to do, but in how we work and live.

> As a prisoner for the Lord, then, I urge you to live a life worthy of the calling you have received. Be completely humble and gentle; be patient, bearing with one another in love. There is one body and one Spirit, just as you were called to one hope when you were called; Make every effort to keep the unity of the Spirit through the bond of peace. So I tell you this, and insist on it in the Lord, that you must no longer live as the Gentiles do, in the futility of their thinking. They are darkened in their understanding and separated from the life of God because of the ignorance that is in them due to the hardening of their hearts. Having lost all sensitivity, they have given themselves over to sensuality so as to indulge in every kind of impurity, and they are full of greed. Therefore each of you must put off falsehood and speak truthfully to your neighbor, for we are all members of one body. "In your anger do not sin": Do not let the sun go down while you are still angry, and do not give the devil a foothold. Anyone who has been stealing must steal no longer, but must work, doing something useful with their own hands, that they may have something to share with those in need. Be kind and compassionate to one another, forgiving each other, just as in Christ God forgave you. (NIV, 2011, Ephesians 4:1–3; 17–19; 25–32)

The purpose in any career and in life is to open the door to fulfillment, wellness and personal growth that emanates from our work when aligned with divine priorities and purpose.

Work as Service—Our Purpose at Work

Lepisto and Pratt (2017) define work as a service that is motivated by the intention to serve others and contribute to the common good. Their concept of work as service is a key component of spirituality in the workplace. Nurses who view their work as service can be motivated to help patients recover and improve their conditions. Teachers who see their work as a service can focus on a variety of life and learning needs to help students perform better. Organizations can embrace the concept of work as service and develop strategies to promote good will among employees by providing opportunities for them to engage in service activities outside of work and creating a culture that values service and encourages employees to see their work as a way of contributing to something beyond themselves.

In Buddhism, the concept of dana or generosity can be applied to work as service, as individuals are encouraged to use their skills and talents to benefit others and contribute to a greater good. Hartnett (2015) examines how the Buddhist concept of bodhisattva, or one who seeks to alleviate the suffering of others, can inform our understanding of work as a form of service to others.

In this way, work is not just a means of personal fulfillment but also a way of caring for others through our personal service, making a positive impact on society.

An Entrepreneurial Mindset

Much of the displeasure in work results from our attitude toward work through an employer, which can be influenced by personal, corporate and environmental factors, whether perceived or real (Ali & Al-Owaihan, 2008; Mitroff & Denton, 1999, 2009). The condition associated with lack of pleasure or fulfillment when working for an employer has often been associated with feelings of burnout (Bakker et al., 2014). Burnout refers to a state of exhaustion and cynicism toward work, compared to engagement which is defined as a positive motivational state of vigor, dedication and absorption. Employees who are engaged in their work are fully connected with their work roles, energetic, dedicated to their work and immersed in their work activities (Bakker, 2011). In this research, although both burnout and work engagement are related to important job-related outcomes, burnout seems to be more strongly related to health outcomes, whereas work engagement is more strongly related to motivational outcomes.

Entrepreneurship offers motivations that are different when compared to traditional agency-type work (see Agency theory as used by scholars in accounting (e.g., Demski & Feltham, 1978), economics (e.g., Spence & Zeckhauser, 1971), finance (e.g., Fama, 1980), marketing (e.g., Basu et al., 1985), political science (e.g., Mitnick, 1986), organizational behavior (e.g., Eisenhardt, 1985, 1988; Kosnik, 1987) and sociology (e.g., Eccles, 1985; White, 1985). The major distinction is that the entrepreneur works for self- versus other-duty fulfillment. In entrepreneurship, a greater focus on personal efficacy is needed to satisfy service for the greater good to ensure sufficient gain from personal profits (Miner, 1997; Olson, 1985). Extensive research has defined the psychology of an entrepreneur in ways that develop faithfulness in their work. Work traits such as focus, purpose, consistency of interest and perseverance (i.e., "grit") are needed to be a successful entrepreneur (Aminuddin et al., 2014; Asante et al., 2022). As a non-exhaustive list of personality traits, Frese and Gielnik (2014) share personality dimensions, such as self-efficacy, the need for achievement, entrepreneurial orientation and alertness as highly associated with entrepreneurship business creation and business success.

Knowledge in areas such as business planning and financial capital and preparation in areas such as practical intelligence, understanding of cognitive biases, goals and visions, personal initiative and passion are noted as required skillsets.

When we consider the inventory of traits and preparedness needed for the successful entrepreneur, we can apply this in a servant-oriented manner to work in general. Whether for personal pursuits or to ensure a faithful response to any work, an entrepreneurial spirit will help focus on the work at hand to ensure both community provision and a rewarding career. In either vocation or career structure, success based on personal efforts for personal gain implies success through faithful service for the entire organization.

God at Work

> There are different kinds of working, but in all of them and in everyone it is the same God at work. There are different kinds of gifts, but the same Spirit distributes them. There are different kinds of service, but the same Lord. There are different kinds of working, but in all of them and in everyone it is the same God at work. Now to each one the manifestation of the Spirit is given for the common good. To one there is given through the Spirit a message of wisdom, to another a message of knowledge by means of the same Spirit, to another faith by the same Spirit, to another gifts of healing by that one Spirit, to another miraculous powers, to another prophecy, to another distinguishing between spirits, to another speaking in different kinds of tongues,[a] and to still another the interpretation of tongues.[b] All these are the work of one and the same Spirit, and he distributes them to each one, just as he determines. (NIV, 2011, 1 Corinthians 12:4–11)

> Whatever you do, work at it with all your heart, as working for the Lord, not for human masters. (NIV, 2011, Colossians 3:23)

We each have a purpose in fulfilling God's provision and purpose for mankind. From the passage as cited, we understand that work is a designed orchestration of activity that comes together to accomplish God's will. When our work is mainly focused on what we want, we live a distorted view of our purpose as we focus on self-directed interests that serve individual needs. When we walk with a divine guide, we participate in service that is in harmony with community efforts to provide for all people. When we operate through a singular focus, we inadvertently create a commodity focus where we or other people function as assets (e.g., as in slave labor, as working on a plantation), poorly treated, misused, working for the benefit of others.

> "Now you are the body of Christ, and each one of you is a part of it. And God has placed in the church first of all apostles, second prophets, third teachers, then miracles, then gifts of healing, of helping, of guidance, and of different kinds of tongues. Are all apostles? Are all prophets? Are all teachers? Do all

work miracles? Do all have gifts of healing? Do all speak in tongues[d]? Do all interpret? Now eagerly desire the greater gifts". (NIV, 2011, 1 Corinthians 12:27–31)

This passage emphasizes the need to view all work and vocation as important parts of a whole body at work, each gift operating with a uniquely divine purpose. No work is to be regarded as menial or less than any other position. Each has its purpose in creating a fully functioning body, a perfectly harmonious community.

It is important for our personal health and provision that we no longer focus on what we do but on how we serve in using our gifts to meet communal needs. What we do is a personal choice that can be made to commit to a path and maintain our identity by aligning career objectives with our vocational gifts. In doing so, we focus on efficacy in preparation for a career path to serve the greater good.

Do not work for food that spoils, but for food that endures to eternal life, which the Son of Man will give you. For on him God the Father has placed his seal of approval. Then they asked him, 'What must we do to do the works God requires?' Jesus answered, 'The work of God is this: to believe in the one he has sent'. (NIV, 2011, John 6:27–29)

Conclusion

As long as it is day, we must do the works of him who sent me. Night is coming, when no one can work. (NIV, 2011, John 9:4)

As humans, we are naturally inclined to focus on temporary goals and purposes—things that satisfy our immediate needs and wants. However, the wisdom literature reminds us that there is more to life than just temporary pursuits. In John 6:27–29 (NIV, 2011), Jesus tells us to work not just for food that spoils, but for food that endures to eternal life. He emphasizes that the work of God is to believe in Him, and this should be our ultimate purpose. In Colossians 3:23, we are reminded to approach our work with a spiritual focus, working with all our heart as if we are working for the Lord and not for human masters. Our work should be a personal reflection of our faith and our dedication to serving God. Finally, in John 9:4 (NIV, 2011), Jesus urges us to use our time wisely, doing the works of God while we still have the chance. Our time on earth is limited, and we should make the most of it by serving and doing His work. In summary, while temporary pursuits are necessary along an initial path, our ultimate purpose should be to serve God and do His work. We should approach any work with a spiritual focus and use our time wisely to fulfill greater purposes.

Just because we are hired for a job today does not mean we will stay in the same career for our entire lives. Research confirms that people change careers several times during a lifespan. If you love the career you are in now and are faithful in serving, feel free to continue to do so. However, if you are feeling discouraged with your current career situation, know that you don't have to stay in the same career for your entire life—especially if the work culture is manipulative or unhealthy. Some work is necessary and even personally sacrificial to serve an immediate need. However, such sacrifice should be regarded as temporary as we work for divine purposes.

Instead of thinking of how much we hate doing work, we can think instead of how much our work will help in our personal development and perhaps help others live a peaceful, fulfilled life. This is an example from military or related public service work where we focus our thoughts on how we choose to serve using our work to help someone else. This is a healthy perspective even when we're given a difficult decision or task. Although we may never know how the work that we're doing will impact others, ultimately, the intent of any job we have can be done for the greater good.

Trusting God in our view of work brings peace and purpose to our labors. As an example, Robertson (1995) shared this prayer from an unknown Confederate soldier, which expresses the humility through which we should seek God's path in our work, yielding to His will:

The soldier wrote:

> I asked God for strength, that I might achieve.
> I was made weak, that I might learn humbly how to obey.
> I asked for health, that I might do greater things.
> I was given infirmity, that I might do better things.
> I asked for riches, that I might be happy.
> I was given poverty, that I might be wise.
> I asked for power, that I might have the praise of men.
> I was given weakness, that I might feel the need of God.
> I asked for all things, that I might enjoy life.
> I was given life, that I might enjoy all things.
> I got nothing that I asked for – but everything I had hoped for.
> Almost despite myself, my unspoken prayers were answered.
> I am, among all men, most richly blessed.

Being open to God's guidance and purpose assures us of the best fulfillment for a life that continues in eternity. In our work, as with other areas of concern, we should remember that our life is found in service and not through a career.

> Whatever you do, work heartily, as for the Lord and not for men, knowing that from the Lord you will receive the inheritance as your reward. You are serving the Lord Christ. (NIV, 2011, Colossians 3:23–24)

References

Ali, A. J., & Al-Owaihan, A. (2008). Islamic work ethic: A critical review. *Cross Cultural Management: An International Journal, 15*(1), 5–19.

Aminuddin, Z. S., Bustaman, U. S. A., & Wahab, K. A. (2014). *Establishing Maqasid al-Shariah principles in Islamic entrepreneurship.*

Asante, E. A., Kurshid, H., Affum-Osei, E., & Antwi, C. O. (2022). Becoming an entrepreneur: How trait grit affects aspiring entrepreneur's opportunity recognition. *Academy of Management Proceedings, 2022*(1). https://doi.org/10.5465/AMBPP.2022.10688abstract

Ashmos, D. P., & Duchon, D. (2000). Spirituality at work: A conceptualization and measure. *Journal of Management Inquiry, 9*(2), 134–145.

Austin, K., & Ecker, D. (2015). The power of perceived experience: Events that shape work as a calling. *Career Development Quarterly, 63*(1), 16–30.

Bakker, A. B. (2011). An evidence-based model of worker engagement. *Current Directions in Psychological Science, 20*(4), 265–269.

Bakker, A. B., Demerouti, E., & Sanz-Vergel, A. I. (2014). Burnout and work engagement: The JD–R approach. *Annual Review of Organizational Psychology and Organizational Behavior, 1*, 389–411.

Basu, A., Lal, R., Srinivasan, V., & Staelin, R. (1985) Sales-force compensation plans: An agency theoretic perspective. *Marketing Science, 4*, 267–291.

Berg, J. M., Grant, A. M., & Johnson, V. (2010). When callings are calling: Crafting work and leisure in pursuit of unanswered occupational callings. *Organization Science, 21*(5), 973–994.

Blanchard, K., & O'Connor, M. (2019). *The 5 essential principles of values-driven leadership.* Berrett-Koehler Publishers.

Bloom, M., Colbert, A. E., & Nielsen, J. D. (2021). Stories of calling: How called professionals construct narrative identities. *Administrative Science Quarterly, 66*(2), 298–338.

Bricker, V. (2020). *Five practical ways to determine God's will for my career.* https://www.ibelieve.com/career-calling/5-practical-ways-to-determine-gods-will-for-my-career.html

Bunderson, S. J., & Thompson, J. A. (2009). The call of the wild: Zookeepers, callings, and the double-edged sword of deeply meaningful work. *Administrative Science Quarterly, 54*(1), 32–57.

Cho, B. (2021). *Being missional, becoming missional: A biblical-theological study of the missional conversion of the Church.* Pickwick Publications.

Conklin, T. A. (2012). Work worth doing: A phenomenological study of the experience of discovering and following one's calling. *Journal of Management Inquiry, 21*, 298–317.

Coulson, J., Oades, L., & Stoyles, G. (2012). Parent's conception and experience of calling in child rearing: A qualitative analysis. *Journal of Humanistic Psychology, 52*, 222–247.

Demski, J. S., & Feltham, G. A. (1978). Economic incentives in budgetary control systems. *Accounting Review*, 336–359.

Dik, B. J., & Duffy, R. D. (2009). Calling and vocation at work: Definitions and prospects for research and practice. *The Counseling Psychologist, 37*, 424–450.

Dik, B. J., Eldridge, B. M., Steger, M. F., & Duffy, R. D. (2012). Development and validation of the Calling and Vocation Questionnaire (CVQ) and Brief Calling Scale (BCS). *Journal of Career Assessment, 20*(3), 293–308.

Dobrow, S. R. (2013). Dynamics of calling: A longitudinal study of musicians. *Journal of Organizational Behavior, 34*(4), 431–452.

Dobrow, S. R., & Tosti-Kharas, J. (2011). Calling: The development of a scale measure. *Personnel Psychology, 64*(4), 1001–1049.

Duchon, D., & Plowman, D. A. (2005). Nurturing the spirit at work: Impact on work unit performance. *The Leadership Quarterly, 16*(5), 807–833.

Duffy, R. D., Bott, E. M., Allan, B. A., Torrey, C. L., & Dik, B. J. (2012). Perceiving a calling, living a calling, and job satisfaction: Testing a moderated, multiple mediator model. *Journal of Counseling Psychology, 59*, 50–59.

Duffy, R. D., Dik, B. J., & Steger, M. F. (2011). Calling and work-related outcomes: Career commitment as a mediator. *Journal of Vocational Behavior, 78*, 210–218.

Duffy, R. D., & Sedlacek, W. E. (2007). The presence of and search for a calling: Connections to career development. *Journal of Vocational Behavior, 70*(3), 590–601.

Eccles, R. (1985). Transfer pricing as a problem of agency. In J. Pratt & R. Zeckhauser (Eds.), *Principals and agents: The structure of business* (pp. 151–186). Harvard Business School Press.

Eisenhardt, K. (1985). Control: Organizational and economic approaches. *Management Science, 31*, 134–149.

Eisenhardt, K. (1988). Agency and institutional explanations of compensation in retail sales. *Academy of Management Journal, 31*, 488–511.

Eisenhardt, K. M. (1989). Building theories from case study research. *Academy of Management Review, 14*(4), 532–550.

Fama, E. (1980). Agency problems and the theory of the firm. *Journal of Political Economy, 88*, 288–307.

Freeney, V. R. (2021). *Difference between purpose and calling* [Blog post]. https://vernettarfreeney.com/difference-between-purpose-and-calling-2021/#:~:text=Purpose%20is%20general%20and%20calling,as%20unique%20as%20our%20fingerprints

Frese, M., & Gielnik, M. M. (2014). The psychology of entrepreneurship. *Annual Review of Organizational Psychology and Organizational Behavior, 1*, 413–438.

Fry, L. W., & Nisiewicz, M. J. (2013). *Maximizing the triple bottom line through spiritual leadership*. Stanford University Press.

Greenhaus, J. H. (2003). Spirituality and work: An overview. In R. A. Giacalone & C. L. Jurkiewicz (Eds.), *Handbook of workplace spirituality and organizational performance* (pp. 15–28). M.E. Sharpe.

Hall, M., Oates, K. M., Anderson, T. L., & Willingham, M. M. (2012). Calling and conflict: The sanctification of work in working mothers. *Psychology of Religion and Spirituality, 4*, 71–83.

Haney, L. D. M., McKenna, R. B., Robie, C., Austin, K., & Ecker, D. (2015). The power of perceived experience: Events that shape work as a calling. *Career Development Quarterly, 63*(1), 16–30.

Hardy, L. (1990). *The fabric of this world*. Eerdmans.

Hartnett, C. (2015). Work and the Bodhisattva Ideal in Theravada Buddhism. *Journal of Buddhist Ethics, 22*, 23–59.

Hasegawa, S. (2017). The concept of right livelihood in Buddhism. *Buddhist Studies Review, 34*(1), 63–83.

Hernandez, E. F., Foley, P. F., & Beitin, B. K. (2010). Hearing the call: A phenomenological study of religion in career choice. *Journal of Career Development, 38*, 62–88.

Hirschi, A. (2012). Callings and work engagement: Moderated mediation model of work meaningfulness, occupational identity, and occupational self-efficacy. *Journal of Counseling Psychology, 59*, 479–485.

Judge, T. A., Erez, A., Bono, J. E., & Thoresen, C. J. (2007). The core self-evaluations scale: Development of a measure. *Journal of Applied Psychology, 92*(2), 295–307.

Karakas, F. (2010). Spirituality and performance in organizations: A literature review. *Journal of Business Ethics, 94*(1), 89–106.

King James Version. (1987). BibleGateway.com. https://www.biblegateway.com/versions/King-James-Version-KJV-Bible/#booklist

Kosnik, R. (1987). Greenmail: A study in board performance in corporate governance. *Administrative Science Quarterly, 32*, 163–185.

Lepisto, D. A., & Pratt, M. G. (2017). Work as service: A review and future directions. *Journal of Management, Spirituality & Religion, 14*(3), 218–239.

Lips-Wiersma, M., & Morris, L. (2009). Discriminating between 'meaningful work' and the 'management of meaning.' *Journal of Business Ethics, 88*(3), 491–511.

Lupton, R. D. (2011). *Toxic charity: How churches and charities hurt those they help*. HarperCollins.

Marsh, D. R., Alayan, A. J., & Dik, B. J. (2020). Answered callings, unanswered callings, or no calling: Examining a nationally representative sample. *Career Development Quarterly, 68*(4), 374–380.

Maslow, A. H. (1943). A theory of human motivation. *Psychological Review, 50*(4), 370–396.

Maupin, E. J. (2007). *Work as a spiritual practice: A practical Buddhist approach to inner growth and satisfaction on the job*. Penguin.

Mearian, L. (2023). The great resignation: Where did the millions who quit their jobs go? *Computerworld*. Retrieved February 10, 2023, from https://www.computerworld.com/article/3686615/the-great-resignation-where-did-the-millions-who-quit-their-jobs-go.html#:~:text=One%2Dthird%20(34%25)%20of,opportunities%2C%20according%20to%20Cengage%20Group

Miller, M. M. (Producer & Director). (2016). *Poverty cure: Poverty, justice, human flourishing* [Film]. Exploration Films. https://www.explorationfilms.com/povertycureglobaledition.html

Miner, J. B. (1997). *A psychological typology of successful entrepreneurs*. Quorum Books.

Mitnick, B. (1986). *The theory of agency and organizational analysis*. Unpublished working paper, University of Pittsburgh.

Mitroff, I., & Denton, E. A. (1999). *A spiritual audit of corporate America: A hard look at spirituality, religion, and values in the workplace*. Jossey-Bass.

Mitroff, I. I., & Denton, E. A. (2009). A study of spirituality in the workplace. *Sloan Management Review, 40*(4), 83–92.

Murray, C. I., & Workman, K. R. (2015). Spirituality and job satisfaction among non-faculty employees of a private Catholic university. *Journal of Catholic Education, 18*(3), 317–345.

New International Version. (2011). BibleGateway.com. http://www.biblegateway.com/versions/New-International-Version-NIV-Bible/#booklist

Oates, K. M., Hall, M., Anderson, T. L., & Willingham, M. M. (2008). Pursuing multiple callings: The implications of balancing career and motherhood for women and the church. *Journal of Psychology and Christianity, 27*, 227–237.

Olson, P. D. (1985). Entrepreneurship: Process and abilities. *American Journal of Small Business, 10*(1), 25–31.

Oswalt, J. N. (2000). *Called to be holy*. Warner Press/Francis Asbury Press.

Placher, W. C. (Ed.). (2005). *Callings: Twenty centuries of Christian wisdom*. Eerdmans.

Robertson, J. (1995, 2019). *Prayer of an unknown Confederate soldier*. Virginia Tech, Civil war series, 52. Retrieved December 12, 2022, from https://www.wvtf.org/civil-war-series/2019-12-15/an-unknown-confederate-soldier

Schabram, K., Nielsen, J., & Thompson, J. (2022). The dynamics of work orientations: An updated typology and agenda for the study of jobs, careers, and callings. *Academy of Management Annals*. Advance Online Publication. https://doi.org/10.5465/annals.2021.0153

Scherer, J. A. (2019). Meaningful work in Buddhism. In D. Shepherd, M. Sisodia, & J. V. M. Holzmann (Eds.), *Conscious capitalism field guide* (pp. 213–219). Harvard Business Review Press.

Smith, B. N., & Vargo, J. (2019). Entrepreneurship, sustainability, and giftedness. *Journal of Business Ethics, 156*(1), 1–12.

Spence, A. M., & Zeckhauser, R. (1971). Insurance, information, and individual action. *American Economic Review, 61*, 380–387.

Steger, M. F., Dik, D. J., & Duffy, R. D. (2012). Measuring meaningful work; The work and meaning inventory (WAMI). *Journal of Career Assessment, 20*(3), 322–337.

Steger, M. F., Pickering, N. K., Adams, E., Burnett, J., Shin, J., Dik, B. J., & Stauner, N. (2010). The quest for meaning: Religious affiliation differences in the correlates of religious quest and search for meaning in life. *Psychology of Religion and Spirituality, 2*, 206–226.

Taylor, M., & McKenzie, B. (2009). Work, spirituality, and organizational values: A study of Canadian health care professionals. *Journal of Business Ethics, 84*(2), 297–311.

Thompson, J. A., & Christensen, R. K. (2018). Bridging the public service motivation and calling literatures. *Public Administration Review, 78*(3), 444–456.

Treadgold, R. (1999). Transcendent vocations: Their relationship to stress, depression, and clarity of self-concept. *Journal of Humanistic Psychology, 39*, 81–105.

Wallace, B. A. (2001). *The Buddha at work: Finding balance, purpose, and happiness at your workplace*. Bantam.

White, H. (1985). Agency as control. In J. Pratt & R. Zeckhauser (Eds.), *Principals and agents: The structure of business* (pp. 187–214). Harvard Business School Press.

Wrzesniewski, A., McCauley, C., Rozin, P., & Schwartz, B. (1997). Jobs, careers, and callings: People's relations to their work. *Journal of Research in Personality, 31*(1), 21–33.

Wrzesniewski, A. (2012). Callings. In K. Cameron & G. Spreitzer (Eds.), *Handbook of positive organizational scholarship* (pp. 45–55). Oxford University Press.

CHAPTER 5

An Analysis of Consumers' Thrifting Practices as an Act of Eudaimonia

Letizia Milanesi, Silvia Biraghi, and Rossella C. Gambetti

Introduction

We turn off the light when we leave a room empty. We arrange food in the fridge according to the best before. We walk and cycle instead of driving whenever we can. We pass over clothes when they are too small for our fast-growing kids. We refill bottles and avoid plastic bags and boxes. We give a second life to old stuff by creatively repurposing them or selling them. Well, not everybody does that, but many consumers are not just depleting value from their consumption objects. Many consumers actively seek ways to increase, extend, and circulate value through small virtuous actions that possess the potential for achieving a more fulfilling state of life based on wise personal growth and societal well-being.

In this chapter, we adopt Arendt's (1958) interpretation of Aristotle's concept of Eudaimonia and virtuous actions to analyze how consumers pursue a state of individual and communitarian well-being by engaging in thrifting practices. According to Arendt, virtuous actions are supposed to be free, plural communicative performances that allow people to begin something anew, and to express their joy at creating something new by interacting with social groups. With the advent of apps and technologies that are making it easier and easier to resell and buy old clothes or items, we see in thrifting practices a context in which consumers publicly and collaboratively construct a more

L. Milanesi (✉) · S. Biraghi · R. C. Gambetti
LABCOM, Università Cattolica del Sacro Cuore, Milan, Italy
e-mail: letizmilanesi@gmail.com

© The Author(s), under exclusive license to Springer Nature Switzerland AG 2023
J. Marques (ed.), *The Palgrave Handbook of Fulfillment, Wellness, and Personal Growth at Work*,
https://doi.org/10.1007/978-3-031-35494-6_5

ethical and sustainable circuit of consumption. In our chapter, then we explore and elaborate how thrifting can represent a realm where consumers pursue the attainment of a eudaimonic state and a flourishing virtuous life.

Eudaimonia and Virtuous Action

Ancient Greek philosophers and Aristotle in particular have long been concerned with questions like what it means to have a moral character and what the links between such character and responsibility are. This morally valuable character trait is traditionally called 'virtue' and is referred to as the set of actions that individuals undertake to pursue the good life (Reis, 2006). According to Aristotle's Nicomachean Ethics, the concept of virtue plays a crucial role in the attainment of happiness, which he calls 'Eudaimonia', meant as the activity of a complete life in accordance with complete virtue as he posits that happiness can be better understood by investigating the field of virtue (Rapp, 2006). Happiness is, then, the actualization of virtuous actions, and according to this perspective, happiness can only come from good activities, from something that functions well and meets high moral standards (Rapp, 2006). Individuals in fact experience Eudaimonia when their life activities match their values, contribute to their life goals, when they learn and grow as individuals, and when they feel integrated into a social setting through their engagements (Ryff, 1989). Eudaimonia then not only includes happiness meant as pleasure attainment and pain avoidance (Ryan & Deci, 2001), as from a hedonic perspective, but also emphasizes vitality, meaning, purposeful engagement, the realization of personal potential, autonomy, mastery, quality ties to others, and self-acceptance (Deci et al., 2001; Ryff, 2019). By focusing on functioning rather than on feeling, eudaimonic well-being highlights the value of actions rather than emotions. The notion of action or better virtuous actions is at the heart of Eudaimonia. It is, in fact, through actions and by aligning their actual and ideal self that people manifest who they are, and attain Eudaimonia (Fabian, 2020). In Aristotelian philosophy, Eudaimonia and the good life are always associated with the human agent's willingness to act and perform virtuous actions.

According to Arendt's reading of Aristotle (1958), actions are activities that are essentially creative and free from the imperatives of necessity (i.e , the production of goods required for material survival) performed in a public space where people can leave behind their domestic and workplace concerns. In Arendt's perspective (1958), actions must be public because the manifestation of the 'daimon' only appears in respect of other people, not just oneself (Arendt, 1958). There are no daimon appearances without people perceiving them (Kulik, 2002). Stories and their unique meanings are the results of action and speech. In a social sense, public actions, words, deeds, and the joy of creating allow people to pursue a good or flourishing life by interacting with social groups (Robinson, 2013).

Building on Arendt's theoretical notion of eudaimonic action, in an empirical study of social labor and cooking, Biraghi et al. (2020) recently showed that individuals engage in digital practices of social labor to display their ethical virtues and live their life at its best by unleashing their own potential and freedom to self-express. In doing so, they achieve a state of Eudaimonia. By studying the representation of cooking practices in social media, the authors illustrate how the cultural agency of consumers to produce, assemble, and share contents while performing identity work actualizes the concept of performativity in Aristotle and Arendt's conceptions in the context of social media. In their study, the authors focus on individuals who, via social media, communicate as conscious subjects animated by a clear self-entrepreneurial ethos (Marttila, 2013) and who—with the support of information, communication, and social technologies (Ashman et al., 2018)—increasingly find their own, unique space of self-governmentality that enables them to conduct their 'life as an enterprise' (Scharff, 2016) in eudaimonic terms. The expression of a self-entrepreneurial ethos in social media enables individuals to form significant—although fleeting and ephemeral—relationships. It also liberates connective energy that gets technologically and affectively intensified (Just, 2019) thanks to communication technologies and provides a shared sense of purpose or direction that binds individuals' otherwise loosely connected networks (Arvidsson, 2011). This combination allows people to pursue a good or flourishing life in interaction with social groups (Robinson, 2013: 77–78) through words, deeds, and the joy of creating in a social sense.

Similarly to what Biraghi et al. (2020) have found in the context of food preparation, in this chapter, we focus on thrifting practices as a setting where the Aristotelian concept of virtuous action can be observed as it unfolds in the technosocial ecosystem of apps and social media that thrifters use to pursue a eudaimonic state and a flourishing life through the creation of a more virtuous circuit of consumption.

The Rise of Thrifting Practices

In this paragraph, we will approach an ever-growing (mass) phenomenon, which shows vividly how individuals are way more than simple consumers and how they can influence brands in society by adopting sustainable shopping practices. We are talking here about thrifting practices. We will then analyze popular thrifting apps and illustrate the key findings of a recent netnographic study conducted in the realm of thriftaholic consumers with the aim to underline how such practice can lead to a continuous process of fulfilling or realizing one's daimon, or true nature, one's virtuous potential and living as one inherently intended to live (Deci & Ryan, 2008). Accordingly, we will elaborate thrifting as a eudaimonic activity as it provides individuals with the opportunity to pursue a eudaimonic state of well-being that occurs when people are holistically, or fully, engaged in pursuing those values, goals, and projects that are most congruent or mesh with their sense of self (Waterman, 1993).

Nowadays, thrifting is the practice of buying and selling secondhand clothing, footwear, and accessories at affordable prices, but its origins date back to the Premodern Ages, when these items were seen as valuable resources both in the perspective of trading them and handing them down to the next generations. At that time there was nothing unseemly in buying secondhand, indeed preserving and conserving goods was a praxis. This perception began to change in the late eighteenth century following massive material and cultural transformations: in particular, the deepening of the medical knowledge brought to light the diffusion mechanisms of diseases, and this led to rising hygiene standards, making people more distrustful of pre-owned apparel (Lozza et al., 2019).

In sum, until the second half of the twentieth century, we are witnessing a polarization (Lozza et al., 2019) of the secondhand market, having on the one hand worthless items sold in questionable flea markets, and, on the other hand, valuable antiques sold in niche market auctions. Instead, from then up to our days, emerging meanings have been tied to cultural aspects: wearing secondhand clothes has taken on a different significance in consumer culture. That since some consumer groups, like hippies or vintage lovers, started using secondhand items to express their detachment from the dominant culture and homologation and from the mainstream market. Furthermore, it should be noted that, at that time, the bond between clothing and identity began to become increasingly tight and today represents an aspect that continues to affect consumption choices.

It is clear that this practice—survived to this day—is now flourishing, partly as a result of sustainability concerns and in part due to the innovative relational and value meanings that it is assuming in new consumption contexts, like the technosocial platforms.

Coming back to the analysis of the thrifting concept, this specific term derives from the English 'thrift shop', used to state charity shops, where secondhand goods were sold to raise money for charitable causes. In fact, 'thrift' literally means 'the careful use of money, especially by avoiding waste' (see 'thrift' in Cambridge Dictionary), the reason why it has then been associated with secondhand shops. However, over time the term has lost its Christian meaning, beginning to be used as a label for buying and selling original and distinctive clothes and accessories eventually inside folkloristic and evocative places. In the last few years, there has been a boom of these kinds of flea markets—both physical (especially in big cities) and virtual (through apps and online platforms)—that has allowed and allows giving a second life to garments, not only the iconic or peculiar ones but to all of them, even fast-fashion brand items. In fact, today thrifting no longer revolves exclusively around vintage or designer pieces but mostly around unsigned or fast-fashion apparel, witnessing a huge shift in consumers' way of perceiving and thinking secondhand. Besides this emerging peculiarity, another new characteristic lies in the fact that in addition to high-level platforms—that provide a huge selection of clothes—merchants and traders, to sell used clothing today are private citizens. If in the past years, only merchants, charities, and enthusiasts' niche dedicated themselves to this trading, nowadays the platforms and apps boom aimed at this activity makes it possible for anyone to exercise it. Therefore, users, while maintaining their consumers' identity, are becoming producers because they 'create the market' inside (of) all these dedicated spaces, assuming consequently the status of prosumers. It was originally Alvin Toffler, an American sociologist and futurologist, in his work 'The Third Wave' (1980), who coined this specific neologism by defining a 'prosumer' as someone who blurs the distinction between a 'consumer' and a 'producer': today, we see prosumers as 'people who produce some of the goods and services entering their own consumption' (Kotler et al., 2010). So thrifters are prosumers because they are consumers who are themselves producers or who contribute to production through consumption. According to what is reported by Wolny (2012), the prosumption phenomenon—made famous by the work of Tapscott and A. Williams as the core business of a new economy ruled by cooperation and pee-to-peer relationships between its participants—began to spread with the advent of Web 2.0., whose portals have become the new economy means of prosumption. Classical examples of this category, as reported by Wolny, include: Wikipedia, where users can create, edit, and update articles and lead a discussion about them; Facebook and other social networking sites where users can both create profiles that include photos and videos, and communicate with each another in order to build a community; eBay and Craigslist, where consumers (along with retailers) create the market.

This last example allows including all the modern thrifting apps and platforms in the prosumption sphere because inside users can create their profile, interact with other thrifters and build communities while creating the market by displaying their apparel on their personal pages. In this specific context, users' creativity and participation lead to a value co-creation process that can be used to nurture a virtuous cycle involving society, the people, and the planet. By joining this thrifting apps and platforms users can actively contribute to extending products' life cycle, reducing their environmental impact, and postponing their controversial disposal. The worldwide sharp rise of these mobile-friendly apps highlights that consumers today are well-aware of sustainability problems, both environmental and social, and data demonstrate that especially new generations are extremely sensitive about these. In fact, according to an estimate by Boston Consulting Group, secondhand clothing, footwear, and accessories are shaping a market segment between 30 and 40 billion dollars worldwide; plus, it is expected to continue to grow in the next 3 years, bringing the secondhand share in the closet from 21 to 27%.

Furthermore, this trend really represents a shift in the mentality of young consumers, who are receptive to economic and environmental problems, and are so realizing that thrifting can be a sustainable and convenient way of shopping. In this regard, The Deloitte Global 2021 Millennial and Gen Z Survey—involving 22,928 respondents from 45 countries across North America, Latin America, Western Europe, Eastern Europe, the Middle East,

Africa, and Asia Pacific—shows that these young individuals, as consumers, 'often put their wallets where their values are, stopping or initiating relationships based on how companies treat the environment, protect personal data, and position themselves on social and political issues'. This means that they are driven to act and thrifting sudden increase is the perfect example of a dialectical shopping context where consumers can negotiate and morally affect the way things go with their consumption choices.

The Context of Our Study: The Thrifting Ecosystem and Its Apps

Following the COVID-19 pandemic, which still creates global imbalances, the habit of shopping online through e-commerce and apps has spread exponentially. The pandemic, in fact, has transformed not only consumption habits but also purchasing methods: in particular, preference for online shopping has depended firstly on the impossibility of physically reaching shops and secondly on the fact that it was—and it is—a procedure that could guarantee not being exposed to the virus, thanks to the absence of contacts. If before the pandemic the 70% of retailers and wholesalers were not organized for online sales, in 2020 European e-commerce reached the value of 757 billion euros, with a +10% growth compared to 2019. Particularly, in relation to the context of secondhand clothing, there has been a boom of online platforms (downloadable also as apps) such as Vestiaire Collective; Depop; ThredUP; Vinted, and Wallapop.

Vestiaire Collective—Home of Pre-loved Fashion

Vestiarie Collective, the secondhand French top player, launched in Paris in October 2009, is definitely one of the first online resale platforms to become famous: self-proclaimed first social shopping site, today has more than 11 million users across 80 countries worldwide with offices in Paris, London, New York, Milan, Berlin, and Hong Kong. This website offers a huge selection of items every week while boosting several projects and showing 'its ability to be a mean that helps people in their life and allows them to make the most of their things, but also to access fashion in a sustainable and conscious way' said CEO Max Bittner in 2020. Moreover, according to Clara Chappaz, Vestiaire's chief business officer, Italy, with increased orders (+85%) since the beginning of 2021, has seen growth not only in buyers but also in sellers, ranking as one of the markets with more sellers and witnessing a real change of mentality in the national context. In fact, Vestiaire responds to the demand for 'slow fashion' and for more sustainable consumption, a need now stronger than ever, distinguishing itself from other platforms not only because it was the first to establish itself/achieve success in the field, but also because it aims to spread the secondhand culture through relevant projects, including the recent 'Vestiaire for change'—that aims to give a voice to sustainable fashion experts on Vestiaire's social community—and collaboration, including those with Alexander McQueen and Mulberry. Furthermore, in 2021, Kering, the luxury giant led by François Pinault, invested 178 million euros in the platform, acquiring its 5% and confirming that circular fashion is not only good for the planet but is also becoming a profitable business. Moreover, Vestiaire has been certified as 'benefit corporation', qualifying as the first fashion resale platform to be. Obtaining a B-Corp certification means being part of a global movement that aims to spread a more advanced business paradigm: basically, this means that a company, to be part of it, in addition to pursuing profit, must try to make its impact on both internal and external stakeholders positive. Vestiaire Collective is simple and intuitive to use, especially in its mobile version, and focuses on a wide selection of products, giving the possibility to talk directly to sellers to negotiate prices and then send offers. Moreover, it guarantees a 'worry-free' shopping experience thanks to its item authentication process, as well as shipping insurance, offering consumers a unique and safe buying and selling journey.

Depop—The Creative's Marketplace

Depop is a marketplace of creative, designed for the new generations and has 30 million users spread over more than 150 countries around the world, where a product is loaded every half second and a fashion item is sold every three seconds: in 2020, Depop sold over a billion items, in a completely virtual environment, without physical stores or warehouse, by simply connecting sellers and buyers through a reliable platform. Founded by the Italian co-founder of PIG magazine and RETROSUPERFUTURE sunglasses, Simon Beckerman, as a social network where PIG's readers could buy items featured in the magazine, it was then re-envisioned with the introduction of the selling function, becoming a global marketplace, then sold for 1.6 billion dollars to Etsy, an American marketplace, in 2021. Today, Depop is an acknowledged mobile space where you can see what your friends and the people you are inspired by are liking, buying, and selling. This ecosystem made Depop 'a global conduit of connection, not only in m-commerce, but culture, design, and creative communities around the world': in fact, since 2019, 90% of its subscribers is under 26 and varied, from young designers to vintage lovers. In an interview for TechCrunch (2019), Maria Raga, CEO of Depop, said that Depop's mission is to 'redefine the fashion industry in the same way Spotify did with music or Airbnb with travel accommodations'. In this sense, Depop differs from other thrifting e-commerce due to the structural creativity of its items, ranking as one of the most popular thrifting apps, precisely thanks to its hybrid nature, halfway between a social network and a marketplace. On Depop items on sale are all linked to specific accounts—with interfaces that recreate the typical social media ones—and it is possible to choose which ones to follow to stay updated on favorite dealers.

ThredUP—An Online Consignment and Thrift Store for Your Closet, Your Wallet, and the Planet

ThredUP, founded in 2009 by James Reinhart, Oliver Lubin, and Chris Homer, is the largest online thrift store in the world—working with more than 35,000 brands—for clothing, shoes, and accessories for women and children. Today ThredUP, which has a workforce of 1,862 employees, promotes the 'belief' that practicing thrifting involves much more than finding your favorite brands at great prices, and that it means buying with intent, rejecting the culture of disposable fashion, and standing for sustainability, stating that 'the clothes we wear have the power to create change'. In this sense, selling on ThredUP is sustainable: before starting it is in fact necessary to have a kit, sold on ThredUP, the so-called clean-out-kit, which includes a 100% recyclable bag, to be used as a shipping box. All clothes must be sent to the collection warehouse, where they are then selected or discarded: at the end of this process, a cash refund or a credit is placed for a subsequent purchase on the site.

The selection criteria are very strict, as the garments must be 'clean, freshly washed; from a name brand; on trend and less than 5 years old; free of tears, stains, and rips; in excellent condition'. Once the clothes entered the platform, they can be purchased through the typical methods of e-commerce.

It is estimated that every day more than 100,000 items are processed thanks to the cutting-edge technologies that the platform uses, including machine learning and artificial intelligence tools to enhance visual recognition, multi-layer algorithms to determine resale prices, and automatic photographs to produce thousands of photos every day. The site, therefore, presents itself as a professional intermediary between buyers and sellers, with the task of ensuring the quality of the service. Among the countless initiatives of the platform, carried out over the years, of considerable interest is resale-as-a-service (RAAS), a service launched in 2018 to allow brands to connect directly to the resale engine and offer their customers thrift experiences.

Vinted and Wallapop

Vinted, the largest European C2C online platform dedicated to second-hand fashion and created in 2008 in Lithuania by Milda Mitkute and Justas Janauskas, was launched in the United States in 2010 and is now available in twenty countries. Originally born as an online swapping platform, today Vinted has more than 45 million users, distinguishing itself for its simplicity of use and for its ability to connect consumers with each other and let them sell their garments, free of charge, except for shipping costs. Unlike ThredUP, Vinted does not receive the products but ensures both the security of the payment and the purchase protection. In fact, Vinted is one of the greatest expressions of prosumption since the users who use the platform are both those who sell the items, generating the content and the raison d'être/reason for being on the site, and the buyers. Plus, Vinted's mission is making secondhand the first choice because, as Milda Mitkune states, 'everything you need is already in circulation' and Vinted represents a win–win solution, offering consumers a quick and easy way to sell their excess clothes—following a social media friendly design—claiming 'take a picture, upload it and sell it without commissions. What you earn is all yours!' and shows itself to be perfect to be used by 'anyone who believes that beautiful clothes deserve to live long'.

The Italian market, lately really interested in thrifting, welcomed first Vinted and right after Wallapop, in 2021. Wallapop, an app along the lines of Vinted, was launched in Spain in 2013, and today, it has 15 million users, differing from Vinted only due to the presence of additional sales categories, including, for example, IT and electronics. In fact, Wallapop was born from the idea of reproducing the flea market model online by developing an application capable of connecting sellers and buyers via geo-localization.

Both applications are extremely easy to use, reason why they are seeing success, and they certainly express the growing interest in a practice that was not previously viewed in the same way.

THRIFTING AS A VIRTUOUS CIRCUIT OF CONSUMPTION

In this section, we will explore the potential connections between the act of thrifting and the attempt to reach Eudaimonia, as intended by Arendt (1958), thanks to new insights from a recent netnographic research, conducted between December 2021 and January 2022. This specific online qualitative research method—developed by Robert Kozinets (2020) and characterized by unique practices, cultural focus, and immersive engagement—was adopted in order to comprehend how thrifting is being perceived on social media, its motivational drivers and which conversational, value-related, ritual and symbolic dynamics characterize it. All data was collected during the 'immersive' phase of the research, which involved preliminarily the analysis of 30 website articles, and then an in-depth content analysis of two Facebook private groups, 10 Instagram personal accounts (nano- and micro-influencers), and 7 videos under the #thrifting on TikTok, led to a total of 103 analyzed posts (see Table 5.1).

Those data were recorded in the 'immersive journal'—a reflexive document that captures the peculiarities of the selected social media ecosystem—together with researchers' fieldnotes: these are researchers' accurate reflections, thoughts, feelings, and impressions that are annotated throughout the entire research path to signpost the key moments of revelatory cultural understanding. The investigative phase conducted on news sites and blogs allowed us to draw important insights about thrifting in general, how it is perceived, what is associated with it, its dark side, the contents that this practice produces

Table 5.1 The data set

Source	Examples	Type of data	Data set
Social network sites	Facebook: I love thrifting; Thrifting Divas. Instagram: @thriftandtangles; @dinasdays Tik Tok: #thrifting; @thatcurlytopp; @imperfectidealist	Texts posts, thread of comments, photographs, and videos	10 personal pages + 2 private groups + 7 videos under the #thrifting on TikTok 103 posts
Website articles and blogs	How thrifting is helping the environment (by THRIFT WORLD); 3 experts shared their top tips for thrifting like a pro (by Brightly Eco)	Texts, archival news, interviews, photos, comments, and videos	30

more on the net and where it is more widespread. Netnography allowed us then to gain an in-depth understanding of the significance of thrifting practices by grounding our analysis on Arendt's notion of virtuous actions.

Given that thrifting practices have nowadays acquired a strong sustainable meaning, it is clear that the secondhand fashion business (Gopalakrishnam & Matthews, 2018) model makes it possible to reduce the use of resources and waste with the support of consumers as main partners and suppliers. In thrifting practices individuals have the power to make things happen as prosumers, who can literally create the market, gaining a crucial role in these kinds of economies and contributing to something bigger, such as Circular economy diffusion, through their single actions (Kirchherr et al., 2016; Prieto-Sandoval et al. 2018; Saidani et al., 2019). According to Arendt, action is the highest form of human activity lies as it is through action that people really become humans and actualize their unique personal identities (Anne-Laure Fayard, 2021). Thanks to action people can express their freedom to be what they want to and thrift shopping fulfills the aspiration to be persons that with their actions contribute to environmental and societal well-being.

In analyzing our data, we identified three practices that support the creation of thrifting as a circuit of virtuous actions with the potential of generating a eudaimonic state of well-being for its participants: (1) self-presentation through cultural curations of outfits' uniqueness that individuals use to express their own identity and construct their life project publicly; (2) ideological commitment against fast-consumption through which consumers engage in thrifting to fight against waste and construct the significance of thrifting as a therapeutic practice for individuals, society, and the whole planet; and (3) virtuous circuits of technosocial collaborations through which the communitarian force of thrifters is channeled toward the construction of a flourishing life in which economic and social gains can coexist.

Self-Presentation Through Cultural Curations of Outfits' Uniqueness

Thrifting has become a real trend and its popularity has made it 'cool': especially for young people, who love to stand out wearing new and creative outfits, 'trend coolness' turns out to be a determining factor, particularly as buying 'used' is an accessible way to get new looks on a budget. Therefore, buying and selling used clothing—very often almost new—responds to the need of these digital natives to have constant outfit turnovers that they can then share as new contents on their social media. The relevance of cultural curations of outfits does not stop here: it also lies in the fact that garments have the power to express one's identity, which in turn can be used to reflect one's core values, making each outfit bearer of a statement. Through used garments, people can express their identities in an unconventional and creative way. In this sense, it emerges as people often go thrift shopping in search of 'odd pieces' or unusual and bizarre items that 'speak' and express a precise value/meaning, which is why we can talk about 'outfit statement'. In fact, fast-fashion brands produce garments that are worn by tons of people, reason why people look for uniqueness: hardly anyone will be able to enter a store to buy what you are wearing if it is something unique. Furthermore, data analysis of the selected online contexts—Instagram, Facebook, and TikTok—has clearly confirmed that thrifting is much more than a simple form of shopping: it is, in fact, a real lifestyle that responds mainly to the need to differentiate ourselves from all others. Thus, for those who go thrifting, finding unique, original, and creative items to create personal outfits seems to be a prerogative, qualifying it as a practice of value expression. It is the same Ayana, founder of 'Thrifting Divas' (a Facebook group), in an interview, to affirm that 'the beauty about thrifting is being able to be confident in your style': in particular, it is stated that by practicing thrifting people are not influenced by fashion and every piece is 'one of a kind' and therefore unique in its kind. Thrifting would be then a way to differentiate oneself: the search for these alternative garments responds to the need to emerge from the crowd and to go against homologation and standardization. Thrifters usually share photos of their outfits as they are truly convinced that clothes are able to reflect their inner self in an effective and unique way. Obviously, the external appearance is just one piece of the bigger picture, but it can be seen as the key to guess one's personality, even before getting to know that specific person. Like a sort of 'business card', second-hand clothing helps people in their attempts to express their life projects and beliefs.

Ideological Commitment Against Fast-Consumption

Beyond aesthetics and self-expression in outfit curations, thrifting has a deeper meaning: it is also an emblem of the fight against fast-fashion brands and the direct expression of sustainability concerns. One of the reasons behind the high increase in used clothes sale-purchase is represented by the interest in environmental and social sustainability. In our analysis, the following benefits are continuously presented and discussed in thrifting conversations: (1) keeping garments away from landfills and combating the accumulation of textile waste impossible to dispose of; (2) providing support to charities; (3) reducing the ecological footprint; (4) conserving water resources; (5) reducing chemical pollution; (6) providing viable purchasing options for less affluent families; (7) bringing people together; and (8) helping to lower the demand for fast-fashion brands. All these benefits along with consumers' aversion to irresponsible consumption habits induced by fast-fashion brands, together with concerns for the environment, become a real motivation that drives people to buy secondhand or to buy new clothes from ethical and sustainable brands and to promote forms of circular fashion. In this sense, buying and selling secondhand clothes represent a manifesto of a social and public commitment that individuals may assume due to several reasons but with the primary aim to make explicit that they fight overconsumption and waste excess. After analyzing conversational threads on Instagram and TikTok, it appears clear that this practice has a symbolic value, acquired among the public of young people and adults belonging to generations Z and Y, i.e., a tool to fight fast fashion, that is also the maximum representation of overconsumption. So, thrifting is really seen as a concrete instrument to improve the world, but to avoid falling into the error of considering it as a mere substitute for traditional shopping, it is fundamental to understand that simply practicing thrifting is not enough to make it valid as a sustainable practice. Numerous green influencers and their followers do thrifting to stand against fast fashion: they firmly highlight the fact that 'you can still fall into overconsumption whilst thrifting' and that we need 'an overall mindset shift away from mindless consumption'. This important insight shows how it is fundamental to distinguish between a 'mindful thrifting' and a 'wasteful thrifting', and how it is necessary, in order to avoid it, for example, to remember to 'be intentional when buying; create a thrift wish list; focus on quality over quantity; stop worrying about thrift FOMO (Fear of Missing Out)'. In sum, it is important to 'understand when something is one-of-a-kind and when it's okay to leave it behind' and by saying it out loud she really helps people who have this kind of tendency to think carefully about their consumption.

The second rule that is vital to remember consists in the fact that even shopping that is not based on the exclusive purchase of sustainable items (and therefore very expensive and inaccessible to most) can be considered sustainable if the garments are worn for many years and taken care of in the best possible way to make them last longer. Sustainable and responsible consumption can be then summed up by the video caption of @imperfectidealist that states: 'I can't afford sustainable fashion, but I buy only what I need and make my clothes last years' 'this is sustainable fashion'. Also, @thatcurlytop shares this philosophy and tries to educate her followers by showing, for example, the 'buyerarchy of needs'. There are many ways to live sustainably, and people need to understand this. Also, @imperfectidealist shares lots of tips to be more conscious and responsible day by day, accepting that is a never-ending challenge, with contents such as '6 ways to care for your clothes sustainably'.

Thus, thrifting becomes the first step to undertake a path where shopping is a transformative journey able to help people and the planet but is also a sort of therapeutic practice. According to the insights from the netnographic research, especially on Instagram and TikTok, in fact, it emerges that thrifting is often considered as the first step to start a life geared toward sustainability: thrifting would be seen as a sort of first antidote to the consumerist culture of excesses, and therefore as a cure for oneself, for society and for the planet, i.e., a form of sustainable 'healing' shopping. In this sense, thrifting is much more than a lifestyle, it is a practice full of value and symbolic meanings that determines the way of being of an individual and influences all her life choices. From this perspective, thrifting can be understood as a cultural practice that could be the expression of what is probably an emerging subculture, where responsible consumers, environmentalists, activists, and all those who decide to detach themselves from the dominant culture to follow ideals at the basis of circular economy, namely 'reuse, reduce, recycle', find their space. Practicing thrifting means having specific beliefs that recall a well-defined value universe: to live by these principles means then pursuing one's own Eudaimonia. Through this research, it appears evident that thrifting is something powerful that generates a sense of well-being due to its beneficial implications for people and the planet. The satisfaction that comes from doing something good for oneself—since the garment is obviously appreciated for its originality/quality—for the planet and for the people gives a strong motivation to individuals. To quote a follower of influencer @thriftsandtangles, 'thrifting is life (…) I always feel good when I do it because I know I'm helping my community and the planet'.

Virtuous Circuits of Technosocial Collaborations

It is attested that individuals buy used clothes also to resell them as resellers, after making changes (upcycling) or simply selecting them among many, for money, and apparently is a fairly lucrative practice. In this sense, the thrifting ecosystem, together with its apps, contributes to the development of a virtuous circle both socially and economically. After analyzing conversational threads on Instagram, TikTok, and Facebook, it appears clear that when individuals buy secondhand, very often the aim is to give a second life to the garments extending their life cycle so that sewing/mending skills or practices such as refashioning, DIY, upcycling and thrift flipping are very popular on the social networks analyzed and are protagonists of thousands of online contents. Given that the creation of this type of contents is a maximum expression of the spread of prosumption, in many cases such videos are not intended to be the simple expression of passion for this 'know-how' (only in Facebook groups it seems to be like so) but are the expression of the will to undertake a path in which these skills are needed to become as autonomous as possible in following the principles of a sustainable life. Therefore, these are tools that have significant value implications for thrifters and for anyone who approaches sustainability: in fact, they provide the key to being able to make a qualitative leap, which is why these activities are associated with sustainability and thrifting. Moreover, being involved in such practices seems to have also a psychological value: taking care of personal garments to give a new life to products makes individuals feel good, not only for a matter of personal satisfaction but also for the implications in terms of reducing their environmental impact. This deepest meaning can be expressed by saying that every single purchase, when viewed from a circular perspective, has much more than just one life to offer.

Anyway, beyond the competencies that may become necessary to improve one's sustainability standards, netnographic analysis revealed that in Italy thrifting is very complex to practice. In fact, in the Italian context, secondhand shops, if any, are in a very limited number, so the scenario is very different from the USA' one—where physical secondhand chains are very widespread—and the implications in terms of cognitive effort and time that Italian people must use to thrift are substantially higher. For this reason, the advent of thrifting apps—Vinted in particular—has proved to be of crucial importance for Italian thrifters. Apps have thus assumed a noteworthy symbolic value.

A significant example is given by a post by @cami_al_naturale, which says: 'I am very happy that Vinted has arrived in Italy. I used it when I was studying in Paris, I have always found it comfortable. (…) Now if I look for / need something, I go and see there (…). From the most technical things (motorcycle jacket) to the most trivial things (covers for the terrace cushions) I have found everything (…)'. Under this IG post, there are several comments supporting this thesis, such as the one stating that 'Vinted was the turning point for me! (…) whenever I need something, I look there and I made crazy deals!' (@carmelitafalcone) and another one confirming 'the turning point for me too, but on the contrary. I sold a lot, things in perfect condition that I didn't use and I felt guilty. Instead, I am so happy to have given those garments new life, and with what I have earned I have made sustainable purchases of bespoke garments. I'm so happy' (@lafede_c).

Furthermore, Vinted gives the possibility to start a new path not only by letting people buy secondhand, but also by letting them sell pre-loved items, starting a massive decluttering of their wardrobe, in order to get rid of the unnecessary, as it can be read in a comment under a post of @not.sogreen about this topic, revealing that ' (…) to me the real challenge - won - of 2021 was a serious and massive decluttering. I can say that on Vinted I got rid of my things that I didn't see myself in anymore to buy others in a 3:1 ratio' (@penelopefizz). The reply by @not.sogreen says 'great !! They seem like excellent foundations to jump into 2022! The decluttering part is hard work, but essential to get started…Holy Vinted'.

Vinted, in fact, together with all the apps that simplify the process of buying and selling pre-loved items, offers the possibility of truly approaching the world of secondhand: it is the symbol of the beginning of a change to which people aspire and finally can really achieve. Vinted is, therefore, fully perceived as a resource, and this is probably also why there has been a boom in its downloads. In a broader sense, in the Italian context in particular, but not only, apps that are made available through technosocial platforms are tools that allow individuals to live accordingly to their ideals and values and consequently achieve fulfillment.

Conclusions

The thrifting practices whether materialized in physical stores, flea markets, garage sales, or in the technosocial web of digital apps offer consumers the opportunity to reembody garments, dresses, accessories, and shoes across space and time. By doing this, thrifters achieve Eudaimonia by extending and empowering their self as a circular force that celebrates uniqueness by blending and bridging taste and style regimes of different cultures, places, and epochs. They also achieve Eudaimonia by putting their cognitive and emotional energies into actions that nurture, expand, and perpetuate the continuity of the material and immaterial resources that actualize sustainable, zero-waste fashion. Finally, they achieve Eudaimonia by stretching their neoliberal ethos in technosocial platforms from the individual aim of self-expression and self-governmentality (Foucault, 2008) to a wider societal aspiration of world-governmentality and world betterment. Through crafting carefully curated affective labor (Carah, 2014) in thrifting digital apps, thrifters shape their own manifesto of virtuous consumption. In line with the prosumption spirit of contemporary times (Ritzer & Jurgenson, 2010), thrifters engage in virtuous consumption actions of secondhand garments, whereby they show their transformative capacity to enrich fashion consumption by blending it with new forms of production, distribution, and sharing. Moreover, thrifters elevate fashion consumption to a form of virtuous social entrepreneurship whereby they fuel a new market without extorting resources from the planet, but by recycling, preserving, respecting, and valorizing them to contribute to a sustainable view of the world to come.

References

Arendt, H. (1958). *The human condition*. University of Chicago Press.
Arvidsson, A. (2011). Ethics and value in customer co-production. *Marketing Theory, 11*(3), 261–278.
Ashman, R., Patterson, A., & Brown, S. (2018). "Don't forget to like, share and subscribe": Digital autopreneurs in a neoliberal world. *Journal of Business Research, 92*, 474–483.
Biraghi, S., Dalli, D., & Gambetti, R. C. (2020). Eudaimonia: The sociocultural value of consumers' social labor. *Marketing Theory, 21*(2), 201–225.
Carah, N. (2014). Watching nightlife: Affective labor, social media, and surveillance. *Television & New Media, 15*(3), 250–265.
Deci, E. L., & Ryan, R. M. (2008). Hedonia, eudaimonia, and well-being: An introduction. *Journal of Happiness Studies, 9*, 1–11.

Deci, E. L., Ryan, R. M., Gagné, M., Leone, D. R., Usunov, J., & Kornazheva, B. P. (2001). Need satisfaction, motivation, and well-being in the work organizations of a former eastern bloc country: A cross-cultural study of self-determination. *Personality and Social Psychology Bulletin, 27*(8), 930–942.

Fabian, M. (2020). The coalescence of being: A model of the self-actualisation process. *Journal of Happiness Studies, 21*(4), 1487–1508.

Fayard, A. L. (2021). Notes on the meaning of work: Labor, work, and action in the 21st Century. *Journal of Management Inquiry, 30*(2), 207–220.

Foucault, M. (2008). *The birth of biopolitics: Lectures at the Collège de France, 1978–1979* (A. I. Davidson & G. Burchell, Trans.). Springer.

Gopalakrishnam & Matthews (2018) in M. A. Dutra Machado et al. (07/2019). Second-hand fashion market: Consumer role in circular economy. *Journal of Fashion Marketing and Management, 23*(3), 283.

Just, S. N. (2019). An assemblage of avatars: Digital organization as affective intensification in the GamerGate controversy. *Organization, 26*(5), 716–738.

Kotler, P., Kartajaya, H., & Setiawan, I. (2010). *Marketing 3.0: From products to customers to the human spirit*. Wiley.

Kozinets, R. V. (2020). *Netnography 3E: The essential guide to qualitative social media research*. Sage.

Kulik, K. (2002). Daimon...the citizen: Arendt and Plato's Socrates. In A. Bove (Ed.), *Questionable returns* (Vol. 12). IWM Junior Visiting Fellows Conferences.

Lozza, E., Cornaggia, C., & Castiglioni, C. (2019). Il recupero di antichi habiti: un'indagine storica e psicologica sul consumo di abbigliamento usato. *Psicologia Sociale, Social Psychology Theory and Research, 2*, 235–258. https://doi.org/10.1482/94267

Marttila, T. (2013). *The culture of enterprise in neoliberalism: Specters of entrepreneurship*. Routledge.

Prieto-Sandoval et al. (2018), Saidani et al. (2019), Kirchherr et al. (2016) in M. A. Dutra Machado et al. (07/2019). Second-hand fashion market: Consumer role in circular economy. *Journal of Fashion Marketing and Management, 23*(3), 283.

Rapp, C. (2006). What use is Aristotle doctrice of the mean? In B. Reis (Ed.), *The virtuous life in Greek ethics*. Cambridge University Press.

Reis, B. (2006). *The virtuous life in Greek ethics*. Cambridge University Press.

Ritzer, G., & Jurgenson, N. (2010). Production, consumption, prosumption: The nature of capitalism in the age of the digital 'prosumer.' *Journal of Consumer Culture, 10*(1), 13–36.

Robinson, R. M. (2013). The philosophy of action and authority in the entrepreneurial ethic. *The BRC Academy Journal of Education, 3*(1), 69–96.

Ryan, R. M., & Deci, E. L. (2001). On happiness and human potentials: A review of research on hedonic and eudaimonic well-being. *Annual Review of Psychology, 52*(1), 141–166.

Ryff, C. D. (1989). Happiness is everything, or is it? Explorations on the meaning of psychological well-being. *Journal of Personality and Social Psychology, 57*(6), 1069–1081.

Ryff, C. D. (2019). Entrepreneurship and eudaimonic well-being: Five venues for new science. *Journal of Business Venturing, 34*(4), 646–663.

Scharff, C. (2016). The psychic life of neoliberalism: Mapping the contours of entrepreneurial subjectivity. *Theory, Culture & Society, 33*(6), 107–122.

The Deloitte Global 2021 Millennial and Gen Z Survey. https://www2.deloitte.com/content/dam/Deloitte/global/Documents/2021-deloitte-global-millennial-survey-report.pdf

Toffler, A. (1980). *The third wave*. Collins.

Wolny, W. (2012). *Prosumption—consumer creativity in e-business*. Prosumption project at University of Economics in Katowice. https://www.ue.katowice.pl/fileadmin/_migrated/content_uploads/13_W.Wolny_Prosumption....pdf

CHAPTER 6

The Role of Dignity in Workplace Well-Being: A Relational Cultural Perspective

Sheldene Simola

Historically, dignity has received scant attention within management scholarship. This likely reflects the fact that dignity connotes the inherent worth of individuals as ends in and of themselves. As such, it is a quality not easily reconciled with conventional economic goals, within which human labor is commercialized as an object of free market exchange, and instrumentalized as a means toward some other end, namely profit maximization (Bal, 2017; Sayer, 2007). However, with the rise of humanistic management, dignity has become an important and growing area of research. Humanistic management focuses on the cultivation of a good and well society. The protection and promotion of human dignity for employees (Melé, 2014) and other stakeholders (Pirson, 2019) are central to this task. Therefore, the purpose of this chapter is three-fold. First, it will elucidate the nature of dignity and its role in fostering employee well-being, development, and vitality. Second, this chapter will interpret dignity within a specific theory of human well-being, development and vitality, relational cultural theory (RCT) (Jordan, 2018; Walker, 2020), and building upon previous research, conceptualize dignity as "mutuality of mattering." Third, the implications of RCT for supporting workplace dignity will be described. Consideration is given to the importance of using co-active power with others (rather than power over others), thereby allowing for

S. Simola (✉)
School of Business, Trent University, Peterborough, ON, Canada
e-mail: ssimola@trentu.ca

© The Author(s), under exclusive license to Springer Nature Switzerland AG 2023
J. Marques (ed.), *The Palgrave Handbook of Fulfillment, Wellness, and Personal Growth at Work*,
https://doi.org/10.1007/978-3-031-35494-6_6

the emergence rather than suppression of both moral emotion and constructive, growth-fostering conflict. Additionally, previous theorizing within RCT will be extended through conceptualization of common employee responses to dignity violations (i.e., Smith, 2008) as psychological, strategic, or politically-engaged forms of resistance (i.e., Gilligan & Snider, 2018). The criticality of enabling resonance for health-sustaining, politically-engaged forms of resistance against dignity violations that comprise disconnections from authentic, growth-fostering, and vital workplace relationships will be discussed.

Nature and Types of Human Dignity

Human dignity has several scholarly connotations. Common among these are notions of both unearned and contingent forms of dignity (Pirson et al., 2016). Unearned dignity refers to the inherent worth of individuals as ends in and of themselves, and in the workplace, requires protection. Contingent or earned dignity refers to dignity associated with living a virtuous life, through which one attempts to fulfill human potential, and more specifically, potential for good and right actions. Contingent dignity requires promotion and is also dependent upon the presence of certain capabilities, which are enabling conditions and opportunities that are commensurate with intrinsic human worth (Nussbaum, 2006). These might include, for example, the availability of education or freedom of self-determination over aspects of one's life. The presence of such capabilities supports social justice; enables development and fulfillment of human capacities as well as human flourishing; and evokes dignifying responses from others, all of which contribute to sense of worth (Westerman-Behaylo et al., 2016).

Role of Dignity in Workplace Well-Being, Purpose, Growth, and Flourishing

In his theory of workplace dignity, Bal (2017) envisioned complex webs of interconnection among and within environmental and human systems, of which business and organizations are parts. Dignity was argued to emerge through responsible and responsive interaction among the elements of these systems, involving multilateral reflection, and dialogue among stakeholders, rather than unilateral implementation of a corporate agenda. This would enable proactive cultivation of values, norms, and principles that support development and fulfillment of the conditions and opportunities that support the dignity, well-being, and flourishing of all.

Workplace dignity also contributes to a sense of human purpose. For example, Folger and colleagues (2005) argued that upholding the dignity of others, even when this is counter to short-term economic interests, reflects connection with a higher order moral motivation. In turn, this both maintains human interconnection and fulfills human needs for purpose or meaning.

Similarly, Pirson (2020, p. 784) proposed a humanistic management model grounded in the core function of ethicality. Within this model, responsible balancing of four human motivations is required to achieve dignity, well-being, and sense of purpose. The four motivations include drives both to acquire and defend the basic forms of sustenance needed for survival and continuation of the human species; as well as the drive to bond by maintaining relationships characterized by mutuality and care; and the drive and to comprehend relationship with the world or discern a sense of "purpose in life."

In a notable contribution on levels of employee treatment in the workplace, Melé (2014) distinguished between high-quality treatment involving various forms of dignity at the highest levels, and problematic treatment involving various forms of indignity and humiliation at the lowest levels. Within this framework, the fundamental requisite for dignity is just, respectful treatment of employees, followed by demonstration of care and responsiveness to legitimate employee concerns. At the highest level, the cultivation of dignity involves fostering employee development and flourishing, within the context of mutual relationships, and in relation to good and right actions.

In addition to a positive focus on supporting workplace dignity, scholars have also highlighted the bivalent nature of dignity and underscored the importance of protecting dignity from the consequences of its opposing dimension, violation through humiliation (Klein, 1991; Lucas and colleagues, 2017; Mann, 1998; Pless et al., 2017; Sayer, 2007). As noted by Hartling et al. (2004, p. 106), the Latin root for humiliation is humus, referring to soil. In its verb form, humiliate means to "cause to be soil," more commonly understood as a form of degradation involving "treating someone like dirt." More formally, humiliation might be understood as the "exercise of power over another that occurs with seeming impunity, in ways that devalue, degrade, and convey the abject and encompassing inadequacy of the other, and which results in ostracism of the other" (Simola, 2022). Hence, humiliation is a tool of social control, both over direct targets and over witnesses. It is most often played out in competitive, win-lose contexts (Klein, 1991), and is, therefore, very common, if not ubiquitous in many varied forms within business and organizations (Czarniawska, 2008). Unlike dignity, which has both a conceptual (Pirson, 2019; Westerman-Behaylo et al., 2016) and empirical (Hojman & Miranda, 2018) association with well-being, humiliation has been associated with a range of negative affective states and serious forms of ill-being (Hartling & Lindner, 2018; Hartling & Luchetta, 1999; Klein, 1991; Leask, 2013). Humiliation not only damages an individual's sense of intrinsic worth, but also constrains possibilities for human flourishing and fulfillment of purpose.

Relational Nature of Dignity and Relevance of RCT

In discussion of workplace dignity, Lucas (2015, p. 638) identified that "affirmations and denials of dignity typically are experienced through communicative interactions. Regardless of the source of dignity...what ultimately affirms or denies those dignities is interaction with others." Indeed, in contrast to conventional management thought, which has tended to be individualist in nature, dignity is recognized as an inherently relational construct (Hartling & Lindner, 2018), and relational considerations characterize discussions of workplace dignity (Bal, 2017; Melé, 2014; Pirson, 2020).

Scholars of behavioral science have identified two dimensions through which dignity is experienced and enacted, comprising relationship with both self and other. For example, Mann (1998) identified that experienced dignity reflects both an internal dimension related to how individuals perceive themselves and an external dimension related to how individuals think that others perceive them. Sayer (2007) identified that enacted dignity involves consideration of both an individual's ability to act autonomously from others, as well as an individual's dependence on others, and noted that these qualities of autonomy and dependence exist in a balanced form of tension. Moreover, when violations of dignity occur, responses to those violations might be internalized within the self as shame and anxiety or externalized in ways that can impact others (Hartling & Lindner, 2016; Smith, 2008).

However, despite the relational nature of workplace dignity (Pirson, 2020; Pless et al., 2017) and the importance of using relational qualities and skills to support it (Melé, 2014), management scholars have yet to contextualize and explore dignity within specific relational theories of human well-being, development, and flourishing. Such theories could offer scholars and practitioners a more nuanced understanding of human dignity and its role in employee well-being, as well as a set of corresponding skills for supporting workplace dignity, and by extension, employee well-being. Consider, therefore, a discussion of RCT (Jordan, 2018; Walker, 2020) and the ways in which dignity might be understood within RCT.

Relational Cultural Theory

Since its inception nearly fifty years ago, RCT has become a leading theory of human well-being and development (Duffey & Trepal, 2016). It has been used as a conceptual lens in various areas of management thought and practice. Examples of these include the role of relational cultural approaches to leadership (Fletcher, 2007, 2012); the use of RCT in employee mentoring (Fletcher & Ragins, 2007; Simola, 2016); and the role of relationality in supporting career empowerment and development (Motulsky, 2010). Unlike conventional models that emphasize separation and self-sufficiency as signifiers of maturity, health, and well-being, RCT recognizes webs of interdependence among self, others, and the natural environment, and asserts the primacy of mutuality within vital, growth-fostering relationships (Hernandez, 2018; Jordan, 2018; Miller, 1986; Prussia, 2018; Walker, 2020). It is through mutual, growth-fostering relationships that "five good things" emerge. These include enhanced clarity about oneself and others in relationship; greater enthusiasm and passion in life; increased ability to undertake meaningful action; elevated desire for deeper connection with others; and greater sense of self-worth (Miller, 1986; Miller & Stiver, 1997).

In contrast, within RCT, the source of human stagnation or decline is chronic disconnection from authentic, vital, and growth-fostering relationship. This occurs through interpersonal violation, carelessness, or injustice, as well as through systemic forms of inequity, violation, and injustice (Jordan, 2018; Miller, 1986; Walker, 2004, 2008, 2020). Chronic disconnection from others can be manifested in an experience called condemned isolation (Jordan, 2008a, 2018; Miller, 1988), in which individuals feel an overwhelming sense of exclusion from human community and simultaneously feel as though others have held them responsible for their own exclusion. As with those who suffer dignity violations (Leask, 2013), those who experience condemned isolation also often lose trust that others will demonstrate empathic responses. They begin to feel unworthy in human relationship and anticipate further ostracism. This loss of trust in possibilities for empathy as well as possibilities for reparation can lead to a downward cycle of withdrawal and isolation associated with a range of substantial, negative impacts on well-being (Gilligan, 2010; Jordan, 2008a).

Conceptualizing Dignity Within RCT: Dignity as Mutuality of Mattering

As previously described, dignity has various dimensions, including that it comprises worth that is intrinsic; worth that is associated with the presence of certain capabilities (i.e., conditions and opportunities for development and fulfillment of human potential); and worth that is associated with fulfilling potential for good and right action (Pirson et al., 2016; Westerman-Behaylo et al., 2016). One way of unifying these dimensions would be consideration of underlying process. An underlying process that is common to all these dimensions of dignity is that of *recognizing* the humanity of others and affirming through actions that others *matter*.

For example, Mann (1998, p. 32) identified that the "common denominator" among different components of dignity is that of "being seen" as well as the "quality of this perception." Islam (2013) argued that workplace recognition is a fundamental building block of workplace dignity. Pless and colleagues (2017) also indicated that recognition and affirmation by others are critical to dignity. Sayer (2007) observed that dignity requires certain affordances from others, including being taken seriously such that it is impossible to maintain dignity if others refuse to acknowledge and give uptake to one's voice. Hicks and Waddock (2016) argued that the primary dignity-related responsibility of leaders is to treat employees as though they mattered.

Within RCT, being seen, recognized, acknowledged, and affirmed require both the mutuality and mattering that are foundational to the vital, growth-fostering relationships through which a sense of worth emerges. Mutuality refers to the engagement, participation, and uptake of both parties to a relationship. Mutuality also reflects the willingness of both parties to become vulnerable through their openness to growth and development (Miller & Stiver, 1997; Walker, 2020). Unlike conventional management approaches that might differentially emphasize the role of leader or manager in fostering the growth or development of "subordinates," mutuality also reflects the converse process. Specifically, through their willingness to be both open to, and affected by a follower, leaders convey that the follower has also made a difference to their own growth, development, or personhood, and therefore, that the follower also matters (Hartling et al., 2004; Jordan, 2018). In addition to being "moved by" followers, leaders also "move with" followers (Hartling et al., 2004, p. 124) by creating the conditions and opportunities necessary for the development and fulfillment of employee potential for good and right action. In other words, there is "mutuality of mattering" that fosters not only inherent sense of worth, but also capability-related and contingent forms of dignity. These, in turn, foster an enhanced sense of relational competence among those who have made a difference; movement toward deeper relationship; and the development of well-being through increasingly vital, growth-fostering relationships (Gilligan, 2010; Jordan, 2008a; Miller, 1986).

Conversely, failures of mutuality can occur in at least two ways. First, failures can occur by omission when one is unwilling or unable to grow through relationship with or by being affected by others. Therefore, one cannot convey to others that they matter. Second, failures can occur by commission, when acts of violation, carelessness, and injustice convey to others that they do not matter. Rather, others become insignificant and disposable entities rather than intrinsically valuable human beings with potential for good actions. Others are, therefore, excluded from mutual, growth-fostering relationships, rather than welcomed into relational communities in which they, too, matter and make a difference. This can result in a sense of condemned isolation in which those who are excluded experience deep shame associated with the perception of having been both rejected and held responsible for these experiences (Hartling & Lindner, 2016). It can also lead to individuals to feel as though they are not worthy of authentic, vital connection, thereby contributing to stagnation or decline (Hartling et al., 2004).

Moreover, individuals who are ostracized in this way might subsequently demonstrate signs of what has been termed the central relational paradox (Miller & Stiver, 1997). Within this paradox, individuals "become so fearful of engaging others because of past neglects, humiliations, and violations…(that they) begin to keep important parts of (their) experiences out of connection"

(Miller & Stiver, 1995, p. 1). Hence, in their desire to remain in relationship, they establish connections that are inauthentic with both self and others. Rather than anticipating possibilities for empathic responsiveness from others, they interact in superficial rather than authentic ways to guard against the potential for additional failures of empathy and reparation. Although such strategies might enable an individual to cope with, or indeed, even survive debasing contexts, the necessity of such strategies also substantially limits the potential for growth, well-being, and flourishing that might stem from authentic relationships.

IMPLICATIONS OF RCT FOR SUPPORTING WORKPLACE DIGNITY

Although it is beyond the scope of the current chapter to discuss each of the interrelated skills within RCT that would support the concept of mutuality of mattering as a foundation for workplace (and other forms) of dignity, two key skills include the use of co-active power with (versus power over) others in ways that allow rather than suppress moral emotion and growth-fostering conflict; and, enablement of resonance and responsiveness to health-sustaining forms of politically-engaged resistance against dignity violations that comprise disconnections from authentic, vital, and growth-fostering workplace relationships.

Use of Co-active Power with Others Versus Power Over Others

In discussions of issues associated with dignity and indignity, various scholars have noted the centrality of power and vulnerability. For example, Sayer (2007) observed that vulnerability is implicit within the interdependencies of human existence from which dignity (or indignity) might arise. Because dignity requires mutual recognition, imbalances of power can comprise substantial impediments to the maintenance of dignity. For example, those who are relatively empowered might expect respectful acknowledgment from subordinates, regardless of whether this is warranted. Conversely, because of their dependence and vulnerability, subordinates cannot necessarily provide authentic recognition, nor therefore, dignity to leaders (Sayer, 2007). Moreover, violations of dignity through exercises of power that humiliate subordinates or others, whether idiosyncratic or systemic, not only perpetuate structures of domination, but also undermine and incapacitate those who object (Kashyap, 2005, as cited by Kashyap, 2009).

Traditionally, power has been understood as the "ability to advance oneself and, simultaneously, to control, limit…the power of others" (Miller, 1986, p. 116), including in ways that perpetuate systemic forms of injustice (Walker, 2020). Such conventional understandings, by virtue of control over and constraint or diminishment of others, implicitly reflect indignity. Yet, within business and organizations, the hierarchical use of power over others is endemic and can comprise indignities of various forms. Examples might include Marxian alienation associated with capitalist modes of production; Durkheimian notions of abuse associated with capitalist competition and expansion; or dehumanization associated with Weberian rationalization (see, for discussion, Hodson, 2001). Examples also include a myriad of interpersonal, organizational, and systemic forms of discrimination and abuse (Czarniawska, 2008; Kożusznik, 2017; Melé, 2014).

In contrast, within RCT, power is understood as the ability to affect change (Miller, 1986). RCT also advocates the use of power with others. In contrast to indignifying, hierarchical uses of power over others in ways that instrumentalize others and constrain the possibilities of who others might be or become, power with others involves mutual engagement and collaboration in support of more creative, expansive, just, dignifying, and health-conferring forms of being and becoming (Jordan, 2018; Walker, 2020). Enacting power with others might involve the use of supported vulnerability through which those who are relatively empowered demonstrate mutual engagement with, support for, and receipt of, the authenticity that others bring to relationship (Jordan, 2008b). Rather than relying upon indignity or humiliation, this requires suspension of the idealized images that individuals hold of their own actions within relationships, as well as suspension of the dominant, often debasing sociopolitical images and narratives that they often hold of others (Walker, 2020). It requires a stance of humility about what can be truly known or understood about others; curiosity in terms of learning about others; and recognition and respect for differences that exist among individuals. Though this might involve discomfort, it can enable the emergence of moral emotions (Simola, 2010) as well as growth-fostering forms of conflict through which new understandings can emerge (Hartling et al., 2004; Walker, 2020). Indeed, defining features of organizational or other cultures that exercise power over others include the suppression of moral emotions through which violations of dignity might be prevented, identified, or repaired (Simola, 2010), as well as the *absence* of disagreement or conflict (Miller, 1986). The prohibition of moral emotion and conflict obscures, maintains, and legitimizes systemic and other power imbalances, inequalities, and injustices. In contrast, allowance of these experiences is a defining characteristic of cultures that enact power with others, and opens possibilities and paths for healthy and health-sustaining growth and vitality (Gilligan & Snider, 2018; Miller, 1986; Simola, 2010).

Enabling Resonance and Responsiveness to Health-Sustaining Forms of Resistance

In relation to the social degradation and anomie that have occurred within the context of neoliberal globalization and exploitation, Smith (2008) identified potential responses that individuals might have to serious violations of dignity involving humiliation. These include acceptance with potential conformity to the expectations of dominant groups; (temporary) escape by holding humiliating experiences perpetrated by others in abeyance; rejection through revenge against those who caused the humiliation; or rejection through (non-vengeful) forms of resistance to humiliation. Within RCT, the task of supporting the workplace well-being of employees who have experienced violations of dignity is the task of responsiveness to healthy and health-sustaining efforts to "resist attempts to control and limit…" and to "escape from a bind that is immobilizing" such that one can "represent oneself authentically…" (Miller, 1986, pp. 117, 143). In other words, within RCT, a central task of supporting well-being is the task of supporting healthy and health-sustaining resistance to indignifying or humiliating treatment from others. An extension of these arguments can be made through consideration of specific types of resistance articulated by Gilligan and Snider (Gilligan, 2010; Gilligan & Snider, 2018). As indicated in column 3 of Table 6.1, all four potential employee responses to indignifying or humiliating treatment might be conceptualized as involving some type of resistance.

For example, as indicated in Table 6.1, within RCT, the response involving acceptance of, and submission to, humiliation by others (Smith, 2008) reflects "movement away" from authentic relationship with others (Horney, 1945 as cited by Hartling et al., 2004, p. 109) with any reinstatement into the group occurring only in a diminished, subordinated, and constrained form (Smith, 2008). Although this might initially be associated with temporary

Table 6.1 Types of resistance reflected within four responses to indignity involving humiliation

Responses to humiliation (Smith, 2008)	Responses as understood within RCT (Hartling et al., 2004, drawing upon Horney, 1945)	Type of resistance reflected in responses (Gilligan & Snider, 2018)
Acceptance	Condemned isolation i.e., "moving away from others" (p. 109) through silence or withdrawal	Psychological: involving loss of knowing
Escape	Central relational paradox and strategies of disconnection from others i.e., "moving toward others" (p. 110) in an effort to cope or survive	Strategic
Rejection with revenge	Relational disconnection i.e., "moving against others" (p. 110) through rage or retaliation	Psychological: involving loss of caring
Rejection through resistance without revenge	Healthy and health-sustaining resistance to disconnection from both self and others i.e., "moving with" self and others (p. 124) through resistance without revenge i.e., supported by leader who is "moved by" and "moves with" supervisees (p. 112)	Politically-engaged requires knowing + caring

relief, individuals might also experience the deep emotional pain associated with either condemned isolation (Jordan, 2008a, 2018; Miller, 1988) or the disavowal of internally held experience and knowledge of the humiliating actions (Gilligan, 2010; Miller & Stiver, 1997). Over repeated occurrences of relational violation in the form of indignity, one might also experience dissociation or loss of knowledge about painful experiences from conscious awareness (Gilligan, 2010; Gilligan & Snider, 2018). Hence, the response of acceptance and submission often comprises a form of *psychological resistance* to loss of growth-fostering relationship that requires *not knowing* what has occurred (Gilligan & Snider, 2018). Ironically, this form of resistance precludes authentic connection with self, and by extension, possibilities for vital, growth-fostering relationship with others.

As indicated in Table 6.1, the second strategy, escape, occurs when individuals separate internally held knowledge of the indignity they have suffered from their outward behavioral responses. Within RCT, this reflects "movement toward" others (Horney, 1945 as cited by Hartling et al., 2004, p. 110) in which individuals retain knowledge of the painful experiences, but do not address these experiences with others, as this would likely lead to further censure and ostracism (Gilligan, 1991). Various strategies of disconnection might emerge to keep these important aspects of the individual's experiences out of relationships with others, thereby enabling the individual to cope or survive in that context (Miller & Stiver, 1995). Hence, the escape response might be understood as a form of *strategic resistance* (Gilligan & Snider, 2018) in which, consciously or non-consciously, individuals separate their deeply held experience and knowledge from their outward actions so that they can fulfill other specific needs, such as coping, maintaining the outward semblance of harmony at work, or even surviving a debasing context. However, the response prohibits authenticity in relationship with others, so over time, it does not support longer term well-being and vitality.

As indicated in Table 6.1, within the third response to humiliation involving rejection through revenge against those who enacted the humiliation, there is "movement against" others (Horney, 1945 as cited by Hartling et al., 2004, p. 110). When ongoing structural, cultural, disciplinary, and interpersonal pressures (Collins, 2000) to retain one's own sense of power and dominance over others are very strong, one might even experience a non-conscious dissociation of, or loss of caring from, one's core identity, and enact violence (Gilligan & Snider, 2018). Hence, the third potential response of rejection through revenge that results in violence shares a quality with the first potential response of acceptance and submission that results in victimization. Specifically, both are forms of psychological resistance (Gilligan & Snider, 2018). However, unlike psychological resistance which requires a *loss of knowing*, psychological resistance involving revenge in the form of violence requires a *loss of caring*. Moreover, the cyclical nature of victimization and violence between parties reflects complementarity in relationship, rather than a healthy mutuality of relationship.

Finally, as indicated in Table 6.1, within RCT, resistance without revenge would be understood as a healthy and health-sustaining action reflecting efforts to stay in authentic, mutual, growth-fostering, and vital relationship with both self and others. It is an effort to resist the internalization of falsely inflicted humiliation (Ward, 2002) or other false, immobilizing constraints or binds (Miller, 1986). It is also an effort to resist the inaccurate conflation of one's value or dignity with notions of competence associated with competitive achievement, or notions of self-esteem in which one is "better than" others. Instead, it relies upon and further develops relational competence (Fletcher, 1999) that can support the dignity, well-being, and flourishing of all. Resistance without revenge therefore reflects efforts to "move with" self and others (Hartling et al., 2004). It is a *politically-engaged resistance* that requires *both knowing* about one's own experiences and *caring* about self and others (Gilligan & Snider, 2018). Unlike conventional forms of employee resistance that might involve various forms of avoidance or sabotage (Hodson, 2001), politically-engaged resistance involves using voice. It is aimed at affirming and upholding one's own value or dignity, while simultaneously working toward the goal of developing healthy and health-sustaining relationships with others. Although such resistance might involve the emergence of health-sustaining, moral emotions (Simola, 2010) or the use of healthy and growth-fostering forms of conflict (Miller, 1986), it can also create possibilities for empathic, relational reparation, and restoration of lost connection and trust. Hence, rather than responding to health-sustaining, politically-engaged forms of resistance as though they were problematic or inflammatory on the part of employees, the cultivation of "resonant spaces" and responsiveness to the voices of those who are resistant to indignity and humiliation is critical (Gilligan & Snider, 2018, p. 120). This would necessitate development of authentic, growth-fostering relational workplace cultures rather than pseudo-relational or individualist workplace cultures that suppress moral emotions and prohibit disagreement or conflict, thereby perpetuating domination over and immobilization of others (Hartling & Sparks, 2008).

Given both historical (Fletcher, 1999) and ongoing (Bal & Dóci, 2018) tendencies of organizations to be founded upon these latter types of individualist or pseudo-relational cultural models, it is perhaps unsurprising the violation of dignity in these contexts has been a norm rather than an exception (Czarniawska, 2008). To the extent to which commitment to relational practice is present, or to which systemic shifts toward authentic relationality occur in the organization of business entities and management practices, a range of specific workplace applications of RCT can be used to promote workplace dignity through mutuality of mattering, and to enable responsiveness to health-sustaining forms of politically-engaged resistance to violation and disconnection (e.g., Fletcher, 1999, 2004, 2007; Simola, 2016; Walker, 2020).

Summary

This chapter elucidated the relational nature of human dignity and its role in fostering employee well-being and vitality. The theoretical lens of RCT (Jordan, 2018; Walker, 2020) was used to explore the meaning of dignity, and, to identify RCT-related skills in support of employee dignity and well-being. Building on previous research within RCT, dignity was conceptualized here as mutuality of mattering that occurs within authentic, growth-fostering relationships. Two interrelated and overarching RCT-related skills in support of employee dignity and well-being were also discussed. The first of these was the use of co-active power with, rather than power over, employees in ways that enabled rather than suppressed the emergence of moral emotion (Simola, 2010) and that allowed use of growth-fostering conflict (Miller, 1986). The second of these involved enabling resonance and responsiveness to healthy and health-sustaining, politically-engaged forms of resistance against dignity violations that comprise disconnections from authentic, growth-fostering workplace relationships.

An important finding within the relational analysis of workplace dignity and well-being offered here is that growth, well-being, and vitality among employees are not something that can be cultivated within employees in top-down, distant and detached, circumscribed ways. Rather, RCT would suggest that it is a process that requires leaders to engage in authentic, mutual relationship with employees, such that leaders might both affect and be affected by employees in ways that reflect and convey mutuality of mattering. In other words, RCT suggests that employee well-being is interdependent with the growth and well-being of organizational leaders and other organizational members. Future research could empirically investigate the conceptual relationships suggested by RCT between relational (versus pseudo-relational and individualist) organizational cultures and perceived mattering by employees, as well as between perceived leader-follower mutuality and employee well-being.

References

Bal, M. (2017). *Dignity in the workplace: New theoretical perspectives*. Palgrave Macmillan.

Bal, M., & Dóci, E. (2018). Neoliberal ideology in work and organizational psychology. *European Journal of Work and Organizational Psychology, 27*(5), 536–548. https://doi.org/10.1080/1359432X.2018.1449108

Collins, P. H. (2000). *Black feminist thought: Knowledge, consciousness, and the politics of empowerment* (2nd ed.). Routledge.

Czarniawska, B. (2008). Humiliation: A standard organizational product? *Critical Perspectives in Accounting, 19*(7), 1034–1053. https://doi.org/10.1016/j.cpa.2007.01.004

Duffey, T., & Trepal, H. (2016). Introduction to the special section on relational-cultural theory. *Journal of Counseling & Development, 94*(4), 379–382. https://doi.org/10.1002/jcad.12095

Fletcher, J. K. (1999). *Disappearing acts: Gender, power, and relational practice at work*. MIT Press.
Fletcher, J. K. (2004). Relational theory in the workplace. In J. V. Jordan, M. Walker, & L. M. Hartling (Eds.), *Complexity of connection* (pp. 270–298). The Guilford Press.
Fletcher, J. K. (2007). Leadership, power, and positive relationships. In J. E. Dutton & B. R. Ragins (Eds.), *Exploring positive relationships at work: Building a theoretical and research foundation* (pp. 347–371). Lawrence Erlbaum Associates.
Fletcher, J. K. (2012). The relational practice of leadership. In M. Uhl-Bien & S. M. Ospina (Eds.), *Advancing relational leadership research: A dialogue among perspectives* (pp. 83–106). IAP Information Age Publishing.
Fletcher, J. K., & Ragins, B. R. (2007). Stone centre relational cultural theory: A window on relational mentoring. In. B. R. Ragins & K. E. Kram (Eds.), *The handbook of mentoring at work: Theory, research, and practice* (pp. 373–399). Sage.
Folger, R., Cropanzano, R., & Godman, B. (2005). What is the relationship between justice and morality? In J. Greenberg & J. A. Colquitt (Eds.), *Handbook of organizational justice* (pp. 215–245). Lawrence Erlbaum Associates.
Gilligan, C. (1991). Womens psychological development: Implications for psychotherapy. In C. Gilligan, A. G. Rogers, & D. L. Tolman (Eds.), *Women, girls & psychotherapy: Reframing resistance* (pp. 5–32). Harrington Park Press.
Gilligan, C. (2010). *Joining the resistance*. Polity Press.
Gilligan, C., & Snider, N. (2018). *Why does patriarchy persist?* Polity.
Hartling, L. M., & Lindner, E. G. (2016). Healing from humiliation: From reaction to creative action. *Journal of Counseling & Development, 94*(4), 383–390. https://doi.org/10.1002/jcad.12096
Hartling, L. M., & Lindner, E. G. (2018). Can systemic humiliation be transformed into systemic dignity? In D. Rothbart (Ed.), *Systemic humiliation in America: Finding dignity within systems of degradation* (pp. 19–51). Palgrave Macmillan.
Hartling, L. M., & Luchetta, T. (1999). Humiliation: Assessing the impact of derision, degradation, and debasement. *The Journal of Primary Prevention, 19*(4), 259–278. https://doi.org/10.1023/A:1022622422521
Hartling, L. M., Rosen, W., Walker, M., & Jordan, J. V. (2004). Shame and humiliation: From isolation to relational transformation. In J. V. Jordan, M. Walker, & L. M. Hartling (Eds.), *The complexity of connection* (pp. 103–128). The Guilford Press.
Hartling, L. M., & Sparks, E. (2008). Relational-cultural practice: Working in a non-relational world. In J. V. Jordan (Ed.), *The power of connection* (pp. 185–188). Haworth Press.
Hernandez, M. A. (2018). Sa Kawanangan: In the cosmos. In D. Gunderson, D. Graff, & K. Craddock (Eds.), *Transforming community: Stories of connection through the lens of relational cultural theory* (pp. 313–319). WholePerson.
Hicks, D., & Waddock, S. (2016). Dignity, wisdom, and tomorrow's business leader. *Society and Business Review, 121*(3), 447–462. https://doi.org/10.1111/basr.12094
Hodson, R. (2001). *Dignity at work*. Cambridge University Press.
Hojman, D., & Miranda, Á. (2018). Agency, human dignity, and subjective well-being. *World Development, 101*(C), 1–15. https://doi.org/10.1016/j.worlddev.2017.07.029
Horney, K. (1945). *Our inner conflicts*. W. W. Norton.

Islam, G. (2013). Recognizing employees: Reification, dignity and promoting care in management. *Cross Cultural Management, 20*(2), 235–250. https://doi.org/10.1108/13527601311313490

Jordan, J. V. (2008a). Learning at the margin: New models of strength. In J. V. Jordan (Ed.), *The power of connection* (pp. 189–208). Haworth Press.

Jordan, J. V. (2008b). Valuing vulnerability: New definitions of courage. *Women & Therapy, 31*(2–4), 209–233. https://doi.org/10.1080/02703140802146399

Jordan, J. V. (2018). *Relational cultural therapy*. American Psychological Association.

Kashyap, R. (2009). Narrative and truth: A feminist critique of the South African Truth and Reconciliation Commission. *Contemporary Justice Review, 12*(4), 449–467. https://doi.org/10.1080/10282580903343100

Klein, D. C. (1991). The humiliation dynamic: An overview. *The Journal of Primary Prevention, 12*(2), 93–121.

Kożusznik, B. (2017). Humiliation: Why we deserve respect at work. In N. Chmiel, F. Fraccaroli, & M. Sverke (Eds.), *An introduction to work and organizational psychology: An international perspective* (3rd ed., pp. 498–505). Wiley.

Leask, P. (2013). Losing trust in the world: Humiliation and its consequences. *Psychodynamic Practice, 19*(2), 129–142. https://doi.org/10.1080/14753634.2013.778485

Lucas, L. (2015). Workplace dignity: Communicating inherent, earned, and remediated dignity. *Journal of Management Studies, 52*(5), 621–646. https://doi.org/10.1111/joms.12133

Lucas, K., Manikas, A. S., Mattingly, E. S., & Crider, C. J. (2017). Engaging and misbehaving: How dignity affects employee work behaviors. *Organization Studies, 38*(11), 1505–1527. https://doi.org/10.1177/0170840616677634

Mann, J. (1998). Dignity and health: The UDHR's revolutionary first Article. *Health and Human Rights, 3*(2), 30–38.

Melé, D. (2014). "Human quality treatment": Five organizational levels. *Journal of Business Ethics, 120*(4), 457–471. https://doi.org/10.1007/s10551-013-1999-1

Miller, J. B. (1986). *Toward a new psychology of women* (2nd ed.). Beacon Press.

Miller, J. B. (1988). *Connections, disconnections, and violations*. Work in Progress, No. 33. Stone Center Working Paper Series.

Miller, J. B., & Stiver, I. (1995). *Relational images and their meanings in psychotherapy*. Work in Progress, No. 74. Stone Center Working Paper Series.

Miller, J. B., & Stiver, I. P. (1997). *The healing connection: How women form relationships in therapy and in life*. Beacon Press.

Motulsky, S. L. (2010). Relational processes in career transition: Extending theory, research, and practice. *The Counseling Psychologist, 38*(8), 1078–1114. https://doi.org/10.1177/0011000010376415

Nussbaum, M. (2006). *Frontiers of justice*. Harvard University Press.

Pirson, M. (2019). A humanistic perspective for management theory: Protecting dignity and promoting well-being. *Journal of Business Ethics, 159*, 39–57. https://doi.org/10.1007/s1055-017-3755-4

Pirson, M. (2020). A humanistic narrative for responsible management learning: An ontological perspective. *Journal of Business Ethics, 162*, 775–793. https://doi.org/10.1007/s10551-020-04426-3

Pirson, M., Goodpaster, K., & Dierksmeier, C. (2016). Human dignity and business. *Business Ethics Quarterly, 26*(4), 465–478. https://doi.org/10.1017/beq.2016.47

Pless, N. M., Maak, T., & Harris, H. (2017). Art, ethics and the promotion of human dignity. *Journal of Business Ethics, 144*, 223–232. https://doi.org/10.1007/s10551-017-3467-9

Prussia, L. (2018). A natural connection: Relational cultural theory and the environment. In D. Gunderson, D. Graff, & K. Craddock (Eds.), *Transforming community: Stories of Connection through the lens of relational cultural theory* (pp. 303–312). WholePerson.

Sayer, A. (2007). Dignity at work: Broadening the agenda. *Organization, 14*(4), 565–581.

Simola, S. (2022). Humiliation and dignity. In D. Poff & A. Michalos (Eds.), *Encyclopedia of business and professional ethics*. Springer. https://doi.org/10.1007/978-3-319-23514-1_1307-1

Simola, S. K. (2010). Anti-corporate anger as a form of care-based moral agency. *Journal of Business Ethics, 94*, 255–269. https://doi.org/10.1007/s10551-011-0755-7

Simola, S. K. (2016). Mentoring the morally courageous: A relational cultural perspective. *Career Development International, 21*(4), 340–354. https://doi.org/10.1108/CDI-01-2016-0010

Smith, D. (2008). Globalization, degradation and the dynamics of humiliation. *Current Sociology, 56*(3), 371–379. https://doi.org/10.1177/0011392107088230

Walker, M. (2004). Race, self and society: Relational challenges in a culture of disconnection. In J. V. Jordan, M. Walker, & L. M. Hartling (Eds.), *The complexity of connection* (pp. 90–102). The Guilford Press.

Walker, M. (2008). Power and effectiveness: Envisioning an alternate paradigm. In J. V. Jordan (Ed.), *The power of connection* (pp. 129–144). Haworth Press.

Walker, M. (2020). *When getting along is not enough: Reconstructing race in our lives and relationships*. Teachers College Press.

Ward, J. (2002). *The skin we're in: Teaching our children to be emotionally strong, socially smart, spiritually connected*. Free Press.

Westerman-Behaylo, M. K., Van Buren, H. J., III., & Berman, S. L. (2016). Stakeholder capability enhancement as a path to promote human dignity and cooperative advantage. *Business Ethics Quarterly, 26*(4), 529–555. https://doi.org/10.1017/beq.2016.46

CHAPTER 7

The Promise and Limits of Self-Employment as a Path to Fulfillment and Well-Being at Work

Albena Pergelova, Jeremy Zwiegelaar, and Shelley Beck

INTRODUCTION

Well-being has been suggested as an important but under-researched outcome in the entrepreneurship literature. High levels of well-being can result in a wealth of psychological resources for entrepreneurs, such as resilience and self-esteem, which in turn can help them to overcome challenges and work toward commercial or social innovations that ultimately contribute to societal well-being (Foo et al., 2009). Wiklund et al. (2019: 582) define entrepreneurial well-being as "the experience of satisfaction, positive affect, infrequent negative affect, and psychological functioning in relation to developing, starting, growing, and running an entrepreneurial venture."

Research suggests that the well-being of entrepreneurs is higher than that of non-entrepreneurs (e.g., Hessels et al., 2018), and the well-being of opportunity entrepreneurs is higher than that of necessity entrepreneurs (Nikolova, 2019; Stephan, 2018). However, research also reports that while in general self-employed persons enjoy greater autonomy and schedule flexibility (which increases their well-being), there are trade-offs between the costs and benefits

A. Pergelova (✉)
Department of International Business, Marketing, Strategy and Law, School of Business, MacEwan University, Edmonton, AB, Canada
e-mail: pergelovaa@macewan.ca

J. Zwiegelaar · S. Beck
Oxford Brookes Business School, Oxford Brookes University, Oxford, UK

© The Author(s), under exclusive license to Springer Nature Switzerland AG 2023
J. Marques (ed.), *The Palgrave Handbook of Fulfillment, Wellness, and Personal Growth at Work*,
https://doi.org/10.1007/978-3-031-35494-6_7

of self-employment (Parasuraman & Simmers, 2001) that may limit the ability of the self-employed[1] to achieve high well-being through their work.

In this chapter, we focus specifically on two groups of entrepreneurs that may face added stressors and challenges in their entrepreneurial paths—women entrepreneurs and immigrant entrepreneurs. The literature has pointed to the structural challenges for self-employed women related to balancing multiple demands (e.g., work and family) due to societal norms (Jennings & Brush, 2013). Similarly, the literature on immigrant entrepreneurship (understood as the pursuit of entrepreneurial activities by immigrants) has discussed added challenges for this group of entrepreneurs due to numerous structural barriers that might limit the career options of immigrants (Dabić et al., 2020). Those added stressors have the potential to affect well-being, and therefore, those groups of entrepreneurs merit focused research attention.

In what follows, we first provide an overview of the literature on self-employment and well-being, then describe some of the key elements that position self-employment as a potential path for achieving better fulfillment at work (the "promise"), followed by some of the limits that an entrepreneurial career poses on people's wellness. We then turn to a discussion of the promise and the limits specifically for women entrepreneurs, and for immigrant entrepreneurs. Subsequently, we review aspects at the intersection of gender and immigrant status as they pertain to well-being for the self-employed. Finally, we present an overview of exciting new research opportunities in the field of entrepreneurship and well-being, and offer a conclusion.

Overview of Self-Employment and Well-Being

Hedonic and Eudaimonic Well-Being

Well-being is a complex construct that characterizes peoples' perceptions about their lives and functioning. Extant research on well-being is based on two general perspectives: hedonic and eudaimonic well-being. According to the hedonic approach, well-being is defined in terms of pleasure attainment and pain avoidance, whereas the eudaimonic approach focuses on self-realization and the degree to which a person is fully functioning (Ryan & Deci, 2001). The literature commonly assesses the hedonic aspect of well-being as positive affect (positive mood), the absence of negative affect (mood), as well as life satisfaction (an evaluative component), which together are summarized as happiness or *subjective well-being* (Diener & Emmons, 1984; Kahneman et al., 1999). The eudaimonic approach, on the other hand, assumes that you cannot equate subjective happiness with well-being, because some outcomes—although pleasure producing—might not be conducive for wellness or be good for the people (Ryan & Deci, 2001). Well-being is thus

---

[1] Because most of the extant literature on entrepreneurial well-being uses self-employment as a proxy for entrepreneurship, in this chapter we use the terms self-employed and entrepreneur interchangeably.

not simply the result of attaining pleasure, but as striving to realize one's potential, which has been termed *psychological well-being* (Ryff, 1995). The eudaimonic perspective emphasizes measures of psychological functioning and focuses on assessment of whether a person is living a fulfilling life, including having *personal growth* (self-realization and achievement of personal potential), *autonomy* (a person is self-determining and independent), *purpose in life* (sense of directedness, meaning in life), *self-acceptance* (positive attitude toward the self, acknowledging multiple aspects of self), *mastery* (competence and master of the environment), and *relationships* with others (trusting relationships with others, concern about the welfare of others) (Ryff, 2019).

Recognizing the importance of variables related to psychological well-being, several recent studies in entrepreneurial well-being (Nikolaev et al., 2020; Shir et al., 2019) build on the premises of self-determination theory (SDT) which is based on three innate psychological needs: autonomy, competence, and relatedness (Ryan & Deci, 2000). Autonomy in SDT refers to experiences of volition, i.e., an individual's need to feel that their actions are self-directed. Competence relates to the experience of effectiveness and mastery, and the ability to engage in activities that use and extend a person's skills and expertise. Relatedness refers to the human need for connectedness with others and feelings of being cared for. SDT posits that the fulfillment of those three basic needs is essential for a person's psychological growth, integrity, and well-being (Ryan & Deci, 2001).

Entrepreneurship and Well-Being

Most research examining entrepreneurship and well-being has focused on the hedonic perspective, especially measures of life satisfaction. However, recent calls and research have increasingly started to recognize the relevance of eudaimonic approaches to well-being, especially given the importance of constructs such as autonomy, self-realization, and personal growth for entrepreneurs (Nikolaev et al., 2020; Ryff, 2019; Shir et al., 2019; Stephan, 2018).

Entrepreneurs/self-employed vs. non-entrepreneurs. A substantial part of research on entrepreneurship and well-being has focused on differences in well-being for entrepreneurs (usually measured as self-employment) vs. employees. Those studies regularly use satisfaction with life and/or work as the outcome variable. The rationale of those studies is usually that entrepreneurs enjoy more decisional freedom, work flexibility, and independence which would lead them to be more satisfied with their work and life, even as they may experience higher stress and longer working hours (Baron et al., 2016). For example, using the British Household Panel Survey, Binder and Coad (2013) found that self-employed individuals have higher life satisfaction scores than individuals in regular employment. However, they caution that in some instances, the self-employed might not enjoy higher life satisfaction because their high job satisfaction (resulting from being self-employed/independent) could mean that they focus too much on their work at the expense of other activities that contribute to high life satisfaction. In another study, using the German Socio-Economic Panel (SOEP) longitudinal data set, Binder and Coad (2016) found that both work and life satisfaction of the voluntarily self-employed (moving from employment to self-employment) were higher than that of their employed counterparts, while being forced into self-employment (moving from unemployment to self-employment) did not provide such benefits. Furthermore, self-employed people were found to be less satisfied with their available spare time compared with employees. Johansson Sevä et al. (2016), using data from 21 countries from the European Social Survey, also found that self-employment was positively related to subjective well-being (measured as life satisfaction), but the effect was more pronounced for self-employed with employees, compared to self-employed without employees. Hessels et al. (2018) used the Eurobarometer data for 28 European countries (2008–2012) and found that self-employed individuals are more satisfied with their lives than paid employees are. Similarly, Benz and Frey (2008) find that self-employment leads to greater autonomy which in turn leads to greater job satisfaction. Parasuraman and Simmers (2001) report that the self-employed had higher levels of job satisfaction but also experienced more work-family conflict, and lower family satisfaction compared to employees.

More recent studies incorporate both hedonic measures of well-being (e.g., life satisfaction) and eudaimonic approaches. In a large-scale study using UK data, Abreu et al. (2019) found that the self-employed have higher levels of job satisfaction (with the effect being persistent over time), and higher subjective well-being (including aspects of eudaimonic well-being). However, the authors show that well-being varies by location with the highest job satisfaction reported for entrepreneurs in semi-urban areas. Shir et al. (2019) also examined both hedonic and eudaimonic measures of well-being and determined that engagement in entrepreneurship is associated with higher levels of well-being compared to engagement in regular employment. Building on self-determination theory (Ryan & Deci, 2000), the authors position the concepts of autonomy, relatedness, and competence as mediating the relationship between engagement in entrepreneurship and well-being, thus highlighting the importance of positive psychological functioning for achieving entrepreneurial well-being. In a similar vein, Nikolaev et al. (2020) place psychological functioning as a mediator in the relationship between engagement in entrepreneurship and subjective well-being, measured as hedonic (positive affect) and evaluative well-being (life satisfaction), while Nikolaev et al. (2022) show how the self-employed achieve higher levels of eudaimonic well-being through a focus on problem-focused coping (proactive behaviors and thoughts that help them overcome challenges). This more recent strand of research points to the importance of attending to the diversity of well-being dimensions and the inclusion of eudaimonic measures that have been linked to entrepreneurial features such as drive for autonomy and self-determination, competence, and sense of purpose and personal growth, among others.

Variations in well-being for different groups of entrepreneurs. While the literature has established, in general, a positive relationship between engagement in entrepreneurship and well-being, it has also offered a more nuanced understanding of the differences in well-being for diverse groups of entrepreneurs. Notably, the benefits of well-being are not equally distributed among entrepreneurs. One of the most prominent differences is the variation established for necessity vs. opportunity entrepreneurs. For instance, despite their overall finding that on average the self-employed have higher life satisfaction than employees, Binder and Coad (2013) found that individuals moving from unemployment to self-employment (arguably "necessity entrepreneurs") were not better off in terms of life satisfaction than individuals moving from unemployment to regular employment. Similarly, Nikolova (2019), utilizing a German longitudinal data to study individuals' switches from unemployment to self-employment (necessity entrepreneurship) and from regular employment to self-employment (opportunity entrepreneurship), found that necessity entrepreneurs experience improvements in their mental health but not physical health, while opportunity entrepreneurs had both physical and mental health gains. While switching from unemployment to self-employment seemed to provide mental health benefits (likely via boosting individuals' self-esteem and avoiding stigma associated with being unemployed), necessity entrepreneurs did not fare as well as their opportunity-motivated counterparts. Following the line of research on well-being variations for different groups of entrepreneurs, in this book chapter, we focus on two specific groups that have received limited attention so far in the entrepreneurial well-being literature: women entrepreneurs and immigrant entrepreneurs.

THE PROMISE OF ENTREPRENEURSHIP AS A PATH TO WELL-BEING

Today, more people than ever before are choosing to be self-employed (Stephan et al., 2020). The drive to be self-employed is different for each person (self-expression, financial independence, or achieving individual dreams) depending on what motivates them (Dawson et al., 2009). Seminal work from Vroom (1964) defined motivation as the expectations that a person has that a specific effort will result in a certain outcome. Literature has focused on classifying these motivations into two distinct categories, namely push and pull factors (Dawson & Henley, 2012; Kirkwood, 2009; McClelland et al., 2005). Push factors can be contextualized as external or personal factors (e.g., not getting a job promotion) and can have a negative connotation (Kirkwood, 2009), while pull factors can be seen as factors that attract people to start their own business and be self-employed (e.g., seeing a gap in the market to take advantage of an opportunity) (Kirkwood, 2009; Segal et al., 2005; Shinnar & Young, 2008). Being self-employed may provide a unique opportunity to enable the fulfillment of basic psychological needs for people (Shir et al., 2019). The fulfillment of the psychological needs has the ability to positively increase a person's well-being (Shepherd & Patzelt, 2017; Williams & Shepherd, 2016). This is further supported by several authors (Abreu et al., 2019; Binder & Coad, 2016; Litsardopoulos et al., 2022; Marshall et al., 2020), that found evidence that people who are self-employed have a greater sense of well-being with their jobs than employees that earn a wage/salary. In this chapter, three drivers of self-employment will be focused on due to their prominence in the literature, namely autonomy, financial gain, and goal fulfillment.

Autonomy

Autonomy can be defined as the preference an individual has to make their own decisions (Douglas & Shepherd, 2002). According to Croson and Minniti (2012), autonomy (also referred to in the entrepreneurial literature as independence) is an important motivator for choosing to be self-employed (Carter et al., 2003; Douglas & Shepherd, 2002; Feldman & Bolino, 2000; Shane et al., 2003). Croson and Minniti (2012) state that when a person leaves organizational employment for self-employment, this allows for the individual to remove the "bonds of obedience and loyalty" that are linked to an employee/employer relationship. The decision to move from organizational employment to self-employment has the ability to directly create autonomy for a person (Croson & Minniti, 2012).

Ryff (2019) states that autonomy is encapsulated in self-determination theory (SDT) and can be seen as the point when core motives and needs are met. A need for autonomy has been found to be associated with higher business start-up intent (Burch et al., 2022; van Gelderen & Jansen, 2006). SDT highlights that work activities which are able to satisfy basic psychological needs (Ryan, 1995) of a person, such as autonomy, competence, and relatedness, can lead to increased motivation and ultimately greater well-being (Deci & Ryan, 2000; Gagné & Deci, 2005; Shir et al., 2019).

Financial Gain

In the literature, financial gain can also be referred to as financial success (Carter et al., 2003). The financial gains a person receives from being self-employed can be seen as the cash payments received from the business (e.g., drawings, salary, and dividends) (Carter, 2011). According to Uddin et al. (2014), some people choose to become self-employed to improve their financial position by making more money and ultimately improve the position of their families. Deng et al. (2011) elaborate further and highlight that individuals are drawn to self-employment for the desire of wealth (financial reward) that is associated with owning a business.

According to Rahman et al. (2016), the financial performance of a business has a positive and significant relationship with subjective well-being. When a person is able to generate enough finances to be in a strong financial position, they are able to engage in activities beyond the fulfillment of the basic needs and therefore advance their well-being (Diener, 2000). Furthermore, Rahman et al. (2016) purport that the ability of a business to be profitable and hence have a financial reward for the business owner could possibly enhance their self-confidence, optimism, and sense of belonging which could aid in the development of a positive outlook for their future and their overall well-being.

Goal Fulfillment

Goals can be defined as targets which people set for themselves that they try and achieve (Hanafiah et al., 2016). These personal goals provide the roadmap and motivation to focus a person's efforts and attention (Locke & Latham, 2006). The attainment of these personal goals is when goal fulfillment occurs. When a person starts or owns a business, business goals are developed which can be similar or different to an individual's personal goals (Hanafiah et al., 2016). Several studies such as Dunkelberg et al. (2013) and Benzing and Chu (2009) suggest that starting or owning a business can accomplish personal goals through the attainment of a higher self-esteem, higher need for achievement, growth, independence, and monetary rewards.

Goal fulfillment from the view of the SDT focuses on an individual's motivation to take action to control their life and act in a way that follows their beliefs and is directed in achieving their goals (Lanivich et al., 2021). According to Vansteenkiste et al. (2004) and Ryan and Deci (2000) goals that are intrinsic in nature are able to satisfy basic (psychological) human needs and therefore are likely to be positively related to psychological well-being.

THE LIMITS TO ACHIEVING WELL-BEING THROUGH SELF-EMPLOYMENT

The following section focuses on key characteristics which have been considered to be limits in the extant literature to the self-employed achieving well-being. They are the long hours, the demand on self-employed, and social support in relation to well-being.

Long Working Hours

The promise of self-employment is that it awards freedom and control (Nikolova, 2019). However, research on the context of work and self-employment supports the view that entrepreneurs may experience more negative working conditions compared to employees who get paid a salary. A key negative working condition is the longer working hours that many entrepreneurs endure. Entrepreneurs work very long hours with a significant amount of time committed to work and entrepreneurs believe that long working hours are a requirement for their business to be successful (Poggesi et al., 2019; Toyin et al., 2019). There is an expectation that entrepreneurs will work long hours to develop their (new) venture (Bae, 2017; Grosch et al., 2006).

Studies investigating working hours point to the importance of recovery processes, meaning the processes of recovering from work demands through disengagement from work and engagement in leisure activities (Sonnentag & Fritz, 2015). For example, Rau et al. (2008) found that the length of vacation time affects well-being positively, while another study compared entrepreneurs' well-being before and after a recovery retreat and found positive outcomes on well-being (Vesala & Tuomivaara, 2015). Yet, it is recognized that entrepreneurs have difficulties separating their personal and professional time, and detaching mentally from work, which introduces the need for targeted recovery practices (Williamson et al., 2021).

Demands on the Self-Employed

Entrepreneurs face high work demands that require strong, consistent effort and concentration (Karasek, 1979). The demands have been shown to negatively affect well-being for self-employed workers (Rau et al., 2008). The demands of being an entrepreneur compared to working as an employee have been characterized to be more "extreme work" as the entrepreneurial activities require both deeper well-being resources and that this subsequently creates more intense stressors (Hahn et al., 2012; Rauch et al., 2018; Stephan et al., 2022). Entrepreneurs are known to be independent and overconfident which leads to them overestimating their likelihood of success in their entrepreneurial venture (Cassar, 2010; Koellinger et al., 2007). They are equally likely to overinflate their abilities to manage the demanding work, typically when they find this work gratifying, satisfying, and energizing, which helps them justify their heightened focus on it (Stephan, 2018). Thus, they have the propensity to amplify their work and "overwork" themselves, thus leading to negative well-being or ill-being (Paye, 2020; Stephan et al., 2022; Williamson et al., 2021). While entrepreneurship offers autonomy and meaningfulness, it also manifests in mental health issues resulting from the pressured nature of their entrepreneurial work, which creates more stressors especially high workload and high levels of uncertainty (Rauch et al., 2018; Stephan, 2018; Wincent et al., 2008), and high levels of accountability. Entrepreneurs also endure the downside of their actions; thus, complications result in great stress, displeasure, feelings of lacking progress, and levels of depression and anxiety (e.g., Stephan et al., 2022; Wach et al., 2021).

Self-employed individuals experience lower levels of family satisfaction (Nguyen & Sawang, 2016; Parasuraman & Simmers, 2001) with family involvement and parental demand being significantly related to Work interference with family (WIF) and Family interference with Work (FIW) (Poggesi et al., 2019). This low family satisfaction and high demand of running a business can explain why many entrepreneurs prefer to stay single or have been divorced, as entrepreneurs explain that their work causes lack of time for family and inability to separate work from life (Toyin et al., 2019). Contributions from other actors such as the spouse and family member work relationships, role relationships in the business, time commitments, and the prior success of the business as a causal indicator have been considered to have a negative bearing on relationships and well-being associated for the family involved or uninvolved with the firm (Stephan, 2018).

Social Support, Isolation, and Well-Being

Social support is positively connected to life satisfaction and well-being among entrepreneurs, where a change in Perceived Social Support (PSS) relates to positive association outcomes in life satisfaction (Alshibani & Volery, 2021; Nguyen & Sawang, 2016). Poggesi et al. (2019) report that social support from the entrepreneur's partner, family, or private/public services help moderate the relationship between family involvement, parental demand, and time committed to family with FIW. Relationships are vital connections throughout the various stages of the entrepreneurial process, from initial concept stage to planning and the implementation stage (Shir & Ryff, 2022).

The social ties which are close to the entrepreneur are considered to be vital for them and the outcome of well-being, as these strong ties help entrepreneurs to endure the stressors of entrepreneurial work (Williamson et al., 2022). A lack of social support and social ties are associated with depression and anxiety for entrepreneurs, and thus ill-being (Ariza-Montes et al., 2017; Stephan et al., 2022). Research suggests that enough time needs to be dedicated for work, family, community, and self in order to have positive well-being (Moen et al., 2008). Entrepreneurs have given accounts where they have experienced feelings of loneliness and isolation as a consequence of working alone or in a small team and trying to meet too many demands (Williamson et al., 2022). The act of entrepreneurial pursuits has thus been shown to be quite a lonely process and could lead to social isolation.

PROMISE AND LIMITS FOR WOMEN ENTREPRENEURS

Little is known about the well-being of women entrepreneurs (e.g.,Hmieleski & Sheppard, 2019; Johansson Sevä et al., 2016). The scant literature on the topic is conflicting. Georgellis and Yusuf (2016) report that men who become self-employed are more satisfied with their job, while Johansson Sevä et al. (2016) found that women who are self-employed (without employees) had higher well-being than their male counterparts. Overall, it is recognized that women entrepreneurs usually have multiple demands (balancing home and work responsibilities) and more restricted access to resources (Brush et al., 2009), which might impact their entrepreneurial well-being differently because structural barriers, societal norms, and contextual limitations can impede their ability to achieve meaningful work and well-being while being self-employed.

The Promise for Women Entrepreneurs

Work-Life Balance and Well-being. The entrepreneurship literature has established that the experience of starting and running a new venture can be substantially different for women compared to men. The differences can stem from, among other factors, gendered socialization that positions entrepreneurship as a male-typed career option (Gupta et al., 2009; Shinnar et al., 2012; Wilson et al., 2007), the desire to balance work and family responsibilities (McGowan et al., 2012), and different initial venturing motivations of women (Jennings & Brush, 2013; Manolova et al., 2012). Those differences in the entrepreneurial experience have the potential to affect differentially the well-being of women entrepreneurs. Specifically, maintaining good work-family balance is a potential benefit from entrepreneurship that draws many women in (Jennings & McDougald, 2007), and being able to achieve such a balance can increase individuals' well-being. Johansson Sevä et al. (2016) propose that women entrepreneurs will benefit more from self-employment compared to men, because self-employment allows them the flexibility to balance career and family responsibilities—a reason more often cited by women who become self-employed. Using European data, Johansson Sevä et al. (2016) find that self-employed women *without* employees enjoy significantly higher life satisfaction (while for self-employed individuals with employees, there was no gender difference).

Sense of Purpose. In addition to providing flexibility to balance different tasks, self-employment has been examined as a way for women entrepreneurs to fulfill their psychological needs for sense of purpose. Bhuiyan and Ivlevs (2019) used the context of micro-borrowers in rural Bangladesh and reported that women micro-borrowers gain satisfaction with their financial security and feelings of achievement in life (an important aspect of eudaimonic well-being). The authors thus conclude that the subjective well-being of women can benefit from microcredit-enabled entrepreneurship. However, their results also caution that micro-borrowers in general have high worry over debt repayment, which leads to reduced life satisfaction.

Chatterjee et al. (2022) investigated marginalized women entrepreneurs and well-being at the base of the pyramid, where the promise of entrepreneurship as emancipation is strong to draw them out of poverty and give them a sense of direction and purpose. Their findings underscore the importance of considering the entrepreneurs' family and social support networks, which are key to women entrepreneurs in this context to be able to achieve flourishing and psychological well-being.

The Limits for Women Entrepreneurs

Work-family conflict and well-being. Comparisons between the self-employed and the traditionally employed show that self-employed individuals report significantly more work-family conflict (WFC) (Bettac & Probst, 2019; Parasuraman & Simmers, 2001). It is seen that as work-family conflict increases, subjective and psychological well-being of entrepreneurs decreases (Nguyen & Sawang, 2016). Although it is reported that self-employed individuals have greater autonomy and flexibility with their work (Parasuraman & Simmers, 2001), job flexibility and time committed to work are significantly related to work-family conflict (Poggesi et al., 2019). Family involvement and parental demand are significantly related to work-family conflict (Poggesi et al., 2019). Poggesi et al. (2019) also found that family plays a crucial role for women entrepreneurs as time devoted to work can mean time subtracted from family, leading to work interference with family. Some characteristics related to entrepreneurship, such as working long hours and high commitment to the entrepreneurial project, can have a negative effect on work-life balance and consequently well-being. In that sense, Parasuraman and Simmers (2001) found that women reported less work-family conflict (presumably because of greater schedule flexibility), but the juggling between work and family led to higher levels of life stress compared to men. In a longitudinal study, Georgellis and Yusuf (2016) revealed that job satisfaction benefits for men entering self-employment persisted over the years, while women transitioning into self-employment experienced only a weak increase in job satisfaction in the first year, which quickly disappeared.

Studies also report that self-employed women experience significantly higher family interference with work (FIW) compared to self-employed men (Hagqvist et al., 2018; Poggesi et al., 2019). When considering perceived social support (PSS), women entrepreneurs have higher levels of PSS compared to male entrepreneurs (Alshibani & Volery, 2021). If women entrepreneurs receive PSS from their partner, their family, or through services, the relationships of family involvement, parental demand, and time committed to family with FIW can be moderated (Poggesi et al., 2019).

Country's level of economic development and well-being. A country's level of economic development has been found to condition the extent to which the relationship between entrepreneurship and well-being holds true, and this can be especially significant for women in economically less developed countries. This is the result of lower economic development leading to more necessity-based entrepreneurs who are deprived of viable work options and are "pushed" into entrepreneurship. For instance, Johansson Sevä et al. (2016) found a significant interaction of self-employment with GDP growth and concluded that a positive macroeconomic environment brings significantly higher well-being benefits from engagement in entrepreneurship. Kwon and Sohn (2017) reported that self-employed individuals were less satisfied with their jobs than employees based on data from the Indonesian Family Life Survey. In the

Indonesian context, the self-employed earned comparatively less; they were also more likely to live in rural areas and be female.

Overall, the results from previous studies suggest a potentially complex pattern of relationships between engagement in entrepreneurship for women and diverse dimensions of well-being. The relationship is not straightforward, but can be dependent on the degree of work-family conflict (Nguyen & Sawang, 2016) or conversely, work-family synergies that create balance (Eddleston & Powell, 2012) and satisfaction. Other factors that can affect this relationship are perceptions of person-work fit (Hmieleski & Sheppard, 2019), and feelings of achievement (Bhuiyan & Ivlevs, 2019). Importantly, however, while some aspects of engagement in entrepreneurship might be conducive to women's well-being (work-life balance, autonomy and self-fulfillment, etc.), others can interfere with women entrepreneurs' ability to achieve well-being (e.g., high stress levels and worry, incompatible demands).

Promise and Limits for Immigrant Entrepreneurs

The promise for immigrant entrepreneurs. Immigrants have been found to have higher levels of self-employment compared to natives in many countries. There are several factors that have been found to influence the higher proportion of self-employed among immigrants compared to natives, namely the ethnocultural milieu, home country traditions, as well as unemployment and discrimination (Andersson & Hammarstedt, 2010; Irastorza & Peña, 2014; Ndofor & Priem, 2011). Many of these factors suggest that there might be a higher proportion of necessity self-employed among immigrants than among natives, which in turn could affect levels of subjective well-being. However, since immigrants come from very diverse ethnocultural backgrounds in terms of entrepreneurial culture (Dana, 1997), and since self-employment might represent a feasible way to become integrated in society, there is also reason to believe that the positive relationship between self-employment and well-being holds for many immigrants.

Financial capital. The benefits of self-employment (life satisfaction) have been found to be significantly greater when there are positive macroeconomic conditions (GDP). It has been found that immigrant entrepreneurs are more likely to be self-employed and have employees which makes it likely they may receive a "substantial booster effect on life satisfaction from economic growth" (Johansson Sevä et al., 2016). According to Hessels et al. (2020), the general health of self-employed individuals increases significantly when their earnings increase. This significant positive relationship between health and earnings for the self-employed suggests that immigrant entrepreneurs experience greater well-being when their business is financially successful.

Social capital. Aldén et al. (2022) investigated the long-term differences between native and immigrant self-employment and found that earnings are similar over time, but capital income decreases for immigrant entrepreneurs with time. The reason for this decrease could be due to a lack of social networks. Therefore, specifically for immigrant entrepreneurs, social capital can be beneficial for building human and financial capital when resources and capabilities are limited. Additionally, a qualitative study involving Thai immigrant-founded restaurants in Malaysia suggested the important role of social capital for immigrant entrepreneurs; specifically, identifying the significant role of family and friends in opportunity discovery and opportunity exploitation for immigrant entrepreneurs (Senik et al., 2022). The concept of ethnic enclaves, or areas that immigrants tend to cluster with other similar immigrants, represents an opportunity for social capital. Within these ethnic enclaves, immigrant entrepreneurs tend to have relationships of reciprocity and increased trust within their in-group communities (Casado et al., 2022), which may facilitate their well-being.

Immigrants encourage and support entrepreneurship among community members; therefore, facilitating networking opportunities with other immigrants can benefit immigrant entrepreneurs (Andersson et al., 2021). The value of immigrant entrepreneurs networking with other immigrants is further supported by a study involving Asian immigrants in New Zealand that found immigrant firms should increase/strengthen managerial networks; specifically, highlighting managerial ties with fellow immigrants from the same country-of-origin or ethnic background to improve products, services, processes, and administrative systems (Chung et al., 2020). A US study on immigrant entrepreneurs found that community social capital is mediated by the individual's agency; however, in general, immigrant entrepreneurs make decisions in an effort to balance the well-being of their ethnic community with the well-being of their business (Gomez et al., 2020).

It has been found that both first- and second-generation self-employed immigrants have higher life satisfaction when they have employees working for them as opposed to no employees—suggesting the significance of human capital for immigrant entrepreneurs (Johansson Sevä et al., 2016). Furthermore, a study found that well-being, satisfaction, and work-life balance were all highest for first-generation immigrants compared to second-generation immigrant entrepreneurs which researchers suggested was due to first-generation choosing to make a major life change (Zbierowski et al., 2019).

The Limits for Immigrant Entrepreneurs

Necessity entrepreneurship. Necessity self-employment has been found to be associated with lower levels of job satisfaction (Block & Koellinger, 2009) and overall life satisfaction (Binder & Coad, 2013). Immigrants often encounter instances of marginalization and discrimination in their host societies which push immigrants to become self-employed as there are no better options, i.e., necessity self-employment (Dana, 1997). Therefore, there is reason to assume that the benefits of self-employment in terms of subjective well-being are less obvious among immigrants than among native-born individuals.

Socio-cultural factors. Limitations due to socio-cultural factors have been found to adversely affect immigrant businesses. Therefore, adaptation was required to develop relational embeddedness within their communities through involvement with its social, structural, and institutional frameworks (Hack-Polay et al., 2020). There may be additional barriers for immigrant entrepreneurs; however, a study involving Chinese immigrants in Australia found that cross-cultural capabilities that include the capability of psychological adaptation (emotion management and positive mindset) and socio-cultural adaptation (cultural learning, language skills, and bicultural flexibility) can be leveraged to create competitive advantage in international markets; specifically, noting that the capability of emotion management helps maintain psychological well-being (Xu et al., 2019).

Intersection of Immigrant Status, Gender, and Entrepreneurship

Research has found that an individual's background, such as human capital, gender, ethnicity, and cultural background, helps explain the likelihood of immigrants becoming entrepreneurs; specifically, compared to self-employed immigrant males, immigrant females are disadvantaged to become self-employed both at entry and in the long term (Sun & Fong, 2022). Similar findings in a study in the USA comparing foreign-born Hispanic and Asian women with native-born Black and White women suggest that gender, race and ethnicity, and family factors interact significantly in the entrepreneurial process (Wang, 2019).

It has been found that spousal support and motivation are important for female immigrant entrepreneurs regardless of whether they were "pushed into entrepreneurship by unemployment or underemployment; attracted by the idea of living in the rural north; or motivated by ideas of independence, flexibility and status"—highlighting the significance of family embeddedness (Munkejord, 2017: 269). Additionally, being unemployed and/or being an immigrant are expected to be the factors most strongly associated with entrepreneurship among mothers (Naldi et al., 2021).

Female Immigrants and Entrepreneurship: Between Personal and Community Well-Being

Women have been found to not rely solely on their earnings to measure to what extent they felt their businesses were successful, but rather "they considered a broad collection of variables such as personal autonomy, job satisfaction, control of their future, the ability to balance work and family, with these measures often personally determined to fit family needs and the desires of the owners" (Patrickson & Hallo, 2021: 5). Some immigrant female entrepreneurs in rural Norway emphasized that "they were motivated by the idea of contributing to place development in their new home region" (Munkejord, 2017: 270). Additionally, an overwhelming majority of the participants in a US study involving immigrant female entrepreneurs stated that giving back to their communities is one of their main goals in running their businesses (Wang, 2019). According to Wang (2019), women entrepreneurs measure their success based on non-financial aspects such as: compatibility with their values, vision, purpose in life, ability to contribute to the community, and flexibility in order to balance work and family. It has been found that well-educated women who arrived in Japan as homemakers were able to redesign themselves to become self-employed and create employment for both native and immigrants (Billore, 2011). Their improving relations with native customers, employees, and suppliers have meant they have become an important source of economic rejuvenation and a strong motivation factor for the population in general (Billore, 2011).

Female Identity: Ethnicity, Culture, and Religion

Perceived gender roles and the impact of those perceptions on female identity are significantly influenced by many factors including ethnicity, culture, and religion of both the country of origin and the destination country. However, a qualitative study involving female immigrant entrepreneurs of Turkish and Moroccan descent found that "these women do not internalize stereotypical roles of gender and ethnicity passively - by engaging in creative identity work, they relate themselves actively to these in creative ways to obtain more female autonomy and to sustain their business ownership identities" (Essers et al., 2013: 1661).

Research suggests that women entrepreneurs live and work under the constraint of social norms and perceived gender roles—notably with culture in the country of origin playing a role for immigrant women business owners in terms of how they view gender's role in family and at work (Wang, 2019). Another study of female entrepreneurs in India found deep-rooted gender bias and family pressures presented major challenges for female entrepreneurs (Aggrawal et al., 2022). A study involving Muslim immigrant businesswomen found that to some extent all women interviewed struggled with the restrictive gender and ethnic rules of their immigrant communities and families; therefore, "restrictive manifestation of female ethnicity urges them either to play down the salience of femininity and ethnicity in their entrepreneurial contexts, or to engage in a continual battle or to distance themselves from the narrow categories of gender and ethnicity" (Essers et al., 2010: 336). Collectively, the results of those studies point to the need to investigate the well-being implications of the entrepreneurial endeavors of immigrant women entrepreneurs, with a special attention to how the intersection of different identities (e.g., woman, immigrant, mother) can affect the experiences of the self-employed.

Discussion: Advancing Research on Self-Employment and Well-Being

While self-employment has been touted as a path to personal fulfillment and well-being, that path is long and winding, and attention needs to be paid to the differences of self-employment experiences for diverse groups of entrepreneurs. In this chapter, we presented arguments for both the "bright" side of self-employment as a way to well-being, and the challenges associated with it. As the field of entrepreneurial well-being is in its early stages, in what follows, we offer several fruitful avenues for future inquiries. Table 7.1 provides a summary of the key future research directions.

The Promise

While several studies have confirmed that self-employment is associated with higher levels of well-being compared to wage employees, the dimensions used to measure well-being have been mainly limited to hedonic measures, such as life satisfaction. A recent stream of research has pointed to the importance of eudaimonic well-being, and several studies have incorporated eudaimonic measures as dependent variables (Nikolaev et al., 2020, 2022; Shir et al., 2019; Stephan et al., 2020). Autonomy has long been considered a key motivator for entrepreneurial behavior (van Gelderen & Jansen, 2006), and it is also a crucial aspect of well-being drivers according to SDT, and a major eudaimonic well-being component (Ryff, 2019). However, other drivers/dimensions such as competence, relationships, purpose in life, self-acceptance, etc. have received relatively little attention. Recent research underscores the importance of understanding how (via) what mechanisms self-employment leads to different measures of eudaimonic well-being (Nikolaev et al., 2022). In line with this research, we encourage research attention on understanding how different measures, e.g., autonomy, competence, and relatedness of eudaimonic well-being impact self-employed/entrepreneurs.

Furthermore, context specificities have rarely been taken into account. While Stephan et al. (2020) investigate eudaimonic well-being for self-employed across 16 European countries, there are potentially many differences in the experience of entrepreneurial well-being across different cultures and geographies. Another important context to consider is the industry context. For instance, high-growth, competitive sectors, such as those related to Science, Technology, Engineering, and Mathematics (STEM), may pose unique challenges and stressors for entrepreneurs (potentially having negative impact on health and/or hedonic well-being measures), but may also offer the possibility of high fulfillment and personal growth, thus increasing eudaimonic well-being. Further, for specific groups of entrepreneurs, e.g., women in STEM, who are underrepresented in the industry and may be subject to constrained expectations due to gendered social norms, the challenges of working in such competitive fields might be compounded, but success

Table 7.1 Advancing research on self-employment and well-being: a summary of future research opportunities

What we need to know more about	Future research directions
The promise *More focus on eudaimonic well-being *Context specificities, e.g., across countries, industry-specific (e.g., women in STEM), intersection of identities, social entrepreneurs *Relationship among different dimensions of well-being, e.g., physical health, mental health, hedonic, eudaimonic	How do different measures, e.g., autonomy, competence, relatedness of eudaimonic well-being impact the self-employed? What are the comparative differences on well-being based on regional/industry-specific, family, social/commercial differences? Longitudinal studies in order to understand the changes over time for the various aspects of well-being
The limits *Context-specific aspects related to the work life balance and ill-being/emotions *Negative aspects of well-being and time spent being entrepreneurial *Contexts for when demand and workload affect feelings of isolation and disconnectedness to others	How can we overcome the positive bias in extant literature on the well-being of entrepreneurs? More work is needed on support for entrepreneurs and aspects of well-being to reduce isolation More longitudinal methods in order to understand the changes over time for the various aspects of ill-being
Women entrepreneurs *Work-life balance and issues related to work-family conflict *Social roles defined based on family commitments and their impact on well-being *Cultural differences in terms of the well-being of women in different countries	How does socialization which reinforces gender differences impact women entrepreneurs' well-being? Qualitative studies context and insights based on dimensions of well-being (family/cultural dynamics)
Immigrant entrepreneurs *Well-being drivers for immigrant entrepreneurs, such as work meaningfulness, autonomy, and sense of community embeddedness/relationships *Intersection of immigrant status and gender	How changes in local embeddedness and relationships along the business lifecycle and effect on immigrant entrepreneurs' well-being How does the intersection of gender and immigrant status impact on entrepreneurial well-being?

in those fields might also lead to a commensurate increase in eudaimonic well-being measures. Further delving into different groups of entrepreneurs, more attention should be paid to differences between "traditional" for-profit entrepreneurs and social entrepreneurs. Are social entrepreneurs better able to achieve well-being because of the nature of their work and the positive societal impact of their ventures, or are they faced with unique challenges that reduce their well-being?

Finally, while a corpus of research has examined a variety of well-being dimensions, we encourage more attention to the relationship between them. For instance, eudaimonic well-being has been positioned as a mediator that leads to hedonic well-being (life satisfaction) (Nikolaev et al., 2020; Shir et al., 2019). However, we know relatively little about the interrelationships among different well-being aspects such as physical health, mental health, hedonic well-being, and eudaimonic well-being.

The Limits

We note that the literature tends to have a "positive bias" when it comes to well-being outcomes of entrepreneurship. However, it is important that (would be) entrepreneurs have a realistic picture of the hardships involved in being self-employed along with the benefits. Demands on the self-employed, such as long working hours and potentially social isolation, can take a heavy toll on various aspects of well-being, such as health, life satisfaction, and positive relationships with others. As entrepreneurs go through various stages of the venture formation process, those experiences may vary, resulting in a differential impact on their well-being (Shir & Ryff, 2022). Future studies should incorporate research methods which are temporal such as longitudinal studies in order to understand the changes over time for the various aspects of well-being/ill-being. Furthermore, how can we overcome the positive bias in extant literature on the well-being of entrepreneurs?

In a review of the literature, Williamson et al. (2022) discuss several negative emotions that can result from entrepreneurship, such as emotional exhaustion, depressive feelings, anxiety, and frustration. Williamson et al. (2021) contend that "entrepreneurship tends to erode boundaries between work and non-work experiences like few other occupations and makes it particularly difficult for entrepreneurs to detach mentally from the stressful aspects of their work" (p. 1308). Thus, more work is needed on support for entrepreneurs and aspects of well-being to reduce isolation and enhance the relationship aspects of well-being. There should be more research in this area on the context and role of working alone and thus the barriers to social connectedness to foster positive well-being for entrepreneurs.

Women Entrepreneurs

The literature on entrepreneurial well-being has not paid sufficient attention to the impact of different entrepreneurial experiences on the well-being of women entrepreneurs. Yet, the unique challenges that many women face (i.e., having to juggle multiple demands such as parental and business demands) have the potential to affect their well-being in different ways. While the literature has explored issues related to work-life balance and work-family conflict, we don't know enough about how those aspects affect different dimensions of well-being, such as physical health, mental health, hedonic well-being, and eudaimonic well-being.

It is well-established that gendered socialization and social norms can affect women's entrepreneurial experiences (e.g., de Bruin et al., 2007; Shinnar et al., 2012). Here, social role theory (Eagly, 2001; Eagly & Wood, 2016; Eagly et al., 2000) could be very useful to examine gendered roles defined based on family commitments and their impact on well-being. Thus, an important future research avenue is how gendered socialization impacts women entrepreneurs' well-being. Such research would need to be contextualized, as gender roles differ across countries/cultures. From that perspective, qualitative studies might be especially useful to understand the context and provide insights based on dimensions of well-being embedded in family/cultural dynamics. Our review of the literature also identified several aspects at the intersection of gender and cultural/immigrant status that need further research. Challenges arising from the intersection of different identities might pose significant constraints on the ability of women entrepreneurs to achieve well-being, and we need a better understanding of strategies and practices that can help reduce stressors for those entrepreneurs.

Immigrant Entrepreneurs

The literature on immigrant entrepreneurship has discussed several benefits for this group of entrepreneurs, but also has underscored the importance of understanding their unique challenges, such as lack of initial social capital, and local knowledge which are crucial for starting a venture. Those challenges can result in various stressors that could manifest more strongly for immigrants compared to native-born entrepreneurs because of potentially limited language skills, relevant local experience, resources, or social embeddedness (Dabić et al., 2020). While immigrants tend to be overrepresented as entrepreneurs, one potential explanation for this is that they may face discrimination on the job market and thus turn to entrepreneurship not as their preferred first choice, but because they need to, i.e., they are potentially engaged in more necessity entrepreneurship than opportunity entrepreneurship. This might have significant implications for their well-being, especially from the point of view of eudaimonic well-being aspects such as feelings of competence, meaningfulness, and personal fulfillment. Therefore, more research is needed to understand the well-being implications of life as an immigrant entrepreneur, especially with regard to eudaimonic well-being.

Furthermore, a dynamic temporal perspective would be especially useful here to understand the variations in well-being throughout the various stages of the business lifecycle. As immigrant entrepreneurs go through the different stages, and build trust and local connections with relevant stakeholders, how does this affect different aspects of their well-being? Longitudinal studies would be especially helpful to bring insights about the interplay of (changes in) local embeddedness, networks, and relationships along the business lifecycle and their effect on immigrant entrepreneurs' well-being.

There are current opportunities which will add to the contextualization of entrepreneurship for minority and gender groups. While the extant literature on well-being has considered the nature and difficulties associated with well-being there is a dearth of research which specifically addresses the complexities such as the nature of entrepreneurial practices and praxis. There is a space to consider and use qualitative research methods to investigate the situated nature and context of the promises and limits of entrepreneurial well-being. To this end, there are further research opportunities which can assist by asking questions which the more quantitative research methods cannot aptly address. A recent special issue by Hlady-Rispal et al. (2021) provides some clear examples of the kinds of qualitative methods that can be applied. Potential questions that can be considered with qualitative research can address the situated nature of well-being. A typical question might be focused not only on when, and how time is spent on balancing work-life issues for the entrepreneurs, but also on the deeper consideration of contextualization factors. These might include the nature of the relationships, the regional complexities, the supports and limits to the types of support available and the reasons/motivations behind the self-employed arrangements. The more pertinent questions might focus not only on the nature of entrepreneurial activities but also the nature of the context for their specific narratives and thus richer insights might be gained to add to theory and knowledge production in the well-being context.

Conclusion

The pathway from being an entrepreneur to achieving high levels of well-being is not necessarily straightforward. There is a promise that entrepreneurship comes with certain benefits for well-being such as autonomy and potential financial independence. However, there are certain limits to the fulfillment of self-employment in terms of entrepreneurial well-being, such as long working hours, high demand, and social isolation. Furthermore, for certain groups, such as for women and immigrant entrepreneurs, there are benefits such as work-life balance and a sense of purpose aiding their well-being. At the same time, we have focused on the limits applied to well-being for women and immigrant entrepreneurs. We have discussed the role of work-family conflict, socio-cultural factors, and the role of motivation such as necessity entrepreneurship. It is our hope that the suggestions for future research which have been specified in the last section will inspire more focused attention to *contextual dimensions* (e.g., how the intersection of gender and immigrant status impacts on entrepreneurs' well-being) and *temporal dynamics* of entrepreneurial well-being (e.g., longitudinal studies in order to understand the changes over time for the various aspects of well-being).

References

Abreu, M., Oner, O., Brouwer, A., & van Leeuwen, E. (2019). Well-being effects of self-employment: A spatial inquiry. *Journal of Business Venturing, 34*(4), 589–607.

Aggrawal, A., Carrick, J., Kennedy, J., & Fernandez, G. (2022). The plight of female entrepreneurs in India. *Economies, 10*. https://doi.org/10.3390/economies 10110264

Aldén, L., Bastani, S., Hammarstedt, M., & Miao, C. (2022). Immigrant-native differences in long-term self-employment. *Small Business Economics, 58*(3), 1661–1697.

Alshibani, S. M., & Volery, T. (2021). Social support and life satisfaction among entrepreneurs: A latent growth curve modelling approach. *International Journal of Manpower, 42*(2), 219–239.

Andersson, L., & Hammarstedt, M. (2010). Intergenerational transmissions in immigrant self-employment: Evidence from three generations. *Small Business Economics, 34*, 261–276. https://doi.org/10.1007/s11187-008-9117-y

Andersson, M., Larsson, J. P., & Oner, O. (2021). Ethnic enclaves and self-employment among Middle Eastern immigrants in Sweden: Ethnic capital or enclave size? *Regional Studies, 55*(4), 590–604. https://doi.org/10.1080/00343404.2020.1839638

Ariza-Montes, A., Arjona-Fuentes, J. M., Law, R., & Han, H. (2017). Incidence of workplace bullying among hospitality employees. *International Journal of Contemporary Hospitality Management, 29*, 1116–1132.

Bae, S.-H. (2017). Work hours of immigrant versus U.S.-born female workers. *Workplace Health & Safety, 65*(10), 478–486. https://doi.org/10.1177/2165079916686358

Baron, R. A., Franklin, R. J., & Hmieleski, K. M. (2016). Why entrepreneurs often experience low, not high, levels of stress: The joint effects of selection and psychological capital. *Journal of Management, 42*(3), 742–768.

Benzing, C., & Chu, H. M. (2009). A comparison of the motivations of small business owners in Africa. *Journal of Small Business and Enterprise Development, 16*(1), 60–77.

Benz, M., & Frey, B. S. (2008). The value of doing what you like: Evidence from the self-employed in 23 countries. *Journal of Economic Behavior & Organization, 68*(3–4), 445–455.

Bettac, E. L., & Probst, T. M. (2019). Work–family conflict, sleep, and health: A comparison of traditional and self-employed workers. *International Journal of Manpower, 42*(2), 240–259.

Bhuiyan, M. F., & Ivlevs, A. (2019). Micro-entrepreneurship and subjective well-being: Evidence from rural Bangladesh. *Journal of Business Venturing, 34*(4), 625–645.

Billore, S. (2011). Female immigrant entrepreneurship: Exploring international entrepreneurship through the status of Indian women entrepreneurs in Japan. *International Journal of Gender and Entrepreneurship, 3*(1), 38–55.

Binder, M., & Coad, A. (2013). Life satisfaction and self-employment: A matching approach. *Small Business Economics, 40*, 1009–1033.

Binder, M., & Coad, A. (2016). How satisfied are the self-employed? A life domain view. *Journal of Happiness Studies, 17*, 1409–1433.

Block, J., & Koellinger, P. (2009). I can't get no satisfaction—Necessity entrepreneurship and procedural utility. *Kyklos, 62*(2), 191–209.

Brush, C. G., De Bruin, A., & Welter, F. (2009). A gender-aware framework for women's entrepreneurship. *International Journal of Gender and Entrepreneurship*, *1*(1), 8–24.

Burch, T., Tocher, N. M., & Murphy, G. (2022). An examination of how personal characteristics moderate the relationship between startup intent and entrepreneurship education. *New England Journal of Entrepreneurship*, *25*(2), 161–182. https://doi.org/10.1108/NEJE-05-2021-0029

Carter, N. M., Gartner, W. B., Shaver, K. G., & Gatewood, E. J. (2003). The career reasons of nascent entrepreneurs. *Journal of Business Venturing*, *18*(1), 13–39.

Carter, S. (2011). The rewards of entrepreneurship: Exploring the incomes, wealth, and economic well-being of entrepreneurial households. *Entrepreneurship Theory and Practice*, *35*(1), 39–55.

Casado, R., Pessoa de Queiroz Falcao, R., & Picanco Cruz, E. (2022). Brazilian immigrant entrepreneurs' support networks and bounded (mis)trust in Western Australia. *Population, Space and Place*, *28*. https://doi.org/10.1002/psp.2489

Cassar, G. (2010). Are individuals entering self-employment overly optimistic? An empirical test of plans and projections on nascent entrepreneur expectations. *Strategic Management Journal*, *31*(8), 822–840. https://doi.org/10.1002/smj.833

Chatterjee, I., Shepherd, D. A., & Wincent, J. (2022). Women's entrepreneurship and well-being at the base of the pyramid. *Journal of Business Venturing*, *37*(4), 106222.

Chung, H. F., Yen, D. A., & Wang, C. L. (2020). The contingent effect of social networking ties on Asian immigrant enterprises' innovation. *Industrial Marketing Management*, *88*, 414–425.

Croson, D. C., & Minniti, M. (2012). Slipping the surly bonds: The value of autonomy in self-employment. *Journal of Economic Psychology*, *33*(2), 355–365.

Dana, L. P. (1997). The origins of self-employment in ethno-cultural communities: Distinguishing between orthodox entrepreneurship and reactionary enterprise. *Canadian Journal of Administrative Sciences/Revue Canadienne des Sciences de l'Administration*, *14*(1), 52–68.

Dawson, C. J., & Henley, A. (2012). "Push" versus "pull" entrepreneurship: An ambiguous distinction? *International Journal of Entrepreneurial Behavior & Research*, *18*(6), 697–719.

Dawson, C. J., Henley, A., & Latreille, P. L. (2009). Why do individuals choose self-employment? *SSRN Electronic Journal*. https://doi.org/10.2139/ssrn.1336091

Dabić, M., Vlačić, B., Paul, J., Dana, L. P., Sahasranamam, S., & Glinka, B. (2020). Immigrant entrepreneurship: A review and research agenda. *Journal of Business Research*, *113*, 25–38.

De Bruin, A., Brush, C., & Welter, F. (2007). Advancing a framework for coherent research on women's entrepreneurship. *Entrepreneurship Theory and Practice*, *31*(3), 323–339.

Deci, E. L., & Ryan, R. M. (2000). The "what" and "why" of goal pursuits: Human needs and the self-determination of behavior. *Psychological Inquiry*, *11*(4), 227–268.

Deng, S., Wang, X., & Alon, I. (2011). Framework for female entrepreneurship in China. *International Journal of Business and Emerging Markets*, *3*(1), 3–20.

Diener, E. (2000). Subjective well-being: The science of happiness and a proposal for a national index. *American Psychologist*, *55*(1), 34.

Diener, E., & Emmons, R. A. (1984). The independence of positive and negative affect. *Journal of Personality and Social Psychology*, *47*(5), 1105.

Douglas, E. J., & Shepherd, D. A. (2002). Self-employment as a career choice: Attitudes, entrepreneurial intentions, and utility maximization. *Entrepreneurship Theory and Practice, 26*(3), 81–90.

Dunkelberg, W., Moore, C., Scott, J., & Stull, W. (2013). Do entrepreneurial goals matter? Resource allocation in new owner-managed firms. *Journal of Business Venturing, 28*(2), 225–240.

Eagly, A. H. (2001). Social role theory of sex differences and similarities. In J. Worell (Ed.), *Encyclopedia of women and gender: Sex similarities and differences and the impact of society on gender*. Elsevier Science & Technology.

Eagly, A. H., & Wood, W. (2016). Social role theory of sex differences. In *The Wiley Blackwell encyclopedia of gender and sexuality studies* (pp. 1–3). Wiley. https://doi.org/10.1002/9781118663219.wbegss183

Eagly, A. H., Wood, W., & Diekman, A. B. (2000). Social role theory of sex differences and similarities: A current appraisal. In *The developmental social psychology of gender* (p. 174). Taylor & Francis. ISBN 9781410605245-12.

Eddleston, K. A., & Powell, G. N. (2012). Nurturing entrepreneurs' work–family balance: A gendered perspective. *Entrepreneurship Theory and Practice, 36*(3), 513–541.

Essers, C., Benschop, Y., & Doorewaard, H. (2010). Female ethnicity: Understanding Muslim immigrant businesswomen in The Netherlands. *Gender, Work & Organization, 17*(3), 320–339.

Essers, C., Benschop, Y., & Doorewaard, H. (2013). Family ties: Migrant female business owners doing identity work on the public-private divide. *Human Resources, 66*(12), 1645–1665.

Feldman, D. C., & Bolino, M. C. (2000). Career patterns of the self-employed: Career motivations and career outcomes. *Journal of Small Business Management, 38*(3), 53–68.

Foo, M.-D., Uy, M. A., & Baron, R. A. (2009). How do feelings influence effort? An empirical study of entrepreneurs' affect and venture effort. *Journal of Applied Psychology, 94*(4), 1086–1094.

Gagné, M., & Deci, E. L. (2005). Self-determination theory and work motivation. *Journal of Organizational Behavior, 26*(4), 331–362.

Georgellis, Y., & Yusuf, A. (2016). Is becoming self-employed a panacea for job satisfaction? Longitudinal evidence from work to self-employment transitions. *Journal of Small Business Management, 54*, 53–76.

Gomez, C., Perera, B. Y., Wesinger, J. Y., & Tobey, D. H. (2020). Immigrant entrepreneurs and community social capital: An exploration of motivations and agency. *Journal of Small Business and Enterprise Development, 27*(4), 579–605.

Grosch, J. W., Caruso, C. C., Rosa, R. R., & Sauter, S. L. (2006). Long hours of work in the U.S.: Associations with demographic and organizational characteristics, psychosocial working conditions, and health. *American Journal of Industrial Medicine, 49*(11), 943–952. https://doi.org/10.1002/ajim.20388

Gupta, V. K., Turban, D. B., Wasti, S. A., & Sikdar, A. (2009). The role of gender stereotypes in perceptions of entrepreneurs and intentions to become an entrepreneur. *Entrepreneurship Theory and Practice, 33*(2), 397–417.

Hack-Polay, D., Igwe, P. A., & Madichie, N. O. (2020). The role of institutional and family embeddedness in the failure of Sub-Saharan African migrant family businesses. *The International Journal of Entrepreneurship and Innovation, 21*(4), 237–249.

Hagqvist, E., Toivanen, S., & Bernhard-Oettel, C. (2018). Balancing work and life when self-employed: The role of business characteristics, time demands, and gender contexts. *Social Sciences, 7*(8), 139.

Hahn, V. C., Frese, M., Binnewies, C., & Schmitt, A. (2012). Happy and proactive? The role of hedonic and eudaimonic well-being in business owners' personal initiative. *Entrepreneurship Theory and Practice, 36*(1), 97–114.

Hanafiah, M. H., Yousaf, Sh. U., & Senik, Z. C. (2016). Satisfaction of goals attainment and intention to restructure among Malaysian SME entrepreneurs. *Journal of Entrepreneurship and Business, 4*(2), 13–29.

Hessels, J., Arampatzi, E., van der Zwan, P., & Burger, M. (2018). Life satisfaction and self-employment in different types of occupations. *Applied Economics Letters, 25*(11), 734–740.

Hessels, J., Rietveld, C. A., & van der Zwan, P. (2020). The relation between health and earnings in selfemployment. *Frontiers in Psychology, 11.* https://doi.org/10.3389/fpsyg.2020.00801

Hlady-Rispal, M., Fayolle, A., & Gartner, W. B. (2021). In search of creative qualitative methods to capture current entrepreneurship research challenges. *Journal of Small Business Management, 59*(5), 887–912.

Hmieleski, K. M., & Sheppard, L. D. (2019). The Yin and Yang of entrepreneurship: Gender differences in the importance of communal and agentic characteristics for entrepreneurs' subjective well-being and performance. *Journal of Business Venturing, 34*(4), 709–730.

Irastorza, N., & Peña, I. (2014). Earnings of immigrants: Does entrepreneurship matter? *The Journal of Entrepreneurship, 23*(1), 35–56.

Jennings, J. E., & Brush, C. G. (2013). Research on women entrepreneurs: Challenges to (and from) the broader entrepreneurship literature? *Academy of Management Annals, 7*(1), 663–715.

Jennings, J. E., & McDougald, M. S. (2007). Work-family interface experiences and coping strategies: Implications for entrepreneurship research and practice. *Academy of Management Review, 32*(3), 747–760.

Johansson Sevä, I., Vinberg, S., Nordenmark, M., & Strandh, M. (2016). Subjective well-being among the self-employed in Europe: Macroeconomy, gender and immigrant status. *Small Business Economics, 46*, 239–253.

Kahneman, D., Diener, E., & Schwarz, N. (Eds.). (1999). *Well-being: Foundations of hedonic psychology.* Russell Sage Foundation.

Karasek, R. A. (1979). Job demands, job decision latitude, and mental strain: Implications for job redesign. *Administrative Science Quarterly, 24*(2), 285–308.

Kirkwood, J. (2009). Motivational factors in a push-pull theory of entrepreneurship. *Gender in Management: An International Journal, 24,* 346–364.

Koellinger, P., Minniti, M., & Schade, C. (2007). "I think I can, I think I can": Overconfidence and entrepreneurial behavior. *Journal of Economic Psychology, 28*(4), 502–527. https://doi.org/10.1016/j.joep.2006.11.002

Kwon, I., & Sohn, K. (2017). Job dissatisfaction of the self-employed in Indonesia. *Small Business Economics, 49,* 233–249.

Lanivich, S. E., Bennett, A., Kessler, S. R., McIntyre, N., & Smith, A. W. (2021). RICH with well-being: An entrepreneurial mindset for thriving in early-stage entrepreneurship. *Journal of Business Research, 124,* 571–580.

Litsardopoulos, N., Saridakis, G., Georgellis, Y., & Hand, C. (2022). Self-employment experience effects on well-being: A longitudinal study. *Economic and Industrial Democracy.* https://doi.org/10.1177/0143831X221086017

Locke, E. A., & Latham, G. P. (2006). New directions in goal-setting theory. *Current Directions in Psychological Science, 15*(5), 265–268.

Manolova, T. S., Brush, C. G., Edelman, L. F., & Shaver, K. G. (2012). One size does not fit all: Entrepreneurial expectancies and growth intentions of US women and men nascent entrepreneurs. *Entrepreneurship & Regional Development, 24*(1–2), 7–27.

Marshall, D. R., Meek, W. R., Swab, R. G., & Markin, E. (2020). Access to resources and entrepreneurial well-being: A self-efficacy approach. *Journal of Business Research, 120,* 203–212.

McClelland, E., Swail, J., Bell, J., & Ibbotson, P. (2005). Following the pathway of female entrepreneurs: A six-country investigation. *International Journal of Entrepreneurial Behavior & Research, 11*(2), 84–107.

McGowan, P., Redeker, C. L., Cooper, S. Y., & Greenan, K. (2012). Female entrepreneurship and the management of business and domestic roles: Motivations, expectations and realities. *Entrepreneurship & Regional Development, 24*(1–2), 53–72.

Moen, P., Kelly, E. L., & Huang, Q. (2008). Work, family and life-course fit: Does control over work time matter? *Journal of Vocational Behavior, 73*(3), 414–425. https://doi.org/10.1016/j.jvb.2008.08.002

Munkejord, M. C. (2017). Immigrant entrepreneurship contextualised: Becoming a female migrant entrepreneur in rural Norway. *Journal of Enterprising Communities: People and Places in the Global Economy, 11*(2), 258–276.

Naldi, L., Baù, M., Ahl, H., & Markowska, M. (2021). Gender (in) equality within the household and business startup among mothers. *Small Business Economics, 56,* 903–918.

Ndofor, H., & Priem, R. L. (2011). Immigrant entrepreneurs, the ethnic enclave strategy, and venture performance. *Journal of Management, 37*(3), 790–818.

Nguyen, H., & Sawang, S. (2016). Juggling or struggling? Work and family interface and its buffers among small business owners. *Entrepreneurship Research Journal, 6*(2), 207–246. https://doi.org/10.1515/erj-2014-0041

Nikolaev, B., Boudreaux, C. J., & Wood, M. (2020). Entrepreneurship and subjective well-being: The mediating role of psychological functioning. *Entrepreneurship Theory and Practice, 44*(3), 557–586.

Nikolaev, B. N., Lerman, M. P., Boudreaux, C. J., & Mueller, B. A. (2022). Self-employment and eudaimonic well-being: The mediating role of problem-and emotion-focused coping. *Entrepreneurship Theory and Practice.* https://doi.org/10.1177/10422587221126486

Nikolova, M. (2019). Switching to self-employment can be good for your health. *Journal of Business Venturing, 34*(4), 664–691.

Parasuraman, S., & Simmers, C. A. (2001). Type of employment, work–family conflict and well-being: A comparative study. *Journal of Organizational Behavior: The International Journal of Industrial, Occupational and Organizational Psychology and Behavior, 22*(5), 551–568.

Patrickson, M., & Hallo, L. (2021). Female immigrant entrepreneurship: The experience of Chinese migrants to Australia. *Administrative Sciences, 11*(4), 145.

Paye, S. (2020). Long work hours in salaried employment and self-employment measures and problems. *Socio-economie du Travail*, 2(6), 119–154. https://doi.org/10.15122/isbn.978-2-406-10053-9.p.0119

Poggesi, S., Mari, M., & De Vita, L. (2019). Women entrepreneurs and work-family conflict: An analysis of the antecedents. *International Entrepreneurship and Management Journal*, 15(2), 431–454. https://doi.org/10.1007/s11365-017-0484-1

Rahman, S. A., Amran, A., Ahmad, N. H., & Taghizadeh, S. K. (2016). Enhancing the wellbeing of base of the pyramid entrepreneurs through business success: The role of private organizations. *Social Indicators Research*, 127, 195–216.

Rauch, A., Fink, M., & Hatak, I. (2018). Stress processes: An essential ingredient in the entrepreneurial process. *Academy of Management Perspectives*, 32(3), 340–357. https://doi.org/10.5465/amp.2016.0184

Rau, R., Hoffmann, K., Metz, U., Richter, P. G., Roesler, U., & Stephan, U. (2008). Gesundheitsrisiken bei Unternehmern. *Zeitschrift fuer Arbeits- und Organisationspsychologie*, 52(3), 115–125.

Ryan, R. M. (1995). Psychological needs and the facilitation of integrative processes. *Journal of Personality*, 63, 397–427.

Ryan, R. M., & Deci, E. L. (2000). Intrinsic and extrinsic motivations: Classic definitions and new directions. *Contemporary Educational Psychology*, 25(1), 54–67.

Ryan, R. M., & Deci, E. L. (2001). On happiness and human potentials: A review of research on hedonic and eudaimonic well-being. *Annual Review of Psychology*, 52(1), 141–166.

Ryff, C. D. (1995). Psychological well-being in adult life. *Current Directions in Psychological Science*, 4(4), 99–104.

Ryff, C. D. (2019). Entrepreneurship and eudaimonic well-being: Five venues for new science. *Journal of Business Venturing*, 34(4), 646–663.

Segal, G., Borgia, D., & Schoenfeld, J. (2005). The motivation to become an entrepreneur. *International Journal of Entrepreneurial Behavior & Research*, 11, 42–57.

Senik, Z. C., Jamaludin, N. A., & Isa, R. M. (2022). Exploring social capital influencing entrepreneurial process among immigrant entrepreneurs in Malaysia. *Jurnal Pengurusan*, 65, 59–69.

Shane, S., Locke, E. A., & Collins, C. J. (2003). Entrepreneurial motivation. *Human Resource Management Review*, 13(2), 257–279.

Shepherd, D. A., & Patzelt, H. (2017). *Trailblazing in entrepreneurship: Creating new paths for understanding the field*. Springer Nature.

Shinnar, R. S., Giacomin, O., & Janssen, F. (2012). Entrepreneurial perceptions and intentions: The role of gender and culture. *Entrepreneurship Theory and Practice*, 36(3), 465–493.

Shinnar, R. S., & Young, C. A. (2008). Hispanic immigrant entrepreneurs in the Las Vegas metropolitan area: Motivations for entry into and outcomes of self-employment. *Journal of Small Business Management*, 46(2), 242–262.

Shir, N., & Ryff, C. D. (2022). Entrepreneurship, self-organization, and eudaimonic well-being: A dynamic approach. *Entrepreneurship Theory and Practice*, 46(6), 1658–1684.

Shir, N., Nikolaev, B. N., & Wincent, J. (2019). Entrepreneurship and well-being: The role of psychological autonomy, competence, and relatedness. *Journal of Business Venturing*, 34(5), 105875.

Sonnentag, S., & Fritz, C. (2015). Recovery from job stress: The stressor-detachment model as an integrative framework. *Journal of Organizational Behavior, 36*(Suppl. 1), S72–S103. https://doi.org/10.1002/job.1924

Stephan, U. (2018). Entrepreneurs' mental health and well-being: A review and research agenda. *Academy of Management Perspectives, 32*(3), 290–322. https://doi.org/10.5465/amp.2017.0001

Stephan, U., Rauch, A., & Hatak, I. (2022). Happy entrepreneurs? Everywhere? A meta-analysis of entrepreneurship and wellbeing across institutional contexts (Version 1). Supplemental material. *Sage Journals.* https://doi.org/10.1177/10422587211072799

Stephan, U., Tavares, S. M., Carvalho, H., Ramalho, J. J., Santos, S. C., & Van Veldhoven, M. (2020). Self-employment and eudaimonic well-being: Energized by meaning, enabled by societal legitimacy. *Journal of Business Venturing, 35*(6), 106047.

Sun, S. B., & Fong, E. (2022). The role of human capital, race, gender, and culture on immigrant entrepreneurship in Hong Kong. *Journal of Small Business & Entrepreneurship, 34*(4), 363–396.

Toyin, A. A., Gbadamosi, G., Mordi, T., & Mordi, C. (2019). In search of perfect boundaries? entrepreneurs' work-life balance. *Personnel Review, 48*(6), 1634–1651. https://doi.org/10.1108/PR-06-2018-0197

Uddin, M. R., Bose, T. K., & Ferdausi, R. (2014). Push and pull factors of entrepreneurs in Khulna City, Bangladesh. *International Journal of Entrepreneurship and Small Business, 21*(1), 101–114.

Van Gelderen, M. W., & Jansen, P. G. W. (2006). Autonomy as a start-up motive. *Journal of Small Business and Enterprise Development, 13*, 23–32.

Vansteenkiste, M., Simons, J., Lens, W., Soenens, B., Matos, L., & Lacante, M. (2004). Less is sometimes more: Goal content matters. *Journal of Educational Psychology, 96*(4), 755.

Vesala, H., & Tuomivaara, S. (2015). Slowing work down by teleworking periodically in rural settings? *Personnel Review, 44*(4), 511–528.

Wach, D., Stephan, U., Weinberger, E., & Wegge, J. (2021). Entrepreneurs' stressors and well-being: A recovery perspective and diary study. *Journal of Business Venturing, 36*(5), 106016. https://doi.org/10.1016/j.jbusvent.2020.106016

Wang, Q. (2019). Gender, race/ethnicity, and entrepreneurship: Women entrepreneurs in a US south city. *International Journal of Entrepreneurial Behavior & Research, 25*(8), 1766–1785. https://doi.org/10.1108/IJEBR-05-2017-0156

Wiklund, J., Nikolaev, B., Shir, N., Foo, M. D., & Bradley, S. (2019). Entrepreneurship and well-being: Past, present, and future. *Journal of Business Venturing, 34*(4), 579–588.

Williams, T. A., & Shepherd, D. A. (2016). Victim entrepreneurs doing well by doing good: Venture creation and well-being in the aftermath of a resource shock. *Journal of Business Venturing, 31*(4), 365–387.

Williamson, A. J., Drencheva, A., & Wolfe, M. T. (2022). When do negative emotions arise in entrepreneurship? A contextualized review of negative affective antecedents. *Journal of Small Business Management.* https://doi.org/10.1080/00472778.2022.2026952

Williamson, A. J., Gish, J. J., & Stephan, U. (2021). Let's focus on solutions to entrepreneurial ill-being! Recovery interventions to enhance entrepreneurial well-being. *Entrepreneurship Theory and Practice, 45*(6), 1307–1338. https://doi.org/10.1177/10422587211006431

Wilson, F., Kickul, J., & Marlino, D. (2007). Gender, entrepreneurial self-efficacy, and entrepreneurial career intentions: Implications for entrepreneurship education. *Entrepreneurship Theory and Practice, 31*(3), 387–406.

Wincent, J., Ortqvist, D., & Drnovsek, M. (2008). The entrepreneur's role stressors and proclivity for a venture withdrawal. *Scandinavian Journal of Management, 24*(3), 232–246. https://doi.org/10.1016/j.scaman.2008.04.001

Vroom, V. H. (1964). *Work and motivation*. Wiley.

Xu, K., Drennan, J., & Mathews, S. (2019). Immigrant entrepreneurs and their cross-cultural capabilities: A study of Chinese immigrant entrepreneurs in Australia. *Journal of International Entrepreneurship, 17*, 520–557.

Zbierowski, P., Brzozowska, A., & Gojny-Zbierowska, M. (2019). Well-being of immigrant entrepreneurs in their entrepreneurial life. *Management Issues, 17*(1), 212–238. https://doi.org/10.7172/1644-9584.81.10

CHAPTER 8

Shepherding Engineering Leadership: A Combined Approach to Leading and Creating Employee Engagement

Ankit Agarwal

INTRODUCTION

Mahatma Gandhi said: "See the good in people and help them." Nelson Mandela said: "For to be free is not merely to cast off one's chains, but to live in a way that respects and enhances the freedom of others." Martin Luther King Jr said: "Darkness cannot drive out darkness; only light can do that. Hate cannot drive out hate; only love can do that."

Why do we hark back to these leaders whom we call 'great?' Why do we refer to what they said when we want to make our point? Why does what they said matter? And many such questions come to my mind when I read such quotes and think about terminologies such as leadership and followership. The common theme in these quotes is focusing on 'people' and our association. These leaders are directing their ideas, their energy, and their significance of existence to *people*. James MacGregor Burns (2012), a Pulitzer Prize-winning historian, examines leaders from Mosses to Machiavelli to Martin Luther King Jr. in his book, *Leadership*. He quotes Mao Zedong (Mao Tse-tung):

> To link oneself with the masses, one must act in accordance with the needs and wishes of the masses.... There are two principles here: one is the actual needs of the masses rather than what we fancy they need, and the other is the

A. Agarwal (✉)
Lecturer in Management and Program Director Bachelor of Business (Management), Adelaide Business School, University of Adelaide, Adelaide, SA, Australia
e-mail: ankit.agarwal@adelaide.edu.au

© The Author(s), under exclusive license to Springer Nature Switzerland AG 2023
J. Marques (ed.), *The Palgrave Handbook of Fulfillment, Wellness, and Personal Growth at Work*,
https://doi.org/10.1007/978-3-031-35494-6_8

wishes of the masses, who must make up their own minds instead of us making up their minds for them.... We should pay close attention to the well-being of the masses, from the problems of land and labour to those of fuel, rice, cooking oil and salt.... We should help them to progress from these things to an understanding of the higher tasks which we have put forward.... Such is the basic method of leadership.

Again... the focus is on 'people,' their needs, their growth, and knowing what 'they' think and not so much what leaders want them to think. Though Mao discusses leadership from times of hunger and the need for compelling and creative leadership, these notions are not much different from the demands of the present time. For example, the Ukraine war has sparked the world's fastest and largest displacement crisis in decades (The United Nations Refugee Agency, 2023). Syria's years of war have triggered a health crisis. Yemen's failed truce failed to mitigate the economic and health consequences of the conflict. Afghanistan's entire population was impoverished (International Rescue Committee, 2023). We could also consider the Iran crisis, where thousands of people were interrogated, unfairly prosecuted, and/or arbitrarily detained solely for peacefully exercising their human rights. Hundreds remained unjustly imprisoned (Amnesty International, 2023). To begin this chapter, I consider it necessary to briefly highlight the 'leadership crisis' that we, planetary colleagues, face. This crisis extends to the organizational problems we find critical to address.

I identify leading or leadership with a mindset that cannot be viewed in silos. For example, Gardner (1993), in his book *On Leadership*, wrote:

> ...leaders, whose task it is to keep a society functioning, are always seeking the *common ground* that will make concerted action possible. They have no choice. It is virtually impossible to exercise leadership if shared values have disintegrated. (p. x)

He also wrote:

> Great things happen nationally when topmost leadership is goaded and supported from below. (p. ix)

Reading the works of Gardner and Burns, I find how the mediocrity or irresponsibility of many people in power indicates today's leadership crisis. Intellectual crisis underlies mediocrity, and so leadership rarely rises to its full potential. In a world where we are familiar with all too many leaders, we are familiar with far too little about leadership (Burns, 2012). Burns (2012) argues that our failure to understand the essence of leadership in the modern age has resulted in us being unable to agree on standards to recruit, measure, and reject leadership. This could be attributed to a common stereotype of leaders being set apart and above others. For example, Goleman (2017) notes that when businesspeople are asked what they believe makes a leader effective or what leaders should do, they respond with a range of sweeping responses, such as the leader sets strategy, motivates employees, creates a mission and culture; or perhaps that their only job is to get results. Largely in the leadership literature, these responses separate leaders from followers. However, Kelley (1998) argues that effective leadership requires the same qualities as effective followers. He advocates in favor of no such thing as a good follower blindly following a leader because the same individual can sometimes exhibit leadership and followership but may perform different roles at different times (Daft, 2014).

The nature and quality of leadership have been discussed for a very long time. Writers often emphasize the importance of leaders (as politicians or higher authority) as being central to the significant issues that impact whole communities (Selznick, 2011). However, some versions of leadership discuss how leading involves empowering others to accomplish extraordinary things in an organization. This refers to the practices leaders use to transform their values into actions, visions into realities, obstacles into innovations, separateness into solidarity, and risks into rewards (Kouzes & Posner, 2006). Kouzes and Porner (2006) argue that creating a climate that fosters success is about leadership creating a culture where people can turn challenges into extraordinary opportunities. We all know leadership is a centuries-old mystery of what leaders can and should do to inspire their people to perform. And this mystery has given rise to industries/organizations devoted to testing and coaching executives (Goleman, 2017). By testing and coaching executives, Goleman (2017) explores how these *leadership experts* work to develop business leaders capable of achieving bold objectives—whether they are strategic, financial, organizational, or a combination of these. However, the challenge is that many leadership practitioners—those who lead organizations—and those who provide professional training and development in leadership—are highly engaged in only one profession, either as trainers or as leaders (Rost, 1991). And business organizations constitute the most significant percentage of these practitioners. Again, seeing what leadership entails from the siloed lens of one particular work domain may not be the way forward when it comes to leading.

Vroom and Arthur (2007) claim that leadership depends on the situation. This statement can be interpreted in many ways, based on what one means by leadership. Some social scientists dispute the validity of this statement (Vroom & Arthur, 2007), but notable work of, for example, Hershey and Blanchard's (1977) Situational Leadership model and Blake et al. (1962) Managerial Grid and others, though being criticized over decades, cast a shadow on such disputes. Bennis and Thomas (2020) raise an interesting question regarding the characteristics of a leader; why do some people possess incomparable confidence, loyalty, and the ability for hard work, while others (with just as much vision and intelligence) stumble repeatedly? Well, I do not see a simple answer to this question. In the behavioral sciences, leadership is considered to be one of the most extensively researched social influence processes (Barrow, 1977). It is undoubtedly one of the most frequently observed phenomena and one of the least understood (Bruns, 2012). Even though the nature of the discussion has persisted, effective leadership remains elusive to many people and organizations (Selznick, 2011). Though in recent years, leadership research has explored how leadership affects follower attitudes and performance (Podsakoff & Podsakoff, 2019) to improve its practical usefulness (Northouse, 2021), definitions of leadership exhibit little convergence (Barrow, 1977). Due to the lack of quantitative evidence, specific leadership behaviors have not been demonstrated to yield positive results. Many leading experts provide advice based on experience, inference, and instinct, and there are times when that advice is right on point, but then there are also times when it is not (Goleman, 2017). For example, some leaders practice management by exception and only intervene when things go wrong. It's their way of leading. But then, in the process, they bend the truth and distort the feedback to create a false impression of positive feedback (Bass, 1985). Sometimes it works, and sometimes it does not. As Selznick (2011) points out, we should not forget that our world is a pluralist society of many large, influential, relatively autonomous groups. At this time of significant disruption, we need to continue the ongoing discussion, reconciling idealistic thinking with pragmatic reasoning and freedom with order (Selznick, 2011).

Many decades ago, Stogdill (1974) observed almost as many variations of the definition of leadership as individuals who have attempted to describe it. It is not much different from today. This creates a danger of popular leadership philosophies, where writers discuss sound advice without any (much) empirical evidence to support their rationale (Chronot-Mason et al., 2019). Due to this, leadership has become ambiguous in its definition and measurement (Pfeffer, 1977). It is a similar case with the concepts of democracy, love, and peace; while we intuitively understand what such words mean, they can have different meanings for different individuals (Northouse, 2021). Pfeffer and Sutton (2006) argue that many leaders fail to use sound evidence and experience poor management practices due to their inability to think clearly. This suggests that leading is a process, an action, and not a position (Hughes, 1993); leading differs from what the term *leadership* entails. Leading is to be understood first. So, in the next section of this chapter, I am not trying to put my version forward to what is and is not understood by 'leading' or leadership. Instead, I am exploring two schools of thought; shepherding and engineering. I discuss the two approaches and attempt to view leading from these two lenses, separately and combined. I do so to understand what leaders can do (or do) to put the focus back on employees while also ensuring looking after what adversely impacts employee performance and what roles leaders can play in minimizing employee adversity at work.

Shepherding

Religious and spiritual literature has widely discussed being a shepherd and shepherd leadership. A quick search for the term "Shepherding Leadership style" in google scholar produced over 23,000 related results within religious and spiritual texts. A similar search in business journals, such as the Academy of Management, produced only three results, while a search in the Leadership Quarterly gave five. I am not pointing out these numbers to suggest how not-religious-focused academic journals must look to research the shepherding style of leading in the leadership arena. I am merely pointing out that shepherding style of leading has much to do with spiritual and religious context. For example, 'herder' is a traditional symbol of many religious traditions. In the Jewish, Christian, and Muslim traditions, God is referred to as the Good Shepherd. In the Levant, these religions emerged out of a herding culture, where good shepherds ensured the safety and unity of their herds. Lord Vishnu's avatar, Krishna, is an important Hindu deity. He worked as a cowherd, a traditional occupation of young men of those times in India. Similarly, in Zen Buddhism, the Ox Herder is a traditional parable. In it, a herder is compared to a man searching for his ox that has gone missing in his quest for spiritual enlightenment (see National Geographic, 2023). According to the Oxford dictionary, shepherding (as a noun) means "the tending of sheep as a shepherd." Also, it means "careful management of resources or an organization." This makes me wonder about the relationship between the two.

Shepherding is based on the idea that sheep can roam wherever they want. They can decide (Altman et al., 2022). But then, the Shepherd ensures that the sheep's decisions do not take them into dangerous territory. Similarly, in managed ecosystems where the central organization does not have authority over community members and are neither employees nor contractually bound suppliers, the organization may provide guidance and boundaries to ensure that the community remains aligned with the organization's objectives (Altman et al., 2022). The book, *Shepherding the Church: Effective Spiritual Leadership in a Changing Culture* by Stowell (1997), examines the core of ministry: those who shepherd the flock. A shepherd is called upon and capable of cultivating a commitment to the ministry's fundamental biblical functions and has the personal character and proficiency required to serve effectively in an increasingly pagan culture. Pagan (Paganus in Latin), *a place with fixed boundaries*, was initially used to refer to a rural district or community but has since evolved to mean *a civilian community*. In historical contexts, Pagan culture is an example of a community or people that observe a polytheistic religion. The practice of paganism is not a matter of belief but rather one of following ritualistic systems. Compared with more ideological religions, paganism is much more tolerant of other beliefs and practices (Dowden & Dowden, 2013, p. 2). Stowell (1997) argues that when ministries fail, it is not because they have not understood or applied the best techniques or programmatic advances but because they either forget or have not realized that the key to every ministry is the quality of the Shepherd who leads. Altman et al., (2022, p. 85) found that "shepherding communities without exploiting them" is one of the capabilities associated with managed ecosystems. They argue that shepherding a community of independent actors is composed of guiding them without having direct authority over them while also maximizing the value of the community's activities by leveraging the community without exploiting its members. Just as sheep are free to roam within certain boundaries, shepherds set those boundaries and enforce them when necessary (Altman et al., 2022). Organizations also use (or can use) this type of control to guide, prod, influence, or steer instead of exerting the more stringent control evident in more onerous contractual relationships (Poppo & Zhou, 2014).

This discussion takes my focus to Greenleaf's (1970) model of Servant Leadership. In theory, servant leadership is, in its nature, inspiring and moral. However, there is a lack of empirical research regarding the effectiveness of servant leadership in the workplace. As an example of the boundaries of servant leadership and to set the stage for systematic empirical research, Graham (1991, p. 105) discusses a "good shepherd" case since both servant leadership and good shepherding are prominent in the Christian Bible as models of responsible leadership. Graham writes that he visited his friends who ran a sheep farm. He asked for their assistance in learning more about servant leadership by examining what good shepherding entails. He stayed in the pasture to observe the sheep, cared for them, and interviewed his friends about sheep and shepherding. In line with Greenleaf's (1970) definition, Graham concluded that good shepherds and servant leaders are not the same. Greenleaf's (1998, p. 24) idea of "servant" is deeply rooted in Judeo-Christian heritage. Greenleaf discusses how, even though we are a low-caring society in general, there are many notable servants among us. However, these servant leaders sometimes seem to lose ground to neutral or non-serving individuals; we do not care enough about our fellow human beings as a general rule (Greenleaf, 1998). When we use sheep as an analogy and try to figure out the role of a shepherd, it is safe to say that sheep herding is not an easy task and is a service that needs recognition. From his experience at a friend's farm, Graham (1991) notes that sheep require considerable attention at inconvenient times and during adverse weather conditions. He observes that sheep are not always cooperative (i.e., easy to lead) and rarely express gratitude for Shepherd's care. This limits the shepherding to leading by demonstrating consideration and initiating structure (Stogdill & Coons, 1957), a concept, perhaps, with which we are all familiar.

Good shepherding is mentioned frequently in the Bible, including in the first book, Genesis. As one of the most appealing books in the Old Testament in contemporary culture, Genesis contains foundational material for Jewish and Christian theology (Moberly, 2009). The Shepherd's life is uncomfortable with exposure to the weather, sleepless nights, and danger from predators and thieves. The Shepherd's role is to keep the flock of sheep from scattering and to look for lost sheep. Lambs who are weary or ill would be carried. Injured sheep were treated by the Shepherd. The metaphor of the relationship between God and people has been made clear in many books of the Christian Bible: for example, Jesus Christ is called the Great Shepherd in the book of Hebrews. Jesus referred to himself as the fine Shepherd with compassion for his sheep. In comparison, the relationship between a leader and followers is much more complex than 'initiating structures and demonstrating consideration for employees.' So, although being a good shepherd to employees would be a possible approach to leading, shepherding alone may not fulfill all of the requirements of a leader.

Many people are hampered by rigid and unyielding mindsets that prevent them from utilizing the knowledge Greenleaf (1970, 1998) discusses. Greenleaf (1998) writes that older people (in the sense of experience) *in charge* may be more likely to be converted into affirmative servants through a *peak* experience, such as a religious conversion, psychoanalysis, or a new vision. Nonetheless, it is worth trying to stem the tide of deterioration for those older individuals who still possess a glimmer of the servant disposition; "Life can be more whole for those who try, regardless of the outcome" (Greenleaf, 1998, p. 23). Biblical leadership is typically depicted as that of a shepherd, and a shepherd's heart will be most evident during times of change. During such times, it is easy to become aggressive, force change, and exert inappropriate pressure on those resisting (Thomas & Wood, 2012). It is also possible to avoid making required changes by not addressing conflict and letting it run its course. However, when a leader fails to act, there is division among some people and a sense of helplessness and frustration among others. Shepherds guide and love their people during difficult times (Thomas & Wood, 2012). Moore (2004, p. 72) argues that "the Shepherd was the most vital to realizing their ideal of an alternate society. The shepherds were in charge of the redeemed community... to develop it to maturity...."

To be effective in shepherding, a shepherd is required to keep their "finger to the wind," adjust their technique, and never take their eyes off the center of the target (Stowell, 1997, p. 12). However, although such awareness and approach may allow shepherds to lead by influence, sometimes shepherds must push from behind to avoid distractions and trouble. Sometimes, shepherds walk alongside their disciples (flock of sheep) to provide guidance (Thomas & Wood, 2012). The Shepherd with a clean conscience can love and lead without being influenced by hidden agendas or hunting for self-deception. The clearer the conscience of a shepherd, the more capable and effective the Shepherd will be (Stowell, 1997). However, concerning humans, the terms 'clear' and 'conscience' remain elusive and subjective, with no empirical evidence of how an individual leader could develop a 'clear conscience' or what 'clear' means when we discuss developing a 'conscience.' This leads me to discuss a branch of knowledge (engineering) with years of evidence behind its processes and rationale concerning why it does what it does. I will discuss engineering in the following section.

Engineering

A significant part of the evolution of engineering has been the influence of trends in politics, society, economics, and technology over the last two centuries. Hence, today's engineer is influenced by the past, shaped by the present, and will continue to be shaped by future trends (Sheppard et al., 2007). Engineering is a field of study that encompasses a wide range of activities, such as software development, construction, aviation, etc. As a result, no *definition of engineering* has been universally accepted as relevant to the various engineering domains. There has been much expansion in the engineering profession over the last few decades (Kirby et al., 1990). As a result, there are now many different definitions of the engineering profession and many different meanings associated with these definitions. Kirby et al. (1990) note that Thomas Tredgold, the British architect who made the first attempt to define engineering in 1828, referred to engineering as "the art of directing the great sources of power in nature for the use and convenience of man" (Marsh, 2019, p. 1). Engineering was so defined in the charter of the Institution of Civil Engineers, led by Thomas Telford. Since then, engineering education has also evolved. In fact, a large part of management and management education can be attributed to engineering. For example, Army engineers were the first professional managers hired to manage railroads (Augier, 2004). Also, in a sense, management training was a product of the engineering mindset. The Canadian Engineering Qualifications Board (1993) defines engineering as follows:

> The 'practice of professional engineering' means any act of planning, designing, composing, evaluating, advising, reporting, directing or supervising, or managing any of the foregoing that requires the application of engineering principles, and that concerns the safeguarding of life, health, property, economic interests, the public welfare or the environment.

Engineering involves various tasks in design and analysis (Brennecke, 2020) and is generally a complex problem-solving activity (Vincenti, 1990). Engineers look for functionality and manufacturability (Liker & Mogran, 2006). They apply their ability to combine elements in different amalgamations that allow them to assemble and manipulate devices in their minds (thinking mechanisms) in ways that are yet to exist for the world in general (Ferguson, 1994). For example, software engineers like to be left alone to experiment with creative ideas when redesigning a system to incorporate enhanced functionalities or enhancements (Raelin, 1989). However, they have to remember that their ideas focus on reducing waste that costs organizations time, money, and resources (Liker & Morgan, 2006). The book, *Engineering and the Mind's Eye* by Ferguson (1994), discusses although often unnoticed, how this critical mode of thinking (i.e., thinking mechanisms) is crucial to understanding engineering. Ferguson (1994) points out that throughout history, nonverbal thinking has created outlines and filled in the details of our physical environment, while technological choices and decisions have shaped our world. For example, architects conceived the pyramids, cathedrals, and rockets not based on geometry, structural theory, or thermodynamics but as first impressions, which got incepted through the visions in their minds (Ferguson, 1994). In the words of Price (1965, p. 123):

> When an engineer, following the safety regulations of the Coast Guard or the Aviation Agency, translates the laws of physics into the specifications of a steamboat boiler or the design of a jet airliner, he is mixing science with a great many other considerations all relating to the purposes to be served. And it is always purposes in the plural—a series of compromises of various considerations, such as speed, safety, economy, and so on.

A common aspect of an engineer's work involves the presence of ambiguities, which frequently require judgment calls (Downer, 2011). Engineers must learn to contend with ambiguities and the external pressures of deadlines and cost-reduction targets while meeting strict safety requirements (Brennecke, 2020). As such, there is pressure to perform as an engineer; failure is not an option when creating constant wins is necessary (Liker & Morgan, 2006). However, it has always been challenging to integrate knowledge, practical skills, and ethical judgment in a setting that is often remote from actual practice (Sheppard et al., 2007). Often this is the case because a large part of a professional engineer's training and early work experience is dedicated to developing their technical skills alone (Slusher et al., 1972). The purpose of engineering as a profession should be to improve the world for the benefit of all. At least, this is how engineering has been discussed in the literature. National Research Council (2009) writes, "Engineers make a world of difference." In addition to developing enhanced engineering skills, engineers are required to learn from the past and acquire specialized knowledge, problem-solving skills, and sound judgment to serve society (Sheppard et al., 2007). Using this approach emphasizes that engineers can accomplish much today because they stand on the shoulders of those who have gone before (Kirby et al., 1990). When engineers look forward to further developing their profession, they must respect the past and the rationale behind its activities. As Sarton (1937, p. 52) puts it, "Reverence without progressiveness may be stupid; progressiveness without reverence is wicked and foolish." While this quote is old, perhaps, many would agree with its implications.

As technology usage increases and software becomes more prevalent, engineers' jobs will become more complex. In one sense, the most significant performance improvements have been achieved by introducing entirely new technologies. The downside, however, is that, as with any significant advancement, reliability may be compromised in the early stages of introduction (Breneman et al., 2022). Studies of the history of engineering provide engineers with an understanding of what is required for national development and what it means to be an engineer. It helps engineers gain insights from the lessons of engineering experiences, enabling them to understand better the complex environment humanity has created (Kirby et al., 1990). Engineers used to believe that what they learned in school would remain relevant throughout their careers. However, any specific practical skills will quickly become obsolete due to advances in the basic sciences. Therefore, an engineer must be trained in these basic sciences to face an unknown future (Price, 1965) or a rapidly changing present competently. Each engineer adds (or learns to add) something to the design, pushes it further (Latour, 1987), and systematically builds a system (Anderson, 2020). An engineer starts with an idea, sometimes distinct, sometimes tentative, which can be thrown onto the mind's screen and observed and manipulated (Ferguson, 1994).

Nevertheless, without conceptual integrity, a system may fail to attract a sufficient user market due to its complexity (Raelin, 1989). It is, therefore, the responsibility of every professional engineer to demonstrate not only intellectual and technical mastery but also gain practical wisdom that combines knowledge and skills to serve humanity most effectively (Sheppard et al., 2007). As Price (1965, p. 32) writes, "when an engineer sets out to build something today, he frequently builds something...never built before." Such a progressive and open mindset broadens the human horizon and liberates it from narrow conceptions (Kirby et al., 1990). Raelin (1987), in his paper, *The '60s kids in the corporation: More than just "Daydream Believers,"* started with a dialogue between Jim, the marketing manager, and Hank, an engineering project leader.

Hank explained that he and his team are not satisfied with the speed of their computer, and it will take six more weeks until the product is ready for display at a sales convention for potential customers to place orders. Jim had aggressively driven sales and pushed Hank to consider doing it early. While the tennis match of argument continued, Jim suggested Hank develop a prototype, even if they were not completely happy with the product, and show it to customers to get customer traction. However, Hank insisted that, as an engineer, he does not work like that. Engineers don't just promise until they can deliver something.

Hank's perspective fits Latour's (1987) example of a dam engineer: a dam engineer would be foolish to imagine that the water would obey his wishes and refrain from flowing over or politely run from bottom to top. The engineer works (should work) on the premise that water will leak away if it can. As a result, solving problems is one of the essential and focal activities of engineering work (Sheppard et al., 2007). For an engineer, doing things early before the product is ready is not one of their concerns (Latour, 1987). In improving performance, systems or their components are often subjected to increasing failures unless adequate countermeasures are taken (Breneman et al., 2022). These failures can be attributed to poor engineering designs, faulty construction, or manufacturing processes. Nevertheless, they are also caused by human error, poor maintenance, inadequate testing and inspection, improper use, and a lack of protection against excessive environmental stresses (Ebeling, 2019, p. 3).

In his book, *Thinking through technology: the path between engineering and philosophy*, Mitcham (2022) discusses Engineering Philosophers. Mitcham contends that engineering philosophers of goodwill can respond to this analysis of failures (see Ebeling, 2019) and improve performance by noting that humanities' emphasis on critical analysis and moral sensitivity may increase the role of bias in decision-making. It can easily conceal irrationality or poor judgment (prone to hide errors, leading to poor decisions) (Hey, 2016). Philosophers of engineering can also appeal to their philosophical counterparts in the humanities, urging them to accept—based on an acknowledgment of the historical character of interpretation—that a common sense understanding has become historically conditioned. As a result, it is necessary to understand the interaction between society and engineering in the present day. The development of knowledge and the knowledge tools fundamental to engineers is equally essential despite their prolific status (Kirby et al., 1990). After all, engineers and engineering have a progressive history involving advancements based on and incorporating previous knowledge (Kirby et al., 1990).

Although we understand the rich history and evidence of what engages and disengages employees at work, I find it necessary to again highlight the challenges to employee engagement before proposing and discussing the combined Shepherding and Engineering approach to leading (SEL) as a plausible solution to leadership challenges.

Leadership Challenges to Creating Employee Engagement

Combining Shepherding and Engineering approaches to leading (SEL) as a proposed solution.

Current leadership frameworks are changing in perspective and practice as workplace knowledge economies become more prevalent and emerging motivational state variables, such as employee engagement, become more widely used (Shuck & Herd, 2012). The research community has been calling for perspectives on leadership, even though shifts in workplace dynamics have occurred in practice for some time, especially in employee engagement. Earlier concepts such as employee satisfaction, employee commitment, and organizational citizenship behavior have formed the basis of employee engagement (Markos & Sridevi, 2010). However, the employee engagement concept has a broader scope. It refers to the relationship between the organization's management and its employees. This makes an organization's leadership crucial to enhancing employee engagement.

Work dynamics have changed and have been continuously changing, especially since the age of globalization. Keeping employees engaged in their work has become one of the primary concerns of managers. It has become increasingly evident to organizational leaders that they can create a more efficient and productive workforce by focusing on employee engagement. However, no leader can improve employee engagement unless employees are willingly involved and engaged in the improvement process (Markos & Sridevi, 2010). The external environment, whether political, economic, sociocultural, technological, ecological, or legal, has a huge role in introducing and forcing such changes. Whether we look at the Russia-Ukraine war, atrocities in Iran, the Syria crisis, the current financial collapse, the introduction of Artificial Intelligence, or changes in rules, regulations, and laws of practice in different countries, an increasing number of controversies across various contexts have led to a growing interest in studying and understanding why individuals engage in behaviors that cause enormous costs to organizations and society (Moore et al., 2012). The changes resulting from these developments have led to many organizations moving from mechanistic to knowledge-intensive work models (Adler, 2001). In light of these facts, leaders pay more attention to their employees' perspectives toward their work and organizations.

Concepts such as employee commitment and organizational citizenship behavior were introduced on the premise that efficiency and productivity can be attributed to employees' commitment and ability (Markos & Sridevi, 2010). This has led to an increase in employees' expectations of participating in organizational decision-making and active participation in organizational activities (Burke & Ng, 2006), so their demand to be treated fairly and with respect in their work environments (Shuck & Herd, 2012). Thus, a totalitarian management style cannot be applied to knowledge workers due to these shifts in employees' perceptions of their work (e.g., having operational autonomy, job satisfaction, fairness, and status) (Markos & Sridevi, 2010). Alvesson and Willmott (1992) argue that by encouraging questions, reflection, and open-mindedness, leaders can minimize anti-emancipatory elements and promote emancipatory impulses (i.e., creating conditions that facilitate human flourishing). A desire to avoid contributing to totalizing thinking can be a more powerful motivation than creating a positive and constructive project (Alvesson & Willmott, 1992). Leaders do not want employees to perceive them as aggressors and agree to their voice (one voice; totalitarianism approach to leading). Unless this approach is corrected, it may become a way for employees to resolve their sense of helplessness and powerlessness in the face of totalitarianism (Kets de Vries, 1994), reducing their engagement at work.

Kahn (1990) conducted an influential study of psychological conditions surrounding employee engagement and work disengagement. As a unique and important motivational concept, he argued that individuals could engage in work roles to varying degrees, describing their engagement as the harnessing of all aspects of an employee, including their physical, cognitive, and emotional energies, to a work role performance (Rich et al., 2010). This has a significant impact on both their work performance and experience (Kahn, 1990). He incorporated several factors into the model, considering that individual, interpersonal, group, intrapersonal, and organizational factors influence people's engagements. Kahn (1990) concluded that observing specific instances of work role performance can be compared to a camera lens zooming in on a distant stationary image and revealing it as a series of innumerable leaps and falls of engagement, whether engaging or disengaging at work. It is safe to assume that generating new, potentially valuable ideas regarding new products, services, manufacturing, and administrative processes is not straightforward. Unless the approach is to nurture employee ideas *and* be transparent about how organizations can support them, though primarily employees may experience a sense of freedom and autonomy in developing new ideas, later, when it comes to applying their ideas, they may find their ideas unimplemented. Perhaps, this is one of the primary concerns of employees being disengaged at work and harboring dissatisfaction or developing a not-so-positive outlook toward organizational leadership. Perhaps one of the reasons behind employees not getting involved in idea generation and assuming such involvement is a disturbance to their work.

There are both benefits and costs associated with enhancing employee engagement (Shuck & Herd, 2012). Thus, leadership and employee engagement have boundaries that should be explored. As discussed in this chapter, shepherding requires leaders to ensure employees know the rigid boundaries that dictate their movements. These boundaries (restrictions) are not in place to curb their independence or autonomy but due to limitations in organizational scope and to protect employees from external threats and internal disappointment through wise guidelines. Simultaneously, leaders need to lead employees through an engineering lens—developing systems that help employees in their daily tasks and idea development, transparently outlining the organization's capability.

CONCLUSION AND SUGGESTIONS FOR FUTURE RESEARCH

Thomas and Wood (2012) write that the nation of Israel was led as faithfully by David (the Shepherd) as he led his flock; "With upright heart, he shepherded them and guided them with his skillful hand" (Psalm 78:72). David did not wait for his flock to decide where they should go; he led and guided them. Following the example of a good shepherd, he led them with skills, competencies, knowledge, and abilities developed over time (Thomas & Wood, 2012). I find this example to illustrate a sense of servant leadership. However, in the context of this chapter, I suggest that this example indicates that SEL is not about giving autonomy and leaving employees on their own to exercise their thinking and come up with great doable ideas. This is not the sense of freedom that SEL advocates. Instead, SEL is about leaders being action-oriented and paving the way for employees to exercise their thinking, within limits; autonomy, and providing a pathway to work together, hand in hand. While autonomy is achieved by giving a sense of freedom, employees need to work within the capability boundaries of their organization. This must be engineered into the employees' minds. To engineer this, a leader needs to unpack the complex organizational climate of growth and development, helping employees to see the leader's and the organization's limitations. This two-way approach of knowing what employees are capable of and how they can exercise their critical and creative thinking, while showing clearly, side-by-side, what support leaders can provide, would help minimize employee agitation and disappointment. This is where leaders can work in the background allowing their employees to work freely while they work to develop supporting systems to implement employees' ideas. Instead of just focusing on supporting employees to develop new ideas, SEL leaders create systems that help idea development and implementation.

Let's assume the leader (taking a Shepherd's role) cannot access the necessary resources, support, or ingredients to carry out their plan. According to Stowell (1997), from a religious context, in that case, the Shepherd must be so closely connected to God that he is willing to relinquish his plans until God can fulfill them in His time or until God can conceive new plans—His plans—and unfold these in the Shepherd's heart and mind. Since organizations have limited timeframes to execute any action plan, differing significantly from the religious and spiritual contexts discussed by Stowell (1997), a leader, as a shepherd, in an organization must continuously develop systems of employee support to minimize this situation of waiting for the right time to implement new ideas. This 'right time' may never come as it may not ever exist. These support systems are supposed to evolve continuously and grow in response to employees' emerging and growing ideas and creative suggestions. In this situation, leaders keep track of but don't control employees' activities, and they implement effective systems that promote creativity within their organization's rigid boundaries. A leader's ability to shepherd (guide transparently—a two-way approach) and engineer (continuously develop evolving systems and processes) their employees are fundamental contributors to their leadership role. The SEL approach is about leaders being caretakers of their employees. Instead of just leading by example or helping employees lead (empowerment), the SEL approach is about leaders continuously being action-oriented, vigilant, and ready to introduce new and/or refined systems to implement creative ideas that are doable within the scope of their organizational work. SEL inverts the lens from what employees can or cannot do to leaders who develop organizational systems to assist employees with their ideas. SEL leaders are continuously working in the background to (1) actively know their employees' ideas, (2) develop new or refine existing systems for idea implementation, (3) be transparent with employees regarding what can or cannot be achieved and not giving false hope or being dismissive of their ideas, and (4) expanding the boundaries within the scope of their organization's work to protect employees from external threats. From the critical discussion, I propose these four principles to SEL leaders.

Interested researchers can study organizational leadership by interviewing leaders on their approaches to supporting employees, not just by helping employees to self-lead, be independent, or enjoy freedom for development, but also by working to build systems that support employees' creative ideas.

Researchers can look at leaders' actions in the background continuously derived from employees' creative ideas and suggestions for improving work processes. Researchers can look at how leaders make themselves visible to employees through their actions in leading the organization (which has been researched extensively) and, at the same time, remain invisible while working to promote employee growth and ensure employee freedom that positively impacts both the company and their employees.

Shepherding Engineering Leading (SEL) is not just an approach to leadership. SEL is a state of leading people.

REFERENCES

Adler, P. S. (2001). Market hierarchy, and trust: The knowledge economy and the future of capitalism. *Organization Science, 12*(2), 215–234.

Altman, E. J., Nagle, F., & Tushman, M. L. (2022). The translucent hand of managed ecosystems: Engaging communities for value creation and capture. *Academy of Management Annals, 16*(1), 70–101.

Alvesson, M., & Willmott, H. (1992). On the idea of emancipation in management and organization studies. *Academy of Management Review, 17*(3), 432–464.

Amnesty International. (2023, March 16). *Iran.* https://www.amnesty.org/en/location/middle-east-and-north-africa/iran/report-iran/

Anderson, R. (2020). *Security engineering: A guide to building dependable distributed systems.* John Wiley & Sons.

Augier, M. (2004). James March on education, leadership, and Don Quixote: Introduction and interview. *Academy of Management Learning & Education, 3*(2), 169–177.

Barrow, J. C. (1977). The variables of leadership: A review and conceptual framework. *Academy of Management Review, 2*(2), 231–251.

Bass, B. M. (1985). Leadership: Good, better, best. *Organizational Dynamics, 13*(3), 26–40.

Bennis, W. G., & Thomas, R. J. (2020). Crucibles of leadership. *Harvard Business Review, 80.*

Blake, R. R., Mouton, J. S., & Bidwell, A. C. (1962). Managerial grid. *Advanced Management—Office Executive, 1*(9), 12–15.

Breneman, J. E., Sahay, C., & Lewis, E. E. (2022). *Introduction to reliability engineering.* John Wiley & Sons.

Brennecke, J. (2020). Dissonant ties in intraorganizational networks: Why individuals seek problem-solving assistance from difficult colleagues. *Academy of Management Journal, 63*(3), 743–778.

Burns, J. M. (2012). *Leadership.* Open Road Media.

Board, C. E. Q. (1993). *Annual Report* (p. 17). Canadian Council of Professional Engineers.

Burke, R. J., & Ng, E. (2006). The changing nature of work and organizations: Implications for human resource management. *Human Resource Management Review, 16*(2), 86–94.

Chrobot-Mason, D., Hoobler, J. M., & Burno, J. (2019). Lean In versus the literature: An evidence-based examination. *Academy of Management Perspectives, 33*(1), 110–130.

Daft, R. L. (2014). *The leadership experience*. Cengage Learning.
Dowden, M. K., & Dowden, K. (2013). *European paganism*. Routledge.
Downer, J. (2011). "737-cabriolet": The limits of knowledge and the sociology of inevitable failure. *American Journal of Sociology, 117*, 725–762.
Ebeling, C. E. (2019). *An introduction to reliability and maintainability engineering*. Waveland Press.
Ferguson, E. S. (1994). *Engineering and the mind's eye*. MIT Press.
Gardner, J. (1993). *On leadership*. Simon and Schuster.
Goleman, D. (2017). *Leadership that gets results (Harvard business review classics)*. Harvard Business Press.
Graham, J. W. (1991). Servant-leadership in organizations: Inspirational and moral. *The Leadership Quarterly, 2*(2), 105–119.
Greenleaf, R. (1970). *The servant as leader*. Indianapolis, In Robert K. Greenleaf Center.
Greenleaf, R. K. (1998). *The power of servant-leadership*. Berrett-Koehler Publishers
Hershey, P., & Blanchard, K. H. (1977). *Management of organizational behavior* (3rd Ed). Englewood Cliffs.
Hey, S. P. (2016). Heuristics and meta-heuristics in scientific judgement. *The British Journal for the Philosophy of Science, 67*(2), 471–495.
Holy Bible, New International Version, NIV. Biblica, Inc. https://www.biblica.com/online-bible/
Hughes, R. L. (1993). *Leadership: Enhancing the lessons of experience*. Irwin Inc.
International Rescue Committee. (2023, March 16). The top 10 crises the world can't ignore in 2023. https://www.rescue.org/article/top-10-crises-world-cant-ignore-2023
Kahn, W. A. (1990). Psychological conditions of personal engagement and disengagement at work. *Academy of Management Journal, 33*(4), 692–724.
Kelley, R. E. (1988). In praise of followers. *Harvard Business Review Case Services, 66*, 142–148.
Kelley, R. (1998). Followership in a leadership world. In L. Spears (Ed.), *Insights on leadership: Service, stewardship, spirit and servant leadership*. John Wiley and Sons.
Kets de Vries, M. F. (1994). The leadership mystique. *Academy of Management Perspectives, 8*(3), 73–89.
Kirby, R. S., Withington, S., Darling, A. B., & Kilgour, F. G. (1990). *Engineering in history*. Dover Publications, Inc.
Kouzes, J. M., & Posner, B. Z. (2006). *The leadership challenge* (Vol. 3). John Wiley & Sons.
Latour, B. (1987). *Science in action: How to follow scientists and engineers through society*. Harvard University Press.
Liker, J. K., & Morgan, J. M. (2006). The Toyota way in services: The case of lean product development. *Academy of Management Perspectives, 20*(2), 5–20.
Markos, S., & Sridevi, M. S. (2010). Employee engagement: The key to improving performance. *International Journal of Business and Management, 5*(12), 89–96.
Marsh, P. (2019). *Governance Handbook 2019–20, Institution of Civil Engineers*. https://policycommons.net/artifacts/1771590/governance-handbook-2019-20/2503236/
Mitcham, C. (2022). *Thinking through technology: The path between engineering and philosophy*. University of Chicago Press.

Moberly, R. W. L. (2009). *The theology of the book of Genesis*. Cambridge University Press.
Moore, C., Detert, J. R., Klebe Treviño, L., Baker, V. L., & Mayer, D. M. (2012). Why employees do bad things: Moral disengagement and unethical organizational behavior. *Personnel Psychology*, 65(1), 1–48.
Moore, S. D. (2004). *Shepherding movement* (Vol. 27). A&C Black.
National Geographic. (2023, March 16). https://education.nationalgeographic.org/resource/herding/
National Research Council. (2009). *Engineering in K-12 education: Understanding the status and improving the prospects*. National Academies Press.
Northouse, P. G. (2021). *Leadership: Theory and practice*. Sage Publications.
Pfeffer, J. (1977). The ambiguity of leadership. *Academy of Management Review*, 2(1), 104–112.
Pfeffer, J., & Sutton, R. I. (2006). Profiting from evidence-based management. *Strategy and Leadership*, 34(2), 35–42.
Podsakoff, P. M., & Podsakoff, N. P. (2019). Experimental designs in management and leadership research: Strengths, limitations, and recommendations for improving publishability. *The Leadership Quarterly*, 30(1), 11–33.
Poppo, L., & Zhou, K. Z. (2014). Managing contracts for fairness in buyer-supplier exchanges. *Strategic Management Journal*, 35(10), 1508–1527.
Price, D. K. (1965). *The scientific estate* (Vol. 253). Harvard University Press.
Raelin, J. A. (1987). The 60s' kids in the corporation: More than just "Daydream Believers." *Academy of Management Perspectives*, 1(1), 21–30.
Raelin, J. A. (1989). An anatomy of autonomy: Managing professionals. *Academy of Management Perspectives*, 3(3), 216–228.
Rich, B. L., Lepine, J. A., & Crawford, E. R. (2010). Job engagement: Antecedents and effects on job performance. *Academy of Management Journal*, 53(3), 617–635.
Rost, J. C. (1991). *Leadership for the twenty-first century*. Greenwood Publishing Group.
Sarton, G. (1937). *The history of science and the new humanism*. Harvard University Press.
Selznick, P. (2011). *Leadership in administration: A sociological interpretation*. Quid Pro Books.
Sheppard, S., Colby, A., Macatangay, K., & Sullivan, W. (2007). What is engineering practice? *International Journal of Engineering Education*, 22(3), 429–438.
Shuck, B., & Herd, A. M. (2012). Employee engagement and leadership: Exploring the convergence of two frameworks and implications for leadership development in HRD. *Human Resource Development Review*, 11(2), 156–181.
Slusher, A., Van Dyke, J., & Rose, G. (1972). Technical competence of group leaders, managerial role, and productivity in engineering design groups. *Academy of Management Journal*, 15(2), 197–204.
Stogdill, R. M. (1974). *Handbook of leadership: A survey of theory and research*. Free Press.
Stogdill, R. M., & Coons, A. E. (Eds.). (1957). *Leader behavior: Its description and measurement* (p. 88). Ohio State University.
Stowell, J. M. (1997). *Shepherding the church: Effective spiritual leadership in a changing culture*. Moody Publishers.
The United Nations Refugee Agency. (2023, March 16). Ukraine emergency. https://www.unhcr.org/en-au/ukraine-emergency.html

Thomas, S., & Wood, T. (2012). *Gospel coach: Shepherding leaders to glorify God*. Zondervan.

Vincenti, W. G. (1990). *What engineers know and how they know it: Analytical studies from aeronautical history*. John Hopkins University Press.

Vroom, V. H., & Jago, A. G. (2007). The role of the situation in leadership. *American Psychologist*, 62(1), 17.

PART II

Wellness

CHAPTER 9

From Organizational Oneness to Organizational Wellness: The Role of Individuals, Teams, and Organizations from a Whole Systems Framework

Duysal Askun

Oneness as a concept is not new. However, it's been overlooked as a subject of scientific and practical exploration therefore expression and action for millennia. The world today is not suffering from the climate change, political unrest, famine, draught, wars, or viruses. It is suffering from the lack of understanding therefore acting on Oneness.

As a term, Oneness has been defined as healthy, whole, or holy (Merriam-Webster's Collegiate Dictionary, 2005). As a hypothesis, it reflects our interrelationships with all others around us. This not only includes human beings, but all living and non-living beings, including all types of creatures, and so forth (Ivanhoe, 2017). This sense of being interrelated connotes 'belongingness' in terms of multi-levels of existence where each level of existence connects to a larger whole (Baumeister & Leary, 1995). In essence, there are two main attributes that identify oneness: *being related and being whole*.

Organizations from a Lens of Oneness

Today, with a few exceptions, organizations still operate on the principle of give and take where the social exchange mechanisms bring financial returns. As a means to survive and thrive, organizations recruit, train, lead, and direct their employees for meeting their end goals which usually center around

D. Askun (✉)
Jones School of Business, Rice University, Houston, TX, USA
e-mail: da47@rice.edu

© The Author(s), under exclusive license to Springer Nature Switzerland AG 2023
J. Marques (ed.), *The Palgrave Handbook of Fulfillment, Wellness, and Personal Growth at Work*,
https://doi.org/10.1007/978-3-031-35494-6_9

profit-making and market share expansion overall. Although in 2019, nearly 200 companies have declared that shareholder value will no longer be their main focus (https://www.cnbc.com/2019/08/19/the-ceos-of-nearly-two-hundred-companies-say-shareholder-value-is-no-longer-their-main-objective.html), employee engagement therefore commitment still poses a significant portion of their problems. The most recent Gallup statistics revealed that globally, employee engagement is at 21% (State of the Global Workplace 2022 report). When we think of the reasons for this considerably low number, we surely could identify multi-factors, starting with the individual level (employees), later on team and departmental levels, and finally the ones at the organizational level. Why is employee engagement so important? Well, employee engagement is argued to be one of the strongest predictors of work performance (Anitha, 2014; Markos & Sridevi, 2010; Motyka, 2018). When we look at the determinants of employee engagement, they also entail a multi-factorial essence. There is individual as well as a social context-related determinants of employee engagement which is a widely explored area in the Organizational Behavior field (Gautam & Kothari, 2021; Mokaya & Kipyegon, 2014; Meswantri & Awaludin, 2018; Sharma Baldev & Anupama, 2010). For the purposes of this chapter and the book, we will focus mostly on the determinants that relate to the oneness principle. The categorization will be the same: Individual, Team/Work unit/Departmental, and Organizational.

Organizational Wellness as an Alternate Outcome

As the world economy has made a shift from being industrial to the digital, there is less of a physical threat in terms of health and safety, but chronic stress is here to stay (Lieberman, 2019). As Lieberman (2019) argues, today, more employers are stressing the importance of mental health which are also reported to be the leading cause of illness and disability. Since the 2019 declaration related to change of focus and shift from shareholders to all stakeholders, we see more companies getting involved in wellness-related programs that target employees' physical and mental health altogether. Sometimes even defined as 'zeitgeist of our age', wellness has gained high popularity among businesses (Jack & Brewis, 2005) working either at the BtoB/BtoC, or CtoC capacities, or all.

Wellness as a term has been equated mostly with 'being healthy'. Therefore, organizational wellness was translated into 'healthy organizations' (Young & Lambie, 2007). Healthy organizations should be made up of healthy individuals and related systems. By definition, healthy individuals should remind us of both physical and emotional health while healthy organizations could be made up of healthy beings and their interrelationships with one another (Maslach, 2001; as cited in Young & Lambie, 2007). Similar to the concept of oneness we have described above, overall organizational health and wellness require healthy players and systems.

Individual Oneness and Wellness Relationship

As any entity, being large or small, individuals are also made up of certain parts. The most visible part is the body, and the less so would be the mind and the soul. Starting with the most visible part, body is an entity also made up of parts. As long as those parts work in harmony, we do not get sick. However, any type of separation or disharmonious operation in and through the body might most likely bring problems, acute or chronic in nature. As an example, if there is an insulin-based imbalance, you most likely become vulnerable to diabetes. Alternatively, if you have a problematic detoxification system concerning your liver, you can start to develop long-term illnesses such as organ failures, immunity problems, or metabolism issues. In either case, separation, and therefore dissonant nature of those relationships between either part of the body, results in illness with changing intensity and duration.

As less visible parts, mind and soul operate similarly but in a less obvious way. As we are still illiterate in terms of the mind and soul's operating mechanisms, here we will rely mostly on analogies for the sake of simplicity and practicality. According to Freud, human mind is made up of the conscious and the unconscious. According to trait theories, personality is made up of several traits. The most recent trait theory is the Big Five which purports that our personalities are made up of 5 distinct traits, starting with Extraversion-Introversion, Conscientiousness, Openness to Experience, Agreeableness, and Neuroticism (McCrae & Costa, 1985). According to cognitive approaches, our mind is composed of several cognitive systems, such as memory, perception, thinking, and intelligence, etc. Whatever our approach to human psyche might be, and however they are being defined, each theory or approach talks about a system of things made up of distinct but related parts. We already know that unconscious and conscious are always related, we know that personality traits co-exist with varying degrees, and we also know that our cognitive systems always relate and benefit from each other such as our perceptions help our memory systems through sensory memory storage, and so on. This all means that whatever the nature of our individual existence, there are distinct parts, and those parts have relationships with one another.

What defines illness/sickness and imbalance is the break of those relationships somehow for some reason. The disconnection therefore separation of any part within the human system results in different types of issues, physical, emotional, or cognitive in nature. When something goes wrong especially in terms of our physical existence, it is more straightforward solution to do something about it. At least we might go and ask a doctor. However, when something goes wrong in our cognitive/emotional or spiritual existence, the solutions somehow lose their visibility therefore accessibility so there is less and less likelihood that we might go and seek help. In any case, imbalance being invisible vs. being visible still brings a lot of discomfort and varying degrees of unrest. This way it might be useful to highlight the importance of our individual selves (physical and non-physical) whatever part they might be composed of, to stay and act in harmony. This state and therefore existence could also be termed as 'individual wellness'.

Given the factors that might relate to individual wellness from oneness perspective, one might naturally ask if it is truly possible to stay in wellness state no matter what. Given life's intricacies, and the fact that the world we live in today is full of turmoil and chaos, it might be bit of a rosy view to expect things to stay healthy as long as they remain in harmony. However, without a critical ingredient of our existence, we are not able to maintain let alone sustain our individual health, therefore wellness. First of all, how do we know everything is working well? How do we also detect if there is a problem? On top of all that, where can we find a way out?

The Role of Individual Consciousness for Health and Well-Being

Consciousness is defined as the quality or state of being aware especially of something within oneself. It is also defined as the totality of conscious states of an individual (Merriam-Webster online dictionary). This way, consciousness seems to have the following functions for human beings to operate in oneness therefore wellness:

- *Observing function* (conscious person is able to look at, see, and make observations on his or her mind, conscious and unconscious processes, thoughts, emotions, and actions)
- *Perceiving function* (conscious person is able to use his/her five and additional senses to perceive what is taking place inside and outside of one's physical self-boundaries)
- *Reflecting function* (conscious person is able to reflect upon his/her perceptions, external and internal experiences)
- *Understanding function* (conscious person is able to make sense of therefore make connections and relationships around whatever he or she observes, perceives, and reflects upon)
- *Analyzing function* (conscious person is able to further analyze what has been taking place in and out of his/her physical self-boundaries therefore is able to create new meanings therefore solutions out of what is being observed and made sense of)

For an individual to be able to operate on his or her consciousness therefore to attain health and well-being in a sustainable way, certain tools are being offered. One of those tools is widely researched in the literature of both psychology and organizational behavior. It is called mindfulness practice. According to Brown et al. (2007), it is being attentive to what is going on inside and outside, with a more mindful manner that involves an active, rather than a passive state (Askun, 2019).

Another way in which one might become more conscious is through an ongoing pursuit of self-knowledge (Ghorbani et al., 2008) which entails: (1) An ongoing sense of self-awareness and (2) Stable mental representations. The definition of self-knowledge is made through one's reflective action concerning both past and present experiences. Ghorbani et al. (2008) therefore coined two terms having different time perspectives: Experiential self-knowledge which represented being aware of what is taking place in the present moment vs. Reflective self-knowledge that encompassed a more stable self-representations (our awareness of what took place before now).

Whatever our tools for becoming more self-conscious might be, it is more important to discuss the relationship of consciousness with healthy and whole selves. If the first step is always to be aware (Wholey, 2017) of what is taking place in both the present and the previous moments, the second step would be to reflect therefore make sense of what is taking place. While the third step would be having an actionable nature that directs toward change if necessary for the maintenance and/or sustainability of one's whole and healthy self. According to Wholey (2017), awareness is always the first step toward living a life in oneness. She contends that acceptance of what is, is a necessary precursor to the action step. The whole catalyst for transformation should happen between those three steps if we are aiming a life of oneness.

As humans are physical, emotional, and cognitive systems, being aware therefore self-conscious at the following levels are deemed most crucial:

- Physical self-awareness (what is going on in our bodies: being hungry vs being full, feeling tired vs energetic, feeling sick vs feeling healthy, etc.)
- Emotional self-awareness (what is going on in terms of our feelings: feeling sad or happy, feeling depressed or the opposite, feeling guilty vs pain-free, etc.)
- Cognitive self-awareness (what is going on in our mind processes: negative vs. positive thought patterns, self-blame vs. the opposite, remembering events and connections to one's conscious being, being aware of our own conscious state (fully conscious, semi-conscious, unconscious, etc.)
- Spiritual self-awareness (what is going on spiritually, feeling a physical vs. non-physical state, feeling one's energy zone vs feeling lack of it, feeling detached from one's spiritual essence vs. feeling connected, etc.).

This way, it can be said that the role of individual consciousness in health and well-being requires a complex but interrelated consciousness processes determined by one's self with varying degrees of intensity and effectiveness. As nobody's consciousness is the same or works the same, the functionality and the degrees differ with so many consequences related to physical, emotional, and cognitive health.

In terms of organizational health and wellness, what this means is that it is the responsibility of each employee/individual partaking in any organization to fulfill the necessary (but may not be sufficient) consciousness-related actions (observing, perceiving, reflecting, understanding, and analyzing) so as to take the first step toward wellness at the individual and organizational level altogether.

The Role of Team Consciousness and the Idea of Consciousness Gap

Team consciousness as a term should not be too different from how we define individual consciousness. Similarly, we are expecting team members to do their necessary consciousness work (observing, perceiving, reflecting, etc.) as part of their self-consciousness practice. However, we also require them to be attentive to something else which might not be always within their personal self-boundaries but between each other. In other words, we are talking about consciousness and awareness of what is taking place in between one another. And to our disappointment, it may not be always as straightforward and visible and even obvious as our work within. Otherwise, there would be no divorces, breakups, or wars, correct? Here, if we dig deep, we find one important competency or skill, however you might name it. It is called Relational Consciousness and it is coined by Hay and Nye (1998). It is the ability to perceive the environment in relational terms. The consciousness here is relational, which exists at both intra- and interpersonal domains (Askun, 2019).

Whoever wrote about team consciousness earlier did so by referring to its practical aspects. As an example, Bennett (2018) talks about an 8-hr training program where employees and managers separately study modules related to policy awareness, stress management, communication, dealing with difficult employees and when to refer a peer to the Employee Assistance Program (EAP). Rather than the content, the process of this training seems to be interactional in scope with many interactive scenarios, games, and role plays being incorporated into the program.

Here, we are mostly referring to the ways in which we can attain more consciousness at the team level. This may mean and require that team members become self-conscious both individually and interpersonally. We have already described and gave some examples of individual consciousness and how it is carried out. In terms of interpersonal consciousness, we do the following in the interpersonal context or arena in which actual relationships take place:

- *Observing function* (both parties are willing and able to observe what is taking place in between one another in terms of action, communication, conflict, feelings, etc.)

- *Perceiving function* (both parties are willing and able to perceive what is taking place in between one another in terms of action, etc. but also are willing to accept the fact that their individual perceptions are only one side of the story or the truth)
- *Reflecting function* (both parties are willing and able to reflect upon what is taking place in addition to being willing and able to listen to the others' reflections which they may or may not agree with)
- *Understanding function* (both parties are willing to understand what is taking place even though they may not be able to understand what is happening. As an example, willing to understand why a conflict might be occurring, what the other feels, etc.)
- *Analyzing function* (Both parties are willing to analyze what is taking place in both the present and the past. They mutually agree on working together on this while willing to join forces and capabilities/competencies in a complementary way to make sense of their relationship and to make it work in a healthy way).

Very similar to individual consciousness, team consciousness operates with the same principles and steps. However, our world is far away from acts that reflect team consciousness. Most of the time, we only widen our gaps in consciousness (Askun, 2020).

As a term, *consciousness gap* forms when we as individuals do not take responsibility for what is taking place in between each other. This is when we are working or living in groups, teams, and communities. According to Askun (2020), consciousness gap widens when our individual consciousness does not expand toward a more interpersonal consciousness; or sometimes a personal need/interest/problem gets in the way of interpersonal consciousness; or a selfish orientation that stems from fear, anxiety or a desire for getting more from the other might lead the individual to contract or become self-protective, reserved, silent, aggressive, or uncooperative. Let alone impaired teamwork and cooperation, many negative consequences might follow because of this. Askun (2020) exemplifies those as follows: reported feelings of being hurt, being misunderstood, and feeling resentful, demotivation, disengagement, mobbing, turnover intention and actual turnover, workplace rumors, project failures, escalating dysfunctional conflict that adds to the negative downward spiral. Depicted as a figure, the consciousness gap in an interpersonal arena looks like this (Fig. 9.1).

Tools for Team Consciousness

Given the importance of team consciousness for both short- and long-term goals and outcomes, it might be useful to talk about some already available tools to enhance consciousness at the team level. Because it requires consciousness at both individual and interpersonal areas, tools that help with team

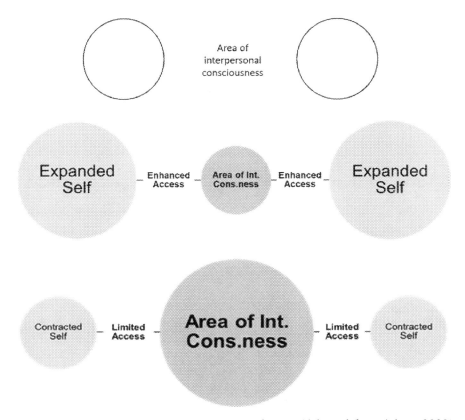

Fig. 9.1 Consciousness gap in an interpersonal arena (Adopted from Askun, 2020)

consciousness could target both levels, although more stress could be given to the interpersonal processes that take place.

a. *Appreciative Inquiry*: Coined by Krahnke & Cooperrider in 2008, appreciative inquiry is a technique that builds on the idea that the reality is being re-created all the time. The space that we share through our relationships are co-created therefore there is no linear approach to whatever is taking place in a relationship. It is unique to the space being formed and to those who create it together. In terms of conversations, discussion and debate are terms to be replaced by dialogue through which there is no competitive nature of relationships but rather, a cooperative one where a new reality is being formed, there is no winner or a loser, and there is a third alternative being explored as part of this mutual exploration.

b. *Awareness of Conversational Styles:* In her analysis of conversational styles which are called overlapping vs. turn-taking, Rehling (2004) suggests that both self and other-awareness practices would help individuals to analyze what is taking place in the interpersonal arena. As an example, as part of self-awareness practice, she recommends that the individual could be invited to recognize the sources of their own conversational style habits, monitor themselves to avoid the downsides of the conversational style that they habitually use with their project teams, apply everyday ethics to their conversational behaviors, and flex their own style to adopt more to others. As part of other-awareness, Rehling (2004) suggests that one should recognize how others, too, express their backgrounds through their conversational styles, recognize others' preferred conversational styles without judging, identify how others define the group or occasion to choose between conversational styles and practice actively listening to others.

c. *We-Awareness based on Shared Intentionality*. According to Tennenberg, Roth, and Socha (2016), communication, as well as its design and interpretation related to the objects and events in the environment, depend on the presumptions that individuals have their own intentions as well as of others, plus, *we-intentions* that they share in that space. Through a computer-supported cooperative work (CSCW), Tennenberg et al. (2016) create case study scenarios to help turn I-Awareness to We-Awareness. In their study, they used a pair programming methodology which is common to software developers. In this methodology, two software developers sit side-by-side to work together to program the same computer, sharing the same input and output streams. Through this practice, they were able to observe the structure of the communicative work that participants carried out. As a result, they concluded that We-Awareness goes beyond an aggregated version of I-Awareness and that there are tools that could be provided through the CSCW methodology to help participants engage more in We-Awareness.

Teams could start with as few as 2 individuals. Understanding the importance of consciousness at the team level could also imply acceptance of the following as inherent nature of teams:

- Formed by interdependent parties
- Share a common/overarching goal
- Perform tasks to reach a goal
- Have a mission/higher objective that they work toward altogether.

As organizations are made up of teams and work units/departments, their consciousness type and levels are imperative for working toward any organizational goal including organizational wellness.

While many organizations try to adopt wellness programs to their day-to-day practices, many of those programs were also reported to fail or at least do not help the organizations reach their end goals. Before we go deep into the realm of organizational wellness, it might be best to first look at some studies that put organizational wellness practices into their focus.

Organizational Wellness Programs Research and Findings

Before outlining the organizational wellness from a consciousness and oneness paradigms, it might be useful to talk about some examples of jobs and workplace that apply wellness principles to their day-to-day practices including wellness programs, wellness-oriented work designs, and outcomes of organizational wellness programs.

Physical Environment of the World of Work

Anthony C. Klotz (2020), in his article on creating jobs and workspaces that energize people, talks about the tremendous importance of work designs which are said to be 'biophilic'. Those types of workplace designs might involve what is called a 'direct immersion in natural elements' such as providing employees an outdoor space to take care of their work-related activities including meetings, phone calls, work-related scheduled activities, etc. On the other hand, there might be designs which could include an indirect exposure to nature though large windows, large TV screens with incredible views of nature, etc. In addition, green rooftop terraces for outdoor breaks were also listed. Some of the companies which applied these types of biophilic designs were many multinationals including but not limited to Samsung, Etsy, Salesforce.com, Amazon, and many others. These types of designs are said to promise many benefits while tapping into all domains for human functioning, as emotional, physical, cognitive, social, including prosocial. This might mean that the more people feel connected to whatever surrounds them, the more they feel energized to help others. In other words, these types of biophilic work environments could lead employees to feel more interconnected with all beings around them.

The Range and Scope of Organizational Wellness Programs

In their meta-analysis study where they explored the impacts of organizational wellness programs, Parks and Steelman (2008) classified those programs into two: fitness-oriented vs. being comprehensive. Fitness-oriented programs are said to provide membership to health clubs. Comprehensive programs include both fitness and educational modalities. Examples could be listed as stress management and nutrition courses.

Parks and Steelman (2008), in their analysis, talk about the reasons underlying the wellness program offerings by the employers. One of the first reasons has been listed as improving employee health therefore decreasing absenteeism due to illnesses. However, they concluded that the research has mixed findings in terms of the relationship between the wellness programs and absenteeism rates.

Another reason was listed as job satisfaction which seems to increase after certain wellness programs are put into place. The main reason underlying this link was that the wellness program could instill a positive attitude which might lead employees to be happier with the organization and therefore to feel more satisfied with their jobs (Gronningsaeter et al., 1992, cited in Parks & Steelman, 2008).

As a result of their meta-analysis of related studies that explored the link between wellness programs and job satisfaction and absenteeism, Parks and Steelman (2008) have found positive links. As a result of their takeaway from the meta-analysis, they also concluded that both individual and organizational factors are at play when we talk about the participation as well as the positive outcomes of the organizational wellness programs. As part of the individual factors they list motivation to exercise, past experience with similar wellness programs, dispositional characteristics. And for the organizational factors, supervisor support, coworker perceptions, and organizational climate are said to play important roles.

Similar to what Parks and Steelman (2008) have found in their meta-analysis study, Berry et al. (2011) contended that fewer absences, improved productivity, worker satisfaction and retention could be promising goals of the organizational wellness programs. She added by stressing the importance of workplace culture as a healthy starting point for all those programs. As an example, she talked about a workplace culture in which high competitiveness is fiercely practiced where no one is literally taking any breaks or hides his or her sickness from others, the first step should be to change that culture.

In their analysis of employee wellness programs, from a return on investment framework, Berry, Mirabito, and Baun (2011) outlined the following pillars of an effective workplace wellness program:

- Multi-level leadership
- Alignment: the program as a natural extension of a firm's identity and goals.
- Scope, Relevance, a-nd Quality
- Accessibility: low or no-cost services to be a priority.
- Partnerships: with internal and external stakeholders.
- Communications: wellness also as a message to be delivered with sensitivity, creativity, etc.

After an extensive research on workplace wellness, Berry et al. (2011) has defined the workplace wellness as 'an organized, employer-sponsored program that is designed to support employees (and sometimes their families) as they adopt and sustain behaviors that reduce health risks, improve quality of life, enhance personal effectiveness, and benefit the organization's bottom line' (p. 4).

Organizational Consciousness Toward Organizational Wellness

When we talk about organizations, we usually understand the following systems:

- Organizational Structures
- Organizational Processes
- Organizational Culture

To be able to enable organizational wellness, all of the above systems need to be supportive. First, let us define what each means from a wellness perspective and then maybe we can offer some alternative methods, approaches for organizational wellness to become a reality.

Organizational Structures Which Support Organizational Wellness

In today's world of work, more and more organizations are organized around non-traditional structures. With the increased importance of Digital Economy and the KPIs (Key Performance Indicators) that come with it, we see more of network, flat, matrix, virtual and related organizational structure types rather than the traditional hierarchical ones where there is one top management made up of a C-suite, functional departments that usually work as silos, and managers leading a group of employees.

As the nature of work becomes more digital and cloud-based, we see fewer rigid structures but mostly structures shaped around projects rather than strict roles or role formations. This does not mean we do not have specialization or function; it mostly means working across specializations and functions (cross-functional work structures). This also means that some teams could be working more autonomously rather than being depending on a manager/leader. This type of organizing around tasks mostly emerged out of necessity rather than a change in consciousness all of a sudden since employees are still seeking a role model, somebody to look up to and to learn from and somebody to teach them the ropes.

As the world of work became flatter and more virtual, the older types of human resources practices such as hiring, training, promoting, evaluating performance, etc. also needed to change. It is this period of change we might be going through at this moment in time. And this is where wellness and related discussion could find a way to express itself.

Since the workplace became more independent, more autonomous, more self-directed, and even more self-paced, the mentality is also shifting toward the types of practices that could support this change in nature. The independence not only came through the use of more technology, but also came as a result of the remote work becoming more common and widespread. This led to changes in how employees spent the whole day, how they carried out their tasks, how they reported information, and how they interacted with one another. Even companies who went back to being fully in-person, still hold many hybrid work formats. Therefore, it is needless to say that remote work is here to stay, it has become our new reality.

Given this new reality, what types of organizational structures or related factors could be helping us to create more wellness at the workplace? We already listed the types of new work structures with an increasing number cutting across many industries and geographic horizons. And it is no coincidence that the new generation fully equipped with technology orientation (if not savviness) are seeking more of those structures which have few or 0 hierarchies, which enable flexible work modalities (remote, in-person, or hybrid could change depending on the nature of the task or the project at the time being), and which do not necessarily require a managerial supervision but rather, leadership that could prove facilitation and guidance from time to time. In addition, the nature of the task is changing. We see more people taking several part-time jobs in the virtual world as compared to those who are seeking permanent roles in some established institution. This new type of work preferences is also called the 'gig economy' where the players and the game change constantly. As the majority of the workforce is shifting in terms of needs and goals, it is time for larger organizations to reconsider their organizing structures, their task/work designs, their physical space, and their performance and reward systems. With the changing trends, no matter what type of work the organization carries out, organizing in more flat structures, with less hierarchy, with less supervision but with more self-directed pace, with more cross-functional project scopes, and with more adaptable rewarding and performance mechanisms seems to be the new requirement when we include wellness into the picture.

Organizational Processes that Support Organizational Wellness

Next to structures, organizational processes also need to be reconsidered with the enormous shift that is taking place in the world of work. The organizational processes need to change with regard to hiring practices, performance appraisals, promotion criteria, managerial inputs and exchanges, meeting times and modalities, KPIs, and departmental or work unit-based evaluations and communication.

Starting with hiring, the new world of work seeks talent everywhere. You can be a candidate for any organization as long as you are able to work with the help of technology. This increased flexibility therefore access to talent also brings with it challenges in terms of deciding whom to hire for best results. Right now, it is not only more important to make the best choice, but also important to create and execute a hiring practice which is fair, free from bias, and carried out with as much objectivity as possible. With the ample opportunities that come with technological solutions provided for the Human Resources, there comes a greater responsibility to act and to select applicants with the best process fairness (Brockner, 2006) that reflects an attitude free from bias, discrimination or all sorts of subjective factors which would blur the hiring process.

Similarly, concerning performance appraisals, responsible authorities need to use the help of technology to collect more data about employee behavior and performance outcomes as well as refrain from explicit or implicit biases when making an evaluation decision. As a manager or a leader doing the evaluation, one has to be aware of his/her stereotypes, subtle biases, and psychological tendencies so as to eliminate any type of subject PA process. As an example, because managers/leaders often overlook the importance of collecting behavioral data, they end up relying on their first impressions or use very recent events (recency effect) to make the performance evaluation of the employee. However, this ends up being faulty and leads to many defensive attitudes by the employee as well as might lead to unfair outcomes leading to turnover and many layoffs.

Again, with the help of today's technology, managers could be spending more quality time with their employees to empower them in their roles. Managers could be doing less, delegating more and training more. In addition to training, managers in their roles could dedicate some time for coaching others. Since the new world of work organizes around more flexible work structures and modalities, managers could find opportunities to carve out more time to spend with their employees, instead of doing more work. The quality of the relationships has a chance to increase such as when a lunch time could be dedicated to human-to-human conversations between two parties rather than being organized around tasks to be done in between. If the majority of work is carried out online for example, more meaningful therefore more valuable activities could be created when the parties come physically together.

Usage of online communication tools such as Zoom, or Microsoft Teams are also part of organizational processes. These tools are sometimes being criticized as leading to more structure, result in less human connection therefore less synergy created. However, some also argues that these tools led to meetings to be held more efficiently and in a more organized fashion. Since the online communication tools do not very much allow for side conversations or it is not as easy to go off the topic, they could be creating a high potential for making the time especially for social purposes. The employees also come to work for social support. Young and Lambie (2007) argued that social support was found to be related to wellness behaviors (Granello, 2001). And they could be strongly yearning for that type of support while working remotely. It might be a helpful organizational process to use the additional time being saved for social connections to go deeper by making them even more enjoyable and even exciting. This practice not only would help toward individual wellness but wellness at the collective level as well.

As for the KPIs, the process fairness should be the ruling factor. When the organizations and departmental units create certain performance indicators for success, they need to make sure it reflects diverse capabilities, cultures, and competencies as much as possible. When an organization decides on a KPI, it has to rely on objective standards and outcomes such as revenue, profits, customer satisfaction rates, employee satisfaction rates, customer engagement measures (now more measurable than ever with the use of enhanced data management tools), peer-to-peer support, and organizational growth metrics, etc. Here the use of traditional tools could still be of value, such as making Balanced Score Sheet as one tool to create KPIs and their timeline with regard to certain long- or short-term goals.

In any case, it is not possible to talk about processes without how the employees see them. The importance of employee perceptions of processes needs to be stressed. This means that consistent and regular assessment of how the employee perceives a current organizational practice is beyond necessity.

This all might mean that the new organizational processes that aim to reflect wellness need to be reconsidered, revisited, or revised to reflect more process fairness, more social interaction, more quality communication, more objective evaluation, and more inclusion of diverse individuals, their viewpoints, personalities, cultures, and capabilities.

Organizational Culture that Supports Organizational Wellness

Organizations start with some beliefs, assumptions, and most importantly, value systems. An organization that does not include idea of 'Wellness' into its core culture principles may not ever realize its wellness-related goals. There are many organizations today which apply various wellness programs, and which try to help employee turnover and absenteeism by providing more programs that reflect wellness. But many also fail the evidence shows. The reason they might fail is not because the programs are useless or do not help employees, in fact they are useful, and they are helpful. However, unless wellness becomes a natural part of an organization, more and more money and effort will be spent on wellness, but less and less long-term outcomes will be achieved. In other words, the organizations need to walk the walk, talk the talk, and walk the talk (Frei & Moriss, 2012). They should not be vacuous (O'Reilly & Pfeffer, 2000) or inconsistent in terms of their wellness-related practices and values. While clarity, consistency, and comprehensiveness are being listed as very important pillars for strong cultures, on a more practical level, how would an organizational culture aimed at wellness look like? What would be some assumptions, values, and practices that could enable and later sustain wellness at the organizational level?

According to Lieberman (2019), organizational culture is the biggest roadblock for employees to feel healthier and happier in their workplace. Edgar Schein (1986) defined culture which is formed as a result of problem-solving approach adopted by a group when it tried to externally adapt while remaining internally integrated. This answers so many questions when we think of wellness also from a oneness perspective. Being one requires interconnectedness with all around us and inside us. While trying to connect, every organism goes through a relational process which might be very transformative. As interconnection requires exchanges and communication between parties, each party will feel the challenge of adaptation while trying to remain integrated or whole, in other words. It is like an individual trying to stay healthy and whole in the face of life's challenges ranging from personal to career or health-related, etc. Similarly, in their journey of existence, organizations also face the task of adaptation and integration. That's why some of them end up failing even in the very beginning. They cannot adapt and/or remain integrated in the face of industrial forces so they die or go out of business too early. On the other hand, some of them continue growing and integrating with some healthy adaptation, but rather stay behind in their mature years. This is also mostly due to their ways of solving problems rather than the adversities surround them. Otherwise, all organizations would come to an end in the face of similar challenges happening at the same time. Thinking of COVID-19 outbreak, and the period would give us an idea. The culture therefore is deemed crucial. It is like the air we breathe, the ocean/sea we swim in, the inside and the outside, the alpha, and the beta… It is all that there is surrounding and filling in the organization. It is beyond structures and processes; it is what creates all of them.

What are some of the characteristics that we could use to define a wellness-oriented culture? With the help of Schein (1986)'s culture triangle, we can use the practices, values, and assumptions framework to categorize some factors. Starting with the assumptions, since they are mostly unconscious and implied, rather than being expressed or being explicit, for a wellness-oriented culture, it might be helpful to bring awareness into the picture. Since they are mostly unrecognized, hard to change, and even understand, some awareness work especially with the most tenured employees would be critical. Without an understanding therefore realization of what types of assumptions are helping the organization remain healthy and balanced vs. which ones hinder its capabilities, it might be impossible to unveil the hidden road to integration, wholeness therefore wellness.

For the values that should reflect wellness, organizations first need to stay away from 'profit first shareholder first' mentality. Whatever they produce and whomever they serve, they need to incorporate wellness into it. When listing their values in their websites, brochures, or whatever platform they use to define themselves, they need to insert keywords associated with wellness such as:

- Physical and Mental Health
- Well-being
- Happiness
- Collaboration
- Positive communication
- Violence-free workplace
- Wholeness

- Productivity
- Satisfaction
- Fulfillment
- Engagement
- Consciousness
- Joy
- Healthy functioning
- Integrated

These keywords could be inside their value framework or also represented in their organizational mottos.

In terms of practices, there are zillion ways in which organizations could incorporate wellness into their practices. But research shows some practices could even be more urgent than others to make the place a wellness-oriented one. We will try to list some of them below.

- *How the employees are being treated.* The treatment of employees is crucial starting with the hiring practices. Fair, objective, inclusive hiring practices help employees adjust easily and stay with their organization longer while showing high performance. In addition to hiring, when the organization spends money, time, and effort on their employees in terms of their self and career development always pays off with less and less absenteeism and turnover and with high performance potential. Including the organization, the managerial style when dealing with employees is invaluable. As an example, if the manager is considerate, respectful, supportive, and empathetic, the employees feel much better with their jobs, and they also yield positive outcomes as listed above. Treating employees with process fairness (see Brockner, 2006) is also an important part of creating wellness as it leads to less burnout, less stress, and more engagement (see also Young & Lambie, 2007).
- *How the decisions are being made.* Decisions as simple as where to conduct the meeting vs what kinds of resources should be spent for the work unit, need to be taken with the inclusion of the employees as much as possible. When employees feel they are being included in the decision-making, minor or major, they become less stressed, more engaged, and more motivated (see also Young & Lambie, 2007).
- *Approaching the task.* When there is enough time to spend on to discuss how the tasks should be approached, with what kinds of resources and budget, with what kinds of information flow and process, there would be less workload imbalance or social loafing, less turnover intentions, less burnout, and more engagement and performance. The way the task is being approached is not only imperative from a performance standpoint, but also from a wellness perspective. If the employees feel they have full control and understanding of their task from start to finish, they

will feel less burdened and happier. The whole demands-resources model talks about the importance of the balance between job demands and job control (see also Young & Lambie, 2007). Another evidence is through research by Worline and Dutton (2017) in which employee performance and well-being increased in environments where there is flexibility around the place and time of work (Lieberman, 2019).

- *Determining the criteria for success.* There are many ways in which the criteria for success could be determined. The KPIs are there for this purpose. However, usually they are given for any employee joining the organization. Unless the employee understands the mentality and the rationale behind those KPIs, they might feel very much like an outsider when it comes to PA talks. If they feel they are being part of the whole process, and that their views are also taken into consideration, then it is more fulfilling for them to complete and perform on a task. Similarly, Young and Lambie (2007) argued that employees experience role stress when they have conflicting or uncertain job expectations, too many responsibilities, or too many different roles. This might lead us to reconsider those roles and their criteria for success if we'd like to talk about wellness-focused organizational practices.
- *Providing opportunities to excel.* Most employees leave jobs and seek employment elsewhere not just because they get bored with their current jobs but mostly because they do not see alternate opportunities for further growth. If today's organizations solely rely on promotion as a way to motivate their workforce, it remains vulnerable to turnover and loss of investment because of the limited number of promotional opportunities available. However, if the organizations allow room for growth around competencies and projects and not necessarily around roles, then the alternatives would be numerous. As an example, if an employee would like additional training programs on leadership, communication skills, or strategic thinking, it would have an additional motivating power to give the training to them. This way, the organization is not just helping the employee on his or her self-development, but also creating opportunities for more commitment and engagement. In addition, if the employee would have alternate opportunities to take part in separate projects that tap into their needs to belong, to self-actualize and to generate ideas, then this would also be an additional step toward wellness-oriented workplace. Through providing more opportunities for employees to express and improve themselves, organizations also benefit from the enhanced well-being of their employees as a result.
- *Presence of Psychological Safety.* Do the employees feel it is ok to express themselves, their feelings, thoughts, and decisions? Is it safe to be 'me' or is it risky? Would an opinion about an issue be open for discussion? Would it be ok to disagree with a managerial decision? Is it ok to express

how one feels with regard to a social exchange? All of the above questions are important to make sure there is felt psychological safety in an organization that is wellness-oriented.

Overall, with all factors included, many effort could be spent to make the workplace a wellness-oriented one. As Lieberman (2019) concluded, we need workplaces of humanity and compassion in which individuals can be present and contribute with their whole selves, including any challenges at the mental or physical level. Employee relationships should center around trust and this way wellness programs can gain power to transform from being unhealthy toward being an integrated human system.

BEYOND ORGANIZATIONS: SOCIALLY INSPIRED WELL-BEING FROM AN INTEGRAL ORGANIZATIONAL WELLNESS FRAMEWORK

According to Bennett (2018), well-being is influenced by a nest of contexts ranging from being national, developmental, social, environmental, and economic. In this type of framework, one's family, social networks, ethnic culture, religious communities, etc. are also important factors at play. And workplaces also operate as part of larger contexts including industry, size, location, etc. In this complex interlocking structures and processes, both individuals and organizations derive influence from multi-factors, stakeholders and all of the surrounding environment. According to Bennett (2018), people thrive in learning environments which are supportive of their well-being. This way, well-being happens within individuals (intrapersonal), their organization (transpersonal), and through coworker relationships which are positive (interpersonal), trustworthy, and triggering a sense of belongingness. Relying on the integral model of health and well-being, Bennett (2018) stresses that wellness is a multi-dimensional construct with physical, spiritual, intellectual, psychological, social, and emotional dimensions having various levels of influential factors operating on them. This model builds on the term *wholeness* to refer to all constructs that represent an individual's health across multiple dimensions, body, mind, and spirit altogether as a whole. Therefore, basic thriving practices are said to be built on three pillars: individual wellness, organizational development and learning, and behavioral health.

Wellness from a Consciousness Perspective with All Quadrants/All Levels Approach

Borrowing Ken Wilber (2001)'s integral model, Bennett (2018) argued that the way individuals and organizations could be helped would be through mutual supportive relationships between those entities. In terms of the role of human consciousness and its derivatives (societal, civilization-based, and technological), it can be viewed from two perspectives, interior (subjective) vs. exterior (objective), and individual (experiential) vs. social (cultural) to make up the four quadrants in the model. Within each, evolution would occur across six levels:

1. I-Subjective experience-What's in it for me? Approach to a more altruistic approach (Organizational citizenship)
2. It-Objective manifestations-from behaviors which are automatic and reactive to those which are synchronized with others
3. We-Intersubjective experience-from experiencing the group as being a place to conform to a community of practice which is promoting health across all levels
4. Its-Cultural/Interobjective manifestations-from data in silos to a broader use of data for the future good of humanity as a whole.

Overall, we tried to discuss and propose a model which encompasses the individual-work unit (teams)-organizations and the surrounding environmental contexts altogether. It seems that consciousness could be both the ingredient and the glue which is irreplaceable. Unless systems operate in consciousness at all levels of existing, organizational wellness would only remain as an oxymoron.

REFERENCES

Anitha, J. (2014). Determinants of employee engagement and their impact on employee performance. *International Journal of Productivity and Performance Management, 63*(3), 308–323. https://doi.org/10.1108/IJPPM-01-2013-0008

Askun, D. (2019). Organizational oneness: A possible vision or an inescapable reality? (pp. 154–167) *The routledge companion to management and workplace spirituality.* In J. Marques (Ed.), Taylor & Francis.

Askun, D. (2020). Leading as one: Inclusive leadership through unity consciousness and the act of oneness (pp. 26–41). *The routledge companion to management and workplace spirituality.* In J. Marques (Ed.), Taylor & Francis.

Baumeister, R. F., & Leary, M. R. (1995). The need to belong: Desire for interpersonal attachments as a fundamental human motivation. *Psychological Bulletin, 117*(3), 497.

Bennett, J. B. (2018). Integral organizational wellness™: An evidence-based model of socially inspired well-being. *Journal of Applied Biobehavioral Research, 23*(4), e12136.

Berry, L., Mirabito, A., & Baun, W. (2011). What's the hard return on employee wellness programs? *Harvard Business Review, 89*, 1–9.

Brockner, J. (2006). It's so hard to be fair. *Harvard Business Review, 84*(3), 122–129.

Brown, K. W., Ryan, R. M., & Creswell, J. D. (2007). Mindfulness: Theoretical foundations and evidence for its salutary effects. *Psychological Inquiry, 18*(4), 211–237.

Frei, F. X., & Morriss, A. (2012). Now multiply it all by culture: Service excellence as a product of organizational design and culture. In *Uncommon service: How to win by putting customers at the core of your business*. Harvard Business Review Press.

Gautam, V., & Kothari, H. V. (2021). Determinants of employee engagement: A study of select information technology firms. *IUP Journal of Organizational Behavior, 20*(4), 62–83.

Ghorbani, N., Watson, P. J., & Hargis, M. B. (2008). Integrative self-knowledge scale: Correlations and incremental validity of a cross-cultural measure developed in Iran and the United States. *The Journal of Psychology, 142*(4), 395–412.

Granello, P. F. (2001). A comparison of wellness and social support networks in different age groups. *Adultspan Journal, 3*(1), 12–22.

Grønningsæter, H., Hytten, K., Skauli, G., Christensen, C. C., & Ursin, H. (1992). Improved health and coping by physical exercise or cognitive behavioral stress management training in a work environment. *Psychology & Health, 7*(2), 147–163. https://doi.org/10.1080/08870449208520016

Hay, D., & Nye, R. (1998). *The spirit of the child*. HarperCollins.

Ivanhoe, P. J. (2017). *Oneness: East Asian conceptions of virtue, happiness, and how we are all connected*. Oxford University Press.

Jack, G., & Brevis, J. (2005). Introducing organizational wellness. *Culture and Organization, 11*(2), 65–68.

Klotz, A. C. (2020). Creating jobs and workspaces that energize people. *MIT Sloan Management Review, 61*(4), 74–78.

Krahnke, K., & Cooperrider, D. (2008). Appreciative inquiry: Inquiring new questions and dreaming new dreams. *Spirituality in business: Theory, practice, and future directions*, 17–34.

Lieberman, C. (2019). What wellness programs don't do for workers. *Harvard Business Review, 14*, 1–7.

Meswantri, M., & Ilyas, A. (2018). Determinant of employee engagement and its implications on employee performance. *International Review of Management and Marketing, 8*(3), 36.

Markos, S., & Sridevi, M. S. (2010). Employee engagement: The key to improving performance. *International Journal of Business and Management, 5*(12), 89.

McCrae, R. R., & Costa, P. T., Jr. (1985). Comparison of EPI and psychoticism scales with measures of the five-factor model of personality. *Personality and Individual Differences, 6*(5), 587–597.

Maslach, C. (2001). What have we learned about burnout and health? *Psychology & Health, 16*(5), 607–611.

Mokaya, S. O., & Kipyegon, M. J. (2014). Determinants of employee engagement in the banking industry in Kenya; Case of Cooperative Bank. *Journal of Human Resources Management and Labor Studies, 2*(2), 187–200.

Motyka, B. (2018). Employee engagement and performance: A systematic literature review. *International Journal of Management and Economics, 54*(3), 227–244.

O'Reilly, C. A., & Pfeffer, J. (2000). *Hidden value: How great companies achieve extraordinary results with ordinary people*. Harvard Business Press.

Parks, K. M., & Steelman, L. A. (2008). Organizational wellness programs: A meta-analysis. *Journal of Occupational Health Psychology, 13*(1), 58.

Rehling, L. (2004). Improving teamwork through awareness of conversational styles. *Business Communication Quarterly, 67*(4), 475–482.

Schein, E. H. (1986). What you need to know about organizational culture. *Training & Development Journal, 40*(1), 30–33.

Sharma Baldev, R., & Anupama, R. (2010). Determinants of employee engagement in a private sector organization: An exploratory study. *Advances in Management, 3*.

Tenenberg, J., Roth, W. M., & Socha, D. (2016). From I-awareness to we-awareness in CSCW. *Computer Supported Cooperative Work (CSCW), 25*, 235–278.

Young, M. E., & Lambie, G. W. (2007). Wellness in school and mental health systems: Organizational influences. *The Journal of Humanistic Counseling, Education and Development, 46*(1), 98–113.

(https://www.cnbc.com/2019/08/19/the-ceos-of-nearly-two-hundred-companies-say-shareholder-value-is-no-longer-their-main-objective.html). Websource, 2019.

Wholey, K. (2017). *Your first step to re-create your life in oneness: Awareness*. Toplink Publishing.

Wilber, K. (2001). *A theory of everything: An integral vision for business, politics, science, and spirituality*. Shambhala Publications.

Worline, M. C., & Dutton, J. E. (2017). 31 how leaders shape compassion processes in organizations. *The Oxford Handbook of Compassion Science*, 435.

CHAPTER 10

Inside Job: Exploring Meaningful Work Through Creative-Spiritual Agency

Jeannel E. King

In the 1970s, American author and historian Louis "Studs" Terkel interviewed thousands of people to gain insight into their everyday working lives. His findings revealed that employees wanted more than just a paycheck; they craved work that offered "daily meaning as well as daily bread, for recognition as well as cash, for astonishment rather than torpor; in short, for a sort of life rather than a Monday through Friday sort of dying" (Terkel, 1974, p. xi). Yet, employers often expected their workers to prioritize the company's needs over their own fulfillment, resulting in a psychological contract that forced employees to compromise their needs for professional paychecks (Rayton et al., 2019). Unfortunately, this agreement has persisted in various forms until the present day. However, the COVID-19 pandemic disrupted the established paradigm of work in the United States and had a fundamental impact on human personalities (Sutin et al., 2022). As a result, people became less extroverted, open, agreeable, and conscientious than they were before the pandemic. In 2022, employees started to alter the terms of their psychological contracts, leading to labor shortages, quiet quitting trends, and a refusal to return to the office (Demirkaya et al., 2022).

After experiencing years of pandemic-related trauma, loss, and mental health issues, workers today value their needs more than ever before. While some employees are fortunate enough to reject the old psychological contract

J. E. King (✉)
Saybrook University, Pasadena, CA, USA
e-mail: jking@saybrook.edu

© The Author(s), under exclusive license to Springer Nature Switzerland AG 2023
J. Marques (ed.), *The Palgrave Handbook of Fulfillment, Wellness, and Personal Growth at Work*,
https://doi.org/10.1007/978-3-031-35494-6_10

in favor of daily meaning, others are not as lucky. Under these conditions, can creative-spiritual agency provide a pathway for individuals to (re)discover meaning in their work?

We have yet to witness the long-term effects of the COVID-19 pandemic on employers and employees, making it challenging to predict the future of work in the Western world. This chapter aims to explore ideas and possibilities in the still-evolving future of work. I introduce creative-spiritual agency (CSA) as a new cross-disciplinary construct for organizational change research and discuss its potential as a pathway for employees to find meaning in their work. I begin by establishing the context for meaningful work and examining two models developed by Western researchers to understand it. From there, I introduce the creative-spiritual agency construct and its theoretical and definitional underpinnings. I then link CSA to the models of meaningful work, provide examples of creative-spiritual agency in action, and suggest ways to cultivate and apply creative-spiritual agency at work. The chapter concludes with possibilities for future study and an invitation to collaborate to explore and shape the future of work.

Work Versus Meaningful Work

The average American spends over 90,000 hours, or one-third of their life, at work (Pryce-Jones, 2010; U.S. Bureau of Labor Statistics, n.d.a, n.d.b). Let that sink in for a moment. Out of 24 hours in a day, one-third of that time on average is spent working and another third on average is spent sleeping. That leaves only eight hours to spend on everything else, from connecting with family and friends to taking care of the house and oneself. In my experience, however, those remaining hours do not often find me at my best after work. My most present, productive, and alert self was applied to my work. By the end of the day, the best I can do sometimes is have dinner and watch the latest episodes of my favorite shows.

As the writer Annie Dillard observed, "how we spend our days is, of course, how we spend our lives" (2007, p. 32). If so much of a person's life is spent at work, how much of their life meaning should come from that work? The subject of meaningful work has fascinated researchers from various fields for decades (Bailey et al., 2019; Weeks & Schaffert, 2019). The work a person does influences how they define part of their sense of self (Weeks & Schaffert, 2019). At the same time, researchers have noted the increasing significance of meaningful work research in the face of ongoing concerns regarding the lack of quality jobs and decent work (Bailey et al., 2019). As a result, ethicists from diverse fields assert that "experiencing meaningful work is a fundamental human need" (Yeoman, 2014, p. 236) and employers are therefore morally obliged to provide their employees meaningful work (Bowie, 2017; Yeoman, 2014) even as employees are ethically obliged to seek out and engage in meaningful work (Aguinis & Glavas, 2019).

What, however, *is* meaningful work? Researchers lack consensus on how to define the construct, presenting challenges for employers and employees alike to know what employers should provide or employees should seek to meet this human need (Weeks & Schaffert, 2019). For organizations to meet the ethical call to provide meaningful work for their employees, organizational leaders must understand how their employees define meaningful work (Weeks & Schaffert, 2019). For the first time, the Western work force is comprised of five different generations: Generation Z, Millennials, Generation X, Baby Boomers, and Traditionalists. Fortunately, workers—regardless of their age or generational cohort appear to define meaningful work in terms of the intrinsic rewards they receive, specifically personal growth and the ability to be true to oneself (Weeks & Schaffert, 2019). Martela and Pessi (2018) advocated for a definition which incorporates work significance, serving a larger purpose or greater good in the world, and self-realization in the forms of personal authenticity, autonomy, and self-expression.

Some researchers have focused on how an employee assigns meaning to their work (Mitra & Buzzanell, 2017; Rosso et al., 2010), emphasizing self-oriented paths such as self-development via inner work, self-expression, the belief that one's work is of service to a larger or higher cause, and a sense of connection to others (Lips-Wiersma & Morris, 2009). Others consider significance and purpose as playing key roles in defining meaningful work (Rosso et al., 2010), as does the distinction of one's work as a personal calling rather than a job (Aguinis & Glavas, 2019; Allan et al., 2019). Moreover, a person brings their sense of self with them to work, including their strengths, preferences, morals, values, and beliefs (Weeks & Schaffert, 2019). Meaningful work supports humanity's basic need for meaning in life (Yeoman, 2014) and becomes a person's moral imperative in action (Weeks & Schaffert, 2019).

One interesting approach to understanding meaningful work was pursued by Bailey and Madden (2019) through their research exploring how and when a person's work is rendered meaningless. Researchers concur that meaningfulness is fundamental human need (Frankl, 1946; Heine et al., 2006; Lips-Wiersma & Morris, 2009), therefore a person's experience of work as meaningless may be perceived as a threat to one's self-existence (Bailey & Madden, 2019). In this light, meaningful work becomes not just a management issue but an existential one.

Frances' Story: Meaningful Work, Lost

What happens when an individual's pathway to meaningful work is out of alignment with what their organization provides? This was the case for Frances, a scientist working in the military defense contracting industry. Frances loved creating elegant solutions to pressing defense problems, but her true joy came from cultivating the people on her team. She had worked in an environment where she could mentor and teach younger team members, helping them grow into their full potential as solution partners and contributing members of the scientific community.

However, once a larger defense contractor purchased Frances' small company, everything changed. She was required to focus on increasing her billable hours to the client, rather than being able to cultivate people or craft elegant solutions to complex problems. This new focus was on gross misalignment with Frances' personal values, and she began to view her work—and eventually her life—as increasingly meaningless. Frances initially found herself dreading going to work, but she was reluctant to leave because of the loss of income she would experience if she left the company. Soon after, she began to experience physical and mental health issues related to her increasing stress, and her mental health issues deepened into a profound depression over the years.

Frances' experience highlights the importance of alignment between an individual's personal values and the work that they do. When there is a misalignment, it can result in negative consequences for both the individual and the organization. In this case, Frances was no longer able to find meaning in her work, and her organization lost a valuable team member because of their inability to provide an environment that aligned with her personal values.

This case study serves as a reminder that organizations should not overlook the importance of meaningful work for their employees. Employees like Frances are essential to the success of an organization, and their well-being should be prioritized to ensure that they can continue to contribute meaningfully.

Two Models for Meaningful Work

Although there is no universal definition for meaningful work, two models for understanding it are commonly found in the literature: Rosso et al.'s (2010) Four Pathways for Meaningful Work (Four Pathways) and Lips-Wiersma and Morris' (2009) holistic development framework, commonly referred to as the Map of Meaningful Work (Map) (Lips-Wiersma & Morris, 2018). Although similar in construction, the Four Pathways and the Map differ in the dimensions, or *axes*, they represent as contributing to meaningful work.

Rosso et al.'s (2010) framework emerged from their review of the literature exploring the various ways meaning might arise from work, such as an individual's values, beliefs, and relationships with others at work, as well as the socio-psychological processes and mechanisms through which work may take on meaning (Scott, 2022). The Four Pathways framework considers meaningful work through two organizing axes: agency versus communion motive and self versus other orientation (Bailey & Madden, 2019; Rosso et al., 2010; Scott, 2022; Weeks & Schaffert, 2019). Agency, according to Rosso et al. (2010), refers to the "drive to differentiate, separate, assert, expand, master, and create", while communion refers to the drive to "contact, attach, connect, and unite" (p. 114). In Rosso et al.'s (2010) model, the self represents a person's self-concept, including their motivations, values, and beliefs about work, while the other represents the relational meaning a person finds in their connections with others, working or otherwise. These two axes combine to provide four pathways to meaningful work: Individuation (self/agency), Contribution (others/agency), Self-Connection (self/communion), and Unification (other/communion) (Fig. 10.1).

Rosso et al. (2010) considered their four pathways and the psychological complexity contained within each to encapsulate the fundamental approaches people took to find meaning in their work. Through the self-agency pathway (individuation), a person may find meaning through personal proficiency and autonomy at work, thereby establishing oneself as valuable to the organization (Scott, 2022). Through the other-agency pathway (contribution), one may discover meaning by making a difference in other people's lives. Through the self-communion pathway (self-connection), one finds meaning by aligning with personal identity, whereas the other-communion pathway (unification) involves a sense of belonging or harmony in the relationships with others.

Lips-Wiersma and Morris' (2009, 2018) Map of Meaningful Work presented subtle differences from the Four Pathways. Arguing that Rosso et al.'s (2010) model axis of self versus other orientation was too similar to Bakan's (1966) descriptions of agency and control, Lips-Wiersma and Morris (2009) used the more action-oriented dimension of being versus doing in lieu of agency and communion (Weeks & Schaffert, 2019). The domains in the Map of Meaningful Work in the Lips-Wiersma and Morris (2009) model

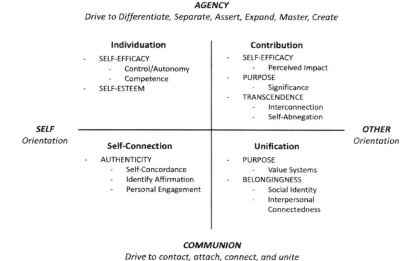

Fig. 10.1 Adaptation of Rosso et al.'s (2010) Four Pathways to Meaningful Work

become Developing and Becoming Self (self/being), Expressing Full Potential (self/doing), Unity with Others (others/being), and Serving Others (others/doing).

Lips-Wiersma and Morris (2009) added another layer of meaning within their framework by including representations of inspiration and reality. Inspiration, in this case, refers to a person's inspiration toward ideal forms of meaning. In early versions of their model, the authors referred to this center point as spiritual coherence (Lips-Wiersma & Morris, 2009). However, their research results indicated that coherence was represented by the totality of the model, while the spiritual aspect provided inspiration of an ideal such as becoming a better version of oneself or making the world a better place. A person's inspiration helps motivate action in the face of reality: one's gloriously imperfect self at work in a gloriously imperfect organization and world.

The Map of Meaningful Work also recognizes the complexity of the external environment and includes the potential for negative experiences in each of its domains, such as one's work being disconnected from personal values or the feeling that work is meaningless or dehumanizing (Lips-Wiersma & Morris, 2009). The holistic perspective of the Map of Meaningful Work aligns with the conceptualization of meaningful work as an integrative construct (Rosso et al., 2010) and may be useful for individuals, managers, and organizations seeking to develop a more comprehensive understanding of the multi-dimensional nature of meaningful work (Fig. 10.2).

A Pause: Frances, Revisited

Let's take a moment to examine Frances' experience through the lens of the two models of meaningful work. Frances found meaning through all four pathways of Rosso et al.'s (2010) model while working at her small company: she found joy in applying her mastery to elegantly solve problems (self/agency), while also aligning with her identity as a mentor and scientist (self/communion), helping elevate her partners above herself (other/agency), and living her values with like-minded colleagues (other/communion). According to the Lips-Wiersma and Morris (2009) model, Frances found meaning by being true to herself and her values (self/being) while creating elegant solutions for her clients and influencing others to do the same (self/doing). She also found meaning by working with others who shared her values (other/being), not only serving her clients' needs but also helping cultivate future generations of talented and thoughtful scientists to make a difference in the world (other/doing). Through her efforts, Frances helped others discover their value and make a difference, ultimately contributing to making the world a better place.

However, when Frances found herself working for a larger company that prioritized financial outcomes over everything else, all her pathways to meaningful work collapsed. The company did not value elegant solutions (self/agency, self/doing) or her mentor/scientist identity (self/being).

Fig. 10.2 Adaptation of Lips-Wiersma and Morris' (2009, 2018) Holistic Development Framework, or Map of Meaningful Work

As her mentoring practice did not immediately generate more revenue for the company, Frances' efforts to foster the growth of her teammates (other/agency, other/communion, self/doing, other/being, other/doing) were prohibited.

Creatively Synthesizing the Two Models

In my study of the above two models, I kept seeing them as complementary rather than contrasting. As I thought about Frances and her painful experience, I couldn't help but wonder what would happen if we combined these two models for meaningful work. Figure 10.3 presents my synthesis of the Four Pathways and the Map of Meaningful Work.

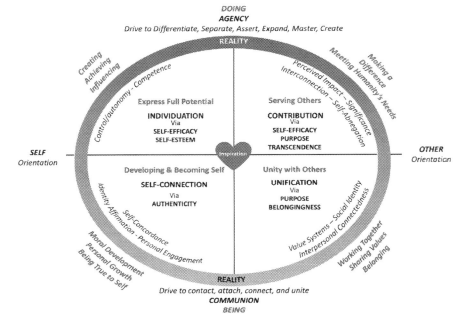

Fig. 10.3 A creative synthesis of Rosso et al.'s (2010) Four Pathways Model and Lips-Wiersma and Morris' (2009, 2018) Map of Meaningful Work. Contributions from Rosso et al.'s (2010) model are represented in black, while contributions from Lips-Wiersma and Morris' (2009) model are represented in red tones

With this synthesized model, I flipped Lips-Wiersma and Morris' vertical axis (Being versus Doing) and quadrant entries to align with Rosso et al.'s (2010) Agency versus Communion structure. When combined in this way, the two models reveal a latent synergy that was not obvious in isolation. Inspiration serves as the motivating heart of both models, and each model is bound by imperfect realities of person, place, and planet. However, each quadrant becomes an engine for internal and external meaning and transformation.

The synthesized model invites further expansion of its dimensions. First, let's consider orientation toward the self. Despite the variations in description, the self is essentially a social and/or personal mythology-construction that implicitly assumes a certain level of *boundary* distinguishing one's self from others and the world (Schneider, 2015). This self-boundary is preserved regardless of whether a person accesses humanity's shared aspects (e.g., the spiritual, the collective unconscious) or has peripersonal, transpersonal, or transcendent experiences. Contrast this concept of self against that of the personality, which tends to remain consistent over time and is comprised of the patterns of a person's internal experiences (e.g., beliefs, thoughts, emotions) and behaviors. Or as Sullivan (1953) defined it, personality is "the relatively enduring pattern of recurrent interpersonal situations which characterize a human life" (p. 110).

Personality flows from, and is secondary to, the self (Schneider, 2015). If agency and communion comprise those "Big Two" dimensions of a person's personality, then creativity and spirituality might be said to represent a similar relationship within humanistic psychology. Agency and communion may be thought of as relatively enduring patterns of being that derive from the self and are activated by one's social interactions within their world...such as getting one's needs met.

If, however, as Dunlop et al. (2020) observed, agency and communion represent the duality of human existence within personality psychology, then creativity and spirituality might be said to represent a similar relationship within humanistic psychology. According to this third force of psychology, all human selves are viewed as creative at their essence, acting with intentionality according to their deeply held values (Krippner & Murphy, 1973). Creativity and spirituality hold esteemed positions within humanistic research, with creativity being referred to as a "bread and butter" issue of humanistic psychology and spirituality researchers evolving a transpersonal psychology dedicated specifically to the study of spirituality, compassionate social action, and transcendence (Schneider, 2015).

Freud explained exceptional human creative and spiritual achievements as products of individuals' abnormal psychology, neuroses, and psychoses (Freud & Strachey, 1964). Rank (1978, 2012), on the other hand, regarded creativity as a continual process of self-creation, one that encompasses the entirety of a person's life, including neuroses and psychoses. According to Rank, human heroism can be defined in terms of taking risks on a larger stage to create oneself. Jung (2019) claimed that a person's spiritual experiences are a part of a never-ending and lifelong process of psycho-spiritual individuation and integration. Jung believed that the self is a richer and less rational construct than the human ego and that its spontaneous wisdom emerges through intuitions, images, and dreams. In Rank's and Jung's view, spirituality provides humans with one of the largest stages upon which a human existence can unfold. Maslow created a mailing list for individuals interested in "the scientific study of creativity, love, higher values, growth, self-actualization, [and] basic needs gratification" (Misiak & Sexton, 1973, p. 111). For Maslow (1962a, 1962b, 1971a, 1971b), creativity was crucial for all individuals as an enabling process for growth, self-actualization, and beyond.

Creativity and spirituality are fundamental aspects of being human and are essential qualities of the human self. While human beings may experience strong desires for material successes and sexual pleasures, these desires are not as strong as their deeper yearning for psychological wholeness and spiritual union (Bradford, 2015). By incorporating creativity and spirituality into our synthesized model, what else becomes possible?

Creativity, Spirituality, and Meaningful Work

Creativity and spirituality have been integral to the human experience since prehistory, and they have been studied as separate areas of research since the twentieth century. Prior to 1950, psychology researchers studied creativity within the larger context of intelligence quotient or IQ (Guilford, 1950). Spirituality, when researched at all, was typically studied as an aspect of religion until its psychologization in the 1990s, where psychology researchers attempted to reduce spirituality to psychological components (Sperry, 2012). Guilford (1950) urged psychology researchers to study creativity as a unique construct to understand how creative promise might be cultivated in young people and creative personalities in adults. Fuller (2001) refocused psychology research to examine spirituality as a construct separate from religion.

As noted earlier in this paper, creativity and spirituality are aspects of self from which the personality qualities of agency and communion derive. However, it is important to recognize that these concepts are not static and that our understanding of them is evolving with the world around us. Therefore, as we review various definitions of creativity and spirituality through the lens of psychology research, it is crucial not to be cavalier and to remain open to the possibility of new understandings that may emerge in the future.

Creativity

Creativity allows people to release emotions, generate passion, and explore their inquisitiveness (Ashbolt, 2018). However, working creatively solely for the sake of being creative has become frowned upon by organizations (Gomez & Smart, 2008). Instead, creative pursuits in organizational settings are evaluated solely on their output, devaluing the holistic process of creativity (Sheridan-Rabideau, 2010). As noted by Adler and Delbecq (2018), beauty has become less valued than efficiency, and businesses often sideline aesthetic creativity, resulting in stagnation rather than growth.

Some creativity researchers have called for a new or renewed understanding of creativity as a way of being (Sheridan-Rabideau, 2010). Creative living and thinking cultivate innovation (Ashbolt, 2018) and the space for possibility and change. By reframing creativity, we may expose ways that existing professional paradigms blind organizations from what is possible (Adler & Delbecq, 2018).

Creativity as Performative Outcome
Creativity has traditionally been studied within psychology as a form of performance that produces high-quality, original, and elegant solutions to complex, novel, ill-defined, or poorly structured problems (Besemer & O'Quin, 1999; Christiaans, 2002; Mumford & Gustafson, 1988). The standard definition of creativity within psychology, which focused on the production of something perceived by others as novel and useful, reinforced this view (Runco & Jaeger, 2012; Stein, 1953). However, this approach has often led organizations to

devalue the holistic process of creativity and to focus solely on the output, leading to a neglect of creativity in organizational settings (Sheridan-Rabideau, 2010). The result has been a narrowing of the humanistic value of creativity to the arts and other areas dedicated to producing beauty, while other aspects of creativity have been sidelined.

Creativity as Being

There is a growing movement to re-evaluate creativity as a way of being (King's College London, 2016; Sheridan-Rabideau, 2010). Living and thinking creatively cultivates innovation (Ashbolt, 2018) and can become an altruistic way to connect with others and have a positive impact on the world (Sheridan-Rabideau, 2010). This view of creativity as a way of being is reflected in the work of philosophers and researchers such as Rollo May (1994), who understood creativity as the process of bringing into being and enlarging human consciousness, and Funk (2000), who argued that the source of creativity lay not in thinking, but in a deeper, more subtle perception of intuition. Adler and Delbecq (2018) advocated for a view of creativity through a lens of beauty, and Richards (2018) proposed that everyday creativity is an aspect of the self, and to live a creative life is to craft what one wants to create value and meaning in one's existence however and with whomever one chooses.

Curiosity, or a person's desire to know, is an important aspect of creativity as being (Russ, 2020). A person's level of curiosity reflects their search for optimal levels of arousal in their environment and motivates them to explore the novel stimuli of their world. Schutte and Malouff (2020) observed people's curiosity through three displayed behaviors: joyous exploration of a scenario, stress tolerance in the face of the new, and a desire to gain more knowledge. People demonstrating elevated levels of curiosity also demonstrated greater experiences of flow during their creative explorations of an activity (Schutte & Malouff, 2020).

Flow is the state where a person optimally experiences both feeling and performance at peak levels (Csikszentmihalyi, 1997). Schutte and Malouff (2020) found that curiosity was strongly correlated with the level of flow a person experienced, and that flow was strongly correlated with creativity. After years of research, Csikszentmihalyi (2004) declared that spontaneous flow states were the secret to happiness. A person's capacity for intense joyful exploration, a high stress tolerance for the new, and a desire to gain knowledge (Schutte & Malouff, 2020) would appear to fuel a person's ability to have spontaneous experiences of optimal feeling and performance (Csikszentmihalyi, 1997, 2004).

These moments of flow align with what Richards (2018) refers to as a world of creative tipping points, be they background flickers or blinding flashes. The everyday creative can approach these tipping points as Aikido masters, intuitively sensing into their energy and working with them to guide and shape their flow (Richards, 2018). Because a creative person is comprised of one's personal features and ongoing style in a setting, a creative person cannot be separated from their press, or environment (Richards, 2018). Creativity, therefore, is not defined by people, products, processes, or presses (that is, environmental conditions supporting creativity) (Rhodes, 1961), but comes alive via one's encounters and interconnections with the objects, ideas, people, projects, situations, ambiguities, and activities of everyday life (Glăveanu & Beghetto, 2021).

Creativity as Experience
Glăveanu and Beghetto (2021) expanded upon the above being understanding of creativity by introducing their non-standard definition of creativity. According to their working definition, creative experience involves (1) a principled engagement with the unfamiliar and (2) a willingness to approach the familiar in unfamiliar ways. This definition shifts creativity from being strictly performative or outcome-oriented to a self-other encounter marked by open-endedness, nonlinearity, pluri-perspectivism, and future orientation. In other words, this definition places the person at the heart of creativity (Credne Creativity, 2021).

Reframing creativity as experience facilitates a significant shift in mindset and expectation. Creative experience recognizes the uniqueness of each person's encounter with what they perceive as other to them (Credne Creativity, 2021). Paradoxically, through their experience with the other, the experiencer may feel a deeper sense of interconnection in which they are part of something bigger than themselves. Additionally, the openness and nonlinearity of creativity as experience removes any need to predict a resulting outcome. Instead, the focus becomes cultivating creative experience rather than evaluating creative action or output, embedding the experience squarely within the heart of living within a living system.

With creativity as being or as lived experience, one needs to cultivate a specific quality of attention. However, in these understandings, creativity is not something one does but something one experiences or is a part of. At this point, creativity as a construct can become transpersonal, extending beyond the individual to encompass the collective.

Creativity as Transpersonal
From a transpersonal psychology perspective, just as a person might access different nonmaterial and transcendent levels and sources of consciousness, they may also access different nonmaterial and transcendent levels and sources of creativity (Funk, 2000). A person's creative product is also thought to reflect the level of consciousness they were in when they produced it (Funk, 2000; Wilber, 1998). Transcendent or transpersonal levels of consciousness (Gebser, 2020; Grof, 1998; Johnson, 2019; Krippner, 2020; Maheshwari, 2021; Miller & Cook-Greuter, 1994; Walsh & Vaughan, 1993) may produce transcendent or transpersonal creative products. Transpersonal creativity occurs within the sacred or liminal space that a person accesses

by means of entering a creative realm (Ver, 2004), sometimes referred to as inspired creativity (Funk, 2000).

Imagination, an aspect of transpersonal creativity, is often studied as a cognitive capacity for reproducing thoughts, experiences, and images. However, imagination does more than just reproduce what a person has sensed or experienced; it creates new combinations and ideas that the person has not had before (Hoff, 2020). In an organizational creativity context, imagination serves as a generative mental power to transcend tacit knowledge (via senses and memory) and imagine something new to produce or create (Thompson, 2018). Inherent in this ability is a person's capacity to transcend reality itself (Hoff, 2020).

Regardless of intention or inner resources, people exist within a larger, interconnected context (Rubenfeld, 2009). This interconnected context profoundly influences the outcomes of one's ventures. Whether one equates that greater context with a spiritual referent (e.g., God, Higher Power) or not, the interconnection holds essential resources for success. To create something new, one must acknowledge and draw from a source greater than the individual self (Rubenfeld, 2009). A creator in this space experiences a drive to wholeness with a sense of awe and the belief that they are connected to something much greater than themselves (Funk, 2000; Rogers, 1993). The resulting integration of inner and outer worlds lies at the heart of creativity (Rubenfeld, 2009). This integration also lies at the heart of spirituality.

Spirituality

The nature of spirituality has been an enduring mystery for philosophers and scholars alike (Skrzypińska, 2018). Spiritual practices have been a part of human cultures throughout the world for over 50,000 years (Henning & Henning, 2021). The history of spiritual practices and ideologies includes vast numbers of evolving approaches that have at times conflicted with or influenced each other, and at other times remained immutable and unchanging. Despite the ubiquity of these practices and traditions in cultures and societies, the reasons behind why and how they developed remain unclear.

Research on spirituality has been contentious, with the construct of spirituality difficult to define (Henning & Henning, 2021; Miller-Perrin & Krumrei Mancuso, 2015; Raney, Cox, & Jones, 2017; Roehlkepartain et al., 2006; Steensland et al., 2018) or left intentionally broad to accommodate the field of study (Benson et al., 2003; Greenway, 2022). The difficulty in defining spirituality is primarily due to the interchangeable use of spirituality, religion, and religiosity in the literature (Hill et al., 2000; Paloutzian & Park, 2021; Skrzypińska, 2018; Zinnbauer et al., 1997, 1999). Spirituality is a complex construct with disparate theories (Henning & Henning, 2021) and meanings (Raney et al., 2017). As an inherently subjective construct, spirituality can imbue many different activities and experiences, leading to challenges in crafting a standard definition.

At its core, spirituality is comprised of a personal collection of beliefs that frame a view of the world (Skrzypińska, 2018) through orientation of an individual to a point of reference (or referent) (Steensland et al., 2018). These beliefs are brought to life or embodied through various practices with the goal of positively transforming one's experience of the world and themselves within it (Henning & Henning, 2021).

Spirituality as Human Response to Subject-Object Duality
According to Henning and Henning (2021), duality requires a complex brain to be experienced. Before human brains were complex, there was no duality of subject or object. The emergence of spirituality appears to align with the emergence of a biological evolutionary mechanism that gives humans the capacity to mentally differentiate between the one who experiences (mental 'me' as 'subject') and what is experienced (mental 'objects'). Biological regulation processes modulate how the brain interprets perceptions of reality in different circumstances to optimize the human's ability to survive and thrive. In addition to being a survival mechanism, this subject-object duality is also the source of humanity's existential problems, including insecurity and questions surrounding personal identity (who am I?), existential loneliness and social insecurities, finding meaningful connection and a sense of belonging, and fear of the unknown, particularly death.

Spiritual practices and traditions emerged as a cultural adaptation and coping mechanism to counterbalance the human mental experience of subject-object duality (Henning & Henning, 2021). Even the term spirituality demonstrates a dualistic worldview, as 'spirit' shares the same root as respiration (spir) and refers to an energy, force, or soul that inhabits and animates the human material form "and looks through our eyes, as if visiting from a special nonphysical 'spiritual realm' before ultimately returning to it" (Henning & Henning, 2021, p. 179).

Spirituality as a Means for Transformation
Spiritual traditions and practices promote a positive and lasting transformation of our experience of self and of the world (Henning & Henning, 2021; Leffel, 2011). Transformation may occur in myriad ways, such as taking a postgraduate course on consciousness and spirituality (Suissa, 2019), having a peak spiritual experience earlier in one's professional career (Flower, 2019), or even participating in bondage, discipline (or domination), sadism, and masochism (BDSM) scenes (Baker, 2018).

Spiritual transformation may occur through the interactions of an individual with their environment (Roehlkepartain et al., 2006). Leffel (2011) advocates that spiritual transformation requires combining upper-level constructs (e.g., reasoning, meaning-making, worldviews) with lower-level qualities (e.g., emotions, intuition) to affect thinking, motivation, and behavior.

Spirituality focuses on how one's inner life affects one's motivations and quality of experience (Carey, 2018). Therefore, spirituality is agent-centric, as a person's focus is on their inner life in terms of ethical thinking and behavior, as opposed to being action-centric or focused on external expression (Carey, 2018). Through a spiritual life, a person seeks to realize an enduring change in their ethical character by transforming the workings of their mind (Carey, 2018).

Creativity and Spirituality as Interrelated Constructs

Having reviewed the historical development of creativity and spirituality, it is time to consider how these constructs are interrelated. While they have emerged as separate research fields, there has been little exploration of their potential links (Gamliel, 2021). Some researchers have proposed a link between creativity and spirituality through terms like "creative-spiritual" (Schmidt, 1995), "spirituality/creativity" (Sinha & Rosenberg, 2013), and "creativity-spirituality construct" (Corry et al., 2013, 2014). However, much of the existing cross-domain research has focused on one construct's influence on the other, rather than their interdependence. For example, some researchers explored how creativity may be used to cultivate spirituality (Beaird, 2006; Buchanan, 2008; Diltz, 2006; Green, 1999; Guarino, 2012; Keener-Wink, 1993; Kelly, 2006; Northcott, 2005; Nusholtz, 2004; Sakaue-Rowan, 1991), while other researchers examined how spiritual practices might improve creativity and the arts (Beaird, 2006; Damianakis, 2006; Das, 2004; Martin, 2007).

Corry et al. (2015) highlighted the interconnections of creativity and spirituality in their Transformative Coping Model. According to the authors, the model was predicated on the premise that spirituality and creativity are intrinsically related and connected because both constructs are expressive languages for the human spirit. Connecting spirituality and creativity is the opportunity for personal growth and positive transformation. Corry et al. (2015) explain both creativity and spirituality as searches for the sacred, with creativity also including a search for oneself. Imbued with transformative power, both creativity and spirituality are paths for a person's search for unity and meaning.

Research on creative and spiritual personalities illuminated shared qualities across types, particularly in a person's level of inquisitiveness (Goldberg et al., 2011; Saucier & Skrzypińska, 2006; Shafranske & Gorsuch, 1984), openness to experience (Johnstone et al., 2012; Saucier & Skrzypińska, 2006), need for individualism and nonconformity, and negative social valence (Goldberg et al., 2011; Saucier & Skrzypińska, 2006). Where the creative individual typically displays a quality of emotional intensity, the spiritual person experiences similar emotionality via their desire for *connection*, or feeling close to another (Gamliel, 2021; Zinnbauer et al., 1997).

The creative person and spiritual person may also share an experience of losing oneself, or one's conscious sense of place and time, while involved in a meaningful activity or cause. In spiritual research, this phenomenon is called *absorption* (Gamliel, 2021; Hamer, 2005; Johnstone et al., 2012;

Saucier & Skrzypińska, 2006), while in creativity research it is referred to as *flow* (Bradfield, 2021; Csikszentmihalyi, 1997; Goslin-Jones, 2010; Sonnenburg & Primus, 2020). With absorption, the emphasis is on the loss of sense of one's self while mentally engaging with a task, while a flow state emphasizes a fully absorbed mental state for creative work (Gamliel, 2021). Both fields are describing a similar construct, however.

Based on my review of the extant review, I believe that creativity and spirituality are two facets of a multifaceted gem, two sides of the same coin. Creativity as experience, as defined by Glăveanu and Beghetto (2021), and spirituality as a means of transcending and transforming the self, as described by Henning and Henning (2021), are interrelated. Both involve a willingness to approach the familiar in unfamiliar ways and can enable transformation and transcendence.

Frances' Story: A Creative-Spiritual Being

Frances describes herself as a creative person who enjoys playing with complexity in unique ways. She approaches familiar problem sets with an unfamiliar perspective and often collaborates with like-minded partners to discover the most elegant solution. Frances is also an amateur musician, sculptor, skillful woodworker, chef, and writer, and can lose herself for hours while working on stimulating projects that fulfill her creative urge. Frances' spirituality is deeply connected to her pursuit of elegance. Although she identifies as an atheist, she is profoundly spiritual and considers the elegant and immutable scientific laws of the universe to be her higher power and the foundation of her spirituality. Through her work, Frances becomes a high priestess of elegant thought, morals, and the elevation of others before self. Her creativity and devotion to elegance are core parts of who Frances is as a creative-spiritual being.

AN EMERGING FRAMEWORK FOR CREATIVE-SPIRITUAL AGENCY AND MEANINGFUL WORK

As we continue to navigate new relationships with and understanding of meaningful work in the context of COVID-19, there is a need for a new approach to work and for meaningful work. This emerging framework considers how creativity and spirituality may be interrelated constructs within a synthesized model for meaningful work (Fig. 10.4).

In this framework, creativity is primarily represented within the domain of the self, as an individual engages in principled engagement with the familiar in unfamiliar ways. The meaning of creativity is also received through social interaction, which is represented through the contribution/serving others quadrant. Creativity provides novel opportunities to connect with oneself and others, resulting in an enhanced sense of meaning from the experience and the work.

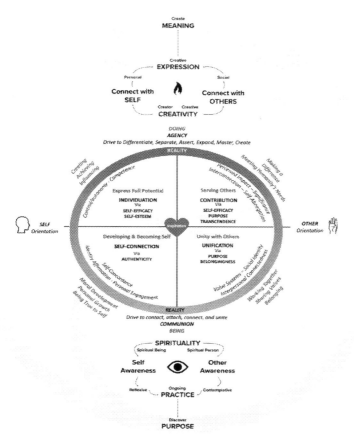

Fig. 10.4 An emerging framework for creative-spiritual agency and meaningful work. In this figure, the yin-yang symbol represents the interconnected nature of creativity and spirituality

Spirituality, on the other hand, is primarily represented within the domain of the other, as most spiritual practices are pursued with a goal to transcend the self and achieve some form of unity with something larger than oneself. Self-reflexive and contemplative practices serve to deepen awareness over time, with the ultimate goal of achieving more profound experiences of unity and self-transcendence to discover the purpose of life and one's existence.

Both creativity and spirituality run through the heart of the model, representing the inspiration to reach an ideal self or ideal world. For both constructs, there is a self and other orientation, as creativity is intentionally paired with agency and doing, while spirituality is paired with communion and being. The creative act engages the creator's unique experience, perspective, and worldview, leading to separation, differentiation, assertion, and creation, while the spiritual path is a means to connect, attach, and unite with others and that which is perceived as greater than oneself.

Overall, this emergent framework suggests that the interrelatedness of creativity and spirituality may be key to unlocking meaningful work in a changing world. By embracing both constructs, individuals may be able to engage in principled and innovative ways of thinking, feeling, and behaving in the workplace, leading to enhanced experiences of agency, communion, and meaning.

Frances' Story: Meaningful Work

What ultimately happened to Frances? After years of working for a large defense company, Frances and her partner had a heart-to-heart conversation about how her job was affecting her. Frances realized that staying in a well-paying but ill-aligned job was not worth the existential torture. She knew that she had value to offer the world, even if her employer tried to convince her otherwise. Frances decided to leave her position at the company to pursue a different path that aligned with her values and beliefs.

The very next day, Frances' company announced layoffs and gave her the option to take early retirement, which she accepted. With newfound freedom, Frances opened a boutique consulting company with like-minded colleagues who shared her commitment to finding the most elegant solutions to problems. Today, she works with a diverse set of clients who value her team's approach to problem-solving. Frances is also healthier, has better personal relationships, and volunteers at local elementary schools to share her passion for creative problem-solving with students. Finally, she has embraced her calling: to help others achieve great things in the world through meaningful work.

REFLECTIONS AND INVITATIONS

Meaningful work is not just a nice-to-have; it's a necessity for a fulfilled and purposeful life. Through the journeys of people like Frances, we've seen how meaningful work can manifest and transform lives. We've explored how creativity, spirituality, agency, communion, and other elements come together to create a meaningful work experience. We've also seen how much more research is needed to fully understand and support individuals on their paths to meaningful work.

As we move forward in this emergent post-pandemic world, let us remember that every person has their own unique path to meaningful work. Employers have a responsibility to create a space for meaningful work to occur, and employees have a right to pursue and find their own meaningful work. Researchers have an opportunity to continue to explore the complex and intertwined factors that contribute to meaningful work.

Ultimately, meaningful work is about finding purpose, connection, and contribution in what we do. It's about discovering and living out our values, passions, and strengths in ways that benefit ourselves, others, and the world. It's about fulfilling our potential and making a positive impact on those around us.

So, let us embrace the challenge and opportunity of finding our own meaningful work, supporting others in finding theirs, and advancing the research on this vital topic. Let us continue to explore and expand our understanding of what meaningful work means and how we can make it a reality for more people. Let us all, in our own way, use our maps, follow our paths, and activate our creative-spiritual agency in the pursuit of meaningful work.

References

Adler, N. J., & Delbecq, A. L. (2018). Twenty-first century leadership: A return to beauty. *Journal of Management Inquiry, 27*(2), 119–137. https://doi.org/10.1177/1056492617710758

Aguinis, H., & Glavas, A. (2019). On corporate social responsibility, sensemaking, and the search for meaningfulness through work. *Journal of Management, 45*(3), 1057–1086. https://doi.org/10.1177/0149206317691575

Allan, B. A., Batz-Barbarich, C., Sterling, H. M., & Tay, L. (2019). Outcomes of meaningful work: A Meta-Analysis. *Journal of Management Studies, 56*(3), 500–528. https://doi.org/10.1111/joms.12406

Ashbolt, K. (2018). Re-evaluating creativity and play: A literature review. *Gestalt Journal of Australia and New Zealand, 15*(1), 54–81.

Bailey, C., & Madden, A. (2019). "We're not scum, we're human": Agential responses in the face of meaningless work. *Scandinavian Journal of Management, 35*(4), 101064. https://doi.org/10.1016/j.scaman.2019.101064

Bailey, C., Yeoman, R., Madden, A., Thompson, M., & Kerridge, G. (2019). A review of the empirical literature on meaningful work: Progress and research agenda. *Human Resource Development Review, 18*(1), 83–113. https://doi.org/10.1177/1534484318804653

Bakan, D. (1966). *The duality of human existence: An essay on psychology and religion*. Rand McNally.

Baker, A. C. (2018). Sacred kink: Finding psychological meaning at the intersection of BDSM and spiritual experience. *Sexual and Relationship Therapy, 33*(4), 440–453. https://doi.org/10.1080/14681994.2016.1205185

Beaird, G. J. (2006). *The experience of transformation in circles of women: Development of voice in a sacred setting* (Doctoral dissertation). https://www.proquest.com/docview/304945057?pq-origsite=gscholar&fromopenview=true

Benson, P. L., Roehlkepartain, E. C., & Rude, S. P. (2003). Spiritual development in childhood and adolescence: Toward a field of inquiry. *Applied Developmental Science, 7*(3), 205–213. https://doi.org/10.1207/S1532480XADS0703_12

Besemer, S. P., & O'Quin, K. (1999). Confirming the three-factor creative product analysis matrix model in an American sample. *Creativity Research Journal, 12*(4), 287–296. https://doi.org/10.1207/s15326934crj1204_6

Bowie, N. E. (2017). *Business ethics: A Kantian perspective*. Cambridge University Press. https://doi.org/10.1017/9781316343210

Bradfield, E. (2021). Subjective experiences of participatory arts engagement of healthy older people and explorations of creative ageing. *Public Health, 198*, 53–58. https://doi.org/10.1016/j.puhe.2021.06.019

Bradford, G. K. (2015). Romantic love as a path: Tensions between erotic desire and security needs. In K. J. Schneider, J. F. Pierson, & J. F. T. Bugental (Eds.), *The handbook of humanistic psychology: Theory, research, and practice* (2nd ed., pp. 667–680). Sage. https://doi.org/10.4135/9781483387864.n52

Buchanan, D. J. (2008). *"Blue tights": Dancing into a life of her own facilitating embodied spirituality for African American adolescent girls* (Doctoral dissertation). https://www.proquest.com/docview/304381472?pq-origsite=gscholar&fromopenview=true

Carey, J. (2018). Spiritual, but not religious? On the nature of spirituality and its relation to religion. *International Journal for Philosophy of Religion, 83*(3), 261–269. https://doi.org/10.1007/s11153-017-9648-8

Christiaans, H. H. C. M. (2002). Creativity as a design criterion. *Creativity Research Journal, 14*(1), 41–54. https://doi.org/10.1207/s15326934crj1401_4

Corry, D. A. S., Lewis, C. A., & Mallett, J. (2014). Harnessing the mental health benefits of the creativity–spirituality construct: Introducing the theory of transformative coping. *Journal of Spirituality in Mental Health, 16*(2), 89–110. https://doi.org/10.1080/19349637.2014.896854

Corry, D. A. S., Mallett, J., Lewis, C. A., & Abdel-Khalek, A. M. (2013). The creativity-spirituality construct and its role in transformative coping. *Mental Health, Religion & Culture, 16*(10), 979–990. https://doi.org/10.1080/13674676.2013.834492

Corry, D., Tracey, A., & Lewis, C. (2015). Spirituality and creativity in coping, their association and transformative effect: A qualitative enquiry. *Religions, 6*(2), 499–526. https://doi.org/10.3390/rel6020499

Credne Creativity. (2021). *Credne seminar: Cultivating the possible: Designing for creativity in education with Vlad Glăveanu.* https://www.youtube.com/watch?v=JMSp0iogi6E

Csikszentmihalyi, M. (1997). *Creativity: Flow and the psychology of discovery and invention.* HarperCollins Publishers.

Csikszentmihalyi, M. (2004). *Flow, the secret to happiness [video].* TED Conferences. https://www.ted.com/talks/mihaly_csikszentmihalyi_flow_the_secret_to_happiness?utm_campaign=tedspread&utm_medium=referral&utm_source=tedcomshare

Damianakis, T. (2006). *The intersection of social work and the arts: Gleanings from creative writers and social workers on spirituality, eros, and creativity for knowledge and practice* (Doctoral dissertation). https://www.proquest.com/docview/304925873?pq-origsite=primo

Das, L. S. (2004). *Letting go of the person you used to be: Lessons on change, loss, and spiritual transformation.* Harmony.

Demirkaya, H., Aslan, M., Güngör, H., Durmaz, V., & Rodoplu Şahin, D. (2022). COVID-19 and quitting jobs. *Frontiers in Psychology, 13*, 916222. https://doi.org/10.3389/fpsyg.2022.916222

Dillard, A. (2007). *The writing life.* HarperCollins e-books.

Diltz, J. (2006). *Writing as threshold to spirit: A phenomenological study of the experience of writing of twelve college women* (Doctoral dissertation). https://www.proquest.com/docview/304914389?pq-origsite=primo

Dunlop, W. L., McCoy, T. P., Hanley, G. E., & Harake, N. R. (2020). *Communion*. In V. Zeigler-Hill & T. K. Shackelford (Eds.), Encyclopedia of personality and individual differences (pp. 765–772). Springer International Publishing. https://doi.org/10.1007/978-3-319-24612-3_1218

Flower, L. (2019). Spiritual experiences of post-performance career ballet dancers: A qualitative study of how peak performance spiritual lived experiences continued into and influenced later teaching lives. *Research in Dance Education, 20*(2), 184–196. https://doi.org/10.1080/14647893.2018.1543260

Frankl, V. E. (1946). Man's search for meaning: Gift edition. *Gift Edition*. Beacon.

Freud, S., & Strachey, J. E. (1964). *The standard edition of the complete psychological works of Sigmund Freud*.

Fuller, R. C. (2001). *Spiritual, but not religious: Understanding unchurched America*. Oxford University Press. https://doi.org/10.1093/0195146808.001.0001

Funk, J. (2000). Inspired creativity. In M. E. Miller & S. R. Cook-Greuter (Eds.), *Creativity, spirituality, and transcendence: Paths to integrity and wisdom in the mature self* (pp. 121–146). Ablex Publishing Corporation.

Gamliel, M. L. (2021). *Divergent minds, convergent molds: Understanding the traits and experiences of creative students in orthodox schooling* (Doctoral dissertation). https://www.proquest.com/docview/2525649686/fulltextPDF/26F4E6906BC74FD3PQ/1?accountid=34120

Gebser, J. (2020). *The ever-present origin*. Ohio University Press.

Glăveanu, V. P., & Beghetto, R. A. (2021). Creative experience: A non-standard definition of creativity. *Creativity Research Journal, 33*(2), 75–80. https://doi.org/10.1080/10400419.2020.1827606

Goldberg, S. J., Pelcovitz, D., & Rosenberg, J. (2011). *Nourishing the adolescent soul: Insights and recommendations to support religious and spiritual growth*. Institute for University-School Partnership.

Gomez, L., & Smart, D. (2008). 'Play' in practice in psychotherapy and education. *European Journal of Psychotherapy & Counselling: Play and Playfulness, 10*(2), 147–158. https://doi.org/10.1080/13642530802076136

Goslin-Jones, T. (2010). *The perceived effects of person-centered expressive arts on one's work experience* (Doctoral dissertation). https://www.proquest.com/docview/753321526/fulltextPDF/90667947E40A4BBFPQ/1?accountid=34120

Green, M. H. (1999). *Opening to the artist within. Reclaiming the inner feminine through the expressive arts: A heuristic study* [Master's thesis, California Institute of Integral Studies]. https://www.proquest.com/docview/230621332/fulltextPDF/C83B207B10CE41EFPQ/1?accountid=34120

Greenway, T. S. (2022). Attending to the multidimensional nature of spirituality and faith: Integrating spiritual development and moral foundations theory. *Christian Education Journal, 19*(1), 47–62. https://doi.org/10.1177/0739891320986162

Grof, S. (1998). *The cosmic game: Explorations of the frontiers of human consciousness*. State University of New York Press.

Guarino, M. S. (2012). *Listen with the ear of the heart: A contemplative ethnography of musical performance, communal religious life, and mystical spirituality among the monks of Weston priory* (Doctoral dissertation). https://www.proquest.com/docview/1037818777/fulltextPDF/DAFDBB68B6E54FBAPQ/1?accountid=34120

Guilford, J. P. (1950). Creativity. *American Psychologist, 5*, 444–454. https://doi.org/10.1037/h0063487

Hamer, D. H. (2005). *The god gene: How faith is hardwired into our genes*. Anchor.

Heine, S. J., Proulx, T., & Vohs, K. D. (2006). The meaning maintenance model: On the coherence of social motivations. *Personality and Social Psychology Review, 10*(2), 88–110. https://doi.org/10.1207/s15327957pspr1002_1

Henning, H., & Henning, M. (2021). Reflections on the nature of spirituality: Evolutionary context, biological mechanisms, and future directions. *Journal for the Study of Spirituality, 11*(2), 174–181. https://doi.org/10.1080/20440243.2021.1955453

Hill, P. C., Pargament, K. I., Hood, R. W., McCullough, J. M. E., Swyers, J. P., Larson, D. B., & Zinnbauer, B. J. (2000). Conceptualizing religion and spirituality: Points of commonality, points of departure. *Journal for the Theory of Social Behaviour, 30*(1), 51–77. https://doi.org/10.1111/1468-5914.00119

Hoff, E. V. (2020). Imagination. In S. Pritzker & M. Runco (Eds.), *Encyclopedia of creativity* (pp. 617–623). Academic Press. https://doi.org/10.1016/B978-0-12-809324-5.21897-X

Johnson, J. (2019). *Seeing through the world: Jean Gebser and integral consciousness*. Revelore Press.

Johnstone, B., Yoon, D. P., Cohen, D., Schopp, L. H., McCormack, G., Campbell, J., & Smith, M. (2012). Relationships among spirituality, religious practices, personality factors, and health for five different faith traditions. *Journal of Religion and Health, 51*(4), 1017–1041. https://doi.org/10.1007/s10943-012-9615-8

Jung, C. (2019). *Memories, dreams, reflections*. William Collins.

Keener-Wink, J. (1993). Shedding the snakeskin: Movement, art, and spirituality. *Women's Studies Quarterly, 21*(1–2), 159.

Kelly, V. (2006). *The arts as catalyst, catharsis, and crucible: Towards a personal philosophy of art* (Doctoral dissertation). https://www.proquest.com/docview/304928739/fulltextPDF/C0BD71D9EAE841CBPQ/1?accountid=34120

King's College London. (2016). *Playing & reality: Winnicott, creativity and play*. https://youtu.be/y5B-TSXe81Y

Krippner, S. (2020). Altered and transitional states. In S. Pritzker & M. Runco (Eds.), *Encyclopedia of creativity* (pp. 29–36). Academic Press. https://doi.org/10.1016/B978-0-12-809324-5.23620-1

Krippner, S., & Murphy, G. (1973). Humanistic psychology and parapsychology. *The Journal of Humanistic Psychology, 13*(4), 3–24. https://doi.org/10.1177/002216787301300402

Leffel, G. M. (2011). Beyond meaning: Spiritual transformation in the paradigm of moral intuitionism. A new direction for the psychology of spiritual transformation. In R. L. Piedmont & A. Village (Eds.), *Research in the social scientific study of religion, volume 22* (pp. 25–125). Brill. https://doi.org/10.1163/ej.9789004207271.i-360.14

Lips-Wiersma, M., & Morris, L. (2009). Discriminating between 'meaningful work' and the 'management of meaning.' *Journal of Business Ethics, 88*(3), 491–511. https://doi.org/10.1007/s10551-009-0118-9

Lips-Wiersma, M., & Morris, L. (2018). *The map of meaningful work: A practical guide to sustaining our humanity* (2nd ed.). Routledge. https://doi.org/10.4324/9781351252065

Maheshwari, A. K. (2021). Higher consciousness management: Transcendence for spontaneous right action. *Journal of Management, Spirituality & Religion, 18*(6), 77–91. https://doi.org/10.51327/CRNG6977

Martela, F., & Pessi, A. B. (2018). Significant work is about self-realization and broader purpose: Defining the key dimensions of meaningful work. *Frontiers in Psychology, 9*, 363. https://doi.org/10.3389/fpsyg.2018.00363

Martin, D. R. (2007). *Can spirituality help individuals discover ideas that creatively resolve their personal problems?* (Doctoral dissertation). https://www.proquest.com/docview/304702634/fulltextPDF/3407225B25A54AB7PQ/1?accountid=34120

Maslow, A. (1962a). *Toward a psychology of being*. D Van Nostrand. https://doi.org/10.1037/10793-000

Maslow, A. H. (1971a). *The farther reaches of human nature*. Viking Press.

Maslow, A. H. (1962b). *Creativity in self-actualizing people*. Princeton. https://doi.org/10.1037/10793-010

Maslow, A. H. (1971b). *Self-actualization*. Psychotherapy Tape Library.

May, R. (1994). *The courage to create*. W. W. Norton.

Miller, M. E., & Cook-Greuter, S. R. (1994). *Transcendence and mature thought in adulthood: The further reaches of adult development*. Rowman & Littlefield.

Miller-Perrin, C., & Krumrei Mancuso, E. (2015). *Faith from a positive psychology perspective* (1st ed.). Springer Netherlands. https://doi.org/10.1007/978-94-017-9436-7

Misiak, H., & Sexton, V. S. (1973). *Phenomenological, existential, and humanistic psychologies: A historical survey*. Grune & Stratton.

Mitra, R., & Buzzanell, P. M. (2017). Communicative tensions of meaningful work: The case of sustainability practitioners. *Human Relations (New York), 70*(5), 594–616. https://doi.org/10.1177/0018726716663288

Mumford, M. D., & Gustafson, S. B. (1988). Creativity syndrome: Integration, application, and innovation. *Psychological Bulletin, 103*(1), 27–43. https://doi.org/10.1037/0033-2909.103.1.27

Northcott, V. D. (2005). *Dialogues and inter-facings: Spirituality and arts-based educational research* (Doctoral dissertation). https://www.proquest.com/docview/305366319/fulltextPDF/52BE6F3E606549AFPQ/1?accountid=34120

Nusholtz, J. E. (2004). *Writing for transformation: Fiction and consciousness. A novella and contextual essay/process journal* (Doctoral dissertation). https://www.proquest.com/docview/305050734/fulltextPDF/57A3957B1AE9460FPQ/1?accountid=34120

Paloutzian, R. F., & Park, C. L. (2021). The psychology of religion and spirituality: How big the tent? *Psychology of Religion and Spirituality, 13*(1), 3–13. https://doi.org/10.1037/rel0000218

Pryce-Jones, J. (2010). *Happiness at work: Maximizing your psychological capital for success*. Wiley-Blackwell. https://doi.org/10.1002/9780470666845

Raney, A., Cox, D., & Jones, R. P. (2017). *Searching for spirituality in the U.S.: A new look at the spiritual but not religious*. Public Religion Research Institute. https://www.prri.org/research/religiosity-and-spirituality-in-america/

Rank, O. (1978). *Will therapy*. Norton.

Rank, O. (2012). *Beyond psychology*. Dover Publications.

Rayton, B., Yalabik, Z. Y., & Rapti, A. (2019). Fit perceptions, work engagement, satisfaction and commitment. *Journal of Managerial Psychology, 34*(6), 401–414. https://doi.org/10.1108/JMP-02-2018-0074

Rhodes, M. (1961). An analysis of creativity. *The Phi Delta Kappan, 42*(7), 305–310. http://www.jstor.org/stable/20342603

Richards, R. (2018). *Everyday creativity and the healthy mind*. Palgrave Macmillan. https://doi.org/10.1057/978-1-137-55766-7
Roehlkepartain, E. C., Benson, P. L., Ebstyne King, P., & Wagener, L. M. (2006). Spiritual development in childhood and adolescence: Moving to the scientific mainstream. In E. C. Roehlkepartain, P. Ebstyne King, L. Wagener, & P. L. Benson (Eds.), *The handbook of spiritual development in childhood and adolescence* (pp. 1–16). Sage. https://doi.org/10.4135/9781412976657.n1
Rogers, N. (1993). *The creative connection: Expressive arts as healing*. Science & Behavior Books Inc.
Rosso, B. D., Dekas, K. H., & Wrzesniewski, A. (2010). On the meaning of work: A theoretical integration and review. *Research in Organizational Behavior, 30*, 91–127. https://doi.org/10.1016/j.riob.2010.09.001
Rubenfeld, F. (2009). Gestalt Creativity. *Gestalt Review, 13*(2), 125–128. https://doi.org/10.5325/gestaltreview.13.2.0125
Runco, M. A., & Jaeger, G. J. (2012). The standard definition of creativity. *Creativity Research Journal, 24*(1), 92–96. https://doi.org/10.1080/10400419.2012.650092
Russ, S. W. (2020). Emotion/affect. In S. Pritzker & M. Runco (Eds.), *Encyclopedia of creativity* (pp. 427–433). Academic Press. https://doi.org/10.1016/B978-0-12-809324-5.21215-7
Sakaue-Rowan, K. (1991). *Art as personal therapy: A pathway toward self-discovery and development* (Master's thesis). https://www.proquest.com/pqdtglobal/docview/303983251/9B6DE48C006C4358PQ/1?accountid=34120
Saucier, G., & Skrzypińska, K. (2006). Spiritual but not religious? Evidence for two independent dispositions. *Journal of Personality, 74*(5), 1257–1292. https://doi.org/10.1111/j.1467-6494.2006.00409.x
Schmidt, V. V. (1995). *Awakening intuition: A Delphi study* (Doctoral dissertation). https://www.proquest.com/docview/304231930/fulltextPDF/B8CC6496D51D4C0DPQ/1?accountid=34120
Schneider, K. J. (2015). Rediscovering awe: A new front in humanistic psychology, psychotherapy, and society. In K. J. Schneider, J. F. Pierson, & J. F. T. Bugental (Eds.), *The handbook of humanistic psychology theory, research, and practice* (2nd ed., pp. 73–81). Sage. https://doi.org/10.4135/9781483387864.n6
Schutte, N. S., & Malouff, J. M. (2020). Connections between curiosity, flow and creativity. *Personality and Individual Differences, 152*, 109555. https://doi.org/10.1016/j.paid.2019.109555
Scott, K. S. (2022). Making sense of work: Finding meaning in work narratives. *Journal of Management & Organization, 28*(5), 1057–1077. https://doi.org/10.1017/jmo.2019.43
Shafranske, E. P., & Gorsuch, R. L. (1984). Factors associated with the perception of spirituality in psychotherapy. *Journal of Transpersonal Psychology, 16*(2), 231–241.
Sheridan-Rabideau, M. (2010). Creativity repositioned. *Arts Education Policy Review, 111*(2), 54–58. https://doi.org/10.1080/10632910903455876
Sinha, J. W., & Rosenberg, L. B. (2013). A critical review of trauma interventions and religion among youth exposed to community violence. *Journal of Social Service Research, 39*(4), 436–454. https://doi.org/10.1080/01488376.2012.730907
Skrzypińska, K. (2018). Existential health concept in a light of the threefold nature of spirituality (TNS) model. In A. Anczyk, H. Grzymała-Moszczyńska, A. Krzysztof-Świderska, & K. Skrzypińska (Eds.), *Religion, spirituality, mental health:*

Current approaches in the psychology of religion (pp. 27–38). https://www.researchg ate.net/profile/Katarzyna-Skrzypinska/publication/318684874_Existential_health_ concept_in_a_light_of_the_Threefold_Nature_of_Spirituality_TNS_model/links/ 5be9e4534585150b2bb2396d/Existential-health-concept-in-a-light-of-the-Threef old-Nature-of-Spirituality-TNS-model.pdf

Sonnenburg, S., & Primus, D. J. (2020). Flow. In S. Pritzker & M. Runco (Eds.), *Encyclopedia of creativity* (pp. 510–515). Academic Press. https://doi.org/10.1016/B978-0-12-809324-5.23754-1

Sperry, L. (2012). Spiritually sensitive psychotherapy: An impending paradigm shift in theory and practice. *Oxford University Press.* https://doi.org/10.1093/oxfordhb/9780199729920.013.0015

Steensland, B., Wang, X., & Schmidt, L. C. (2018). Spirituality: What does it mean and to whom? *Journal for the Scientific Study of Religion, 57*(3), 450–472. https://doi.org/10.1111/jssr.12534

Stein, M. I. (1953). Creativity and culture. *The Journal of Psychology, 36*(2), 311–322. https://doi.org/10.1080/00223980.1953.9712897

Suissa, D. (2019). A journey of transformation: A lived experience of students of an online postgraduate program in transpersonal psychology. *Journal of Transformative Learning, 3*.

Sullivan, H. S. (1953). *The interpersonal theory of psychiatry*. W. W. Norton.

Sutin, A. R., Stephan, Y., Luchetti, M., Aschwanden, D., Lee, J. H., Sesker, A. A., & Terracciano, A. (2022). Differential personality change earlier and later in the coronavirus pandemic in a longitudinal sample of adults in the United States. *PLoS ONE, 17*(9), e0274542. https://doi.org/10.1371/journal.pone.0274542

Terkel, S. (1974). *Working: People talk about what they do all day and how they feel about what they do*. The New Press.

Thompson, N. A. (2018). Imagination and creativity in organizations. *Organization Studies, 39*(2–3), 229–250. https://doi.org/10.1177/0170840617736939

U.S. Bureau of Labor Statistics. (n.d.a). *National longitudinal surveys: NLSY79 percent of weeks employed from age 18 to age 54 in 1978–2018 by educational attainment, race, and Hispanic or Latino ethnicity.* https://www.bls.gov/nls/graphics/news-releases/nlsy79-percent-employed-ages-18-54.htm

U.S. Bureau of Labor Statistics. (n.d.b). *National longitudinal surveys: NLSY97: Percent of weeks employed from age 18 to age 34 in 1998–2019, by educational attainment, race, and Hispanic or Latino ethnicity.* https://www.bls.gov/nls/graphics/news-releases/nlsy97-percent-employed-ages-18-34.htm

Ver, J. M. (2004). *Transpersonal creativity: The alchemy of Indigenous art and craft* (Doctoral dissertation). https://www.proquest.com/docview/305049453/fulltextPDF/3712ED4AFF05495EPQ/1?accountid=34120

Walsh, R., & Vaughan, F. (1993). The art of transcendence: An introduction to common elements of transpersonal practices. *Journal of Transpersonal Psychology, 25*(1), 1–9.

Weeks, K. P., & Schaffert, C. (2019). Generational differences in definitions of meaningful work: A mixed methods study. *Journal of Business Ethics, 156*(4), 1045–1061. https://doi.org/10.1007/s10551-017-3621-4

Wilber, K. (1998). *The essential Ken Wilber*. Shambhala Publications.

Yeoman, R. (2014). Conceptualising meaningful work as a fundamental human need. *Journal of Business Ethics, 125*(2), 235–251. https://doi.org/10.1007/s10551-013-1894-9

Zinnbauer, B. J., Pargament, K. I., Cole, B., Rye, M. S., Butter, E. M., Belavich, T. G., Hipp, K. M., Scott, A. B., & Kadar, J. L. (1997). Religion and spirituality: Unfuzzying the fuzzy. *Journal for the Scientific Study of Religion, 36*(4), 549–564. https://doi.org/10.2307/1387689

Zinnbauer, B. J., Pargament, K. I., & Scott, A. B. (1999). The emerging meanings of religiousness and spirituality: Problems and prospects. *Journal of Personality, 67*(6), 889–919. https://doi.org/10.1111/1467-6494.00077

CHAPTER 11

Embracing Inclusive Leadership for Collaborative Healthcare Work Environments: Fostering Wellness in Ambivalent Situations

Aikaterini Grimani and George Gotsis

INTRODUCTION

Workplace inclusion is a multi-layered construct. Prime et al. (2020) identify the multi-dimensional nature of this concept. *First and foremost*, inclusion is person-centred, substantiated in our relationships with others; thus, inclusive leadership is grounded in adaptiveness and flexibility. *Second*, inclusion is multi-layered and systemic, presupposing skills and practices pertinent to inclusive leaders. *Third*, inclusion involves intrapersonal attributes, based on the self-awareness of inclusive leaders. *Finally*, inclusion is balancing organizational paradoxes, incorporating apparently contradictory elements and as such, it necessitates a capacity for complexity and for harmonizing distinct, sometimes opposing, mindsets and practices.

Al-Omoush et al. (2022) posit that collaborative endeavours significantly affect organizational sustainability, mainly through developing new knowledge through collaborative innovation which in turn promotes sustainability in these unprecedented situations. Their findings confirmed that social capital, which generates bonds of trust, commitment, and cohesiveness within business environments, plays a pivotal role in improving productivity, increasing

---

A. Grimani (✉)
Warwick Business School, University of Warwick, Coventry, UK
e-mail: grimaniaik@phs.uoa.gr

G. Gotsis
Department of History and Philosophy of Science, National and Kapodistrian University of Athens, Athens, Greece

© The Author(s), under exclusive license to Springer Nature Switzerland AG 2023
J. Marques (ed.), *The Palgrave Handbook of Fulfillment, Wellness, and Personal Growth at Work*,
https://doi.org/10.1007/978-3-031-35494-6_11

profitability, and enhancing corporate reputation during such unprecedented crises. Beyond corporate entities, the healthcare environment is increasingly becoming more complex; thus, healthcare organizations are in need for seeking exceptional leaders. Leaders whose abilities have been so far relied on enacting top-down directives in conformity to rigid control mechanisms, have been proved quite ineffective in addressing unpredictable challenges. Concomitantly, different skills are now required for enhanced performance and growth of healthcare organizations. More specifically, in the aftermath of the COVID-19 pandemic, the cultivation of such new competencies is elevated to a core organizational imperative.

Inclusive health care seeks to meet the needs of underprivileged groups in the provision of high-quality, accessible healthcare services employing various innovative approaches. However, inclusive health care should be viewed as a rather non-linear, adaptable process intended to align the organizational functions and leadership with the ideal conditions for adoption, advocacy, and sustainability of innovative and collaborative efforts in each unique context. Whelehan et al. (2021) contend that to cope with occupational fatigue, transformational leadership remains a valuable resource that ensures work engagement in terms of vigour, dedication, and absorption. Jha (2021) elaborates a functional leadership model of practice during pandemic crisis that is expected to realize effective patient outcomes, develop a compassionate organizational culture, and enhance professional satisfaction within healthcare teams. Visionary leaders can undoubtedly realize this substantial paradigm shift, given that healthcare institutions need to make fundamental transformations in their operating methods to navigate through these unpredictable situations. Leadership style, organizational culture and successful implementation are inextricable parts of sustainable interventions to support healthcare workers' well-being (Crain et al., 2021; Obrien et al., 2021). Leading with compassion and authenticity is paramount to improved quality of health care, acting jointly with organizational collaborations to meet novel challenges (Graham & Woodhead, 2021).

This study is intended to demonstrate the importance of leader inclusiveness as a core competence required by healthcare leaders who seek to be more resilient, innovative, adaptive to new circumstances, and inspiring collaborative mindsets across teams, departments, and organizations. The aim of this chapter is to elaborate on inclusive leadership as a construct invested with a strong potential to promote humane, compassionate, and collaborative organizations. Inclusive leadership is primarily rooted in the primary human need for both belongingness and uniqueness, and as such is highly respectful of social identities and personal beliefs and commitments.

The present study is intended to expand on this perspective by providing a tentative framework of assessing the role of leader inclusiveness in informing collaborative healthcare work environments in times in which the intrinsic worthiness of the human person is highly at stake. Inclusive leaders envisage a more collaborative and participative workplace, so much needed in healthcare sector in times of unprecedented public health crisis. In so doing, inclusive leaders have an innate potential to enhance positive perceptions of medical staff, by making them experience feelings of wellness, personal growth, and self-fulfilment in accomplishing their occupational tasks. Emphasis is placed upon inclusiveness practices that mitigate social disadvantage, alleviate human suffering, and make patients feel that they are appreciated and valued in a state of vulnerability. Inclusive leadership embodies a major shift in healthcare leadership styles towards a more collaborative, humane, and compassionate work environment, especially in a post-COVID ambiguous reality.

Collaborative Leadership in Health Care

Collaboration thrives in synergistic work environments in which multiple parties work together based on shared healthcare management practices and processes. Collaboration facilitates a deeper understanding of distinct cultures, promotes social integration and interdependencies by fostering shared vision, values, and organizational objectives. Shaping collaborative environments presupposes nurturing collaborative leadership, a unique style of leadership perceived as a transformation leadership style, not so much frequently employed within a healthcare setting. By designing and implementing collaborative practices, leaders can elaborate upon diverging ideas, goals, and objectives arising from a rich diversity of employee perspectives. Leaders are thus bearing the responsibility for accommodating a variety of stakeholder interests to yield positive and constructive outcomes through renegotiating power relations and fostering collaborative partnerships among health organizations (Dickinson et al., 2022; Griewatz et al., 2020; Nyström & Strehlenert, 2021; VanVactor, 2012).

Collaborative leadership strategies should be employed by healthcare leaders to ensure that patients enjoy enhanced access to healthcare services. Okpala (2020) focused on determining the impact of collaborative leadership skills on patients' access to quality healthcare services. The study demonstrated that different collaborative leadership initiatives can affect the factors that determine individual access to quality healthcare services. Moreover, healthcare leaders should facilitate the adoption of patient-centred inter-organizational collaboration strategies to effectively manage healthcare costs, such cost-reduction effectiveness not being secured to the detriment of enhanced healthcare quality delivery (Okpala, 2018; Wang, 2018).

Okpala (2019) suggests that healthcare managers should act jointly with other stakeholders in developing enhanced disease awareness, increased disease screening, and team-based self-management to cope with the negative consequences of chronic health conditions. Accordingly, appropriate collaborative leadership approaches pursued by healthcare managers are highly beneficial to alleviate the detrimental effects of chronic diseases to patients' overall well-being. Orchard et al. (2017a) demonstrated that nurse leaders displayed a capacity to influence integration of inter-professional collaborative practices with other health professionals within their leadership areas. In so doing, they employed strategies that advocated for a change in the very meaning of nursing leadership, this resulting in a substantial shift from task orientation to an individualized and comprehensive patient-focused care (Orchard et al., 2017b). Collaborative leadership initiatives have been also suggested as ensuring healthcare providers' commitment to a culture of psychological safety (MacPhee et al., 2009).

Shu and Wang (2021) investigated the mechanisms through which collaborative leadership enhanced collective action in community governance in an area located near Wuhan during the COVID-19 pandemic. Their findings showed that collaborative leadership was able to prevent internal diffusion and eliminate spread of public panic by effectively integrating local knowledge, employing modern information technologies as well as promoting the realization of collective action aiming at epidemic prevention and control. In respective importance, collaborative leadership was found to initiate constructive responses to emergencies based on shared understanding, trust building, commitment to process, institutional design, conflict resolution, empowerment, system context, and allocation priorities, all of which enabled collective multi-stakeholder engagements for sustainable solutions in the face of extreme adversity (Agbodzakey, 2021).

Collaborative leadership is thus supportive of healthy work environments and best practices to achieve desirable outcomes. Shirey et al. (2019) claimed that high-performing inter-professional collaborative practices were contingent upon compassionate, authentic leaders who were devoted to helping their teams thrive amidst complexity. Grandy and Holton (2013) explored the possibility of a collaborative approach to leadership development programmes involving the need for encouraging collaborative leadership, the role of partnerships in leadership development, and the specific need for proper mentoring and coaching. This endeavour necessitates leadership development processes akin to determining the competences required to secure desired and sustainable change (Macphee et al., 2014). North (2020) demonstrated that local health systems need entry-level clinicians who possess excellent non-technical abilities to contribute to collaborative practice outcomes, as well as specific competencies for an enhanced performance assessment. More specifically, adoption of collaborative leadership by decision and policymakers involving in ameliorating integrated health care, is highly contingent upon contextual factors that collaborative and participatory leadership structures need to take into due consideration (Sibbald et al., 2021).

Inclusive Leadership

Inclusive leadership emphasizes that everyone matters, thus, employees feel that they have equal opportunity to contribute to the change process (Younas et al., 2021). In the extant literature, we can identify multiple definitions of leader inclusiveness. Carmeli et al. (2010) defined inclusive leadership as "leaders who exhibit visibility, accessibility, and availability in their interactions with followers" (p. 250). Nembhard and Edmondson (2006) defined inclusive leadership as "words and deeds by a leader or leaders that indicate an invitation and appreciation for others' contributions" (p. 947). According to Booysen (2014), inclusive leadership is "an ongoing cycle of learning through collaborative and respectful relational practice that enables individuals and collectives to be fully part of the whole, such that they are directed, aligned, and committed toward shared outcomes, for the common good of all, while retaining a sense of authenticity and uniqueness" (p. 306).

Nishii and Leroy (2020) define inclusive leadership as a set of leader behaviours that shape inclusive climates. They in turn argue that inclusive leadership involves the emergence of shared motivation, norms, and accountability structures that clarify for the precise meaning of inclusion for employees, enumerate the potential benefits from inclusion as well as the employee attitudes needed for co-creating their own and others' experiences of inclusion. Inclusive leadership is processual, shared and distributed throughout the organizational system. Responsible inclusive leaders should cultivate high-quality interactions, re-examine dominant practices, and avoid adopting a binary "either/or perspective". Accordingly, responsible inclusive leadership originates in a joint collective relational practice dispersed throughout the entire organizational system, permeating strategy, structure, culture, systems, and processes (Booysen, 2020).

Furthermore, inclusive leadership refers to behaviours that collectively facilitate group members' perceptions of belongingness to the work group and that encourage group members contributing their uniqueness to achieving positive group outcomes. Such behaviours could be the following: supporting individuals as group members, ensuring justice and equity within the group, promoting individuals' diverse contributions to the group, helping followers fully provide their unique perspectives and abilities to the workgroup (Randel et al., 2018). Inferentially, inclusive leadership has minimal overlap with existing conceptualizations of leadership and the core tenets of inclusive leadership are not fully captured by other leadership styles (Gotsis & Grimani, 2016).

Veli Korkmaz et al. (2022) propose a multilevel model of inclusive leadership behaviour consisting of four dimensions. The first dimension is related to fostering employee's uniqueness, such as promoting diversity, supporting employees as individuals, empowering employees, employees, employee's learning and development. The second dimension of inclusive leadership refers to the strengthening of belongingness within a team by ensuring equity, building relationships, and sharing decision-making. The dimension of showing appreciation refers to leaders' reaction to recognize efforts and contributions attained either by individuals themselves or by the team. The fourth dimension of inclusive leadership is related to supporting organizational efforts by promoting organizational mission on inclusion and being open to organizational change.

Inclusive leadership has not received due attention, while there is a lack of agreement about what it involves and how it should be measured. In the extant body of research on leader inclusiveness, evidence has shown a positive relationship between inclusive leadership and employee perceptions of psychological safety, which in turn predicted employees' creativity. Empirical work has also revealed that inclusive leadership is positively related to unit performance, innovative work behaviour through psychological empowerment, and change-oriented organizational citizenship behaviour via behavioural integrity and trust in leadership. Inclusive leaders also exhibit attributes such as openness, availability, and accessibility (Choi et al., 2017; Javed et al., 2019; Randel et al., 2016; Shore et al., 2018).

There are individual characteristics, such as pro-diversity beliefs, humility, and cognitive complexity, which have the potential to increase an individual's propensity to engage in inclusive leadership behaviours. Inclusion, such as belongingness and uniqueness, have a positive impact on work group identification and psychological empowerment, which in turn should lead to positive behavioural outcomes (Ashikali et al., 2021; Gotsis & Grimani, 2017). Moreover, inclusion climate as a corollary of genuine inclusive leaders is shaped not only by the shared experiences of group members but also by their unique identities (Mor Barak et al., 2022). Leader inclusion is invaluable especially for employees with marginalized social identities because of the emergence of psychological mechanisms beneficial to vulnerable groups. These psychological mechanisms accompanying experiences of inclusion consist of psychological safety, psychological empowerment, and work group identification (Shore & Chung, 2022a). Inclusive leadership encourages an inclusive climate in ethnic and cultural diverse teams, so much needed to manage affective responses ensuing from social categorization processes. Inclusive leadership is a prerequisite for diverse teams to shape an inclusive climate in which different team members are valued for their unique contribution to work practices.

Researchers have consistently demonstrated that simply having diversity on a team alone does not automatically lead to desired outcomes of greater productivity or creative thinking (Booysen, 2014). In an inclusive culture where employees experienced high support from their leadership, employees challenged the current situation by showing innovative work behaviour. Inclusive leadership is a more powerful and relevant conducive leadership style for employees' ideation, promotion, and implementation (Carmeli et al., 2010). Inclusive leadership has also been found to significantly affect psychological well-being of older workers, acting jointly with mature-age HR practices (Teo et al., 2022).

Inclusive leadership is an important situational factor that plays a significant role in fostering change-oriented organizational citizenship behaviour. Inclusive leaders practice fairness regarding employee needs, communicate openly, and develop constructive relations with subordinates. For instance, managers should take the responsibility for failures instead of blaming employees to prevent employees from under-performing in the future. In addition, managers should exhibit acts of kindness and empathy towards their employees, while employees should be given constructive feedback, which will ensure enhanced productivity and commitment. Managers should elicit trust by initiating quality relationships based on mutual obligation, the maintenance of long-term relationships, higher level of confidence, and open communication. Furthermore, inclusive leaders share their power with followers, so that the latter perceive that leadership has faith in their abilities, which in turn promotes trust in leadership (Javed, et al., 2019; Younas et al., 2021). Encouraging inclusive leadership behaviours holds promise for improving the work experience of all members and the effectiveness of their groups and organizations.

Inclusive Leadership and Collaboration in Health Care

Inclusive leadership remains an invaluable resource in ameliorating healthcare quality services. Kalina (2020) claims that in those unprecedented times of global health crisis, healthcare leaders are in need to focus on their vision, fully adhering to their organization's mission, culture, and core values. Healthcare workers can thus experience a feeling that meaningful participation-can save lives. This can happen only when leaders display the capacity to embrace staff across hierarchies and accommodate personal identities so that healthcare staff will be able to engage in improvement efforts of services' quality. Inclusive leaders are expected to encourage authentic participation of healthcare personnel by employing constructive patterns of managing work and occupational tensions, thus positively affecting healthcare outcomes (Bradley, 2020). Ahmed et al. (2021) found that inclusive leadership can promote coping mechanisms that improve the psychological safety of employees in the long run, thus significantly reducing psychological distress. Leader inclusiveness is also deemed beneficial in more rigid environments in which offering suggestions, raising concerns, reporting errors, or even disagreeing with those in more senior positions is discouraged as ethically and culturally inappropriate behaviour (Lee & Dahinten, 2021).

Uman et al. (2022) suggest that emphasizing differences and similarities, culture-related tensions within the team can be reduced. In addition, work groups appear to become more cohesive in environments that meaningful interactions are stimulated, resulting in more effective team functioning, conflicts and misunderstandings reduction, and increased team ability to focus on patients' needs rather than on team dynamics. Furthermore, establishing engagement structures in the team, based on leaders' ability to communicate clear expectations, is an important facilitator of well-functioning teams in the workplace.

Inclusive leadership can undoubtedly mitigate employees' concerns through shaping such a psychologically safe work environment in pandemic crisis (Zhao et al., 2020). The delivery of high-quality, compassionate care still remains an imperative for healthcare systems, an endeavour that necessitates more humane, compassionate, and inclusive leadership as a prerequisite to foster an inclusiveness culture in healthcare settings (Edwards et al., 2018). Inclusive leaders employ the most effective strategies to foster collaborative, collective, and inclusive attitudes that facilitate staff engagement, the rise of proficient practitioners, and the articulation of a clear vision for collaborative practice. In terms of physician associates, such an approach will improve substantially collaborative practice and create the supportive, motivated environment needed to facilitate the recruitment of physician associates (Edwards & Till, 2019).

Inclusive leadership is invested with a unique potential in informing synergistic and collaborative practices. As already indicated, inclusive leadership requires practising self-awareness, articulating a shared vision, building relationships, and creating change (Barton, 2021). Read et al. (2016) employ a framework of inclusive leadership intended to nurture social change in nursing environments. Nurse educators can adopt a social change model insofar as it is able to promote equity, social justice, self-knowledge, service, and collaboration. Such a framework is extremely helpful to students who seem not to be adequately experienced with, but display a sense of commitment to change that can be cultivated by leadership development programmes intended to promote health equity through a set of best practices. Pyo (2020) employed collaborative team approach intervention akin to occupational therapists in inclusive environments. The study underscored the beneficial effects of the implementation of collaborative team intervention in inclusive environments, as well as the need for supporting such initiatives and addressing factors that could impede such an endeavour.

Inclusion consists of collaborative work arrangements and conflict resolution procedures designed to involve employees of marginalized groups in organizational processes, thus requiring multilevel synergy and collaboration (Roberson, 2006). Belongingness and inclusiveness can inform collaborative and participative practices required to achieve positive transformational effects (Bryer, 2020). Inclusive leadership embodies rationales for promoting the common good and creating a positive and collaborative organizational culture (Ketikidou & Saiti, 2022). DeMatthews (2021) identified a set of leadership practices critical to shaping inclusive organizations. These practices comprised the construction of a culture of change-oriented collaboration, collaborative inquiry, evaluating, building capacity, and seeking for effective plans.

A stream of literature elaborates upon these challenges and explores how leader skills and competencies can address issues of vulnerability and integrity (e.g. Wasserman, 2020) Inclusive leadership is grounded in leaders' beliefs about inalienable human dignity, personalized connectedness, and individualized development that influence critical components of psychological empowerment (self-worth, self-competency, self-determination and shared meaning) of the more vulnerable group members. More specifically, leaders' beliefs about dignity as a stimulus for a capability approach centred on personal connectedness fostered subordinates' perceptions of their *self-worth*; reflecting core competencies such as self-confidence and self-mastery. This empowering perspective triggered employees' sense of shared meaning, so as to achieve their desired objectives (Fujimoto & Uddin, 2021). Worthy to mention is the entwinement between leader inclusiveness and sustainability in the sphere of organizational behaviour (Fang et al., 2021) in an effort to remove barriers to inclusion at micro (individual), meso (relational), and macro (institutional) levels (Shyamsunder, 2020). Inclusive leadership is in a position to advance an inclusive society insofar as this leadership style is expected to enable equity, diversity, and inclusion in organizations, local communities, and society in general (Meehan, 2020).

Equally importantly, Swaffield and Major (2019) specified a number of inclusive strategies intended to foster collaboration in educational settings. Such strategies were imbued by core co-operative values such as democratic participation, solidarity, equality, equity, self-help, and self-responsibility. Gardiner and MacLellan (2021) found that a process of adaptation and resilience through collaborative teamwork, a strong sense of purpose, and role validation of nursing staff during the COVID-19 pandemic in the UK, was enabled by an inclusive leadership style. Patterson (2020) indicated the importance of developing inclusive and collaborative business spaces that ensure progression. This necessitates a change of focus, from the micro to the macro level of organizational change to enable inclusion as an integral part of the processes and outcomes of such collaborative spaces. Inclusive leadership offers followers invaluable support that facilitates proper functioning and enhanced performance in healthcare teams, manifest in efficient responses to unprecedented challenges.

Discussion

Contribution and Implications for Wellness Research

Inclusive leadership is intrinsically participative and as such, it encourages collaboration even in difficult situations, in the case of entirely diverse work groups. Inclusive leadership encourages team members to contribute to decision-making, thus engendering team cohesion, collaborative mindsets, information sharing and ultimately team effectiveness (Minehart et al., 2020). van Knippenberg and van Ginkel (2022) integrate insights from two complementary perspectives on diversity leadership, inclusive leadership, and leadership for diversity mindsets in view of targeting extant asymmetries on inclusion of marginalized groups. They thus advance a comprehensive view on how leadership is expected to mitigate strict demarcations originating in different identity groups, by stimulating both inclusion and synergy from diversity, thus capitalizing on synergistic benefits and outcomes due to diverse team members. High inclusive leadership combined with prevention of social exclusion is expected to entail more positive and mitigate negative employee outcomes (Shore & Chung, 2022b).

Inclusion-based collaborative outcomes are highly beneficial at the group, organizational, and societal levels, insofar as inclusive leaders foster an inclusiveness climate that facilitates information sharing, constructive exchange of diverse opinions and ideas, mutual understanding, as well as collaborative processes that enhance group and organizational efficiency. Our findings are consistent with those of Roberson and Perry (2022) according to which inclusive leadership encourages a shared identity and a sense of collaboration. Collaboration stems from a type of relational leadership that prioritizes relating to, and showing a genuine interest in, other team members.

The COVID-19 pandemic has shed light to a set of critical deficiencies in the healthcare sector regarding infection control, communication, and supportive care provision. Runacres et al. (2022) introduced a collaborative model that was both reactive and proactive in caring for several residents at different stages of COVID-19 infection. This innovative model of integrating high-quality services through the utilization of telehealth platforms, allowed for the provision of individualized care, as well as for invaluable interaction with our beloved ones in these unprecedented times. Inclusive leadership generates such behaviours that affirm team and organizational diversity through proper responses to individual needs, as well as by allowing spaces for constructive employee voice. Healthcare organizations may substantially benefit from such environments in which members share and build upon others' perspectives, thus leaders should create spaces for leveraging individual contributions to decision-making process, even when certain suggestions tend to diverge from established norms.

Inclusive leadership elicits best performance of team members, thus realizing the full potential of inter-professional teams to provide enhanced quality care for patients. Luu (2019) found that disability inclusive HR practices were strengthening the effects of benevolent leadership on job and personal resources. Moreover, inclusive leaders suggest coping mechanisms to address unpredictable challenges and secure effective procedures of conflict resolution, thus mitigating tensions that threaten collaborative dynamic. Beyond organizational level, collaborative outcomes are manifest in the inter-organizational and societal levels because of the participative potential with which inclusive leadership is invested. Kegler et al. (2019) offer permeating insights into the challenges of collaborating in view of advancing health equity through inclusive processes and shared goals to unravel social determinants of health. Beyond typical multi-sectoral coalitions, community organizing and building resident power are strategies intended to reduce health inequities through community collaboration.

In the case of healthcare organizations, inclusive leaders promote collaborative outcomes across teams, groups, and departments. This positive dimension of leader inclusiveness is entrenched in the leader competency of openness to others that ensures constructive dialogue and reduces the possibility of rigid decision-making processes. Health professionals, nurses, and patients appear highly benefited from this inclusive climate that is respectful of otherness and accepts human person in its wholeness.

In this respect, the two principal dimensions of inclusive leadership, its ability to address both needs for belongingness in a health team and uniqueness of each individual contribution to attaining positive results, are highly related to collaboration synergies, without which the effort of both staff and patients would appear as totally fragmented, thus subverting individual contribution to overall well-being. There is new evidence that collaborative governance and distributive leadership can provide an effective framework for benefiting from new opportunities for collaboration and innovation through transformative learning and empowered participation (Lindsay et al., 2021). This is of the utmost importance in public emergencies in which policymakers seek to cope with public health crisis such as COVID-19, as well as with the major economic and labour market crisis that this pandemic engenders.

Affirming the contribution of each member to providing higher quality of healthcare leadership is intertwined with inclusive leadership that alleviates human vulnerability and mitigates social disadvantage. In addition, social exclusion evidenced in pandemic times is reduced through leader inclusiveness which fosters multilevel cooperation with health agencies, government officials, and authority structures, so much needed in these unprecedented times of pandemic crisis. Local communities need to leverage their collaborative capacity to capture the needs of the most vulnerable segments of population, by advocating for an equitable and just emergency response for all, in particular for the most afflicted (Azevedo et al., 2022). Inclusive leadership is thus a unique resource in considering voices and experiences of the needy.

Inter-professional health care teams are increasingly urged to cope with complex problems through innovative solutions. Caver and Livers (2021) employ the organizational metaphor of seed and soil to denote, among others, the benefits reaped through inclusive leadership. Inclusive leadership ameliorates team innovation; furthermore, it is required as part of multilevel efforts to improve pandemic preparedness and encourage constructive responses to conflict perils, thus mitigating their gendered impacts (Meagher et al., 2020). Inclusive leadership is strongly supportive of the virtues of compassion and humaneness, without which healthcare organizations would be degenerated into loci of profitable exploitation of the human pain. In such a case, focusing solely on collaborative leadership in health care would appear as no more than an instrumental attempt to manage efficiency in healthcare service delivering, without considering the experience of suffering that accompanies the patients' personal odyssey in stabilizing their health. Humane responses to human pain on the contrary, necessitate a joint type of collaborative and inclusive leadership that stems from our shared humanity to treat others with dignity, as persons deserving of our innate respect.

Implications for Practice and Conclusions

Healthcare systems are increasingly engaging in improving best practices centred on patient experience and narratives of care, general population health, avoiding exorbitant prices for care, and ensuring work-life balance of clinicians. This approach is aligned with management education principles and competencies of health systems science, which revolves around population health, high-quality services, effective leadership, teamwork, collaboration, and systems thinking. In this respect, collaboration and communication between healthcare professionals have been identified as core mechanisms for ensuring quality of patient care. Moreover, implementing resident wellness program can substantially promote well-being and work performance. By engaging in similar initiatives, healthcare institutions can secure a culture of wellness among residents and the greater workforce (Rath et al., 2022).

Lapalme and Doucet (2018) showed the indirect effects of perceived distributive justice, perceived similarity and leader inclusiveness towards agency workers on employees' cooperation behaviours through group identification processes. Inclusive leadership meets medical staff's emotional needs for approval through supportive behaviour, affiliation, and esteem, thus entailing increased commitment and reciprocating behaviours of employees by exhibiting enhanced work engagement. Ahmed et al. (2020) suggest that inclusive leaders should shape more open and engaging environment for nurses that in turn, would facilitate employees' vigour, focus, and work engagement while simultaneously reducing risk of persistent psychological distress. Accordingly, managers of care facilities seeking to foster collaboration among their workforce, should have to create work environments conducive to a more inclusive identity.

The concept of inclusive health focuses on overall well-being, fact that entails equitable, affordable, and efficacious healthcare services. Creating equitable access to mainstream healthcare services and ensuring inclusive responses to healthcare management is deemed an effective means of addressing health disparities, especially in certain indigenous contexts. For instance, Adebisi et al. (2021) comment on the need for more inclusive responses to public health crisis in African contexts, resorting to typical COVID-19 cases. Africa's responses to such emergencies should consider the need for individualized care, with respect to marginalized and vulnerable groups, which face additional barriers to healthcare services. Jayasinghe et al. (2022) suggested certain reasons for the effectiveness of a makeshift collaborative networked hierarchy in public healthcare delivery during the new pandemic that prioritized leadership, creativity, and flexibility. This public endeavour reflected the articulation of new patterns of collaborative working, namely, organizational values, beliefs, and ideas that were consonant to the Sri Lankan public service provision (Uman et al., 2022).

In this respect, inclusive, strategic, and proactive responses to specific societal needs require efforts intended to strengthen the indigenous healthcare systems through overt political commitment, increased funding of healthcare sector, collaboration and cooperation among multiple stakeholders, and inclusive leadership development. An inclusive and diverse public health workforce substantially improve health outcomes, thus public authorities have to encourage policy interventions that promote a diverse and inclusive public health workforce (Böbel, 2021). Kumar et al. (2020) move a step forward by elaborating on a collaborative framework based on AI and the internet of things to address multiple (operational, resource-based, organizational, and external healthcare) challenges faced by medical staff during the epidemic outbreak.

Diverse teams need to avoid a sub-optimal performance to help build more effective organizations in view of optimizing healthcare delivery and value to patients. Inclusive healthcare leadership models should be founded on the principles of equity, efficiency, and person-centred care by considering the needs, preferences, and values of medical staff. Such principles are universally held, dictated by inherent dignity and respect for employees, embodying them into the transmission of information and participation in decision-making, thus enabling respectful and responsible treatment (Ito & Tsutsumi, 2022).

The development of collaborative practices to confront the COVID-19 pandemic is more than necessary, given that the emphasis on communication, interaction, and cooperation is critical to enhance the quality of healthcare services. Such collaborative practices were invaluable to the proper functioning of teams who were facing occupational fatigue, fear of contamination, and internal tensions or conflict. Creating new opportunities for a more holistic leadership development presupposes a transparent, caring, collaborative ethical culture based on empathy, sincerity, and inclusivity, so much needed in these unprecedented times of global pandemic.

Blake (2021) argues that, to build hospital systems and processes that provide more efficient care, as well as ensure healthy work environments, we have to develop: skilled communication, genuine collaboration, effective decision-making, appropriate staffing, authentic leadership, and meaningful recognition. Not unexpectedly, Mete et al. (2022) found that leadership behaviours of physician supervisors have a strong relationship to their team members' burnout, professional fulfilment, and intent to leave. Leaders should thus elaborate on a genuine follower/leader relationship which helps to build a psychological safety climate, by fostering a sense of value, autonomy, mastery, and purpose among followers (Weber et al., 2022). Inclusive leadership can significantly support such positive affective states through psychological safety climates that in turn motivate healthcare employees to display higher levels of creativity (Fu et al., 2022).

Responses to a severe public health crisis involve certain constructive aspects, yet as the pandemic continues, occupational fatigue and frustration among frontline physicians may entail worsening burnout that threatens professional fulfilment (Melnikow et al., 2022). In a longitudinal evaluation of healthcare professionals' wellness during the pandemic, Kerlin et al. (2022)

found that symptoms of burnout and depression increased, whereas personal fulfilment has decreased during the course of the pandemic. To address new challenges related to depression, anxiety, stress, burnout, and professional fulfilment, wellness programmes in health care should focus on sustaining and developing targeted mental health resources that are widely accessible, as well as on employing effective strategies for creating awareness regarding these resources (Kannampallil et al., 2020). Medical staff's wellness must be deemed an important factor in healthcare delivery systems, a need reaffirmed in the aftermath of the COVID-19 pandemic. Fostering inclusive environments devoid of demeaning behaviours is likely to shape a workforce that is intrinsically motivated, seeks resilient well-being, and pursues purpose and meaning, all of which promote thriving and self-fulfilment.

Accordingly, role fulfilment, a sense of shared purpose, collective coping strategies, and preparedness for effective problem-solving, comprise positive and inclusive experiences that nurture wellness in healthcare settings. Liu et al. (2022) lend support to a culturally sensitive, sustainable, and holistic program focusing on shaping compassionate communities of healthcare grounded on strong collaborative leadership, social connectedness and increasing commitment to support the needy throughout the COVID-19 pandemic. Cultivating an inclusive and resilient learning environment that encourages belonging and inclusivity significantly improves staff engagement, motivation, retention, and satisfaction (Dowling et al., 2021; Veli Korkmaz et al., 2022). In addition, a sense of shared mission to promote health equity and wellness provides the symbolic resources that allow for collaborative efforts between clinicians, administration, and stakeholders to improve community well-being.

We are thus in need of inclusive and compassionate leadership styles, consonant to more synergistic and collaborative perspectives to healthcare management (Pelley, 2021). In the post-COVID-19 context, the inclusion of team and organizational resilience to healthcare training interventions designed to optimize the potential of collaboration, could positively influence healthcare professionals' well-being, and support equity issues in healthcare settings (Khalili et al., 2021). Developing conditions supportive of mutually respectful interactions between group members seems to be an essential aspect of actualizing inclusion in healthcare teams. We would thus like to encourage research on inclusive leadership in healthcare organizations, with respect to its potential to foster collaborative behaviours in diverse teams, in such times of unpredictable challenges to healthcare systems. In the absence of leader inclusiveness, collaborative mindsets and attitudes that promote patients and staff's wellness will be less likely to emerge, especially in the case of highly diversified teams and heterogeneous organizational entities.

REFERENCES

Adebisi, Y. A., Ekpenyong, A., Ntacyabukura, B., Lowe, M., Jimoh, N. D., Abdulkareem, T. O., & Lucero-Prisno, D. E. (2021). COVID-19 Highlights the need for inclusive responses to public health emergencies in Africa. *The American Journal of Tropical Medicine and Hygiene, 104*(2), 449–452.

Agbodzakey, J. K. (2021). Leadership in collaborative governance: The Case of HIV/AIDS Health Services Planning Council in South Florida. *International Journal of Public Administration, 44*(13), 1051–1064.

Ahmed, F., Zhao, F., & Faraz, N. A. (2020). How and when does inclusive leadership curb psychological distress during a crisis? Evidence from the COVID-19 outbreak. *Frontiers in Psychology, 11*. https://doi.org/10.3389/fpsyg.2020.01898

Ahmed, F., Zhao, F., Faraz, N. A., & Qin, Y. J. (2021). How inclusive leadership paves way for psychological well-being of employees during trauma and crisis: A three-wave longitudinal mediation study. *Journal of Advanced Nursing, 77*(2), 819–831.

Al-Omoush, K. S., Ribeiro-Navarrete, S., Lassala, C., & Skare, M. (2022). Networking and knowledge creation: Social capital and collaborative innovation in responding to the COVID-19 crisis. *Journal of Innovation and Knowledge, 7*(2). 100181.

Ashikali, T., Groeneveld, S., & Kuipers, B. (2021). The role of inclusive leadership in supporting an inclusive climate in diverse public sector teams. *Review of Public Personnel Administration, 41*(3), 497–519.

Azevedo, L., Bell, A., & Medina, P. (2022). Community foundations provide collaborative responses and local leadership in midst of COVID-19. *Nonprofit Management and Leadership, 32*(3), 475–485.

Barton, A. J. (2021). Inclusive leadership in nursing education. *Journal of Nursing Education, 60*(5), 247–248.

Böbel, S., Bormans, M., Siepmann, I., Tirekidis, I., Wall, K., & Kalaitzi, V. (2021). Diverse and inclusive leadership teams in public health schools: The change agents for sustainable and inclusive public health education. *South Eastern European Journal of Public Health, 2021*(Special Issue 3).

Blake, N. (2021). Building a new, better normal after COVID-19. *Nursing Management, 52*(6), 20–23.

Booysen, L. (2014). *The development of inclusive leadership practice and processes*. In B. M. Ferdman & B. R. Deane (Eds.), *The professional practice series. Diversity at work: The practice of inclusion* (p. 296–329). Jossey-Bass/Wiley.

Booysen, L. A. E. (2020). Responsible inclusive leadership: A whole system collective process outcome. In B. M. Ferdman, J. Prime, & R. E. Riggio (Eds.), *Inclusive leadership: Transforming diverse lives, workplaces, and societies* (pp. 195–211). London; Taylor and Francis.

Bradley, E. H. (2020). Diversity, inclusive leadership, and health outcomes. *International Journal of Health Policy and Management, 9*(7), 266–268.

Bryer, A. (2020). Making organizations more inclusive: The work of belonging. *Organization Studies., 41*(5), 641–660.

Caver, K., & Livers, A. (2021). The paradox of the seed and soil: Cultivating inclusive leadership for a "new normal." *Leadership, 17*(1), 18–31.

Carmeli, A., Reiter-Palmon, R., & Ziv, E. (2010). Inclusive leadership and employee involvement in creative tasks in the workplace: The mediating role of psychological safety. *Creativity Research Journal, 22*(3), 250–260.

Choi, S. B., Tran, T. B. H., & Kang, S. W. (2017). Inclusive leadership and employee well-being: The mediating role of person-job fit. *Journal of Happiness Studies, 18*(6), 1877–1901.

Crain, M. A., Bush, A. L., Hayanga, H., Boyle, A., Unger, M., Ellison, M., & Ellison, P. (2021). Healthcare leadership in the COVID-19 pandemic: From innovative preparation to evolutionary transformation. *Journal of Healthcare Leadership, 13*, 199–207.

DeMatthews, D. (2021). Undoing systems of exclusion: Exploring inclusive leadership and systems thinking in two inclusive elementary schools. *Journal of Educational Administration, 59*(1), 5–21.

Dickinson, H., Brown, A., Robinson, S., Parham, J., & Wells, L. (2022). Building collaborative leadership: A qualitative evaluation of the Australian Collaborative Pairs trial. *Health & Social Care in the Community, 30*(2), 509–518.

Dowling, T., Metzger, M., & Kools, S. (2021). Cultivating inclusive learning environments that foster nursing education program resiliency during the covid-19 pandemic. *Journal of Professional Nursing, 37*(5), 942–947.

Edwards, L. D., & Till, A. (2019). Leading the integration of physician associates into the UK health workforce. *British Journal of Hospital Medicine, 80*(1), 18–21.

Edwards, L. D., Till, A., & McKimm, J. (2018). Meeting today's healthcare leadership challenges: Is compassionate, caring and inclusive leadership the answer? *BMJ Leader, 2*(2), 64–67.

Fang, Y., Ren, Y., Chen, J., Chin, T., Yuan, Q., & Lin, C. (2021). Inclusive leadership and career sustainability: Mediating roles of supervisor developmental feedback and thriving at work. *Frontiers in Psychology, 12*. https://doi.org/10.3389/fpsyg.2021.671663

Fu, Q., Cherian, J., Ahmad, N., Scholz, M., Samad, S., & Comite, U. (2022). An inclusive leadership framework to foster employee creativity in the healthcare sector: The role of psychological safety and polychronicity. *International Journal of Environmental Research and Public Health, 19*(8). 4519.

Fujimoto, Y., & Uddin, J. (2021). Inclusive leadership for reduced inequality: Economic–Social–Economic cycle of inclusion. *Journal of Business Ethics, 181*, 563–582.

Gardiner, S., & MacLellan, J. (2021). Delivering covid-19 research during the UK pandemic: Experiences of a local research taskforce. *Journal of Advanced Nursing*. https://doi.org/10.1111/jan.15103

Gotsis, G., & Grimani, K. (2016). Diversity as an aspect of effective leadership: Integrating and moving forward. *Leadership and Organization Development Journal, 37*(2), 241–264.

Gotsis, G., & Grimani, K. (2017). The role of spiritual leadership in fostering inclusive workplaces. *Personnel Review, 46*(5), 908–935.

Grandy, G., & Holton, J. (2013). Leadership development needs assessment in healthcare: A collaborative approach. *Leadership and Organization Development Journal, 34*(5), 427–445.

Graham, R. N. J., & Woodhead, T. (2021). Leadership for continuous improvement in healthcare during the time of COVID-19. *Clinical Radiology, 76*(1), 67–72.

Griewatz, J., Yousef, A., Rothdiener, M., Lammerding-Koeppel, M., Fritze, O., Dall'Acqua, A., & Koenig, S. (2020). Are we preparing for collaboration, advocacy and leadership? Targeted multi-site analysis of collaborative intrinsic roles implementation in medical undergraduate curricula. *BMC Medical Education, 20*(1). https://doi.org/10.1186/s12909-020-1940-0

Ito, M., & Tsutsumi, M. (2022). A call to action for an inclusive model of shared decision making in healthcare. *Nursing and Health Sciences, 24*(1), 3–6.

Javed, B., Abdullah, I., Zaffar, M. A., ul Haque, A., & Rubab, U. (2019). Inclusive leadership and innovative work behavior: The role of psychological empowerment. *Journal of Management Organization, 25*(4), 554–571.

Javed, S., & Chattu, V. K. (2021). Strengthening the COVID-19 pandemic response, global leadership, and international cooperation through global health diplomacy. *Health Promotion Perspectives, 10*(4), 300–305.

Jayasinghe, K., Wijesinghe, C., Wijethilake, C., & Prasanna, R. (2022). Collaborative public service provision archetypes in healthcare emergencies: A case of COVID-19 administration in Sri Lanka. *Journal of Public Budgeting, Accounting and Financial Management, 34*(3), 391–410.

Jha, M. K. (2021). An integrated framework of leadership for healthcare organizations to navigate through COVID-19 crisis. *Asia Pacific Journal of Health Management, 16*(3), 16–20.

Kalina, P. (2020). Resilient and inclusive healthcare leadership: Black swans, COVID-19, and beyond. *International Journal of Health Planning and Management, 35*(6), 1611–1613.

Kannampallil, T. G., Goss, C. W., Evanoff, B. A., Strickland, J. R., McAlister, R. P., & Duncan, J. (2020). Exposure to COVID-19 patients increases physician trainee stress and burnout. *PLoS ONE, 15*(8). e0237301.

Kegler, M. C., Wolff, T., Christens, B. D., Butterfoss, F. D., Francisco, V. T., & Orleans, T. (2019). Strengthening our collaborative approaches for advancing equity and justice. *Health Education & Behavior, 46*(1_suppl): 5S–8S.

Kerlin, M. P., Silvestri, J. A., Klaiman, T., Gutsche, J. T., Jablonski, J., & Mikkelsen, M. E. (2022). Critical care clinician wellness during the COVID-19 pandemic: A longitudinal analysis. *Annals of the American Thoracic Society, 19*(2), 329–332.

Ketikidou, G., & Saiti, A. (2022). The promotion of inclusive education through sustainable and systemic leadership. *International Journal of Leadership in Education.* https://doi.org/10.1080/13603124.2022.2032368

Khalili, H., Lising, D., Kolcu, G., Thistlethwaite, J., Gilbert, J., Langlois, S., & Pfeifle, A. (2021). Advancing health care resilience through a systems-based collaborative approach: Lessons learned from COVID-19. *Journal of Interprofessional Care, 35*(6), 809–812.

Kumar, S., Raut, R. D., & Narkhede, B. E. (2020). A proposed collaborative framework by using artificial intelligence-internet of things (AI-IoT) in COVID-19 pandemic situation for healthcare workers. *International Journal of Healthcare Management, 13*(4), 337–345.

Lapalme, M., & Doucet, O. (2018). The social integration of healthcare agency workers in long-term care facilities: A cross-sectional study. *International Journal of Nursing Studies, 82*, 106–112.

Lee, S. E., & Dahinten, V. S. (2021). Psychological safety as a mediator of the relationship between inclusive leadership and nurse voice behaviors and error reporting. *Journal of Nursing Scholarship, 53*(6), 737–745.

Lindsay, C., Pearson, S., Batty, E., Cullen, A. M., & Eadson, W. (2021). Collaborative innovation in labor market inclusion. *Public Administration Review, 81*(5), 925–934.

Liu, C., Huang, S., & Wang, S. S. (2022). Implementation of compassionate communities: The Taipei experience. *Healthcare (Switzerland), 10*(1), 177.

Luu, T. T. (2019). The well-being among hospitability employees with disabilities: The role of disability inclusive benevolent leadership. *International Journal of Hospitality Management, 80*, 25–35.

MacPhee, M., Espezel, H., Clauson, M., & Gustavson, K. (2009). A collaborative model to introduce quality and safety content into the undergraduate nursing leadership curriculum. *Journal of Nursing Care Quality, 24*(1), 83–89.

Macphee, M., Chang, L., Havaei, F., & Chou, W. (2014). A descriptive account of an inter-professional collaborative leadership project. *Administrative Sciences, 4*(3), 373–399.

Meagher, K., Singh, N. S., & Patel, P. (2020). The role of gender inclusive leadership during the COVID-19 pandemic to support vulnerable populations in conflict settings. *BMJ Global Health, 5*(9). e003760.

Meehan, D. (2020). How to develop and support leadership that contributes to a more equitable, diverse, and inclusive society. In B. M. Ferdman, J. Prime, & R. E. Riggio (Eds.), *Inclusive leadership: Transforming diverse lives, workplaces, and societies* (pp. 407–418). Taylor & Francis.

Melnikow, J., Padovani, A., & Miller, M. (2022). Frontline physician burnout during the COVID-19 pandemic: National survey findings. *BMC Health Services Research, 22*(1), 365.

Mete, M., Goldman, C., Shanafelt, T., & Marchalik, D. (2022). Impact of leadership behavior on physician well-being, burnout, professional fulfilment and intent to leave: A multicentre cross-sectional survey study. *BMJ Open, 12*(6). e057554.

Minehart, R. D., Foldy, E. G., Long, J. A., & Weller, J. M. (2020). Challenging gender stereotypes and advancing inclusive leadership in the operating theatre. *British Journal of Anaesthesia, 124*(3), e148–e154.

Mor Barak, M. E., Luria, G., & Brimhall, K. C. (2022). What leaders say versus what they do: Inclusive leadership, policy-practice decoupling, and the anomaly of climate for inclusion. *Group and Organization Management, 47*(4), 840–871.

Nembhard, I. M., & Edmondson, A. C. (2006). Making it safe: The effects of leader inclusiveness and professional status on psychological safety and improvement efforts in health care teams. *Journal of Organizational Behavior: The International Journal of Industrial, Occupational and Organizational Psychology Behavior, 27*(7), 941–966.

Nishii, L. H., & Leroy, H. L. (2020). Inclusive leadership: Leaders as architects of inclusive workgroup climates. In B. M. Ferdman, J. Prime, & R. E. Riggio (Eds.), *Inclusive leadership: Transforming diverse lives, workplaces, and societies* (pp. 162–178). Taylor and Francis.

North, S. E. (2020). Health care system leadership views on competencies for a collaborative-ready health workforce. *Journal of Interprofessional Education and Practice, 20*, 100351.

Nyström, M. E., & Strehlenert, H. (2021). Advancing health services collaborative and partnership research comment on "experience of health leadership in partnering with university-based researchers in Canada: A call to re-imagine research." *International Journal of Health Policy and Management, 10*(2), 106–110.

Obrien, N., Flott, K., & Durkin, M. (2021). COVID-19: Leadership on the frontline is what matters when we support healthcare workers. *International Journal for Quality in Health Care, 33*(1), mzaa153.

Okpala, P. (2018). Balancing quality healthcare services and costs through collaborative leadership. *Journal of Healthcare Management, 63*(6), e148–e157.

Okpala, P. (2019). Harnessing the power of collaborative leadership in the management of chronic health conditions. *International Journal of Healthcare Management, 12*(4), 302–307.

Okpala, P. (2020). Increasing access to quality healthcare through collaborative leadership. *International Journal of Healthcare Management, 13*(3), 229–235.

Orchard, C. A., Sonibare, O., Morse, A., Collins, J., & Al-Hamad, A. (2017a). Collaborative leadership, Part 1: The nurse leader's role within interprofessional teams. *Nursing leadership (Toronto, Ont.), 30*(2), 14–25.

Orchard, C. A., Sonibare, O., Morse, A., Collins, J., & Al-Hamad, A. (2017b). Collaborative leadership, part 2: The role of the nurse leader in interprofessional team-based practice: Shifting from task-to collaborative patient/family-focused care. *Nursing Leadership, 30*(2), 26–38.

Patterson, N. (2020). Developing inclusive and collaborative entrepreneuring spaces. *Gender in Management, 35*(3), 291–302.

Pelley, C. (2021). We need inclusive and compassionate leadership. *Nursing Management, 28*(1), 13.

Prime, J., Ferdman, B. M., & Riggio, R. E. (2020). Inclusive leadership: Insights and implications. In B. M. Ferdman, J. Prime, & R. E. Riggio (Eds.), *Inclusive leadership: Transforming diverse lives, workplaces, and societies* (pp. 421–429). Taylor & Francis.

Pyo, Y. H. (2020). Inquiry into collaborative team approach intervention experiences and support plans of special educators and occupational therapists in inclusive environments. *Korean Journal of Physical, Multiple and Health Disabilities, 63*(2), 141–169.

Randel, A. E., Galvin, B. M., Shore, L. M., Ehrhart, K. H., Chung, B. G., Dean, M. A., & Kedharnath, U. (2018). Inclusive leadership: Realizing positive outcomes through belongingness and being valued for uniqueness. *Human Resource Management Review, 28*(2), 190–203.

Randel, A. E., Dean, M. A., Ehrhart, K. H., Chung, B., & Shore, L. (2016). Leader inclusiveness, psychological diversity climate, and helping behaviors. *Journal of Managerial Psychology, 31*(1), 216–234.

Rath, C. G., Lapetina, P. E., Reed, J., Vogt, E., & Brown, M. (2022). Roadmap to resilience: Incorporating a wellness program into the pharmacy residency curriculum. *Currents in Pharmacy Teaching and Learning, 14*(6), 751–757.

Read, C. Y., Betancourt, D. M. P., & Morrison, C. (2016). Social change: A framework for inclusive leadership development in nursing education. *Journal of Nursing Education, 55*(3), 164–167.

Roberson, Q. M. (2006). Disentangling the meanings of diversity and inclusion in organizations. *Group and Organization Management, 31*(2), 212–236.

Roberson, Q., & Perry, J. L. (2022). Inclusive leadership in thought and action: A thematic analysis. *Group and Organization Management, 47*(4), 755–778.

Runacres, F., Steele, P., Hudson, J., Bills, M., & Poon, P. (2022). 'We couldn't have managed without your team': A collaborative palliative care response to the COVID-19 pandemic in residential aged care. *Australasian Journal of Ageing*, 41(1), 147–152.

Shirey, M. R., White-Williams, C., & Hites, L. (2019). Integration of authentic leadership lens for building high performing interprofessional collaborative practice teams. *Nursing Administration Quarterly*, 43(2), 101–112.

Shore, L. M., & Chung, B. G. (2022a). Inclusive leadership: How leaders sustain or discourage work group inclusion. *Group and Organization Management*, 47(4), 723–754.

Shore, L M., & Chung, B.G. (2022b). Enhancing leader inclusion while preventing social exclusion in the work group. *Human Resource Management Review*, 33(1), 100902.

Shore, L. M., Cleveland, J. N., & Sanchez, D. (2018). Inclusive workplaces: A review and model. *Human Resource Management Review*, 28(2), 176–189.

Shu, Q., & Wang, Y. (2021). Collaborative leadership, collective action, and community governance against public health crises under uncertainty: A case study of the Quanjingwan Community in China. *International Journal of Environmental Research and Public Health*, 18(2), 598.

Shyamsunder, A. (2020). Inclusive leadership: Driving multilevel organizational change. In B. M. Ferdman, J. Prime, & R. E. Riggio (Eds.), *Inclusive leadership: Transforming diverse lives, workplaces, and societies* (pp. 236–247). Taylor and Francis.

Sibbald, S. L., Hall, R. E., Embuldeniya, G., Gutberg, J., & Wodchis, W. P. (2021). Foundations, functions and current state of collaborative leadership: A case of newly developing integrated care in Ontario. *Healthcare Quarterly*, 24(3), 60–67.

Swaffield, S., & Major, L. (2019). Inclusive educational leadership to establish a co-operative school cluster trust? Exploring perspectives and making links with leadership for learning. *International Journal of Inclusive Education*, 23(11), 1149–1163.

Teo, S. T., Bentley, T. A., Nguyen, D., Blackwood, K., & Catley, B. (2022). Inclusive leadership, matured age HRM practices and older worker wellbeing. *Asia Pacific Journal of Human Resources*, 60(2), 323–341.

Uman, T. Edfors, E., Padoan, S., & Edberg, A. K. (2022). Contribution of an inclusive climate to the work of culturally diverse healthcare teams: A qualitative descriptive design. *Nordic Journal of Nursing Research*. https://doi.org/10.1177/20571585211070381

van Knippenberg, D., & van Ginkel, W. P. (2022). A diversity mindset perspective on inclusive leadership. *Group and Organization Management*, 47(4), 779–797.

VanVactor, J. D. (2012). Collaborative leadership model in the management of health care. *Journal of Business Research*, 65(4), 555–561.

Veli Korkmaz, A., van Engen, M. L., Knappert, L., & Schalk, R. (2022). About and beyond leading uniqueness and belongingness: A systematic review of inclusive leadership research. *Human Resource Management Review*, 32(4), 100894.

Wang, B. S. (2018). Practitioner application: Balancing quality healthcare services and costs through collaborative leadership. *Journal of Healthcare Management*, 63(6), e157–e158.

Wasserman, I. C. (2020). Inclusive leadership in complex times: Leading with vulnerability and integrity. In B. M. Ferdman, J. Prime, & R. E. Riggio (Eds.), *Inclusive leadership: Transforming diverse lives, workplaces, and societies* (pp. 83–98). Taylor & Francis.

Weber, L. A., Bunin, J., & Hartzell, J. D. (2022). Building individual and organizational wellness through effective followership. *Journal of Healthcare Leadership, 14*, 47–53.

Whelehan, D. F., Algeo, N., & Brown, D. A. (2021). Leadership through crisis: Fighting the fatigue pandemic in healthcare during COVID-19. *BMJ Leader, 5*, 108–112.

Younas, A., Wang, D., Javed, B., & Zaffar, M. A. (2021). Moving beyond the mechanistic structures: The role of inclusive leadership in developing change-oriented organizational citizenship behaviour. *Canadian Journal of Administrative Sciences, 38*(1), 42–52.

Zhao, F., Ahmed, F., & Faraz, N. A. (2020). Caring for the caregiver during COVID-19 outbreak: Does inclusive leadership improve psychological safety and curb psychological distress? A cross-sectional study. *International Journal of Nursing Studies, 110*. https://doi.org/10.1016/j.ijnurstu.2020.103725

CHAPTER 12

Empathy as a Wellness Driver in the Workplace

Jody A. Worley

EMPATHY AS A WELLNESS DRIVER IN THE WORKPLACE

Interpersonal relationships constitute the foundation on which human society is based. The human capacity to form enduring social relationships is central to individual and collective mental health in a society. These relationships can manifest as "care for others," whether parental care in parent–child dyads, care within kinship relationships, altruistic helping behaviors toward friends and even strangers, or prosocial workplace relations with coworkers. Given that adverse childhood experiences (ACEs) have been linked to long-term negative health consequences (Anda et al., 2006; Felitti et al., 1998), a reasonable proposition is that being present and attending to the well-being of others (empathy) may be a wellness driver for all parties in the exchange. Consideration of this proposition in the context of the professional workplace is the premise for this brief expository essay.

This chapter focuses on a few small aspects of a single question: What is the role of empathy as it relates to wellness? Initially, the emphasis is on defining and offering alternative explanations for the function of empathy in interpersonal, group, and team interactions in the workplace for creating a supportive and healthy workplace climate. This is considered within the framework of organizational behavior and organizational dynamics—human relations. Then, the emphasis shifts to focus on wellness as the primary outcome of interest

J. A. Worley (✉)
University of Oklahoma, Norman, OK, USA
e-mail: jworley@ou.edu

and how empathy might get us there as a contributing factor, along with other necessary but perhaps not sufficient drivers of wellness. Therefore, the ideas presented in this chapter are intended to provide fragments of a partial answer to that question about empathy as a wellness driver. The fragments represent a sample of possible ideas rather than conclusive evidence of a cause-effect association between empathy and wellness. The available evidence is inconclusive, and more work needs to be done if we are to make stronger claims for empathy as a wellness driver. The small number of words in the chapter may be somewhat balanced by the large number of references in published studies across a broad range of disciplines including cognitive and social neuroscience, psychology, sociology, neurobiology, philosophy, ethics, organizational leadership, and management studies.

Although they might with justice claim that I have extracted lessons from their writing and thus teachings that are not what they intended, the authors of my source references have contributed substantially to the perspectives that are presented here on empathy as a wellness driver. Because of all the terrific insights gained from these source references, I feel compelled to note that any imperfections in the incomplete ruminations on the ideas rather than thorough expositions of them are mine.

Empathy Defined

Empathy is a concept used broadly to refer to thoughts and feelings of an individual in response to observed experiences (usually emotional experiences) of another individual (Cf. Davis, 1983; Woltin et al., 2011). However, a specific definition is debatable and difficult to operationalize. Although there are probably as many different ways of describing empathy as there are people who are working on the topic, there is at least general consensus that empathy reflects an ability to perceive and be sensitive to the emotional states of others combined with a drive to care and show concern for them. Empathy is distinct, however, from care and caregiving. A brief statement on this distinction is presented later. In an attempt to define empathy for understanding its role in wellness, it is valuable to consider that empathy is a neural (brain) process.

There is an abundance of evidence that empathy is neurobiologically supported by a triangulation of neural circuitry. In other words, empathy is not just a socially constructed concept. Rather, there is physiological, biological, and anatomical evidence for empathy. Empathy connects neurocircuitry (brain wiring) for social behavior, physical pain, and the ability to represent both the self and another (Cikara & Van Bavel, 2014; Decety & Jackson, 2004, 2006; Vignemont & Singer, 2006). The overarching goal of this section of the paper is to relate these connections between empathy and brain structures, including the influence of hormones, with general health and wellness. The aim is not to present a technical explanation or description of the anatomy and physiology of brain functioning as it relates to wellness. Rather, this review aims to integrate the understanding of empathy as a neural process with the understanding of empathy as a catalyst for social behavior—the ability to understand and foster connections with others as a wellness driver as we navigate and negotiate our work and nonwork lives.

There appears to be widespread agreement on the importance of empathy in human relations. Unfortunately, there also appears to be an equally widespread lack of agreement on a suitable definition. Some of the questions about the meaning and components of empathy arises from the subjective nature of the concept, the complexity of the empathic process (how it operates and works in relationships), and at times, the incomplete conceptualization of empathy in the published literature. One consequence of this ambiguity is a body of confusing literature, confounded by the contradictory views of many researchers. Some researchers believe that empathy has several attributes. Others define empathy in a more narrow and particularistic way. Therefore, in this effort to understand the role of empathy as a wellness driver, empathy is considered as a multidimensional concept for social cognitive ability. That is, in addition to the emotional or affective component, empathy as a wellness driver is understood to also include cognitive, behavioral, and moral components that have significant associations with wellness.

Affective (emotional) component—This component of empathy reflects the perspective-taking and sense-making that is responsible for understanding and relating with experiences or points of view of another person, even if that experience, perspective, or point of view is discrepant from one's own (e.g., trait empathy). In other words, empathy is functional in the context of emotional processing, which is a wellness driver in the sense that it has evolved to guide behavior. Empathy is also an interpersonal communication system that elicits response from others, helps to determine priorities within relationships, and holds people together in social groups (Decety, 2015). The affective component of empathy reflects the ability to perceive and be sensitive to the emotional states of others as a mechanism to promote wellness.

Cognitive component—This component of empathy reflects our ability for pattern recognition (e.g., how to respond and/or treat others contingent upon context). This is sometimes referred to as *state empathy*. The ability to represent, monitor, and control cognitive processes helps us perform many tasks when working alone and when working with others. The cognitive component of empathy and our related abilities to recognize, discriminate, interpret, and broadcast representations of concern for others depends somewhat on cultural learning and may be adaptive. Neural networks involved in empathy are activated by perceptions of others in distress or pain. This, of course, depends on some level of subjective interpretation of events. However, there is evidence that empathy is not merely a consequence of passive observation of emotional cues but that it is subject to contextual appraisal and modulation through cognitive processing (Vignemont & Jacob, 2012; Vignemont & Singer, 2006). The neurobiological connections for social behavior in our brains (as well as physical pain and the ability to understand social distress or pain in others) promote understanding of social distress or pain in others and experience that distress very much as though the feeling was generated within oneself. This neurobiological mechanism promotes social affiliation and behavior, which seeks to reduce the display of stress in others. Furthermore, the limbic system which is partly responsible for empathy has been co-opted for other forms of affiliation as well, including pair bonding behaviors (Insel, 1997; Insel & Fernald, 2004) or affiliation among friends (Taylor et al., 2003).

Behavioral component—This component of empathy reflects our ability for communicative response (e.g., listening, hearing, feeling, and emoting) to convey understanding of another's perspective (e.g., how to "express" empathy so that it is recognized as such (Cf. Morse et al., 1992). So, this component of empathy is responsible for the ability to understand and communicate one's understanding of another person's emotion (Vignemont & Singer, 2006). Consider that empathy is an ability-based, interactional relationship-building process, rather than strictly as a subjective, affective-based emotional concept. Therefore, empathy is not simply a feeling that we have for others, but also a responsive action that we share with others in working relationships with them. As such, it is a catalyst for social behavior. In fact, it has been proposed that "empathy is *the* competence for beneficial social interaction and communication" (Olderbak et al., 2014, p. 11).

Moral component—This component of empathy reflects a learned internal motivating force that influences the altruistic practice of empathy (e.g., moral predisposition and intuition). Empathy is thought to play a foundational role in morality and understanding why it is wrong to harm others. Support for such a role comes from multiple sources of evidence. For instance, a study conducted with a large sample of neurotypical participants reported a significant relationship between moral judgment and empathic concern (Gleichgerrcht & Young, 2013). Blair et al. (2005) argued that a lack of empathy during early development results in a lack of morality. There is also evidence that people with empathy deficits are more likely to display aggressive, antisocial behaviors toward others (Hoffman, 2001). Although there is an observable relationship between empathy and morality, these two concepts should not be used interchangeably. They are related, but distinct. Empathy can be motivated and regulated (Zaki, 2014). However, empathy is also socially influenced, sometimes without any cognitive awareness. For this reason, empathy is not always a direct path to moral or prosocial behavior because, at times, empathy can interfere with moral decision-making by introducing partiality (favoritism, for instance) and implicit bias for family, friends, and other in-group members (Decety, 2021). Yet, empathy does provide the affective, cognitive, and behavioral prompt to sense, recognize, and act on behalf of a victim's suffering, irrespective of group membership and social hierarchies. For example, after separation from their parents by U. S. Customs and Border Protection agents near the U.S.-Mexico border, photographs of unknown crying children prompted sympathy and moral outrage in many people, and evoked criticism from across the political spectrum. This example illustrates how empathy, as an affective reaction, increases cognitive and behavioral responses and subsequent likelihood for moral concern and compassion for other people as a core aspect of humanity.

Therefore, the brain mechanisms supporting empathy are flexible and amenable to behavioral interventions that can promote caring beyond family, friends, and acquaintances, including workplace relations. Literature on empathy supports its strong role in affective social functioning. Empathy is related to various prosocial behaviors such as helping (e.g., Batson et al., 1989, 1991, 1997) and cooperation (e.g., Eisenberg & Miller, 1987). In health care settings, for example, patients recover more quickly when interacting with empathic physicians (e.g., Van Dulmen & Bensing, 2002), and empathy improves intergroup relations (e.g., Dovidio et al., 2010).

The role that empathy plays in concern for others among humans has been documented as early as 6–8 months of age and continues to develop through adulthood. Not only are very young children capable of making pain attributions, but studies on comforting behavior demonstrate that young children also respond to a variety of distress cues, and they direct their comforting behavior in ways that are appropriate to the distress of other people (Davidov et al., 2013). For example, Roth-Hanania et al. (2011) observed moderate levels of empathic concern (indicated by facial expressions, vocalizations, and gestures reflecting concern), and attempts to explore and comprehend the others' distress are already present at 8 and 10 months of age. Hepach et al. (2012) presented evidence suggesting that children as young as two years old are not motivated to help others by a drive to benefit themselves through reciprocity or because they are interested in engaging with the task, but rather by a desire to see the person be helped. These empathic responses continue to develop across the life span. It is reasonable to assume that empathic concerns responsible for affective social functioning may contribute to wellness later in life for self and others.

Two Roles of Empathy as a Wellness Driver

The components of empathy (affective, cognitive, behavioral, and moral components) have significant associations that play a vital role in social functioning. We empathize for social and developmental wellness (vitality). House et al. (1988) presented a compelling statement supported by research evidence establishing both a theoretical basis and strong empirical evidence for a causal impact of social relationships on health. Prospective studies, which control for baseline health status, consistently show increased risk of death among persons with low quantity, and sometimes low quality, of social relationships (House et al., 1988). There are two major roles that empathy plays in social functioning as a wellness driver—an epistemological role and a social role.

First, the mechanisms in our brain responsible for empathy provide information about future actions of other people and other environmental factors.

This is an epistemological role of empathy (Vignemont & Singer, 2006). Empathy might not be the more direct route to understanding other people's emotions, but it is a faster route for prediction of subsequent behavior. The shared emotional networks operating in our brain that are responsible for empathy provide a more precise and direct estimate of what other people may feel and how they may act (Vignemont & Singer, 2006). That is, by sharing the emotional state of others, we also share their emotional and motivational significance (Perry, 2001).

Empathy also provides knowledge about important environmental factors other than direct interaction with people. For example, social learning and vicarious learning from observing or hearing about someone else's experience are powerful tools that are possible, in part, due to our ability to empathize. We learn through empathy to assign negative "avoidance" to dangerous environmental factors without having to experience pain or suffering ourselves (Keysers et al., 2004). In this sense, empathy is an efficient computation tool for acquiring knowledge about the values of the world around us (Preston & de Waal, 2002). As such, empathy might contribute to wellness (vitality) indirectly by resulting in personal distress and thereby motivate self-related helping behaviors, such as avoidance and withdrawal, instead of other-related prosocial behavior (Batson & Shaw, 1991) in times when self-preservation takes precedence for wellness in the long view. Awareness and understanding of others and the dynamics of the relational interdependence we have with them have contributory value for wellness and well-being.

The second role that empathy plays in social functioning as a wellness driver is a social role responsible for cooperation and prosocial behavior, as well as help with social communication effectiveness. Empathy is often emphasized more in literature as related to having a moral sense, altruism, justice, prosocial behavior, and cooperation (Batson & Shaw, 1991; Eisenberg & Morris, 2001; Hoffman, 2001).

Overall, there is strong research support for the notion that empathic concern and other emotional reactions play a pivotal role in guiding prosocial behavior. However, the relation between empathy and moral judgment is not always clear (Decety, 2015). It remains to be shown whether individual differences in empathic brain responses also predict subsequent prosocial behavior. Empathy can interfere with moral judgment and may even lead to amoral behavior (Decety & Cowell, 2014). Therefore, in an effort to avoid the risk of promoting neuro-hype, questions concerning the interplay between empathy, sympathy, and prosocial behavior will need to wait for a better understanding of the neural signature underlying specific emotions and empathy before distinguishing between empathic and sympathetic affective brain responses. That said, the ability to share other people's emotional experiences and react to them in a fine-tuned manner might facilitate social communication and create social coherence.

EMPATHY FACILITATES SOCIAL INTERACTION

Empathy facilitates social interactions in many ways as a driver of wellness for self and others. Some examples for the functional role of empathy in social interaction includes pair bonding (including parent–child and adult partnerships), social affiliation, empathic concern and caring, and prosocial behaviors as discussed earlier. Genetics and environmental factors (nature and nurture) contribute to the association between prosocial behavior and empathy (Knafo et al., 2008). The association between prosocial behavior and the single receptor for oxytocin (OXTR) has been shown to be mediated by empathic concern and perspective-taking, which are important components of human empathy (Christ et al., 2016). Consequently, a prosocial drive is experienced when an empathic response is coupled with a motivation to act (Decety et al., 2016), and therefore, empathy facilitates social interaction.

This functional nature of empathy helps us understand why we have empathy for others and how it emerged. Social neuroscientists and neurobiologists believe that empathy is a driving factor promoting parental care and bonding between caregiver and infants, enables prosocial behaviors, and plays a role in inhibiting aggression (Decety & Svetlova, 2012; Swain et al., 2012). There is empirical and anecdotal evidence that people prefer to interact with others who are experiencing similar emotional states. This emotional similarity is associated with an assortment of benefits including greater cooperation and less conflict among group members (Cikara & Van Bavel, 2014). Consistent with this idea, research demonstrates that sharing a threatening situation with a person who is in a similar emotional state buffers individuals from experiencing the heightened levels of stress (reducing cortisol response) that typically accompany threat (Townsend et al., 2014). This supports the notion that there are some positive benefits for some people who engage in social support groups, and similar mechanisms may be at play in social clubs and the desire to spend leisure time with friends or colleagues. Empathy facilitates the drive and motivation to interact with others who are experiencing similar emotional states.

Empathic concern has also been consistently shown to predict helping behavior (Ho et al., 2014). Myers et al. (2014) found that imagining oneself in another person's situational experience leads to a greater sense of consciously perceived connection to and overlap with the other person, which in turn is associated with a greater likelihood of helping another person in need. In fact, listening is a basic social behavior and one of the most fundamental features of satisfying social interaction (Rogers, 1962).

Again, to the extent that the quality of our life is contingent upon the quality of our relationships; the quality of our relationships is contingent upon the quality of our communication—and empathy is instrumental in facilitating social communication and social coherence. The ability to adopt other people's postures, gestures, and mannerisms was found to create social affiliation and fondness (Lakin & Chartrand, 2003). Similarly, perceiving another person's empathy for oneself is likely to increase affiliation and strengthen the emotional bond with that person.

Social Contact Improves Health and Wellness in the Workplace

Evidence indicates that social contact improves health and well-being and decreases the risk of mortality (House et al., 1988). Researchers have assumed that the positive correlations between social contact, health, and wellness are due to the responsiveness that is received, and to the social support made available by the relationship. As described by House and his colleagues, "investigators ... leaped almost immediately to the interpretation that what was consequential for health about social relationships was their supportive quality," (p. 541) consistent with established clinical views of the importance of social support for psychological adjustment. Despite prominent acclaim for the social support hypothesis, empirical assessments have not always been positive (e.g., Thoits, 1982), and some studies have demonstrated that receiving support can be harmful (e.g., Brown & Vinokur, 2003; Hays et al., 1997; Seeman et al., 1996). A meta-analysis of the link between social support and health outcomes revealed only a small effect of receiving social support (Smith et al., 1994). Therefore, results are mixed on the role of social contact and wellness, but what about empathy?

Care is, after all, an emerging topic in organizational management and work processes. Kahn (1993) was among the first to identify dimensions and articulate the mechanisms for generating and actually providing care within an organizational context. One of the eight dimensions that Kahn named was empathy (p. 544) along with a proposed model for how the eight dimensions of care diffuse throughout organizational systems.

Stiehl et al. (2018) also propose a model of care flow—defined as a multilevel work process through which care feelings and actions are generated and spread throughout an organization to address member needs. The model distinguishes between the generation of care and the spread of care. According to this model, there are three specific stages of care that are cyclical and multivalve mechanisms (dyadic, collective, and organizational system level) through which caregivers and care recipients act together to enhance flow in a work system. They argue that care is inherently rational *and* emotional at the same time. They also strongly emphasize that the reproduction of care is shaped through collaboration between caregivers and care recipients (beneficiaries). They claim that this reciprocity exchange addresses a gap that is overlooked by organizational theorists.

Care is similar but distinct from empathy in a number of important ways. Both are strongly rooted in reciprocity and grounded in relationships and focused on needs of others and motivated by concern for others (care recipients; Waerness, 1984, 2009; Pattern recognition and perspective-taking; Morse et al., 1992). However, authentic empathy is distinct from the types of behavioral and emotional labor that Arie Hochschild named in her 1983 book, *Managed Heart*, where behaviors and attitudes of expressing concern are a part of the job. Empathy is a powerful motivator for caring and helping behaviors among humans and other species. However, the experience of empathy is distinct from consequent behaviors such as cooperation, helping someone in distress, and other prosocial behaviors (Decety et al., 2016). Empathy is the neural ability to perceive and be sensitive to emotional states of others, which can be but is not necessarily combined with a drive to care for their well-being (Decety, 2015). Authentic empathy fosters independence and autonomy of people who receive empathy in similar ways with servanthood leadership (Cf. Greenleaf's work on servanthood leadership and the subscale for empathy in assessing servant leader behaviors). Empathy, unlike emotional labor and paid caregiving, helps people who receive it to move toward their ideal selves in a way that is consistent with their goals and not someone else's, thus promoting strengths of dignity, identity, and agency (willpower).

Opportunities for authentic empathy, or the expression of empathic concern, that promote or hinder perceived relationship quality span most aspects of people's lives because most employees spend a large portion of each day communicating and relating with others. Perceived responsiveness in relationships has been shown to lessen pain sensitivity (Oishi et al., 2013) and reports of physical symptoms (Lun et al., 2008). A study of coworker perceptions found that active listening and perceived responsiveness affected social influence over and above the effect of verbal expressiveness (Ames et al., 2012). The association between empathy and social interactions that foster wellness and well-being can be observed in interpersonal contexts in the workplace including interactions that involve conflict (disagreements).

The manager-employee relationship, for example, can be undermined when a performance feedback conversation feels threatening to either party (Kluger & DeNisi, 1996). When either party feels threatened, a typical response is defensiveness. A defensive reaction often reduces the likelihood that an employee will adapt in response to performance feedback, thereby potentially hindering future performance. Alternatively, managers who enact positive listening behaviors and empathic concern may reduce employee defensiveness (Itzchakov & Kluger, 2018). Likewise, coworkers often disagree with each other, and other social interactions may include tension and conflict at times. When partners in social interactions do not feel understood or heard, they are less likely to resolve disagreements amicably (Livingstone et al., 2020). However, when people actively listen to each other in exchange relationships, people are more likely to feel understood (Reis et al., 2017). Moreover, hostile or extreme attitudes are less extreme when people feel listened to and heard (Bruneau & Saxe, 2012; Itzchakov & Kluger, 2017). These are a few examples of how social contact with empathy might improve health and wellness in the workplace.

COMPARISON OF TOPICS ON EMPATHY IN THE WORKPLACE

There are a few reasonable explanations for why empathy has not received more attention in the organizational and workplace literature. First, empathy involves idiosyncratic interactions and exchanges. This makes it difficult to measure empathy in objective ways that would allow comparisons across individuals or workplace contexts. Many factors will vary from one specific situational context to another and often cannot be controlled for in research studies. Second, there is a tendency to think that the relationship between empathy, empathic leadership, and wellness or well-being in the workplace is a relationship based on reciprocity—and perhaps it is. However, another reasonable consideration is that empathy as a wellness driver has less to do with how and how much empathy is received from external sources and has more to do with how empathic one is toward oneself and to others. That is, there is a shift in the locus of focus. This is the case regardless of leadership status.

Much of what has been written on empathy in the workplace is directed at what people in formal leadership positions are, or are not, doing to create and sustain empathy in the workplace (remotely or otherwise). A summary comparison of topics on empathy in the workplace is presented in Table 12.1. Most of the work on empathy in the workplace has presented a more positive than negative message. One alternative suggestion has been that empathy in the workplace is a finite and limited resource that may impair judgment and drain our mental and emotional energy if we overuse it (Waytz, 2016). In any event, published research on empathy in the workplace can be organized into four distinct but related topical categories. Empathy in the workplace has been presented as it relates to leadership and organizational climate, occupational health and wellness, quality of care (e.g., health care, social services, and helping professions), and the ethics of care.

Leadership and Organizational Climate. Representative work on empathy in the workplace as it relates to leadership and organizational climate focuses on the role of empathy in leadership and recognizing differences between management, leadership, and leaders. A common thread or goal among the studies in this topical category is to describe variations across observed organizational dynamics and gain insight on how to develop workplace relationships (Cf. Choi, 2006; Holt & Marques, 2012; Holt et al., 2017; Jian, 2022; Kellett et al., 2006; Marques, 2010, 2011; Sadri et al., 2011; Worley, 2019). The predominant level of analysis is at the individual or organizational level. In the leader-centered approach to understand empathy and its role in creating supportive organizational climate, for example, researchers often present empathy as a key element for positive leadership outcomes (Kellett et al., 2006; Sadri et al., 2011) and an essential component for authentic (Mortier et al., 2016) and transformational leaders (Choi, 2006). Other studies have also offered some insight into the role of communication and

Table 12.1 Comparison of topics on empathy in the workplace

	Leadership and organizational climate	Occupational health and wellness	Quality of care (e.g., health care, social services, and helping professions)	Ethics of care
Representative work	Choi (2006), Jian (2022), Holt and Marques (2012), Holt et al. (2017), Kellett et al. (2006), Marques (2010, 2011), Sadri et al. (2011), Worley (2019)	Majercsik (2021), Martino et al. (2017)	Kelley et al. (2014), Mercer and Reynolds (2002), Morse et al. (1992), Mortier et al. (2016)	Gilligan (1982), Hoffman (2001), Noddings (1984, 2010), Tronto (2005), Wærness (1984, 2009)
Focus	Role of empathy in leadership. Recognizing differences between management, leadership, and leaders	The power and influence of social connections and the quality of relationships for personal health and wellness	Role of empathy in the therapeutic relationship	The responsibility of caregivers to recognize and address actual needs
Goal	To describe organizational dynamics and gain insight on how to develop workplace relationships	To describe and explain the significance of healthy habits and socially supportive connections as a foundation for health and wellness	To describe and understand the complexity and multidimensional nature of empathy in workplace contexts where there is concern for others	To enhance understanding of various ideas of caring and ethical provision of care
Level of analysis	Individual and organizational	Individual	Multilevel	Relationships where the care provider generally does not expect care in return

discourse in developing empathy as a relational leadership practice (Holt et al., 2017). However, the leader-centered approach to understand the role of empathy in the workplace this way may fall short of appreciating the full reciprocal dynamic of empathy among all actors in non-administrative (not formal) leadership positions. Not everyone who holds a formal leadership position is a leader, of course, and not all leaders have the status or positional power of someone in an administrative leadership role. Furthermore, the leader-centered approaches that do link relational leadership with empathy have only a limited number of concrete suggestions for leading by relating through empathy as a wellness driver.

Occupational Health and Wellness. Although the literature on occupational health and wellness has a strong and popular representation of studies on work engagement, work-life integration, work-related stress, demands and resources, and interventions at the individual and organizational levels, there has also been some interest in the role of empathy in workplace health and wellness (Cf. Majercsik, 2021; Martino et al., 2017). The focus on empathy in the context of occupational psychology has focused on the power and influence of social connections and the quality of relationships for personal health and wellness. These studies help describe and explain the significance of healthy habits and social supportive connections as a foundation for health and wellness (Martino et al., 2017).

Quality of Care. There are also studies that focus on the role of empathy in therapeutic relationships across a variety of workplace contexts (e.g., health care, social services, and helping professions). The perspectives on empathy presented from this focal area help describe and understand the complexity and multidimensional nature of empathy in workplace contexts where concern for others is part of the job role (Cf. Kelley et al., 2014; Mercer & Reynolds, 2002; Mortier et al., 2016). Whereas topics on empathy as it relates with leadership, workplace climate, occupational health, and wellness are often presented at the individual or organizational level of analysis, discussions of the role of empathy in the context of quality of care provision often require a multilevel perspective.

Ethics of Care. A related but distinct area of focus is on the ethics of care in relationships where the care provider generally does not expect care in return (Cf. Gilligan, 1982; Hoffman, 2001; Noddings, 1984, 2010; Tronto, 2005; Wærness, 1984, 2009). "The ethics of care takes our responsibilities within relationships as the foundation for moral values" (Waerness, 2009, p. 139). The guiding thought is that the quality of one's life is contingent upon the quality of one's relationships. The quality of one's relationships is contingent upon the quality of communication with and caring for others vis-à-vis attentiveness, responsibility, competence, and responsiveness—the four stages of core values of the ethic of care (Cf. Tronto, 1993, 2005). Again, as mentioned earlier, care is similar but distinct from empathy in several important ways.

What is missing is the role that being empathic has on individual health and wellness (i.e., mental, physical, and emotional stability) at the intra-individual level. Exploring the role of cognitive, affective, behavioral, and moral components of empathy in workplace wellness initiatives would be valuable. This topic for future research is pertinent given recent modifications in the structure and function of workplace environments following the global COVID-19 pandemic.

Conclusion

Empathic concern, including listening and responding to concerns of others, takes place in multiple relationship domains. In workplace relationships between managers and employees, coworkers, and exchanges with customers, for example, individuals may experience a sense of being understood and responded to when others exhibit their grasp of an expressed concern. In relationships that are closer, and in relationships where individual differences are more extreme, attention to positive intentions may be more important as a means to avoid misunderstandings. There is value in taking personal time to identify emotions and emotional triggers that may drive behavior (and wellness) for oneself and others in relationships. Reflecting on one's own position on issues that arise in relationships creates an opportunity to build empathy. Exploring our perceptions of others' views and their possible experiences in the relationship creates an opportunity for understanding one another. The reflection and exploration of one's own and others' perspectives can nurture a relationship context or workplace climate that fosters a sense of "knowing" or consciousness that there is mutual respect for personal identities even in the context of disagreements or tension. This way, even if something is spoken or enacted that could be misinterpreted, the impact is buffered by the "knowing" that there is no malicious intent. Research is needed to further understand how comprehension can be effectively signaled in such relationships and how to integrate those insights into training and development practices.

One of the challenges in understanding the role of empathy as a wellness driver in social relationships is the task of measuring empathy. Therefore, this chapter on empathy as a wellness driver concludes with some recommended source references for different approaches that have been used in survey research to assess and evaluate empathy. Table 12.2 presents a list of 18 different self-report measures that can be used to identify various components of empathy at an individual level. The list of these 18 self-report measures is based on published research in peer-reviewed journals. There are at least two caveats that must be emphasized with regards to this list. First, all of the reviewed publications were in English language. It is likely that there are other high-quality measures in languages other than English that are not included on this list. Second, and related to the first comment, this list is not intended to represent a complete or comprehensive list of available measures. The primary objective of this chapter was to offer some insight and understanding of empathy as a wellness drive. A comprehensive review of the measurement of empathy across contexts, cultures, languages, and the like, far exceeds the scope of the current project. In any event, this list of source references to some of the valuable measures of empathy that are available may contribute to meeting the objectives of offering insight and understanding on empathy as a wellness driver. Although it is generally accepted that empathy is a universal human trait that is accessible for people who are neurotypical, there are individual differences supported by evidence that the level of empathy and

Table 12.2 Empathy self-report questionnaires

1. Measure of Emotional Empathy (Mehrabian & Epstein, 1972)
2. Emotional Intelligence Scale (EES; Schutte et al., 1998)
3. Hogan Empathy Scale (HES; Hogan, 1969)
4. Perth Empathy Scale (PES; Brett et al., 2022)
5. Impulsiveness and Venturesomeness (IVE—Empathy subscale; Eysenck & Eysenck, 1978)
6. Interpersonal Reactivity Index (IRI—Empathic Concern subscale; Davis, 1980, 1983)
7. Empathy Quotient (EQ; Baron-Cohen & Wheelwright, 2004; Lawrence et al., 2004)
8. Basic Empathy Scale (BES; Jolliffe & Farrington, 2006)
9. Toronto Empathy Questionnaire (TEQ; Spreng et al., 2009)
10. Empathy Assessment Index (EAI-26; Gerdes et al., 2011)
11. Empathy Assessment Index (EAI-17; Lietz et al., 2011)
12. Questionnaire of Cognitive and Affective Empathy (QCAE; Reniers et al., 2011)
13. Emotion Specific Empathy (ESE; Olderbak et al., 2014)
14. Adolescent Measure of Empathy and Sympathy (AMES; Bloom & Lambie, 2020; Vossen et al., 2015)
15. Affective and Cognitive Measure of Empathy (ACME; Vachon & Lynam, 2016)
16. Empathy Index (EI; Jordan et al., 2016)
17. Empathic Experience Scale (EES; Innamorati et al., 2019)
18. Empathy Components Questionnaire (ECQ; Batchelder et al., 2017)

Note This list of 18 self-report measures is based on a search of peer-reviewed journals published in English language and is not intended to represent a complete or comprehensive list of available measures

its communicative expression may vary across situational contexts and over time. This suggests that empathy may also be state-specific. If true, then one implication is that empathy can be improved and successfully taught.

Based on evidence from neurobiology and social neuroscience that empathy is not simply a subjective feeling that we have for others, but also a responsive action that we share with others in the workplace and in human relations with them, this chapter reviews current literature to explore how empathy may function as a multiplier for wellness. Empathy facilitates social interaction in many ways that are linked to positive health outcomes. Empathy is thought to also play a foundational role in morality, supporting the notion of empathy as a wellness driver for self and others.

References

Ames, D., Maissen, L. B., & Brockner, J. (2012). The role of listening in interpersonal influence. *Journal of Research in Personality, 46*, 345–349.

Anda, R. F., Felitti, V. J., Bremner, J. D., Walker, J. D., Whitfield, C. H., Perry, B. D., Dube, S. R., & Giles, W. H. (2006). The enduring effects of abuse and related adverse experiences in childhood. *European Archives of Psychiatry and Clinical Neuroscience, 256*(3), 174–186.

Baron-Cohen, S., & Wheelwright, S. (2004). The empathy quotient: An investigation of adults with Asperger syndrome or high functioning autism, and normal sex differences. *Journal of Autism and Developmental Disorders, 34*, 163–175.

Batchelder, L., Brosnan, M., & Ashwin, C. (2017). The development and validation of the empathy components questionnaire (ECQ). *PLoS ONE, 12*(1), e0169185.

Batson, C. D., Batson, J. G., Griffitt, C. A., Barrientos, S., Brandt, J. R., Sprengelmeyer, P., & Bayly, M. J. (1989). Negative-state relief and the empathy—Altruism hypothesis. *Journal of Personality and Social Psychology, 56*, 922–933.

Batson, C. D., Batson, J. G., Slingsby, J. K., Harrell, K. L., Peekna, H. M., & Todd, R. M. (1991). Empathic joy and the empathy-altruism hypothesis. *Journal of Personality and Social Psychology, 61*, 413–426. https://doi.org/10.1037/0022-3514.61.3.413

Batson, C. D., Polycarpou, M. P., Harmon-Jones, E., Imhoff, H. J., Mitchener, E. C., Bednar, L. L., Klein, T. R., & Highberger, L. (1997). Empathy and attitudes: Can feeling for a member of a stigmatized group improve feelings toward the group? *Journal of Personality and Social Psychology, 72*, 105–118.

Batson, C. D., & Shaw, L. L. (1991). Evidence for altruism: Toward a pluralism of prosocial motives. *Psychological Inquiry, 2*, 107–122.

Blair, J., Mitchell, D., & Blair, K. (2005). *The psychopath: Emotion and the brain.* Blackwell Publishing.

Bloom, Z. D., & Lambie, G. W. (2020). The adolescent measure of empathy and sympathy in a sample of emerging adults. *Measurement and Evaluation in Counseling and Development, 53*, 89–103.

Brett, J. D., Becerra, R., Maybery, M. T., & Preece, D. A. (2022). The psychometric assessment of empathy: Development and validation of the Perth Empathy Scale. Assessment, published online April 18, 2022. https://doi.org/10.1177/10731911221086987

Brown, S. L., & Vinokur, A. D. (2003). The interplay among risk factors for suicidal ideation and suicide: The role of depression, poor health, and loved ones' messages of support and criticism. *American Journal of Community Psychology, 32*(1–2), 131–141.

Bruneau, E. G., & Saxe, R. (2012). The power of being heard: The benefits of 'perspective-giving' in the context of intergroup conflict. *Journal of Experimental Social Psychology, 48*, 855–866.

Choi, J. (2006). A motivational theory of charismatic leadership: Envisioning, empathy, and empowerment. *Journal of Leadership and Organizational Studies, 13*, 24–43.

Christ, C. C., Carlo, G., & Stoltenberg, S. F. (2016). Oxytocin receptor (OXTR) single nucleotide polymorphisms indirectly predict prosocial behavior through perspective taking and empathic concern. *Journal of Personality, 84*, 204–213.

Cikara, M., & Van Bavel, J. J. (2014). The neuroscience of intergroup relations: An integrative review. *Perspectives on Psychological Science, 9*, 245–274.

Davidov, M., Zahn-Waxler, C., Roth-Hanania, R., & Knafo, A. (2013). Concern for others in the first year of life: Theory, evidence, and avenues for research. *Child Development Perspectives, 7*(2), 126–131.

Davis, M. H. (1980). A multidimensional approach to individual differences in empathy. *JSAS Catalog of Selected Documents in Psychology, 10*, 85.

Davis, M. H. (1983). Measuring individual differences in empathy: Evidence for a multidimensional approach. *Journal of Personality and Social Psychology, 44*, 113–126.

Decety, J. (2015). The neural pathways, development and functions of empathy. *Current Opinion in Behavioral Sciences, 3*, 1–6.

Decety, J. (2021). Why empathy is not a reliable source of information in moral decision making. *Current Directions in Psychological Science, 30*, 425–430.

Decety, J., Bartal, I. B. A., Uzefovsky, F., & Knafo-Noam, A. (2016). Empathy as a driver of prosocial behaviour: Highly conserved neurobehavioural mechanisms across species. *Philosophical Transactions of the Royal Society B: Biological Sciences, 371*, 1–11. https://doi.org/10.1098/rstb.2015.0077

Decety, J., & Cowell, J. M. (2014). The complex relation between morality and empathy. *Trends in Cognitive Science, 18*, 337–339.

Decety, J., & Jackson, P. L. (2004). The functional architecture of human empathy. *Behavioral and Cognitive Neuroscience Reviews, 3*, 71–100.

Decety, J., & Jackson, P. L. (2006). A social-neuroscience perspective on empathy. *Current Directions in Psychological Science, 15*, 54–58.

Decety, J., & Svetlova, M. (2012). Putting together phylogenetic and ontogenetic perspectives on empathy. *Developmental Cognitive Neuroscience, 2*(1), 1–24.

de Vignemont, F., & Jacob, P. (2012). What is it like to feel another's pain? *Philosophy of Science, 79*(2), 295–316.

de Vignemont, F., & Singer, T. (2006). The empathic brain: How, when and why? *Trends in Cognitive Sciences, 10*(10), 435–441.

Dovidio, J. F., Johnson, J. D., Gaertner, S. L., Pearson, A. R., Saguy, T., & Ashburn-Nardo, L. (2010). Empathy and intergroup relations. In M. Mikulincer & P. R. Shaver (Eds.), *Prosocial motives, emotions, and behavior* (pp. 393–408). American Psychological Association.

Eisenberg, N., & Miller, P. A. (1987). The relation of empathy to prosocial and related behaviors. *Psychological Bulletin, 101*, 91–119.

Eisenberg, N., & Morris, A. S. (2001). The origins and social significance of empathy-related responding. A review of empathy and moral development: Implications for caring and justice by M. L. Hoffman. *Social Justice Research, 14*, 95–120.

Eysenck, S. B., & Eysenck, H. J. (1978). Impulsiveness and venturesomeness: Their position in a dimensional system of personality description. *Psychological Reports, 43*(3_suppl), 1247–1255.

Felitti, V. J., Anda, R. F., Nordenberg, D., Williamson, D. F., Spitz, A. M., Edwards, V., & Marks, J. S. (1998). Relationship of childhood abuse and household dysfunction to many of the leading causes of death in adults: The Adverse Childhood Experiences (ACE) Study. *American Journal of Preventive Medicine, 14*(4), 245–258.

Gerdes, K. E., Lietz, C. A., & Segal, E. A. (2011). Measuring empathy in the 21st century: Development of an empathy index rooted in social cognitive neuroscience and social justice. *Social Work Research, 35*, 83–93.

Gilligan, C. (1982). *In a different voice: A psychological theory and women's development.* Harvard University Press.

Gleichgerrcht, E., & Young, L. (2013). Low levels of empathic concern predict utilitarian moral judgment. *PLoS ONE, 8*(4), e60418.

Hays, J. C., Saunders, W. B., Flint, E. P., Kaplan, B. H., & Blazer, D. G. (1997). Social support and depression as risk factors for loss of physical function in late life. *Aging & Mental Health, 1*(3), 209–220.

Hepach, R., Vaish, A., & Tomasello, M. (2012). Young children are intrinsically motivated to see others helped. *Psychological Science, 23*(9), 967–972.

Ho, S. S., Konrath, S., Brown, S., & Swain, J. E. (2014). Empathy and stress related neural responses in maternal decision making. *Frontiers in Neuroscience, 8*(Article 152), 1–9.

Hochschild, A. R. (1983). *Managed heart: Commercialization of human feeling.* University of California Press.

Hoffman, M. L. (2001). *Empathy and moral development: Implications for caring and justice.* Cambridge University Press.

Hogan, R. (1969). Development of an empathy scale. *Journal of Consulting and Clinical Psychology, 33*, 307–316.

Holt, S., & Marques, J. (2012). Empathy in leadership: Appropriate or misplaced? An empirical study on a topic that is asking for attention. *Journal of Business Ethics, 105*, 95–105.

Holt, S., Marques, J., Hu, J., & Wood, A. (2017). Cultivating empathy: New perspectives on educating business leaders. *The Journal of Values-Based Leadership, 10*, 1–26.

House, J. S., Landis, K. R., & Umberson, D. (1988). Social relationships and health. *Science, 241*(4865), 540–545.

Innamorati, M., Ebisch, S. J., Gallese, V., & Saggino, A. (2019). A bidimensional measure of empathy: Empathic Experience Scale. *PLoS ONE, 14*(4), e0216164.

Insel, T. R. (1997). A neurobiological basis of social attachment. *American Journal of Psychiatry, 154*, 726–735.

Insel, T. R., & Fernald, R. D. (2004). How the brain processes social information: Searching for the social brain. *Annual Review of Neuroscience, 27*, 697–722.

Itzchakov, G., & Kluger, A. N. (2017). Can holding a stick improve listening at work? The effect of listening circles on employees' emotions and cognitions. *European Journal of Work & Organizational Psychology, 26*, 663–676.

Itzchakov, G., & Kluger, A. N. (2018). The power of listening in helping people change. *Harvard Business Review.* https://hbr.org/2018/05/the-power-of-listening-in-helping-people-change

Jian, G. (2022). From empathic leader to empathic leadership practice: An extension to relational leadership theory. *Human Relations, 75*, 931–955.

Jolliffe, D., & Farrington, D. P. (2006). Development and validation of the Basic Empathy Scale. *Journal of Adolescence, 29*(4), 589–611.

Jordan, M. R., Amir, D., & Bloom, P. (2016). Are empathy and concern psychologically distinct? *Emotion, 16*, 1107.

Kahn, W. A. (1993). Caring for the caregivers: Patterns of organizational caregiving. *Administrative Science Quarterly, 38*, 539–563.

Kellett, J. B., Humphrey, R. H., & Sleeth, R. G. (2006). Empathy and the emergence of task and relations leaders. *The Leadership Quarterly, 17*, 146–162.

Kelley, J. M., Kraft-Todd, G., Schapira, L., Kossowsky, J., & Riess, H. (2014). The influence of the patient–clinician relationship on healthcare outcomes: A systematic review and meta-analysis of randomized controlled trials. *PLoS ONE, 9*(4), e94207. https://doi.org/10.1371/journal.pone.0094207

Keysers, C., Wicker, B., Gazzola, V., Anton, J. L., Fogassi, L., & Gallese, V. (2004). A touching sight: SII/PV activation during the observation and experience of touch. *Neuron, 42*(2), 335–346.

Kluger, A. N., & DeNisi, A. (1996). The effects of feedback interventions on performance: A historical review, a meta-analysis, and a preliminary feedback intervention theory. *Psychological Bulletin, 119*, 254–284.

Knafo, A., Zahn-Waxler, C., Van Hulle, C., Robinson, J. L., & Rhee, S. H. (2008). The developmental origins of a disposition toward empathy: Genetic and environmental contributions. *Emotion, 8*, 737–752.

Lakin, J. L., & Chartrand, T. L. (2003). Using nonconscious behavioral mimicry to create affiliation and rapport. *Psychological Science, 14*, 334–339.

Lawrence, E. J., Shaw, P., Baker, D., Baron-Cohen, S., & David, A. S. (2004). Measuring empathy: Reliability and validity of the Empathy Quotient. *Psychological Medicine, 34*, 911–920.

Lietz, C. A., Gerdes, K. E., Sun, F., Geiger, J. M., Wagaman, M. A., & Segal, E. A. (2011). The Empathy Assessment Index (EAI): A confirmatory factor analysis of a multidimensional model of empathy. *Journal of the Society for Social Work and Research, 2*, 104–124.

Livingstone, A. G., Fernández Rodríguez, L., & Rothers, A. (2020). "They just don't understand us": The role of felt understanding in intergroup relations. *Journal of Personality and Social Psychology, 119*, 633–656.

Lun, J., Kesebir, S., & Oishi, S. (2008). On feeling understood and feeling well: The role of interdependence. *Journal of Research in Personality, 42*, 1623–1628.

Majercsik, E. (2021, May 20). Building the foundation for mental wellness in the workplace. *Forbes Human Resources Council*. https://www.forbes.com/sites/forbeshumanresourcescouncil/2021/05/20/building-the-foundation-for-mental-wellness-in-the-workplace/?sh=1312a8057ee3

Marques, J. (2010). Spirituality, meaning, interbeing, leadership, and empathy: SMILE. *Interbeing, 4*(2), 1–13.

Marques, J. (2011). Five principles that will determine the new mainstream: Spirituality, meaning, inter-being, leadership and empathy: SMILE. *Human Resource Management International Digest, 19*, 39–42.

Martino, J., Pegg, J., & Frates, E. P. (2017). The connection prescription: Using the power of social interactions and the deep desire for connectedness to empower health and wellness. *American Journal of Lifestyle Medicine, 11*, 466–475.

Mehrabian, A., & Epstein, N. (1972). A measure of emotional empathy. *Journal of Personality, 40*, 525–543.

Mercer, S. W., & Reynolds, W. J. (2002). Empathy and quality of care. *British Journal of General Practice, 52*(Suppl), S9–S12.

Morse, J. M., Anderson, G., Bottorff, J. L., Yonge, O., O'Brien, B., Solberg, S. M., & McIlveen, K. H. (1992). Exploring empathy: A conceptual fit for nursing practice? *Image: The Journal of Nursing Scholarship, 24*(4), 273–280.

Mortier, A. V., Vlerick, P., & Clays, E. (2016). Authentic leadership and thriving among nurses: The mediating role of empathy. *Journal of Nursing Management, 24*, 357–365.

Myers, M. W., Laurent, S. M., & Hodges, S. D. (2014). Perspective taking instructions and self-other overlap: Different motives for helping. *Motivation and Emotion, 38*, 224–234.

Noddings, N. (1984). *Caring: A feminine approach to ethics and moral education.* University of California Press.

Noddings, N. (2010). Complexity in caring and empathy. *Abstracta, 6*, 6–12.

Oishi, S., Schiller, J., & Gross, E. B. (2013). Felt understanding and misunderstanding affect the perception of pain, slant, and distance. *Social Psychological and Personality Science, 4*, 259–266.

Olderbak, S., Sassenrath, C., Keller, J., & Wilhelm, O. (2014). An emotion-differentiated perspective on empathy with the emotion specific empathy questionnaire. *Frontiers in Psychology, 5*, 653–666. https://doi.org/10.3389/fpsyg.2014.00653

Perry, J. (2001). *Knowledge, possibility, and consciousness.* MIT Press.

Preston, S. D., & De Waal, F. B. (2002). Empathy: Its ultimate and proximate bases. *Behavioral and Brain Sciences, 25*, 1–20.

Reis, H. T., Lemay, E. P., & Finkenauer, C. (2017). Toward understanding understanding: The importance of feeling understood in relationships. *Social and Personality Psychology Compass, 11*, e12308. https://doi.org/10.1111/spc3.12308

Reniers, R. L., Corcoran, R., Drake, R., Shryane, N. M., & Völlm, B. A. (2011). The QCAE: A questionnaire of cognitive and affective empathy. *Journal of Personality Assessment, 93*, 84–95.

Rogers, C. R. (1962). The interpersonal relationship: The core of guidance. *Harvard Educational Review, 32*, 416–429.

Roth-Hanania, R., Davidov, M., & Zahn-Waxler, C. (2011). Empathy development from 8 to 16 months: Early signs of concern for others. *Infant Behavior and Development, 34*(3), 447–458.

Sadri, G., Weber, T. J., & Gentry, W. A. (2011). Empathic emotion and leadership performance: An empirical analysis across 38 countries. *The Leadership Quarterly, 22*, 818–830.

Schutte, N. S., Malouff, J. M., Hall, L. E., Haggerty, D. J., Cooper, J. T., Golden, C. J., & Dornheim, L. (1998). Development and validation of a measure of emotional intelligence. *Personality and Individual Differences, 25*, 167–177.

Seeman, T. E., Bruce, M. L., & McAvay, G. J. (1996). Social network characteristics and onset of ADL disability: MacArthur studies of successful aging. *The Journals of Gerontology Series b: Psychological Sciences and Social Sciences, 51*(4), S191–S200.

Smith, C. E., Fernengel, K., Holcroft, C., Gerald, K., & Marien, L. (1994). Meta-analysis of the associations between social support and health outcomes. *Annals of Behavioral Medicine, 16*(4), 352–362.

Spreng, R. N., McKinnon, M. C., Mar, R. A., & Levine, B. (2009). The Toronto Empathy Questionnaire: Scale development and initial validation of a factor-analytic solution to multiple empathy measures. *Journal of Personality Assessment, 91*, 62–71.

Stiehl, E., Ernst Kossek, E., Leana, C., & Keller, Q. (2018). A multilevel model of care flow: Examining the generation and spread of care in organizations. *Organizational Psychology Review, 8*, 31–69.

Swain, J. E., Konrath, S., Brown, S. L., Finegood, E. D., Akce, L. B., Dayton, C. J., & Ho, S. S. (2012). Parenting and beyond: Common neurocircuits underlying parental and altruistic caregiving. *Parenting, 12*(2–3), 115–123.

Taylor, S. E., Klein, L. C., Gruenewald, T. L., Gurung, R. A., & Fernandes-Taylor, S. (2003). Affiliation, social support, and biobehavioral responses to stress. *Social Psychological Foundations of Health and Illness*, 314–331.

Thoits, P. A. (1982). Conceptual, methodological, and theoretical problems in studying social support as a buffer against life stress. *Journal of Health and Social Behavior*, 145–159.

Townsend, S. S., Kim, H. S., & Mesquita, B. (2014). Are you feeling what I'm feeling? Emotional similarity buffers stress. *Social Psychological and Personality Science, 5*, 526–533.

Tronto, J. C. (1993). *Moral boundaries: A political argument for an ethic of care*. Routledge.

Tronto, J. C. (2005). Care as the work of citizens: A modest proposal. In M. Friedman (Ed.), *Women and citizenship*. Oxford University Press.

Vachon, D. D., & Lynam, D. R. (2016). Fixing the problem with empathy: Development and validation of the affective and cognitive measure of empathy. *Assessment, 23*, 135–149.

Van Dulmen, A. M., & Bensing, J. M. (2002). Health promoting effects of the physician-patient encounter. *Psychology, Health & Medicine, 7*, 289–300.

Vossen, H. G., Piotrowski, J. T., & Valkenburg, P. M. (2015). Development of the adolescent measure of empathy and sympathy (AMES). *Personality and Individual Differences, 74*, 66–71.

Wærness, K. (1984). The rationality of caring. *Economic and Industrial Democracy, and International Journal, 5*, 185–210.

Wærness, K. (2009). Ethics of care. In J. Peil & I. van Staveren (Eds.), *Handbook of economics and ethics*. Edward Elgar Publishing.

Waytz, A. (2016). The limits of empathy. *Harvard Business Review, 94*, 68–73.

Woltin, K. A., Corneille, O., Yzerbyt, V. Y., & Förster, J. (2011). Narrowing down to open up for other people's concerns: Empathic concern can be enhanced by inducing detailed processing. *Journal of Experimental Social Psychology, 47*, 418–424.

Worley, J. A. (2019). The role of empathy in the professional workplace. In J. Marques (Ed.), *Routledge companion to management and workplace spirituality*. Routledge.

Zaki, J. (2014). Epathy: A motivated account. *Psychological Bulletin, 140*, 1608–1647.

CHAPTER 13

Making a Workplace a Happy One: Benefits and Risks of Remote Work in a Socio-Philosophical Perspective

Edyta Janus and *Agnieszka Smrokowska-Reichmann*

Introduction

Humankind today lives in a situation of constant change. The fluidity of postmodernity identified by Zygmunt Bauman (Bauman, 2013) is associated with the coexistence of two forms of life: traditional, which undergoes gradual destruction, and modern, which undergoes continuous construction. Postmodernity and the modifications characteristic of it force individuals to adapt to a new way of functioning, which consists in departing from constancy toward permanent transformations. The transition from modernity to postmodernity is one of the clearest turning points in sociohistorical development. It is believed that modernism and postmodernism are separate cultural epochs, or even more broadly, civilizational epochs (Szahaj, 2001: 12).

The beginnings of modernity are associated with the beginnings of capitalism, that is, the second half of the eighteenth century, whereas postmodernity began to take shape in the 1970s, accompanying the final transformation of industrial society into postindustrial society. Modernity in the Western world is the era of a rapid development of science and technology, followed by an economic reorganization of society. The "civilization of coal and steel" (Szahaj, 2001: 13) is developing, and it is accompanied by social phenomena described, for example, by Max Weber: rationalization and intellectualization,

E. Janus (✉) · A. Smrokowska-Reichmann
Department of Occupational Therapy, Institute od Applied Sciences, University of Physical Education in Krakow, Kraków, Poland
e-mail: edytajanus3@wp.pl

© The Author(s), under exclusive license to Springer Nature Switzerland AG 2023
J. Marques (ed.), *The Palgrave Handbook of Fulfillment, Wellness, and Personal Growth at Work*,
https://doi.org/10.1007/978-3-031-35494-6_13

and the belief that "all things can – in principle – be mastered by calculation" (Weber, 1989: 47). The modern era ends with the emergence of a postindustrial society (Bell, 1976). In a postindustrial society, we no longer observe the civilization of "coal and steel;" instead, the information civilization comes to the fore. Physical work is increasingly replaced by intellectual work. The importance of education is growing (primarily of higher education). The importance of the white-collar class is also increasing (at the expense of the blue-collar class). The service sector is developing rapidly, and capital is globalized. The production paradigm, which creates the structure of the industrial society in the modern era, in the postindustrial society of the postmodern era is replaced by the consumption paradigm. There is no doubt that only a society which, thanks to the advancement of technological progress, has become a postindustrial society can enter postmodernity. The affirmation of the beginning of postmodernism is also the admission that there has been a transition from the scientific-technical age to the technological age (Zimmerli, 1988).

Typical of modernism was the belief that humankind can, through instrumental action, master both nature and society (Szahaj, 2001: 14). Modernity was an optimistic era because it was characterized by faith in progress and the power of science and technology. However, already in modernity, certain processes began to be marked, which later intensified in postmodernity. This includes: approval of change and pluralism, emphasizing individualism, a decentralized vision of the world, and a new division of labor. Postmodernity is distrustful and skeptical about the existence of one truth and one discourse, as well as about a single strong Cartesian Cogito. Instead, antilogocentrism and intertextualism appear in the philosophy of postmodernism, as along with metaphors of nomad and transversal reason (Deleuze & Guatari, 1988; Welsch, 1998). This in turn means the continuous creation of new meanings in the process of recombination of the existing ones (Derrida, 1993). This constant differentiation also creates certain problems. Admittedly, as enthusiasts of postmodernism note, "postmodern pluralism by no means signifies discretion, but only defends the multiplicity and variety of obligations" (Welsch, 1998: 215). However, there are also alarming opinions that indicate that extreme phenomena appear in postmodernism, e.g., the cult of changeability favoring disorientation, the cult of individualism bordering on social atomism, the cult of pluralism reaching as far as questioning the possibility of meeting in a single discourse, axiological decentralization, flexibility turning into fluidity and lack of anchorage, and, lastly, tolerance turning into indifference. Thus, even philosophers who are otherwise identified with postmodernism are critical of postmodernism, such as Gianni Vattimo, Odo Marquardt, or, first and foremost, Jean Baudrillard.

The ambivalence of postmodern volatility and fluidity is noticed not only in speculative philosophy, but also in economics and management sciences based on hard empiricism. For example, the term VUCA is used to describe a business environment characterized by rapid changes (Bennett & Lemoine, 2014). It is an acronym for: Volatile, Uncertain, Complex, and Ambiguous. By inverting this vector, one can also say that in a postindustrial and postmodern society, the reality of VUCA nowadays reaches not only the corporate and business space, but also the space of the individual, resulting in helplessness in trying to understand and unambiguously define the surrounding world. Ubiquitous transformations also determine changes related to the sphere of employment and forms of work.

The historical, social, and economic changes outlined above motivate us to ask the important questions: what does the slogan "Making a Workplace a Happy One" mean today? What factors determine this process? And finally, is this goal achievable at all?

The Transformation of Work: From Ancient Greece to Modern Forms of Remote Work

Work is an interdisciplinary issue, and its definition differed between historical periods. In ancient Greece and Rome, work had a dual nature, that is, it was distinguished into mental work (belonging to a higher level; thus, people who performed it enjoyed prestige) and physical work. The transformation of views on work took place largely due to Christian doctrine. Work began to be interpreted as a source of virtues as well as moral improvement related to, i.e., helping others. In the Middle Ages, working was treated as a means of salvation, and not working (laziness) as a source of evil (Majka, 1982). Work, therefore, played both an educational and a penitential role until the Reformation, when Martin Luther assessed the importance of work for salvation higher than living in asceticism and contemplation. Johannes Calvin's views can be treated as announcements of changes related to capitalism—that is, working in a rational and orderly manner. The nineteenth century brought the industrial revolution and birth of the working class. Class divisions were treated as the necessary but negative effects of socioeconomic development. At the beginning of the twentieth century, work had acquired the status of both a value and a moral duty of the individual. The transformations of work were also closely related to the market economy, which equated work with the product being exchanged between the seller and the customer. In the industrial era, work was primarily assigned to industry. Finally, in postindustrial society, which is particularly interesting to us, work is embedded in the sphere of services and computerization, which means that its character is increasingly complex and technical (Kolasińska, 2011). It is no coincidence that in the five components of postindustrial society presented by David Bell, particular attention is paid to work. Namely:

1. In the area of the economy, there has been a shift from producers of goods to the service sector. In particular, services related to health, education, research, and administration have developed. In these areas, a "new intelligentsia" has emerged in postindustrial society.

2. With respect to the work structure, the first place has been taken by technical and scientific professions. At the same time, the number of clerks has exceeded the number of laborers.
3. Theoretical knowledge has become the starting point and principle of society. In the past, changes took place first, after which theories were adapted to them. In a postindustrial society, the opposite is true: universities first develop theories, and only then do changes arise.
4. The goal is to raise the standard of living through constant economic development. Therefore, technical progress is planned, based on the assumption that it will be possible to create the future more consciously.
5. "New Intellectual Technology" has become a method of managing highly complex systems and keeping them operational. Problems in postindustrial society are solved by both rules and intuition.

Contemporary society takes the postindustrial and, at the same time, postmodern form. In a publication of the eminent theoretician of contemporary societies, Niclas Luhmann, we can find an alarming observation. Namely, according to Luhmann, each modern society is a complex structure, which is associated not only with a higher efficiency of action and functioning, but also greater susceptibility to disorders. In such a society, the individual has more opportunities than they are capable of grasping. This applies in a special way to the category of work (Luhmann, 1984). In the era of postmodernity, work has gained a new form and quality: it has become a specific style of professional life. There are non-standard forms of work, including remote working. As Drucker (2002: 452) notes, because this type of work requires expertise, those who perform it are called *knowledge workers*.

The term *remote work* is not new, nor is the term *telework*. As early as 1962 in Great Britain, the company F International employed women who worked at home in programming services (Wyrzykowska, 2014: 3803). The creator of the concept of remote work is considered to be Jack Nilles, who (due to the energy crisis and the sharp increase in fuel prices) in 1973 carried out the first experimental teleworking project (Szluz, 2013: 254). He defined it as work that allows its results to be transmitted through information technology such as telecommunications and computers, rather than the physical movement of workers (Nilles, 1976: 87). A special role in popularizing the notion of teleworking was played by Alvin Toffler (2001), who described it in the context of an "electronic village," pointing to computers as the heart of the Third Wave infrastructure, and Francis Kinsman (1988), a futurologist who analyzed the factors influencing the short-term development of teleworking based on organizations such as Rank Xerox I F International. He also predicted a dynamic development of this form of work and its potential impact on the lives of future workers. In 1995, the European Commission recognized that teleworking could become part of future working life. As a result of the telecommunications and IT revolution, there is now a wide range of new, flexible modes of working, including the possibility of partially or completely relocating it outside the traditional office (Nojszewski, 2004). Teleworking is considered to be a form of flexible employment (Piątkowski, 2011: 433), and one of the most popular forms of remote work is to work from home using modern information technologies.

Consequently, remote work has been in use as a "new" mode of work for several dozen years. This is, of course, related to the aforementioned development of modern technologies. It should be noted, however, that current knowledge about remote work urgently needs to be revised due to the COVID-19 pandemic. Most of our knowledge of remote work was generated from within a context where it was only practiced occasionally or infrequently and was only considered by some, but not all or most, of the employees in an organization.

From the Production Paradigm to the Consumption Paradigm

The analysis of the transformation of industrial society into a postindustrial, and thus postmodern, one, should only be supplemented with one more change, which also affects the category of work; namely, the change from the production paradigm to the consumption paradigm, which is analyzed in the postmodern society by philosophy in particular. One must be aware that postmodernity is not received by everyone with enthusiasm and optimism. A crowning example here is Jean Baudrillard, who describes postmodernity as "a process of dramatic change and mutation" (Kellner, 1994: 1), referring to changes not only in the social sphere and political economy, but also within the subjects (the individuals) themselves.

According to Baudrillard, the organization of society in modernity was based on the production and consumption of goods, while in postmodernity, it involves the simulation and play of images and signs (Kellner, 1994). Baudrillard argues that the reality of production has now disappeared. This does not mean that individuals have stopped producing (quite the opposite), but that the category of work has changed significantly. Currently, according to Baudrillard, information processing is replacing traditional production work. The main purpose of work today is not to produce, but to provide information about the social status and the degree of integration of the individual performing the work in society. Furthermore, the wage is not related to the work performed by the individual and thus becomes a simulation. The wages only confirm that the person is playing the game, conforming to the system. As a result, instead of exchange value and use value (to use these old Marxist concepts), we now have sign value. The point of consumption in a postmodern society is not so much to meet needs as it is to constantly recombine the signs. (Baudrillard, 1995). This is how Baudrillard explains the fact that there are no limits to consumption (Oosterling, 1990). The production paradigm involves the duty of working and producing, and as such, is typical of the inner-control modern individual. On the other hand, the consumption paradigm is associated with the compulsion to consume and is typical of the postmodern outside-control individual (Riesman, 1996).

Baudrillard's views on the paradigm shift take on a new meaning in the context of remote work and raise the following questions: is remote working more compatible or more appropriate to the consumer society (i.e., postindustrial and postmodern) than to the productive society (i.e., industrial and modern)? Does the category of sign value, the constant recombination of signs, and the lack of limits for consumption favor the creation of more and more new places and jobs in remote working? If we agree with Baudrillard's other observation, namely that for the postmodern individual, the reality of new technologies is much more interesting than interpersonal relationships (Lane, 2001), then additional questions can be asked: does remote work foster indifference to interpersonal ties? Does remote work entail focusing more on the reality of technology than the reality of human interaction? Baudrillard claims that the world of technological objects and processes becomes for the postmodern subject a support stronger than interpersonal bonding. Subjects create their identity based on the structure of objects (Baudrillard, 1990). This raises another question: does remote work lead to the disappearance of the "Human Factor," at least in direct experience? Perhaps remote work requires an urgent revision not only in the context of the COVID-19 pandemic, but also in the context of the postmodern condition of the individual and society.

Postmodern Nomadism in the Twenty-First Century

When, in the last decades of the twentieth century, theorists of postmodernism created the metaphor of the mobile subject, whether as a nomad or as a transversal reason, no one could have imagined that the twenty-first century would see the subject immobilized by the COVID-19 pandemic.

Undoubtedly, the mobility of the subject of the postmodern era must be interpreted symbolically. The mobility of the postmodern subject means moving freely between meanings, values, and discourses. It is a logical consequence of the fundamental upheaval that took place at the very beginning of postmodernism. This refers, of course, to the explicit abandonment of great narratives (e.g., the Enlightenment's belief in progress) and one Truth in favor of the pluralism of small individual narratives, each presenting its own valuable truth (Lyotard, 1997). One truth and one narrative have been associated by postmodernism with totality/totalitarianism. Postmodernism affirms difference rather than unity; dispute rather than agreement. According to Lyotard, the price for the pursuit of unity and wholeness was the terror that abounded in the twentieth century (Lyotard, 1996: 43).

Thus, a nomad has become the postmodern ideal of a person. There are no fixed roads in the life of a nomad; a nomad does not move along designated routes. Yes, a nomad does leave traces, but these traces, like those on sand, quickly fade away and disappear. The postmodern nomadic subject has no permanent abode, is on the road all the time, which also means that they do not inhabit anything, colonize anything, or appropriate anything. The metaphor of nomadism is completed by the metaphor of the rhizome. Here, instead of Cartesian reason (central root), we have a pluralistic postmodern reason (rhizome). This means that the modernist applies opposition in their thinking, uses dialectics, and seeks one truth. Conversely, postmodern thinking means wandering along the branches of the rhizome through successive narratives, truths, values, and meanings (Deleuze & Guattari, 1988). By functioning from change to change, the life of the postmodern subject that, as postmodern theorists say, the primal state of reality is multiplicity, not unity. Unity was imposed on the world by force. Therefore, the fragmentation of the world is a return to its original and optimal state (Lyotard, 1997). In addition to the symbolism of postmodernism, we may say that pluralism has indeed become something obvious even in the most practical dimensions of modern human life. Today, no one is surprised by frequent changes in profession, living and working environment, place of residence and work, or even changes in gender and identity.

Postmodern fluidity and pluralism are usually received positively. Consequently, the importance of freedom, the affirmation of individuality, and the flexibility of life forms are emphasized above all. Both in academic discourse and public life, we are not surprised today by the metaphors of nomads or tourists, or even separate fields of science, such as the sociology of mobility (Urry, 2009). Baumann claims that the metaphor of human life as a pilgrimage was only possible in a society with a relatively rigid structure. That is why the role model of modernism is the Pilgrim, while in the world of postmodernism, characterized by volatility and fluidity, where signposts have been replaced by change, other role models have appeared: the Stroller, Vagabond, Tourist, and Player (Baumann, 1994: 12–13). As with all cultural and social phenomena, many people also fear that the excessive intensification of pluralism may lead to a lack of a feeling of support and roots, and that it may cause confusion, including axiological confusion. A postmodern mobile subject may become destabilized, in the negative sense of the word. "Since life ceased to be a pilgrimage and has become to a much greater degree a kind of tourism – following various types of seasonal goals, the failure of which may be the cause of, at most, an unsuccessful trip (…) the 'I' seems to be drifting" (Kołacka, 1998: 42).

In the world after the COVID-19 pandemic, however, a completely different question arises, which, for obvious reasons, the earlier critics of postmodernism could not have posed. Namely, was it not the postmodern subject—freely moving between narratives, values and relationships—that, perhaps paradoxically, dealt with the pandemic in the best possible way? The postmodern subject, immersed in the virtual space and constantly looking for new meanings and discourses, was actually perfectly prepared for the situation in which, as a result of the pandemic, only virtual reality was left at one's disposal. As John Urry rightly pointed out, nomadism can only be imagined alongside virtual mobility (Urry, 2009: 13). What was taken to be the weakness of the postmodern nomad—"drifting" in the Web—was found to be their strength in pandemic conditions. The necessity to transfer to the virtual mode of interpersonal contacts, both social and professional, was a challenge that the postmodern man, in general, was able to meet.

Mobility resulting from the IT revolution allows one to master space and time, just as new lands and seas were mastered in the past. In the COVID-19 era, only virtual mobility was available for a period of time. Of course, we may always look for other aspects of the discussion. For example: since IT mobility is dimensionless, will it not create problems for humans as dimensional beings? Or: since IT mobility runs lightning fast, will not the communication based on it be so fast that it becomes worthless? Regardless of this type of discussion, one thing seems certain: the emergence of postmodernity is conducive to remote work in many dimensions. Above all, the following aspects should be mentioned here: (1) Possibilities given to the subject by new technologies; (2) Dealing with the dimensionlessness and speed of information movement by the subject; (3) Individualization of the subject; and (4) Willingness of the subject to embrace change (frequent changes of the workplace and no attachment to the workplace).

Remote Work in the Era of the COVID-19 Pandemic

The outbreak of the pandemic in 2019 in the city of Wuhan caused dramatic changes in the functioning of societies around the world. Initially, it seemed that the coronavirus would be local and short-lived. Unfortunately, the virus has left an imprint in everyone's life. Likewise, the pandemic has caused revolutionary changes in the socioeconomic area.

Restrictions in mobility, the risk of infection, the need for isolation, closure of nurseries and kindergartens, and global market changes (decline in GDP and economic downturn) have forced the introduction of a number of changes in the functioning of enterprises, in particular, in the modes and forms of work in some sectors and industries. It was necessary to switch to remote work. Prior to COVID-19, most workers had little experience with working remotely; neither they nor their organizations were prepared to support this practice. The outbreak of the COVID-19 pandemic in 2020 has turned millions of people around the world into remote workers (Kniffin et al., 2020). Remote work became the "new standard" almost overnight, even though many organizations were insufficiently prepared for it, much like their employees. A significant portion of remote work prior to the pandemic was voluntary, which means that individuals chose to do it at their own discretion. In the era of the pandemic, remote work has become a necessity, rather than a choice (Wang et al., 2020).

To better characterize remote work in the context of COVID-19, it is worth referring to the Work Characteristics as Antecedents in the Context of Remote Work approach (Wang et al., 2020). Remote work is understood as a context or environment (Bailey & Kurland, 2002). This approach focuses on the relationship between the characteristics of virtual work and work experience. It has important theoretical and practical implications. This trend is derived from the perspective of socio-technical systems (Trist, 1981), in which remote work is treated as a context, rather than an independent variable. It is argued that the characteristics of remote work should conform to the new mode of working in order to achieve better results and well-being (Bélanger et al., 2013). Unintended consequences may appear when the characteristics of the virtual work do not meet the individual and/or task requirements. This is exemplified by conflicts between work and family, which can arise when work demands are high and the workers' autonomy is limited by household obligations. According to a study by Wang et al. (2020), challenges regarding remote work reflect the direct psychological experiences of employees related to the performance of tasks, interpersonal cooperation, and social interactions with family and friends. In the context of working remotely during a pandemic, researchers point to four factors that have a detrimental effect on the efficiency of work and well-being of individuals. These are: procrastination, ineffective communication, work-at-home disruptions, and loneliness. Procrastination is common in the office workplace (Kühnel et al., 2016) and can be even worse when people work from home due to the difficulty of self-regulation. Loneliness means fewer face-to-face interactions with others. Of course, this refers to real contact, rather than contact via electronic tools and the Internet. Disruptions in working at home result from the multitude of roles and the need to combine them when one's home also becomes one's workplace. Communication difficulties mean a limited possibility of transmitting messages outside modern information and communication technologies. An important aspect of the contextual model are the features of virtual work: social support, professional autonomy, monitoring, and workload. Individual factors are equally important; among these, self-discipline can be considered the most important.

Remote working resulting from the changes related to the pandemic is provided mainly in knowledge-based enterprises, i.e., those that produce intangible products based on their know-how and employee competences. The second category of enterprises are those in which some of the work performed has high teleworkability. This term refers to a specific scope of activities, the effects of which are easily quantifiable and are subject to simple assessment, and thus, performing this work outside the office is not difficult. An example is working in a call center (Jarczewska-Gerc et al., 2021). The lowest share in remote work was recorded in industries such as the hotel industry and catering (Lewiatan Confederation Report, 2021).

The year 2022 is the "end of the pandemic" in many countries, manifested by attempts to take root in the new reality. Research shows that as many as ¾ of companies do not plan for all employees to obligatorily return to offices (Castrillon, 2020), and ¾ of employees want to continue working in the hybrid model. According to Barrero et al. (2021), the trend toward a more flexible workplace and working hours will continue. This is indicated by the following economic arguments:

1. Companies want to reap the benefits of out-of-office investments made in recent months;
2. There is a wave of technological innovations supporting work from home (applications for videoconferencing, work monitoring, teamwork, etc.), which makes it, on the one hand, cheaper and, on the other hand, better suited to needs;
3. Recruiting employees for remote work can open up access to a more qualified pool of talent.

Benefits and Limitations of Remote Working

Switching to a remote work mode requires an employee to reorganize their thinking and change their habits. The positive and negative effects of this situation will largely depend on both the organization of remote work by the employer and the employee themselves. In the case of the employee, the following factors will have an effect: their experience and training in remote work, working conditions, as well as certain personality traits, e.g., determination, honesty, conscientiousness, and time management skills. Previous research on the benefits and limitations of remote work has focused mainly on the links between working remotely and employee performance. Employees' professional experience and their subjective perception of work were taken into account only to a small extent (Pérez et al., 2003).

A comparative analysis was performed between the benefits and limitations of remote work based on data available in subject literature, with particular emphasis on the context of the pandemic. It is also worth noting that both the benefits and the limitations have a twofold meaning. Each benefit may also have a number of limitations; likewise, the limitations of remote work may also be perceived by some individuals as advantages.

According to available studies (Dolot, 2020; Felstead & Henseke, 2017; Jarczewska-Gerc et al., 2021), the general benefits of remote work include many aspects that should be briefly characterized.

The first advantage of remote work is the possibility to better balance work and personal life (including family life). Working from home allows one to spend more time with the family, which results, among others, in time saved on commuting between home and work. In addition, in the era of lockdowns and the change in the mode of broadly defined education from stationary to remote, individuals with families are able to carry out their professional tasks in the presence of other household members. On the one hand, these circumstances may affect the declarations of the respondents collected by researchers of this issue, and on the other hand, it should be remembered that the presence of household members may also be an important distracting factor.

The aforementioned time saving related to lack of commuting, treated as a benefit of remote work, is also associated with spending less money on fuel, tickets, etc.

Decreased mobility due to remote work is also connected with the aspect of environmental protection. Research on the correlation between remote work and ecology has been conducted for years. The issue gained particular importance in the era of the pandemic: it was noted that the current situation related to remote work (or its hybrid form, which means alternating between working from home and from the company's premises) may, for example, reduce the degradation of the urban environment (Maipas et al., 2021).

Remote work allows for greater flexibility in planning one's activities, adjusting them to the individual rhythm of the day and the way of working. In addition, researchers show that working remotely improves the respondents' productivity, efficiency, and satisfaction (Beno, 2021).

In addition to the benefits associated with remote work, researchers show a number of negative consequences (Dolot, 2020; Felstead & Henseke, 2017; Jarczewska-Gerc et al., 2021).

The blurring of the boundary between work and private life is shown to be a significant negative effect related to remote working. In addition, remote workers often report a sense of being constantly at work, which is associated with reduced comfort, because their apartment has a dual function, both residential and as a space for performing professional tasks.

According to Eurofound research (2020), one of the most burdened groups in terms of work-life balance is parents. The pandemic additionally created them new difficulties for them related to, i.e., combining work with the organization of distance learning for their children. According to the employees who were also parents working remotely, family matters made it difficult for them to devote time to work and to concentrate. Women, who more often than men report problems with providing childcare and assistance in organizing remote education, are in a more difficult situation in terms of reconciling work and family roles during remote work (International Labor Organization, 2020). Researchers also show that remote work is often depreciated as "staying at home," which negatively affects the employees themselves and may contribute to the disorganization of their work (Jarczewska-Gerc et al., 2021).

The negative consequences related to remote work also include the lack of direct contact with colleagues and a feeling of lack of support on their part (feeling of isolation, loneliness, and alienation and no possibility of building informal relationships). Working and being part of an organization is not limited to performing professional duties; it is also an area for maintaining social relationships that play an important role in the functioning of an employee in a company (Dolot, 2020). The limitations of remote work also include limited access of the employee to the resources of the organization understood as not only technical elements, but also the area of sharing knowledge with other people.

The listed benefits and limitations of remote work, as already mentioned, intermingle. Knowledge on this subject should constitute the basis for organization managers to take effective management actions, paying attention not only to the economic dimension, but above all to the human factor.

Conclusions

Analyzing changes in work, in particular remote work, indicates that this form, even though it has been known for many years, is currently undergoing significant transformations. This becomes especially visible during the pandemic, when providing work in this mode has become the norm for many sectors and industries. The importance of remote work will certainly not be marginalized after the end of the coronavirus epidemic, at the very least because many companies limit the rented office space or even stop using it altogether due to the popularization of remote working. The development of remote work is also fostered by the interest in it on the part of employees themselves. Researchers forecast that in future, hybrid solutions combining stationary and remote work will be the most popular (Smoder, 2021).

To summarize the analyses undertaken in this chapter, it can be stated that we are seeing a breakthrough in the modes of work, which in particular concerns remote work. Although, as shown above, remote work does not only bring positive effects, ignoring, let alone combating, this new form of work would be akin to "Neo-Luddism"[1] and would have to be assessed negatively as irrational behavior. We are the heirs of the IT revolution. Our life—and our work belonging to it—takes place in a postindustrial and postmodern society. These are obvious facts; it would be nonsensical to deny them. In a dimensionless virtual space, where more and more information is received and sent faster and faster, the subject has been dynamized in a specific manner, including when the subject does not physically leave home. The more insightful observers of the uninterrupted development of new technologies should not be surprised by the new forms that work has taken. It was to be expected. In fact, nothing new has happened in the world of employers and employees, except that individuals have adapted to the new technological opportunities that appeared with the advent of postindustrial society. Such a reaction of adapting to the objective and indisputable fact of technological (and civilizational) progress should be regarded as the most rational behavior.

The development of technology and the related change in the functioning of society observed between the industrial and postindustrial era led to the

---

[1] Luddism—a movement of British workers, cottage workers, and craftsmen related to the destruction of factory machines (especially weaving workshops), being a response to the changes taking place as a result of the industrial revolution. The first incident—the destruction of weaving workshops—took place in Sheffield. The riots were caused by the fear that the machines introduced at that time into the weaving industry would lead to poverty and unemployment among factory workers and the collapse of craft and cottage workshops. The leader of the movement was known as King Lud (PWN Encyclopedia).

emergence of postmodernism. However, on the philosophical level, postmodernism is the heir of the critical and unmasking thought of Wittgenstein, Nietzsche, Heidegger, and Sartre. The postmodern critique of Cartesian rationality, one truth, or one narrative only means taking a step further than these philosophers. There are even opinions that, from the philosophical point of view, postmodernism is a recipe for cultivating philosophy in the conditions of a postindustrial society. Perhaps postmodernism is another attempt to find an answer to the question: "Who is the contemporary man?" (Czerniak & Szahaj, 1996: 15, 17). Thus, postmodernism in the philosophical and social layer can be presented not as a revolutionary movement, but as an evolutionary movement. It seems that Wolfgang Welsch went the furthest, referring to Immanuel Kant himself as a precursor of the postmodern vision of pluralistic reason (Welsch, 1998: 403). Kant's analysis of practical reason, theoretical reason, and the power of judgment became Welsch's main inspiration in his project of transversality, and ultimately allowed him to formulate the thesis: "Reason for us today (…) is the ability to connect and switch between forms of rationality" (Welsch, 1998: 405). The creator of the concept of transversal reason believes that postmodernism is a transformation of modernity directed toward the future (Welsch, 1998: 149). True, postmodernism radicalizes the achievements of philosophy and goes beyond its past limitations, but does not reject this heritage. The frame of postmodern thinking about humankind and the world includes the continuation and further development of human thought. Postmodernism remains open to new ways of thinking, including those that have been dismissed by traditionalists as anti-intellectual. However, postmodernism is still based on tradition. And again—as with technological and economic changes—we may say that it was to be expected.

Thus, in the dimension of empiricism and practice, as well as in the dimension of abstraction and theory, changes are taking place that constitute the next stage of the evolution of our society and our civilization. However, this phenomenon should not be interpreted in terms of determinism. Rather, socioeconomic evolution and its inevitable changes should be seen as an opportunity. Our task is to observe and analyze these changes, and then draw constructive conclusions from it, intensifying the positives and reducing the negatives. This also applies, and perhaps especially so, to such specific manifestations of socioeconomic life as remote work. We have to accept that remote work creates a new permanent form of workplace while objectively and rationally assessing both its pros and cons. Whether we are able to make this new special workplace a happy one depends on an objective and rational approach.

References

Bailey, D. E., & Kurland, N. B. (2002). A review of telework research: Findings, new directions and lessons for the study of modern work. *Journal of Organizational Behavior, 23*(SpecIssue), 383–400. https://doi.org/10.1002/job.144

Barrero, J. M., Bloom, N., & Davis, S. J. (2021). Why working from home will stick (Working Paper Nr 28731). National Bureau of Economic Research.
Baudrillard, J. (1990). *Fatal strategies*. Pluto.
Baudrillard, J. (1995). *Symulakry i symulacja*. Wydawnictwo Sic!
Bauman, Z. (2013). *Ponowoczesność jako źródło cierpień*. Wydawnictwo Sic!
Baumann, Z. (1994). *Dwa szkice o moralności ponowoczesnej* (pp. 12–13). Instytut Kultury.
Bélanger, F., Watson-Manheim, M. B., & Swan, B. R. (2013). A multi-level socio-technical systems telecommuting framework. *Behaviour and Information Technology*, 32(12), 1257–1279.
Bell, D. (1976). *The coming of post-industrial society*. Penguin Books.
Bennett, N., & Lemoine, J. (2014). What VUCA really means for you. *Harvard Business Review*, 92(1/2), 27.
Beno, M. (2021). The advantages and disadvantages of E-working: An examination using an ALDINE analysis. *Emerging Science Journal*, 5, 11–20. https://doi.org/10.28991/esj-2021-SPER-02
Castrillon, C. (2020). *This is the future of remote work in 2021*. Forbes.
Czerniak, S., & Szahaj A. (1996). *Postmodernizm a filozofia. Wybór tekstów*. IFiS PAN.
Deleuze, G., & Guattari, F. (1988). Kłącze. *Colloquia Communia*, 1–3
Derrida, J. (1993). *Pismo filozofii*. inter esse, Kraków.
Dolot, A. (2020). Wpływ pandemii COVID-19 na pracę zdalną – perspektywa pracownika. *E-mentor*, 83(1), 35–43. https://doi.org/10.15219/em83.145
Drucker, P. (2002). *Myśli przewodnie Druckera*, Wydawnictwo MT Biznes.
Encyklopedia.pwn.pl/haslo/luddyzm.
Eurofound. (2020). *Living, working and COVID-19, COVID-19 series*. Publications Office of the European Union.
Felstead, A., & Henseke, G. (2017). Assessing the Growth of Remote Working and its Consequences for Effort, Well-Being and Work-Life Balance. ORG: Other Change Management & Organizational Behavior (Topic).
ILO. (2020). *Teleworking during the COVID-19 pandemic and beyond: A practical guide*. International Labour Organization.
Jarczewska-Gerc, E., Filiciak, M., & Brach, B. (2021). *Modele pracy w nowej (nie)normalności*. CD Projekt Red, Uniwersytet SWPS.
Kellner, D. (Ed.). (1994). *Baudrillard: A critical reader*. Wiley-Blackwell Publishing.
Kinsman, F. (1988). *The telecommuters*. Wiley.
Kniffin, K. M., Narayanan, J., Anseel, F., Antonakis, J., Ashford, S. P., Bakker, A. B., Bamberger, P., Bapuji, H., Bhave, D. P., Choi, V. K., Creary, S. J., Demerouti, E., Flynn, F. J., Gelfand, M. J., Greer, L. L., Johns, G., Klein, P. G., Lee, S. Y., & van Vugt, M. (2020). COVID-19 and the workplace: Implications, issues, and insights for future research and action. *American Psychologist*. https://doi.org/10.1037/amp0000716
Kołacka, D. (1998). Odwrotna strona pluralności. In A. Zeidler-Janiszewska (red.), *Problemy ponowoczesnej pluralizacji kultury. Wokół koncepcji Wolfganga Welscha* (p. 42). Wydawnictwo Fundacji Humaniorum.
Kolasińska, E. (2011). Praca jako cenna wartość. In D. Duraj (Ed.), *Przemiany pracy, postaw i ról zawodowych*. Wydawnictwo Uniwersytetu Łódzkiego.
Kühnel, J., Bledow, R., & Feuerhahn, N. (2016). When do you procrastinate? Sleep quality and social sleep lag jointly predict self-regulatory failure at work. *Journal of Organizational Behavior*, 37(7), 983–1002.

Lane, R. J. (2001). *Jean Baudrillard*. Routledge.
Lewiatan, K. (2021). *Raport improved social dialogue in Poland: A model for initiating social dialogue by employer organisations*. Konfederacja Lewiatan.
Luhmann, N. (1984). *Soziale systeme. Grundriss einer allgemeinen theorie*. Suhrkamp.
Lyotard, J.-F. (1996). Odpowiedź na pytanie, co to jest postmoderna. In S. Czerniak & A. Szahaj (Eds.), *Postmodernizm a filozofia. Wybór tekstów* (p. 43). IFiS PAN.
Lyotard, J.-F. (1997). *Kondycja ponowoczesna*. Aletheia.
Maipas, S., Panayiotides, I. G., & Kavantzas, N. (2021). Remote-working carbon-saving footprint: Could COVID-19 pandemic establish a new working model with positive environmental health implications? *Environmental Health Insights, 15*, 11786302211013546. https://doi.org/10.1177/11786302211013546
Majka, J. (1982). *Etyka życia gospodarczego*. Wydawnictwo Wrocławskiej Księgarni Archidiecezjalnej.
Nilles, J. M. (1976). *The telecommunications—Transportation trade off: Options for tomorrow*. Wiley.
Nojszewski, D. (2004). Telepraca. *E-metor, 3*(5).
Oosterling, H. (1990). *Philosophie als Scheinmanöver, Methamorphose und Ironie in den späteren Arbeiten Baudrillards*. www.henkoosterling.nl/pdfs/art-baud-dts-1990.pdf
Pérez Pérez, M., Martínez Sánchez, A., & Pilar de Luis Carnicer, M. (2003). The organizational implications of human resources managers' perception of teleworking. *Personnel Review, 32*(6), 733–755. https://doi.org/10.1108/00483480310498693
Piątkowski, M. (2011). Znaczenie form zatrudnienia w funkcjonowaniu przedsiębiorstw. *Zeszyty Naukowe Uniwersytetu Szczecińskiego, Ekonomiczne Problemy Usług, 73*, 431–442.
Riesman, D. (1996). *Samotny tłum*. MUZA.
Smoder, A. (2021). Remote work in pandemic conditions—Selected issues. *Polityka Społeczna, t. XLVIII*(5–6). https://doi.org/10.5604/01.3001.0015.2582
Szahaj, A. (2001). *Postmodernizm w kulturze współczesnej. Wykłady z humanistyki*. Instytut Nauk Humanistycznych i Ekonomicznych Akademii Techniczno-Rolniczej w Bydgoszczy.
Szluz, B. (2013). Telepraca – nowoczesna, elastyczna forma zatrudnienia i organizacji pracy. Szansa czy zagrożenie? *Modern Management Review, 4*, 253–266.
Toffler, A. (2001). *Trzecia fala*. Państwowy Instytut Wydawniczy.
Trist, E. L. (1981). The evolution of socio-technical systems In A. H. V. de Ven & W. F. Joyce (Eds.), *Perspectives on organization design and behavior*. Wiley.
Urry, J. (2009). Socjologia mobilności. *PWN, 44*, 13.
Wang, B., Liu, Y., Qian, J., & Parker, S. K. (2020). Achieving effective remote working during the COVID-19 pandemic: A work design perspective. *Applied Psychology*. https://doi.org/10.1111/apps.12290
Weber, M. (1989). Nauka jako zawód i powołanie. In M. Weber (Ed.), *Polityka jako zawód i powołanie* (p. 47). Nowa.
Welsch, W. (1998). *Nasza postmodernistyczna moderna* (p. 215). Oficyna Naukowa.
Wyrzykowska, B. (2014). Przedsiębiorstwo bez pracowników – telepraca. *Logistyka, 4*, 3801–3813.
Zimmerli, W. (1988). Das antiplatonische experiment. Bemerkungen zur technologischen Postmoderne. In W. Zimmerli (Ed.), *Technologisches Zeitalter oder Postmoderne?* (pp. 13–36). Wilhelm Fink Verlag.

CHAPTER 14

Coping with Stress: The Importance of Individual Resilience and Work Tasks Complexity and Unpredictability

Simona Leonelli and *Emanuele Primavera*

INTRODUCTION

After the first cases of COVID-19 were diagnosed at the beginning of 2019 in Rome (Italy), the Italian National Institute of Health and the Ministry of Health started investigating the diffusion of the phenomenon stating some guidelines to protect the population. As a result, healthcare companies were confronted with the need to reorganize hospital structures and create new pavilions, wards, and hospitals dedicated to COVID-19 patients (Leonelli & Primavera, 2022a, 2022b). These sudden changes have radically transformed all workers' professional lives, particularly those in the healthcare industry, powerfully affecting their perception of stress and workload (Leonelli et al., 2022; Primavera & Leonelli, 2022a, 2022b). Healthcare workers were at the frontline against COVID-19: they fought with the possibility of being infected and faced long working hours, stress, exhaustion, and burnout (Primavera & Leonelli, 2020). Moreover, even if the COVID-19 pandemic is declining, its effect on healthcare workers is always touchable.

In this chapter, we will analyze the perceived stress as a first consequence of working in the healthcare sector during the pandemic. Perceived stress

---

S. Leonelli (✉)
Department of Economics and Management "M. Fanno", University of Padova, Padova, Italy
e-mail: simona.leonelli@unipd.it

E. Primavera
"Spirito Santo" Hospital, Pescara, Italy

© The Author(s), under exclusive license to Springer Nature Switzerland AG 2023
J. Marques (ed.), *The Palgrave Handbook of Fulfillment, Wellness, and Personal Growth at Work*,
https://doi.org/10.1007/978-3-031-35494-6_14

refers to an individual judgment about stressful situations and events and negatively affects an individual's well-being, particularly when individuals recognize that the requests overreach their ability to cope (Teoh et al., 2020). In the healthcare context, perceived stress negatively impacts nurses' quality of life and well-being (Leonelli & Primavera, 2022b; Mroczek & Almeida, 2004; Mukhtar, 2020) and, in extreme cases, perceived stress can be the cause of organizational inefficiency because of high rates of displacement, absence due to illness, and increasing costs to maintain the high quality of care services (Babyar, 2017; Stimpfel et al., 2019; van Schothorst-van Roekel et al., 2020).

The first aim of this study is to investigate how individual resilience can reduce perceived stress levels. Individual resilience refers to the ability to adapt to and cope with adversity and stress (Hart et al., 2014). Previous studies show that individual resilience has both a direct and an indirect effect on decreasing stress perception, particularly for nurses (Britt et al., 2021; Delgado et al., 2017; Hegney et al., 2015; Shoss et al., 2018; Yu et al., 2019). However, only a few studies analyze this relationship during an intense crisis such as the pandemic (e.g., Heath et al., 2020).

The second aim of this study is to understand how the characteristics of the work tasks can improve or worsen the relationship between individual resilience and stress perception. The work task characteristics can have positive or negative vibes on the staff, depending on individual personality, abilities, experience, etc., (Schoellbauer et al., 2022). This study considers two characteristics of the work tasks: complexity and unpredictability, analyzing the differences in nurses working in COVID-19 (i.e., higher complexity and unpredictability) and non-COVID-19 wards (i.e., lower complexity and unpredictability).

281 Italian nurses are surveyed between April and May 2020, and results show that individual resilience negatively relates to nurses' stress perceptions. Furthermore, this relationship appears to be more damaging in non-COVID-19 wards than in COVID-19 wards.

This chapter theoretically contributes to organizational behavior and human resource management literatures. In the first case, focusing on individual characteristics of employees, the contribution is linked to the first result that shows that individual resilience can be "idealized" as a coping strategy or resource investment to cope with perceived stress, particularly in periods of crisis. While in the second case, focusing on the work task characteristics, the contribution refers to managing complexity and unpredictability that can strongly impact employees' well-being. Finally, the chapter identifies practical interventions that can improve individual resilience and prevent the phenomenon of burnout.

BACKGROUND

Perceived Stress

Perceived stress is related to negative feelings about lack of control and unpredictability concerning the existence of actual stressors (Teoh et al., 2020). This means that perceived stress is a self-reported judgment of stressful situations and events in an individual's life (Hilcove et al., 2020). Perceived stress at work can cause physical problems, irritability, and depression, impacting work performance and interpersonal relationships (Bliese et al., 2017). Numerous studies underline that healthcare professionals experience the highest stress levels in the work setting (Hilcove et al., 2020; Rodwell et al., 2009). In a study involving five countries, Glazer and Gyurak (2008) show that the factors influencing nurses' stress are linked to a scarcity of resources, issues in the leadership dynamics, lack of staff, high quantitative workload, and issues related to their relationship with co-workers. Regarding culture-specific stressors, death, inadequate communication, and psychological strain are particularly relevant in Hungary and Israel. Staff skillset is usually indicated as a stressor in UK and Israel. Disorganization and time pressure are important stressors in Italy, the UK, and the US. Moreover, US nurses report that low rewards and poor consideration of their prestigious work affect their stress levels. Finally, nurses' stress level generally increases because of prolonged exposure to patient suffering, heavy workloads, staffing deficiencies, and peer conflict (Hetzel-Riggin et al., 2020). However, prolonged exposure to high-stress levels can lead to burnout (Di Trani et al., 2021; Hilcove et al., 2020).

Individual Resilience

Resilience is a broad concept belonging to different fields, such as psychology, management, physics, ecology, engineering, and economics. In general, resilience refers to the ability to "bounce back" from adversity remaining focused and optimistic about the future (Hart et al., 2014). Individual resilience is a personal attitude related to the ability to address difficulties, elicit positive emotions in negative circumstances, and resist and recover from stressors (Ong et al., 2006). According to Bonanno (2004), resilient individuals are more capable of maintaining an emotional equilibrium during stressful events.

Individual resilience in nursing refers to nurses' attitude to cope with workplace adversities and difficult requests (Delgado et al., 2017). Nurses' high levels of resilience are associated with increased well-being, psychological health, and job satisfaction (Gabriel et al., 2011; Grabbe et al., 2020). In fact, nurses with higher levels of resilience are able to preserve positive emotions even if they are not satisfied with their task performance. Moreover, resilience improves work relationships and professional quality of life (Hegney et al., 2015; Zhao et al., 2016). In this chapter, we propose that nurses who possess higher levels of individual resilience will experience lower levels of perceived stress. This is because resilient individuals unconsciously know how to face challenges or difficulties. Hence, we state:

H1: Individual resilience is negatively related to nurses' perceived stress.

Work Tasks' Complexity and Unpredictability

Knowledge-intensive jobs are generally characterized by complex and unpredictable changing work tasks (Schoellbauer et al., 2022). By complexity, we mean the individuals' perception of the challenging nature of the work (Dóci & Hofmans, 2015). At the same time, unpredictability implies a lack of control at work and mastery expectancies related to the abovementioned complexity (Schoellbauer et al., 2022).

Crisis, like pandemics, substantially impact the complexity and unpredictability of work tasks, particularly for healthcare workers (De Bloom, 2020). Work task complexity suddenly increased for those working with COVID-19 patients; the disease and treatments were unknown (López-Cabarcos et al., 2020). Even work task unpredictability suddenly increased; for healthcare workers was difficult to predict which work tasks they would have to accomplish in a day and the prioritization they should follow (Bowers et al., 2001; Pavedahl et al., 2022). Moreover, with the increasing task complexity and unpredictability, healthcare workers encountered difficulties in anticipating the task completion process, that is, identifying the suitable method and time needed to perform the work activities and prevent any problems that may come up in the work process.

Previous studies show that work task complexity and unpredictability are negatively related to stress perception (Dóci & Hofmans, 2015; Rana et al., 2020; Schoellbauer et al., 2022). However, to the best of our knowledge, none of them focused on his moderator role. In this sense, we hypothesize that work task characteristics (i.e., complexity and unpredictability) can decrease the beneficial role of individual resilience on stress perception. This is because even if resilient individuals know how to cope with complexity and unpredictability; these circumstances can undermine their resilience levels, slightly decreasing their beneficial effects. Hence, we state:

H2: Work task characteristics moderate the relationship between nurses' individual resilience and perceived stress.

Materials and Methods

Sample and Procedure

The study was constructed using a descriptive cross-sectional design, considering a sample of nurses who voluntarily participated. Nurses enrolled in the study were required to meet the subsequent inclusion criteria: being Italian and working as professionals in care services facilitating direct contact with patients. Retired nurses or those working in healthcare administration management without direct contact with patients (such as sterilization and laboratories) were excluded.

The survey was administered during April and May 2020. Because of the social distancing measures during that lockdown period, the questionnaire was administered online via Facebook, the most widely used social network in the world. A brief introduction to the study and the link to the questionnaire were posted on three Facebook pages where many nurses are registered. Since it is difficult to identify a starting sample when administering online questionnaires, in agreement with Houser (2016), we calculated the total initial sample considering the actual number of people who viewed the post using the Brand24 tool. Out of a total of 956 views, 285 nurses answered the questionnaire (29.4% response rate). However, due to the occurrence of some missing data and biases, 281 were complete and eligible.

Ethical Considerations

This study did not need the approval of the local research ethics committee. Participants were informed about the objective of the study and signed an informed consent form. No economic incentives were offered or envisaged to complete the questionnaire. The ethical principles enshrined in the Declaration of Helsinki were always observed.

Measures

The scales used in this study were originally in English. We administered the questionnaire in Italian, and to ensure an accurate translation, we employed a rigorous back-translation technique (Brislin, 1980).

Perceived stress was measured using the Perceived Stress Scale (PPS) (Cohen et al., 1983). The PPS is the most widely used psychological instrument for measuring stress perception. The scale comprises 10 items that explore the degree to which some life situations appear stressful. Questions are related to "how often do you feel stress about…" and the answers follow the 5-point Likert scale rules where zero means "never" and four "always." The higher the results derived from the sum of the score, the higher the perceived stress.

Individual resilience was measured using the Connor-Davison resilience Scale (Revised), consisting of 10 items (Connor & Davidson, 2003). Answers follow a 5-point response scale where zero means "strongly disagree" and four "strongly agree." The total score ranges from 0 to 40, with higher scores reflecting greater resilience. We have used the official Italian adaptation of the scale (Connor & Davidson, 2003).

Work task characteristics were measured considering the complexity and unpredictability of work tasks based on the work of Schoellbauer et al. (2022). For this reason, we asked if nurses worked in COVID-19 or non-COVID-19 wards. In fact, in COVID-19 wards, nurses encountered high levels of complexity and unpredictability in performing their tasks. Conversely, those who worked in non-COVID-19 wards experienced lower complexity and unpredictability in completing their task. Therefore, the dummy variable assumes the value of one if nurses worked in COVID-19 wards (i.e., higher complexity and unpredictability) and zero otherwise (i.e., lower complexity and unpredictability).

Consistent with the extant literature, we have also included a number of control variables that have been found by prior studies to be correlated with perceived stress and phycological resilience. Specifically, we controlled for *gender*, *age*, g*eographical area*, and w*ard type*.

Data Analysis

Data were analyzed using quantitative techniques employing Stata 16 as the statistical software. Descriptive statistics are also shown to present the main sample characteristics. Finally, to test our hypotheses, linear regression models were employed.

RESULTS

Table 14.1 presents the characteristics of the sampled survey. The sample is predominantly composed of female nurses (84.3%), aged between 30 and 39 years old (32.8%), mainly working in the Medical area (48.4%) and COVID-19 ward (71.2%), and in hospitals principally located in the Northwest of Italy (32.7%).

Descriptive statistics and Spearman's correlations of the examined variables are presented in Table 14.2. Spearman's Rank-Order Correlation is useful to measure the strength and direction of the association between continuous and categorical variables. Results show that all the correlation values of our variables lie below 0.50. Thus, we can state that a small correlation exists between them. We have controlled for multicollinearity and common method variance using the Variance Inflation Factor (non-reported here but available from request), and results show that all the values of the variables are close to 1, which means they are almost completely uncorrelated to one another and no common method variance affected our model (Kock, 2015).

Before running our regressions, we checked differences in individual resilience and stress perception in nurses working in COVID-19 and non-COVID-19 wards, performing T-tests. T-test is generally used to compare the

Table 14.1 Full sample characteristics

		n	%
Gender		237	84.3
	Female	44	15.7
	Male		
Age		47	16.7
	<30 years old	92	32.8
	30–39 years old	86	30.6
	40–49 years old	56	19.9
	>50 years old		
Ward's type		136	48.4
	Medical area	79	28.1
	Critical area	41	14.6
	Surgery area	25	8.9
	Others		
COVID-19 ward		192	71.2
	COVID-19	89	28.8
	Non-COVID-19		
Geographical area		83	29.5
	Northeast	92	32.7
	Northwest	49	17.5
	Center	57	20.3
	South and Islands		

Note N = 281

Table 14.2 Descriptive statistics and correlations for study variables

Variable	n	M	SD	1	2	3	4	5	6	7
1. Perceived stress	281	29.62	4.71	–						
2. Individual resilience	281	23.20	7.67	–0.28**	–					
3. Age	281	2.54	0.99	–0.14*	0.05	–				
4. Gender[a]	281	0.15	0.36	–0.14*	0.14*	0.03	–			
5. Ward's type	281	2.52	0.85	–0.08	0.04	0.06	0.00	–		
6. Work task characteristics[b]	281	0.68	0.47	–0.06	0.02	0.13*	0.09	0.02	–	
7. Geographical area	281	2.00	0.91	–0.03	0.07	0.05	0.03	0.10⁺	0.01	–

[a] 0 = Woman and 1 = Man
[b] 0 = lower complexity and unpredictability (i.e., non-COVID-19 ward) and 1 = higher complexity and unpredictability (i.e., COVID-19 ward)
⁺ $p < 0.1$; * $p < 0.05$; ** $p < 0.01$

means of a normally distributed interval variable for two independent groups (Kim, 2015). As we expected, there was no statistical difference in the individual resilience and stress perception of nurses working in COVID-19 and those in non-COVID-19 wards.

Table 14.3 presents the results of the proposed linear model. Column 1 shows the results of the full sample, while columns 2 and 3 present the results of the cross-sectional analysis. In detail, column 2 considers nurses working in COVID-19 wards, thus characterized by higher complexity and unpredictability of work tasks. Instead, column 3 considers nurses working in non-COVID-19 wards, thus characterized by lower complexity and unpredictability of work tasks.

Hypothesis 1 suggests that individual resilience negatively affects nurses' perceived stress. Results support this hypothesis, given the existence of a negative and significant relationship between individual resilience and perceived stress ($\beta = -0.21$, $p < 0.001$). While regarding Hypothesis 2, which suggested

Table 14.3 Regression Analysis results differentiating by COVID-19 and non-COVID-19 wards

DV: Perceived Stress	Full sample	Higher complexity and unpredictability (COVID-19 wards)	Lower complexity and unpredictability (non-COVID-19 wards)
Intercept	37.02***	35.42***	40.36***
	(33.88, 40.16)	(31.59, 39.26)	(34.73, 45.98)
Control Variables			
Gender	−1.23+	−1.25	−0.66
	(−2.70, 0.23)	(−3.10, 0.60)	(−3.25, 1.93)
Age	−0.80**	−0.86**	−0.86+
	(−1.34, −0.27)	(−1.51, −0.22)	(−1.88, 0.16)
Ward's type	−0.19	−0.10	−0.36
	(−0.81, 0.43)	(−0.82, 1.03)	(−1.24, 0.52)
Geographical area	0.02	−0.29	−0.48
	(−0.56, 0.60)	(−0.43, 1.00)	(−1.55, 0.59)
Explanatory Variable			
Individual Resilience	−0.21***	−0.18***	−0.29***
	(−0.29, −0.14)	(−0.28, −0.09)	(−0.43, −0.15)
Work task characteristics	0.26	–	–
	(−0.89, 1.41)		
n	281	192	89
R-sq	0.14	0.11	0.22
Adj. R-sq	0.12	0.08	0.16
RMSE	4.45	4.42	4.56

+$p < 0.1$; *$p < 0.05$; **$p < 0.01$; ***$p < 0.001$
DV= Dependent Variable

that work task characteristics moderate the relationship between nurses' individual resilience and perceived stress, results support this hypothesis showing that, in COVID-19 wards, the beneficial effect of individual resilience on stress perception is lower ($\beta = -0.18$, p < 0.001) than for nurses working in non-COVID-19 wards ($\beta = -0.29$, p < 0.001).

Discussion

The results of this chapter showed that when individuals possess higher levels of resilience; they perceive decreasing stress levels. However, this beneficial effect decreases when work tasks become more complex and unpredictable. These results contribute to the literature on human resource management and organizational behavior.

In detail, the first result of the chapter shows that individual resilience is negatively related to perceived stress, meaning that as resilience increases, stress decreases. This result is in line with previous studies showing that resilience is an intrinsic ability that enables individuals to cope with stress or work conflict when facing crisis situations (Gillespie et al., 2007). Furthermore, other authors show that higher levels of resilience defend individuals from emotional exhaustion and provide personal accomplishment (Hetzel-Riggin et al., 2020). Entering into the debate about the importance of personality and abilities in the workplace and showing that even these individual characteristics can help employees reach high levels of well-being, we directly contribute to the organizational behavior literature.

The second result of the chapter shows that work task characteristics—complexity and unpredictability—strongly impact employees' stress perception. This is an important result because it underlines that crisis contexts negatively affect work tasks causing damage to employee well-being. Moreover, even the beneficial effect of individual resilience is lowered by those dynamics. This result contributes to the organizational behavior literature, underlining the importance of implementing some actions that allow minimizing the complexity and unpredictability, particularly in the healthcare context.

Practical Contributions

This study has practical implications that go well beyond the current pandemic and can be generalizable for each crisis and different industries. COVID-19 has twofold impacted individuals' psychological well-being and stress perception. In particular, in the healthcare industry, employees had to change their work tasks in order to cope with the crisis, but even their relationships with peers, superiors, and patients suffered. Spreading knowledge and building relationships was very difficult in this period. However, with this chapter, we want to propose some practical implications that can tangibly help human resource managers and governments, and policymakers to increase employees' well-being.

Since in some contexts, such as the healthcare one, there are more complex and unpredictable work tasks than in others, in order to contain these detrimental effects, we propose human resource managers (i) practice a fair and reasonable distribution of employees in order to have an equally distributed and manageable workload for all them; (ii) to keep an eye on employees' stress perception because it affects the quality of their work, their mental stability, and, in extreme cases, can cause burnout and economic efficiencies for the overall organization. Practically, this could be acted through two interventions: (i) increase salaries, benefits, and part-time possibilities (when it is possible) because this allows for decreasing perceived stress; (ii) enhance interventions focused on increasing workers' individual resilience. For instance, human resource managers can promote mindfulness classes, psychological assistance, and the identification of spaces inside the organization that allows workers to relax and decrease stress, thanks to the availability of sofas, books, music, lights, and aromatherapy.

Finally, governments and policymakers should not identify one-time interventions to deal with employees' hard work and stress (i.e., promise incentives for nurses who have worked in COVID-19 Wards) but develop policy packages that provide long-term solutions. For example, policymakers should work to bridge the clear evidence of nursing shortage in many countries, and governments should create strategies and strongly invest in valuing the essential role of nurses in the healthcare system.

Limitations and Future Research

The chapter has some limitations that may offer promising directions for future research. First, self-reported data were collected at a single point in time, which might raise some issues regarding causality among the investigated variables. Second, the study's sample focuses on Italian nurses and thus limits the generalizability of our findings. Previous studies show that individual resilience and stress perception may vary across different geographies and cultures. Further research is therefore needed to investigate the relationships we examined in a global context.

Conclusion

COVID-19 have radically transformed all workers' professional lives, particularly those in the healthcare industry, powerfully affecting their perception of stress and workload. The necessary reorganization inside hospitals has also impacted the complexity and unpredictability of their work tasks. As a result, healthcare workers have faced a very new and critical situation, which caused them higher stress levels. Results showed that when individuals possess higher levels of resilience; they perceive lower stress levels. However, this beneficial effect decreases when work tasks become more complex and unpredictable that is when the work in COVID-19 wards, for instance. The study extends prior research on stress perception, considering the impact of individual abilities and work task characteristics.

REFERENCES

Babyar, J. C. (2017). They did not start the fire: Reviewing and resolving the issue of physician stress and burnout. *Journal of Health Organization and Management, 31*(4), 410–417.

Bliese, P. D., Edwards, J. R., & Sonnentag, S. (2017). Stress and well-being at work: A century of empirical trends reflecting theoretical and societal influences. *Journal of Applied Psychology, 102*(3), 389–402.

Bonanno, G. A. (2004). Loss, trauma, and human resilience: Have we underestimated the human capacity to thrive after extremely aversive events? *American Psychologist, 59*(1), 20–28.

Bowers, B. J., Lauring, C., & Jacobson, N. (2001). How nurses manage time and work in long-term care. *Journal of Advanced Nursing, 33*(4), 484–491.

Brislin, R. W. (1980). Translation and content analysis of oral and written material. In H. C. Triandis & J. W. Berry (Eds.), *Handbook of cross-cultural psychology: Methodology* (pp. 349–444). Allyn and Bacon.

Britt, T. W., Adler, A. B., & Fynes, J. (2021). Perceived resilience and social connection as predictors of adjustment following occupational adversity. *Journal of Occupational Health Psychology, 26*(4), 339–349.

Cohen, S., Kamarck, T., & Mermelstein, R. (1983). A global measure of perceived stress. *Journal of Health and Social Behavior, 24*, 386–396.

Connor, K. M., & Davidson, J. R. (2003). Development of a new resilience scale: The Connor-Davidson resilience scale (CD-RISC). *Depression and Anxiety, 18*(2), 76–82.

De Bloom, J. (2020). How to recover during and from a pandemic. *Industrial Health, 58*(3), 197–199.

Delgado, C., Upton, D., Ranse, K., Furness, T., & Foster, K. (2017). Nurses' resilience and the emotional labour of nursing work: An integrative review of empirical literature. *International Journal of Nursing Studies, 70*, 71–88.

Di Trani, M., Mariani, R., Ferri, R., De Berardinis, D., & Frigo, M. G. (2021). From resilience to burnout in healthcare workers during the COVID-19 emergency: The role of the ability to tolerate uncertainty. *Frontiers in Psychology, 12*, 646435.

Dóci, E., & Hofmans, J. (2015). Task complexity and transformational leadership: The mediating role of leaders' state core self-evaluations. *The Leadership Quarterly, 26*(3), 436–447.

Gabriel, A. S., Diefendorff, J. M., & Erickson, R. J. (2011). The relations of daily task accomplishment satisfaction with changes in affect: A multilevel study in nurses. *Journal of Applied Psychology, 96*(5), 1095–1104.

Gillespie, B. M., Chaboyer, W., Wallis, M., & Grimbeek, P. (2007). Resilience in the operating room: Developing and testing of a resilience model. *Journal of Advanced Nursing, 59*(4), 427–438.

Glazer, S., & Gyurak, A. (2008). Sources of occupational stress among nurses in five countries. *International Journal of Intercultural Relations, 32*(1), 49–66.

Grabbe, L., Higgins, M. K., Baird, M., Craven, P. A., & San Fratello, S. (2020). The community resiliency model® to promote nurse well-being. *Nursing Outlook, 68*(3), 324–336.

Hart, P. L., Brannan, J. D., & De Chesnay, M. (2014). Resilience in nurses: An integrative review. *Journal of Nursing Management, 22*(6), 720–734.

Heath, C., Sommerfield, A., & von Ungern-Sternberg, B. S. (2020). Resilience strategies to manage psychological distress among healthcare workers during the COVID-19 pandemic: A narrative review. *Anaesthesia, 75*(10), 1364–1371.

Hegney, D. G., Rees, C. S., Eley, R., Osseiran-Moisson, R., & Francis, K. (2015). The contribution of individual psychological resilience in determining the professional quality of life of Australian nurses. *Frontiers in Psychology, 6*(1613), 1–8.

Hetzel-Riggin, M. D., Swords, B. A., Tuang, H. L., Deck, J. M., & Spurgeon, N. S. (2020). Work engagement and resiliency impact the relationship between nursing stress and burnout. *Psychological Reports, 123*(5), 1835–1853.

Hilcove, K., Marceau, C., Thekdi, P., Larkey, L., Brewer, M. A., & Jones, K. (2020). Holistic nursing in practice: Mindfulness-based yoga as an intervention to manage stress and burnout. *Journal of Holistic Nursing*, 0898010120921587.

Houser, J. (2016). *Nursing research: Reading, using and creating evidence*. Jones & Bartlett Learning.

Kim, T. K. (2015). T test as a parametric statistic. *Korean Journal of Anesthesiology, 68*(6), 540–546.

Kock, N. (2015). Common method bias in PLS-SEM: A full collinearity assessment approach. *International Journal of e-Collaboration (IJeC), 11*(4), 1–10.

Leonelli, S., Morandi, F., & Di Vincenzo, F. (2022). La propensione al knowledge sharing dei medici durante la pandemia: Uno studio empirico sul ruolo della resilienza e del commitment. *Prospettive in Organizzazione, 19*, 22–29.

Leonelli, S., & Primavera, E. (2022a). Everything gonna be alright: Antecedents to nurses' change adaptability in the COVID-19 Era. In *Leadership after COVID-19: Working together toward a sustainable future* (pp. 347–359): Springer.

Leonelli, S., & Primavera, E. (2022b). Narcissism and perceived stress among Italian hospital nurses during COVID-19: The moderator role of age. *International Journal of Healthcare Technology and Management, 19*(3–4), 260–279.

López-Cabarcos, M. Á., López-Carballeira, A., & Ferro-Soto, C. (2020). New ways of working and public healthcare professionals' well-being: The response to face the covid-19 pandemic. *Sustainability, 12*(19), 8087.

Mroczek, D. K., & Almeida, D. M. (2004). The effect of daily stress, personality, and age on daily negative affect. *Journal of Personality, 72*(2), 355–378.

Mukhtar, P. S. (2020). Mental wellbeing of nursing staff during the COVID-19 outbreak: A cultural perspective. *Journal of Emergency Nursing, 46*(4), 426–427.

Ong, A. D., Bergeman, C. S., Bisconti, T. L., & Wallace, K. A. (2006). Psychological resilience, positive emotions, and successful adaptation to stress in later life. *Journal of Personality and Social Psychology, 91*(4), 730–749.

Pavedahl, V., Muntlin, Å., Summer Meranius, M., von Thiele Schwarz, U., & Holmström, I. K. (2022). Prioritizing and meeting life-threateningly ill patients' fundamental care needs in the emergency room—An interview study with registered nurses. *Journal of Advanced Nursing, 78*(7), 2165–2174.

Primavera, E., & Leonelli, S. (2020). Un'indagine sulla percezione del carico assistenziale tra gli infermieri italiani, nell'era del COVID-19. *Nsc Nursing, 4*(4), 57–83.

Primavera, E., & Leonelli, S. (2022). "OSS! Ti piacerebbe farlo?" Uno studio trasversale per conoscere mansioni, competenze complementari e carico assistenziale percepito dagli OSS. *Journal of Biomedical Practitioners, 6*(1).

Rana, W., Mukhtar, S., & Mukhtar, S. (2020). Mental health of medical workers in Pakistan during the pandemic COVID-19 outbreak. *Asian Journal of Psychiatry, 51,* 102080.

Rodwell, J., Noblet, A., Demir, D., & Steane, P. (2009). The impact of the work conditions of allied health professionals on satisfaction, commitment and psychological distress. *Health Care Management Review, 34*(3), 273–283.

Schoellbauer, J., Sonnentag, S., Prem, R., & Korunka, C. (2022). I'd rather know what to expect ... Work unpredictability as contemporary work stressor with detrimental implications for employees' daily wellbeing. *Work & Stress, 36*(3), 274–291. https://doi.org/10.1080/02678373.2021.1976881

Shoss, M. K., Jiang, L., & Probst, T. M. (2018). Bending without breaking: A two-study examination of employee resilience in the face of job insecurity. *Journal of Occupational Health Psychology, 23*(1), 112–126.

Stimpfel, A. W., Djukic, M., Brewer, C. S., & Kovner, C. T. (2019). Common predictors of nurse-reported quality of care and patient safety. *Health Care Management Review, 44*(1), 57–66.

Teoh, K. R. H., Hassard, J., & Cox, T. (2020). Individual and organizational psychosocial predictors of hospital doctors' work-related well-being: A multilevel and moderation perspective. *Health Care Management Review, 45*(2), 162–172.

van Schothorst-van Roekel, J., Weggelaar-Jansen, A. M. J. W. M., de Bont, A. A., & Wallenburg, I. (2020). The balancing act of organizing professionals and managers: An ethnographic account of nursing role development and unfolding nurse-manager relationships. *Journal of Professions and Organization, 7*(3), 283–299. https://doi.org/10.1093/jpo/joaa018

Yu, F., Raphael, D., Mackay, L., Smith, M., & King, A. (2019). Personal and work-related factors associated with nurse resilience: A systematic review. *International Journal of Nursing Studies, 93,* 129–140.

Zhao, F., Guo, Y., Suhonen, R., & Leino-Kilpi, H. (2016). Subjective well-being and its association with peer caring and resilience among nursing vs medical students: A questionnaire study. *Nurse Education Today, 37,* 108–113.

CHAPTER 15

Precarious Workers' Wellbeing: Identity Development Through Online Discourses of Quiet Quitting

Gerben Wortelboer and Martijn Pieter Van der Steen

INTRODUCTION

Organizations typically serve as identity workspaces (Petriglieri & Petriglieri, 2010), which provide cultural scripts and other resources (Menzies, 1960) for workers to construct a meaningful identity at work (Pratt, 2000). However, a considerable stream of research has highlighted the increasing precariousness of work (e.g. Kalleberg & Vallas, 2017; Petriglieri et al., 2019; Zamponi, 2019), which denotes a trend in which less-secure employment arrangements replace more conventional employment relationships (Lewchuk & Dassinger, 2016). Precarious work may prevent workers to forge strong attachments to an organization, making it challenging to create and sustain a stable workplace identity (Petriglieri et al., 2019). Hence, precarious work may undermine the organization's role as a site for identity construction and put workers' identity construction under pressure.

A need exists to understand how workers respond to such lack of resources for identity sensemaking in precarious work, because a well-developed workplace identity is directly associated with wellbeing (Aldridge et al., 2016). An inability to engage in identity work, which is an interpretive activity involved in reproducing and transforming identity (Alvesson & Willmott, 2002), may result in ontological insecurity—a threatened sense of professional continuity

G. Wortelboer · M. P. Van der Steen (✉)
Faculty of Economics and Business,
University of Groningen, Groningen, Netherlands
e-mail: m.p.van.der.steen@rug.nl

© The Author(s), under exclusive license to Springer Nature Switzerland AG 2023
J. Marques (ed.), *The Palgrave Handbook of Fulfillment, Wellness, and Personal Growth at Work*,
https://doi.org/10.1007/978-3-031-35494-6_15

(Ashman & Gibson, 2010). A poorly developed workplace identity limits security and self-esteem at work (Alvesson & Willmott, 2002). By contrast, well-developed identities influence wellbeing in a positive manner as they satisfy fundamental desires for uncertainty reduction (Hogg & Terry, 2000), belonging (Baumeister & Leary, 1995), and autonomy (Deci & Ryan, 2013). Therefore, precariousness reduces workers' abilities to create workplace identities, and this is likely to be detrimental to the wellbeing they experience (Kalleberg & Hewison, 2013; Lewchuk & Dassinger, 2016).

Confronted with fewer cultural resources, workers may seek to construct a meaningful worker identity outside the workplace, for example, through the mobilization of online discourses (Petriglieri et al., 2019; Zhang et al., 2017). Recent debates surrounding "quiet quitting", "the great resignation", and "anti-workism" exemplify these online discourses. However, it is unclear *how* precarious workers make sense of their workplace identity in online fora and this chapter seeks to explore this knowledge-gap. Understanding precarious workers' identity sensemaking in online fora is important, because, as noted, their ability to create and make sense of workplace identities is closely related to personal wellbeing.

Advancing this understanding provides multiple contributions. It stresses workers' resilience in coping with their precariousness through online "identity workspaces" (Petriglieri & Petriglieri, 2010), and it demonstrates workers' ability to develop these identity workspaces in a spontaneous and self-organized manner. In the process of utilizing these online identity workspaces, workers construct meaningful identities while simultaneously detaching from the workplace as a crucial locale for such identity development. As such, we provide a novel understanding of the identity development of precarious workers. We argue that, in their attempts to regain a sense of control over an increasingly precarious position, the diversion to online fora offers alternative resources for the collective construction of a more desirable "precarious worker" identity.

Accordingly, the next section explains the theory informing this study, while Sect. 3 outlines the research methods. Section 4 presents the findings, and Sect. 5 provides a discussion of these findings. The final section concludes this work.

Theoretical Background

This section first outlines the importance of identity for wellbeing at work. Then, the section explains how precarious work challenges workers' ability to create a meaningful workplace identity. Finally, the section suggests that online fora may serve as alternative sites for identity work.

Identity Creation at Work: Implications for Wellbeing

Identity constitutes an answer to the question "who am I?" or "who are we?" (Pratt & Foreman, 2000). Individuals and groups define their selves based on their core and distinctive characteristics, including the values, the beliefs, and the expectations they embrace (Albert & Whetten, 1985). Social Identity Theory suggests that people tend to classify themselves and others in social categories, such as organizational membership, gender, and age cohort (Tajfel & Turner, 1985). There is a large literature which examines the ways in which a well-developed social identity contributes to wellbeing. Examples include examinations of wellbeing in relation to gender (Cassidy, 2009; Sahu & Rath, 2003), racial identities (Franklin-Jackson & Carter, 2007; Prelow et al., 2006), and ethnic identities (Umaña-Taylor et al., 2008; Vignoles et al., 2006). In organizations, individuals are motivated to assume social identities (identities based on shared group attributes) as these identities provide a balance amid various needs for inclusion, differentiation, and an overall need for belonging (Brewer, 1991). The neglect of such needs has harmful implications for wellbeing and may provoke anxiety, low self-esteem, and depression (Waller, 2020).

The workplace is important for identity development, because it provides a sense of community, support, and contributes to workers' personal goals, sense of self, life satisfaction, and overall sense of belonging (Willis, 2009). Individuals may identify with their organization to satisfy these needs (Pratt, 2000). Well-developed workplace identities are important determinants of positive workplace outcomes and personal wellbeing (Horton et al., 2014; Riketta, 2005). In addition, the workplace provides cultural and social resources for the development of social identity, further contributing to workers' wellbeing (Dutton et al., 2010). For example, organizational ties, such as relations to supervisors, include access to resources and conferral of social identity (Podolny & Baron, 1997). Individuals tend to invest in workplaces as identity workspaces, the latter of which are defined as "institutions that provide a holding environment for individuals' identity work" (Petriglieri & Petriglieri, 2010, p. 44) that may facilitate sensemaking to create and stabilize social identities. Thus, work is important for wellbeing, because it provides an important basis for identity construction. However, in recent years, under the heading of "precarious work", more attention has been given to the changing nature of work and the workplace.

The Identity Implications of Precarious Work

Precarious work refers to uncertainty and insecurity in employment which are brought about by a variety of employment arrangements (Chang, 2009). Employers' demands on workers have strongly increased, but, simultaneously, many employers are reducing their commitment to their workforce. Consequently, workers experience an unwillingness of employers to "deliver their side of the bargain" as they shift to insecure, short-term, and flexible employment arrangements (Lewchuk & Dassinger, 2016). Precarious work arrangements include less-secure arrangements such as putting-out systems, dispatched workers, in-house contracted labor, and irregular and casual employment (Kalleberg & Hewison, 2013). As a consequence of precarious *work*, precarious *workers* tend to experience a low degree of certainty, a lack of control over work, a lack of social protection, and an inability to secure a well-developed occupational identity (Hanappi, 2013). The resulting precarious worker experiences work as being exploited in and outside the workplace and the hours of work (Standing, 2014).

Since the 1980s, precarious employment has grown more rapidly than overall employment in most OECD countries (Busby & Muthukumaran, 2016). In a European context, it is clear that while the quantity of European jobs has increased, the quality of these jobs has lagged behind—precarious work is spreading (ETUC, 2007). Similar observations have been made about the nature of work in the United States (Blustein et al., 2020).

Precarious work affects workers' abilities to develop occupational or workplace identities as it limits the cultural resources it provides for identity work. It tends to deprive a worker from strong attachments to an organization, and as a consequence, attaining and sustaining a stable workplace identity is challenging (Petriglieri et al., 2019). This is difficult to overcome and may give rise to a growing mass of people in states that can be described as anxious, frustrated, alienated, anomic, or prone to anger (Standing, 2011). Generally speaking, among the many adverse effects of precarious work on workers' wellbeing, one is notably related to the ways it impedes identity work at the workplace.

A focus on workplace identity and identity work is important, because identity likely mediates the relation between precarious work and wellbeing. Precarious work impedes workers' identity work which negatively affects wellbeing. However, as the next subsection illustrates, people may be able to divert to *online* identity workspaces[1]. Examples of these identity workspaces include weblogs (Richards & Kosmala, 2013) and online fora (Proferes et al., 2021).

Online Communities as Identity Workspaces

As traditional employment arrangements are declining, it is important to understand the ways in which workers make sense of their precarious position. We argue that online communities constitute attractive identity workspaces where workers mobilize specific discourses to construct a "precarious worker" identity. Online communities are spaces where individuals interact through written text visible to all members of the community (Danescu-Niculescu-Mizil et al., 2013). The choice of what people choose to talk about in these

---

[1] We define an online identity workspace as a holding environment, accessible on the internet, for individuals' identity work.

communities serves as a primary signal of social identity (Zhang et al., 2017). Prior studies demonstrate how online spaces, such as weblogs or online fora facilitate information sharing and mutual support. Workers in precarious work conditions may use social network sites to address the negative emotions associated to this precarity (Patrick-Thomson & Kranert, 2021; Peticca-Harris et al., 2015).

However, little is known about the processes by which workers use these online communities to make sense of their workplace identity, especially when their employment arrangements no longer provide them with the social and cultural resources to do so in more traditional ways. Online communities can be viewed as identity workspaces that provide space to engage in identity work (Boyd, 2013). Therefore, we posit that, confronted with fewer traditional resources, workers seek to construct an alternative worker identity through the mobilization of discourses in online identity workspaces. Online communities are attractive for the development of such discourses because members may share similar ambitions, interests, and problems, and as a consequence, identify with other members (Nabeth, 2009; Van Weele et al., 2018). Generally speaking, online communities provide workers with identity workspaces when precarious work arrangements restrict their ability to construct identities at the place of work.

Recently, a particular online identity workspace has emerged around the notion of quiet quitting—an online community self-organized around a common concern with precarious work. Quiet quitting is a term that denotes that workers fulfill only the minimum requirements of their job. More specifically, quiet quitting entails workers being increasingly disengaged emotionally from their work and fulfill only the terms of their employment contract, but refuse to offer employers additional time or effort (Alfes et al., 2022). Quiet quitting is a widespread phenomenon, as a recent poll reported that 50% of today's employees have chosen to limit their commitment to their jobs (Mahand & Caldwell, 2023). On online fora, heated debates about quiet quitting are held and we consider the online communities in which these debates take place identity workspaces for workers in precarious work arrangements.

As precarious work makes it more difficult to construct a meaningful workplace identity, it is likely that workers engage in identity work in online communities. However, it is unclear how these workers make sense of their workplace identity through these online communities. Therefore, this chapter asks the following research question: *how do online discourses of quiet quitting affect the construction of a precarious worker identity?*

Methodology

Data Description & Collection

We conducted an inductive qualitative study to examine how online discourses of quiet quitting affect the construction of a precarious worker identity. The data for this study consist of posts and comments taken from the Reddit internet forum. Reddit is a popular forum where users engage in discussion-based communities, referred to as subreddits. Subreddits are designated by "r/", followed by the subreddits topic, such as "r/jobs". Within these subreddits, users post content which "often spark vibrant lengthy discussions in thread-based comment sections" (Zhang et al., 2017, p. 380). The website contains many active subreddits with millions of daily worldwide users. These subreddits span an extremely rich variety of topical interests, several of which are of interest to this chapter, including: "r/antiwork", "r/workreform", and "r/workersstrikeback". As such, Reddit provides a large dataset containing discursive data, which is well suited for our research question.

Importantly, identity construction can be examined through the study of "stories in which individuals encode their identity and poetically embellish facts for effect [...] the storyteller expresses opinions, makes connections, displays feelings, and casts him/herself as a character in a meaningful narrative" (Gabriel, 1999, p. 196). Hence, Reddit represents an ideal landscape in which to examine closely how online discourses of quiet quitting affect the construction of a precarious worker identity.

The data from Reddit was scraped utilizing the Apify web-scraper, returning a collection of 34,052 items, consisting of posts and comments on these posts. The data includes all threads (each of which containing a single post plus all its comments) in which there was at least one mention of "quiet quitting", because this term was particularly central to online discourses regarding precarious work. The resulting dataset consists of a total of 34,052 unique items from 23,237 unique Reddit users. Table 15.1 summarizes the data. The data spans a timeframe of three and a half months, with the first item dated at August 1, 2022, and the last post scraped on November 14, 2022.

Table 15.1 Summary of data scraped from Reddit

Total unique users[2]	22,198
Total unique posts and comments	34,052
Total number of subreddits	139
Timeframe of posts and comments	08-01-2022 – 11-14-2022
Date of data scraping	11-14-2022

---

[2] 1,040 users deleted their account before we scraped the data. We are unable to confirm if these users are unique.

Data Analysis

The data was analyzed using Wordstat. This computer software package can simultaneously analyze multiple corpora of texts (Pollach, 2011). We used Wordstat especially for data-reduction purposes. We generated frequency histograms, word clouds, and topic models that were used to exclude items that were not relevant to our research question. For example, all items related to the Wordstat-generated topic "game play" were excluded, because a visual inspection revealed that this topic was mostly about playing computer games. By contrast, the items organized in the Wordstat-generated topics "great resignation" and "hustle culture" were included, as they were highly relevant for an examination of discourses and identity work of workplace selves. More generally, items were included in the dataset when they fit in one of four general categories: (1) remarks about precarious work; (2) discussions of wellbeing; (3) expressions of defiance; and (4) mentions of identity. For example, an item including the phrase *"A lot of people make their job their identity and neglect their life, health, family or friends" (r/civilengineering)* was deemed relevant under the broad theme of identity. Similarly, the item *"It's the same companies that promote wellness/mindfulness that expect you to stay on late, do extra days, and go outside the scope of your role" (r/antiwork)* was deemed relevant under the broad theme of discussions of wellbeing.

We use the "Gioia method" (Gioia et al., 2013) for analyzing the data as it allows for a systematic presentation of both first-order analysis, derived from informant-centric terms or codes, and second-order analysis, derived from researcher centric concepts, themes, and dimensions (Gehman et al., 2018; Van Maanen, 1979). Our approach is rather novel, because the Gioia method is typically applied in case-studies. Our dataset consists of posts and comments made by 23,237 unique Reddit users. However, like interview data, our dataset contains emerging categories originating from informants' discourses and narratives, and therefore, we consider the Gioia method an appropriate approach. Accordingly, supported by Wordstat, we labeled the categories emerging from the empirical data as first-order concepts. After examining similarities and differences between these emerging categories, we constructed theoretical concepts, or, second-order themes. We went back and forth between the empirical first-order concepts and the theoretically meaningful second-order themes to construct aggregate dimensions, which are the basic building blocks for our theory explaining how online discourses of quiet quitting are related to the construction of a precarious worker identity.

This process of going back and forth between data and theory was consistently undertaken until theoretical saturation occurred; the point at which no new insights were obtained and no new themes were identified (Bowen, 2008). We ultimately obtained a set of 39 first-order concepts, which resulted in twelve second-order themes, out of which we created four aggregate dimensions. The resulting data structure is depicted in Fig. 15.1.

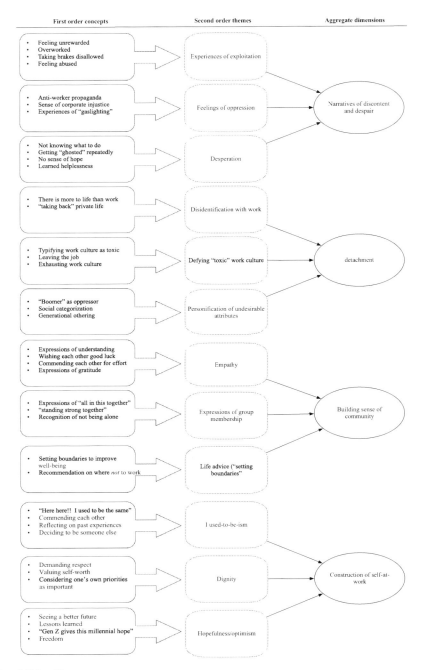

Fig. 15.1 Data structure

Findings

This section is structured into four subsections explaining how online discourses of quiet quitting affect the construction of a precarious worker identity. The first subsection explains how precarious work has generated narratives of discontent. These narratives outlined the threats to workplace identities that workers encountered. The second subsection explains how Redditors engaged in discourses of detachment—seeking to reduce the ontological insecurity resulting from these identity threats. The third subsection explains how workers built a sense of community among quiet quitters, stressing how they all formed a fellowship, who "were in this together". Finally, the fourth subsection explains how this community collectively worked to understand what it means to be a "precarious worker".

Narratives of Discontent

Redditors indicated that they were drawn to Reddit as a platform to express discontent with the conditions in which they worked. More precisely, they engaged in narratives expressing discontent through emotional stories: experiences of exploitation, sentiments of oppression, and feelings of desperation.

> The thing that bums me out, is that I try to take pride in my work, and genuinely try to help things run smoothly, but somehow always feel unappreciated when I go that extra mile—r/antiwork

These feelings of exploitation were often not related to pay, but rather to a lack of employer reciprocity:

> Quiet quitting isn't quitting. It isn't *anything*. But so many workplaces have become accustomed to hustle culture and employees giving 110% that 'I'm going to do my job to the best of my ability during my standard work hours' sounds like slacking. So many workplaces have spent the last 2 decades cutting corners and working with skeleton crews of people desperate for a paycheck, any paycheck, while reaping the profits, and they now think that that is standard—r/askwomen

Sentiments of exploitation were sometimes expressed in small examples that were meaningful to the Redditor:

> It was ridiculous how often I was expected to work for free and take no breaks […]. They wanted me to never take bathroom breaks/lunch and stay late […]—r/askwomen

Combined with these sentiments of exploitation, Redditors felt that they had few recourses for resistance, due to what they perceived as instances of corporate oppression. They suspected coordinated attempts by employers to manipulate discourses about work. This was especially clear when they interacted about the nature of quiet quitting, the concept that bound these Redditors together. To some, quiet quitting was part of oppressive corporate speak:

> Quiet quitting is a corporate term for 'we want people to do more work for free, even though we are already not paying them enough to live a stable life'—r/antiwork

> Quiet Quitting - Shitty made up term by companies to guilt their workers into doing a bunch of free shit they are not being paid for—r/askreddit

For others, the concept was more neutral, but still indicating a vulnerable position under specific working conditions—corporate power versus individual fragility:

> The short answer is that quiet quitting is when workers do exactly what's required of them but stop going above and beyond for various reasons. It's usually a combination of burnout, overwork, underpayment in the face of massive inflation, or mediocre to absent raises while companies report record profits and executive bonuses—r/sysadmin

Instances of experienced oppression were not limited to corporate speak of quiet quitting, but took different forms, such as workplace bullying and gaslighting; the latter of which is manipulating someone into questioning their own sanity.

> I was at their home office working in IT for 5 years and they treat everyone like shit. Gaslighting, bullying, favoritism are all commonplace and if they like you they'll big you up but as soon as they get bored with you or you make one slight mistake they'll be done with you and trying everything to get rid—r/askreddit

The resulting sense of injustice that accompanied these expressions of workplace oppression, led to a sense of despair.

> It's really just like an abusive relationship. It doesn't just start all at once. And then once you realize wtf is happening you're really entrenched and it's difficult, sometimes impossible, to even see that there's a way out, much less be able to take advantage of it—r/askreddit

For the Redditors in the data set, this was a particularly destructive combination of narratives that featured exploitation experienced in the workplace, suspected workplace oppression through corporate speak, coupled with feelings of inaptness to resolve this situation. The consequential feelings of despair were illustrated by the following item:

> Estranged from family. No way to get education without going into debt. No way to afford a down payment on a house. The only community we have are other people in the same desperate situations as us—r/workreform

This and other expressions of despair highlight how these Redditors believed they had few alternatives to change this situation. In this vein, despair was particularly oriented toward "being trapped" in a situation from which they could not expect to escape. Overall, workers on Reddit engaged in narratives of discontent due to a variety of negative experiences. They were not engaged in identity work per se, but they were instead making sense of their current situation as identity threats. That is, their situation was undesirable as it did not enable them to affirm a valued workplace identity:

> Companies don't take care of their employees properly anymore. Work is becoming more and more soul crushing and bureaucratic. Simultaneously, we're all being taught that it's okay to take care of ourselves and to value our health above economic contribution, and we're no longer able/willing to swallow the lie that your job should be your identity anymore—r/onguardforthee

The next subsection outlines how these Redditors sought to detach themselves from a variety of "identity anchors"; the increasingly defunct symbols of identification that used to constitute the cultural resources for constructing a meaningful self-at-work.

Detachment

Redditors evaluated the increasingly problematic relationship with their workplace as identity threats, because, as indicated in a variety of posts and comments, they had experienced difficulties in realizing who they wanted to be in the workplace. The resulting ontological insecurity needed resolving.

> For many of us, we SHOULD NOT conflate our work with our identity, and we SHOULD NOT live into expectations that our job is allowed to take over our lives. It is good that our culture has shifted away from our jobs being the most important things about us as humans (emphasis in original)—r/oregon

One way in which these Redditors sought to resolve this insecurity was through narratives that aimed to detach personal identity from work. Specifically, they did so through (1) expressions reflecting personal disidentification with work, (2) defying the culture of the workplace, and (3) personifying undesirable workplace attributes in, mostly, generational groups.

The workers on Reddit distanced their selves from work and the workplace, but also from many material and symbolic objects that are commonly associated to work, such as pay and career:

> It is the realization that life is more than work, and that happiness and identity does not come from money nor from a career—r/antiwork

Work, careers and money were presented as diametrically opposite to having good health and fulfilling social relations:

> This is 100% real! A lot of people make their job their identity and neglect their life, health, family or friends for a company that would replace them in a heartbeat lol—r/civilengineering

These statements reflected a belief that the workplace can no longer be a resource for identification, because such identification would come at the expense of health and social relations. Such detachment between identity and work was also made clear in statements concerning work culture. These statements reframed cultural resources for constructing a meaningful self-at-work as toxic and ways for employers to manipulate workers into submission:

> Corporate culture' has it you have to work more than you agreed to, more than your contracted hours, more than you are paid for, to impress the employer, to "show you care" and other bullshit like that. People are gradually waking up to the realisation that this is all unacceptable—r/askreddit

To these Redditors, work culture had become suspect, as they argued they had exposed an agenda of worker identity regulation:

> Employees "going above and beyond" is something they have baked into corporate culture. Seeing this recede is a problem for big companies so they are trying to reshape the narrative and add some new corp-agenda—r/antiwork

Escaping the totalizing influence of a "toxic" work culture on identity led some Redditors to note that leaving the organization was the only recourse left:

> I think the problem is the culture and management. Probably these folks are leaving because it's easier to change a job than change a toxic culture when they are not in a position of powe—r/sysadmin

However, other instances of detachment were less dramatic and involved the personification of undesirable attributes. Specifically, Redditors categorized social groups that they did *not want to be part of*. A particular significant element in Redditors' stories was the social categorization of generational differences. They differentiated their selves from others in generational terms—"GenXer", "millennial", "boomer", and "GenZer"—to make sense of their current situation and to personify undesirable attributes:

Boomer/Gen X'ers will publicly slate you for not going above and beyond in a job. Many were/are brainwashed into the whole 110% work, head down and don't ask questions culture—r/unitedkingdom

Ever talk to a boomer? This is their whole attitude. My boomer parents have always pushed garbage like going above and beyond and all that. [...]—r/onguardforthee

In line with Social Identity Theory, these categorizations were especially used to affirm the social identity of the precarious generation, which arguably, generated a sense of control over their lives outside a context of work:

Hi Gen-X er here: we invented slacking. We relished in it. Our entire music and identity revolved around it. We were the Boomers first abuse victims and we reacted by collectively stopping to give any shits—r/antiwork

These quotes and related expressions of social categorization call attention to how these Redditors perceived themselves as different from other groups. Redditors publicly detached from cultural resources provided by the workplace—through disidentification with work, work culture, and specific generational groups. In this process of detachment, however, they constructed potential new resources for identity work that were not based on the attributes of work, but rather on their sense of *detachment from work*. The next subsection discusses how Redditors constructed a community around this sense of detachment that was brought about by the precarity of their work.

Building a Sense of Community

For Redditors, the platform appeared not to simply represent a public address system as a means of expressing their problematic situation. Rather, they utilized the platform as a means to establish membership of the newly forming group of quiet quitters. More precisely, Redditors engaged in building a sense of community among quiet quitters through three types of supportive stories: empathy and voice, supportive expressions of group membership, and life advice.

Redditors expressed a high degree of empathy toward each other, especially through highlighting that they could relate to the plight of others:

I'm just so tired of the hours and hours I spend after school doing all this work that should really be for a teacher or two. Being the head of an orchestra program in a ton of schools must be even more draining. I'm sorry you're going through it. It's nice that at least someone can connect with what I'm going through—r/teachers

Empathy was also expressed through Redditors' mutual support and wishes of good fortune:

> Sorry you're going through this buddy, at least place is not terrible to stay around until something better come up. Wish you the best of luck with your job hunting!—r/ama

In other cases, Redditors showed empathy through commending each other for their efforts.

> Well done! It's kind of amazing to see all of these stories of penny pincher managers and CEOs that don't realize they are the ones coming out ahead if they just...treat their employees like adults and don't hawk over the clock—r/maliciouscompliance

Others reciprocated and expressed gratitude for the advice and empathy toward each other's struggles.

> Thank you for giving things to me straight, I appreciate the reality check. I know you're right, and that perspective helps me value my contributions more—r/careeradvice

In all cases, the Redditors exchanged stories that were laden with emotions toward each other. They validated each other's emotions in response to the changed nature of work and this validation came especially in the form of empathy and support. For these Redditors, as the workplace had lost some of its traditional function as a basis for identification, the Reddit platform represented a social collectivity which could potentially serve as an alternative for social identification at work. Redditors were quite outspoken about the fact that quiet quitters formed a community that was based on shared experiences.

> Sounds like a place I left not long ago. You're definitely not alone—r/conservative

Community members not only shared their own experiences, but as part of their membership, they provided advice on how to respond to these experiences. This advice especially included health-related advice, such as recommendations to set "healthy" boundaries, but also practical recommendations about what *not* to do:

> I'm pushing 59 years old and I want to tell EVERY SINGLE ONE OF YOU. There is NO SUCH THING as a company that is loyal to their employees. I've been 'let go', 'restructured out', and so on. Do your job and nothing more, use the experience as a bullet point on your resume, and keep jumping jobs. It's really the only way to get ahead these days. Damn the man (emphasis in original)—r/workreform

In these ways, community building of quiet quitters through Reddit was accomplished by sharing and responding to emotional stories and providing subsequent advice. As sensemaking of elapsed experience tends to be a social accomplishment (Weick et al., 2005), Redditors could make sense of their struggles to realize a meaningful work identity in this community.

The next and final subsection outlines this process of identity sensemaking and how this community was helpful for Redditors' identity work as precarious workers—a sense of self which was both based on emotions associated with a position at the periphery of the labor force and forward looking and hopeful in nature.

The Construction of Self at Work

By participating in story-telling, the quiet quitters made sense of their perceived position at the periphery of the labor market and their emerging identity as "precarious workers". This section explains how they engaged in identity work through three types of forward-looking stories: I-used-to-be-isms, stories of dignity, and hopefulness/optimism.

I-used-to-be-isms are narratives highlighting one's current self as distinct from a past self, pointing to the shedding of identity attributes and disidentification with this former self:

> I used to be that guy too. I was never late, rarely took a personal day, never caused any drama [...]. I prided myself on having a good work ethic. You know what it got me? Not a damn thing because I didn't kiss the plant manager's ass. So I quietly quit—r/askreddit

These and other related stories highlighted Redditors' reflection on past experience and their subsequent rejection of past identity attributes—a feature of a newly emerging identity as precarious worker.

Another identity attribute that was foregrounded was a strong personal sense of self-worth that required validation in the workplace. Some Redditors interpreted this as a greater emphasis on personal dignity and self-respect. To this end, the term quiet quitting was given a meaning that was oriented to wellbeing and was very different from the meaning that was attributed to employers' use of the term (see above):

> Quiet quitting is just healthy work-life boundaries—r/askreddit

Another example is the following item:

> It ain't quiet quitting, it's self love—r/science

The precarious worker was a worker who celebrated self-love not only as a personal, but also as a workplace concern. The Redditors in the community emphasized personal wellbeing in the workplace as inherent part of the identity of a precarious worker. These kinds of expressions highlight that the precarious worker identity privileged personal wellbeing over an identity that was based on increasingly precarious work.

By contrasting the past to the present and the future, an optimistic and hopeful tone was struck; one that highlighted the new possibilities afforded by being in a community of precarious workers:

> Gen Z gives this millennial hope. You are the allies I've been waiting for because too many of my generation want compromise or think there is another way out. It seems to me that your generation see the writing on the wall and are prepared to resist. I am proud of your showing [...] and I'm looking forward to working towards a better future with you all—r/antiwork

In This Community, Redditors Speculated About Positive Changes for the Role of Work in Modern Society:

> Hopefully we start to see some turning tides in labour laws as people start realizing the rich keep getting richer whether an employee is treated with dignity or not—r/teachers

These statements suggest hopes for a positive future. Arguably, these hopes were fueled by the collective sense quiet quitters made of their precarious position, through the identity-in-progress of the precarious worker.

Over all, through the Reddit internet forum, workers self-organized around the notion of quiet quitting and engaged in identity work, outside of the confines of the workplace, which resulted in a better understanding of what it meant to be a precarious worker. Arguably, the outcomes included workers for whom the concept of quiet quitting had become a badge of honor and a vignette of what could, over time, become a fully formed workplace identity:

> I 100,000% have quiet quit and embrace it wholeheartedly—r/teachers

DISCUSSION

This chapter suggests several contributions to the understanding of wellbeing and identity work in online identity workspaces.

One contribution emphasizes workers' resilience when they are faced with the loss of cultural resources for the construction of a workplace identity. Prior studies have shown that precariousness tends to lead to lower wellbeing at work (e.g. Hanappi, 2013; Lewchuk & Dassinger, 2016). However, we show that workers are not acquiescent; they resist. Admittedly, much of this resistance may be considered symbolic, but even symbolic resistance, through narratives and stories, provided workers with an extra-workplace community in which to engage in identity work. In this vein, workers demonstrated their resilience and ability to deal with challenging work conditions. The implication is that, if the stability of the workplace is under pressure, people may create online identity workspaces that can provide the means to deal with their precariousness. In this vein, precarity may still lead to lower wellbeing *at work*, but, as the Reddit community has shown; workers may depreciate the importance of such wellbeing in favor of their wellbeing outside the workplace.

Consequently, online identity workspaces may arise spontaneously when a sufficient number of workers rally around a salient topic. Thus far, identity workspaces (e.g. Petriglieri et al., 2019) are considered to be designed for specific purposes. Similar suggestions have been made for online identity workspaces, such as online fora (Boyd, 2013). However, akin to online activism, workers can form online identity workspaces in spontaneous and self-organized ways outside the workplace. In this way, they may escape employers' attempts for identity regulation (Alvesson & Willmott, 2002) and regain control over their workplace identities. Since such identity work takes place outside the scope of the organization, workers may escape employers' influence on the identities they aspire to realize. Through the creation of a community of quiet quitters, the need for belonging to a work community could be separated from the work organization. Online identity workspaces, such as Reddit, provide the resources that precarious work can no longer offer.

At a macro level, prior work has shown that workers in many countries in the Western hemisphere have experienced work of declining quality (e.g. Blustein et al., 2020; ETUC, 2007), and fewer means to resist precarious employment arrangements (e.g. Kalleberg & Hewison, 2013; Standing, 2011). Our suggestion that workers may develop a precarious worker identity outside the workplace is particularly salient here, because the detachment from the workplace as an important site for identity development may have implications for possible labor reforms. As noted, this detachment relaxes employers' control over worker identity and highlights the divergent interests between workers and employers. At the surface, quiet quitting has overtly symbolic overtones and may be considered a "decaf" form of resistance, because it provides resistors only with the illusion of autonomy (Fleming & Spicer, 2003). However, some of our quotes suggest that the extra-workplace organization of these workers may potentially evolve into a movement that aims to provoke substantive labor law reforms. Its symbolic overtones notwithstanding, quiet quitting as an organizing principle has generated its own infrastructure and several identity attributes of the precarious worker. In this vein, quiet quitting is not simply a symbolic response to precarious labor conditions, but rather a collective accomplishment of community building and identity work outside the employers' purview.

Conclusion

We must address a few limitations of this study, which may perhaps yield further opportunities for study. First, future research may examine a longer period of Reddit data, which may uncover in more depth the longitudinal evolution of precarious worker's discourses and processes of identity construction. Second, future studies may consider the analysis of interview data to arrive at a better understanding of workers' motivations for engaging in identity work through online identity workspaces. Finally, since leaders tend to have a disproportionate influence on identity sensemaking (Petrigliere et al., 2019), future research may consider the identity effects of formal (e.g. moderator-roles) and informal leadership roles of users in online identity workspaces. Thus far, despite their likely significance, leadership roles have largely been ignored.

These limitations notwithstanding, this chapter has explored the unfolding of the construction of a precarious worker identity through online discourses of quiet quitting. In this way, the chapter has laid the groundwork for further contributions and a greater understanding of precarious workers' wellbeing and their identity work in online identity workspaces.

References

Albert, S., & Whetten, D. (1985). Organizational identity. *Research in Organizational Behavior, 7*, 263–295.

Aldridge, J. M., Fraser, B. J., Fozdar, F., Ala'i, K., Earnest, J., & Afari, E. (2016). Students' perceptions of school climate as determinants of wellbeing, resilience and identity. *Improving Schools, 19*(1), 5–26. https://doi.org/10.1177/1365480215612616

Alfes, A., Beauregard, C., & Muratbekova-Touron. (2022). New ways of working and the implications for employees: A systematic framework and suggestions for future research. *The International Journal of Human Resource Management, 33*(22), 4361–4385.

Alvesson, M., & Willmott, H. (2002). Identity regulation as organizational control: Producing the appropriate individual. *Journal of Management Studies, 39*(5), 619–644.

Ashman, I., & Gibson, C. (2010). Existential identity, ontological insecurity and mental well-being in the workplace. *Contemporary Readings in Law and Social Justice, 2*(2), 126–147.

Baumeister, R. F., & Leary, M. R. (1995). The need to belong: Desire for interpersonal attachments as a fundamental human motivation. *Psychological Bulletin, 117*(3), 497–529.

Blustein, D. L., Perera, H. N., Diamonti, A. J., Gutowski, E., Meerkins, T., Davila, A., Erby, W., & Konowitz, L. (2020). The uncertain state of work in the U.S.: Profiles of decent work and precarious work. *Journal of Vocational Behavior, 122*, 103481. https://doi.org/10.1016/j.jvb.2020.103481

Bowen. (2008). Naturalistic inquiry and the saturation concept: A research note. *Qualitative Research, 8*(1), 137–152.

Boyd. (2013). Online discussion boards as identity workspaces: Building professional identities in online writing classes. *The Journal of Interactive Technology & Pedagogy, 4*.

Brewer, M. B. (1991). The social self: On being the same and different at the same time. *Personality and Social Psychology Bulletin, 17*(5), 475–482. https://doi.org/10.1177/0146167291175001

Busby, & Muthukumaran. (2016). Precarious positions: Policy options to mitigate risks in non-standard employment. *CD Howe Institute Commentary.*

Cassidy. (2009). ullying and victimisation in school children: The role of social identity, problem-solving style, and family and school context. *Social Psychology of Education, 12,* 63–76.

Chang. (2009). Informalising labour in Asia's global factory. *Journal of Contemporary Asia, 39*(2), 161–179.

Danescu-Niculescu-Mizil, C., West, R., Jurafsky, D., Leskovec, J., & Potts, C. (2013). No country for old members: User lifecycle and linguistic change in online communities. *Proceedings of the 22nd International Conference on World Wide Web,* 307–318.

Deci, E., & Ryan, R. (2013). *Intrinsic motivation and self-determination in human behavior.* Springer Science & Business Media.

Dutton, R., & Bednar. (2010). Pathways for positive identity construction at work: Four types of positive identity and the building of social resources. *Academy of Management Review, 35*(2), 265–293.

ETUC. (2007). *Quality of jobs at risk.* ETUC.

Fleming, P., & Spicer, A. (2003). Working at a cynical distance: Implications for power. Subjectivity and resistance. *Organization, 10*(1), 157–179. https://doi.org/10.1177/1350508403010001376

Franklin-Jackson, D., & Carter, T. R. (2007). The relationships between race-related stress, racial identity, and mental health for Black Americans. *Journal of Black Psychology, 33*(1), 5–26.

Gabriel, Y. (1999). Beyond happy families: A critical reevaluation of the control-resistance-identity triangle. *Human Relations, 52*(2), 179–203.

Gehman, J., Glaser, V. L., Eisenhardt, K. M., Gioia, D., Langley, A., & Corley, K. G. (2018). Finding theory-method fit: A comparison of three qualitative approaches to theory building. *Journal of Management Inquiry, 27*(3), 284–300. https://doi.org/10.1177/1056492617706029

Gioia, D. A., Corley, K. G., & Hamilton, A. L. (2013). Seeking qualitative rigor in inductive research: Notes on the Gioia methodology. *Organizational Research Methods, 16*(1), 15–31. https://doi.org/10.1177/1094428112452151

Hanappi. (2013). Precarious work: Agenda and implications for corporate social responsibility. *Encyclopedia of Corporate Social Responsibility,* 1880–1885.

Hogg, M. A., & Terry, D. J. (2000). Social identity and self-categorization processes in organizational contexts. *The Academy of Management Review, 25*(1), 121–140.

Horton, K. E., Bayerl, S. P., & Jacobs, G. (2014). Identity conflicts at work: An integrative framework. *Journal of Organizational Behavior, 35*(1), 6–22.

Kalleberg, A. L., & Hewison, K. (2013). Precarious work and the challenge for Asia. *American Behavioral Scientist, 57*(3), 271–288. https://doi.org/10.1177/0002764212466238

Kalleberg, A. L., & Vallas, S. P. (Eds.). (2017). Probing precarious work: Theory, research, and politics. In *Research in the sociology of work* (Vol. 31, pp. 1–30). Emerald Publishing Limited. https://doi.org/10.1108/S0277-283320170000031017

Lewchuk, W., & Dassinger, J. (2016). Precarious employment and precarious resistance: "We are people still." *Studies in Political Economy, 97*(2), 143–158. https://doi.org/10.1080/07078552.2016.1211397

Maanen, V. (1979). The fact of fiction in organizational ethnography. *Administrative Science Quarterly, 24*(4), 539–550.

Mahand, T., & Caldwell, C. (2023). Quiet quitting—Causes and opportunities. *Business and Management Research, 12*(1).

Menzies, I. (1960). A case-study in the functioning of social systems as a defence against anxiety: A report on a study of the nursing service of a general hospital. *Human Relations, 13*(2), 95–121.

Nabeth. (2009). Social web and identity: A likely encounter. *Identity in the Information Society, 2*, 1–5.

Patrick-Thomson, & Kranert. (2021). Don't work for free: Online discursive resistance to precarity in commercial photography. *Work, Employment and Society, 35*(6), 1034–1052.

Peticca-Harris, W., & McKenna. (2015). The perils of project-based work: Attempting resistance to extreme work practices in video game development. *Organization, 22*(4), 570–587.

Petriglieri, G., Ashford, S. J., & Wrzesniewski, A. (2019). Agony and ecstasy in the gig economy: Cultivating holding environments for precarious and personalized work identities. *Administrative Science Quarterly, 64*(1), 124–170. https://doi.org/10.1177/0001839218759646

Petriglieri, G., & Petriglieri, J. L. (2010). Identity workspaces: The case of business schools. *Academy of Management Learning & Education, 9*(1), 44–60.

Podolny, & Baron. (1997). Resources and relationships: Social networks and mobility in the workplace. *American Sociological Review*, 673–693.

Pollach. (2011). Software review: Wordstat 5.0. *Organizational Research Methods, 14*(4), 741–744.

Pratt, M. (2000). The good, the bad, and the ambivalent: Managing identification among Amway distributors. *Administrative Science Quarterly, 45*(3), 456–493.

Pratt, M., & Foreman, P. (2000). Classifying managerial responses to multiple organizational identities. *Academy of Management Review, 25*(1), 18–42.

Prelow, M., & Bowman. (2006). Perceived racial discrimination, social support, and psychological adjustment among African American college students. *Journal of Black Psychology, 32*(4), 442–454.

Proferes, N., Jones, N., Gilbert, S., Fiesler, C., & Zimmer, M. (2021). Studying reddit: A systematic overview of disciplines, approaches, methods, and ethics. *Social Media + Society, 7*(2), 20563051211019004. https://doi.org/10.1177/20563051211019004

Richards, J., & Kosmala, K. (2013). 'In the end, you can only slag people off for so long': Employee cynicism through work blogging. *New Technology, Work and Employment, 28*(1), 66–77. https://doi.org/10.1111/ntwe.12004

Riketta. (2005). Organizational identification: A meta-analysis. *Journal of Vocational Behavior, 66*, 358–384.

Sahu, F.M., & Rath, S. (2003). Self-efficacy and wellbeing in working and non-working women: The moderating role of involvement. *Psychology and Developing Societies, 15*(2), 187–200.

Standing, G. (2011). *The precariat: The new dangerous class*. Bloomsbury academic.

Standing, G. (2014). The Precariat. *Contexts, 13*(4), 10–12. https://doi.org/10.1177/1536504214558209

Tajfel, H., & Turner, C. J. (1985). The social identity theory of intergroup behavior. Worchel. *Psychology of Intergroup Relations. Nelson-Hall, Chicago, 2.*

Umaña-Taylor, V.-C., & Garcia, D. C., & Gonzales-Backen. M. (2008). A longitudinal examination of Latino adolescents' ethnic identity, coping with discrimination, and self-esteem. *The Journal of Early Adolescence, 28*(1), 16–50.

Weele, V. M. A., & Steinz, j. H., & Van Rijnsoever, J. F. (2018). Start-up communities as communities of practice: Shining a light on geographical scale and membership. *Tijdschrift Voor Economische En Sociale Geografie, 109*(2), 173–188.

Vignoles, R., Manzi, G., & Scabini. (2006). Beyond self-esteem: Influence of multiple motives on identity construction. *Journal of Personality and Social Psychology, 90*(2), 308–333.

Waller. (2020). Fostering a sense of belonging in the workplace: Enhancing wellbeing and a positive and coherent sense of self. *The Palgrave Handbook of Workplace Well-Being,* 1–27.

Weick, K. E., Sutcliffe, K. M., & Obstfeld, D. (2005). Organizing and the process of sensemaking. *Organization Science, 16*(4), 409. https://doi.org/10.1287/orsc.1050.0133

Willis. (2009). From exclusion to inclusion: Young queer workers' negotiations of sexually exclusive and inclusive spaces in Australian workplaces. *Journal of Youth Studies, 12*(6), 629–651.

Zamponi, L. (2019). The "precarious generation" and the "natives of the ruins": The multiple dimensions of generational identity in italian labor struggles in times of crisis. *American Behavioral Scientist, 63*(10), 1427–1446. https://doi.org/10.1177/0002764219831740

Zhang, J., Hamilton, W., Danescu-Niculescu-Mizil, C., Jurafsky, D., & Leskovec, J. (2017). Community identity and user engagement in a multi-community landscape. *Proceedings of the International AAAI Conference on Web and Social Media, 11*(1), 377–386. https://doi.org/10.1609/icwsm.v11i1.14904

CHAPTER 16

Significant Measures of Ancient Indian Ethos Towards Wellness and Growth in the Workplace

Nidhi Kaushal

INTRODUCTION

Vedic Sanskriti depicted in *Vedic* literature has fruitfully recognized the *Vedic* society as an idyllic community of people with a significant impression of their ritualistic traditions, practices, and work-life environment (Thapar, 1982). Their traditional behaviour is called virtue, which is culture-driven and expands with humanity and raises mutual respect, and the concept of peace includes respect for humanity and responsibility for social justice (Abidi, 2002). Tolerance is a guiding official and public behaviour, while happiness is the name of peace in the mind and heart. Similarly, gentleness is synonymous with honesty, and Vedas called it dharma to follow. Dharma sustains all and protects the humanity of individuals (Shastri, 2018), which is a fortification of truth and natural principles, so its dynamism has been overshadowed by all philosophies, literature, and arts (Mishra, 2008). The inner sense (Chitt) is the cause of initializing every deed (Chakrabarti, 1999), and it has been identified as an ideational insight in the *Ramcharitmanas* (an Indian scripture) (Leaman, 2002). The Indian mythology is affluent in its context, which has impactful power of change because its stories are not typical and hold a valuable position in the psychological development of people (Wig, 2004), which asserts that factors like habits, recency, vividness, and emotional congruity are related to their ethical thought processes (James, 1984). The imperatives of leadership

N. Kaushal (✉)
Leadership Practitioner/Researcher, Yamunanagar, India
e-mail: nidhi.k3333@gmail.com

© The Author(s), under exclusive license to Springer Nature Switzerland AG 2023
J. Marques (ed.), *The Palgrave Handbook of Fulfillment, Wellness, and Personal Growth at Work*,
https://doi.org/10.1007/978-3-031-35494-6_16

include a spiritual commitment to the welfare of the people, communicativeness or ability to express, courage to sacrifice a small goal for a bigger one, expertness and clear preferences, trust in decision-making, and awareness of the external and internal environment (Swamy, 2013), and these features reflect the distinctiveness of workers and enrich the standards of the workplace as well.

The environment of peace, harmony, and affection has become the very first necessity and demand of every human living in the present hurry-scurry culture. The act of maintaining happiness involves a significant contribution of people apart from the perspective measures at the societal and organizational level, and it is concerned with the psychological upliftment of the people involved and related to it. The high rising aspirations, demands, goals, and culmination, including the craving to get more, often serve as the probable reasons for rebellion and strife in their life. They adhere to an ideology to get peace after achieving everything has a contradictory effect that never lets them enjoy life's small valuable moments, possessions, and relationships. This kind of mind-set becomes one of the reasons for their anxiety or conflict, and it is a myth only that has not any tangibility. In today's changing materialism era, the country-wide efforts of various institutions are not enough, and new ideas and unique strategies are constantly being identified for conflict resolution as well as peace-making in every field. In this phenomenon, the universal effectiveness of ancient spiritual approaches and *Vedic* solutions has a significant role in awakening humans to make harmony within the self and outer world. It also requires the development of their inner conscience, wisdom, and steadiness through self-realization and self-restraining.

The field of virtue encompasses a very thorough study, developed aptitude, and guidelines, which are beneficial for the meaningful growth of individuals and signify the need and importance of good conduct and behaviour in the workplace. Every culture emphasizes the practice of virtue which expresses that it is necessary to bring changes to the depths of the inner self to create a virtuous environment at the workplace because there is a lot of difference in the behavioural mechanisms of people and their living perspectives. Scholars have highlighted the significance of moral values, but there is no morality without the spirit of virtuous conduct because success brings egotism along, while good behaviour keeps it well-regulated. Virtue refers to the progress and wellness of cultured beliefs, and the morality of a particular person represent the depth of his cultural values. In the context of work-life fulfilment and happiness, the implication of aspects like the power of tolerance, moral Ideology, virtuous conduct, respect and gratefulness, and purification of the mind is referred from the ancient Indian *Vedic* and mythological texts, which show the prosperity and richness of the Indian civilization. This chapter has been written off as considerably related to the ethos of the workplace and includes five parts such that (1) Developing the Power of Tolerance; (2) Make Changes in the Trend of Thinking (Ideology); (3) Intensifying the Moral Self through an Observation of Virtues; (4) Being Respectful towards Gifts of Nature and Diligence; (5) The inevitable Designation of Peace and Purification of Mind in happiness.

Literature Review

Tolerance is a cultural and indispensable moral ideal for working in a society that demands respect for the right of the people (Furedi, 2014) and signifies an individual's attitude or character trait, which is transitive or intransitive (Oberdiek, 2001). It has the intent of patience, endurance, fortitude, and forbearance as virtues required for harmonious living with mindfulness (Witenberg, 2019). It fosters the peaceful simultaneous existence of different ethnic groups in the organization or society and assures their self-realization through the development of emotional intelligence (Jurs & Samusevica, 2018). Tolerance makes harmony in the difference of opinions and exalts through wisdom, freedom, sharing of ideas, and conviction (Abidi, 2002). When tolerance becomes an attitude or practice, it represents dignity and counts for social justice (Brown & Forst, 2014). The ethical standard of tolerance developed through the identification of various cultural parameters is extremely relevant and strategically impactful in dealing with conflicts (Moreno-Riaño, 2016). A judicious person understands the virtue of tolerance and its principle, which is mostly required and not merely expedient (Bowlin, 2019). Individuals and societies must aspire to tolerance as a positive response to diversity (Hjerm et al., 2020), and organizational culture must have moral and ethical discussion practices (Martin & Hafer, 2017).

The word dharma has been used in a broad sense in the scriptures, which define an act of restraining on mind, word, and deed as austerity (Nirala, 2008). It leads to the accomplishment of both prosperity and unreliable advent (Awasthi, 1974). The two forms of dharma include paths of instinct and retirement, and to get happy and fulfil every duty faithfully is called Pravritti Marga, and for the attainment of liberation, Jnana Yoga, Bhakti Yoga, and Dhyana Yoga are called Nirvriti Marga (Premeshananda, 2011). *Sanatan Dharma* or *Sanatan Samhita* has such a formula of wisdom that embracing it raises the standard of life, removes negativity, and people learn to never complain of injustice and lack in life (Swamy, 2013). It is in the values of the Indian cultural tradition of wisdom and moral consciousness and leads humans to self-realization through its observation (Sharma & Sharma, 2001). Virtue is Supreme dharma, and its protection shields the human being while wealth leads to dharma and it leads to happiness, so humanity should follow virtue (Vaidh, 2008). It has the traditional rules of morality (Mishra, 2008).

The concept of well-being has been profoundly interpreted in the ancient Hindu scriptures *Charaka Samhita* as well (Sinha, 1990). A core ancient Indian concern that has pan-human relevance to well-being includes the synchronization of nutrition (Aahar), leisure (Vihar), and thoughts (Vichar) (Dalal, 2011). *Vedic Hindu* ideology has the wisdom and dynamism to develop people as cosmic citizens with values of truth, prosperity donation, offering, respect, and help and service as their dharma (Dhungana, 2014). Courage and valour are the gems of virtue and through which duality is attained where ethos protects the culture (Gupt, 1994). The enlightenment of thought leads to intelligent behaviour, forms the basis of life's actions, and develops its magnificence, so one should use enough words and give more attention to thoughts and actions, be punctual and patient, make heart and mind pure, and maintain self-confidence and self-respect to get success (Tiwari, 2021). Valuing diversity emphasizes the appreciation of human differences where everyone feels esteemed, and tolerance highlights respect towards civility and is an effective tool for solving intractable conflict (Bergen & Collier, 2013).

The context of Ideology has the programmes for the advancement of society with an explanation of facts (Roucek, 1944), and the ideology of dignity highlights the workplace identity and enriches the standard of the individual (Levin, 2009). The workplace dignity has the perspective of equality, positive contribution, openness, and responsibility to make it noble, and organizations should honour the dignity of workers without any obligation to change (Bal, 2017). Judgements of moral accountability concern the divergent inferences about intention, knowledge, and mindfulness (Ditto et al., 2009). Virtue is an ethical disposition, and people should adhere to moral beliefs in their judgements and not get subjective through moral flexibility (Bartels et al., 2014). Every organization expects its workers to be proficient at psychological, social, and cultural levels while in their behaviour (Robbins et al., 1999). The kind of exposure of individuals influences their judgement abilities during ethical dilemmas (Johari et al., 2020). Situationists have emphasized risks relative to benefits, absolutists on the riskiness of the procedures, and exceptionists on the magnitude of costs (Forsyth & Pope, 1984).

A particular social self is the honour and recognition of a person (James, 1984). Highly relativistic individuals relate moral actions to circumstances, and people with low-relativism relate morality to principles, norms, or laws (Ismail, 2014). A person's outer conflict includes his real inner struggle between his past and future aspirations (Pandey, 2011). Universalism involves the existence of ideological barriers because people's policy views are correlated (Enke et al., 2020). The intent of the corporate to make a profit and the responsibility for the well-being of the employees does not negate its importance and aspects of values and motivation (Weissman, 1981). Organizations need to employ positive qualities in their employees and should be allowed to integrate their moral self with the organizational self (McFerran et al., 2010). Imaginative vision, activism, and honesty or integrity are the three essential conditions of leadership, and its training and skills in the progress of an individual, nation, and society determine his true identity, inspiration, goal, and a clear plan to achieve it (Swamy, 2013). Genuineness maintains the confidence and values the importance of cooperation with others and the approach of relational leaders to complete their incompleteness (Gauthier, 2014).

The ancient Indian civilization's lifestyle behavioural patterns reflect the practice of maintaining discipline, peace, and harmony in the family and society and explain the specialty of unity in diversity (Tiwari & Pandey, 2013). Vedas have phrases that signify that trend of thinking is responsible for deeds and show the significance of humanity (Arka, 2018), and these texts are authoritative scriptures of experiences written by ancient Indian sages (Long, 2019), which states that Dharma is a means or manner of enlightenment (Sangharakshita, 1998). Similarly, *Ramcharitmanas* is an epic written by Goswami Tulsidas (1532–1623), an Indian Saint, is a depository of moral ideals and has a bizarre arrangement of events and the fineness of the language (Shastri, 2018), and It has eternal values and mechanisms not only for intelligence transformation skills of human beings but also for the intelligence development process (Beniwal, 2019).

Developing the Power of Tolerance

Tolerance as virtue is an ancient idea of ethics, including a reflection of positiveness (Fiala, 2005), and it is an intangible and influential Skill or a gentle personal quality, one who acts judiciously (Brown & Forst, 2014). It defines enduring hardship without failing, and developing its culture is the responsibility of all individuals to create a peaceful and harmonious environment (Abidi, 2002). Tolerance is the meaning of social acceptance and equal behaviour towards others and its observation (Golebiowska, 2014), and it manifests itself as a virtue and concept and a universal notion of people, including relationships at the personal and social levels (Bowlin, 2019). Developing tolerance requires a consistent belief in a moral principle that affirms individual autonomy (Furedi, 2014), and its concept endorses the respect that every individual possesses inherent values and affirms the belief-system (Bergen & Collier, 2013). It is a proactive attitude that does not mean not empathy and involves principles of morality with universal freedom (Abidi, 2002).

The ancient Indian model of society has excellent concepts regarding the versatile development of an individual, which are able to transform the people or organizations through wisdom (Tiwari & Pandey, 2013). The concept of responsibility defines moral respect for the individual, while tolerance involves an acceptance of moral values. Tolerance in theory and practice can be challenging, but the toleration of workplace rudeness also reflects leaders' incapability to resolve conflicts at the organizational level and strain the valuable resources of employees (Aljawarneh & Atan, 2018). Employees tend to become pessimistic due to the rise in unethical and opportunistic behaviour patterns in modern competitive organizational cultures. So, an organizational structure should have a paradigm of understanding towards values and tolerance for human rights because values play an influential role in maintaining a culture of peace (Rivera, 2008). A philosophical understanding of tolerance helps to analyse possibilities of an appropriate intelligent change (Oberdiek,

2001) because it is effectively cognitive and intimates patience in confronting diversity (Moreno-Riaño, 2016). Diverse work culture enhances the power of tolerance and collaboration among workers.

Tolerance means patience and the main four parts of sensibility in this context are conflict tolerance, elan-tolerance, transcendence tolerance, and ultimate tolerance.

1. Another meaning of conflict tolerance is the knowledge of the nature of vicissitudes of life. Happiness and sorrow are not particularly related to materialistic objects, rather their source is in one's mind, and where there is the experience of adversity or lack, there is sorrow, and where there is no experience of compatibility or lack, there is happiness. A human being sees compatibility in the attainment of the objective in which there is passion and in the destruction or absence of the object in which there is hatred, and similarly, there is adversity in the attainment of an unpleasant thing and appears to be animosity in the destruction or absence of the object of passion.
2. To stop the velocity of wicked feelings like anger, greed, pride, passion, enmity, or violence arising in the mind due to ignorance and ego and not being under their control is called elan-tolerance. Their pace should be tolerated with thoughtful patience because their flow is very strong, and getting swept away in it, many great misfortunes and crimes may happen, so a thoughtful endurance leads to the well-being of people. The fine way to cope with these odd emotions is detachment from pleasures and affection for God. The significant aspect of tolerance and its value in human life has been magnificently described in verse 23 of chapter 5 in the *Shrimad Bhagavad Gita*.

    i. *shaknotīhaiva yaḥ soḍhuṁ prāk śarīra-vimokṣhaṇāt*
    ii. *kāma-krodhodbhavaṁ vegaṁ sa yuktaḥ sa sukhī naraḥ [5.23]*

    b. A person who can tolerate or stop the velocity arising from the kama (desire) and krodha (anger), even before they leave the body, is appropriate and peaceful in the world. The impulse (vega) of wicked feeling should be controlled mindfully to prevent prospective hazardous situations.

3. Seeing the progress, wealth, or strength of others and not being jealous, rather having happiness, is called transcendence tolerance, and this quality can be individual, societal, communal, and country or terrain according to the extent of selfishness and attachment. Out of ignorance, living within the limits of petty ego and wishing for the degradation or destruction of others is certainly a great sin. There is nothing alien in the world, but everything belongs to God, so everybody should be ecstatic while performing life chores. According to the season, every tree flourishes, and one should be pleased with the hope that in the same manner, when his season comes, he will also flourish.

4. Not keeping any hatred towards humans, communities, or castes of opposite opinions and having love towards every creature is called ultimate congenial tolerance. The world is the work of nature, and it creates it only by being heterogeneous, and that is why no one in the world has specifically the same shape, nature, or interest, and this is the beauty of the world. A person who sees the eternal, omnipresent, unchangeable, imperishable, immovable divine in various forms and expressions has recognized the real humanity in the true sense. So, virtuous conduct is to respect others' points of view and appreciate and acknowledge each other acceptable sentiments (Goswami, 2014).

According to all these parameters, tolerance can have many connotations, but they all insist on conflict resolution through the development of forbearance and integrity with a strong mind and inner strength. It is an intrinsic force that works all-round in human development. It represents a significant feature of steely strength within a person, which enables him to endure the biggest blow like a rock. It marks his culmination of meditation which can also be advanced because it is not an innate quality but an art of maintaining peace through conscience, in constant struggle, internal conflict, and making harmony with the surrounding environment. Its practice certainly builds up the sharp intellect and personality of human beings.

Make Changes in the Trend of Thinking (Ideology)

Ideology means a system of detailed ideas in the light of certain concepts of life outlook (Roucek, 1944). Ancient Indian ideology states that everything has a manifestation of the Supreme Being, and people should develop consciousness in thoughts and acts for unity (Sinha, 2014). The context of Ideology in the organization describes the role and appropriate behaviour of the worker and customer and their respective standings towards each other (Robbins et al., 1999). Its concept justifies the value of human dignity in his behaviour (Budd & Bhave, 2008). Idealistic people believe in the possible achievement of good results (Forsyth & Pope, 1984) because the well-being of employees includes mutual concern, and it should be in precedence of the organization for efficient management processes (Zawadzki, 2018). Cultural ideology refers to the approach of ethical thinking and the existence of autonomous values and norms of an individual or group (Narvaez et al., 1999). Ethical judgement includes moral reasoning and sensitivity with an understanding of respective cultural ideologies (Jurković et al., 2018). Elite Ideology has the main place in the synergetic philosophy, and cultures inspire people to behave under rules and regulations, which have a similar effect on the ethical climate of an organization (Johari et al., 2020).

Human nature is naturally downward, and if the effort is not made to rise and grow continuously, then it tends to fall. It always requires awareness and conation to avoid the reduction (Poddar, 2005). The whole world may be different, including the dissimilar castes, beliefs, worship, practices, languages, behaviour, and food habits, but the urge to find happiness and wellness, and the desire to avoid misery, are found everywhere equally. The more the gold is heated, the purer it will be, and similarly, the more a person with a stoic talent gets involved in conflicts, the more powerful and socially useful he strikes with rocky intentions. Sorrow or conflict is hard to bear, but happiness is very difficult to digest wisely, and it only comes in life to test patience because whenever there is contempt, neglect, humiliation, there is an acceleration in the workflow or conduct of a person, and when one path is blocked by the opponents, then his conscience starts looking for other paths. Accordingly, the respect doesn't lead him ahead, while the disgrace doesn't let him stop. His goal is to rise above pleasure and distress and enter into the divine bliss where they have no access because it has been well explained in the *Vedic* scriptures that respect and disrespect are of the body only and not of the inner self-consciousness. Therefore, he should rise above all these difficulties and should be able to maintain inner peace through connecting with the Supreme Being (Chaitanya, 2019).

Ethics intensifies emotional intelligence because the right ideology always gives the desired result (Jennings et al., 2014). An ethical ideology of the business firm should include Integrity in every dealing, responsibility of decisions and strategies, fairness towards buyers and sellers, respect and dignity of stakeholders, and transparency in every marketing operation (Lončarić & Balent, 2019). Workers have a pluralistic attitude towards society, while workplace ideology has a unitarist outlook (Geare et al., 2009). Moral behaviour has moral norms of judgement and moral identity (Reynolds & Ceranic, 2007), while moral thoughts are a putative global form of ideology (Harcourt, 2000). Every community workplace reflects its perspective and distinct ideology, and the concept of dignity has relevance in individuals' perceptions and analysing their perspectives on the competitive domain of the workplace (Bal, 2017). Work-life ideologies are individualistic beliefs (Leslie et al., 2019), and the ancient ideologies based on the moral values and virtues of human behaviour are fruitful enough for analysing the management practices and work policies of the modern organization in the contemporary and changing environment (Budd & Bhave, 2008).

The field of mythology apprehends the approaches of culture, including its leadership styles, shrewdness, and preferences (Kessler & Wong-MingJi, 2009), and its contexts are helpful in understanding the customs and civilizations of any era extensively. The elements presented in Indian scriptures have been confirmed by examples because they are historical and fictional and are corroborated by taking the basis of stories (Anubhavananda, 2010). The psychological impact of the trend of thinking and ideology of well-being has been identified in the story given below:

Once, there was an Emperor called Ajitsen of Kashi (an ancient Indian city). He frequently strode to know about the wellness and interest of the people. One day, his ride was passing through the middle of the city, and his people had applauded him, and the city's sandalwood merchant Manibhadra was also standing in that crowd and looking at him furiously. He was worried about his warehouse full of sandalwood, and as soon as he saw the Emperor, he thought that all the sandalwood could be utilized in his cremation ceremony. At the same time, that royal leader also saw him, and he got upset immediately and considered him his enemy. He did not understand his perception and ordered his minister to find the reason behind the sudden change in his mind-set.

The minister was a very wise person and scholar of psychology. He initiated his probe through proper planning and befriended the merchant to analyse his ideology of thinking. He realized that his evil thoughts had invisibly affected the Emperor, which led to a negative change in his mind-set. He decided to protect the interests of both persons and suggested him of using the sandalwood for the new palace and buys all the goods from the warehouse. As soon as the wood had been sold, thinking of Manibhadra got changed, blessings started pouring into his mind, and he wished for the Emperor's long life, who too felt a sense of affection towards the merchant while seeing him again.

He again asked his minister the actual reason behind the sudden change in his thoughts. He explained that it was the psychological effect of ideology because people's perceptions of each other influenced the state of their minds. So, one should always keep his perspectives right and think positive because good feelings have fruitful reactions and consequences (Khemka, 2020).

According to personal feelings, attitude, and imagination towards life, a person's life path can be soft or rough, and happiness, sorrow, prosperity and kindness, generosity, and narrowness are the two roles of human nature, good, and bad. The realization of these two is mostly dependent on the personal ideals, beliefs, mental attitudes, environment, and education-direction of an individual, and through imbibing good thoughts and inviting them, he nurtures and grows his personality. To create a new feeling is to take a new step in the path of self-realization, and by changing the thoughts, he should change the permanent frequency of self-consciousness. In this aspect, benevolence is always beneficial, and through its spirit, he can develop life as he can and utilize it properly in the same way.

He gets the impetus of progress only because of the bad situation, the opportunity of adversity, and obstacles, and in such cases; the unusual valour of man has manifested. If he does not get the opportunity to provoke a reaction, then the secret powers will never appear because these energies reside at such a high level that they do not have any effect on them due to ordinary reasons, so such motives are expected and needed, whoever hurts at the heart place. Just as one can make the body strong by exercise, so in the same way, the power of reasoning, comparison, memory, writing, poetry, including enthusiasm and willpower can be developed, and through moving forward in the spirit of well-being and creates the association and circumstances favourable to him, then surely there will be a remarkable change all around (Mahendra, 2007). Everybody should always observe his thoughts as well as his trend of thinking because it has a direct impact on his behaviour.

Intensifying the Moral Self Through an Observation of Virtues

The conduct of a soulful and self-aware person is called virtue. To purify the inner self, one has to do selfless action, worship, and self-reflection in a sequence, and this process is called the virtuous practice (Saraswati, 2013). Dharma is *Vedic* in its context (Awasthi, 1974), and it has been regarded as the source of virtue, which develops the values of self-confidence, self-improvement, self-realization, self-discipline, and self-reliance in an individual (Chaube, 2004). It is a quality of human nature, and the spirit of the Supreme Being is inherent in all humans, which is their nature or identity (Masih, 2008). In the context of *Sanatan Dharma*, *Sanatan* means eternal, and *Dharma* is the confirmation of human actions (Mishra, 2018). It depicts that there is a whole universe for spiritual search and has the value of renunciation and selfless sacrifice and the art of being equal in happiness and sorrow (Swamy, 2013). In the Indian philosophical view of life, the development of personality at the personal and social level has been signified by ancient scholars of *Vedic Sanskriti* (Sharma & Sharma, 2001). These philosophical thoughts and religious practices have created a special kind of *Sanskars* in the mind of all Indian human beings, which develop their points of view /insights which decide the values of life and give honour to others' opinions (Nirala, 2008). Virtue is connected with truth and bliss, which means good conduct and behaviour, and its importance has been glorified in *Vedic* texts and set up as an ideal for the welfare of the people or society.

Well-being is a popular parlance expression and possesses the aspects of personality and cultural values (Sinha, 1990). It defines the circumstances of a person's life and experiences. Ancient Indian mythological texts have asserted that well-mindedness and virtue lead to achieving every possible gain while dissemination of virtue from intellect and conscience leads to dissolution (Tiwari, 2021). The development of the mind cannot take us even one step towards excellence unless there is a call for restraint and suppression of the senses, and a person who pays attention to the teachings of his conscience, does not do any work against them, his soul becomes very strong. It acts as a guide for him and saves him from being downtrodden or losing (Mahendra, 2015). The absurdity of thoughts leads to the unethical performance of the work, and despite having a proper understanding of the undue duty, he does the wrong deeds, so a person whose mind is pure his judgement is always good (Nirala, 2008), so all the saints and great men of the world have considered virtue as one of the best qualities of human beings through which one can achieve spiritual and material heights. The *Sanatan* tradition is a flowing ideology, a simple way of life, as vast and deep as a stream of continuity, and exemplifies an ethical and virtuous ancient culture. It teaches the art of living and mandatory qualities of humanity, tolerance, and, benevolence for the well-being of humankind.

Every culture has a series of stories that explain the involved changes from past to present, and its customs and deities have played a significant role in it (Sanders, 1998). The narrative paradigm is a mechanism of cross-cultural communication for people and sets a common ground to build social relationships (Barker & Gower, 2010). All stories are narratives, and their intent of knowledge sharing helps to stimulate and disseminate effective action in the organization with the art of storytelling (Sole & Wilson, 2002). Ethos is the presence of folk life, but its history gives a glimpse of the past and indicates its utility in the future. It includes a set of folk rites, folk customs, and taboos and has long-term existence (Gupt, 1994). A story showing the importance of virtuous conduct is given here:

In the olden times of India, despite the large markets, some merchants used to sell goods from house to house, and there was a virtuous small trader of bangles among them. He had a horse to sell the goods and roamed everywhere in the villages with him. He followed an amazing way to drive him and would always pamper him, pat him and communicate with him very lovingly and never scold him. People were often surprised to see his impressive behaviour towards that animal and asked him the reason behind it.

He said that his job was to sell the bangles, and most of the customers were included the women, and he had to be among them throughout the day. If he employed the wrong words while communicating with the horse, then his tongue would also get used to abusing language, and this practice would turn out to be his habit. Now, all girls and daughters-in-law of the villages consider me as their father, and in that condition, someday, even among all the women, suddenly abusing words could be part of his dialectal. This habit might lead to losing his employment and respect as well. So, he always talked to his horse with affection in the same language through which he communicated to his sisters and daughters and escaped himself from wrong deeds. Hence, being a small trader, he had a big standard and great value for the art of living a virtuous life. He was a man of real virtues.

People carelessly indulge in destructive practices and allow bad things to come into their life, which turns out to be their habits and harm them, and they can't escape from their effects even after trying to avoid them. The only prerequisite here is to make a habit of avoiding unethical behavioural routines and develop virtues for making life significant and respectful (Khemka, 2020). An individual's personality enriches itself according to the circumstances of his environment, and his sense of responsibility motivates him to perform his duty. The following verse defines the value of a virtuous life:

> Ashtadasa puraneshu vyasasya vachana dvayam |
> Paropakaraya punyaya papaya parapeedanam ||

Doing benevolence is a virtue and suffering others because of oneself is immorality (Sharma, 2010). The concept of a meaningful life is beyond the success of personal gains, and people's exchanges should be balanced with nature for a prosperous life because serving and developing each other with knowledge, skill, and intelligence leads to self-satisfaction (Badaaya, 2021).

The psychological desire to get happiness remains in the subconscious mind of people. For the pleasure of the senses, the eyes want to see beautiful sights, the ears like to listen to sweet music, the tongue wants to taste delicious food, and the nose likes the pleasant fragrance, but the real happiness lies in the welfare of humanity because giving happiness to others destroys the tendency of one's own happiness (Sharma, 2021).

Being Respectful Towards Gifts of Nature and Diligence

It has been written in the ancient literary scriptures that one should respect everybody, value everything, enjoy each moment, and maintain relationships that have been given as a divine life's treasure. The main cause of the disturbance, conflict, and dissatisfaction of individuals' life is their perspective to misuse or disrespect the achieved possessions. The objects which are near and on which a person has ownership; he is neither interested in nor did he understand their importance, benefits, and utility (Mahendra, 2007). The senses are ruled by the mind, but through the intellect, an individual should always understand himself, and when he respects the available entities, the memory of three types has awakened such as the memory of duty, the memory of the self, and the memory of the divine, which proliferate dutifulness, reliability, and affinity. Through this approach, the rights of others are protected and lead to mutual unity and an increase of affection and trust among them, which builds a beautiful workplace (Sadhvi, 2019).

Exhibiting respect and giving honour to each other is the fundamental duty of every living being in this global world, and this notion of respect has been analysed by scholars concerning the humanistic, materialistic, and spiritual aspects and impacts. The term respect holds a prominent place and value in terms of its practicality and psychological beliefs, and the approach of understanding the necessity for respecting everybody, everything, and every relationship has been perfectly-acknowledged in the Indian mythological text Ramcharitmanas. Aggarwal (2005) has observed that it has an epic teaching virtue and is very helpful to a person in living a happy, contented and virtuous life. It is a spiritual narrative that has enthralled Indian "cognitive and communicative sensibility" through times (Beniwal, 2019), and a manual of folk education, folk motivation, folklore, folk behaviour, and ethos. It ascertains that all living entities have a common inheritance from the Supreme Being, and they can have divine living through divine deeds and universal brotherhood. It has values and ethics combined with responsibility and duty and includes the purpose of value-based contemplation.

The character of King Rama indicates his virtuous and pious conduct, integrity, and goodness. He showed a sense of equality and respect towards everyone through his behaviour and justice without any preferences. Since ancient times of India, the qualities and characteristics of his great personality have been enlightened and articulated through tales and also as traditional and cultural mythological stories to educate folks about the importance of virtue in life and to develop respect for humanity. The manner through which he functioned and organized his state works and acknowledged every small to big deed of all ministers, princes, and servants, and fulfilled their interests is exceptional and exemplary. In this spiritual text, his virtues have fruitfully reflected his personality as an ideal leader, and the depiction of his well-ordered, well-governed, and prosperous society indicates his personality of *Satchidananda* means supreme bliss and *Sadacharan* means corresponding virtuous conduct. This piece of Indian literature illustrates his notable behaviour mechanism of humanity, and two sagas about respect have been specified here:

In one of the incidents in *Ramcharitmanas*, when Hanuman Ji (an important head of Shri Rama's troops) had incinerated the Lanka and traced Sita Mata (his wife), and came back to him, then he immediately appreciated and heartily blessed him (Pandey, 2012). And also, when he gave the information about task accomplishment and narrated the message of Sita Mata to him, he got overwhelmed and stated that the work that he had done was difficult even for the deities, and he couldn't repay this favour (Gupt, 2017). Tulsidas Ji has shown the gratefulness of Shri Rama in the *Sunderkand* of *Ramcharitmanas* as follows:

> Sunu kapi tohi saman upakari | Nahin kou sur nar muni tanudhari ||
> Prati upakar karaun ka tora | Sanamukh hoi n sakat man mora ||

With a feeling of gratitude towards Hanumanji, Shri Rama said that he couldn't compensate for his courteous service (Pandey, 2009). He not only admired the significant achievement of all his connected great personalities but also gave the honour to the little contribution of every small living being.

In another instance, during wartime, a massive group of bears and monkeys was engaged in building a bridge on the sea for the conquest of Lanka, and they were collecting big rocks and trees for it. At that time, a squirrel also came down from the tree to help in their work, but neither the branch of the tree nor could the rock rise from the little squirrel. So after bathing in the seawater, she would have rolled in the sand, ran on the bridge, removed all the sand from her body, and continued her work uninterruptedly.

No one else was paying attention to that petty creature, but Shri Rama was watching the squirrel's efforts. He signalled to Hanuman Ji to bring her, and after caressing her while keeping it in his hand, he asked about her work and fearless behaviour. The squirrel got excited with joy and said that despite everyone's hard work; the land of the bridge was not getting levelled even after planting huge boulders, and he would have trouble walking on high and low ground, so she was trying to fill the small pits with the sand. He was pleased with her simplicity, very lovingly patted her on the back, and gave her the blessing and compliment that no one could achieve in the world, and since then, three lines were formed as a sign of Lord Rama's fingers on her back. (Lakkad, 2022). Because of his compassionate heart, he always gave credit and recognition to others and appreciated their work.

Maryada Purushottam Shri Rama engaged in the worldly conduct of dharma as the responsibility to set standards of morality and had executed every task virtuously to enlighten and educate the people. His kingdom was beautiful, and there was progress in everyone's life because they were satisfied, and their spirits were *sattvik* (morally true) (Pandey, 2012). He recognized the true value of humanity and life and was respectful towards every resource and support. Trust and trustworthiness affect every social interaction (Gjoneska et al., 2019). Genuineness is a combination of authenticity, confidence, humility, and translucence that reflects a true identity while performing any task or in any condition (Gauthier, 2014). An adherence to gratitude is a personal human construct that enhances the strength to manage emotions, so an organization should have a culture of respect and ethos. Gratefulness is an effective measure towards maintaining wellness and growth in the workplace.

Through analysing prudently, it has been observed that even in the house of the underprivileged person, despite his poverty, adversity, and conflict; the gracious Lord has provided many things which can provide peace and happiness to him. So, in the present highly competitive and demanding world, he should learn to respect the achieved position and affluence and demonstrates his talents, abilities, and qualities with the help of those simple entities, which certainly leads to his happiness and wellness (Mahendra, 2007). The honesty, justice, love, reverence, faith, and honesty of a person get reflected through his virtuous conduct. Therefore, the magnificence of organizational culture depends on his exquisiteness, and he can make it significant by enriching himself with all these qualities (Sadhvi, 2019). Accordingly, every person must associate virtue with the propensity of dharma.

The Inevitable Designation of Peace and Purification of Mind in Happiness

Peace is a state of mind and related to the conscience. When the conscience is satisfied, the peace of mind remains stable, and if it gets violated by any unjust reasoning, greed, bribery, lie, deceit, tyranny, or incest, then the peace of mind is disturbed. It is not to be found by searching in the outer world rather; it is a balanced state, living in the secret region of the mind (Mahendra, 2007), and it refers to the continued freedom of progress in orderly socio-cultural order (Abidi, 2002). Affection and thoughts are essential for the purification of the heart because by renouncing body pride by thought and surrendering himself to the Supreme Lord, one comes to the state of fairness, and the absence of all kinds of desires is the ultimate purification of the conscience (Maharaj, 2020). Good thoughts influence the mind because they accelerate a person's tendency to auspicious work (Poddar, 2005).

A peaceful and mindful person is always self-supporting, but a dependent person can never remain that happy because he assumes out of ignorance that he will be blissful if he gets great authority or wealth. However, as his glory increases, his dependence, fear, disease, indulgence, and hardness also increase, which is evidently due to his distress. So, he should get rid of all beneficence of society and nature by serving with wealth and power and dedicating himself to Almighty God. In this way, he gets deliverance from all kinds of debts and becomes supremely pure. It can be a way to live life peacefully and consciously (Maharaj, 2020). The process of purification of the mind is related to a person's actions and adequate use of his acquired abilities. He should understand the meaning of past events, make benefit from the present, and not anticipate the future. In this way, by sacrificing vain efforts and contemplation with caution and fulfilling the necessary resolutions, the time and strength that he gets are acted as the power that gets him to his goal (Poddar, 2005). So, only by wisdom, the inferiority complex, the evil instinct, blasphemous and vile desires are pacified, and he gets free from opposing mentality by having good contemplation and becoming an inner seer (Mahendra, 2007).

In today's era, there is turmoil in all the fields, and everywhere a call for peace and happiness has been heard. Despite being wealthy and prosperous, the number of people's discontent, internal disturbance, and mental distress is on the increase, and even after having all the worldly pleasures, they are in desolation and feel absent-minded. The main reason for all these peculiarities is the bonded attachment and tying oneself with the worldly web. Therefore, being free from it, not indulging in worldly things, sacrificing them, believing in spiritual divinity, and considering it as the root of their happiness—is to go in the lap of peace. A person's attitude always takes different forms and becomes evident from his behaviour, and whatever he is good-bad, calm-disturbed, happy-depressed from the inside, so he is in the outer world, and the inner state of mind is manifested on his face, and who has been freed from selfishness is calm, engrossed, and feel no sorrow in renouncing the world.

The purification of the mind leads to a state of concentration or resolute and without doubt and provides independence and power. An individual must not make such resolutions, whose fulfilment can be delayed by someone else or which he cannot fulfil, and should obey the necessary resolutions that he can but should not boast of their accomplishment According to his ability and interest, he should adopt such means in which any person, substance, place, other than himself, or there is no need for the cooperation of the situation and which is completely free. It also requires equality in behaviour with all and the power of forgiveness (Poddar, 2005). He should keep on examining his own mind without looking at the faults of others and possess prudence and awareness because a person with anger and hatred feels pleasure in seeing the flaws of people and in praising, and condemning them, and employing hopeless, bitter, and harmful speeches, which lead to the destruction of his inner happiness.

Accordingly, the main reason for the internal distraction of a person is not to relish his life's gifts. It is an irony of today's world that needs to be resolved, and he should sensibly understand the difference between his preferences, desires, and needs. Liberation from psychosis and selfishness gives birth to the light of knowledge within the mind, removes the image of ignorance, and shows a righteous path of ethics. Keeping all these facts in mind, an individual must make himself self-reliant because his right ideology, tolerance, policies, and truth while facing the conflicts and contradictions empowers him to reach his goal.

Thus, an organization can make the work and workplace effective by orienting and developing the employees through knowledge and understanding of all the stated measures of gratefulness and toleration, purification of thoughts and trend of thinking, and virtues and ethos. These are fundamental factors based on personality development and are inherently inclusive to the well-being of the organization's people, which also have represented a coordinated dimension for maintaining harmony, progress, happiness, and wellness in life and work.

Conclusion

Assimilation and practice of proficient approaches such as inculcating tolerance power, change in perspectives, purification of mind, valuing every object and relation, and enlightening the inner self to make prudent choices act as the power of a person in establishing a cultured organization and workplace of wellness and fulfilment. The reference works of Indian mythological texts have approaches to virtuous conduct, which are exemplary for comprehending the ethics of working. This literary work has highlighted the significant aspects of these features and their impact on the growth of human personality and has reflected their vital contribution and influence in conflict resolution, peacemaking, and maintaining happiness in the workplace. Ancient Indian ethos has an impressive framework and standard for learning the organization's behaviour and decency, which can improve employees' perspectives on work to become dynamically manageable in diverse organizational cultures.

References

Abidi, S. (2002). *Living beyond conflict for peace and tolerance*. ABETO.
Aggarwal, G., & Aggarwal, M. (2005). *Diamond nibandh evem patra lekhan*. Diamond Pocket Books (P) Ltd.
Aljawarneh, N. M. S., & Atan, T. (2018). Linking tolerance to workplace incivility, service innovative, knowledge hiding, and job search behavior: The mediating role of employee cynicism. *Negotiation and Conflict Management Research*, 11(4), 298–320. https://doi.org/10.1111/ncmr.12136
Anubhavananda, S. (2010). *Mere kanhaiya: Sapta khanda*. Indra Publishing House.
Arka, S. (2018). Understanding of Wellbeing through Ancient Indian Spiritual Texts *International Journal of Social Work and Human Services Practice*, 6(3), 101–105.
Awasthi, V. B. (1974). *Rāmacaritamānasa para paurāṇika prabhāva*. Delhi, India Dillī Pustaka Sadana.
Badaaya, V. P. (2021). Jeevan safal hi nahi sarthak bhi ho. *Kalyan*, 15(10), 1–50.

Bal, P. M. (2017). Introducing workplace dignity to management studies. *Dignity in the workplace: New theoretical perspectives* (pp. 97–128). Springer International Publishing.

Barker, R. T., & Gower, K. (2010). Strategic application of storytelling in organizations: Toward effective communication in a diverse world. *Journal of Business Communication, 47*(3), 295–312. https://doi.org/10.1177/0021943610369782

Bartels, D. M., Bauman, C. W., Cushman, F. A., Pizarro, D. A., & McGraw, A. P. (2014). Moral judgment and decision making. In G. Keren & G. Wu (Eds.), *The Wiley Blackwell handbook of judgment and decision making* (pp. 478–530). Blackwell.

Beniwal, A. S. (2019). Theory in story: The pedagogical potentials of Tulsidas'Sri-Ramcharitmanas in theory classroom. *Maharshi Dayanand University Research Journal ARTS, 18*(1), 1–19.

Bergen, C. W. V., & Collier, G. (2013). Tolerance as civility in contemporary workplace diversity initiatives. *Administrative Issues Journal Education Practice and Research,* 86–97.https://doi.org/10.5929/2013.3.1.6

Bowlin, J. R. (2019). *Tolerance among the Virtues*. Princeton University Press.

Brown, W., & Forst, R. (2014). A debate between Wendy Brown and Rainer Forst. In L. D. Blasi & C. F. E. Holzhey (Eds.), *The power of tolerance: A debate. New directions in critical theory* (pp. 9–70). Columbia University Press.

Budd, J. W., & Bhave, D. (2008). Values, ideologies, and frames of reference in employment relations. In N. Bacon, P. Blyton, J. Fiorito, & E. Heery (Eds.), *Sage handbook of industrial and employment relations* (pp. 92–112). Sage.

Chaitanya, T. (2019). Sukh-Dukh Ki Teh Me. *Kalyan, 13*(10), 1–50.

Chakrabarti, K. K. (1999). *Classical Indian philosophy of mind: The Nyaya dualist tradition*. State University of New York Press.

Chaube, S. P. (2004). *Kuch paścimī deśoṃ aura Bhārata meṃ śikṣā*. Concept Publishing Company.

Dalal, A. K. (2011). Psychology of health and well-being: Emergence and development. In A. K. Dalal & G. Misra (Eds.), *New directions in health psychology* (pp. 1–46). Sage.

Dhungana, R. K. (2014, August 10–15). Peace education: A Hindu perspective. *25th International Peace Research Association (IPRA) General Conference on Uniting for Peace: Building Sustainable Peace through Universal Values* in Istanbul/Turkey, pp. 1–14.

Ditto, P. H., Pizarro, D. A., & Tannenbaum, D. (2009). Motivated moral reasoning. In D. M. Bartels, C. W. Bauman, L. J. Skitka, & D. L. Medin (Eds.), *Moral judgment and decision making* (pp. 307–338). Elsevier Academic Press. https://doi.org/10.1016/S0079-7421(08)00410-6

Enke, B., Rodríguez-Padilla, R., & Zimmermann, F. (2020). *Moral universalism and the structure of ideology* (National Bureau of Economic Research, Working Paper No. 27511, pp. 1–45).

Fiala, A. (2005). *Tolerance and the ethical life*. Bloomsbury Publishing.

Forsyth, D. R., & Pope, W. R. (1984). Ethical ideology and judgments of social psychological research: Multidimensional analysis. *Journal of Personality and Social Psychology, 46*(6), 1365–1375.

Furedi, F. (2014). *On tolerance: A defence of moral independence*. Bloomsbury Publishing.

Gauthier, V. (2014). *Leading with sense: The intuitive power of savoir-relier*. Stanford University Press.

Geare, A., Edgar, F., & McAndrew, I. (2009). Workplace values and beliefs: An empirical study of ideology, high commitment management and unionisation. *The International Journal of Human Resource Management, 20*(5), 1146–1171. https://doi.org/10.1080/09585190902850331

Gjoneska, B., Liuzza, M. T., Porciello, G., Caprara, G. V., & Aglioti, S. M. (2019). Bound to the group and blinded by the leader: Ideological leader–follower dynamics in a trust economic game. *Royal Society Open Science, 6*, 1–12. https://doi.org/10.1098/rsos.182023

Golebiowska, E. A. (2014). *The many faces of tolerance: Attitudes toward diversity in Poland*. Taylor & Francis.

Goswami, C. L. (2014). *Bhavrog Ki Ramban Dawa*. Gita Press.

Gupt, N. (1994). *Bundel*. Retrieved from Ignca. https://ignca.gov.in/coilnet/bun del10.htm

Gupt, M. L. (2017). *Adhyatma Ramayan*. Gita Press.

Harcourt, E. (2000). Introduction. In E. Harcourt (Ed.), *Morality, reflection, and ideology* (pp. 1–20). Oxford University Press.

Hjerm, M., Eger, M. A., Bohman, A., & Fors Connolly, F. (2020). A new approach to the study of tolerance: Conceptualizing and measuring acceptance, respect, and appreciation of difference. *Social Indicators Research, 147*(1), 897–919. https://doi.org/10.1007/s11205-019-02176-y

Ismail, S. (2014). Effect of ethical ideologies on ethical judgment of future accountants: Malaysian evidence. *Asian Review of Accounting, 22*(2), 145–158. Emerald Group Publishing Limited. https://doi.org/10.1108/ARA-08-2013-0052

James, W. (1984). *Psychology, briefer course*. Harvard University Press.

Jennings, P. L., Mitchell, M. S., & Hannah, S. T. (2014). The moral self: A review and integration of the literature. *Journal of Organizational Behavior, 36*, 104–168. https://doi.org/10.1002/job.1919

Johari, R., J., Rosnidah, I., Nasfy, S. S. A., & Hussin, S. A. H. S. (2020). The effects of ethical orientation, individual culture and ethical climate on ethical judgement of public sector employees in Malaysia. *Economics and Sociology, 13*(1), 132–145.https://doi.org/10.14254/2071-789X.2020/13-1/9

Jurković, R., Jurković, S., & Jambrešić, M. (2018). Ethical decision making in business—Overview of some antecedents of individual ethical judgment. *International Journal of Digital Technology & Economy, 3*(1), 11–22.

Jurs, P., & Samusevica, A. (2018). The perspective of tolerance in the context of youth civic attitude. *International Journal on Lifelong Education and Leadership, 4*(2), 1–7.

Kessler, E. H., & Wong-MingJi, D. J. (2009). Introduction to cultural mythology and global leadership. In E. H. Kessler & D. J. Wong-MingJi (Eds.), *Cultural mythology and global leadership* (pp. 1–30). Edward Elgar.

Khemka, R. (2020). *Bodhkatha-Ank*. Gita Press.

Lakkad, P. P. (2022). *Kripanubhuti Ank*. Gita Press.

Leaman, O. (2002). *Key concepts in eastern philosophy*. Taylor & Francis.

Leslie, L. M., King, E. B., & Clair, J. A. (2019). Work-Life ideologies: The contextual basis and consequences of beliefs about work and life. *Academy of Management Review, 44*(1), 72–98. https://doi.org/10.5465/amr.2016.0410

Levin, A. (2009). Dignity in the workplace: An enquiry into the conceptual foundation of workplace privacy protection worldwide. *ALSB Journal of Employment and Labor Law, 11*(1), 63–103.
Lončarić, D., & Balent, M. (2019). The impact of ethical ideologies on the judgment of online marketing communications ethics in the tourism market—Tourism students' perspective. *Zbornik Veleučilišta u Rijeci, 7*(1), 127–147. https://doi.org/10.31784/zvr.7.1.5
Long, J. D. (2019). Religious experience, Hindu pluralism, and hope: Anubhava in the tradition of Sri Ramakrishna. *Religions, 10*(210), 1–17.
Maharaj, S. (2020). Prasannata Ka Rahasya. *Kalyan, 14*(11), 1–50.
Mahendra, R. (2007). *Amrit Ke Ghoont*. Gita Press.
Mahendra, R. (2015). *Amrit Ke Ghoont*. Gita Press.
Martin, T., & Hafer, J. C. (2017). Managerial tolerance of insider information sabotage acts and how different organizational cultures might influence such tolerance. *Journal of Behavioral and Applied Management, 17*(3), 254–274. https://doi.org/10.21818/jbam.15.3.6
Masih, Y. (2008). *Tulnatamak Dharma-Darshan*. Motilal Banarsidass Publishers Pvt. Limited.
McFerran, B., Aquino, K., & Duff, M. (2010). How personality and moral identity relate to individuals' ethical ideology. *Business Ethics Quarterly, 20*(1), 35–56.
Mishra, D. (2018). *Aalekh Sangrah*. Rajmangal Publishers.
Mishra, V. (2008). *Hindu dharma: Jeevan mein sanatan ki khoj*. Rajkamal Prakashan.
Moreno-Riaño, G. (2016). Tolerance in the twenty-first century: An introduction. In G. Moreno-Riano (Ed.), *Tolerance in the twenty-first century: Prospects and challenges* (pp. 1–10). Lexington Books.
Narvaez, D., Getz, I., Rest, J. R., & Thoma, S. J. (1999). Individual moral judgment and cultural ideologies. *Developmental Psychology, 35*(2), 478–488.
Nirala, S. T. (2008). *Sampooran kahaniyan: Suryakant Tripathi Nirala*. Rajkamal Prakashan.
Oberdiek, H. (2001). *Tolerance: Between Forbearance and Acceptance*. Rowman & Littlefield Publishers.
Pandey, N. (2009). *Jahiram pad neh*. Prabhat Prakashan.
Pandey, A. (2011). Psychotherapy and Indian thought. In A. K. Dalal & G. Misra (Eds.), *New directions in health psychology* (pp. 259–282). Sage.
Pandey, P. R. (2012). *Anand Ramayan*. Rupesh Thakur Prasad Prakashan.
Poddar, H. P. (2005). *Ek Mahatma ka prasad*. Gita Press.
Premeshananda, S. (2011). Sri *Shankara charit*. Advaita Ashrama.
Reynolds, S. J., & Ceranic, T. L. (2007). The effects of moral judgment and moral identity on moral behavior: An empirical examination of the moral individual. *Journal of Applied Psychology, 92*(6), 1610–1624.
Rivera, J. (2008). Introduction. In J. de Rivera (Ed.), *Handbook on building cultures of peace* (pp. 1–10). Springer New York.
Robbins, S. P., Chatterjee, P., & Canda, E. R. (1999). Ideology, scientific theory, and social work practice. *Families in Society: The Journal of Contemporary Human Services, 80*(4), 374–384. https://doi.org/10.1606/1044-3894.1217
Roucek, J. S. (1944). A history of the concept of ideology. *Journal of the History of Ideas, 5*(4), 479–488. https://doi.org/10.2307/2707082
Sadhvi, A. (2019). Apni Aur Niahro. *Kalyan, 13*(10), 3–50.

Sanders, T. I. (1998). *Strategic thinking and the new science: Planning in the midst of chaos complexity and change*. Free Press.
Sangharakshita. (1998). *What is Dharma? The essential teachings of the Buddha*. Windhorse Publications Limited.
Saraswati, S. P. (2013). *Sadachar*. Central Chinmaya Mission Trust.
Sharma, B. D., & Sharma, S. K. (2001). *Contemporary Indian English novel*. Anamika Publishers & Distributors (P) LTD.
Sharma, A. (2010). *Puran darshan samagra drishti part (Puran ka vedatva)*. Jagadguru Ramanadacharya Rajasthan Sanskrit University.
Sharma, R. C. (2021). Sukh Ki Khoj Me. *Kalyan, 15*(10), 1–50.
Shastri, G. P. B. (2018). *Aadikavya aur Bauddh sahitya: Ramayan avam Jatak kathayen*. Educreation Publishing.
Sinha, D. (1990). Concept of psycho-social well-being: Western and Indian perspectives. *NIMHANS Journal, 8*(1), 1–11.
Sinha, J. B. (2014). *Psycho-social analysis of the Indian mindset*. Springer India.
Sole, D., & Wilson, D. G. (2002). Storytelling in organizations: The power and traps of using stories to share knowledge in organizations. *LILA, Harvard, Graduate School of Education*, 1–12.
Swamy, S. (2013). *Hindutva evam rashtriya punarutthan*. Prabhat Prakashan Pvt Ltd.
Thapar, R. (1982). Ideology and the interpretation of early Indian history. *Review (Fernand Braudel Center), 5*(3), 389–411. https://doi.org/10.1177/053901848 102000201
Tiwari, S. C., & Pandey, N. M. (2013). The Indian concepts of lifestyle and mental health in old age. *Indian Journal of Psychiatry, 55*(2), 288–292. https://doi.org/10.4103/0019-5545.105553
Tiwari, M. (2021). *Jeevan tatva vivechan*. Blue Rose Publishers.
Vaidh, L. C. (2008). *Ashtanghridayam of Shrivagbhattavirachitam sarvangsundri vyakhya vibhushitam*. Motilal Banarsidass Publishers Pvt. Limited.
Weissman, A. (1981). Ideology in the workplace. *Social Work, 26*(4), 342–343. https://doi.org/10.1093/sw/26.4.342-a
Wig, N. (2004). Hanuman complex and its resolution: An illustration of psychotherapy from Indian mythology. *Indian Journal of Psychiatry, 46*(1), 25–28.
Witenberg, R. T. (2019). *The psychology of tolerance: Conception and development*. Springer Singapore.
Zawadzki, M. (2018). Dignity in the workplace. The perspective of humanistic management. *Journal of Management and Business Administration. Central Europe, 26*(1), 171–188. https://doi.org/10.7206/jmba.ce.2450-7814.224.

CHAPTER 17

Entrepreneurship: An Auspicious Context for Examining Its Connection to Wellbeing

Nazha Gali and Susanna L. M. Chui

INTRODUCTION

The purpose of this chapter is to examine the connection between entrepreneurship and wellbeing whereby we adopt a holistic approach in examining different aspects of wellbeing. The following sections will discuss important themes in the interconnections of entrepreneurship and wellbeing, yet the consideration of wellbeing in entrepreneurship research is still nascent. Entrepreneurship is about acting forth to bring new ideas, novel and sometimes wild, to generate value (McMullen & Shepherd, 2006; Shane & Venkatraman, 2000). To do this, entrepreneurs act with a sense of urgency to address immediate challenges in their communities and generate opportunities amid the uncertainty (Fisher et al., 2020).

Wellbeing is an integral element of living a positive and fulfilling life and is closely related to one's capacity to work, to experience positive emotions, and to maintain positive relationships with others (Diener et al., 2010; Ryan & Deci, 2000). Wellbeing is defined as "the experience of satisfaction, positive affect, infrequent negative affect, and psychological functioning in relation

---

N. Gali (✉)
Strategy and Entrepreneurship Department, Odette School of Business, University of Windsor, Windsor, ON, Canada
e-mail: nazha.gali@uwindsor.ca

S. L. M. Chui
Department of Management Hang Shin Link, School of Business, The Hang Seng University of Hong Kong (HSU), Siu Lek Yuen, Hong Kong

© The Author(s), under exclusive license to Springer Nature Switzerland AG 2023
J. Marques (ed.), *The Palgrave Handbook of Fulfillment, Wellness, and Personal Growth at Work*,
https://doi.org/10.1007/978-3-031-35494-6_17

to developing, starting, growing, and running an entrepreneurial venture (Wiklund et al., 2019, p. 581)." Several global leaders are launching initiatives to place wellbeing as an essential societal goal. This represents a profound shift in attitudes toward ensuring socio-economic progress rather than solely focusing on economic growth (Wiklund et al., 2019). Thus, wellbeing has become a popular outcome to be studied in entrepreneurship research apart from the traditional financial metrics (Wiklund et al., 2019).

The Importance of Examining Wellbeing Post COVID

The COVID-19 pandemic is a public health and global economy breakdown and has impacted every facet of society, in which at the individual level the pandemic has led to a myriad of long-term psychological stressors and negative effects on mental health and life satisfaction as well as psychosocial stressors such as social distancing and decreased family and social support that are integral for emotion regulation and for ensuring financial security (Gruber et al., 2021). Thus, following the COVID-19 pandemic the importance of ensuring and maintaining wellbeing has become more critical than ever. International organizations have advocated the integration of psychosocial support and mental health into the COVID-19 response (Moreno et al., 2020).

Hedonic and Eudaimonic Wellbeing

Modern psychology offers two main theoretical perspectives on wellbeing (hedonic and eudaimonic). The hedonic approach to wellbeing emphasizes positive life evaluations and positive feeling states, such as happiness and life satisfaction. Thus, the hedonic approach refers to the subjective wellbeing and consists of affective appraisals of emotions and cognitive judgments of satisfaction (Diener et al., 1999).

On the other hand, the eudaimonic approach emphasizes multiple facets of wellbeing such as autonomy, self-acceptance, self-actualization (Maslow, 1968), self-determination (Ryan & Deci, 2000), personal development (Erikson, 1959), and realization of one's potential. Even though these two approaches (hedonic and eudaimonic) are positively correlated, they are empirically distinct (Keyes et al., 2002; Ring et al., 2007). Striving to realize one's potential and for reaching personal growth may be demanding and stressful and may not always be conducive to being content and to feelings of happiness, yet both perspectives on wellbeing are core components of wellbeing representing positive psychological functioning as well as positive feelings and evaluations.

Increasing Interest in Wellbeing in Entrepreneurship Research

Due to its widespread relevance across scientific fields, empirical research on wellbeing has exponentially increased in recent years (Ryff, 2017). Entrepreneurship and management scholars are becoming increasingly interested in the antecedents and consequences of wellbeing (Shepherd & Patzelt, 2017; Stephan, 2018; Uy et al., 2013; Wiklund et al., 2017, 2019). As such wellbeing is not only an important outcome but also an antecedent of many important outcomes (Ryff, 2019). Individuals who are happier tend to be more satisfied at work, live healthier and longer lives (Wiest et al., 2011), and they tend to be more psychologically fulfilled in their lives (Erdogan et al., 2012; Helliwell et al., 2013). Further, they tend to be more creative and socially connected (De Neve et al., 2013). Thus, psychological wellbeing is an important element of workplace cooperation and enhanced productivity.

Recently, there has been an increase in the number of studies that examine wellbeing in entrepreneurship research as wellbeing is a relevant construct to consider in entrepreneurship. Entrepreneurs are often considered to be visionary who are deeply passionate about their work and have an innate connection with the products and services that they create. Entrepreneurship embodies the process of self-actualization of one's potential through authentic, self-organized, and self-purposeful endeavors that help lead to a fulfilling and fully functioning life (Shir et al., 2019). Individuals pursue entrepreneurship for personal purposes. In this sense, entrepreneurship can be a source of life satisfaction and personal fulfillment as it provides entrepreneurs with a sense of control and freedom to work around any adversity or disabilities that they may have. Thus, it is logical that the field of entrepreneurship is able to contribute to the growing international movement and interdisciplinary conversation around wellbeing in a meaningful and unique way.

Dependent Variable in Entrepreneurship Research: Wellbeing

A recent review has shown that entrepreneurship research since 2000 has focused on firm-level outcomes such as firm performance or growth (Shepherd et al., 2019). The reason for this is that policymakers and entrepreneurship scholars tend to assume that entrepreneurship is inherently good and that what benefits the entrepreneur should benefit other stakeholders; there are universal positive spillover effects from entrepreneurial activity to stakeholders, such as customers, suppliers, employees, and family members.

However, recently, other dependent variables such as wellbeing are being considered, and the relative percentage of papers that are using performance as the dependent variable are decreasing. Entrepreneurship is a complex phenomenon involving different emotional states, uncertainty, risk taking, and opportunity recognition and exploitation.

Individuals choose to engage in entrepreneurship, start or fail a new business venture for a variety of reasons. As there is diversity in entrepreneurship, it is also important that there is greater diversity in outcomes that are studied by scholars (Shepherd, 2015). Yet, there is still little research that interlinks entrepreneurial phenomena to psychological constructs such as wellbeing or psychological disorders such as ADHD (Attention Deficit Hyperactivity Disorder) (Wiklund et al., 2016, 2019; Yu et al., 2021). Wellbeing/lack of wellbeing is an important construct that should be considered in entrepreneurship research.

ADHD and Entrepreneurship

Neurodiverse[1] individuals are inherently attracted to entrepreneurship because the position offers them autonomy to shape their work in a way that leverages their idiosyncratic strengths while safeguarding their weaknesses (Wiklund et al., 2018). However, entrepreneurship is demanding and stressful and can lead to a negative impact on wellbeing (Stephan, 2018), especially among neurodiverse individuals who are susceptible to being vulnerable to stress (Harpin, 2005). There has been an increasing interest in the relationship between entrepreneurship and neurodiversity symptoms such as ADHD (impulsivity/hyperactivity) symptoms.

ADHD, a trait that has been associated with negative implications, has been argued to be functional in the entrepreneurship context (Antshel, 2018) which has conveyed advantages in entrepreneurship in terms of greater entrepreneurial entry and performance (Wiklund et al., 2017; Yu et al., 2021). Previous research has indicated that ADHD symptoms are interrelated with higher entrepreneurial behaviors among small business owners (Wismans et al., 2020). Individuals with ADHD have been argued to be able to pay better attention to novel and innovative opportunities (Yu et al., 2021), have a stronger sensitivity to potential rewards, underestimate potential losses in risky decision-making (Shoham et al., 2016), and exhibit high alertness, readiness to change, and openness to new experiences (Nigg et al., 2005).

ADHD symptoms are related to boredom, quick action without considerable deliberation, and sensation seeking (Barkley, 1997; Miller et al., 2003) and these resonate with EO (entrepreneurial orientation). EO is considered to be a strategic orientation which has been mostly researched as a firm-level phenomenon that consists of three dimensions (innovativeness, proactiveness, and risk taking) until recently whereby it was conceptualized as a multi-level phenomenon exhibited as a top management team style as well (Wales et al., 2020). Innovativeness reflects the tendency of focusing on new ideas and

---

[1] The term neurodiversity has been termed to provide a strengths-based approach to neurological differences among individuals that traditionally were associated with psychiatric diagnoses, such as ADHD, Dyslexia, and Autism.

experimentation with new products and services. Proactiveness is the forward-looking dimension of EO which involves anticipating future demand and establishes first-mover advantages. Risk taking is the willingness to commit large amount of resources and the willingness to accept the uncertainty that is inherent to entrepreneurship with the probability of large losses and failure (Covin & Slevin, 1989; Miller, 1983).

Entrepreneurship has been an attractive endeavor for individuals with ADHD symptoms, in which individuals with ADHD exhibit higher entrepreneurial intentions (Verheul et al., 2015) and actions (Lerner et al., 2019; Wiklund et al., 2017). Recently, researchers have shown that ADHD symptoms of entrepreneurs, aligned with the three dimensions of EO (innovativeness, proactiveness, and risk taking), positively influence firm performance (Yu et al., 2021).

While ADHD symptoms have been positively interrelated with entrepreneurial pursuit and performance, these very symptoms are negatively linked to wellbeing (Tran et al., 2021). Thus, neurodiverse individuals with ADHD may perform well and exhibit high entrepreneurial performance but may not feel well.

There has been research that has examined how the presence of ADHD may impact entrepreneurial team functioning and how entrepreneurial team conflict, influenced by ADHD symptoms and gender, impacts wellbeing and performance of entrepreneurs (Tran et al., 2022). Even though ADHD symptoms have been linked with higher entrepreneurial intentions and higher levels of creativity and risk taking, this may promote entrepreneurs with ADHD to come up with divergent and out of the box opinions. ADHD symptoms such as lack of attention, procrastination, and interruptions of others will lead to emotional and cognitive team conflicts. Thus, neurodiversity brought by ADHD may be considered as a double-edged sword. Further, while teams with members with ADHD may incline the team to experience team conflict, having women on the team may lead to less team conflict as women entrepreneurs are less likely to confront with conflict.

Previous researchers have also examined the relationship between ADHD symptoms and wellbeing and the moderating effect of gender, in which it was found that ADHD symptoms have a negative relationship with wellbeing and that negative effect is aggravated for women entrepreneurs (Tran et al., 2021). The reason is that entrepreneurship is more common among men whereby "entrepreneurship" has male connotations (Sullivan & Meek, 2012). Further, ADHD is male gendered whereby ADHD symptoms of hyperactivity, impulsivity, and lack of attention run counter to female stereotypes (Gaub & Carlson, 1997). Thereby, women entrepreneurs with ADHD face two behavioral stereotypes. The challenging of stereotypes takes a toll on women in terms of their wellbeing.

The COVID-19 outbreak has created several stressors for individuals and individuals exhibit different levels of vulnerability. Individuals with ADHD have been shown to be more vulnerable to the challenges created by the

COVID-19 outbreak and may need better care and attention (Pollak et al., 2022). Higher levels of ADHD symptoms have been found to predict higher psychological distress, lower life satisfaction, and lower adaptation to the COVID-19 outbreak through the indicators: financial status, adherence to preventive measures, and mental health. Thus, ADHD symptoms have been shown to be correlated with higher perceived risk of COVID-19 and lower adaptation to the COVID-19 outbreak.

Stressors in Entrepreneurship

Entrepreneurs are known to experience stressors such as extended working hours, increased work effort, unpredictable, and volatile external environment and this negatively impacts their wellbeing. Entrepreneurs are known to persevere and to persist when faced with implausible and difficult tasks.

Uncertainty is inherent in the process of creating and implementing new products/services which define entrepreneurship (Alvarez & Barney, 2007). As entrepreneurs are propelled to make decisions under conditions of uncertainty, time pressures, and they are not endowed with historical references to provide them with a guideline (Baron, 2008), emotions are important to consider within entrepreneurship.

The entrepreneurial journey does not follow a smooth path, in which the entrepreneur may experience an emotional rollercoaster with time periods characterized with fulfillment and other time periods that are stressful and whereby resources may be depleted (McMullen & Dimov, 2013). The majority of new business start-ups have been shown to fail and even if a start-up venture survives in its early stages such ventures suffer from a liability of newness with lack of resources and network; in turn, they need to seek external relationships with suppliers, distributors, customers, and to develop internal relationships with their employees.

While the entrepreneurial journey may be filled with stressors, entrepreneurs may use various mechanisms of recovery in order to re-energize. The entrepreneurship journey is stressful and uncertain but not all entrepreneurs would experience a similar journey. As such, previous research has shown that novice and experienced entrepreneurs react differently to entrepreneurial stressors. Among experienced entrepreneurs, entrepreneurial stressors had a direct sleep impairing effect whereas among novice entrepreneurs the same stressors had an indirect effect on sleep by leading to an increase in work-home interference and as a result leading to an increase in insomnia. While both novice and experienced entrepreneurs experience insomnia when dealing with entrepreneurial stressors, the underlying mechanisms differ (Kollmann et al., 2019).

The Emotional State in the Entrepreneurial Journey

Entrepreneurs are known to likely be influenced by their wellbeing/emotional state in which positive affect has been shown to be interlinked with creativity and innovation (Baron & Tang, 2011), risk perceptions and preferences (Podoynitsyna et al., 2012), and opportunity evaluation (Grichnik et al., 2010). Yet, there is a lack of focus on the impact of negative emotional states or lack of wellbeing on entrepreneurial actions. Highly activated emotions (whether they have a positive or negative valence) are associated with more entrepreneurial actions (Foo et al., 2015). In comparison with individuals with high dispositional positive affectivity, those with high dispositional negative affectivity are more likely to pursue higher risk taking by starting their own business venture (Nikolaev et al., 2018). Thus, even negative affectivity can promote entrepreneurial behavior.

Necessity Versus Opportunity Entrepreneurs

There is research that has indicated that there are different types of entrepreneurs with regard to their mental health and wellbeing, in which there is a distinction that is drawn between necessity and opportunity entrepreneurs (Stephan, 2018). Necessity entrepreneurs pursue entrepreneurship because they have few occupational alternatives and are forced into entrepreneurship while opportunity entrepreneurs pursue entrepreneurship because of the rewards that it offers. Opportunity entrepreneurs have been argued to experience greater wellbeing in comparison with necessity entrepreneurs in line with psychological theory.

Opportunity entrepreneurs report higher family and health satisfaction because of the alignment between their internal motivation and outward activities (Carree & Verheul, 2012). On the other hand, necessity entrepreneurs may be faced with resource constraints especially if self-employment occurred due to a job loss or lack of job satisfaction. Yet, both types of entrepreneurs experience higher dissatisfaction due to the lack of leisure time (Binder & Coad, 2016).

Previous researchers have provided evidence of the physical and mental health consequences of switching from unemployment to self-employment (necessity entrepreneurs) and from regular employment to self-employment (opportunity entrepreneurs), and they found that necessity entrepreneurs experienced improvements in their mental health but not physical health whereas opportunity entrepreneurs experienced benefits in their mental and physical health (Nikolova, 2019).

The Role of Prosocial Motivation on the Entrepreneur's Wellbeing

The number of ventures that are driven by a social mission or environmental concerns has grown. Contrary to for-profit ventures, social ventures do not only focus on income-generating activities but are also driven by their social mission which focuses on improving the societal welfare. Recent research in entrepreneurship has highlighted the important role of prosocial motivation as a factor that benefits society and improves the entrepreneur's wellbeing (Shepherd, 2015).

An entrepreneur who is prosocially motivated engages in new venturing activities that create value in their community and help to alleviate the suffering of people facing challenges (Williams & Shepherd, 2016). The majority of entrepreneurship research that has examined prosocial motivation focuses on social entrepreneurs whose venture's main mission is to help others in their communities (Dacin et al., 2011; Zahra et al., 2009). Yet, commercial entrepreneurs also exhibit varying degrees of prosocial motivation even when their social goals are not part of their venture's mission (Shepherd, 2015).

Recent studies have raised the possibility that prosocial motivation may negatively impact the entrepreneur's psychological wellbeing as well as their performance. The reason for this is that the burden of helping others may outweigh the entrepreneur's desire to fulfill their immediate job responsibilities. Thus, the entrepreneur may take on too much which contributes to work overload and job stress (Bolino & Grant, 2016).

As the entrepreneur is driven to help others, they may pursue too many activities which then depletes their personal resources (Baumeister et al., 2007). Recent authors have argued that an entrepreneur's prosocial motivation may be difficult to sustain in a self-directed manner (Kibler et al., 2019; Weinstein & Ryan, 2010). The inability of the entrepreneur to fulfill both prosocial as well as financial goals can create a stressful experience and negatively impact wellbeing (Shepherd, 2015). Yet, previous research has found that even though prosocial motivation may harm subjective wellbeing of the entrepreneur because of conflicting goals (financial vs. prosocial), the entrepreneur's level of intrinsic motivation (their desire to put in more effort into their venture because of the enjoyment of the work itself) (Ryan & Deci, 2000) and their perceived control of the external work environment (degree of autonomy that they perceive upon completing their daily tasks) (Deci & Ryan, 2000) impact the relationship between prosocial motivation and subjective wellbeing.

Work-Life Balance in Entrepreneurship

An associated area to work-life balance is the spillover effects from the entrepreneur to their family members. The entrepreneurial journey requires a high commitment financially and emotionally and thus it is bound to impact family relationships (Stephan, 2018). In ongoing businesses, there are work-family crossovers or spillover (Song et al., 2011), yet in entrepreneurship research there has been a limited number of studies that have examined the relationship between work-family interface and hedonic and eudaimonic wellbeing of entrepreneurs.

Job characteristics have been found to impact work-family facilitation or the involvement in one domain can positively influence the functioning of the other domain (Wayne et al., 2007), such that jobs with more variety and autonomy (i.e., entrepreneurially oriented jobs) have been found to promote higher levels of work-family facilitation (Grzywacz & Butler, 2005).

Gender Differences in Entrepreneurial Wellbeing

New venture formation is often considered to be a masculine activity that requires assertiveness, taking risks, competitiveness, and independence (Ahl, 2006). Role congruity theory considers that members of a gender will be positively evaluated when their characteristics align with the social roles that are assigned to that gender (Eagly & Karau, 2002). Women are expected to act in ways that are consistent with communal characteristics (nurturing, affiliation). On the other hand, men are expected to behave consistent with agentic characteristics (independence, leadership, or dominance).

A recent study found that contrary to expectations, when women exhibit masculine or agentic characteristics such as high creativity, they experience greater wellbeing and performance benefits. Whereas men achieve higher levels of wellbeing and performance outcomes when they exhibit feminine characteristics such as teamwork. Thus, this study reveals the benefits of going against one's gender stereotypes (Hmieleski & Sheppard, 2019). When female entrepreneurs consider themselves as being well-suited for their job and exhibit a perceived fit with the demands of new venture creation and with the role of an entrepreneur, their perceptions of person-work fit will in turn lead to high levels of subjective wellbeing (low work-family conflict and high work satisfaction) and enhanced new venture performance.

Entrepreneurship and Wellbeing: Future Research Avenues and Practical Implications

Work can be a great way for personal fulfillment and for fueling one's creativity. However, work can also negatively impact one's potential. While some entrepreneurs are able to work around their disabilities and challenging tasks and are able to reach their potential leading to a fulfilled life, many other entrepreneurs are unable to do so and yet are not captured in the research. Thus, there is a major survivor bias whereby individuals who may have more severe ADHD symptoms are unable to be included in one's target population when examining entrepreneurship and wellbeing (Yu et al., 2021).

Even though there is a growing body of work on the wellbeing of entrepreneurs, there is still limited research investigating wellbeing as a resource or trigger for entrepreneurial action. Recent studies to date have focused on the hedonic dimension of wellbeing. On the other hand, eudamonic wellbeing (multidimensional approach to wellbeing) has received less attention. Thus, more research should investigate the six dimensions of eudamonic wellbeing (autonomy, purpose in life, self-acceptance, personal growth, positive relationships, and environmental mastery) (Ryff, 2019). Due to the self-directed nature of entrepreneurship, it would be beneficial to move beyond the hedonic and embrace the eudaimonic aspects of wellbeing, leading to a more holistic understanding of wellbeing in entrepreneurship.

Additionally, while interest in prosocial motivation and wellbeing has grown in entrepreneurship research, it is less known under which conditions and how prosocial motivation impacts subjective wellbeing in the context of social versus commercial entrepreneurship. Future research comparing social to commercial entrepreneurs and whether prosocial motivation has a differential impact on wellbeing from each of those samples would be beneficial (Kibler et al., 2019).

While past research has examined grief of entrepreneurs following venture failure, less entrepreneurship research has examined work and family effects and crossovers such as the spillover effects from entrepreneurs to their family members and employees. Thus, it is important to broaden the scope beyond the entrepreneurs' wellbeing to consider the wellbeing of other stakeholders such as employees and family members since the high emotional and financial commitment of entrepreneurs is likely to impact their relationships with their family members and other stakeholders. Previous entrepreneurship research has focused on positive emotions as critical psychological resource leading to various entrepreneurial outcomes, yet negative emotions can be equally powerful as well.

There are also practical implications of more wellbeing and entrepreneurship research being pursued and this is useful in grooming new entrepreneurs in both the commercial and social entrepreneurship sectors as the two fields have crossovers with young rising entrepreneurs having to face multiple demands in trying to achieve their double bottom line. Further, it would help give insights into whether entrepreneurship would be a lucrative career choice for neurodiverse individuals. It can also help inform policy and decision makers whether investing in an entrepreneur who is neurodiverse, with high risk taking, innovativeness, and proactiveness behaviors, might be more appropriate in certain industries such as dynamic, volatile, and high-tech industries. Lastly, since neurodiverse individuals have been shown to be more vulnerable to the challenges created by the COVID-19 pandemic, they deserve more care and attention, therapeutic discourse, and mental counseling which would be vital to foster their healthy lifestyle.

Conclusion

The path to entrepreneurship can be a stressful long journey, but at the same time, this journey may bring joy and satisfaction. The field of entrepreneurship can contribute to the accelerating movement and interdisciplinary conversation around wellbeing. Entrepreneurship often leads to a positive change in the community and may even provide breakthrough and novel commercial as well as social innovations that contribute to societal wellbeing. Entrepreneurship is known to positively contribute to growth and personal development (Stephan, 2018). Unlike fixed income wage earners, entrepreneurs enjoy a level of freedom and control which enables them to derive more meaning from their work, to engage in purposeful activities through self-directed work, and to fulfill their innate abilities (Shir et al., 2019). When entrepreneurs experience higher levels of wellbeing because they are fulfilling themselves through their entrepreneurial journey, this can recharge their psychological resources (self-esteem, resilience) and will energize them to continue and persevere when dealing with challenging tasks that others may consider impossible (Foo et al., 2009). Thus, entrepreneurship can be a force for positive change in society enhancing both individual and societal wellbeing. It is vital to study wellbeing as a key outcome in entrepreneurship research complementing the traditional outcomes, such as performance and growth.

References

Ahl, H. (2006). Why research on women entrepreneurs needs new directions. *Entrepreneurship Theory and Practice, 30*(5), 595–621.

Alvarez, S. A., & Barney, J. B. (2007). Discovery and creation: Alternative theories of entrepreneurial action. *Strategic Entrepreneurship Journal, 1*(1–2), 11–26.

Antshel, K. M. (2018). Attention deficit/hyperactivity disorder (ADHD) and entrepreneurship. *Academy of Management Perspectives, 32*(2), 243–265.

Barkley, R. A. (1997). Behavioral inhibition, sustained attention, and executive functions: Constructing a unifying theory of ADHD. *Psychological Bulletin, 121*(1), 65.

Baron, R. A. (2008). The role of affect in the entrepreneurial process. *Academy of Management Review, 33*(2), 328–340.

Baron, R. A., & Tang, J. (2011). The role of entrepreneurs in firm-level innovation: Joint effects of positive affect, creativity, and environmental dynamism. *Journal of Business Venturing, 26*(1), 49–60.

Baumeister, R. F., Vohs, K. D., & Tice, D. M. (2007). The strength model of self-control. *Current Directions in Psychological Science, 16*(6), 351–355.

Binder, M., & Coad, A. (2016). How satisfied are the self-employed? A life domain view. *Journal of Happiness Studies, 17*(4), 1409–1433.

Bolino, M. C., & Grant, A. M. (2016). The bright side of being prosocial at work, and the dark side, too: A review and agenda for research on other-oriented motives, behavior, and impact in organizations. *Academy of Management Annals, 10*(1), 599–670.

Carree, M. A., & Verheul, I. (2012). What makes entrepreneurs happy? Determinants of satisfaction among founders. *Journal of Happiness Studies, 13*, 371–387.

Covin, J. G., & Slevin, D. P. (1989). Strategic management of small firms in hostile and benign environments. *Strategic Management Journal, 10*(1), 75–87.

Dacin, M. T., Dacin, P. A., & Tracey, P. (2011). Social entrepreneurship: A critique and future directions. *Organization Science, 22*(5), 1203–1213.

De Neve, J.-E., Diener, E., Tay, L., Xuereb, C. (2013). The objective benefits of subjective well-being. In J. Helliwell, R. Layard, & J. Sachs (Eds.), *World happiness report 2013*. UN Sustainable Development Solutions Network.

Deci, E. L., & Ryan, R. M. (2000). The "what" and "why" of goal pursuits: Human needs and the self-determination of behavior. *Psychological Inquiry, 11*(4), 227–268.

Diener, E., Suh, E. M., Lucas, R. E., & Smith, H. L. (1999). Subjective well-being: Three decades of progress. *Psychological Bulletin, 125*(2), 276.

Diener, E., Wirtz, D., Tov, W., Kim-Prieto, C., Choi, D. W., Oishi, S., & Biswas-Diener, R. (2010). New well-being measures: Short scales to assess flourishing and positive and negative feelings. *Social Indicators Research, 97*, 143–156.

Eagly, A. H., & Karau, S. J. (2002). Role congruity theory of prejudice toward female leaders. *Psychological Review, 109*(3), 573–598.

Erdogan, B., Bauer, T. N., Truxillo, D. M., & Mansfield, L. R. (2012). Whistle while you work: A review of the life satisfaction literature. *Journal of Management, 38*(4), 1038–1083.

Erikson, E. H. (1959). Identity and the life cycle: Selected papers. *Psychological Issues, 1*, 1–171.

Fisher, G., Stevenson, R., Neubert, E., Burnell, D., & Kuratko, D. F. (2020). Entrepreneurial hustle: Navigating uncertainty and enrolling venture stakeholders through urgent and unorthodox action. *Journal of Management Studies, 57*(5), 1002–1036.

Foo, M. D., Uy, M., & Baron, R. (2009). Affect and entrepreneurial efforts. *Journal of Applied Psychology, 94*(4), 1086–1094.

Foo, M. D., Uy, M. A., & Murnieks, C. (2015). Beyond affective valence: Untangling valence and activation influences on opportunity identification. *Entrepreneurship Theory and Practice, 39*(2), 407–431.

Gaub, M., & Carlson, C. L. (1997). Gender differences in ADHD: A meta-analysis and critical review. *Journal of the American Academy of Child & Adolescent Psychiatry, 36*(8), 1036–1045.

Grichnik, D., Smeja, A., & Welpe, I. (2010). The importance of being emotional: How do emotions affect entrepreneurial opportunity evaluation and exploitation? *Journal of Economic Behavior & Organization, 76*(1), 15–29.

Gruber, J., Prinstein, M. J., Clark, L. A., Rottenberg, J., Abramowitz, J. S., Albano, A. M., Aldao, A., Borelli, J. L., Chung, T., Davila, J., Forbes, E. E., Gee, D. G., Hall, G. C. N., Hallion, L. S., Hinshaw, S. P., Hofmann, S. G., Hollon, S. D., Joormann, J., Kazdin, A. E., ... & Weinstock, L. M. (2021). Mental health and clinical psychological science in the time of COVID-19: Challenges, opportunities, and a call to action. *American Psychologist, 76*(3), 409–426.

Grzywacz, J. G., & Butler, A. B. (2005). The impact of job characteristics on work-to-family facilitation: Testing a theory and distinguishing a construct. *Journal of Occupational Health Psychology, 10*(2), 97–109.

Harpin, V. A. (2005). The effect of ADHD on the life of an individual, their family, and community from preschool to adult life. *Archives of Disease in Childhood, 90*(suppl_1), i2–i7.

Helliwell, J., Layard, R., & Sachs, J. (2013). *World happiness report*.

Hmieleski, K. M., & Sheppard, L. D. (2019). The Yin and Yang of entrepreneurship: Gender differences in the importance of communal and agentic characteristics for entrepreneurs' subjective well-being and performance. *Journal of Business Venturing, 34*(4), 709–730.

Keyes, C., Shmotkin, D., & Ryff, C. (2002). Optimizing well-being: The empirical encounter of two traditions. *Journal of Personality and Social Psychology, 82*(6), 1007–1022.

Kibler, E., Wincent, J., Kautonen, T., Cacciotti, G., & Obschonka, M. (2019). Can prosocial motivation harm entrepreneurs' subjective well-being? *Journal of Business Venturing, 34*(4), 608–624.

Kollmann, T., Stöckmann, C., & Kensbock, J. M. (2019). I can't get no sleep—The differential impact of entrepreneurial stressors on work-home interference and insomnia among experienced versus novice entrepreneurs. *Journal of Business Venturing, 34*(4), 692–708.

Lerner, D. A., Verheul, I., & Thurik, R. (2019). Entrepreneurship and attention deficit/hyperactivity disorder: A large-scale study involving the clinical condition of ADHD. *Small Business Economics, 53*, 381–392.

Maslow, A. H. (1968). *Toward a psychology of being* (2nd ed.). Van Nostrand.

McMullen, J. S., & Dimov, D. (2013). Time and the entrepreneurial journey: The problems and promise of studying entrepreneurship as a process. *Journal of Management Studies, 50*(8), 1481–1512.

McMullen, J. S., & Shepherd, D. A. (2006). Entrepreneurial action and the role of uncertainty in the theory of the entrepreneur. *Academy of Management Review, 31*(1), 132–152.

Miller, D. (1983). The correlates of entrepreneurship in three types of firms. *Management Science, 29*(7), 770–791.

Miller, J., Flory, K., Lynam, D., & Leukefeld, C. (2003). A test of the four-factor model of impulsivity-related traits. *Personality and Individual Differences, 34*(8), 1403–1418.

Moreno, C., Wykes, T., Galderisi, S., Nordentoft, M., Crossley, N., Jones, N., Cannon, M., Correll, C. U., Byrne, L., Carr, S., Chen, E. Y. H., Gorwood, P., Johnson, S., Kärkkäinen, H., Krystal, J. H., Lee, J., Lieberman, J., López-Jaramillo, C., Männikkö, M., ... Arango, C. (2020). How mental health care should change as a consequence of the COVID-19 pandemic. *The Lancet Psychiatry, 7*(9), 813–824.

Nigg, J. T., Stavro, G., Ettenhofer, M., Hambrick, D. Z., Miller, T., & Henderson, J. M. (2005). Executive functions and ADHD in adults: Evidence for selective effects on ADHD symptom domains. *Journal of Abnormal Psychology, 114*(4), 706–717.

Nikolaev, B. N., Boudreaux, C. J., & Palich, L. (2018). Cross-country determinants of early-stage necessity and opportunity-motivated entrepreneurship: Accounting for model uncertainty. *Journal of Small Business Management, 56*, 243–280.

Nikolova, M. (2019). Switching to self-employment can be good for your health. *Journal of Business Venturing, 34*(4), 664–691.

Podoynitsyna, K., Van der Bij, H., & Song, M. (2012). The role of mixed emotions in the risk perception of novice and serial entrepreneurs. *Entrepreneurship Theory and Practice, 36*(1), 115–140.

Pollak, Y., Shoham, R., Dayan, H., Gabrieli-Seri, O., & Berger, I. (2022). Symptoms of ADHD predict lower adaptation to the COVID-19 outbreak: Financial decline, low adherence to preventive measures, psychological distress, and illness-related negative perceptions. *Journal of Attention Disorders, 26*(5), 735–746.

Ring, L., Höfer, S., McGee, H., Hickey, A., & O'BOYLE, C. A. (2007). Individual quality of life: can it be accounted for by psychological or subjective well-being? *Social Indicators Research, 82*, 443–461.

Ryan, R. M., & Deci, E. L. (2000). Self-determination theory and the facilitation of intrinsic motivation, social development, and well-being. *American Psychologist, 55*(1), 68.

Ryff, C. D. (2017). Eudaimonic well-being, inequality, and health: Recent findings and future directions. *International Review of Economics, 64*, 159–178.

Ryff, C. D. (2019). Entrepreneurship and eudaimonic well-being: Five venues for new science. *Journal of Business Venturing, 34*(4), 646–663.

Shane, S., & Venkataraman, S. (2000). The promise of entrepreneurship as a field of research. *Academy of Management Review, 25*(1), 217–226.

Shepherd, D. (2015). Party on! A call for entrepreneurship research that is more interactive, activity based, cognitively hot, compassionate, and prosocial. *Journal of Business Venturing, 30*(4), 489–507.

Shepherd, D. A., & Patzelt, H. (2017). *Trailblazing in entrepreneurship: Creating new paths for understanding the field.* Palgrave Macmillan.

Shepherd, D. A., Wennberg, K., Suddaby, R., & Wiklund, J. (2019). What are we explaining? A review and agenda on initiating, engaging, performing, and contextualizing entrepreneurship. *Journal of Management, 45*(1), 159–196.

Shir, N., Nikolaev, B. N., & Wincent, J. (2019). Entrepreneurship and well-being: The role of psychological autonomy, competence, and relatedness. *Journal of Business Venturing, 34*(5), 105875.

Shoham, R., Sonuga-Barke, E. J., Aloni, H., Yaniv, I., & Pollak, Y. (2016). ADHD-associated risk taking is linked to exaggerated views of the benefits of positive outcomes. *Scientific Reports, 6*(1), 34833.

Song, Z., Foo, M. D., Uy, M. A., & Sun, S. (2011). Unraveling the daily stress crossover between unemployed individuals and their employed spouses. *Journal of Applied Psychology, 96*(1), 151–168.

Stephan, U. (2018). Entrepreneurs' mental health and well-being: A review and research agenda. *Academy of Management Perspectives, 32*(3), 290–322.

Sullivan, D. M., & Meek, W. R. (2012). Gender and entrepreneurship: A review and process model. *Journal of Managerial Psychology, 27*(5), 428–458.

Tran, M. H., Wiklund, J., & Yu, W. (2022). Entrepreneurial team conflict—The associations with ADHD, gender, well-being and firm performance. In *Academy of management proceedings* (Vol. 2022, No. 1, p. 13437). Academy of Management.

Tran, M. H., Wiklund, J., Yu, W., & Perez-Luño, A. (2021). The impact of psychological vulnerabilities, gender and venturing stage on entrepreneurial wellbeing. In *Academy of management proceedings* (Vol. 2021, No. 1, p. 15987). Academy of Management.

Uy, M. A., Foo, M. D., & Song, Z. (2013). Joint effects of prior start-up experience and coping strategies on entrepreneurs' psychological well-being. *Journal of Business Venturing, 28*(5), 583–597.

Verheul, I., Block, J., Burmeister-Lamp, K., Thurik, R., Tiemeier, H., & Turturea, R. (2015). ADHD-like behavior and entrepreneurial intentions. *Small Business Economics, 45*, 85–101.

Wales, W. J., Covin, J. G., & Monsen, E. (2020). Entrepreneurial orientation: The necessity of a multilevel conceptualization. *Strategic Entrepreneurship Journal, 14*(4), 639–660.

Wayne, J. H., Grzywacz, J. G., Carlson, D. S., & Kacmar, K. M. (2007). Work–family facilitation: A theoretical explanation and model of primary antecedents and consequences. *Human Resource Management Review, 17*(1), 63–76.

Weinstein, N., & Ryan, R. M. (2010). When helping helps: Autonomous motivation for prosocial behavior and its influence on well-being for the helper and recipient. *Journal of Personality and Social Psychology, 98*(2), 222.

Wiest, M., Schüz, B., Webster, N., & Wurm, S. (2011). Subjective well-being and mortality revisited: Differential effects of cognitive and emotional facets of well-being on mortality. *Health Psychology, 30*(6), 728.

Wiklund, J., Hatak, I., Patzelt, H., & Shepherd, D. A. (2018). Mental disorders in the entrepreneurship context: When being different can be an advantage. *Academy of Management Perspectives, 32*(2), 182–206.

Wiklund, J., Nikolaev, B., Shir, N., Foo, M. D., & Bradley, S. (2019). Entrepreneurship and well-being: Past, present, and future. *Journal of Business Venturing, 34*(4), 579–588.

Wiklund, J., Patzelt, H., & Dimov, D. (2016). Entrepreneurship and psychological disorders: How ADHD can be productively harnessed. *Journal of Business Venturing Insights, 6*, 14–20.

Wiklund, J., Yu, W., Tucker, R., & Marino, L. D. (2017). ADHD, impulsivity and entrepreneurship. *Journal of Business Venturing, 32*(6), 627–656.

Williams, T. A., & Shepherd, D. A. (2016). Victim entrepreneurs doing well by doing good: Venture creation and well-being in the aftermath of a resource shock. *Journal of Business Venturing, 31*(4), 365–387.

Wismans, A., Thurik, R., Verheul, I., Torrès, O., & Kamei, K. (2020). Attention-deficit hyperactivity disorder symptoms and entrepreneurial orientation: A replication note. *Applied Psychology, 69*(3), 1093–1112.

Yu, W., Wiklund, J., & Pérez-Luño, A. (2021). ADHD symptoms, entrepreneurial orientation (EO), and firm performance. *Entrepreneurship Theory and Practice, 45*(1), 92–117.

Zahra, S. A., Gedajlovic, E., Neubaum, D. O., & Shulman, J. M. (2009). A typology of social entrepreneurs: Motives, search processes and ethical challenges. *Journal of Business Venturing, 24*(5), 519–532.

CHAPTER 18

Motivating Latin American Employees in the Twenty-first Century

Jesus Juyumaya

Introduction

In this chapter, you will learn some valuable concepts for academics, researchers, managers, and practitioners to motivate Latin American employees. The first part of this chapter will define transformational leadership and work engagement and then analyze these variables considering the Latin American context. In the second part, this chapter will examine the moderating role of Latin American cultural practices in the relationship between digital work characteristics and work design. Furthermore, this chapter proposes solutions that can allow positive results in employee task performance.

I hope that these theoretical studies are of practical and academic interest. This chapter presents key insights to build better strategies for managing human resources in the digital era. The principal aim of this chapter is to give valuable insights to motivate Latin American employees in the twenty-first century.

J. Juyumaya (✉)
Escuela de Ingeniería Comercial, Facultad de Economía y Negocios, Universidad Santo Tomás, Santiago, Chile
e-mail: jesusjuyumayafu@santotomas.cl

© The Author(s), under exclusive license to Springer Nature Switzerland AG 2023
J. Marques (ed.), *The Palgrave Handbook of Fulfillment, Wellness, and Personal Growth at Work*,
https://doi.org/10.1007/978-3-031-35494-6_18

Transformational Leadership for Latin American Employees

Transformational Leadership

Prior research suggests that Latin American employees suffer from a significant lack of motivation and engagement at work (Gallup, 2020), which explains, for instance, the poor historical performance of agricultural businesses (Markos & Sridevi, 2010).

Latin American countries developed certain traits, behaviors, and values that helped frame their identity based on the agricultural business's contractual relationship. In Latin America, the boss and the employee were paternalistic, focused on protection and obedience. The paternalistic relationship built on reciprocity helped manage the power structure by assigning the leader a benevolent role in the social exchange, entitling them to decision-making power over personal and work-related matters in business for social protection (Martinez, 2005).

The protective role of the leader included an interest in employees' health and a preference for long-term employment (Elvira & Davila, 2005). The social bond behind this employment relationship enhanced a sense of community and reciprocity within the social system, which helped organize social jobs in the nineteenth century (Davila & Elvira, 2012). However, empowered human capital is crucial for twenty-first-century firms and businesses (World Economic Forum, 2021).

This chapter suggests that learning to practice transformational leadership and work engagement will positively move Latin American companies to increase well-being and task performance in Latin American employees. Transformational leadership and work engagement results have been associated with higher productivity and long-term satisfaction, which are predictors of an organization's effectiveness and performance.

In transformational leadership theory, the leader works with followers beyond their immediate self-interest to recognize needed change, building a vision to guide the change through influence, inspiration, and executing the change in tandem with committed members of a group (Bass & Steidlmeier, 1999). This self-interest change elevates the follower's maturity, ideals, and concerns for achievement and task performance (Juyumaya & Torres, 2023a)

Thus, transformational leadership occurs when leader behaviors influence followers and inspire them to perform beyond their perceived capabilities. Transformational leaders inspire people to achieve better results through higher performance. It gives employees autonomy over specific jobs and the authority to make decisions once trained. This induces a positive change in followers' attitudes and the organization. Transformational leaders typically perform four distinct behaviors, also known as the "four I's." These behaviors are inspirational motivation, idealized influence, intellectual stimulation, and individualized consideration (Bass & Steidlmeier, 1999).

Transformational leadership is crucial for a diverse range of task performance. For instance, Koh et al. (2019) performed a meta-analysis using 127 studies. They found a positive relationship between transformational leadership and creative performance. They suggest that employees' innovative behavior is enhanced if leaders have an idealized influence, are inspiring, and intellectually stimulate their employees.

Leaders provide managers with several mediator mechanisms to suppress or facilitate their intrinsic work motivation for creativity. Employees acquire knowledge and creativity skills by observing the work and skills of transformational leaders (Eisenbeiß & Boerner, 2013; Jaussi & Dionne, 2003). Employees whose leaders are transformational tend to have visions and goals similar to those of their leaders, enhancing the organizational performance (Qu et al., 2015).

The Latin American Context

Increasingly, managers are finding themselves leading diverse workforces with employees scattered across dozens of nations. And for all the global companies to remain competitive, they need to retain their top talent and increase human capital performance. Naturally, retaining talent is more accessible when workers feel good about their jobs and are engaged with their organizations. Additionally, when employees feel positive about their workplaces, they are less likely to be searching for greener pastures elsewhere. Consequently, a key challenge for Latin American companies is figuring out how to motivate best and satisfy a workforce that is not only diverse in terms of geographic location and cultural values but, as a result, also diverse in what they need and want from their jobs (Gelade et al., 2008).

Despite Latin America's growing economic importance globally, limited research has been conducted to explain the unique aspects of leadership in Latin American countries (Romero, 2004). Hofstede (1984) mentions that the organizational culture of Latin American firms has been characterized as highly paternalistic, collectivist, and with little tolerance of uncertainty. This description of Latin American organizations significantly differs from other Western cultures, such as the United States or the United Kingdom (House et al., 2004). However, few studies describe how transformational leadership shapes work engagement and task performance within Latin American organizations.

Currently, transformational leadership is widely regarded as one of the most effective leadership styles (Judge & Piccolo, 2004). However, the relationship between transformational leadership and task performance could differ in countries with lower productivity and innovation, like Latin American countries. Latin American employees' most common leadership style is autocratic and paternalistic (Romero, 2004). As mentioned, Latin America is a high-power-distance culture in which employees mostly give instructions to their subordinates and expect them to follow those instructions without much questioning.

Leadership in Latin America tends to be paternalistic because the apparent rigidity of hierarchy and formalism is tempered to some degree by a relatively casual approach to rules and regulations. Consequently, transformative leaders should manage paternalism and a sense of extended family, essential Latin American management styles. In Latin America, transformative leaders must issue instructions to subordinates politely and respectfully (Romero, 2004).

The description of Latin American culture significantly differs from other Western cultures (Bandura, 2002; Hauff et al., 2014; Schein, 2004). Unfortunately, there is a lack of studies describing the role of leadership styles in Latin American businesses and organizations.

Furthermore, the Latin American cultural traits have permeated firms' organizational cultures. Latin American corporate cultures promote employees who respect authority (House et al., 2004). Employees tend to accept an unequal power distribution and feel comfortable with highly structured environments with great certainty (Dickson et al., 2012). The Latin American firms' organizational culture thus be characterized as a sizeable power-distance culture just as it happens with Latin American culture.

The characteristics of Latin American culture are explained before describing an essential historical context, as those characteristics affect work-related relationships and behaviors grounded in deep assumptions about reality and jobs. This chapter suggests that Latin American employees have particular reasons to seek transformational leadership leaders, and transformational leadership becomes a crucial job resource to work engagement.

But what is work engagement? Work engagement is a positive, fulfilling, work-related state of mind characterized by vigor, dedication, and absorption (Bakker & Demerouti, 2017). To understand work engagement, Job Demands and Resources (JD-R) offer a profound explanation about how employees engage in the workplace. We can understand, explain, and predict employee well-being and performance with JD-R theory (Bakker & Albrecht, 2018). Two broad categories of work-related conditions can be identified, named job demands and resources, that apply to three occupations: employees work with things, information, or people.

In JD-R theory, all job characteristics can be classified into job demands and job resources. Job demands are the physical, psychological, social, or organizational aspects that require sustained physical and mental effort and are associated with specific physiological and psychological costs (Demerouti et al., 2001). Examples are high work pressure and emotionally demanding interactions with clients or customers.

Job resources refer to the physical, psychological, social, or organizational aspects of the job that are functional in achieving job goals, reducing job demands and the associated physiological and psychological costs, or stimulating personal growth, learning, and development. Examples of job resources are autonomy, performance feedback, transformational leadership, and growth opportunities.

Transformational leadership is the new style of leadership that Latin American employees need to achieve better task performance through work engagement. Due to the complex and digital challenging world scenario, Latin American employees need more autonomy and motivation at the workplace. Hence, transformational leadership becomes a critical job resource to increase work engagement and task performance.

Practical Implications for Management

This chapter suggests that the elements of Latin American culture help understand Latin American human capital behaviors since they are usually overlooked in most organizational behavior and human resources management theories, for instance, in transformational leadership and work engagement theories (Gabel-Shemueli et al., 2019; Juyumaya, 2019).

As mentioned, transformational leadership helps Latin American employees foster work engagement and task performance. Hence, integrating transformational leadership and work engagement models (e.g., JD-R theory) can provide researchers and managers valuable insights into developing leadership training in Latin American organizations.

This chapter suggests that learning to practice transformational leadership will positively move companies, increasing Latin American employees' work engagement and task performance. These key constructs have been associated with higher productivity and long-term satisfaction, which are predictors of an organization's effectiveness and financial performance (Wells & Welty-Peachey, 2011).

Nowadays, Latin American employees prefer transformational leaders over transactional or autocratic leaders (Gallup, 2020). In this vein, this chapter suggests that employees seek transformational leadership from leaders and autonomy to feel more empowered, which helps them feel more engaged and increases their task performance.

Therefore, this chapter proposes that evidence-based leadership training should be taught in Latin American graduate courses (e.g., MBA, Managerial Training Programs, Executive Courses) and technical institutions, ideally based on empirical evidence provided by theories that have already been tested in the Latin American context.

Following Romero (2004), this chapter encourages using this analysis to (1) discuss the effects of this leadership practice with employees, (2) try to understand the mechanisms or circumstances that make this behavior more effective (e.g., type of industry, the corporate culture of the firm, organizational climate and organizational structure, among others), and (3) ask people how they view different levels of autonomy in the workplace to understand better how an employee's autonomy may alter the effect of transformational leadership and work engagement on task performance in Latin American employees.

Leadership theories have been an essential topic in the last few centuries. However, a vital avenue of advancement is discussing leader behavior in the larger context of modernization, cultural homogenization, and global complexity. Moreover, Latin America can be a fruitful scenario to test cross-cultural leadership hypotheses. For example, provide the opportunity to test these theories in other parts of the world. The insights delivered helped to a profound theoretical understanding of the role of leadership in Latin American employees.

CULTURAL PRACTICES SHAPE LATIN AMERICAN WORK DESIGN

Job Characteristics and the Culture as a Moderator

Work design concerns the content and organization of tasks, activities, relationships, and responsibilities (Parker, 2014). Previous literature argues that job characteristics shape work design. Following Hackman and Oldham (2007), work characteristics implement enriching jobs in organizational settings. Furthermore, work design research supports the notion that the effect of job characteristics on individual reactions will be affected by the national or regional culture in which the organization is embedded. Thus, culture has been recognized as a moderator of the relationship between job characteristics and work design (Grant et al., 2011).

However, a complication comes about because although the findings on job characteristics in the context of culture are promising, research on work design needs more theoretical development and systematic studies about the effect of particular job characteristics on specific outcome variables considering different cultures and a wide range of macroscopic contexts (Grant et al., 2011).

Some studies have supported the notion that the effect of job characteristics on individual reactions will be affected by the national culture in which the organization is embedded. For instance, scholars have argued that autonomy is a universal psychological need across cultures differentiated from individualism and independence. Autonomy involves choice, whereas individuality and independence involve separation from other people (Chirkov et al., 2003). Other researchers, however, have argued that autonomy is still more critical in individualistic than collectivistic cultures (Chua & Iyengar, 2006). Future research is needed to resolve this debate and other recent questions about work design.

As was previously mentioned, Latin America has unique social, cultural, and economic conditions that offer management researchers valuable opportunities to test theories and investigate phenomena with the purpose of theory building within a context that allows us to challenge implicit assumptions often present in ideas created in the United States and other developed countries (Vassolo et al., 2011).

The unique Latin American culture reflects the complexity of the region's history, mainly for indigenous and European cultures. Latin American cultural traits can be described as paternalistic, collectivist, and high-power-distance culture (Hofstede et al., 2010). For instance, employees primarily receive instructions from their leaders and expect to follow them without question.

The article of Aguinis et al. (2020) states that in terms of cultural and demographic characteristics, Latin America is more homogeneous than Asia, Africa, and Europe because countries share a similar colonial history that is reflected in their familiar languages (Spanish and Portuguese), religion (Roman Catholic), and legal structures. These similarities facilitate communication and business across national borders, as does the presence of relatively few military and religious conflicts, few cross-country rivalries relative to other parts of the world, and steady consolidation of relatively young democracies (Goenaga, 2016).

Nevertheless, there are significant challenges to doing business in Latin America, including vulnerable institutions, weak market infrastructures, high levels of corruption and volatility, populism, and income inequity (World Bank, 2019). Thus, Latin America is a region of paradoxes (Cuervo-Cazurra & Dau, 2009). These are precisely these unique conditions that allow scholars and practitioners to test theories, challenge implicit assumptions, and investigate new phenomena.

Digital Work Design in Latin America

In the past four decades, research on work design has played a critical role in building a bridge between scholars and practitioners. Prominent theories such as the job characteristics model (Hackman & Oldham, 2007) have stimulated much of the research in the field. As a result, researchers have accumulated extensive insight into the diverse tasks, knowledge, and physical characteristics of jobs. Moreover, past research has studied the psychological and behavioral impacts of work design, the mediating mechanisms that explain these effects, and the individual and contextual factors that moderate these relationships (Grant et al., 2011).

Past studies appear to paint a comprehensive portrait of the nature, antecedents, mechanisms, consequences, and boundary conditions of work design and provide a clear, robust set of guidelines for managers to promote employee performance and well-being. However, several scholars have recently pointed out that current theoretical models and empirical studies of work design no longer reflect, and have yet to integrate, the impact of the dramatic changes in work contexts that have occurred over the past few decades (Grant & Parker, 2009). This situation has driven a significant reduction in interest among researchers in exploring issues in work design, stemming from a shared belief that most of the essential theoretical and practical questions in job design research have been answered.

This chapter aims to build a theoretical analysis highlighting the importance of culture as a moderator variable between digital-related work characteristics and work design, considering the particular Latin American context and the associated cultural practices.

This effort is essential because the urgency to reskill employees for the era of intelligent machines is especially acute for Latin America. In Latin America, there are many jobs at risk. The World Economic Forum (2021) estimates that 27% of Latin Americans employed in the formal economy are in positions where most of their time is spent on repetitive tasks. More than 40% are in jobs with a moderate everyday job. For that reason, a significant proportion of Latin American managers and employees need to reskill and upskill the new or modified jobs created by intelligent technologies in digital environments (World Economic Forum, 2021).

Without decisive action, employees displaced by automation could wind up in a regular job or problematic necessity entrepreneurship practices. Further depressing wage rates at the low end of the income ladder threaten Latin America's precious progress in reducing informality and inequality. A vicious cycle of informality, soft skills, and low productivity could nullify the growth potential that intelligent technologies offer the region. Fortunately, this bleak scenario is avoidable.

Based on the makeup of Latin American employees, the region has half as many high-skilled employees as Europe and the United States and 50% more low and middle-skilled employees. However, the advent of intelligent systems could also be an opportunity to narrow the gap with advanced economies. Indeed, the nature of the skills needed in intelligent machines may favor Latin American organizations. Specific technical skills are vulnerable to automation. In contrast, behavioral, cognitive, and social skills take on new importance.

Creativity, collaboration, resilience, and risk-taking are all skills that Latin American cultures have cherished and nurtured; they have been essential to building agility in the face of volatile conditions. With investments in retraining, these cultural traits and tendencies can be turned into the skills that firms will seek and priorities for future employees and all the workforce.

Furthermore, these softer skills are not restricted to the rich or the well-educated and well-connected, opening opportunities for a more extensive section of society. This could be a chance for Latin American companies to train and develop skills in their employees (World Economic Forum, 2021).

A Work Design Model for Latin America

Parker and Grote (2020) propose a central role for work design in understanding the effects of digital technologies. The course of action to address these concerns entails analyzing digital work characteristics and the moderating role of cultural practices in Latin America to understand work design. This chapter uses Parker and Grote's (2020) study about digital work characteristics to do this aim.

Parker and Grote's (2020) article gives examples of how new technologies can positively and negatively affect job characteristics: (1) job resources (autonomy/control, skill use, job feedback, relational aspects) and (2) job demands (e.g., performance monitoring), with consequences for employee well-being, work motivation, work engagement, and task performance.

On the other hand, to analyze Latin American culture, this chapter uses six of the nine cultural practices dimensions from Global Leadership & Organizational Behavior Effectiveness (GLOBE) 2020. This chapter had focused on the more work-related cultural practices dimensions. Table 18.1 includes the definition of these six cultural practices dimensions.

The GLOBE investigation identified nine cultural competencies and grouped the 62 countries into ten convenient societal clusters. The GLOBE, Latin America cluster, consists of the most significant number of countries of all the GLOBE clusters. This supports the notion that Latin Americans have a unique cultural context. The Latin American cluster includes Brazil, Guatemala, Argentina, Ecuador, El Salvador, Colombia, Bolivia, Costa Rica, Venezuela, and Mexico. The societies belonging to this cluster are unique from most other groups, reflecting relatively high scores of In-group Collectivism's societal and cultural practices dimensions. Overall, these societies maintain close family ties, and individuals express pride and loyalty in organizations and families.

These societies do not expect power to be distributed evenly among citizens, instead of accepting authority, power differentials, status privileges, and social inequality. The dimensions of human orientation are approximately average. Its scores are relatively low on several other sizes, including Future Orientation, Institutional Collectivism, and Uncertainty Avoidance.

Performance orientation is among the lowest scores in comparison to other clusters. Interestingly, Latin American countries score high on In-group

Table 18.1 GLOBE 2020 definitions of cultural practices dimensions

Dimension	Definition
Humane orientation	The degree to which a collective encourages and rewards individuals for being fair, altruistic, generous, caring, and kind to others
Future orientation	The extent to which individuals engage in future-oriented behaviors such as delaying gratification, planning, and investing in the future
Uncertainty avoidance	The extent to which a society, organization, or group relies on social norms, rules, and procedures to alleviate the unpredictability of future events
Institutional collectivism	The degree to which organizational and societal institutional practices encourage and reward collective distribution of resources and collective action
In-group collectivism	The degree to which individuals express pride, loyalty, and cohesiveness in their organizations or families
Performance orientation	The degree to which a collective encourages and rewards group members for performance improvement and excellence

Collectivism and lowest on Institutional Collectivism. The high In-group Collectivism scores suggest that they generally express pride and cohesiveness in their families and organizations. They, however, do not strongly endorse societal and institutional practices with the goals of collective distribution of resources or rewards (GLOBE, 2021).

Considering the Latin American cultural reality, we can match the six digital work characteristics proposed by Parker and Grote (2020) and the six cultural practices from GLOBE (2021). Table 18.2 analyzes the possible effects of digital work characteristics and cultural practices on work design.

Additionally, this chapter complements the analysis, proposing six potential training and development solutions that can moderate the impact of the previous interaction. Managing these solutions is an exciting challenge to human resources managers and practitioners to integrate and promote a digital workplace in Latin America.

For instance, big data and machine learning support decision-making as the first digital work design characteristic. The analysis matches this characteristic with the cultural practice dimension named humane orientation.

Due to Latin Americans having low levels of humane orientation, a positive effect can be using information from big data and machine learning to support the decision-making process. This process may be facilitated because the low humane interaction disposition goes on the line with the intensive use of algorithms and machine learning in the decision-making process.

On the other hand, an adverse effect may be that automated decision-making replaces human judgment. Thus, to boost the positive impact (and avoid negative results), it is necessary to understand and manage big data and machine learning limitations. Managers need to manage algorithms. Setting goals and having the ethical lens of human behavior and demographic characteristics may be the start point in the enterprise.

Finally, this chapter presents a model of work design considering the individual level of analysis. Figure 18.1 shows the moderate effects of Latin American cultural practices on work design considering digital work characteristics.

It proposes potential training and development solutions for facing the negative impact of the interaction between digital work characteristics and cultural practices. Thus, work design can achieve positive results for Latin American employees.

The model's left side depicts digital work characteristics (e.g., big data and machine learning to support decision-making and skill variety). Cultural practice dimensions (e.g., humane orientation and uncertainty avoidance) strain digital work characteristics and shape work design. The right half of the model illustrates the positive results under the moderate condition of the presumed training and development solutions.

Solutions based on cultural practices can moderate the challenging relationship between twenty-first-century digital work characteristics and their positive/adverse effects on work design in Latin America. These potential

Table 18.2 Possible effects of digital work characteristics and cultural practices in Latin America on work design and potential solutions

Digital work characteristics	Cultural practice	Positive effects	Negative effects	Potential solutions
Big data and machine learning to support decision-making	Low humane orientation	Information from big data and machine learning to support decision-making	Automated decision-making that replaces human judgment	Understand and manage the limitations
Choice over where and when to job	Low future orientation	Technology-enabled virtual/remote and other forms of flexible job	Algorithmic management that pressures employees about when and how much to job	Promote hybrid and flexible job
Skill variety	Low uncertainty avoidance	Replacement of routine cognitive and physical tasks	Automation-caused a decline in active use of skills with increased monitoring	Upskilling and reskilling strategies
Job feedback	Low institutional collectivism	Algorithmic management and provision of "objective" feedback	Algorithmically mediated feedback that is punitive, idiosyncratic, and biased	Consider ethic and long-term implications
Social and relational	High in-group collectivism	Information communication technologies that enhance coordination and team working	Technology-mediated communication that impairs connections and coordination, removes empathy	Promote social relationships and team-job
Job demands	Low-performance orientation	Increased cognitive demands due to automating simpler tasks	Variation in workload due to automation	Boost work engagement and job crafting strategies

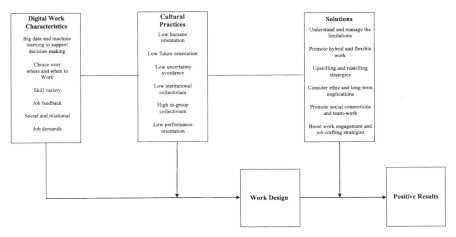

Fig. 18.1 A work design model in a context of digital work characteristics and cultural practices in Latin America

solutions can be arranged considering the specific organizational culture of Latin American companies.

This model can be helpful for managers working in Latin American firms. Practitioners aim to do that using human resources practices. Human resources managers may develop distinctive culture-based human resource management systems focused on empowering and engaging employees. For example, job crafting or self-design might better align the position with the Latin American employee's personal needs, goals, abilities, and skills.

Conclusions

This Latin American-focused chapter revised the critical concepts of transformational leadership, work engagement, and work design. These variables are essential to consider when managers work with Latin American employees. Cultural analysis may complement other crucial studies (e.g., institutional, economic, financial, societal) (Gomez-Mejia & Palich, 1997).

Thanks to advances in cultural studies, we can be clear about Latin American cultural traits, which will allow us to make diagnoses and generate more effective human resources solutions. Culture is a moderating variable that we must include, theoretically and methodologically, in current human resources management models.

Considering the intense investment of time, capabilities, and resources that companies put into retaining talent, it's essential to realize that management practices to improve employee retention may be culture-specific. For instance, investing in team training to improve working relationships may do wonders for managers in feminine cultures who hope to strengthen commitment and retention but have little impact on retaining talent in more masculine cultures. The challenge is even more significant if we consider the present digital changing scenario, strongly influenced by automation, and the irruption of new job demands and resources in the workplace (Juyumaya & Torres, 2023b). To follow this theoretical analysis, the model presented in Fig. 18.1 can be helpful in this aim.

Overall, this research is critical in understanding how cultural differences can affect managers' ability to build engagement and retain their employees in Latin America. Managers in global companies are likely to realize that the answer to this question depends on culture and other factors. Before companies implement resource-intensive programs to keep their talent, managers would be wise to ask which cultures are situated.

This chapter contributes to delivering insights to motivate Latin American employees in the twenty-first century. Taken together, their suggestions might compensate, at least in part, for corporate blind spots in the area of human resources management and organization development and change by ensuring that cultural concepts' consequences are reviewed with a focus on digital work characteristics and their impact on work design. This chapter encourages revising the presented analysis to make an organizational diagnosis and human resources practices and strategies that shape a cheerful twenty-first-century work design in Latin America.

This chapter aims to motivate Latin American employees and build more successful organizations in managerial practice. Successful strategic human resources management will bring greater fulfillment, wellness, and personal growth at work, and turn employees into an internal source of competitive advantage by creating unique strategic business capabilities and increased task performance.

References

Aguinis, H., Villamor, I., Lazzarini, S. G., Vassolo, R. S., Amorós, J. E., & Allen, D. G. (2020). Conducting management research in Latin America: Why and what's in it for you? *Journal of Management, 46*(5), 615–636.

Bakker, A. B., & Albrecht, S. (2018). Work engagement: Current trends. *Career Development International, 23*(1), 4–11.

Bakker, A. B., & Demerouti, E. (2017). Job demands–resources theory: Taking stock and looking forward. *Journal of Occupational Health Psychology, 22*(3), 273–285.

Bandura, A. (2002). Social cognitive theory in cultural context. *Applied Psychology: An International Review, 51*(2), 269–290.

Bass, B. M., & Steidlmeier, P. (1999). Ethics, character, and authentic transformational leadership behavior. *Leadership Quarterly, 10*(2), 181–217.

Chirkov, V., Ryan, R. M., Kim, Y., Kaplan, & U. (2003). Differentiating autonomy from individualism and independence: A self-determination theory perspective on internalizing cultural orientations and well-being. *Journal of Personality and Social Psychology, 84*, 97–109.

Chua, R. Y. J., & Iyengar, S. S. (2006). Empowerment through choice? A critical analysis of the effects of selection in organizations. In B. Staw & R. M. Kramer (Eds.), *Research in Organizational Behavior, 27* (pp. 41–79). Elsevier.

Cuervo-Cazurra, A., & Dau, L. A. (2009). Structural reform and firm exports. *Management International Review, 49*(4), 479–507.

Davila, A., & Elvira, M. M. (2012). Humanistic leadership: Lessons from Latin America. *Journal of World Business, 47*(4), 548–554.

Demerouti, E., Bakker, A. B., de Jonge, J., Janssen, P. P. M., & Schaufeli, W. B. (2001). Burnout and engagement at work as a function of demands and control. *Scandinavian Journal of Work Environment and Health, 27*(4), 279–286.

Dickson, M., Castaño, N., Magomaeva, A., & Den Hartog, D. (2012). Conceptualizing leadership across cultures. *Journal of World Business, 47*, 483–492.

Elvira, M. M., & Davila, A. (2005). *Managing human resources in Latin America: An agenda for international leaders*. Routledge.

Eisenbeiß, S. A., & Boerner, S. (2013). A double–edged sword: Transformational leadership and Individual Creativity. *British Journal of Management, 24*(1), 54–68.

Gabel-Shemueli, R., Westman, M., Chen, S., & Bahamonde, D. (2019). Does cultural intelligence increase work engagement? The role of idiocentrism–allocentrism and organizational culture in MNCs. *Cross-Cultural & Strategic Management, 26*, 46–66.

Gallup. (2020). *State of the global employees: Employee engagement insights for business leaders worldwide*.

Gelade, G. A., Dobson, P., & Auer, K. (2008). Individualism, masculinity, and the sources of organizational commitment. *Journal of Cross-Cultural Psychology, 39*(5), 599–617.

Global Leadership & Organizational Behavior Effectiveness. (2021). *The GLOBE Latin America cluster*. Retrieved October 18, 2021, from https://globeproject.com/results/clusters/latin-america?menu=list#list

Goenaga, A. (2016). *Democracy in Latin America*. Oxford University Press.

Gomez-Mejia, L. R., & Palich, L. E. (1997). Cultural diversity and the performance of multinational firms. *Journal of International Business Studies, 28*, 309–335.

Grant, A. M., & Parker, S. K. (2009). Redesigning work design theories: The rise of relational and proactive perspectives. *The Academy of Management Annals, 3*(1), 317–375.

Grant, A. M., Fried, Y., & Juillerat, T. (2011). Work matters: Work design in classic and contemporary perspectives. In S. Zedeck (Ed.), *APA handbook of industrial and organizational psychology, Vol. 1. Building and developing the organization* (pp. 417–453). American Psychological Association.

Hackman, J. R., & Oldham, G. R. (2007). How job characteristics theory happened. In K. G. Smith & M. A. Hitt (Eds.), *Great minds in management: The process of theory development* (pp. 151–170). Oxford University Press.

Hauff, S., Richter, N. F., & Tressin, T. (2014). *Culture's role in the job characteristics and job satisfaction relationship: An empirical analysis of GLOBE's culture scores*. Hamburg University of Technology (TUHH). Retrieved October 18, 2021, from http://papers.ssrn.com/sol3/papers.cfm?abstract_id=2407574

Hofstede, G. (1984). The cultural relativity of the quality of life concept. *Academy of Management Review, 9*(3), 389–398.

Hofstede, G., Hofstede, G. J., & Minkov, M. (2010). *Cultures and organizations: Software for the mind*. McGraw-Hill.

House, R. J., Hanges, P. J., Javidan, M., Dorfman, P. W., & Gupta, V. (2004). *Culture, leadership, and organizations: The GLOBE study of 62 societies*. Sage.

Jaussi, K. S., & Dionne, S. D. (2003). Leading for creativity: The role of unconventional leader behavior. *Leadership Quarterly, 14*(4), 475–498.

Judge, T. A., & Piccolo, R. F. (2004). Transformational and transactional leadership: A meta-analytic test of their relative validity. *Journal of Applied Psychology, 89*(5), 755–768.

Juyumaya, J. (2019). Escala utrecht de work engagement en Chile: Medición, confiabilidad y validez. *Estudios de Administración, 26*(1), 35–50.

Juyumaya, J., & Torres, J. P. (2023a). Effects of transformational leadership and work engagement on managers' creative performance. *Baltic Journal of Management, 18*(1), 34–53.

Juyumaya, J., & Torres, J. P. (2023b). A managers' work engagement model in a digital era. *Frontiers in Psychology, 14*, 1009459.

Koh, D., Lee, K., & Joshi, K. (2019). Transformational leadership and creativity: A meta-analytic review and identification of an integrated model. *Journal of Organizational Behavior, 40*(6), 625–650.

Markos, S., & Sridevi, M. (2010). Employee engagement: The key to improving performance. *International Journal of Business and Management, 5*(12), 89–96.

Martinez, P. (2005). Paternalism as a positive form of leadership in the Latin American context: Leader benevolence, decision–making control and human resource management practices. In M. M. Elvira & A. Davila (Eds.), *Managing human resources in Latin America: An agenda for international leaders* (pp. 75–93). Routledge.

Parker, S. K. (2014). Beyond motivation: Job and work design for development, Health, Ambidexterity, and More. *Annual Review of Psychology, 65*(1), 661–691.

Parker, S. K., & Grote, G. (2020). Automation, algorithms, and beyond: Why work design matters more than ever in a digital world. *Applied Psychology, 71*, 1171–1204.

Qu, R. J., Janssen, O., & Shi, K. (2015). Transformational leadership and follower creativity: The mediating role of follower relational identification and the moderating role of leader creativity expectation. *Leadership Quarterly, 26*(2), 286–299.

Romero, E. J. (2004). Latin American leadership: El patrón & el líder moderno. *Cross Cultural Management: An International Journal, 11*(3), 25–37.

Schein, E. (2004). *Organizational culture and leadership*. Jossey-Bass.

Vassolo, R. S., De Castro, J. O., & Gomez-Mejia, L. (2011). Managing in Latin America: Common issues and a research agenda. *Academy of Management Perspectives, 25*, 22–36.

Wells, J. E., & Welty-Peachey, J. (2011). Turnover intentions: Do leadership behaviors and satisfaction with the leader matter? *Team Performance Management: An International Journal, 17*(1), 23–40.

World Bank. (2019). *World development report 2019: The changing nature of work*. Overview booklet. World Bank.

World Economic Forum. (2021). *Here's why Latin Americans will thrive in the age of robots*. Retrieved November 29, 2021, from https://www.weforum.org/agenda/2018/03/here-s-why-latin-americans-will-thrive-in-the-age-of-the-robots/

CHAPTER 19

Embracing Stigma? Finding Workplace Dignity in Dirty Work

Ariana Chang and Ying-Tzu Lin

INTRODUCTION

The term *dirty work* refers to work occupations and tasks that are usually viewed as dangerous, demeaning, disgusting, and degrading (Hughes, 1958). In the workplace setting, it is very challenging for dirty workers to establish a positive sense of self due to the stigma attached (Ashforth & Kreiner, 1999) and such work links with physical (e.g., danger, death, waste), social (e.g., subservient relationships, tainted clients), and/or moral (e.g., sinful, immoral) issues (Ashforth & Kreiner, 1999; Hughes, 1951, 1958; Simpson et al., 2012). Dirty workers have been marginalized in our society and the dirty work discourse has been neglected in organizational literature (Ashforth & Kreiner, 1999). Especially, dirty work has been disregarded in the disciplines of organization studies and the sociology of work (Ashforth & Kreiner, 1999; Dick, 2005). Differed greatly from one another, dirty work occupations include garbage collector, funeral director, prison guard, security guard, construction

A. Chang (✉)
Bachelor's Program in Interdisciplinary Studies, Fu Jen Catholic University, New Taipei, Taiwan
e-mail: 140517@mail.fju.edu.tw

Y.-T. Lin
Department of Business Administration, Fu Jen Catholic University, New Taipei, Taiwan

© The Author(s), under exclusive license to Springer Nature Switzerland AG 2023
J. Marques (ed.), *The Palgrave Handbook of Fulfillment, Wellness, and Personal Growth at Work*,
https://doi.org/10.1007/978-3-031-35494-6_19

worker, social worker, and exotic dancer (Ashforth & Kreiner, 2014). Generally seen as deviant, these workers often experience severe stigma and are excluded from mainstream society. Of note, occupations such as sex work are tainted by multiple stigmas. However, sex workers can be both the stigmatized and stigmatizers (Toubiana & Ruebottom, 2022).

In examining the question as to whether and how sex workers experience dignity in the context of work that has multiple taints, this study seeks to explore the dynamics of workplace dignity and the stigmas that are encountered by workers in the special service clubs in Taiwan. In special service clubs, it is mainly catered to men seeking drinks and companionship. The hostesses are hired to drink, engage, and have a pleasant time with their clients (Bedford & Hwang, 2011). These clubs are legal adult entertainment establishments in which clients go for drinks and have a good time with female accompaniment (Chang, 2022).

Our findings reveal that the positive identity of female sex workers can be constructed through reframing to attain dignity at work. Research has shown that sex workers can use the embracing strategy by treating their work as a profession through fabricating narratives that highlight their role in providing emotional support (Sanders, 2005). Once the embracing strategy is adopted, collective reframing can be utilized as a strategy to depict the multiple roles of the worker. Dignity can be cultivated through collective reframing as a means to manage stigma. Thus, it is easier for sex workers who work in top-tier clubs to adopt collective reframing. This research contributes to the growing literature on stigma and dirty work in the Asian context, which has been paid with scant attention.

Dirty Work and Stigma

A stigma is a negative social judgment that undervalues a person or a group (Kreiner et al., 2022), and it is an attribute that is "deeply discrediting" that leaves the bearer tainted (Goffman, 1963). For individuals, organizations, and industries, extensive amount of work has directed stigma to negative implications (Ruebottom & Toubiana, 2021). In stigmatized industries, dirty workers are also the targets of those who devalue their identities and impose sanctions that restrict their relationships and opportunities (Ashforth & Kreiner, 1999; Galvin et al., 2005; Hughes, 1958; Simpson et al., 2012). Rather than being innately linked to a specific practice, behavior, or structure, contemporary viewpoints on stigma pinpoint that stigma is actually socially constructed by observers (Link & Phelan, 2001). The attachment of stigma has substantial restrictions for dirty workers. For dirty workers, Anspach (1979) found that stigmatized individuals use available resources to combat stigma and shape their own identities. In the case of dirty work, workers are frequently labeled as "dirty workers" because stigma is transferred from the job to the people who do it (Ashforth et al., 2017).

Worldwide, violence against sex workers of all genders has become prevalent (Argento et al., 2021). Sex workers may be hesitant to seek health care due to fear of harassment by healthcare providers (Shahmanesh et al., 2018; Shannon et al., 2009). One issue related to the well-being of sex workers is the lack of access to services, such as health care. Many sex workers face barriers to accessing health care due to stigma and discrimination, as well as lack of knowledge and awareness about their rights. Research has shown that sex workers who have access to health care and other services, such as counseling and harm reduction programs, have better health outcomes and are less likely to experience violence and abuse (Shahmanesh et al., 2018; Shannon et al., 2009).

The sex industry is defined by a three-part core stigma (Ashforth & Kreiner, 2014; Mavin & Grandy, 2013; Wolfe & Blithe, 2015). Sex work is deemed corruptive, immoral, seedy (Voss, 2015) and perceived as a "risky business" because of the services provided (Sanders, 2005). Most media portrayals of prostitutes reinforce stereotypes of women as dangerous or deviant (Dunn, 2012). When one becomes involved in the sex industry, personal stigmas such as "whore" become attached to the worker (Weitzer, 2010). In order for sex workers to rectify and negate stigma, they must find ways to manage it. Sigma management strategies for sex workers include: distancing and embracing (Choi & Lai, 2021). For "psychological survival," sex workers adopt strategies to separate themselves from their work and maintain a clear separation between work sex and non-work sex (Brewis & Linstead, 2000; McKeganey & Barnard, 1996). Conversely, sex workers can use the embracing method to ascertain the importance of sex work (Brewis & Linstead, 2000; Sanders, 2005).

Sex Work and Workplace Dignity

The identity of sex workers is a complicated and many-sided problem that has generated much discussion. Although dirty workers are imprinted with stigma and would have a hard time forming a positive identity (Ashforth & Kreiner, 1999), research has shown that they maintain high level occupational esteem (e.g., Hong & Duff, 1977; McIntyre, 1987; Steward, 1978). Dignity can be understood in various ways (Lucas, 2017) and the concept of workplace dignity remains as an "ambiguous" subject (Bolton, 2007). Generally, it refers to a person's sense of worth, value, or esteem (Hodson, 2001; Lee, 2008). The fundamental means by which intrinsic human dignity is upheld is through respect, which can be demonstrated through greetings, civility, self-worth, and kindness (Lucas, 2017; Otis, 2008; Stievano et al., 2012). In order to ensure well-being, dignity is required to achieve self-worth, self-respect, and gain the recognition by others (Hodson, 2001). Our self-respect greatly depends on how others treat us, especially those with whom we frequently interact (Sayer, 2007). Thus, how one perceives and experiences dignity is influenced by organizational cultures and culture at large (Lucas et al., 2013). Organizations, whether intentionally or unintentionally, can increase worker vulnerability and create additional barriers to the quest of dignity.

Through providing decent work, people's dignity can be recognized (Lucas, 2017). To achieve dignity in the workplace, methods include the development of skills and competencies, the creation of a sense of community among coworkers, management, and clients (Otis, 2008). There are objective and subjective factors in recognizing dignity (Noronha et al., 2020). Objective factors include providing secure terms of employment with safe and healthy working conditions (Noronha et al., 2020). This sense of worth acquired from secure employment is strengthened by sufficient staffing and resources, availability of professional development, and advancement opportunities (Buzzanell & Lucas, 2013; Otis, 2008). Contrarily, the social process that shapes the subjective realm of dignity is interactive, relational, and contextual (Rodriquez, 2011).

Sex work is a type of erotic or sexual labor with a wide range of activities (Mavin & Grandy, 2013) and has been characterized as one of the "dirtiest" professions (Ashforth & Kreiner, 2014; Blithe & Wolfe, 2017). It is anticipated that sex workers have to engage in not only sexual but aesthetic and emotional labor as well (Chen, 2008). Forged by cultural and social norms, dignity is a subjective experience (Howard & Donnelly, 1986). Decent employment not only gives people with enough financial resources, but also provides them with recognition, respect, autonomy, and esteem by involving them in meaningful tasks—these are subjective characteristics of dignity (Bolton, 2007; Bolton et al., 2016). Even for stigmatized groups, dignity can be discursively constructed (Hamilton et al., 2017). The ability to decipher how work is performed and conducted generates meaning and offers a sense of accomplishment (Buzzanell & Lucas, 2013; Cockburn-Wootten, 2012; Stacey, 2005). By so doing, employees' sense of self-worth can be boosted and serve as the foundation for others' recognition (Lucas, 2017).

Research Methodology

An inductive qualitative approach was utilized to analyze the data (Denzin, 2000). Adopting an exploratory perspective (Bryman, 1988; Patton, 1990), the qualitative research is a suitable approach to examine regions that have not yet been classified (Patton, 2002). The data in this research were collected between March 2022 and February 2023. The primary data are based on field interviews and field observations. The ethical protocol of the research is marked with confidentiality of the informants.

A total of 12 conversational interviews were conducted with hostesses, friends of the hostesses, administrative staff, and male clients. To develop a richer and more in-depth understanding of the phenomenon being studies, conversational interviews can be utilized to investigate experiential narrative material to grasp participants' experiences from their viewpoints (Noronha et al., 2020). For the informants, the hostesses are aged between 20 and 32 and the male clients are regular visitors to these hostess clubs. To triangulate the data collected, they are supplemented with on-site visits. Observations were made at a private special service club and a conventional hostess club in the Eastern district of Taipei city. Notes were immediately taken down after each visit to the clubs.

Research Setting

Generally, the two traditional sectors in the sex industry can be categorized into *mai shen* (body selling) and *mai xiao* (pleasure selling) in Taiwan. In the pleasure-selling sector, it caters to the diverse needs of the clients, and therefore, sex is not always involved (Chen, 2008). Thus, it takes place in legal, urban, and modern entertainment venues in which women are hired to accompany their clients (Chen, 2006). In these establishments, personal engagement may include drinking, singing karaoke, playing games, dancing, and flirting.

Cases

"Special service clubs" or hostess clubs can be found in both regular affluent neighborhoods and red-light districts in Taiwan. The clientele of these special service clubs are mainly businessmen and politicians (Bedford & Hwang, 2011; Hwang, 2003). These clubs are staffed by young women (referred to as "hostesses") who urge male clients to consume alcohol while attempting to grasp their attention. Although the personal interaction between the hostess and client is sexual in nature, intercourse is not usually provided (Hwang & Bedford, 2003). Of note, forms of sexual transaction can be agreed upon outside the club.

The identities of the special service clubs examined have been concealed and have been code-named East and West. East is a hostess club that begins to operate in the early afternoon and known for having young (average of 20 years old) top-tier hostesses. Mainly catered to businessmen, East claims that many of its hostesses are educated with the status of college students. The dress code for workers in the East includes tank tops or sleeveless tops paired with mini-skirts and high heels. Thus, most of the tops are low-cut that shows a lot of cleavage. Also catered to businessmen, West is a private hostess club that only operates in the evening that are exclusive to members or by invitation only. Many of the hostesses who work at West also have daytime jobs. The dress code for workers in the West includes formal dresses and evening gowns with high heels. In addition to private rooms, there is a piano bar in the communal area.

Findings

As mentioned, we would like to examine how dignity is constructed for dirty workers such as those who work in the sex industry in Taiwan. There occupations are regarded as "dirty" because entail physically, socially, or morally taint that the society views as disgusting (Chenault & Collins, 2019). As we analyzed our data, we found that there is a pattern to how stigma is being managed. We began to realize that reframing is evoked as a strategy to negate negative features of dirty work through immersing in dignity work. Furthermore, the firm's stakeholders collectively assist the hostesses to reframe. We call this phenomenon "collective reframing" and define it as stakeholders who try enhance the reframing process of the hostesses. The attainment of dignity work is constructed through positive narratives with the help of the firm's stakeholders.

Often, the embracing strategy is applied so that the society can recognize the value of sex work (Sanders, 2005). For sex workers, they experience loss of dignity at some point in their careers. However, dirty work is a type of necessary evil that still needs to be conducted (Kreiner et al., 2006). In spite of having to fulfill and satisfy the demands of clients, hostesses can reframe their work as a "necessary evil" that is deemed professional work. For example, garbage must be collected, funeral home directors must deal with the deceased and inmates must be guarded.

According to Ashforth and Kreiner (1999), dirty workers attempt to modify the meaning of their stigmatized profession by "reframing" through covering the negative features of their work. In a study by Choi and Lai (2021), they found that sex workers from Hong Kong frequently compared themselves to psychiatrists, health workers, and marital counselors—claiming that they were providing an outlet for married men's frustrations and stress and alleviating the burden of marriages. In Taiwan, we found that clients, friends of hostesses, agents, and other stakeholders collectively help hostesses reframe their work.

This entails instilling positive value in the stigmatized component of their work or negating the negative connotations. For example, prostitutes can claim to be providing a therapeutic service rather than selling their bodies (Ashforth & Kreiner, 1999). This study has found that reframing is constantly adopted by the hostesses in order to contend with unruly interactions. As a part of her everyday work, her role fluctuates from time to time. On top of performing aesthetic labor, the discursive constructions of dignity through reframing espouse multiple roles for these workers. In this context, the women are "professionals" who are economically successful and provide services to the community. They believe that the work they provide is of immense value.

Finding Dignity in Sex Work

To achieve a sense of dignity is not an easy task. Employees could be susceptible to the subjective effects of unedifying workplace encounters due to the material restrictions of the organizational structure (Lucas et al., 2013). In all facets of society, sex work is stigmatized and perceived as a sign of shame, social dishonor, and/or corrupted identity. Derogatory terms such as "hookers" and "whores" are often used to describe workers in this industry. Stigmas associated with sex work is sometimes referred to as the "whore" or "prostitution" stigma (Benoit & Unsworth, 2022). To protect self-worth, workers can infuse work with meaning through engaging in identity work (Buzzanell & Lucas, 2013; Lucas, 2011). Notwithstanding, even stigmatized groups can discursively construct dignity (Hamilton et al., 2019), and dignity can be experienced through quality of work with a strong sense of high morality (Noronha et al., 2020). Moral standards are a method for workers to maintain dignity, and it serves as an alternative function to economic success (Lamont, 2001).

Berg and Frost (2005) conceptualized dignity through the three pillars: economic stability, fair treatment, and satisfying work. Accordingly, how employees' experiences of dignity will thus be influenced by how they are treated at work. Although the main tasks for hostesses are to entertaining clients through conversation and hospitality, there are more stringent rules for clients to follow in higher-tier hostess clubs. Workers in lower-tier clubs are more prone to exploitations due to the demographics of the clientele. What the workers encounter is contingent on the social demographics of the working-class clientele level.

In the Asian context, dignity is based on the perception of others and employees know that their experiences of dignity are dependent on their relationships with others in the work setting (Lucas et al., 2013). A person's worth is based on what others think of him or her (Kim & Cohen, 2010) and dignity could be at the disposal of others because it can be given or taken away (Brennan & Lo, 2007). In short, dignity is contingent and dependent on others. Contesting the notion that sex workers are primarily victims of sexual violence or primarily from dysfunctional families, the women who were interviewed were not forced or manipulated to enter this industry. Many stated that they entered the industry because they have financial issues and can generate income more easily.

Sex Work as Professional Work

Often, the workers serve as "facilitators" because bonding over alcohol in hostess clubs is an integral part of doing business in Taiwan. Previous research has found that entrepreneurial, business (from advertising, publicity, and choosing a suitable location), and organizational skills are of great importance when operating a sex work business (Choi & Lai, 2021). In terms of personal branding, these workers work toward having an irreproachable presentation so they can leave an indelible image in the minds of clients to stand out. In this industry, an impeccable presentation is required to differentiate from other workers. It is the combination of skills, experiences, and personal branding that makes each hostess unique.

To become as successful and great hostess, one needs to be able to immediately establish a connection to get recurring clients.

In addition to performing femininity, workers in the pleasure-selling sector have to engage in both aesthetics labor and emotional labor. The skills that hostesses need include but are not limited to composure, confidence, charm, interpersonal, and people skills. Many of these young women no longer deny that they lack professional skills as previous research has indicated.

> I know how to market myself so that my clients like me. I am a responsible citizen. I am not a thief and I don't steal. I make ends meet. Being a hostess is legal.
>
> (Former hostess)

These sex workers know that it is vital to upkeep their personal brand because they are greatly responsible for the first impression that clients have on the club. Anticipating the demands and meeting the needs of interlocutors, they need to be responsive and dynamic. In addition, they need to meet the requests of clients by depth listening and learning to expressing themselves. Aside from exuding confidence, manners, and verbal skills, these need to have the ability to maintain composure.

> My job is to make the clients feel comfortable and important. They are the king of the world.
>
> (Former hostess)

It is of utmost importance that the hostesses establish connections with their clientele on an emotional level so they leave a lasting positive impression. The hostesses cannot show any signs that can imply rudeness during their work.

Aesthetics Labor

Sex work, in all of its manifestations, is a part of the service industry and is susceptible to exploitation (Tremblay, 2021). The mainstream discourse in Taiwan comprehends that sex work lacks professionalism because it is something any woman can do, however, there are many labor dimensions of sex work (Chen, 2008).

As recorded in our field notes:

> I spend a lot of my money on self-grooming. A huge part of the business is having the "it" looks. I pamper myself with facials, massages, hair washes, manicures, and pedicures. I need to look nice. That is the number one requirement to be in this industry. Everyone here is pretty. I have to make sure that I look my best at all times so I can get customers.
>
> (Hostess)

Not only confined to sex work, it is also common in the service economy to carry out femininity (Chen, 2008). For the clientele, it is the hostess's duty to play out her femininity and bond with her respective clients. It is vital that the hostess look her best at all times. At the two sites, all of the hostesses were as immaculate as ever—they all have a neat and tidy appearance.

> The girls here need to maintain their figure and stay in shape. Being skinny is a must.
>
> (Administrative Staff)

> All of the girls here are young, you will be surprise at how beautiful they are. Many of them are even better looking than celebrities. We are lavished with attention.
>
> (Male client)

The men who were interviewed stated that they visit these establishments because they enjoy the company of the hostesses. It is a place where men can feel relaxed and have a good time with the company of beautiful women. In addition, there is a preference toward "young women" with college degrees.

Emotional Labor

Most importantly, the hostess must pander to her clients' demands (Chen, 2017). Aside from negotiable physical contact (Bedford & Hwang, 2011) such as fondling, the engagement between hostesses and customers includes karaoke singing and playing drinking games. On top of being scantily clad, the main objectives of the hostess are not only to keep the patron company but also to make the patron order more alcohol and satisfy his demands. There is pressure of turning clients into regular customers. In terms of social class, a sexual hierarchy is built among Taiwanese men: the affluent patronize the services in the pleasure-selling sector while the underprivileged are relegated to the body-selling sector (Chen, 2017). Of note, hostess clubs are known to be pricey and clients have to pay an exorbitant amount to receive company. Nonetheless, many businessmen still think that it is worth the cost. Especially, these clubs are positioned to foster better networks with both business partners and potential business partners.

> All of my business negotiations and deals are conducted in these clubs.
>
> (Male client)

> I gain business knowledge. People come here to talk about businesses. It is where people build relationships and close deals. With my help, businesses can go more smoothly. Many of the clients who come here are wealthy business owners. I can say that I am learning while working.
>
> (Hostess)

The typical activities include: serving and pouring drinks while conversing with the customer, engaging in fun, flirtatious conversation, and ensuring that the customers have a good time, whether that means doing exciting things like playing games or singing to help take their mind off work or just being a good listener. In the midst of the hostesses' company, men discuss business with coworkers, associates, and business partners.

> Unless you have infinite money to spend at these clubs, I wouldn't actually fall in love with the hostesses. It is part of their plan to drain your money, they just want to tease you. I just have fun, no need to get serious. You would be stupid to fall in love with them. I know their tactics.
>
> (Male Client)

Reframing as a Means to Manage Stigma

To transform the meaning of stigmatized work, three commonly adopted ideological techniques include reframing, recalibrating, and refocusing (Ashforth & Kreiner, 1999). There are two forms of reframing: infusing and neutralizing. In *infusing*, stigma is inculcated with positive worth that can eventually transform into a badge of honor (Ashforth & Kreiner, 1999). From our analysis, we found that the reframing strategy is adopted through the help of customers, employers, friends, colleagues, and other relevant stakeholders. We call this phenomenon "collective reframing" in which stakeholders of the special service clubs coalesce to help the employees adjust to distasteful tasks by reframing through imbuing positive value. By reaffirming the benefits of sex work, these workers are reassured that their work is indeed professional. To normalize taint, managers have a vital role to play of those in stigmatized occupations (Shantz & Booth, 2014).

The reason why socioeconomic and cultural positioning influences stigmatized identity management may be due to individuals' proclivity to rely on their environment to make sense of their own experiences, explain their behavior, and present a convincing self-narrative to others around them (Choi & Lai, 2021).

In this context, the workers constructed positive identities through reframing to attain workplace dignity. Outside of work, these workers frequently disclose that they work in field of media and communications. Many dirty workers take an ambivalent stance regarding their work in an attempt to establish positive identity since their sense of self is dependent on the affirmation of others (Albert et al., 2000; Ashforth, 2000).

> If she is smart, she would use this opportunity to build networks, find a rich man, marry and come clean.
>
> (Male client)

The hostesses make great facilitators. The hostesses can use their job as an advantage. In these top tier clubs, the hostesses can meet a lot of wealthy men and learn a lot. If they are smart, they will reach out to the elite customers and establish long-term relationships. Many of them actually fall in love with the hostesses. They can even come clean, save up and buy a house.

(Administrative Staff)

I mull between keep on working in this industry or not. I don't like my work but there are pros and cons to this job. It helps pay for my expenses. I can't afford the lifestyle I have now if I leave this job. I tell people I work in media relations.

(Former hostess)

Why would you pity these women? When many of them actually have income more than that of a typical university professor.

(Male Client)

While being attractive is required to work at a hostess club, it takes more than just have the right appearance to keep clients to come back for more. For example, there are essential skills such as communication, active listening, depth listening, and persuasive skills that need to be mastered. Since most of the clients here are businessmen. You need to stay up-to-date with current events. There are some tips on how to be a better active and better listener. You nod from time to time, make eye contact, and smile.

(Former Hostess)

The aim of a special service club caters to men seeking drink, attentive conversation, and companionship. It's also crucial that a hostess makes her clients feel valued because it is her job to satisfy the requests of her clients. For hostesses, there are both constraints and rewards to sex work. Many of them are constrained by unemployment or financial difficulties so they perceive sex work as a means to survive and make ends meet. On the other hand, they still believe that they have a fair share of advantages. These include having the ability to generate more income than a typical worker, receiving special treatment and lavish presents from clients. For the occupational mission, the hostesses assert that they work in media communication. In reaction to stigma, some sex workers claim that they offer a type of educational and therapeutic service rather than selling their bodies (Thompson & Harred, 2003).

In this case, the stigma is promulgated with positive value which can transform into a badge of pride. Our study has found that collective reframing is adopted by sex workers in the pleasure-selling sector of Taiwan to deflect stigma by embracing it. The meaning of work is provided collectively and concurrently by those who surround the sex worker such as the agent, colleagues, family members, and friends. It is interesting to note that the workers with support and acknowledgment from family members were able to reclaim dignity (Fig. 19.1).

Fig. 19.1 Collective reframing in sex work

Conclusion

In closing, the well-being of stigmatized workers is a critical issue that has important implications for the health and productivity of employees. Our study indicates that sex workers encounter structural (i.e., support programs) and social (i.e., stigma) barriers. This underscores that we need a better understanding into how the special service clubs are structured. Given the stigma imprinted on sex workers, they are confronted with demands resulting from the incompatible expectations of a wide array of audience. Research has shown that stigmatization can lead to a wide array of negative outcomes, including lower job satisfaction, increased stress and burnout, and diminished mental and physical health. The well-being of sex workers is also closely related to their working circumstances, such as their level of liberty and control over their job, as well as the level of aggression they encounter. Working in the sex industry is not just menial work due to the large spectrum of atypical situations that can arise. The informants challenged the stereotype that sex work is an easy job that requires no training. Our findings highlight a critical need for bespoke services and programs to address the intersecting aspects of stigma and sex work.

References

Albert, S., Ashforth, B. E., & Dutton, J. E. (2000). Organizational identity and identification: Charting new waters and building new bridges. *Academy of Management Review,* 25(1), 13–17.

Anspach, R. R. (1979). From stigma to identity politics: Political activism among the physically disabled and former mental patients. *Social Science & Medicine. Part A: Medical Psychology & Medical Sociology, 13*, 765–773.

Argento, E., Win, K. T., McBride, B., & Shannon, K. (2021). Global burden of violence and other human rights violations against sex workers. In *Sex work, health, and human rights* (pp. 41–59). Springer, Cham.

Ashforth, B. (2000). *Role transitions in organizational life: An identity-based perspective*. Routledge.

Ashforth, B. E., & Kreiner, G. E. (2014). Dirty work and dirtier work: Differences in countering physical, social, and moral stigma. *Management and Organization Review, 10*(1), 81–108.

Ashforth, B. E., & Kreiner, G. E. (1999). "How can you do it?": Dirty work and the challenge of constructing a positive identity. *Academy of Management Review, 24*(3), 413–434.

Ashforth, B. E., Kreiner, G. E., Clark, M. A., & Fugate, M. (2017). Congruence work in stigmatized occupations: A managerial lens on employee fit with dirty work. *Journal of Organizational Behavior, 38*(8), 1260–1279.

Bedford, O., & Hwang, S. L. (2011). Flower drinking and masculinity in Taiwan. *Journal of Sex Research, 48*(1), 82–92.

Benoit, C., & Unsworth, R. (2021). COVID-19, stigma, and the ongoing marginalization of sex workers and their support organizations. *Archives of Sexual Behavior*, 1–12.

Berg, P., & Frost, A. C. (2005). Dignity at work for low wage. *Low Skill*.

Blithe, S. J., & Wolfe, A. W. (2017). Work–life management in legal prostitution: Stigma and lockdown in Nevada's brothels. *Human Relations, 70*(6), 725–750.

Bolton, S. (Ed.). (2007). *Dimensions of dignity at work*. Routledge.

Bolton, S., Laaser, K., & Mcguire, D. (2016). Quality work and the moral economy of European employment policy. *JCMS: Journal of Common Market Studies, 54*(3), 583–598.

Brennan, A., & Lo, Y. S. (2007). Two conceptions of dignity: Honour and self-determination. *Perspectives on human dignity: A conversation*, 43–58.

Brewis, J., & Linstead, S. (2000). 'The worst thing is the screwing'(1): Consumption and the management of identity in sex work. *Gender, Work & Organization, 7*(2), 84–97.

Bryman, A. (Ed.). (1988). *Doing research in organizations*. Routledge.

Buzzanell, P. M., & Lucas, K. (2013). Constrained and constructed choices in career: An examination of communication pathways to dignity. *Annals of the International Communication Association, 37*(1), 1–31.

Chang, A. (2022). The impact of COVID-19 on social responsibility in stigmatized occupations. In *Comparative CSR and Sustainability* (pp. 87–106). Routledge.

Chen, M. H. (2006). Selling bodies/selling pleasure: The social organisation of sex work in Taiwan. In *International approaches to prostitution* (pp. 165–184). Policy Press.

Chen, M. H. (2008). Sex and work in sex work: negotiating intimacy and commercial sex among Taiwanese sex workers. *East Asian sexualities: Modernity, gender and new sexual cultures*, 104–122.

Chen, M. H. (2017). Crossing borders to buy sex: Taiwanese men negotiating gender, class and nationality in the Chinese sex industry. *Sexualities, 20*(8), 921–942.

Chenault, S., & Collins, B. (2019). It's dirty work but someone has to do it: An examination of correctional officer taint management techniques.
Choi, S. Y., & Lai, R. Y. (2021). Sex work and stigma management in China and Hong Kong: The role of state policy and NGO advocacy. *The China Quarterly*, 247, 855–874.
Cockburn-Wootten, C. (2012). Critically unpacking professionalism in hospitality: Knowledge, meaningful work and dignity. *Hospitality & Society*, 2(2), 215–230.
Denzin, N. K. (2000). Aesthetics and the practices of qualitative inquiry. *Qualitative inquiry*, 6(2), 256–265.
Dick, P. (2005). Dirty work designations: How police officers account for their use of coercive force. *Human Relations*, 58(11), 1363–1390.
Dunn, J. C. (2012). It's not just sex, it's a profession: Reframing prostitution through text and context. *Communication Studies*, 63(3), 345–363.
Galvin, T. L., Ventresca, M. J., & Hudson, B. A. (2004). Contested industry dynamics. *International Studies of Management & Organization*, 34(4), 56–82.
Goffman, E. (1963). Stigma. Notes on the management of spoiled identity, reprint 1986 edn. *Harmondsworth, Penguin*.
Hamilton, P., Redman, T., & McMurray, R. (2019). 'Lower than a snake's belly': Discursive constructions of dignity and heroism in low-status garbage work. *Journal of Business Ethics*, 156, 889–901.
Hodson, R. (2001). *Dignity at work*. Cambridge University Press.
Hong, L. K., & Duff, R. W. (1977). Becoming a taxi-dancer: The significance of neutralization in a semi-deviant occupation. *Sociology of Work and Occupations*, 4(3), 327–342.
Howard, R. E., & Donnelly, J. (1986). Human dignity, human rights, and political regimes. *American Political Science Review*, 80(3), 801–817.
Hughes, E. C. (1951). Work and the self. In J. H. Rohrer & M. Sherif (Eds.), *Social psychology at the crossroads* (pp. 313–323). Harper & Brothers.
Hughes, E. C. (1958). *Men and their work*. Free Press.
Hwang, S. L. (2003). Masculinity and Taiwan's flower-drinking culture. *Taiwan She Hui Xue*, 5, 73.
Hwang, S. L., & Bedford, O. (2003). Precursors and pathways to adolescent prostitution in Taiwan. *Journal of Sex Research*, 40(2), 201–210.
Kim, Y. H., & Cohen, D. (2010). Information, perspective, and judgments about the self in face and dignity cultures. *Personality and Social Psychology Bulletin*, 36(4), 537–550.
Kreiner, G. E., Ashforth, B. E., & Sluss, D. M. (2006). Identity dynamics in occupational dirty work: Integrating social identity and system justification perspectives. *Organization Science*, 17(5), 619–636.
Kreiner, G., Mihelcic, C. A., & Mikolon, S. (2022). Stigmatized work and stigmatized workers. *Annual Review of Organizational Psychology and Organizational Behavior*, 9, 95–120.
Lamont, M. (2001). The dignity of working men: Morality and the boundaries of race, class and immigration. *Symbolic Interaction*, 24(4), 505–508.
Lee, M. Y. K. (2008). Universal human dignity: Some reflections in the Asian context. *Asian Journal of Comparative Law*, 3, 1–33.
Link, B. G., & Phelan, J. C. (2001). Conceptualizing stigma. *Annual Review of Sociology*, 27(1), 363–385

Lucas, K. (2011). Blue-collar discourses of workplace dignity: Using outgroup comparisons to construct positive identities. *Management Communication Quarterly, 25*(2), 353–374.

Lucas, K. (2015). Workplace dignity: Communicating inherent, earned, and remediated dignity. *Journal of Management Studies, 52*(5), 621–646.

Lucas, K. (2017). Workplace dignity. In C. R. Scott, (Ed.), *The international encyclopedia of organizational communication*. Chichester: Wiley.

Lucas, K., Kang, D., & Li, Z. (2013). Workplace dignity in a total institution: Examining the experiences of Foxconn's migrant workforce. *Journal of Business Ethics, 114*, 91–106.

Mavin, S., & Grandy, G. (2013). Doing gender well and differently in dirty work: The case of exotic dancing. *Gender, Work & Organization, 20*(3), 232–251.

McIntyre, L. J. (1987). *The public defender: The practice of law in the shadows of repute*. University of Chicago Press.

McKeganey, N. P., & Barnard, M. (1996). *Sex work on the streets: Prostitutes and their clients*. Open University Press.

Noronha, E., Chakraborty, S., & D'Cruz, P. (2020). 'Doing dignity work': Indian security guards' interface with precariousness. *Journal of Business Ethics, 162*(3), 553–575.

Otis, E. M. (2008). The dignity of working women: Service, sex, and the labor politics of localization in China's city of eternal spring. *American Behavioral Scientist, 52*(3), 356–376.

Patton, M. Q. (1990). *Qualitative evaluation and research methods*. SAGE Publications, inc.

Patton, M. Q. (2002). *Qualitative research & evaluation methods*. sage.

Rodriquez, J. (2011, June). "It's a dignity thing": Nursing home care workers' use of emotions 1. In *Sociological forum* (Vol. 26, No. 2, pp. 265–286). Blackwell Publishing Ltd.

Ruebottom, T., & Toubiana, M. (2021). Constraints and opportunities of stigma: Entrepreneurial emancipation in the sex industry. *Academy of Management Journal, 64*(4), 1049–1077.

Sanders, T. (2005). 'It's just acting': Sex workers' strategies for capitalizing on sexuality. *Gender, Work & Organization, 12*(4), 319–342.

Sayer, A. (2007). What dignity at work means. In S. C. Bolton (Ed.), *Dimensions of dignity at work* (pp. 17–29). Butterworth-Heinemann.

Shantz, A., & Booth, J. E. (2014). Service employees and self-verification: The roles of occupational stigma consciousness and core self-evaluations. *Human Relations, 67*(12), 1439–1465.

Shannon, K., Bright, V., Alexson, D., & Shoveller, J. (2009). Social and structural violence and power relations in mitigating HIV risk of drug-using women in survival sex work. *International Journal of Drug Policy, 20*(4), 367–372.

Shahmanesh, M., Clowes, P., & Mooney-Somers, J. (2018). "It's not just a physical thing": The impact of structural violence on the health of female sex workers. *Culture, Health & Sexuality, 20*(3), 327–342.

Simpson, R., Slutskaya, N., & Hughes, J. (2012). Gendering and embodying dirty work: men managing taint in the context of nursing care. In *Dirty Work* (pp. 165–181). Palgrave Macmillan.

Stacey, C. L. (2005). Finding dignity in dirty work: The constraints and rewards of low-wage home care labour. *Sociology of Health & Illness, 27*(6), 831–854.

Stewart, E. (1978). *Perry*. Dirty work and the pride of ownership. University of California Press.

Stievano, A., Marinis, M. G. D., Russo, M. T., Rocco, G., & Alvaro, R. (2012). Professional dignity in nursing in clinical and community workplaces. *Nursing Ethics, 19*(3), 341–356.

Thompson, W. E., Harred, J. L., & Burks, B. E. (2003). Managing the stigma of topless dancing: A decade later. *Deviant Behavior, 24*(6), 551–570.

Toubiana, M., & Ruebottom, T. (2022). Stigma hierarchies: The internal dynamics of stigmatization in the sex work occupation. *Administrative Science Quarterly*.

Tremblay, F. (2021). Labouring in the sex industry: A conversation with sex workers on consent and exploitation. *Social Sciences, 10*(3), 86.

Voss, G. (2015). *Stigma and the shaping of the pornography industry*. Routledge.

Weitzer, R. (2010). The movement to criminalize sex work in the United States. *Journal of Law and Society, 37*(1), 61–84.

CHAPTER 20

Why Workplace Peer Coaching Groups Are Vital for the Corporate Culture of the Future

Roman Terekhin and Maria Feddeck

Introduction

Well-being and personal growth at work have recently become increasingly important for employees, and hence, for the organizations that now consider these factors important goals for developing corporate culture and management practices of the future. While many alternative definitions of organizational culture exist, scholars assume that organizational cultures are best understood by attributed sets of beliefs and values (Denison, 1996; O'Regan & Oster, 2005). These underlying values serve as drivers of organizational behavior. It should be emphasized that organizational culture refers to a fundamental layer that remains stable even when organizational practices are changed (Albert et al., 2000). The Competing Values Framework (Quinn & Rohrbaugh, 1981) was further developed by Quinn and Kimberly (1984) into a theory that differentiates organizational culture types. Its purpose was defined as to "explore the deep structure of organizational culture, the basic assumptions that are made about such things as the means of compliance, motives, leadership, decision making, effectiveness, values, and organizational forms" (Quinn & Kimberly, 1984, p. 298). Due to its broad applicability, the Competing Values Framework can be used to explore practical aspects of organizational culture, such as "the relationship between organizational culture

R. Terekhin (✉) · M. Feddeck
Weatherhead School of Business, Case Western Reserve University, Cleveland, Ohio, US
e-mail: roman.terekhin@case.edu

© The Author(s), under exclusive license to Springer Nature Switzerland AG 2023
J. Marques (ed.), *The Palgrave Handbook of Fulfillment, Wellness, and Personal Growth at Work*,
https://doi.org/10.1007/978-3-031-35494-6_20

and organizational outcomes (e.g., effectiveness)" (Langer & LeRoux, 2017, p. 460). As positioned by the Competing Values Framework, developmental culture focuses on organizations' ability to manage their environment and effectively adapt to new factors (Langer & LeRoux, 2017). The developmental culture quadrant is directed toward external orientation and organizational flexibility (Davies et al., 2007), and organizations with developmental cultures aim for expansion, transformation, and change. The ideological compliance of developmental culture suggests that all organizational members should realize the strategic importance of their tasks and achieve growth visible to an external observer (Denison & Spreitzer, 1991). Hence, the key motives of developmental culture include variety, creativity, and stimulation, as well as leadership roles in developmental organizations associated with risk-taking, innovation, and entrepreneurship (Langer & LeRoux, 2017). Organizational effectiveness is measured in developmental cultures against resource acquisition, dynamism, visibility, acquisition of legitimacy, growth indicators, external support, ratings of productivity, and shorter waiting time.

However, the complexities of the current and future business environment render developmental culture only a part of the solution. We are at a crossroads due to the universal power stress and motivation crisis experienced in the world today. The past decade has brought a global pandemic, financial crisis, and a war in Europe that profoundly impacted organizations and the people working in them (Chatrakul Na Ayudhya et al., 2019). During the pandemic, the dissolution of the face-to-face workplace led to a new, more digital than ever "normal" (Bondarouk & Ruël, 2009) where employees could work at home, spend more time with their families, and devote more time to well-being and hobbies (Zacher & Rudolph, 2021). As pandemic restrictions lessen and employees return to work, the once familiar "in-person" work environment has drastically shifted to include more remote options. Unfortunately, remote work can increase feelings of isolation (Antonacopoulou & Georgiadou, 2021), while returning to work after being online and having time with family can also be isolating. This post-pandemic catch-22 may exacerbate even further if organizational cultures focus more on performance than their employees' well-being or development.

Organizations' singular focus on performance has already prompted scholars to call for agility (Bal & Izak, 2021) and a more employee-centered culture in the future (Haddon & Brynin, 2005; Kulik, 2022). For example, focusing on performance rather than compassionate care has been proven to reduce the likelihood of long-term growth and behavior change (Boyatzis et al., 2019). Focus on compassion, however, allows for prioritizing caring and compassionate relationships and facilitates mutual commitment to change, development, and well-being at work (Boyatzis et al., 2019).

As such, we posit that the solution to this isolation is a culture that promotes community, cooperation, continuous development, and compassion. The course of action for facilitating this culture is the implementation of peer coaching groups (PCGs). Below, we explain what we mean by the four pillars of the culture of the future—community, cooperation, continuous development, and compassion—and talk about the mechanisms of action that peer coaching groups provide to support the four pillars of the culture of the future.

THE FOUR PILLARS OF THE CULTURE OF THE FUTURE

Pillar One: Compassion

Compassion involves noticing another's needs, empathizing, and acting to enhance their well-being (Boyatzis et al., 2013). Three sub-processes characterize compassion at the individual level: noticing another's pain, experiencing an emotional reaction to the pain, and acting in response to the pain (Kanov et al., 2004). Based on these sub-processes, Kanov et al. (2004) conceptualize "organizational compassion" as something which exists when members of a system collectively notice, feel, and respond to pain experienced by members of that system. That article identifies a range of characteristics, including culture, systems, leadership, and technology, which appear to enable the collective processes of noticing, feeling, and responding to the pain of others, thereby facilitating organizational compassion. Finally, the authors suggest that further study of organizational compassion could raise awareness of the positive potential inherent in human organizations and the human organizing processes. Underscoring the importance of studying organizational compassion, scholars note how organizations that support and encourage individual expressions of compassion build capacities for collectively noticing, feeling, and responding to pain, which can be instrumental in replenishing and strengthening individuals' emotional resources (Frost, 2003; Worline et al., 2004).

Compassion as a leadership quality. Research has established how leaders' empathetic attitudes and dispositions positively influence organizational functions for improved performance (Arghode et al., 2022). However, further research is needed to explore how employees' and supervisors' behaviors and interactions can create an empathic organizational culture.

Effects of compassion. Compassion has a notable effect on emotional well-being (Boyatzis et al., 2019). For example, compassion from managers is more effective in easing workers' anxiety. At the same time, the support of coworkers is more effective at fostering a happy emotional state at work, as research has found that people who have a sense of friendship with their coworkers are more likely to care for and be supportive of them (Bakker, 2022). More importantly, participants felt that their coworkers understand them better than their supervisors. Therefore, compassion toward one's colleagues can foster positivity in one's workplace environment, which is necessary for enjoying job satisfaction, having high levels of job performance, and being a healthy employee overall (Bakker, 2022).

For example, compassion in the workplaces of public servants has a significant role in determining their job performance, productivity, and efficiency

(Eldor, 2018). Furthermore, by promoting employees' physical and mental health, compassion can increase productivity and improve customer satisfaction (Eldor, 2018). These findings pose a strong case for public sector managers and policymakers to make a concerted effort to cultivate compassionate workplaces.

Organizations with compassionate leaders can be more efficient, productive, and profitable (George, 2014). They can attract talented employees seeking to work in an environment where they are valued and respected. These types of organizations also tend to have higher morale than their counterparts, which leads to increased productivity. Additionally, compassionate organizations allow for better employee retention, which can be attributed to organizations placing a high value on their employees.

For instance, compassion practices are significantly and positively associated with hospital ratings and the likelihood of a recommendation (McClelland & Vogus, 2014). In addition, providing compassionate care allows hospitals to improve the quality of their patient interactions, improving patient satisfaction and physician trust and reducing medical errors among healthcare providers (McClelland & Vogus, 2014).

Pillar Two: Community

Community is a significant factor in flourishing organizational cultures, as illustrated by the concept of "organizational embeddedness" (Mitchell et al., 2001). Rather than focusing on why employees leave their jobs, the organizational embeddedness framework pinpoints the factors that keep employees at their firms. The three critical aspects of job embeddedness are:

1. the extent to which people have links to other people or activities
2. the extent to which their jobs and communities are similar to or fit with the other aspects of their living spaces
3. the ease with which links can be broken—what they would give up if they left, especially if they had to physically move to other cities or homes.

Mitchell et al.'s (2001) seminal study showed that job embeddedness predicts the key outcomes of both intent to leave and "voluntary turnover" and explains significant incremental variance over and above job satisfaction, organizational commitment, job alternatives, and job search. The authors posit that being embedded in an organization, and a community is associated with reduced intent to leave and reduced actual leaving. Their analysis suggests that employers' focus on money and job satisfaction as the levers for retention may be too limited, while community could play a more significant role in retention.

The concept of change-oriented citizenship. Three key sources of support in work contexts make up a community: leaders, coworkers, and the organization (Ng & Feldman, 2012; Ng & Sorensen, 2008; Tekleab & Chiaburu, 2011). A meta-analytic study based on 131 independent samples and 38,409 employees investigated how these three types of support from employees' social context at work predict change-oriented citizenship. Change-oriented citizenship behavior is defined as proactive actions to identify and implement changes in work processes, products, and services.

Results demonstrated positive relationships between the three social context antecedents and change-oriented citizenship, exhibiting effect sizes around 0.30 and emerging as essentially equal predictors. Moreover, results remained robust after controlling for three previously demonstrated predictors: job satisfaction, organizational commitment, and intention to quit. Moreover, as revealed by the relative importance analyses, the source of support did not make a significant difference when predicting change-oriented citizenship. Thus, the findings suggest that none of the sources of support emerges as a clear "winner" over the others. These results build upon prior studies demonstrating the importance of social exchanges and context as predictors of affiliative citizenship in the workplace (Cardona et al., 2004; Cohen & Keren, 2008; Zagenczyk et al., 2008).

Effect on unity, belonging, and job security. A sense of community among coworkers fosters a more united work environment (Garrett et al., 2017). This unity among workers can ensure workers' feelings of security and safety regarding their future in the company while also helping to develop an environment where employees can communicate more easily. A sense of community provides security and comfort for employees working in groups with others they know and trust (Nistor et al., 2015). As employees interact regularly, they foster a sense of community that allows them to grow professionally as they work with their peers on projects or initiatives (Nistor et al., 2015).

Emotional effect and investment of employees. Employees with a sense of community are emotionally attached to their employers and highly involved in their jobs (Markos & Sridevi, 2010). As a result, they are willing to go the extra mile to ensure their success. This commitment is not only to display an employee's hard work but because they genuinely care about the success of their employer, allowing the employees to feel part of a family and have a sense of belongingness toward the company (Markos & Sridevi, 2010).

Pillar Three: Cooperation

Interactions with coworkers are important (Love & Dustin, 2014), and levels of cooperation with each other predict the ability to take charge or exhibit leadership behaviors. Cooperation can also impact employees' proactive behavior for change. Having higher quality social exchanges with the members of one's work group and valuing a sense of collectivism increase the likelihood that individuals will engage in taking charge behaviors in their organization (Love & Dustin, 2014).

Cooperation is often considered an outcome of team flow; a positive team state that can facilitate team performance and members' well-being (van Oortmerssen et al., 2022). Wang and Zatzick (2019) explain that collaborative work practices have many benefits, including improving productivity, quality, and customer satisfaction. This positive effect is because when employees work together; they can share ideas and solve problems that would not be possible if they were working alone or as part of a small team. Collaborative work practices also help an organization make better decisions by giving everyone input into what should be done or how it should be done (Wang & Zatzick, 2019). Moreover, collaborative work practices foster innovation by allowing employees to learn new skills, such as managing different projects.

Cooperation benefits both employers and employees (Abou Elnaga & Imran, 2014). The individuals involved will have better job satisfaction and improved profitability if they work together because they know their colleagues are dependable, trustworthy, and committed to completing tasks on time. In addition, the organization will achieve its goals more efficiently if all employees are committed to doing their parts. This practice can lead to improved profitability for the company and increased productivity for individual employees who rely on cooperation among coworkers to succeed in their jobs (Abou Elnaga & Imran, 2014).

Cooperative behavior has benefited individuals and organizations (Schuh et al., 2014). Cooperation among coworkers is a way to share information, make decisions, and solve problems, increasing productivity or output per input unit (Schuh et al., 2014). Cooperative employees communicate effectively with each other and improve their efficiency by sharing knowledge and skills. Cooperative work can also help increase productivity by allowing workers to accomplish more tasks in less time (Schuh et al., 2014).

Pillar Four: Continuous Development

Both men and women are the agents of their education and development. Most adults embark upon one or two learning journeys in a year, and there are many ways of learning and changing for adults that can be considered as development. Changes in adults, in general, are a natural part of social and cultural change. Still, major problems in organizations and society cannot be solved without changes and the development of groups and individuals (Tough, 1971, p. 31). Development is a crucial pillar of any organization at the individual, team, and organizational levels. Imagine if individuals in an organization did not strive for learning and development: organizations' leaders would not seek to understand the problems that they need to solve, and employees receiving promotions would not take the time to learn the new skills they need to acquire. The motivation to learn and develop stems from having lifelong learning as a core value. Organizations that encourage continuous development—for example, by hiring executive coaches—exemplify this pillar of the organization of the future. Thus, peer coaching groups (PCGs) can facilitate continuous development by democratizing coaching and making it accessible to all levels of the organization.

Peer Coaching Groups as a Tool to Support the Four Cs

Scholars suggest two types of coaching: coaching for compassion and coaching for compliance (Boyatzis et al., 2019). Coaching for compassion enables the client to be open to new ideas by engaging the positive emotional attractor (PEA). The PEA is a physiological and emotional state where one's body is in parasympathetic arousal, and the mind is more open to learning, development, and new ideas. Coaching for compliance, on the other hand, evokes the negative emotional attractor: a psychophysiological state where the body is in sympathetic arousal and the individual is focused on short-term improvement prescribed externally (Boyatzis & Jack, 2018). Notably, talking about compliance closes individuals off to new ideas and induces sympathetic nervous system arousal, which puts individuals at a higher risk of burnout (Taylor & McGraw, 2004). Given that growth and development form the ideological basis of developmental culture (Langer & LeRoux, 2017), we propose that the future workplace be preoccupied not with compliance but with compassion.

Coaching for compassion is an empirically proven tool that can help professional development, well-being, and goal achievement at an individual level (Boyatzis et al., 2022; De Haan et al., 2019). However, Mirvis (2012) observes that developmental culture needs to be engaged at both the corporate and individual levels. Therefore, we propose peer coaching groups as a way to affect both levels of developmental engagement.

A plethora of literature defines peer coaching as relationships between colleagues of equal status at work who choose to support each other developmentally and professionally through a formalized network (Parker et al., 2018). PCGs support the 4Cs through four distinct mechanisms. Firstly, PCGs create the perfect conditions for resonant relationships to flourish (Boyatzis et al., 2013). Secondly, PCGs allow for status equalization regardless of seniority differences in the group (Terekhin, 2023). Thirdly, PCGs encourage vicarious learning (Trinh, 2020). Fourthly, PCGs evoke an emotion-physiological state known as the positive emotional attractor (Boyatzis et al., 2019).

Mechanism One: Resonant Relationships

The intentional change theory posits a framework for professional and personal development where one goes through various discoveries (Boyatzis et al., 2013). It offers an approach to coaching that engages one's dreams and allows for connection to a strong sense of purpose. The whole process is supported by and impossible without the presence of resonant relationships.

Resonant relationships are characterized by team-member exchange, coworker support, and psychological collectivism (Love & Dustin, 2014). Resonant relationships are necessary for our well-being in the workplace. High-quality connections both support and motivate us to move forward, while low-quality connections are energy-depleting (Dutton & Heaphy, 2003). Resonant relationships are vital in coaching with compassion (CWC) (Boyatzis et al., 2013). CWC is an approach to engaging a person's dreams and sense of purpose, building on resonant and caring relationships that activate neural, hormonal, and psychological states of openness to new ideas, people, and possibilities. PCGs can use CWC to facilitate resonant relationships, as CWC can raise social and emotional intelligence skills (Boyatzis et al., 2019). Additionally, the competency of other awareness increases compassion. Resonant relationships in coaching drive the motivation for intentional change that contributes to continuous development (Boyatzis et al., 2013).

Helping others in this way is very inspirational and, thus, an essential way to develop resonant relationships. CWC is an approach to coaching that engages one's dreams, allows for connection to a strong sense of purpose, and focuses on building resonant relationships. Neural, hormonal, and psychological states of openness to new ideas, people, and possibilities are all the result of CWC. Humans feel more connected when they can help and when their attempts to help are successful. Peer coaching groups of six to eight people, where individuals discuss topics such as vision and values, are perfect opportunities to foster resonant relationships. Moreover, resonant relationships increase a sense of community and cooperation through increased interaction (Love & Dustin, 2014).

Mechanism Two: Status Equalization

The equal status of participants (that is, being peers) is an inherent characteristic of PCGs (Boyatzis et al., 2019; Hopkins et al., 2022; Parker et al., 2008). It secures a lack of power imbalance or the presence of an appraiser for other peers in the group. Elsewise, such power disbalance or the presence of a perceived appraiser would harm psychological safety and openness in the group (Edmondson, 1999), both of which are vital characteristics of a learning environment in a PCG (Ladyshewsky, 2007). Status equalization contributes to community and cooperation. Peer coaching groups formed with members of an equal status encourage a sense of community in the organization through deep collective reflections on professional development. PCGs also have the power to connect people through a joint vision that will likely increase team flow and organizational embeddedness.

Mechanism Three: Vicarious Learning

PCGs involve vicarious learning from shared experience. This element can be inferred through Albert Bandura's Social Learning Theory, which proposes that we learn through observational learning (1961; 1977). While sometimes people use models to replicate their behaviors intentionally, people often serve as indirect models in that they are not trying to influence behavior. Bandura identifies four cognitive mediational processes which drive learning from observation: Attention, Retention, Motor Reproduction, and Motivation.

Initially, the person must be paying attention to the model (attention). The observer needs to be able to remember the behavior that has been observed (retention). The observer must be able to replicate the behavior or action (motor reproduction). Finally, the observer must have some motivation that will make them want to model the behavior that they have observed.

The motivation to imitate behavior depends on several factors (Bandura et al., 1961): consistency, degree of identification with the model, rewards/punishment through vicarious reinforcement, and degree of liking the model. If the model reacts consistently across settings (e.g. always being compassionate), the observer is more likely to imitate the model. We tend to imitate models resembling us, whether in physical appearance, social status, age, or social identity. Bandura suggests that people can learn from the consequences that others face from their actions through vicarious reinforcement. Liking the model is important in whether an observer will be motivated to replicate their behavior. For instance, Yarrow et al. (1970) found that children were more likely to learn altruistic behaviors from people they knew to be friendly than from people they did not know at all. In this study, participants often described how they wanted to copy what they saw as "good" coaching practices.

Mechanism Four: Tapping into the PEA

The PEA is a physiological and emotional state where one's body is in parasympathetic arousal and is more open to learning, development, and new ideas. Conversely, the negative emotional attractor is a psychophysiological state where the body is in sympathetic arousal, and the individual is focused on short-term improvement prescribed externally (Boyatzis & Jack, 2018). Physiologically, the PEA evokes peripheral nervous system activation and activation of the default mode neuronal network (Lvc, Vs, na, pcDPC brain areas). Emotionally, the PEA evokes positive emotions, openness to possibilities, learning, improvement, and recognition of strengths.

Compliance-based coaching, as opposed to compassion-based coaching, stifles PEA activation. By closing off members to new ideas and inducing sympathetic nervous system arousal, coaching for compliance greatly reduces organizations' capacity to foster either cooperation or community. Conversely, coaching with compassion induces PEA, allowing participants to cultivate cooperative mentalities of openness and improvement that also align with a sense of community.

Opportunities for Future Research

Despite the growing interest of the practitioners, existing research on PCGs is scarce. Thus, there are many opportunities to advance research in the field. Among the key elements of PCGs discussed earlier in the paper (vicarious learning, status equalization, resonant relationships, and PEA activation), equal status can be confidently considered at the beginning of the group's formation. While the other three elements emerge in PCGs over time, the conditions for them to emerge, as well as possible catalysts, have not been sufficiently studied. The effect of each of the four PCGs elements theorized in this paper should also be explored further through empirical studies. We posit possible research questions for future empirical studies, such as: How do PCGs contribute to creating a sense of belonging (or community) in the organization? Do PCGs positively impact the cooperative environment in the organization at large? What makes PCGs effective for continuous employee development in an organization? How can PCGs spread compassionate culture across organizations?

As digitalization becomes a common attribute of modern organizations, the effect of automation on PCGs would also be a subject of interest. For example, a study could investigate if a high level of automation within an organization and the increased complexity of required skills change the nature of learning and knowledge exchange in the groups.

The effect of virtual workplaces on relationships in PCGs is particularly interesting with the possible growth of virtual teams in the future. Additionally, decentralizing offices can add challenges to PCG beyond the virtual setting, such as diversity of skills and knowledge requirements, less shared experience, and less understanding in the groups. Some global corporations, like Microsoft, have successfully implemented PCGs for distributed teams. Still, there needs to be scholarly evidence for the factors that make such groups successful and if this effect is sustainable over time. In addition, practical studies of how psychological well-being is being affected by participation in PCGs are ongoing (Feddeck, 2023; Terekhin, 2022). Finally, the relationships theoretically discussed in this article are shown in Fig. 20.1 and need to be studied empirically.

Implications for Practitioners

A growing number of organizations have started to embrace an employee-centered culture, and we hope this trend continues. In order to facilitate the building of an employee-centered culture in an organization, we provide specific elements that such a culture should have and explain how they can be nurtured using peer coaching groups.

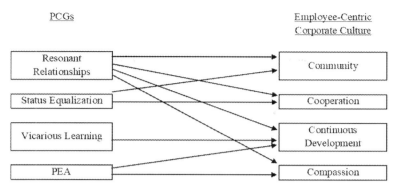

Fig. 20.1 Effect of PCGs on corporate culture

Thousands of global organizations have implemented varying designs of PCGs, including the World Bank, Google, Adidas, Cleveland Clinic, and KPMG. In the absence of sufficient scholarly research on PCGs, the practitioners design PCGs intuitively and experiment with them, thanks to the low cost of their implementation. Moreover, many organizations benefit from PCGs that the employees created as grassroots initiatives with minimal or no support from the organization's leadership.

According to recent studies, the design of an effective, sustainable PCG should consider the following main elements: matching the group members (to avoid conflict of interests and provide desirable diversity of experiences), organized process (emphasizing coaching instead of advice-giving), and trusted relationships among all the participants (Feddeck, 2022; Terekhin, 2022). In addition, the groups should conduct discussions in a safe, respectful environment and provide support not only with professional challenges but also with salient issues from personal life.

Conclusion

Discussion about the workplace of the future cannot exclude compassion, community, cooperation, and continuous development as elements of employee-centric culture. Organizations spend years or even decades implementing technological innovations or digitalization that can completely change their environment and become a state-of-the-art competitive advantage. Building the corporate culture of the future is similarly laborious yet similarly beneficial for an organization. Such a culture can increase employee engagement, retention, and effectiveness. Above all, organizations that care about the employees' well-being and development will increasingly be perceived as necessary by the customers as an element of a sustainable policy, contributing to the organization's bottom line. However, proper implementation and cultivation of developmental culture require effort at every level of the organization. PCGs, an emerging phenomenon in scholarly literature, can become a shortcut to building such a culture due to benefits such as status equalization in the group, opportunities for vicarious learning, and evoking PEA and resonant relationships instrumental both for individual development and organizational change. Furthermore, as PCGs are a low-cost and accessible tool for employee development (Hopkins et al., 2022), they can be easily scaled to provide learning, coaching, and support for all the employees in the organization at a lower cost than executive coaching. Once, the skills and coaching conversations are happening daily; PCGs will induce positive emotions and even physiological changes across the organization, contributing to the competitive advantage of future organizations, both in competition for clients and talent.

References

Abou Elnaga, A., & Imran, A. (2014). The impact of employee empowerment on job satisfaction theoretical study. *American Journal of Research Communication, 2*(1), 13–26.

Ayudhya, C. N., & U., Prouska, R., & Beauregard, T. A. (2019). The impact of global economic crisis and austerity on quality of working life and work-life balance: A capabilities perspective. *European Management Review, 16*(4), 847–862. https://doi.org/10.1111/emre.12128

Albert, S., Ashforth, B. E., & Dutton, J. E. (2000). Organizational identity and identification: Charting new waters and building new bridges. *Academy of Management Review, 25*(1), 13–17. https://doi.org/10.5465/amr.2000.2791600

Antonacopoulou, E. P., & Georgiadou, A. (2021). Leading through social distancing: The future of work, corporations and leadership from home. *Gender, Work & Organization, 28*(2), 749–767. https://doi.org/10.1111/gwao.12533

Arghode, V., Lathan, A., Alagaraja, M., Rajaram, K., & McLean, G. N. (2022). Empathic organizational culture and leadership: Conceptualizing the framework. *European Journal of Training and Development, 46*(1/2), 239–256. https://doi.org/10.1108/EJTD-09-2020-0139

Bakker, K. (2022). *Compassion in organisations from supervisors and co-workers: Do size and nature of the organisation matter?* (Master's Thesis), University of Twente. https://purl.utwente.nl/essays/89340

Bal, P. M., & Izak, M. (2021). Paradigms of flexibility: A systematic review of research on workplace flexibility. *European Management Review, 18*(1), 37–50. https://doi.org/10.1111/emre.12423

Bandura, A., Ross, D., & Ross, S. A. (1961). Transmission of aggression through imitation of aggressive models. *The Journal of Abnormal and Social Psychology, 63*, 575–582. https://doi.org/10.1037/h0045925

Bandura, A., & Walters, R. H. (1977). *Social learning theory* (Vol. 1). Prentice Hall.

Bondarouk, T. V., & Ruël, H. J. M. (2009). Electronic human resource management: Challenges in the digital era. *The International Journal of Human Resource Management, 20*(3), 505–514. https://doi.org/10.1080/09585190802707235

Boyatzis, R. E., Hullinger, A., Ehasz, S. F., Harvey, J., Tassarotti, S., Gallotti, A., & Penafort, F. (2022). The grand challenge for research on the future of coaching. *The*

Journal of Applied Behavioral Science, 58(2), 202–222. https://doi.org/10.1177/00218863221079937

Boyatzis, R. E., & Jack, A. I. (2018). The neuroscience of coaching. *Consulting Psychology Journal: Practice and Research, 70*(1), 11.

Boyatzis, R. E., Smith, M. L., & Beveridge, A. J. (2013). Coaching with compassion: Inspiring health, well-being, and development in organizations. *The Journal of Applied Behavioral Science, 49*(2), 153–178. https://doi.org/10.1177/0021886312462236

Boyatzis, R. E., Smith, M. L., & Van Oosten, E. (2019). *Helping people change: Coaching with compassion for lifelong learning and growth*. Harvard Business Press.

Cardona, P., Lawrence, B. S., & Bentler, P. M. (2004). The influence of social and work exchange relationships on organizational citizenship behavior. *Group & Organization Management, 29*(2), 219–247. https://doi.org/10.1177/1059601103257401

Cohen, A., & Keren, D. (2008). Individual values and social exchange variables: Examining their relationship to and mutual effect on in-role performance and organizational citizenship behavior. *Group & Organization Management, 33*(4), 425–452. https://doi.org/10.1177/1059601108321823

Davies, H. T. O., Mannion, R., Jacobs, R., Powell, A. E., & Marshall, M. N. (2007). Exploring the relationship between senior management team culture and hospital performance. *Medical Care Research and Review, 64*(1), 46–65. https://doi.org/10.1177/1077558706296240

De Haan, E., Gray, D. E., & Bonneywell, S. (2019). Executive coaching outcome research in a field setting: A near-randomized controlled trial study in a global healthcare corporation. *Academy of Management Learning & Education, 18*(4), 581–605. https://doi.org/10.5465/amle.2018.0158

Denison, D. R. (1996). What is the difference between organizational culture and organizational climate? A native's point of view on a decade of paradigm wars. *Academy of Management Review, 21*(3), 619–654. https://doi.org/10.5465/amr.1996.9702100310

Denison, D. R., & Spreitzer, G. M. (1991). Organizational culture and organizational development: A competing values approach. *Research in Organizational Change and Development, 5*(1), 1–21.

Dutton, J., & Heaphy, E. D. (2003). The power of high-quality connections. In K. Cameron, J. Dutton, & R. E. Quinn (Eds.), *Positive organizational scholarship: Foundations of a new discipline* (pp. 263–278). Berrett-Koehler Publishers.

Edmondson, A. (1999). Psychological safety and learning behavior in work teams. *Administrative Science Quarterly, 44*(2), 350–383.

Eldor, L. (2018). Public service sector: The compassionate workplace—the effect of compassion and stress on employee engagement, burnout, and performance. *Journal of Public Administration Research and Theory, 28*(1), 86–103. https://doi.org/10.1093/jopart/mux028

Feddeck, M. (2022). *Helping you helping me: Forging Meaningful connections at a distance*: Unpublished.

Feddeck, M. (2023). *Peer coaching groups in surgical residency programs*: Forthcoming, unpublished manuscript.

Frost, P. J. (2003). *Toxic emotions at work: How compassionate managers handle pain and conflict*. Harvard Business School Press.

Garrett, L. E., Spreitzer, G. M., & Bacevice, P. A. (2017). Co-constructing a sense of community at work: The emergence of community in coworking spaces. *Organization Studies*, *38*(6), 821–842. https://doi.org/10.1177/0170840616685354

George, J. M. (2014). Compassion and capitalism: Implications for organizational studies. *Journal of Management*, *40*(1), 5–15. https://doi.org/10.1177/0149206313490028

Haddon, L., & Brynin, M. (2005). The character of telework and the characteristics of teleworkers. *New Technology, Work and Employment*, *20*(1), 34–46. https://doi.org/10.1111/j.1468-005X.2005.00142.x

Hopkins, K., Meyer, M., Afkinich, J., Bialobrzeski, E., Perry, V., & Brown, J. (2022). Facilitated peer coaching among women human service professionals: Leadership learning, application and lessons learned. *Human Service Organizations: Management, Leadership & Governance*, *1–18*,. https://doi.org/10.1080/23303131.2021.1961963

Kanov, J. M., Maitlis, S., Worline, M. C., Dutton, J. E., Frost, P. J., & Lilius, J. M. (2004). Compassion in organizational life. *American Behavioral Scientist*, *47*(6), 808–827. https://doi.org/10.1177/0002764203260211

Kulik, C. T. (2022). We need a hero: HR and the 'next normal' workplace. *Human Resource Management Journal*, *32*(1), 216–231. https://doi.org/10.1111/1748-8583.12387

Ladyshewsky, R. K. (2007). A strategic approach for integrating theory to practice in leadership development. *Leadership & Organization Development Journal*, *28*(5), 426–443. https://doi.org/10.1108/01437730710761733

Langer, J., & LeRoux, K. (2017). Developmental culture and effectiveness in nonprofit organizations. *Public Performance & Management Review*, *40*(3), 457–479. https://doi.org/10.1080/15309576.2016.1273124

Love, M. S., & Dustin, S. L. (2014). An investigation of coworker relationships and psychological collectivism on employee propensity to take charge. *The International Journal of Human Resource Management*, *25*(9), 1208–1226. https://doi.org/10.1080/09585192.2013.826712

Markos, S., & Sridevi, M. S. (2010). Employee engagement: The key to improving performance. *International Journal of Business and Management*, *5*(12), 89–96.

McClelland, L. E., & Vogus, T. J. (2014). Compassion practices and HCAHPS: Does rewarding and supporting workplace compassion influence patient perceptions? *Health Services Research*, *49*(5), 1670–1683. https://doi.org/10.1111/1475-6773.12186

Mirvis, P. (2012). Employee engagement and CSR: Transactional, relational, and developmental approaches. *California Management Review*, *54*(4), 93–117. https://doi.org/10.1525/cmr.2012.54.4.93

Mitchell, T. R., Holtom, B. C., Lee, T. W., Sablynski, C. J., & Erez, M. (2001). Why people stay: Using job embeddedness to predict voluntary turnover. *Academy of Management Journal*, *44*(6), 1102–1121. https://doi.org/10.5465/3069391

Ng, T. W. H., & Feldman, D. C. (2012). Employee voice behavior: A meta-analytic test of the conservation of resources framework. *Journal of Organizational Behavior*, *33*(2), 216–234. https://doi.org/10.1002/job.754

Ng, T. W. H., & Sorensen, K. L. (2008). Toward a further understanding of the relationships between perceptions of support and work attitudes: A meta-analysis.

Group & Organization Management, 33(3), 243–268. https://doi.org/10.1177/1059601107313307

Nistor, N., Daxecker, I., Stanciu, D., & Diekamp, O. (2015). Sense of community in academic communities of practice: Predictors and effects. *Higher Education, 69*(2), 257–273. https://doi.org/10.1007/s10734-014-9773-6

O'Regan, K., & Oster, S. M. (2005). Does the structure and composition of the board matter? The case of nonprofit organizations. *The Journal of Law, Economics, and Organization, 21*(1), 205–227. https://doi.org/10.1093/jleo/ewi009

Parker, P., Hall, D. T., & Kram, K. E. (2008). Peer coaching: A relational process for accelerating career learning. *Academy of Management Learning & Education, 7*(4), 487–503. https://doi.org/10.5465/amle.2008.35882189

Parker, P., Hall, D. T., Kram, K. E., & Wasserman, I. C. (2018). *Peer coaching at work: Principles and practices*. Stanford University Press.

Quinn, R. E., & Kimberly, J. R. (1984). Paradox, planning, and perseverance: Guidelines for managerial practice. In R. E. Quinn & J. R. Kimberly (Eds.), *Managing organizational transitions* (pp. 295–313). Irwin.

Quinn, R. E., & Rohrbaugh, J. (1981). A competing values approach to organizational effectiveness. *Public Productivity Review, 5*(2), 122–140. https://doi.org/10.2307/3380029

Schuh, G., Potente, T., Wesch-Potente, C., Weber, A. R., & Prote, J.-P. (2014). Collaboration mechanisms to increase productivity in the context of Industrie 4.0. *Procedia CIRP, 19*, 51–56. https://doi.org/10.1016/j.procir.2014.05.016

Taylor, T., & McGraw, P. (2004). Succession management practices in Australian organizations. *International Journal of Manpower, 25*(8), 741–758. https://doi.org/10.1108/01437720410570045

Tekleab, A. G., & Chiaburu, D. S. (2011). Social exchange: Empirical examination of form and focus. *Journal of Business Research, 64*(5), 460–466. https://doi.org/10.1016/j.jbusres.2010.03.005

Terekhin, R. (2022). Peer coaching groups to bring development for everyone. *Academy of Management Proceedings, 2022*(1). https://doi.org/10.5465/AMBPP.2022.14783abstract

Terekhin, R. (2023). Peer coaching groups as a natural space for intergenerational and lifelong learning. In F. Ince (Eds.), *Leadership perspectives on effective intergenerational communication and management* (pp. 36–52). IGI Global. https://doi.org/10.4018/978-1-6684-6140-2.ch003

Tough, A. (1971). *The adult's learning projects: a fresh approach to theory and practice in adult learning*: Ontario Institute for Studies in Education.

Trinh, M. P. (2020). Peer coaching: a holistic experiential learning process in online leadership classes. In *Handbook of teaching with technology in management, leadership, and business* (pp. 129–140). Edward Elgar Publishing.

van Oortmerssen, L. A., Caniëls, M. C. J., Stynen, D., & van Ritbergen, A. (2022). Boosting team flow through collective efficacy beliefs: A multilevel study in real-life organizational teams. *Journal of Applied Social Psychology, 52*(10), 1030–1044. https://doi.org/10.1111/jasp.12910

Wang, T., & Zatzick, C. D. (2019). Human capital acquisition and organizational innovation: A temporal perspective. *Academy of Management Journal, 62*(1), 99–116. https://doi.org/10.5465/amj.2017.0114

Worline, M., Dutton, J., Frost, P., Janov, J., Lilius, J., & Maitlis, S. (2004). *Creating fertile soil: The organizing dynamics of resilience*. University of Michigan School of Business.

Yarrow, M. R., Campbell, J. D., & Burton, R. V. (1970). Recollections of childhood a study of the retrospective method. *Monographs of the Society for Research in Child Development*, 35(5), iii–83. https://doi.org/10.2307/1165649

Zacher, H., & Rudolph, C. W. (2021). Individual differences and changes in subjective wellbeing during the early stages of the COVID-19 pandemic. *American Psychologist*, 76, 50–62. https://doi.org/10.1037/amp0000702

Zagenczyk, T. J., Gibney, R., Murrell, A. J., & Boss, S. R. (2008). Friends don't make friends good citizens, but advisors do. *Group & Organization Management*, 33(6), 760–780. https://doi.org/10.1177/1059601108326806

CHAPTER 21

Leading Individual and Collective Well-being for Planetary Health

Wanda Krause

INTRODUCTION

From a 2017 Gallup poll using analytics from 160 countries on the global workplace, 33% of employees were engaged, 51% were not engaged, and 16% were actively disengaged. Engagement rates were relatively unchanged for over a decade. In 2021, fluctuations were observed and in 2022, we saw these fluctuations move to decline whereby 60% of people reported being emotionally detached at work and 19% as being miserable (actively disengaged). Here, again, only 33% reported feeling engaged. In the USA specifically, 50% of workers reported feeling stressed at their jobs on a daily basis, 41% as being worried, 22% as sad, and 18% angry (Gallup, 2022). In 2022, in Canada, 20–30% of employees started their day feeling sad or angry (Forbs, 2022). Kincentric (2022) tracked global employee engagement between 2019 to 2022 including 12 million employees across 125 markets. Similarly, Kincentric's (2022) research on engagement was at 67% over 2019, rose to a high close to mid-2021 with 73%, although averaging 69% during the year, and then saw a decline to 62% in 2022. The questions this chapter seeks to reflect on are: What might we learn from the experiences related to these years to contemplate how we may lead better post-COVID-19? As engagement is used as a measure of workplace well-being the following considers engagement as

W. Krause (✉)
Royal Roads University, MA Global Leadership Program, School of Leadership Studies, Victoria, BC, Canada
e-mail: wanda.1krause@royalroads.ca

© The Author(s), under exclusive license to Springer Nature Switzerland AG 2023
J. Marques (ed.), *The Palgrave Handbook of Fulfillment, Wellness, and Personal Growth at Work,*
https://doi.org/10.1007/978-3-031-35494-6_21

a factor but points to others as well. The assumption is that we are entering an era where we will have to recognize that we are not going back to the same ways of working as we did pre-COVID-19. What do experiences during these years of chaos brought on largely by the pandemic tell us in the scope of well-being, individually and collectively more broadly in aligning to planetary health?

The author's differential experience with higher levels of engagement is the impetus for this chapter's revisiting the heavy emphasis on engagement driven by both leadership studies and popular research on engagement in the workplace. The Gallup (2022) report states:

> Wellbeing and engagement interact with each other in powerful ways. When employees are engaged and thriving, they experience significantly less stress, anger and health problems. Unfortunately, most employees remain disengaged at work. In fact, low engagement alone costs the global economy $7.8 trillion. The relationship between wellbeing and engagement is vital because how people experience work influences their lives outside work, and overall wellbeing influences life at work. (finding six)

The report consequently affirms: "Organizations need to think about the whole person, not just the worker" (2022, finding 6). Although satisfaction and well-being may be connected to higher levels of engagement, individual and collective well-being can also be compromised by higher levels of engagement. Further, Gallup's polls are often referenced to emphasize the correlation of engagement to not only greater levels of satisfaction but also productivity. However, other even more significant determinants are often neglected. As such, we might ask if engagement levels might actually also be productive of higher levels of dissatisfaction and burnout, and under what conditions. Because burnout is simultaneously tracked as increasing or, at least fluctuating, within the years where COVID-19 presented most significantly to date, higher engagement may not be such a great thing at all times.

The anomaly more specifically close to mid-2021 tracked in the Kincentric (2022) report seems to be ignored in google searches on engagement and in the recent literature. Higher engagement continues to be presented as the thing for which we ought to be striving. In fact, with a hyper-focus on engagement, specific instruments have been created to measure it. The Work Engagement Scale-17 is one of the most commonly utilized tools to measure work engagement globally. Yet, Song et al. (2021) found that it did not reflect the level of work engagement adequately in their case study and more significantly in attempting to understand male and female participants proved to express inadequate differentiation between males and females.

The following seeks to nuance the view that engagement correlates to greater satisfaction and well-being. The chapter advocates bringing largely siloed perspectives together to understand, first, the meaning of well-being. It does so by connecting to the framework of planetary health. Such is, in fact, critical as we are faced with multiple and compounded global challenges moving forward in what we refer to as post-COVID-19. In 2023, COVID-19 infections were still present globally; however, for the sake of differentiating the era of mobility after physical distancing measures and enforcement of COVID-19 policies, we will refer to this period as post-COVID-19. Using reflective analysis through differential observations from within leadership, the following also interrogates the assumption that productivity is, in fact, a key goal we ought to keep at the forefront of planning and the reason for engaging.

Engagement is but one variable and not even the key variable. Others, such as Kulikowski (2022), similarly point out that engagement as a central construct for well-being at work is problematic. Kulikowski (2022) argues, in fact, the current understanding of engagement overlooks what people consider as engagement, arguing for the need for understanding engagement from the employee point of view. Following an interrogation of the assumptions around engagement, my argument is that well-being must also be understood in a holistic, decolonized manner. Recognizing that planetary health is a broad term and ill-defined, at least in western neoliberal and secular frameworks, what follows is a working definition, resting on both western and traditional knowledge. The chapter follows with a discussion and recommendations on leading individual and collective well-being in the post-COVID-19 era.

Planetary Health

"Planetary health" is a relatively new concept to the scientific community in the west, elevated in 2015 to greater awareness in western research by the Rockefeller Foundation, although earlier discussed in the 1970s. It has, however, been a central philosophy and practice of Indigenous communities globally for millennia. In the western lexicon, in brief, it conceptually connects the individual to the planet (Prescott & Logan, 2019). In this recent framing, planetary health has served to expand and broaden the term "public health" that has dominated the discourse over the past two decades (Jamison et al., 2013) to "one health" and now to planetary. In capturing and lifting the definition to a broader perspective, the planetary health manifesto and the Rockefeller Foundation–Lancet Commission on Planetary Health defined planetary health as:

> ... the achievement of the highest attainable standard of health, wellbeing, and equity worldwide through judicious attention to the human systems—political, economic, and social—that shape the future of humanity and the Earth's natural systems that define the safe environmental limits within which humanity can flourish. Put simply, planetary health is the health of human civilisation and the state of the natural systems on which it depends. (2015, p. 1978)

In addressing the empathy failures, inequity, and engaging across diverse worldviews, it is important to bridge western and non-western thought, or Global North and Global South perspectives and ways of being, doing, and seeing. A means to do so is through decolonizing lenses and approaches. Decolonial planetary health aspires to center the diversity and importance of Indigenous thought and stewardship (Hoogeven et al., 2023). "Indigenous" refers to those who identify their ancestry with original inhabitants of countries worldwide (Wilson, 2008). Principles from traditional knowledges (TK), in general, can support a more inclusive and relational approach to inform leadership thinking and practice to go further in, if not rediscover, being more integral in several significant ways (Krause, 2023). Traditional knowledge can be defined as "all that is known about the world around us and how to apply that knowledge in relation to those beings that share the world" (Bennet et al., 2014). As such, it is more accurate to acknowledge the concept of "planetary health" has been around for millennia in various forms of thinking and practice, as found in traditional knowledges.

Hoogeven et al. (2023) advocate "highlighting intercultural thinking to promote an anti-colonial, anti-racist, and reciprocal approach to climate change and global health inequities across geographical space and within planetary health discourse" (para. 1), considering how rigorous engagement with epistemic and geographical diversity can strengthen and advance planetary health. Ubalijoro and Lee (2022) argue "[i]t is noteworthy that hunter-gatherer societies have practiced for millennia situational and inclusive leadership only relatively recently (re)discovered in modern leadership theories such as servant leadership, transformational leadership and holocracy" (p. 52). Current challenges in planetary health and decolonization are necessarily related to the COVID-19 pandemic (Hoogeven et al., 2023, para. 7).

The Rockefeller Foundation–Lancet Commission (2015) offered three categories of challenges that would need to be addressed to both maintain and enhance human health. These are conceptual and empathy failures, the failure to account for future health and environmental harms over present-day gains, and the disproportionate effect of those harms on the poor and those in developing nations. The field of planetary health recognizes human impacts on the environment, and specifically, the impacts that the exploitative practices initiated by colonialism and maintained by capitalism have on the natural systems of the planet, ultimately threatening human health. The Commission argued that "a population attains a given level of health by exploiting the environment unsustainably then it is likely to be doing so at the expense of other populations—now or in the future, or both" (2015, p. 1978).

Not only has exploitation occurred around the planet's resources but the colonizing and exploiting of people for social, economic, and political gain and dominance. Hence, it is impossible to talk about creating human health in relation to environmental health without considering human health as relates to individual and collective well-being at all levels and with the lens of inequity (Krause, 2022). As such, we must consider the realms of the social, political, and organizational from an intersectional lens, as well the interconnections between political, social, and environmental discourses in shaping human perceptions, decision-making, and behavior, as well leadership behavior.

Essentially, planetary health is also an approach to life which attempts to address inequalities, with the objective that all people on the globe have the ability to enjoy health and well-being (Gostin et al., 2018), and leave no one behind (Holst, 2020; UN Committee for Development, 2018). We can consider how changing how we lead at policy levels, within organizations, and how we conduct ourselves can change the trajectory of colonization in its old and modern forms and top-down non-inclusive hierarchies to greater inclusion and equity. We can do so through efforts at decolonization and transformation of systems. In this, we must recognize the power and agency we hold, both as leaders and followers, to re-define societal values to promote justice, equity, and inclusion. Through changing discourses, choices, and practices, we can shift collective value systems, and promote individual and planetary health from the grassroots or organizational levels upwards. From this perspective, while we seek to protect biological diversity, we must also seek to protect not only cultural diversity but nurture equity and caring relationships as means for advancing individual and collective health and well-being.

Hence, how can planetary health leadership transform power relations in promoting and protecting well-being from the individual and grassroots to the broader collective and global levels? It is important, therefore, to recognize and understand how power has been exercised to lead to a state of burnout and active disengagement, and enable a gap between the rich and poor, among various intersectionalities. From the grassroots up, inclusive of organizations, civil society and communities, it is imperative to, thus, secure diversity, equity, and inclusion and address unfair treatment within organizations, too.

The Rockefeller Foundation–Lancet Commission (2015) identifies the importance of changing human behavior as the connection to human progress and well-being. In line with a focus on human behavior, the WISER framework advocates interventions that consider or can help contribute to well-being, inclusivity, sufficiency, empowerment, and resilience. These five categories can encompass the 17 interlinked sustainable development goals (SDGs) listed below. The authors of the WISER framework define well-being as "the degree to which people can flourish as a whole, as characterized by being happy and surrounded by resources that are necessary to ensure an optimal life expectancy." Building on "the degree to which people can flourish as a whole," it is also important to understand flourishing holistically. Such encompass the emotional, mental, physical, and spiritual, as also aligned to Indigenous and TK epistemologies.

Basso and Krpan (2023) offer the following SDGs, as focus, to support the WISER framework:

- SDG2: end hunger, achieve food security and improved nutrition, and promote sustainable agriculture;

- SDG3: ensure healthy lives and promote well-being for all at all ages;
- SDG6: ensure availability and sustainable management of water and sanitation for all; and
- SDG7: ensure access to affordable, reliable, sustainable, and modern energy for all.

Basso and Krpan (2023) suggest that a behavioral intervention can be reviewed to consider the following questions: "does this intervention bring people the resources, whether material or immaterial, that they are missing (1) to live more healthily, (2) to live more sustainably, and (3) that contribute to their well-being" (2023, para. 4)? These questions align well with the focus on the four SDGs above as interventions that leaders can consider in their work to empower and support. The planetary health lens, described here, seeks to empower and support people's emotional, mental, and spiritual needs, more explicitly, and from a greater understanding of intersectionality. In addressing power relations and imbalances, it is important, then, to include empowerment of marginalized voices and advance practices as part of a decolonized planetary health lens, thereby promoting well-being individually and collectively as aligned to context and place. It must also be situated as the lens of those who are central to their own agency; as such, sees interventions as a collective effort, if not necessarily so, through the partnerships and engagements with those who must have a say in what matters to them in any intervention. As Prescott and Logan (2019, p. 1) argue, the role of beliefs, expectations, and agency are core in linking narrative and planetary health.

Three further categorizations Basso and Krpan (2023) connect to the categorization above of well-being are as follows: inclusivity through SDG1, SDG5, SDG10, SDG16; sufficiency through SDG12, SDG14, SDG15, empowerment through SDG4, SDG8, SDG17, and resilience through SDG9, SDG11, SDG13. They, too, note where possible, it is important to include the local actors (empowerment) to nurture behavioral change in the long run (resilience) based on the diversity of the needs of the actors involved in the community (inclusivity). The complexity of interrelated psychological, social, and ecological problems that dynamically interact to drive the currently developing challenges cannot be understood or responded to appropriately by using compartmentalized, specialized, and partial thinking (Wahl, 2006). The SDGs are not the only means or even necessarily the best means to capture globally interconnected goals founded upon individual and collective well-being (Krause, 2023). However, the UN's framework for sustainable development goals is one way of presenting the interconnections, especially in regard to behavior, between micro-level, meso-level, and macro-level determinants for planetary health. Redvers et al. (2022) introduce an Indigenous concensus perspective, for example, to define the determinants of planetary health, with three overarching levels of interconnected determinants, in addition to ten individual-level determinants. The overarching levels are: Mother-Earth level determinants, interconnecting determinants, and Indigenous People's determinants. The authors emphasize that it is critical to conceptualise the determinants of planetary health from an Indigenous perspective by embracing and advancing Indigenous-specific methods of knowledge from around the globe.

What Does Engagement Mean in the Scope of Planetary Health?

As remote or work from home has increased over the years reviewed here, so has the blurring between work and home life. The blurring of work and home, the increased pressures to manage chaos as a result of COVID-19, and the lack of direction among some workplaces, during these times of uncertainty, certainly impact well-being. Such leads to problems fulfilling work and family tasks and responsibilities, which in turn further impacts health (Forbs, 2022). Consequently, while working from home may have many upsides, it does not mean that stress did not increase simultaneously. In early 2020, I resolved to establish more frequent engagement with others. Believing that extending greater support was of benefit, I correlated that sense of purpose to my greater personal satisfaction and fulfillment. Engaging with others to think through new challenges, largely presented by COVID-19, mostly felt supportive. On the other hand, like many others, work-related hours were not only even longer but compounded with more challenges to address, and, indeed, challenges of greater complexity and, taken together with the responsibility to family. Double-booking meetings became a means to fit increasing demands and tasks in the same span of space. Replenishing of self and relations became more challenging.

The experience of feeling stretched through longer hours and the need to attend to greater and multiple demands are a necessary phase on which to reflect and examine how leaders can better support individual and collective well-being for the prospect of planetary health now and into the future, in a post-COVID-19 era. More significantly, "[t]his is an Era of Opportunity that provides businesses with an inflection point unmatched in history" (Kinsentric, 2022, p. 3)—for any type of organization or civil society activism. Even though the concept of employee engagement has been discussed for the past decade, employee engagement surveys among most corporations still continue to show an overall decline in engagement levels among employees worldwide (Kuok & Taormina, 2017).

Revisiting the correlations attributed to higher engagement is not to dismiss the merit of engagement, nor to argue that engagement should not be somewhere on the priority list for planning effective leadership strategies for workplace well-being. However, given the decoupling of higher levels of engagement from higher levels of satisfaction during this time impacted by COVID-19, given that despite the value placed on engagement workplaces are generally seeing a decline in engagement nonetheless, and given that post-COVID-19 has in fact also evolved to a time referred to as the Great Resignation, whereby higher numbers of people in the USA are quitting jobs,

I argue for a pause to reflect. This is both a time of new learnings to take forward on understanding what engagement means in the scope of planetary health when working focusing on individual and collective well-being.

It is established that COVID-19 can be attributed as a key variable in the levels of stress and burnout experienced in the workplace and life in general. However, it is not just the hours, work-life balance, or workplace location that have left workers dissatisfied. What matters is how they experience that work, in other words how they are managed, treated, and coached (Forbs, 2022). Gallup research has also found that the number one reason for job dissatisfaction is "unfair treatment at work." This means that the lack of a culture that emphasizes respect, diversity and inclusiveness, community, and acknowledgment of contribution will negatively impact a sense of well-being. Gallup reports mistreatment by coworkers, inconsistent compensation, biases and favoritism are top examples of "unfair treatment." In addition, beyond unfair treatment, job dissatisfaction correlates with lack of manager support, unclear communication from management, and unreasonable time pressures—all are indicators of burnout and job dissatisfaction (Forbs, 2022). How, then, can we lead better?

Leading Individual and Collective Well-Being

If "unfair treatment" is found to be a leading reason for dissatisfaction, then inequity ought to be higher on a leader's priority list for addressing or supporting well-being in the organization. After all, how we engage is determined by our biases for and toward individuals, groups, agendas, and assumptions of what goals are most important. Inequity and exclusion persist across systems; that is, within organizations, society, and in view of increasing global challenges, globally. As such, leaders have a critical role to play to support planetary health through the individual and collective levels in ways that are cognizant of bias and, I will further argue, short-sighted goals. In December 2021, the WHO World Health Assembly established an International Negotiating Board (INB) to reach a global cooperative agreement on future pandemic preparedness by 2024. One of their areas of focus is the human–environment interactions that contribute to pandemic risk. As the Lancet Planetary Health (2023) affirms, "The Pandemic Treaty therefore represents an important opportunity to take an integrated whole-environment approach to strengthening global health" (para. 1). Therefore, that taking a holistic view of well-being is critical, and in this vein, considering how we are leading individual and collective well-being not merely for efficiency or productivity but in relation to an integrated, interdependent whole-environment.

As leaders are in positions to develop and implement interventions at organizational levels, too, and given what we may learn from a global challenge affecting human and global health, we can reflect on how best to move forward, considering how to manage, treat, and coach (Forbs, 2022) or, in other words, lead employees or followers. Our workplaces are increasingly seeing burnout and stress manifesting in many ways, as the Gallup and Kincentric reports demonstrate. We might consider, as Basso and Krpan (2023) suggest, that a behavioral intervention within communities and at the organizational level is led with questions, such as: "does this intervention bring people the resources, whether material or immaterial, that they are missing (1) to live more healthily, (2) to live more sustainably, and (3) that contribute to their well-being?" Organizational leaders need to also create culturally safe, equitable, and inclusive environments as part of well-being. Organizational leaders, therefore, require the systems thinking and strategies for interventions within their organizations also for a positive impact on the larger social and planetary systems (Krause, 2022).

Addressing the behavioral intervention, and the question: Does this intervention bring people resources, whether material or immaterial, that they are missing? People need more support to get work done, when there are concerns relating to insufficient resources and staffing levels (Kincentric, 2022). In the Kincentric (2022) study, 50% of people globally felt they had their staffing needs met, meaning 50% did not. It is not surprising that despite the emphasis on engagement, studies are seeing an overall trend toward lower levels of engagement. If one feels stretched to do the work that could better be supported by further staff one might not welcome engagement that would take time away from completing tasks and risk burnout. Interventions that bring resources for greater efficiency do not necessarily lead to more time for the individual and, in fact, the opposite can result whereby the freed time has already been allocated to with other tasks. The intent for efficiency, as facilitated by leaders, is not for greater work-life balance but usually for greater productivity.

Even before COVID-19, a decrease in work-life balance has been found among studies, leading the Kincentric (2022) study to conclude "it isn't surprising that they are feeling underappreciated and underpaid" (p. 5). Without systems thinking and strategies for interventions within their organizations also for a positive impact on the larger social and planetary systems, it will be difficult to put people first. Currently, even when a people first statement is made by leadership, there is a disjuncture to practice. Equal treatment and social justice must be leadership practices not merely taught in the leadership literature but practiced among leaders if well-being and satisfaction are part and parcel of an organization's success. The 23rd IUHPE World Conference on Health Promotion held in Rotorua, Aotearoa New Zealand in April 2019, had the theme "Waiora: promoting planetary health and sustainable development for all." Representing global Indigenous and traditional knowledges, it called for a reorientation of health awareness toward planetary health and sustainable development while also focusing on equity and social justice (Krause, 2023). Messages included raising awareness that western approaches are culturally bound and tend to further the interests of the neoliberal agenda (Krause, 2023).

The kind of engagement matters. Engagement around process matters but it can also feel challenging to engage in conversations and meetings around process when the vision is not clear, beforehand fully understood, not modeled, and demonstrated by leadership, or the vision is not co-created. Kincentric (2022) found that engagement is eight times higher when senior leaders make people feel excited about the future. However, while communicating vision is emphasized if people do not buy into, co-create, and see the words behind the vision lived and practiced by leaders, the vision can carry little motivational quality. In fact, the demonstration of misalignment to vision or lip service to values underlying a vision can erode trust in the vision and trust in leadership preaching to the vision.

Leaders, both executive and senior, need to ask themselves why they are seeking to engage and whether higher levels of engagement at a minimum during times of greater stress is helpful, and to whom. Leaders need to be aware of seeking to engage encompasses some form of communicating one way, whether communicating developments, new directions, changes, or additional tasks. Over-communicating versus under-communicating might benefit in the long term in that employees feel they are on the right track, and such minimizes the chances of having to retrace steps, revisit, or redo tasks on the leader's and follower's side. However, leaders need to be cognizant of the possible impacts of over-communicating, the side effects, or unintended consequences. When communication becomes routinely one-directional, such communication can land as being told or commanded, rather than collaborative and opinions valued.

Inquiry and deep listening become critical forms of leadership in engagement. These are competencies that leaders need to further, particularly in turbulent times. However, these are leadership competencies that are critical to nurture relationships and build trust over longer periods of time. These entail effectively holding space for those they lead as a routine leadership and engagement practice. Leaders can practice inquiry by asking open-ended or semi-open-ended questions with genuine curiosity. The leadership imperative is to seek guidance from others, particularly being attuned to including marginalized voices, and actively responding to opinions, grievances, goals, and desires expressed. Deep listening is letting go of all distractions and holding heart-centered focus on the person you are listening to, remaining grounded, present, clear, attentive, open, observant, and curious. When deep listening, one drops down from thinking to attention on the heart and listens from this space of awareness and being (Krause, n.d.). This practice can be understood as empathetic listening as listening entails seeking to truly hear and understand the other. Such is leading from the heart, the place from which connections for engagement are created, an endeavor that is impossible from the place merely of mind. Such practice also involves cultural competencies as different worldviews will be expressed.

COVID-19 served to create not only physical but also social distance, felt much more strongly by some than others. Leaders are not immune to stress at the least. Where isolation or burnout was likely felt more strongly by some than others, these often competing needs among different leaders require different responses and planning by executive leadership. Where leaders and followers are feeling isolated or they have a greater need to connect with others specifically in the workplace, opportunities to connect need to be presented. In many Global North cultures, community is not found outside the home as more prevalent and present for those in the Global South (Ife, 2016)—in most, although, as my previous research (2009, 2012) found not all instances, particularly for marginalized and racialized people in those contexts. Gallop's research found that both Europe and South Asia (including India) dropped five percentage points in well-being in 2021, with South Asia at the lowest in well-being in the world at 11%. In these regions, people felt that their current life is worse than it had been previously. Hope in the future had also dropped (Gallup, 2022).

The challenge to leaders is that they sometimes attach to that role identity and understanding of resilience that is superhuman. In key respects, leaders have gotten to their positions through hard work, determination, and grit. Many of us women have been taught by our especially racialized family in advocating for our success and happiness that we have to work much, much harder. No doubt male leaders in the workplace are socially expected to lead in a way where vulnerability is also a taboo to show in leadership, particularly in hard times. Gallup (2022) found that while almost half of the world's workers felt the burden of stress, working women in the US and Canada region were among the most stressed employees globally. Executive and senior leadership do need to be aware of these vulnerabilities as related to individual circumstance and intersectionalities where higher levels of engagement may be leading to burnout and not communicated due to internalized expectations of what leadership and the role entails. Leadership need to provide tangible resources, including time away. Time away, as a tangible resource, is, however, improbable when 50% of workers already do not have adequate staffing support. Therefore, one intervention on its own will not work unless the impacts of that intervention are fully understood and mitigated.

Relying on a concept of planetary health that seeks to bridge Indigenous and western lenses, it is imperative to consider individual and collective interventions and support from a holistic and epistemologically inclusive lens. For planetary health, as a concept, to truly provide a way forward that supports the health of the planet sustainably, it will also be necessary to go beyond dominant western worldviews that continue to contribute a capitalist mindset, whether subtly or overtly as in one that extracts from the planet that which exclusively benefits "man and human communities" (Redvers et al., 2020). Burnout and compromised well-being cannot be addressed sustainably from a worldview and mindset shaped by capitalist, extractive mindsets, and worldviews. A shifting in thinking must be informed by a worldview that truly centers caring, relationship, equity, and justice.

CONCLUSIONS

The author's differential experience with higher levels of engagement is the impetus to this inquiry. There is a heavy emphasis on engagement as a leadership value and practice, particularly discussed in the literature regarding leadership and followership within organizations. Gallup's polls are often referenced in discussions around engagement and used as the critical indicator of how people feel in their workplaces as relates to their well-being and satisfaction. Gallup (2022), however, points to other factors that can be seen as indicators of well-being. As Gallup (2022) has also found, it's not just the hours, work-life balance, or workplace location that lead to dissatisfaction and unhappiness. The report, in fact, has demonstrated that disengagement has risen with remote work or work from home. The significance of this chapter's inquiry, therefore, is manifold. I have striven to address the question of under what conditions higher engagement levels are productive of higher levels of dissatisfaction and burnout. I asked, what might we learn from these experiences to contemplate how we may lead better post-COVID-19? What do these experiences tell us in the scope of well-being, individually and collectively more broadly in aligning to planetary health?

Because burnout is simultaneously tracked as increasing over these years in review, particularly in 2021 and during COVID-19, higher levels of engagement may actually not be such a great thing at all times. Particularly where insufficient material and immaterial supports are not present, such higher levels of engagement may actually lead to burnout. We ought, instead, to consider centering the factors, such as, insufficient supports along with higher levels of engagement, the focus on productivity over deep listening as part of engagement in the organizations, engaging in a lop-sided one-directional manner over inquiry into the needs, ideas, and goals of individuals, and significantly inequality in treatment. If we are to navigate the issue of sustained stress to achieve the goals and changes we say we want to see, and not get sick, our well-being is priority.

In leading better, we might also see post-COVID-19 as the era for revisiting some of the assumptions around higher levels of engagement that have (1) not led to leadership practice that has actually been shown to increase engagement over time and (2) been shaped by thinking, being, doing, and seeing from a colonizing paradigm that leads to us becoming disengaged from ourselves, not just others, and sick. Now is the time to shift our thinking and practices in the way we lead with more holistic and inclusive paradigms, as advanced by traditional knowledge systems, such as Indigenous ways of being, doing, and seeing.

By becoming more resilient, adapting better, doing work more efficiently and more effectively, we may not end up as a civilization where we want to be (Krause, n.d.). The significance of exploring the various, and especially marginalized wisdom traditions, is to cultivate insights into how to support individual and collective well-being to align to and advance planetary health.

This inquiry is particularly critical as we contemplate how to create transformations at a time that demands that we work in ways that are different to pre-COVID-19. The way forward for better leadership involves cultivating individual and collective well-being that aligns with planetary health. This approach must (1) link the inner being to the outer world and in relationship, (2) foster inclusion and equity, and (3) bridge Indigenous wisdoms and traditional knowledges to support a holistic and integral perspective for larger systems alignment (Krause, 2023). Traditional knowledges can be learned from various sources globally. The significance of these wisdoms is the emphasis on symbiotic relationships whereby individual thriving is understood as related to collective thriving and part of the web of interconnections of all life held within our planetary system.

References

Basso, F., & Krpan, D. (February 2023). The Wiser framework of behavioural change interventions for mindful human flourishing. *The Lancet Planetary Health, 7*(2). https://doi.org/10.1016/S2542-5196(22)00336-9

Bennett, T. C. B., Maynard, N., Cochran, P., Gough, R., Lynn, K., Maldonado, J., Voggesser, G., Wotkyns, S., & Cozzetto, K. (2014). Chapter 12: Indigenous peoples, lands, and resources: Climate change impacts in the United States: The third National Climate Assessment. In J. M. Melillo, T. C. Richmond, & G. W. Yohe (Eds.), *Climate change impacts in the United States: The third national climate assessment* (pp. 297–317). USA Global Research Program.

Forbs. (June 2022). *Gallup shows what drives engagement (with E. Mosely)*. https://www.forbes.com/sites/ericmosley/2022/06/14/gallup-shows-what-drives-engagement/?sh=65c2428a3734

Gallup. (2022). *State of the global workplace 2022 report: The voice of the world's employees*. Washington, DC: Employee engagement and life evaluation. Gallop.

Gostin, L., Meier, B., Thomas, R., Magar, V., & Ghebreyesus, T. (2018). 70 years of human rights in global health: Drawing on a contentious past to secure a hopeful future. *Lancet, 392*(10165), 2731–2735. https://doi.org/10.1016/S0140-6736(18)32997-0

Holst, J. (2020). Global health—Emergence, hegemonic trends and biomedical reductionism. *Globalization and Health, 16*(1), 42. https://doi.org/10.1186/s12992-020-00573-4

Hoogeveen, D., et al. (February 2023). On the possibility of decolonising planetary health: Exploring new geographies for collaboration. *The Lancet Planetary Health, 7*(2). https://doi.org/10.1016/S2542-5196(22)00336-9

Ife, J. (2016). *Community development in an uncertain world: Vision, analysis and practice* (2nd ed). Cambridge University Press.

Jamison, D., Breman, J., Measham, A., Alleyne, G., Claeson, M., Evans, D., et al. (2013). Global health 2035: A world converging within a generation. *Lancet, 382*(9908), 1898–1955. https://doi.org/10.1016/S0140-6736(13)62105-4

Kincentric. (2022). *Stability is an illusion—Take a closer look*. Global trends in employee engagement 2022: Research highlights. A Spencer Stuart Company. https://www.kincentric.com/

Krause, W. (2022). Diversity, equity and inclusion as a Fertile Foundation for workplace well-being, optimal performance, and planetary health. In J. Marques & S. Dhiman (Eds.), *Diversity, equity and inclusion as a leadership strategy* (pp. 263–279). Springer. https://doi.org/10.1007/978-3-030-95652-3_16

Krause, W. (2023). Global leadership practices for planetary health. In S. Dhiman, J. Marques, J. Schmieder-Ramirez, & P. G. Malakyan (Eds.), *Handbook of global leadership and followership: Integrating the best leadership theory and practice.* Springer.

Krause, W. (n.d). http://wandakrause.com

Kulikowski, K. (2022). Measuring the personal perspective on work engagement: An empirical exploration of the self-anchoring work engagement scale in Poland. *Evidence-based HRM: A global forum for empirical scholarship.*

Kuok, A. C. H., & Taormina, R. J. (2017). Work engagement: Evolution of the concept and a new inventory. *Psychological Thought, 10*(2), 262–287. https://doi.org/10.23668/psycharchives.1866

Lancet Planetary Health. (March 2023). Pandemic preparedness on all fronts. *The Lancet Planetary Health, 7*(2). https://doi.org/10.1016/S2542-5196(23)00030-X

Prescott, S., & Logan, A. (2019). Narrative medicine meets planetary health: Mindsets matter in the Anthropocene. *Challenges, 10*(17), 1–26. https://doi.org/10.3390/challe10010017

Redvers, N. et al. (2022). The determinants of planetary health: An Indigenous consensus perspective. *Lancet Planet Health, 6*(2), e156–e163. https://doi.org/10.1016/S2542-5196(21)00030-5

Redvers, N., Poelina, A., Schultz, C., Kobei, D. M., Githaiga, C., Perdrisat, M., Prince, D., et al. (2020). Indigenous natural and first law in planetary health. *Challenges, 11*(2), 29. MDPI AG. https://doi.org/10.3390/challe11020029

Song, H.-D., Hong, A. J., & Jo, Y. (2021). Psychometric investigation of the Utrecht work engagement scale-17 using the Rasch measurement model. *Psychological Reports, 124*(3), 1384–1411. https://doi.org/10.1177/0033294120922494

Ubalijoro, E., & Lee, S. (2022). Homo Ubuntu leadership for the twenty-first century. In G. Perruci (Ed.), *The study and practice of global leadership* (pp. 51–66). Emerald Insight.

UN Committee for Development. (2018). Policy, report on the twentieth plenary session. Supplement No. 13 (E/ 2018/33). United Nations. https://sustainabledevelopment.un.org/content/documents/2754713_July_PM_2_Leaving_no_one_behind_Summary_from_UN_Committee_for_Development_Policy.pdf

Wahl, D. C. (2006). Design for human and planetary health: A transdisciplinary approach to sustainability. In *Management of natural resources, sustainable development and ecological hazards.* D. C. Wahl Centre for the Study of Natural Design, University of Dundee, Scotland, UK. WIT Transactions on Ecology and the Environment (Vol. 99). WIT Press. https://doi.org/10.2495/RAV060281

Whitmee, S., Haines, A., Beyrer, C., Boltz, F., Capon, A. G., & Dias, B. (2015). Safeguarding human health in the Anthropocene epoch: Report. Lancet commission. *The Rockefeller Foundation-Lancet Commission on Planetary Health, 386*(10007-P19732028). https://doi.org/10.1016/S0140-6736(15)60901-1

Wilson, S. (2008). *Research is ceremony: Indigenous research methods.* Fernwood Publishing.

CHAPTER 22

Employee Boundary Management Practices and Challenges

Amy Tong Zhao

INTRODUCTION

Conceptualizations of Boundary Management and Blurring Boundary

Boundary management refers to the strategy of making decisions and taking actions in order to deliberately separate or blur the lines both time and location among different domains of one's life (Allen et al., 2014; Ashforth et al., 2000; Olson-Buchanan & Boswell, 2006; Rothbard & Ollier-Malaterre, 2016). With limited time and attention, employees have to make decisions about how to divide personal and professional domains. Employees navigate the boundary between work and non-work-related activities, such as assigning different keys and calendars (Nippert-Eng, 1996) or temporally segment the work-home boundaries with rigorous tight schedules (Kreiner et al., 2009); in contrast, employees blur the boundary by integrating work and non-work issues, for instance, placing family photos at the workplace (Byron & Laurence, 2015), bringing the family to an annual corporate picnic, responding to a client's urgent request via email during weekends (Ticona, 2015), or engaging in social interactions with colleagues (Dumas et al., 2013).

Nonetheless, individuals only have limited autonomy over their boundaries (Clark, 2000) since their employers' expectations may be different from

---

A. T. Zhao (✉)
Department of Organization & Strategic Management, Guanghua School of Management, Peking University, Beijing, China
e-mail: amyzhaotong@pku.edu.cn

© The Author(s), under exclusive license to Springer Nature Switzerland AG 2023
J. Marques (ed.), *The Palgrave Handbook of Fulfillment, Wellness, and Personal Growth at Work*,
https://doi.org/10.1007/978-3-031-35494-6_22

employees' personal priorities (Capitano & Greenhaus, 2018; Derks et al., 2015; Huyghebaert-Zouaghi et al., 2022), thereby leading to a commonplace of boundary blurring. At present, the most popular online social networks (OSNs), such as Facebook, Twitter, Instagram, and WeChat, are widespread in both personal and business settings (Leonardi & Vaast, 2017; Ollier-Malaterre et al., 2013, 2019; Song et al., 2019; Thomala, 2023; Utz, 2015; Wilson et al., 2012), which has made professional/personal boundary become more blurred (Bartels et al., 2019).

Origins of Boundary Management

Role Theory. Human beings naturally segment and maintain domains by different boundaries in daily lives (Nippert-Eng, 1996; Zerubavel, 1993). Prior studies have mostly relied on role theory to understand the blurring boundaries between work and family issues (Biddle, 1986; Kahn et al., 1964; Katz & Kahn, 1978). Typically, roles are confined to specific locations and times, and are more relevant at particular times and days of the week. For instance, during the weekdays, the role of being an employee is more likely to be played in the office, while the role of being a family member happens at home during evenings and weekends. By clearly defining the expected behaviors for each role and building the basis for communications with others, boundaries around work and family can be a source of order for individuals. However, the boundaries can also create conflict by complicating the transition between roles. When the roles associated with belonging to one group conflict with those associated with belonging to another group, inter-role conflict occurs (Kahn et al., 1964).

Boundary theory is concerned with the transitions between roles. A number of studies have examined how role identities can be navigated across domains (Ashforth et al., 2000; Nippert-Eng, 1995), so that one integrates or segments with all roles at work or home similarly (Rothbard & Ollier-Malaterre, 2016). Ashforth et al. (2000) characterized role transitions into micro and macro dimensions. Micro transitions are periodic shifts that occur often (such as daily commute between home and work), as opposed to macro transitions, which are unusual and radical shift (such as a job promotion). Studies have consistently revealed that role conflict is detrimental, and it is associated with outcomes of negative emotion (Fisher & Gitelson, 1983; Kahn et al., 1964; Kreiner et al., 2006), emotions of anxiety (Zhao & Yu, 2023), and even embarrassment, if employees are obliged to cope with or maintain multiple roles (Gross & Stone, 1964). These studies are based on the assumption that role blurring can create tensions and intrusions that exacerbate the transition difficulty in highly integrated roles (Ashforth et al., 2000; Rothbard et al., 2005).

Self-presentation Theory. Until recently, scholars began to use self-presentation theory to explain online blurring boundary when social media is permeated in people's everyday life (Zhao & Yu, 2023). Self-presentation theory (Goffman, 1959) posits that people are self-selected to present the content to others; humans are actors who present themselves to various audiences on a daily basis and they utilize tactics of managing their impressions to maintain coherence among different situations. The term "front-stage" refers to interactions with others in public or professional occasions, while "back-stage" enables people to become relaxed and leisurely. Being front-stage differs from being back-stage for most individuals, for front-stage may cause employees to feel uneasy regarding how to deal with and expose personal lives and emotions.

According to Goffman, the boundaries between the front-stage and the back-stage of daily life self-representation begin to blur. However, self-presentation in daily life must be placed in the context of a specific boundary, that is, people adopt different impression management strategies in different contexts. This is correlated with another key concept "audience segregation", which is also proposed by Goffman. Audience segregation is the idea that when people are confronted with one or a group of people to present themselves, they do not want another person or a different group of people to barge in. Ideally, successful audience segregation requires at least two specific prerequisites: one is that the audience is identifiable; and the second is that the audience can be segregated. In everyday life, these two preconditions are often manageable. However, in the social media era, both of these specific premises are being threatened and challenged. Boundary management in the form of awareness, effort, and competence is needed if employees attempt to ensure specific disclosure reaching the right audiences across the proper boundaries (Hogan, 2010).

Goffman argues that the primary motivation for impression management is, on the one hand, conformity to social or expectations of social approval and control over the outcome of the interaction, so that the interpersonal interaction goes smoothly, and on the other hand to obtain appreciation or evaluation in one's favor (Tedeschi et al., 1971). Through impression management, people aim to make others perceive their public identity that is in line with their desired self-image (Baumeister et al., 1989). It has also been argued that people performing impression management are motivated by exerting interpersonal influence, constructing personal identity and maintaining self-esteem; At the same time, to influence others in order to achieve their purposes, such as gaining appraisal, friendship, reputation, etc. (Leary & Kowalski, 1990).

An individual reveals his or her self-image to others in a way of self-presentation (Muraven et al., 2000). People have the desire to reveal themselves in order to gain acceptance and establish interpersonal relationships. The desire to communicate identity signals is an important way to satisfy self-presentation. However, online blurring boundaries without segmenting audiences challenges the consistent role's identity and self-presentation images. When different interpersonal relationships and interaction situations in daily life are brought together in the super social platform such as on Facebook or

WeChat, employees not only have to self-present to friends at the same time and try to make consistent images of themselves, but also have to deal with the possible conflicts between multiple self-images to different audiences. In this way, when employees post to their WeChat "moment", they will have difficulty adjusting audience reaction and consequent performance obstacles, which will lead to a series of "embarrassing" events for the themselves.

Key Antecedents and Outcomes of Boundary Management

Previous studies have investigated both antecedent and outcome variations in boundary practices. From individual level, they have different preferences for work-home domain segmentation, which will affect employee outcomes such as work-home conflicts, job satisfaction and stress (Kossek & Lautsch, 2012; Kreiner et al., 2006; Methot & LePine, 2016; Rothbard et al., 2005).

From organization level, companies are different in their segmenting policies and job demands, which will influence the level of person-situation fit (Adkins & Premeaux, 2014; Capitano & Greenhaus, 2018), and thus bring difficulties for employees to manage boundaries (Olson-Buchanan & Boswell, 2006). An employee who is regularly on and off work will generally have a high degree of segmentation between the duties at home and at work. Employees may be required to be on call at specific times under the formal rules of their employers. In addition, informal norms are found outside of formal policies. Companies may provide communication devices to employees that expand an informal norm while also adding formal work norms. Companies set the expectation that employees will be available at all times when they give employees communication tools. Richardson and Benbunan-Fich (2011) have investigated the effect of organizational deployment of wireless email devices and laptops. According to their findings, when the company provides or paid for the communication device, employees utilized it more frequently and for longer periods of time than they otherwise would have. Thus, the level of an employee's work-life integration may depend on workplace expectations and rules as well as personal preferences. The Internet and other technology mediated devices may assist the transitions between borders or even blur the boundaries between work and home.

Besides demands and regulations of the workplace, as well as individual choices, some country-level factors could also dictate the level of segmentation versus integration. For example, Ashforth et al. (2000) suggested that an individual's culture may have an impact on how roles are segmented and integrated, as well as how roles are transitioned between one to another. That is, individuals from collectivism, low masculine, high-uncertainty-acceptance, and/or low-power-distance cultures tend to integrate than to segment roles, which can be specifically predicted by the culture where an individual is embedded.

Forms of Blurring Boundary

Blurring Boundary Between Workplace and Home

Foremost, scholars investigated blurring boundary to have a fundamental understanding of how work and family responsibilities are intertwined, and much of the extant studies on boundary management are anchored on the line between off-site personal and work life (e.g., Leonardi & Vaast, 2017; McFarland & Ployhart, 2015; Otonkorpi-Lehtoranta et al., 2022). The boundary between home and work may result in a segmented environment where the work environment is separate from the home environment in terms of time and place, or it may result in an integrated environment where an employee works from home and mixes family obligations with work.

Boundary management is needed when an employee's capacity to handle the demands of family life is compromised by the demands of the workplace. Researchers have looked at a variety of elements that may cause blurring boundary between workplace and home, such as work schedules, family obligations, and job features (see Eby et al., 2005 for a review). Among them, the most related concept is work-family-conflict. Kahn et al. (1964) and Greenhaus and Beutell (1985) defined work-family conflict as a particular type of inter-role conflict when work and family boundary are mutually incongruent. Research on work-family conflict has dominated the literature on work-family relationships, and one strategy for reducing work-family conflict is adapting to successful role transitions.

Extant studies have also explained the variations of employee preferences for managing the work/nonwork boundary between off-site personal and work life, such as work-from-home (e.g., Leonardi & Vaast, 2017; McFarland & Ployhart, 2015; Otonkorpi-Lehtoranta et al., 2022). However, blurring boundary makes it difficult for one to disengage from one role completely to focus on another, leading to difficulties in decoupling the roles psychologically. For example, Derks and Bakker (2014) found blurring boundary between life roles undermines employees' psychological detachment that leads to burnout, and they are hard to recuperate from work. As such, blurring boundary may impede employees' concentration on immersion in work related activities by their duties as employees and duties of family members (Leroy, 2009). This is also in line with Greenhaus and Beutell's (1985) study which showed that the overlap between work and personal issues is associated with lower work satisfaction and performance. These imply that the self-presentation intentions and strategies of social media users are closely related to their psychological feelings.

Blurring Boundary Between Online and Offline

The tensions not merely between professional and personal life place, but also occur from offline to online domains (Greenhaus & Beutell, 1985; Kossek et al., 2012; Nippert-Eng, 1996; Park et al., 2011; Rothbard et al., 2005).

The use of communication devices has made it possible to complete job tasks outside of conventional office environments and out of conventional working hours. The capability of employees to combine work and personal life is affected in a variety of complex, sometimes conflicting ways by this flexibility and shift in connectivity. On the one hand, employees can easily access to work through work from home and outside of regular business hours, which may minimize work-related conflicts with family members because the degree of the incompatibility of responsibilities for family life and the office time are lower (e.g., Greenhaus & Beutell, 1985). For instance, an employee may work from home in the evening after taking time off for a children's school play, while awaiting house repairs which regularly in the afternoons. As a result, the Internet and other communication technologies may significantly improve a worker's capability to make a balance between work and personal life. On the other hand, there are also some border keepers who carefully guard work-family borders, and communication technologies may break their own rules to define boundary between the work and family issues without time borders, which may also bring negative responses from blurring boundary.

Online social networks (OSNs), such as Facebook, Twitter, Instagram, and WeChat, are widely used in both personal and business settings (Leonardi & Vaast, 2017; Ollier-Malaterre et al., 2013, 2019; Song et al., 2019; Utz, 2015; Wilson et al., 2012). This has profoundly changed professional/personal boundary management practices (Bartels et al., 2019). The online blurring of boundary can have mixed influences on employees' interrelationship and offline behaviors at workplace, since there are advantages, such as providing access to sharing private life after work with coworkers for a richer multiplex relationship (Haythornthwaite, 2001; Pratt & Rosa, 2003), social capital (Adler & Kwon, 2002; Huang & Liu, 2017), and newcomer socialization (Gonzalez et al., 2013).

Online social networks have made it more challenging for employees to navigate boundary online given that the popularity of people is more connected to social media (Kossek & Lautsch, 2012; Mazmanian et al., 2013). Technology and Internet conditions make it more normative that people exchange ideas and socialize via OSNs (Ollier-Malaterre et al., 2019; Park et al., 2011). By default, self-presentation on social media isn't tailored to the specific context or individual (McFarland & Ployhart, 2015; Ollier-Malaterre et al., 2013; Shi et al., 2014). Thus, the untailored self-disclosure not intended for a particular individual or the customs of the professional context is often associated with privacy concerns and anxiety (Reynolds, 2015). It's also perilous because employees don't have control over everything that is exposed online (Boyd, 2014). In sum, blurring boundary online enhances one's psychological burden and anxiety to maintain a good and consistent image.

Blurring the boundary online by adding a coworker, especially one's leader, to the social network platform is quite different from other informal off-site interactions (i.e., dinner or drinks). First, social media connecting is a timely instant interaction way. Due to the convenience of the Internet, social media make it easier to blur the temporal boundaries between work and nonwork time (Ollier-Malaterre et al., 2019). Second, spatial boundaries have also become vaguer because hierarchy among coworkers is less visible on social media (Bartels et al., 2019). For example, after adding one's leader to OSNs, an employee may not notice how much of their personal information is disclosed due to the unseen audience. Employees find it a dilemma to socialize with their coworkers or maintain exclusively professional connections online (Pillemer & Rothbard, 2018). Third, prior studies have shown that interrelations on personal social media can have a long-term social impact than a simple talk or greeting at the workplace because individuals would like to present more vivid and rich information about their unique personality and preference on social media (Phillips & Young, 2009; Song et al., 2019). Social media scholars have incorporated these features into studies and investigated the dilemma incurred by adding coworkers to OSNs (e.g., Frampton & Child, 2013; Huang & Liu, 2017; Marder et al., 2016).

However, few studies have investigated to underpin the consequences incurred by online boundary blurring (Rothbard et al., 2022). This is an important omission because the blurring of online boundary with coworkers may change their relationships at workplace and off-site work performance (Landers & Callan, 2014; Ollier-Malaterre et al., 2013). Ellison et al. (2007) found that many boundary-management behaviors have been observed across multiple domains for people who use social media intensively in a personal context, because the increasing self-disclosure may lead to the awareness of differences (e.g., values, attitudes, habits; Dumas et al., 2013; Harrison et al., 1998; Phillips et al., 2009). In addition, the greater the formal hierarchy gap is, the greater the visibility of other social media interactions (Leonardi & Vaast, 2017) could further exacerbate the concerns from the blurring boundary online (Liao et al., 2008). For example, Ellison and Boyd (2013) found that social media such as Twitter and Facebook imply fewer formal expectations than traditional business communications.

In sum, different from blurring boundary between workplace and home, which is more related to location boundary, the blurring boundary between online and offline is more concerned about time borders. Benefits include the flexibility to work overtime from home rather than at work, the flexibility to work from home while taking care of family obligations, and improved work-family balance. On the negative side, employees also claimed that family time was sacrificed for work and that the online connection devices are obtrusive. In line with this, Batt and Valcour (2003) discovered that while technology helps employees balance work and family obligations, it also causes more disturbances in the family sphere.

Concerns and Challenges About Blurring Boundary in the Workplace

Nowadays, social media deeply influences the boundary between work and life. The blurring of boundary can have concerns, such as bringing about privacy anxiety (Dumas et al., 2013; Methot et al., 2016), ruining one's professional evaluation among colleagues (Pillemer & Rothbard, 2018), and even impacting employees' career path (i.e., not being promoted or being fired; Ollier-Malaterre & Rothbard, 2015; Valentine et al., 2010). The use of communication technologies may make it easier for a person to move between domains, but excessive use may blur the lines between online and offline activities, especially if the person prefers a minimal degree of integration between the domains.

WeChat is the most frequently used OSN for both private and work-related activities in China (Thomala, 2023; Wang, 2016). An online survey conducted in 2021 suggested that around 80% of 2,566 people in China aged 16–64 are using WeChat, over half of them normally spend at least two hours a day on it, and one-quarter of them even spend more than four hours per day (Thomala, 2023). Compared with other OSNs, employees could have connections via WeChat for all sorts of purposes. People can upload text, pictures, or short videos on a social feature called "Moments" on WeChat and their friends can comment or "like" the post. In contrast, other OSNs may provide limited functions, which hinders the scope of our investigation. Finally, compared to other OSNs, real names are used more frequently on WeChat (Wang, 2016). In the following parts, I conclude some of the most cited concerns and challenges comes from the blurring boundary in the workplace.

First, blurring boundaries caused by the use of social media can bring psychological social media anxiety, a negative psychological state, which have been investigated as a key mechanism to influence employees' productivity and performance (Brown et al., 2005; Mulki et al., 2015; Staw & Barsade, 1993). Zhao and Yu (2023) recognized that an employee's psychological state of social media anxiety plays a key contingency mechanism between the online blurring boundary and work engagement, which is a delightful state that is associated with emotions of vigor, dedication, and immersion in one's job (Schaufeli & Bakker, 2004; Schaufeli et al., 2006). Employee work engagement is an important outcome and it has been studied widely in organizational and psychological research. Employees are more likely to do so if they felt that responding to coworkers outside of work hours was expected of them. The use of communication technology by employees has also been shown to mirror that of their managers and to correspond with their perceptions of organizational norms (Turner et al., 2006).

However, social media anxiety results from intrusions are resource-depleting which amplifies its negative effect on employees' work performance (Metiu & Rothbard, 2013). Anxiety represents an employee's experience of undesirable emotions (Seabrook et al., 2016), thus an employees' social media anxiety will distract employee attention from concentrating on their work when their life and work blend together, and thereby will reduce their work engagement. Since Facebook and WeChat allow individuals to post photos of social gatherings and to tag the "friends" accompanying them, anxiety caused by this public disclosure becomes more salient to others. When other colleagues are aware of other coworkers' friendships online, they are likely to fall into the emotion of envy and mental breaks, resulting in a distraction from work that they are inundated with information from using OSNs at work (Krasnova et al., 2013; Tandon et al., 2021). Further, employee's social media anxiety results from information distraction for the use of social media in nonwork-related areas. The widespread use of social media from the leisure to the work domain has influenced the internal organization and work practices (Leonardi & Vaast, 2017; Orhan et al., 2021). Leftheriotis and Giannakos (2014) demonstrated that social media is a noise to insurance personnel who use social media extensively for both pleasure and business purposes, which impairs their engagement in work.

Second, blurring boundary intensities employee's role conflicting and brings them difficulties in roles transition. Turkle (2011) has demonstrated how kids and teenagers worry about their parents' scarce attention when they pick them up after school, having dinner, or participating sporting activities because parents are on their phones. Parents are under pressure to respond job emails and other messages. This emphasizes the necessity to reconsider how organizational regulations and expectations concerning employees' availability and communication tools are used. Employees' devotion of time and effort to maintaining social relationships with coworkers on social media may blur employees' identification with the organization (Bartels et al., 2019), and thereby socioemotional goals may compromise pragmatic goals (Bridge & Baxter, 1992; Hobfoll, 2002). This logic is well supported by the study of Weiss and Cropanzano (1996), which posits that the negative emotions elicited by adverse working conditions demotivate and distract employees from doing their jobs (Elfenbein, 2007; Wajcman & Rose, 2011).

Last but not least, employees who are struggling with blurring boundary often encounter emotion and stress problems (e.g., Desrochers & Sargent, 2004; Kahn et al., 1964). Negative psychological well-being is the primary mechanism through which social media anxiety develops, which is particularly the case when the use of social media raises burnout or distraction in the workplace (Coker, 2011; Ninaus et al., 2021). Negative emotional experiences function as signals that things went wrong (Clore et al., 2001), therefore stimulating employees' cognitive processing in an attempt to address the problem and tackle their unpleasant emotions. (Lazarus, 1991). An increasing body of evidence suggests that negative emotions have harmful consequences for people's encouragement and behavior, including their persistence, effort, and job performance (Mulki et al., 2015; Seo et al., 2004; Staw & Barsade, 1993). As employees become focused on "fixing" their bad sentiments and consequently distracted from deliberate goal pursuit, the probability of their work engagement reduction increases when they continue to make cognitive efforts (Frijda, 1986; Keller et al., 2020; Schmidt et al., 2016). activating social media anxiety and by infusing negative emotion with resource depletion (Metiu & Rothbard, 2013).

Boundary Management Tactics

The growing use of social media enables boundary blurring to be a default setting, especially for knowledge-based employees (Holtgrewe, 2014; Kolb et al., 2012; Leonardi & Vaast, 2017; McFarland & Ployhart, 2015; Saura et al., 2022), thus personal and relational boundary blurring management skills will become even more important. Below I summarize some helpful tactics for individuals to smartly cope with blurring boundary and integrating roles based on existing studies.

Employee Personal Control

The control to manage technological disruptions was investigated as a mediator of the association between blurring boundary and work-family conflict (Adkins & Premeaux, 2014). Kossek et al. (2006) found that higher levels of segmentation and control over where and how work was conducted resulted in better levels of wellbeing for employees. Similarly, Kossek et al. (2012) discovered that people's methods for regulating the work-home border significantly differed. They discovered that the three main factors linked with boundary management were cross-role disruption behaviors, perceived control of borders, and identity centrality of work and family roles. For example, individuals differ in preference of blending work and personal issues (Mazmanian et al., 2013; Tammelin, 2018) or individuals who are excel at time management (Ollie-Malaterr et al., 2013) find blurring boundary online may not bring about social media anxiety. Employees who have more self-control over social media may have lower anxiety caused by the blurring boundary (Orhan et al., 2021) and thus, they are more likely to be engaged in their job. Specifically, people can have separate keys and contact books for work and home (Nippert-Eng, 1996) and can organize "no-disturbing slot" in their calendars (Kreiner et al., 2009). Some people maintain strict boundaries between work and home, with family members turning their communication devices off when they don't want to be interrupted, leaving cell phones behind, or simply not answering them (Wajcman et al., 2008). Moreover, employees may opt to withhold their phone numbers, limit their phone use to specific hours, or refrain from using their phones after working hours (Towers et al., 2006). Hughes and Parkes (2007) found the association between long-time working hours and job that interferes with family has been demonstrated to be moderated by personal control over work hours; in contrast, inability or unwillingness to control these interruptions will exacerbate negative outcomes of blurring boundary and intensity work-family conflicts.

Based on qualitative research with priests, Kreiner et al. (2009, p. 704) identified four categories of tactics people may use to design their ideal level of integration and style of work-home balance: behavioral, temporal, physical, and communication. Utilizing others (e.g., asking for help), utilizing technology (e.g., setting up multiple email contacts books), implementing category (e.g., prioritizing), and limiting differential intimacy (e.g., picking the particular aspects of personal family time that will/will not be intruded) are examples of behavioral tactics. Temporal tactics include managing work time (such as cutting off specific periods of time) and seeking relief (such as taking a big break from work/home commitments). Changing physical boundaries (such as establishing or removing barriers between the work and home realms), altering physical space (such as increasing or decreasing the physical distance between job and family issues), and controlling physical artifacts are examples of physical strategies. Communication methods include setting expectations, such as notifying people of expectations prior to boundary infractions, and addressing offenders (e.g., asking disrupters of boundaries during or after a boundary invasion).

Except for controlling the time and place of technology devices use, to achieve a desired boundary management, employees can also learn to regulate the emotions after work, especially when they experience unpleasant things or meet obstacles at work (i.e., emotion regulation; Gross, 1998). That is, boundary management tactics can also draw from theory on self-regulation to gain a deeper comprehension of employees' psychological state and transition. The strength model of self-control explains how exerting self-control depletes limited resources and influences the individual's performance of subsequent behaviors that supported by self-control (Baumeister et al., 2007). Generally, employees can use a variety of strategies to have a beneficial synergistic impact that lessens work-family conflict and the negative effect from blurring boundary (Kreiner et al., 2009).

Managing Relational Partners

Boundary management cannot be fully understood without considering the relational partner in which it occurs (Rothbard et al., 2022; Trefalt, 2013). Relationships at the workplace are essential as they not only function as ends in themselves (Gersick et al., 2000) but also the means through which job task is often completed. Employees can also manage boundary issues through proactive ways in working with related partners. For example, employees can express that they prefer to be contacted by e-mails rather than cell phones during weekends and off-work time. In comparison to using cell phones, using e-mails stay linked to work-related issues may be less intrusive to employees. The former is regarded to require more immediate attention and may make employees feel less in control, while the latter are thought to be depending on employee's choice of when to respond to the e-mail. Besides, employee-leader relationships (i.e., their perceived leader support for help to cope with emotional reactions; Eisenberger et al., 2002) may also have an impact on employee performance by acting as a boundary condition on the proposed relationship between blurring boundary and work engagement (Jehn & Shah, 1997). Perceived leader support is associated with personal exchanges, and is expected to provide sentiment comfort (Soares & Mosquera, 2019; Toegel et al., 2013).

Sturges (2012) proposed the proactive, self-initiated, and goal-oriented actions as "crafting" behaviors. Physical, cognitive, and relational crafting activity were recognized as three distinct types. Physical crafting includes time crafting (e.g., getting off work in time for family gathering), locational crafting (e.g., working from home to handle job-related issues), seeking for a job (e.g., choosing a job that supports work-home balance), and reducing travel time (e.g., relocating close to one's place of employment to shorten distance). Cognitive crafting includes chasing work-life balance (for example, by telling others it can be achieved), prioritized (for example, by justifying time spent at work), and reach via compromise (e.g., sacrificing balance now for future gain). Managing connections at work (such as utilizing relationships with coworkers to promote work-family balance) and managing relationships outside of work, e.g., using relationships with family to promote work-home balance, are both examples of relational craftsmanship.

Organizational Support

Organizations may provide kind advice among co-workers on work-life balances and on OSNs use between business contexts and personal life segmentations. For example, organizations could encourage employees to use the Enterprise WeChat (a version of WeChat for enterprise use) at work and personal WeChat after work, which may facilitate to better control the strength of employees' anxiety caused by blurring boundary online. Although online social media such as Facebook, Twitter, WhatsApp, and WeChat allow rich textual and visual connections between employees and their leaders, they also clearly highlight the mix of casual and professional role identities. Managers nowadays are frequently expressing their concerns about the downsides of OSNs use on employees' well-being and productivity (Luqman et al., 2021; Zhao & Yu, 2023). As a result, the way to utilize social media wisely so that employees can manage it rather than be dominated by it needs further exploration. Therefore, boundary management online becomes such a vital skill that deserves much attention (Jämsen et al., 2022; Kossek et al., 2021; Oksanen et al., 2021). As many organizations and professions impose norms or policies regarding work-life integration to their employees (Foucreault et al., 2016) or encourage employees to respond instantly through social media (Ticona & Mateescu, 2018), I suggest that organizations raise awareness among employers and organizations of the challenges of managing blurring boundary between workplace and home, and between offline and online as well.

Following Park et al. (2011), people who used technology less at home also reported feeling more psychologically detached from their jobs, which has been linked to a number of advantageous outcomes (Sonnentag, 2012). In other words, the more technology devices a person possesses, the more methods there are for them to stay linked to their jobs, preventing work-life separation. Another practical implication for organizations is to set rules on how much technology use is mandatory or encouraged outside of work hours.

Measures of Blurring Boundary

Extant research has developed many scales to capture blurring boundary. As an example, to evaluate the blurring of roles, Desrochers et al. (2005) designed The Work-Family Integration-Blurring Scale (WFIBS), with sample items such as "It is frequently difficult to distinguish where my work life ends and my family life begins" and "I tend to combine my job and family obligations when I work at home." The WFIBS has been utilized in various research to capture integration and segmentation implement (Ilies et al., 2009; Kossek et al., 2012).

The work-family role integration-blurring scale has been used in several research to measure integration and segmentation (Ilies et al., 2009; Kossek et al., 2012; Li et al., 2013). The frequency of transitions between the family and work domains has been examined in a number of research on boundary management. A measure of interdomain transitions was developed by Matthews et al. (2010) to count the frequency of physical and mental transitions. They contended that interdomain transition should take the place of permeability since it is a concept that is better theoretically supported. Moreover, they proposed that flexibility should allow for the movement across borders and, as such, act as a precursor to interdomain transitions. The amount of physical and mental changes from one domain to another is how they define interdomain transitions. They use questions like "How frequently have you considered family obligations while at work?" or "How often have you gone to work on the weekend to meet work responsibilities?".

Some scholars have looked into concepts related to boundary management so-called interruptions or distractions (e.g., Cardenas et al., 2004; Kossek et al., 2012). Intrusions from one role into another are referred to as interruptions. The two types of interruptions were measured by Kossek et al. (2012) using a scale developed by Kossek and Lautsch (2008) and originally named as work-family integration. A sample item depicting nonwork-to-work interruptions is "I respond to personal communications (e.g., email, texts, and phone calls) during work," and a sample item describing work interrupting non-work is "I regularly bring work home." In fact, there are various ways to evaluate interruptions. Some other scholar's evaluations concentrated on the quantity or kind of interruptions. For instance, Glavin and Schieman (2012) utilized the following example item to demonstrate how role blurring is measured: "How frequently do coworkers, managers, supervisors, customers, or clients contact you regarding work-related issues after hours? Add all calls from your phone, mobile phone, beeper, pager, fax, and email that require a response." These items are similar to those who used to record interruptions and a lack of psychological distance from one's job.

Other scales measure how people react to cross-role interruptions (e.g., items such as "When I work at home, distractions often make it difficult to attend to my work"; Desrochers et al., 2005). Olson-Buchanan and Boswell (2006) examined response to interruptions in two directions (e.g., "I get upset or annoyed when I am interrupted by my personal/family life at work," and "I get upset or annoyed when I am interrupted by work-related problems during my 'off-work' hours").

Besides, enactment of integration and segmentation has been evaluated in a variety of ways. To capture actual behavior rather than desire, Powell and Greenhaus (2010) changed the items created by Kreiner (2006) (e.g., "I keep work life at work"). In addition, a 12-item questionnaire was created by Kossek et al. (2006) to evaluate their border management method ("the degree to which one strives to separate boundaries between work and home roles"; p. 350). Examples of items include "I prefer to not discuss about my family concerns with most individuals I work with," and "I only take care of personal demands at work when I am 'on break' or during my lunch hour.". More recently, Zhao and Yu (2023) developed a 4-item scale adapted from the Facebook Blurring Scale (Rothbard et al., 2022) to directly measure participants' perception of online blurring boundary when interacting with their immediate leader on WeChat. The wording of the scale was modified from "*adding coworkers onto Facebook*" to "*interacting with my immediate leader on WeChat*". An example item was "Interacting with my immediate leader on WeChat blurs my personal and professional life".

DISCUSSIONS AND CONCLUSIONS

Conclusions

This chapter reviewed the boundary management literature by using the construct of blurring boundary, and its antecedents and outcomes. Two forms of blurring boundaries are identified and some concerns and challenges about blurring boundaries are discussed. Extant literature has identified the importance of boundary management to employees' performance and how social media use has changed employees' work-life balance. This chapter addressed the role of blurring boundary to employees' psychical and psychological well-being by identifying constructs of work-family conflict and social media anxiety. With this outcome, the challenge for most organizations is the implementation of work-from-home and the use of OSNs. However, the challenge of blurring boundary can be overcome by using some tactics including increasing employee personal control, managing relational partners and offering organizational support. The blurring boundary can result in role transition difficulty and social media anxiety for the employee, which may lead to psychological stress, loss of work engagement, and a threat to productivity. Workplace spirituality can lead to lack of spiritual intelligence and spiritual capital. Identifying and managing blurring boundaries will not only foster workplace engagement but also enhance employee performance and productivity for the organization.

The development of metrics that more accurately capture and discriminate the physical, behavioral, and psychological components of integration/segmentation may be important as research on boundary management tactics and methods progresses. One example of a particular segmentation technique within the psychological realm is psychological separation from one's job. Throughout these several aspects, people may have distinct preferences and tendencies to enforce limits. A global evaluation may be helpful in certain situations, but there may also be instances when more specific data is required, just as there were in the examples of job satisfaction and work-family conflict.

Future Research Directions

Most quantitative studies on the dynamics of work and family boundaries has been conducted in single-source, cross-sectional settings, except for work on psychological detachment from job, which is mostly related to the stress and recovery literature. There is a need for research that more accurately depicts the changing nature of boundary management. Inspired by naturalistic observation research (Campos et al., 2009), studies that based on events and capture boundary transitional phases would be very promising in this sense.

Moreover, the extant literature on boundary management has largely ignored the relational partner to whom employees disclose personal lives, which is a pity because boundary management strategy is relying on the relationship basis (Trefalt, 2013). For example, employees are more likely to interact online with their peer workers than with their supervisors, and compared with male supervisors, employees tend to disclose more to their female supervisors (Rothbard et al., 2022). As such, other members of the social system can influence how well people are able to use their preferred boundary-management techniques, e.g., employee's spouse, supervisor, coworkers, and team members. As an example, Hahn and Dormann (2013) found a negative correlation between one spouse's preference for integration and the other spouse's detachment. Moreover, the presence of children buffered the relationship.

Finally, although there is a growing body of recent research that focuses on cross-national and cross-cultural work-family research (Poelmans et al., 2013), research on boundary practices and challenges has only been discussed in Western countries. Personal blurring boundary management and its application to well-being and employees' performance is as complex as they are important to individuals and organizations in different contexts (Berkelaar & Buzzanell, 2015; Cao et al., 2016; Leftheriotis & Giannakos, 2014; Van

Zoonen et al., 2016). Thus, future research can identify the difference of boundary management practices across countries and cultures.

References

Adkins, C. L., & Premeaux, S. A. (2014). The use of communication technology to manage work-home boundaries. *Journal of Behavioral and Applied Management*, 15(2), 82–100.

Adler, P. S., & Kwon, S. W. (2002). Social capital: Prospects for a new concept. *Academy of Management Review*, 27(1), 17–40.

Allen, T. D., Cho, E., & Meier, L. L. (2014). Work–family boundary dynamics. *Annual Review of Organizational Psychology and Organizational Behavior*, 1(1), 99–121.

Ashforth, B. E., Kreiner, G. E., & Fugate, M. (2000). All in a day's work: Boundaries and micro role transitions. *Academy of Management Review*, 25(3), 472–491.

Bartels, J., Van Vuuren, M., & Ouwerkerk, J. W. (2019). My colleagues are my friends: The role of Facebook contacts in employee identification. *Management Communication Quarterly*, 33(3), 307–328.

Batt, R., & Valcour, P. M. (2003). Human resources practices as predictors of work-family outcomes and employee turnover. *Industrial Relations: A Journal of Economy and Society*, 42(2), 189–220.

Baumeister, R. F., Tice, D. M., & Hutton, D. G. (1989). Self-presentational motivations and personality differences in self-esteem. *Journal of Personality*, 57(3), 547–579.

Baumeister, R. F., Vohs, K. D., & Tice, D. M. (2007). The strength model of self-control. *Current Directions in Psychological Science*, 16(6), 351–355.

Berkelaar, B. L., & Buzzanell, P. M. (2015). Online employment screening and digital career capital: Exploring employers' use of online information for personnel selection. *Management Communication Quarterly*, 29(1), 84–113.

Biddle, B. J. (1986). Recent developments in role theory. *Annual Review of Sociology*, 12(1), 67–92.

Boyd, D. (2014). *It's complicated: The social lives of networked teens*. Yale University Press.

Bridge, K., & Baxter, L. A. (1992). Blended relationships: Friends as work associates. *Western Journal of Communication*, 56(3), 200–225.

Brown, S. P., Westbrook, R. A., & Challagalla, G. (2005). Good cope, bad cope: Adaptive and maladaptive coping strategies following a critical negative work event. *Journal of Applied Psychology*, 90(4), 792–798.

Byron, K., & Laurence, G. A. (2015). Diplomas, photos, and tchotchkes as symbolic self-representations: understanding employees' individual use of symbols. *Academy of Management Journal*, 58(1), 298–323.

Campos, B., Graesch, A. P., Repetti, R., Bradbury, T., & Ochs, E. (2009). Opportunity for interaction? A naturalistic observation study of dual-earner families after work and school. *Journal of Family Psychology*, 23(6), 798.

Cao, X., Guo, X., Vogel, D., & Zhang, X. (2016). Exploring the influence of social media on employee work performance. *Internet Research*, 26(2), 529–545.

Capitano, J., & Greenhaus, J. H. (2018). When work enters the home: Antecedents of role boundary permeability behavior. *Journal of Vocational Behavior*, 109, 87–100.

Cardenas, R. A., Major, D. A., & Bernas, K. H. (2004). Exploring work and family distractions: Antecedents and outcomes. *International Journal of Stress Management, 11*(4), 346.
Clark, S. C. (2000). Work/family border theory: A new theory of work/family balance. *Human Relations, 53*(6), 747–770.
Clore, G. L., Gasper, K., & Garvin, E. (2001). Affect as information. In J. P. Forgas (Ed.), *Handbook of affect and social cognition* (pp. 121–144). Lawrence Erlbaum Associates Inc.
Coker, B. L. S. (2011). Freedom to surf: The positive effects of workplace internet leisure browsing. *New Technology, Work and Employment, 26*(3), 238–247.
Derks, D., & Bakker, A. B. (2014). Smartphone use, work–home interference, and burnout: A diary study on the role of recovery. *Applied Psychology, 63*(3), 411–440.
Derks, D., Van Duin, D., Tims, M., & Bakker, A. B. (2015). Smartphone use and work–home interference: The moderating role of social norms and employee work engagement. *Journal of Occupational and Organizational Psychology, 88*(1), 155–177.
Desrochers, S., Hilton, J. M., & Larwood, L. (2005). Preliminary validation of the work-family integration-blurring scale. *Journal of Family Issues, 26*(4), 442–466.
Desrochers, S., & Sargent, L. D. (2004). Boundary/border theory and work-family integration1. *Organization Management Journal, 1*(1), 40–48.
Dumas, T. L., Phillips, K. W., & Rothbard, N. P. (2013). Getting closer at the company party: Integration experiences, racial dissimilarity, and workplace relationships. *Organization Science, 24*(5), 1377–1401.
Eby, L. T., Casper, W. J., Lockwood, A., Bordeaux, C., & Brinley, A. (2005). Work and family research in IO/OB: Content analysis and review of the literature (1980–2002). *Journal of Vocational Behavior, 66*(1), 124–197.
Eisenberger, R., Stinglhamber, F., Vandenberghe, C., Sucharski, I. L., & Rhoades, L. (2002). Perceived supervisor support: Contributions to perceived organizational support and employee retention. *Journal of Applied Psychology, 87*(3), 565–573.
Elfenbein, H. A. (2007). Emotion in organizations: A review and theoretical integration. *Academy of Management Annals, 1*(1), 315–386.
Ellison, N. B., & Boyd, D. (2013). Sociality through social network sites. In W. H. Dutton (Ed.), *The Oxford handbook of internet studies* (pp. 151–172). Oxford University Press.
Ellison, N. B., Steinfield, C., & Lampe, C. (2007). The benefits of Facebook "friends": Social capital and college students' use of online social network sites. *Journal of Computer-Mediated Communication, 12*(4), 1143–1168.
Fisher, C. D., & Gitelson, R. (1983). A meta-analysis of the correlates of role conflict and ambiguity. *Journal of Applied Psychology, 68*(2), 320–333.
Foucreault, A., Ménard, J., & Stevens, C. (2016). A diary study on work-related perseverative cognition and employees' need for recovery: The role of emotional support from family and neuroticism. *International Journal of Psychological Studies, 8*(4), 1–77.
Frampton, B. D., & Child, J. T. (2013). Friend or not to friend: Coworker Facebook friend requests as an application of communication privacy management theory. *Computers in Human Behavior, 29*(6), 2257–2264.
Frijda, N. H. (1986). *The emotions*. Cambridge University Press.

Gersick, C. J., Dutton, J. E., & Bartunek, J. M. (2000). Learning from academia: The importance of relationships in professional life. *Academy of Management Journal*, 43(6), 1026–1044.

Glavin, P., & Schieman, S. (2012). Work–family role blurring and work–family conflict: The moderating influence of job resources and job demands. *Work and Occupations*, 39(1), 71–98.

Goffman, E. (1959). *The presentation of self in everyday life*. Anchor Books.

Gonzalez, E. S., Leidner, D. E., Riemenschneider, C., & Koch, H. (2013). The impact of internal social media usage on organization socialization and commitment. *Proceedings of the 34th International Conference on Information Systems* (ICIS2013), Milan.

Greenhaus, J. H., & Beutell, N. J. (1985). Sources of conflict between work and family roles. *Academy of Management Review*, 10(1), 76–88.

Gross, E., & Stone, G. P. (1964). Embarrassment and the analysis of role requirements. *American Journal of Sociology*, 70(1), 1–15.

Gross, J. J. (1998). The emerging field of emotion regulation: An integrative review. *Review of General Psychology*, 2(3), 271–299.

Hahn, V. C., & Dormann, C. (2013). The role of partners and children for employees' psychological detachment from work and well-being. *Journal of Applied Psychology*, 98(1), 26.

Harrison, D. A., Price, K. H., & Bell, M. P. (1998). Beyond relational demography: Time and the effects of surface-and deep-level diversity on work group cohesion. *Academy of Management Journal*, 41(1), 96–107.

Haythornthwaite, C. (2001). Exploring multiplexity: Social network structures in a computer-supported distance learning class. *The Information Society*, 17(3), 211–226.

Hobfoll, S. E. (2002). Social and psychological resources and adaptation. *Review of General Psychology*, 6(4), 307–324.

Hogan, B. (2010). The presentation of self in the age of social media: Distinguishing performances and exhibitions online. *Bulletin of Science, Technology & Society*, 30(6), 377–386.

Holtgrewe, U. (2014). New new technologies: The future and the present of work in information and communication technology. *New Technology, Work and Employment*, 29(1), 9–24.

Huang, L. V., & Liu, P. L. (2017). Ties that work: Investigating the relationships among coworker connections, work-related Facebook utility, online social capital, and employee outcomes. *Computers in Human Behavior*, 72, 512–524.

Hughes, E. L., & Parkes, K. R. (2007). Work hours and well-being: The roles of work-time control and work–family interference. *Work & Stress*, 21(3), 264–278.

Huyghebaert-Zouaghi, T., Morin, A. J., Fernet, C., Austin, S., & Gillet, N. (2022). Longitudinal profiles of work-family interface: Their individual and organizational predictors, personal and work outcomes, and implications for onsite and remote workers. *Journal of Vocational Behavior*, 134, 103695.

Ilies, R., Wilson, K. S., & Wagner, D. T. (2009). The spillover of daily job satisfaction onto employees' family lives: The facilitating role of work-family integration. *Academy of Management Journal*, 52(1), 87–102.

Jämsen, R., Sivunen, A., & Blomqvist, K. (2022). Employees' perceptions of relational communication in full-time remote work in the public sector. *Computers in Human Behavior*, 132, 107240.

Jehn, K. A., & Shah, P. P. (1997). Interpersonal relationships and task performance: An examination of mediation processes in friendship and acquaintance groups. *Journal of Personality and Social Psychology, 72*(4), 775–790.
Kahn, R. L., Wolfe, D. M., Quinn, R. P., Snoek, J. D., & Rosenthal, R. A. (1964). *Organizational stress: Studies in role conflict and ambiguity*. Wiley.
Katz, D., & Kahn, R. L. (1978). *The social psychology of organizations* (Vol. 2, p. 528). Wiley.
Keller, A. C., Meier, L. L., Elfering, A., & Semmer, N. K. (2020). Please wait until I am done! Longitudinal effects of work interruptions on employee well-being. *Work & Stress, 34*(2), 148–167.
Kolb, D. G., Caza, A., & Collins, P. D. (2012). States of connectivity: New questions and new directions. *Organization Studies, 33*(2), 267–273.
Kossek, E. E., Dumas, T. L., Piszczek, M. M., & Allen, T. D. (2021). Pushing the boundaries: A qualitative study of how stem women adapted to disrupted work–nonwork boundaries during the COVID-19 pandemic. *Journal of Applied Psychology, 106*(11), 1615–1629.
Kossek, E. E., & Lautsch, B. A. (2008). *CEO of me: Creating a life that works in the flexible job age*. Pearson Prentice Hall.
Kossek, E. E., & Lautsch, B. A. (2012). Work–family boundary management styles in organizations: A cross-level model. *Organizational Psychology Review, 2*(2), 152–171.
Kossek, E. E., Lautsch, B. A., & Eaton, S. C. (2006). Telecommuting, control, and boundary management: Correlates of policy use and practice, job control, and work–family effectiveness. *Journal of Vocational Behavior, 68*(2), 347–367.
Kossek, E. E., Ruderman, M. N., Braddy, P. W., & Hannum, K. M. (2012). Work–nonwork boundary management profiles: A person-centered approach. *Journal of Vocational Behavior, 81*(1), 112–128.
Krasnova, H., Wenninger, H., Widjaja, T., & Buxmann, P. (2013). Envy on Facebook: A hidden threat to users' life satisfaction? *Proceedings of the 11th International Conference on Wirtschaftsinformatik* (WI2013), Universität Leipzig, Germany.
Kreiner, G. E. (2006). Consequences of work-home segmentation or integration: A person-environment fit perspective. *Journal of Organizational Behavior, 27*(4), 485–507.
Kreiner, G. E., Hollensbe, E. C., & Sheep, M. L. (2006). On the edge of identity: Boundary dynamics at the interface of individual and organizational identities. *Human Relations, 59*(10), 1315–1341.
Kreiner, G. E., Hollensbe, E. C., & Sheep, M. L. (2009). Balancing borders and bridges: Negotiating the work-home interface via boundary work tactics. *Academy of Management Journal, 52*(4), 704–730.
Landers, R. N., & Callan, R. C. (2014). Validation of the beneficial and harmful work-related social media behavioral taxonomies: Development of the work-related social media questionnaire. *Social Science Computer Review, 32*(5), 628–646.
Lazarus, R. S. (1991). Cognition and motivation in emotion. *American Psychologist, 46*(4), 352–367.
Leary, M. R., & Kowalski, R. M. (1990). Impression management: A literature review and two-component model. *Psychological Bulletin, 107*(1), 34.
Leftheriotis, I., & Giannakos, M. N. (2014). Using social media for work: Losing your time or improving your work. *Computers in Human Behavior, 31*, 134–142.

Leonardi, P. M., & Vaast, E. (2017). Social media and their affordances for organizing: A review and agenda for research. *Academy of Management Annals, 11*(1), 150–188.

Leroy, S. (2009). Why is it so hard to do my work? The challenge of attention residue when switching between work tasks. *Organizational Behavior and Human Decision Processes, 109*(2), 168–181.

Li, Y., Miao, L., Zhao, X., & Lehto, X. (2013). When family rooms become guest lounges: Work–family balance of B&B innkeepers. *International Journal of Hospitality Management, 34*, 138–149.

Liao, H., Chuang, A., & Joshi, A. (2008). Perceived deep-level dissimilarity: Personality antecedents and impact on overall job attitude, helping, work withdrawal, and turnover. *Organizational Behavior and Human Decision Processes, 106*(2), 106–124.

Luqman, A., Talwar, S., Masood, A., & Dhir, A. (2021). Does enterprise social media use promote employee creativity and well-being? *Journal of Business Research, 131*, 40–54.

Marder, B., Joinson, A., Shankar, A., & Thirlaway, K. (2016). Strength matters: Self-presentation to the strongest audience rather than lowest common denominator when faced with multiple audiences in social network sites. *Computers in Human Behavior, 61*, 56–62.

Matthews, R. A., Kath, L. M., & Barnes-Farrell, J. L. (2010). A short, valid, predictive measure of work–family conflict: Item selection and scale validation. *Journal of Occupational Health Psychology, 15*(1), 75.

Mazmanian, M., Orlikowski, W. J., & Yates, J. (2013). The autonomy paradox: The implications of mobile email devices for knowledge professionals. *Organization Science, 24*(5), 1337–1357.

McFarland, L. A., & Ployhart, R. E. (2015). Social media: A contextual framework to guide research and practice. *Journal of Applied Psychology, 100*(6), 1653–1677.

Methot, J. R., & LePine, J. A. (2016). Too close for comfort? Investigating the nature and functioning of work and non-work role segmentation preferences. *Journal of Business and Psychology, 31*, 103–123.

Methot, J. R., Lepine, J. A., Podsakoff, N. P., & Christian, J. S. (2016). Are workplace friendships a mixed blessing? Exploring tradeoffs of multiplex relationships and their associations with job performance. *Personnel Psychology, 69*(2), 311–355.

Metiu, A., & Rothbard, N. P. (2013). Task bubbles, artifacts, shared emotion, and mutual focus of attention: A comparative study of the microprocesses of group engagement. *Organization Science, 24*(2), 455–475.

Mulki, J. P., Jaramillo, F., Goad, E. A., & Pesquera, M. R. (2015). Regulation of emotions, interpersonal conflict, and job performance for salespeople. *Journal of Business Research, 68*(3), 623–630.

Muraven, M., & Baumeister, R. F. (2000). Self-regulation and depletion of limited resources: Does self-control resemble a muscle? *Psychological Bulletin, 126*(2), 247.

Ninaus, K., Diehl, S., & Terlutter, R. (2021). Employee perceptions of information and communication technologies in work life, perceived burnout, job satisfaction and the role of work-family balance. *Journal of Business Research, 136*, 652–666.

Nippert-Eng, C. (1995). It's about time. *Qualitative Sociology, 18*(4), 479–485.

Nippert-Eng, C. (1996). Calendars and keys: The classification of "home" and "work." *Sociological Forum, 11*, 563–582.

Oksanen, A., Oksa, R., Savela, N., Mantere, E., Savolainen, I., & Kaakinen, M. (2021). COVID-19 crisis and digital stressors at work: A longitudinal study on the Finnish working population. *Computers in Human Behavior, 122*, 106853.

Ollier-Malaterre, A., Jacobs, J. A., & Rothbard, N. P. (2019). Technology, work, and family: Digital cultural capital and boundary management. *Annual Review of Sociology, 45*, 425–447.

Ollier-Malaterre, A., & Rothbard, N. P. (2015). Social media or social minefield? Surviving in the new cyberspace era. *Organizational Dynamics, 44*(1), 26–34.

Ollier-Malaterre, A., Rothbard, N. P., & Berg, J. M. (2013). When worlds collide in cyberspace: How boundary work in online social networks impacts professional relationships. *Academy of Management Review, 38*(4), 645–669.

Olson-Buchanan, J. B., & Boswell, W. R. (2006). Blurring boundaries: Correlates of integration and segmentation between work and nonwork. *Journal of Vocational Behavior, 68*(3), 432–445.

Orhan, M. A., Castellano, S., Khelladi, I., Marinelli, L., & Monge, F. (2021). Technology distraction at work: Impacts on self-regulation and work engagement. *Journal of Business Research, 126*, 341–349.

Otonkorpi-Lehtoranta, K., Salin, M., Hakovirta, M., & Kaittila, A. (2022). Gendering boundary work: Experiences of work–family practices among Finnish working parents during COVID-19 lockdown. *Gender, Work & Organization, 29*(6), 1952–1968.

Park, Y., Fritz, C., & Jex, S. M. (2011). Relationships between work-home segmentation and psychological detachment from work: The role of communication technology use at home. *Journal of Occupational Health Psychology, 16*(4), 457.

Phillips, D., & Young, P. (2009). *Online public relations: A practical guide to developing an online strategy in the world of social media* (2nd ed.). Kogan Page Publishers.

Phillips, K. W., Rothbard, N. P., & Dumas, T. L. (2009). To disclose or not to disclose? Status distance and self-disclosure in diverse environments. *Academy of Management Review, 34*(4), 710–732.

Pillemer, J., & Rothbard, N. P. (2018). Friends without benefits: Understanding the dark sides of workplace friendship. *Academy of Management Review, 43*(4), 635–660.

Poelmans, S., Greenhaus, J., Maestro, M. L. H., & Maestro, M. L. H. (Eds.). (2013). *Expanding the boundaries of work-family research: A vision for the future*. Springer.

Powell, G. N., & Greenhaus, J. H. (2010). Sex, gender, and the work-to-family interface: Exploring negative and positive interdependencies. *Academy of Management Journal, 53*(3), 513–534.

Pratt, M. G., & Rosa, J. A. (2003). Transforming work-family conflict into commitment in network marketing organizations. *Academy of Management Journal, 46*(4), 395–418.

Reynolds, N. S. (2015). Making sense of new technology during organizational change. *New Technology, Work and Employment, 30*(2), 145–157.

Richardson, K., & Benbunan-Fich, R. (2011). Examining the antecedents of work connectivity behavior during non-work time. *Information and Organization, 21*(3), 142–160.

Rothbard, N. P., & Ollier-Malaterre, A. (2016). *Boundary management*. Oxford University Press.

Rothbard, N. P., Phillips, K. W., & Dumas, T. L. (2005). Managing multiple roles: Work-family policies and individuals' desires for segmentation. *Organization Science, 16*(3), 243–258.

Rothbard, N. P., Ramarajan, L., Ollier-Malaterre, A., & Lee, S. S. (2022). OMG! My boss just friended me: How evaluations of colleagues' disclosure, gender, and rank shape personal/professional boundary blurring online. *Academy of Management Journal, 65*(1), 35–65.

Saura, J. R., Ribeiro-Soriano, D., & Saldaña, P. Z. (2022). Exploring the challenges of remote work on Twitter users' sentiments: From digital technology development to a post-pandemic era. *Journal of Business Research, 142*, 242–254.

Schaufeli, W. B., & Bakker, A. B. (2004). Job demands, job resources, and their relationship with burnout and engagement: A multi-sample study. *Journal of Organizational Behavior, 25*(3), 293–315.

Schaufeli, W. B., Bakker, A. B., & Salanova, M. (2006). The measurement of work engagement with a short questionnaire: A cross-national study. *Educational and Psychological Measurement, 66*(4), 701–716.

Schmidt, G. B., Lelchook, A. M., & Martin, J. E. (2016). The relationship between social media co-worker connections and work-related attitudes. *Computers in Human Behavior, 55*, 439–445.

Seabrook, E. M., Kern, M. L., & Rickard, N. S. (2016). Social networking sites, depression, and anxiety: A systematic review. *JMIR Mental Health, 3*(4), e50.

Seo, M. G., Barrett, L. F., & Bartunek, J. M. (2004). The role of affective experience in work motivation. *Academy of Management Review, 29*(3), 423–439.

Shi, Z., Rui, H., & Whinston, A. B. (2014). Content sharing in a social broadcasting environment: Evidence from Twitter. *MIS Quarterly, 38*(1), 123–142.

Soares, M. E., & Mosquera, P. (2019). Fostering work engagement: The role of the psychological contract. *Journal of Business Research, 101*, 469–476.

Song, Q., Wang, Y., Chen, Y., Benitez, J., & Hu, J. (2019). Impact of the usage of social media in the workplace on team and employee performance. *Information & Management, 56*(8), 103160.

Sonnentag, S. (2012). Psychological detachment from work during leisure time: The benefits of mentally disengaging from work. *Current Directions in Psychological Science, 21*(2), 114–118.

Staw, B. M., & Barsade, S. G. (1993). Affect and managerial performance: A test of the sadder-but-wiser vs. happier-and-smarter hypotheses. *Administrative Science Quarterly, 38*(2), 304–331.

Sturges, J. (2012). Crafting a balance between work and home. *Human Relations, 65*(12), 1539–1559.

Tammelin, M. (2018). Work-family border styles and mobile technology. In M. Tammelin (Ed.), *Family, work and well-being* (pp. 91–103). Springer.

Tandon, A., Dhir, A., Islam, N., Talwar, S., & Mäntymäki, M. (2021). Psychological and behavioral outcomes of social media-induced fear of missing out at the workplace. *Journal of Business Research, 136*, 186–197.

Tedeschi, J. T., Schlenker, B. R., & Bonoma, T. V. (1971). Cognitive dissonance: Private ratiocination or public spectacle? *American Psychologist, 26*(8), 685.

Thomala, L. L. (2023, February 11). *Average daily time spent on WeChat in China 2021*. Statista. https://www.statista.com/statistics/668386/china-amount-of-time-users-spent-on-wechat-daily/. Accessed February 12, 2023.

Ticona, J. (2015). Strategies of control: Workers' use of ICTs to shape knowledge and service work. *Information, Communication & Society, 18*(5), 509–523.

Ticona, J., & Mateescu, A. (2018). Trusted strangers: Carework platforms' cultural entrepreneurship in the on-demand economy. *New Media & Society, 20*(11), 4384–4404.

Toegel, G., Kilduff, M., & Anand, N. (2013). Emotion helping by managers: An emergent understanding of discrepant role expectations and outcomes. *Academy of Management Journal, 56*(2), 334–357.

Towers, I., Duxbury, L., Higgins, C., & Thomas, J. (2006). Time thieves and space invaders: Technology, work and the organization. *Journal of Organizational Change Management, 19*(5), 593–618.

Trefalt, Š. (2013). Between you and me: Setting work-nonwork boundaries in the context of workplace relationships. *Academy of Management Journal, 56*(6), 1802–1829.

Turkle, S. (2011). *Alone together: Why we expect more from technology and less from each other*. Basic Books.

Turner, J. W., Grube, J. A., Tinsley, C. H., Lee, C., & O'Pell, C. (2006). Exploring the dominant media: How does media use reflect organizational norms and affect performance? *The Journal of Business Communication, 43*(3), 220–250.

Utz, S. (2015). The function of self-disclosure on social network sites: Not only intimate, but also positive and entertaining self-disclosures increase the feeling of connection. *Computers in Human Behavior, 45*, 1–10.

Valentine, S., Fleischman, G. M., Sprague, R., & Godkin, L. (2010). Exploring the ethicality of firing employees who blog. *Human Resource Management, 49*(1), 87–108.

Van Zoonen, W., Verhoeven, J. W., & Vliegenthart, R. (2016). How employees use Twitter to talk about work: A typology of work-related tweets. *Computers in Human Behavior, 55*, 329–339.

Wajcman, J., Bittman, M., & Brown, J. E. (2008). Families without borders: Mobile phones, connectedness and work-home divisions. *Sociology, 42*(4), 635–652.

Wajcman, J., & Rose, E. (2011). Constant connectivity: Rethinking interruptions at work. *Organization Studies, 32*(7), 941–961.

Wang, X. (2016). The social media landscape in China. *Social media in industrial China* (1st ed., pp. 25–56). UCL Press.

Weiss, H. M., & Cropanzano, R. (1996). Affective events theory: A theoretical discussion of the structure, causes and consequences of affective experiences at work. *Research in Organizational Behavior, 18*(1), 1–74.

Wilson, R. E., Gosling, S. D., & Graham, L. T. (2012). A review of Facebook research in the social sciences. *Perspectives on Psychological Science, 7*(3), 203–220.

Zerubavel, E. (1993). *The fine line*. University of Chicago Press.

Zhao, A. T., & Yu, Y. (2023). Employee online personal/professional boundary blurring and work engagement: Social media anxiety as a key contingency. *Computers in Human Behavior Reports, 9*, 100265.

CHAPTER 23

Strategic Changes Toward Engagement, Wellness, and Growth

Peter Mutuku Lewa and Susan K. Lewa

INTRODUCTION

Today all kinds of organizations operate in dynamic contexts. The dynamism is underlined by the phenomenon of Change. In common parlance, change implies moving from one position to a new position. This may also mean to replace or use a modified thing or process or may imply the onset of new things (Collins COBUILD Dictionary, 1987). The term change is thus nebulous. We hear people today often talking of the era of dynamic or radical change; change is a constant; and if you do not change then change will change you. Other phrases used to denote the nature of change today include dynamism and rapidity. Change is thus a fundamental element affecting all organizations that operate in dynamic or turbulent business operating environments or contexts. Ideally no organization is a Robinson Crusoe, existing and operating in a remote environment without close interactions with other organizations or other independent elements for that matter. It can be said that even the mythological Crusoe interacted with the insects, birds, animals, and the elements on the remote environment, and later on with other human beings that he taught, among other things, the value of work ethics. Ehlers

---

P. M. Lewa (✉)
University of Kwazulu Natal, Durban, South Africa
e-mail: LewaP@ukzn.ac.za

S. K. Lewa
Jomo Kenyatta University of Agriculture and Technology, Nairobi, Kenya
e-mail: lewa.susan@jkuat.ac.ke

© The Author(s), under exclusive license to Springer Nature Switzerland AG 2023
J. Marques (ed.), *The Palgrave Handbook of Fulfillment, Wellness, and Personal Growth at Work*,
https://doi.org/10.1007/978-3-031-35494-6_23

and Lazenby (2010: 58) observed in their book that "strategic leadership" is always needed for successful competition in a turbulent business environment. This emphasizes the need for strategic change management today.

Change must be managed strategically for success to be realized in the future. Strategic change management can be described as the process that prepares us for the uncertain future by enabling us to create and empower organizations to take responsibility for their desired future state. They must have a clear mission in dealing with the change problem (Nickols Fred, 2012). Strategic changeis futuristic. It has therefore to be managed well with "tomorrow" or the "future" in mind. Strategic change has been defined as all the efforts and actions that are involved in moving an organization from its present position toward a desired future state to increase its competitive position and its profitability. For the non-profits, we can say that strategic change will involve moving the organization to its desired future state of success in their operations that involve pursuit of mostly social goals.

Today's nature of change is what Igor Ansoff & McDonnell (1990) described as "turbulent", meaning the degree of rapidity and changeability of change. COVID-19 and other infectious diseases such as Ebola and Bird flu have impacted workers and hence the dynamics of the workspace everywhere in fundamental ways. There are other changes too affecting the world of work arising from changing dynamics in the political, economic, socio-cultural, technological, legal, and Competitive (PESTELCO) arenas of business. Global business competition has increased the complexities experienced today in the workspace. For example, geopolitics has assumed new dimensions mostly because of the rise of some countries such as China, and also global terrorism, depletion of resources, and climate change among other factors. There have been major changes in the economic sphere as well as in other spheres. Today as ever anyway, change is a reality that we need to embrace and accept. We need to be comfortable with it because we have little or no control over it. Change has been described in management and related disciplines as a "constant" since it is always present. In the past change was slow. Today it is rapid and its "changeability", and "surprise", in the words of the late US Professor Igor Ansoff, are things to be wary of so that we can plan not in the ordinary sense but in a strategic sense. This implies managing change in order to take responsibility for the future of the organization.

It is a truism that in today's world, every organization operates in a changing context. Change today, and especially due to the pandemic, shows the world gravitating to trends yet to be developed and awakened. It has been argued in many quarters that this scenario requires awakened leaders who generally maintain and advocate an open mind, allowing for interventions that address new and novel yet intricate phenomena (Marques & Dhiman, 2018). The changing business context has brought to the fore how work happens in the workspace in the company office or away from the office or at home while working remotely, what workers feel about their welfare and the adjustments they see as necessary in their today's mondus operandi in order to make work more meaningful in the face of change. These and other concerns have underlined the need for considering the issues of employee engagement, wellness, and growth. This in turn has engendered the need for the design and implementation of strategic change management strategies in the organization to address the workspace challenges and new opportunities engendered by change.

There are fundamental changes in the labor and employment sectors everywhere that have affected workers, their wellness, and orientation. These include finding different occupations; marked change of occupations by most people; increased remote working accelerated by the pandemic; higher use of technology; expanded data collection, new marketing and distribution styles, business analytics, and big data management; need for better employee engagement and inclusion and many other related factors and disruptions in the workspace to say the least. There is need for reskilling than there was before COVID-19; increased use of automation, and a fast rise in virtual transactions within expanding e-commerce space. Many of these changes have been captured in recent reports by renown organizations, agencies, and writers such as Mackinsey (Ellingrud, 2021), Gartner Baker (2021), Hannon (2016), US Bureau of Labor and Statistics (2021), Society for Strategic Human Resource Management (2017), and Reddy (2020). There are many other contributors to the phenomenon of change today brought largely by the COVID-19 pandemic. What these changes imply is the need for a strategic approach since they will not only affect organizations today but in future as well with probably quite serious consequences if the issues are not handled strategically. We can no longer do business the way it has been done in the past. Changes have come and these must be managed with tomorrow in mind as their major consequences will be felt mostly in the future. We must embrace the paradigm of strategic change.

But what is the meaning of strategic change? Strategic change is a paradigm that can be defined in different ways but there is an established consensus that it includes all the efforts and actions that the Top Management Team (TMT) implements in order to move an organization from its current or present state toward the desired future state. This future state is usually captured in an organization's vision and to some extent in the mission (Ehlers & Lazenby, 2010). There is, therefore, the need for strategic change management. The process of strategic management has well developed conceptual tools and skills created over the years whose effective use brings about good results especially when strategizing for the future of the organization.

Strategic change management can simply be described as the management's use of processes and tools that are utilized to prepare organizations for the uncertain future by enabling them to create and empower them to take responsibility for their desired future. Creating and empowering organizations is a strategic process (Mutuku & Mutuku, 2005). It generally involves asking very basic strategic approach questions: Where are we now? Where are we going? How do we go there? These questions are basic in any strategic moves an organization may wish to make in deciding how to move forward into the future under rapid change and under intense competitive situations. The questions help organizations to carry out situation analyses of both the internal and external environments to establish their current positioning in the environment; give opportunity for the TMT to consider how they want the future of the organization to be, and what frameworks, strategies, or blue prints they might formulate or design and implement to help them navigate toward their future in a sustainable way.

Strategic Change Management (SCM) can be represented in our own developed model (in an equation form) as **SCM = C X C X O X M X A** (Context or situation or environment X Challenges X Opportunity X Motivation X Ability).

In other words, Strategic Change management involves examining factors such as the context (C) situation or context or environment, Challenges (C), Opportunities (O) available in the operating environment, the Motivation (M) of the TMT to put into place strategies to manage change, and the Ability (A) of the organization to manage change. The equation shows what we consider the critical factors in strategic change management (SCM) process. It is a function of the factors provided in the equation; the sum total of all the interplay of the factors in the equation and other related ones that may arise in analysis.

Strategic management requires strategic leadership. This is the type of leadership that helps organizations to compete successfully in the turbulent and unpredictable environments of today (Ehlers & Lazenby, 2010). It involves the ability of the managers in an organization to anticipate, set, and share a common vision, think strategically, and work with others to initiate change that will create a viable future for the organization. Thus, in addition to the change caused by external forces, managers within an organization must create change from within in order to be successful.

Key Forces of Change in the Workspace Today

Today our lives are undergoing transformation in an unprecedented way (Naisbitt, 1984). The world of work is facing unprecedented changes that require implementation of strategic change interventions. These changes, as identified earlier, have been brought about by a multiplicity of factors, including COVID-19, ICT, climate change, and globalization. These changes have challenged organizations in terms of some critical aspects in the workspace such as employees' happiness at work, engagement, inclusiveness, wellness, and growth. Generally, today the overall result of the changes in the workspace is lack of fulfillment at work and glaring impediments to employee commitment, engagement, wellness, and growth. These engender the need for strategic interventions to engage employees more, improve their wellness, and growth among other benefits.

The US workforce experience probably depicts the kind of situation found everywhere in the globe. The US Bureau of Labor and Statistics reports that over 4 million Americans quit their jobs in November 2021, and more than 40% of the global workforce stated that they are "likely to consider leaving their current employer" (https://www.bls.gov/news.release/jolts.nr0.htm). Resignation rates among mid-career managers have increased more than 20% since the onset of the COVID-19 pandemic. The Rosie report makes the following observation that captures the essence of change brought about by COVID-19 and the changing dynamics at work as they have always been known traditionally (https://www.hbr:org/2021/09/who-is-driving-the-great-resignations?).

> "As this inaugural report was underway, the global COVID-19 pandemic broke out at global scale, initiating the largest work-from-home experiment in human history. While The Rosie Report is authored in pursuit of sustainable business evolution, COVID-19 is recognized as a wake-up call to the imperative of remote work readiness, and hopefully an accelerant to this new, more enlightened, and fully flexible work paradigm we strive every day to manifest". (Rosie Report, 2020)

Change is here with us and we must manage it strategically for future success. The ideas in the Rosie report apply everywhere in the work environment. There are new employee concerns, aspirations, and orientation that must be addressed. Today we need strategic leaders who must act differently from how they did in the past before the changes being witnessed today. Professor Sydney Finkelstein of the Tuck School, speaking at a seminar organized by the Coursera Leadership Academy on the 7th April 2022, talked of the need for "Super Bosses" (Leaders) who must today inspire workers, communicate a truly compelling vision, and unleash creativity in organizations. He spoke at length about talent retention today in the midst of change. He observed that workers are going to leave their jobs and so the goal of leaders should be how to retain talent, as well as the search for new talent. These are generally seen in many quarters as critical challenges today especially in regard to the remote work environment.

Because of high integration of employee concerns and practices what happens in one place on the globe happens in another in more or less the same way. Today's world is highly integrated. Marques & Dhiman (2018: 3) observe that when one looks at the "speeding trend in which we are exposed to different ways of acting, thinking, and relating, we can say that our world is more interdependent than ever before". One result of this has been increased knowledge sharing. Education and knowledge have increased. Because of the increased levels of education among populations, values and expectations among employees have shifted more or less in the same way all over the world. The shifts have resulted in the emphasis on increased inclusion, engagement, and participation of employees at all levels in the organization as well as a focus on individual health and wellness to improve the quality of work life. Health has become a truly universal rights issue.

Nowadays we are witnessing the era of knowledge management and learning. Today most employees seek knowledge and new meaning outside the support of their leaders and their managers at work. They invest time outside the office in learning skills that will help them grow and contribute to the company. Many engage in studies for courses that support their personal growth and the work they do. They read articles, book chapters, and texts that they wish to master in order to achieve their set goals. The senior management loves this as the company does not have enough resources to support everyone to advance their skills. There is probably no known organization that has ever had adequate resources for employee's personal development because available company resources are never adequate. However, a key challenge today is how to achieve more employee engagement, wellness, and growth.

Strategic Change Management Interventions to Support Employee Engagement, Wellness, and Growth

Strategic change management is an important factor in the process of strategic management. An organization's Strategy is the management's action plan or blue print for running the business and conducting operations. Managing the company's strategy is called Strategic management. This has been defined as the process whereby all organizational functions and resources are integrated and coordinated to implement formulated strategies, mostly stable and growth, which are aligned with the environment and therefore gain a competitive advantage through adding value for the stakeholders in order to achieve the long-term goals and plans of the organization (Ehlers & Lazenby, 2010). The key elements in strategic management process have been studied and established in many quarters and management practice as:

1. Setting the vision and mission of the organization. This provides strategic direction to the organization.
2. Conducting environmental analysis that includes both internal environmental analysis and external environmental analysis.
3. Strategy formulation to come up with long-term goals and competitive strategies (both grand and functional strategies), alignment of strategy with industry demands and life cycle, and strategic analysis and choice (Ehlers & Lazenby, 2010).
4. Strategy implementation necessary to implement the chosen strategies. This requires examination of available driving forces (drivers) that include leadership, culture, reward systems, organizational structures, and resources deployment.
5. Strategy evaluation and control is seen as the last component and stage in the process. It involves taking actions to seek continuous improvements. Evaluation and control benefits from such tools as the Balanced Score

Card (BSC), Total Quality Management (TQM), and other tools utilized in Monitoring and Evaluation (M&E) techniques.

The above processes and elements must be managed well. This helps the members of the top management to be futuristic in their orientation. One has to pay close attention to the factors in the strategic change management process. There is consensus in many quarters that change management involves the task of managing change or an area of professional practice, or a sector, where change is planned, or as a body of knowledge where the content or subject matter, that is models, methods, and techniques, tools, skills, and other forms of "change knowledge" are studied. Change management is therefore the attempt to develop and apply strategic management to both inevitable and desired organizational changes. The first step is to develop a clear assessment of the current reality of the organization and then identify the primary change drivers and finally identify the desired future state. Using this information to identify the forces driving the change and the creative forces needed to create those specific changes is the common view of what leading change management in an organization should entail.

Many other contributors have made substantial contributions in this area. They include Kotter (1996) and his models of leading change, Bennis et al. (1969) in the planning of change, Beckhard and Harris (1987) on organizational transitions and management of complex change, Senge (1990) on the Learning Organization, Lewin (1958) and his seminal contribution on Group Decisions and Social change, and Schuler (2003) on the key issue of resistance to change as a natural process that occurs when adjustments from the normal way of doing things have to be made.

Resistance to change is one of the biggest problems to any organization that is changing today and careful attention must be paid to this phenomenon. Ansoff & McDonnell (1990) defined resistance to organizational change as a multi-faceted phenomenon, which introduces unanticipated delays, costs, and instabilities into the process of strategic change. This results in unforeseen implementation delays and inefficiencies, which slow down the change. If sabotage occurs, there are performance lags or employees try to make efforts to go back to the pre-change status by striking or being absent. This leisure is no longer available given today's degree of the changeability and the rapidity of change. Many organizations today are involved in issues to do with how best to create customer value under changing dynamics. They are involved in the search for new ways to perform research and development, production, distribution, and logistics in general, human capital development, financial management, and risk management among other considerations. A key question appears to be: How do we create new customer value under changed or changing dynamics? For example, in the area of ICT a big question is: How do we implement digital marketing in meeting customer needs? What are the best available options in the social media space for us today? And: What new skills do we acquire or develop in order to remain relevant in our market space?

Kotter (1996) explains the reasons as to why change fails by arguing that the management tries to manage change instead of leading it; apparently changes do not alter behavior he observes. Kotter (1996) identifies the common errors that hinder change as follows: allowing too much complacency, failing to create a sufficiently powerful guiding coalition, underestimating the power of vision, under-communicating the new vision, permitting obstacles to block the new vision, failing to create short-term wins, declaring victory too soon, and neglecting to anchor changes firmly in the corporate culture. As a result of the errors mentioned above; new strategies are never well implemented, acquisitions do not achieve expected synergies, reengineering takes too long and costs too much, downsizing does not get costs under control, and quality programs do not deliver promised results. This implies that things have to be done differently.

Understanding resistance to change therefore calls for a clear understanding of the reasons as why people resist change (Wasserman et al., 2008). Schuler (2003) outlines ten reasons as to why people resist change. First, the risk of change is seen as greater than the risk of standing still. This is because people decide to move in the unknown direction on the promise of better things. Thus, making change requires a kind of leap of faith. Secondly, people feel connected to other people who are identified with the old way. Since people are social species, they like to remain connected to those people they know, those who have taught them, and those with whom they are familiar. Thirdly, people have no role models for new activity. For most people seeing is believing, thus it is hard for them to comprehend things that they have not seen. Fourth, people fear that they lack the competence to change. Some people will feel that they would not be able to make it through the transition since organization change may necessitate change in skills, life styles, and may even impact the workspace in diverse ways.

The fifth reason is that people feel overloaded and overwhelmed. Fatigue can easily kill a change effort even when people believe in the wisdom of the idea of accepting change. Sixth, people have a healthy skepticism and want to be sure that the new ideas are sound. This occurs since few changes are conceived in their final best form at the outset. Seventh, people fear hidden agenda among would-be reformers or change agents. This is common because some reformers may not be trusted since they share a blemished past. Eight, people feel that the proposed change threatens their notions of themselves. Sometimes change on job may be right or wrong with the people's sense of identity. Nine, people anticipate a loss of status or quality of life. Change brings with it a reshuffling of the deck which may cause some people to be winners and other losers. Finally, people genuinely believe that the proposed change is a bad idea. Sometimes people may not be afraid of the change but they just see it as wrong or as halfway wrong.

The above fears will need to be confronted by organizations as they try to strategically manage changes brought about by the pandemic and other factors.

Overcoming Resistance to Change

For the management to implement change, it must appreciate that change may bring with it some resistance hence the management should device ways of overcoming resistance in order for the change to be successful. To overcome resistance to change, management must educate and communicate well with the staff, involve them and let them participate in the change process, negotiate on some variables as much as possible to reach a consensus or agreement on how the change will be and get help from those supporting the change to influence the resisting ones and offer support at all times (Ansoff & McDonnell, 1990).

Above all else, management should lead the change by creating a shared need for the change, shaping the vision, mobilizing commitment, changing the systems and structure as needed, monitoring progress, and giving continuous feedback to ensure that the change lasts. Kotter (1996) developed eight stages for creating major positive change within an organization.

These steps are; establishing a sense of urgency, creating the guiding coalition, developing a vision and strategy, communicating the change vision, empowering broad-based action, generating short-term wins, consolidating wins and producing more change, and finally anchoring new approaches in the culture.

To overcome resistance, one needs to understand how to estimate change. Thus, the model developed by Beckhard & Harris (1987) comes in handy when studying change as illustrated in the following equation.

$$C = \{A + B + D\} \succ X$$

where C denotes change, A denotes level of dissatisfaction with the status quo, B denotes desirability of the proposed change and end state, D denotes practicality of the change (minimal risk and disruption), and finally X denotes cost of changing. For change to successfully occur, then the sum of A, B, and D must outweigh the perceived cost (X). This formula can help managers develop or create strategies for enhancing the degree of receptivity to change. Finally, to overcome resistance to change the management needs to understand that some employees may be putting their own welfare first thus they are uncommitted to the change efforts. Therefore, the management should come up with effective ways of communicating and creating a conducive environment for its employees. This is the challenge to management today in the face of changing employee dynamics and the growing need among employees everywhere for wellness and personal growth and development.

Employee Engagement, Wellness and Growth

Today's employee is a "wellness and happiness seeking one" and yearns for more and more inclusiveness and engagement in the workplace. Fulfillment in the workspace underlies the key issues of employee engagement, wellness, and growth. By fulfillment, we mean that feeling we have when we're working in line with our natural motivations and with a sense of purpose. As work-life boundaries continue to blur, employees increasingly want to explore and pursue opportunities that give them that purpose.

A new PwC/CECP study shows that meaning and fulfillment at work is the new standard employees expect of their work experience, and one that companies need to embrace if they want to cultivate the best workforce, now and in the future (PwC, 2016) (https://www.pwc.com/us/meaningatwork). Some key findings from this study reveal that companies must rethink how they can contribute to the employee experience becoming more meaningful if they want to increase productivity and remain competitive. The employee experience is related to engagement and inclusion of employees and what happens to them in their occupations at work.

According to the above study, a large majority (96%) of employees believe that achieving fulfillment at work is possible, and 70% say they would consider leaving their current role for a more fulfilling one. This desire for fulfillment at work today is so strong that one out of three employees say they would consider lower pay for a more fulfilling job. In the recent PwC survey, 83% of employees identified "finding meaning in day-to-day work" as a top priority.

Another key factor is that, contrary to common view, employees recognize they must lead in making work more meaningful for themselves with nearly 80% of them willing to find their own path to fulfillment. However, the findings of the PwC suggest that one third of employees find senior leaders as a barrier to them finding fulfillment. Neuroscience reveals that the three hallmarks that really create that fulfilling work experience are relationships that help in pushing one toward their goal, impact that is realized as we make progress toward a goal we believe in, and growth implying personal challenge that we overcome giving us new experiences and learning at work. Social support systems of the past have died out and communal support of individuals especially in Asia and Africa has died out. One consequence of this is that human beings have become more individualistic. They see themselves growing in their individual capacities in the work place, and have become more aware and more conscious of the need for personal self-development and self-actualization. Also because of changes and the impact of modernization people have become more self-focused and a key question today is "what is in this for me"? Proper employee engagement strategies assist organizations to address this question among other questions that are prominent today in the workspace.

Employee engagement has emerged as a critical driver of business success in today's highly competitive marketplace. The concept of employee engagement relates to the level of an employee's commitment and connection to the company. It is the strength of the mental and emotional connection employees feel toward their places of work leading to the willingness and ability to contribute to the organization's success. Employee psychological investment is also part of employee engagement. Engagement requires effective leadership. This kind of leadership is seen as the current perspective of leadership characterized by inclusiveness (Metcalfe et al., 2008). The ideas on inclusiveness and engagement are captured well in the published works of various authors who have contributed to a book on engaged leadership and transformation through future-design-thinking edited by Marques and Dhiman (2018).

High levels of engagement promote retention of talent, employee commitment, loyalty, productivity, foster customer loyalty and improve organizational performance, organizational reputation, and stakeholder value (Marques & Dhiman, 2018). Increasingly, organizations are turning to well-established policies in Human Resources (HR) to set the agenda for employee engagement. The organization should consider the strategic implications of various HR practices and determine which are more important and merit greater investment today in the midst of rapid change to enhance engagement levels. There is a strong case for the application of business analytics and big data management in the design of new HR policies. These should be linked to the organization's key performance measures, such as profitability, productivity, quality, customer satisfaction, and customer loyalty as well as to the key factors in the external environment of the organization. In addition, the organization should endeavor to create an "engagement culture" and "inclusion culture". This can be done by communicating the value of engagement in key policy documents as well as in the vision and mission statements of the organization.

Literature found in various sources suggests several employee engagement strategies that might be relevant today. These include seven strategies that we have found in various sources commonly recommended by various authors and organizations. These will definitely undergo modification and reform as rapid change continues to occur.

1. Today, it is challenging to plan for the long term because of the rapidity and changeability of change. However, it is important for the organization to develop as a matter of priority a strategy for success with a well stated purpose for the organization's existence to be captured in the company mission. The vision should be a mental picture of how the organization sees itself positioned in the future when doing its best. Today because of change it is not easy to clearly see the future but efforts can be expended toward scenario building and this is likely to give a good idea of what is likely to happen in the future.
2. Use of performance management, collaboration at work to share experiences, and confront challenges in a team spirit and appreciation of effort has been recommended (Holt, 2018). It appears that today in the midst of rapid change it is important for managers to keep asking for the opinion of employees in terms of how they feel work should be done. This effort certainly makes employees feel valued, engaged, esteemed, and respected.

3. Today more than ever before, organizational communication has assumed a more prominent role. Old habits and many others in different aspects of the organization have to be broken down. It is no longer business as usual. New and novel ways of two-way communication with employees have to be developed. Participation and inclusion in decision-making must be shared between top management and the other employees. It is no longer practical and wise for the TMT to speak at employees. They must speak to and with them.
4. Performance management and recognition of achievements through pursuit of performance targets leads to improvements in the bottom lines and encourage and motivate employees to perform better (Rao, 2018). Employees everywhere engage better and deliver their maximum potential where they are recognized and rewarded. Experiences from the recent past and indeed today suggest that employees everywhere are demanding to be engaged and included in the decisions affecting them and their welfare in particular.
5. Employees should be supported in their growth and development. Training opportunities should be availed to them and adequately budget for especially today where new learning and knowledge seeking have become mandatory. Employees need to learn the new techniques demanded by remote working. They need to learn and advance their skills in artificial intelligence, machine learning, big data management, and business analytics. This is the new normal in the world of work. Retaining talent is going to be more challenging especially in dealing with millennials whose expectations at work are so different from those of the past generation workers. One piece of good news is that most employees today are known to be investing their own efforts and money to seek for new knowledge. Companies need to pay more attention to learning and knowledge management. These are indeed the days of knowledge seeking and continuous learning.
6. Today's employees demand effective engagement at work and not lip service. This can be achieved by preparing the managers to know the techniques for better engagement. The TMT members are the bridge between the employees and the Board and they therefore need capacity building in order to perform and achieve the bar as expected. Gallup's chairman, Jim Clifton, *once said:*

> Employees—especially the stars—join a company and then quit their manager. It may not be the manager's fault so much as these managers have not been prepared to coach the new workforce.

7. Training and hiring capable managers are extremely important for organizations that want to become more competitive in their operating environments. These require carefully worked out strategies for human resource development and recruitment of talent.

The above outline of relevant strategies today is not and will definitely not be exhaustive per se over time as change continues to occur, and different industries discover more suitable and relevant strategies to apply within their contexts and within the broad frameworks suggested above. The key point is worker inclusion that requires management to take into account the critical issues that meet the employee expectations today (Pelled et al., 1999).

Employee Wellness is about employee health and productivity. Issues such as employee health screening, health coaching, health presentations, community wellness events, health changes to the environment, virtual wellness challenges, proper nutrition, and related concerns are all geared toward improvement of employee wellness. Some common wellness strategies recommended to address employee welfare have been suggested in different quarters.

Organizations must engage the services of nutritionists in order to educate employees about healthy eating and healthy living. Gym managers and psychologists must find more space in today's organizations. It is widely believed that managers who take a lead in identifying good restaurants with good heathy food choices, within a close proximity of their company premises, improve healthy eating among their employees and this has a positive impact on productivity. Moreover, relevant food supply chains can be identified and collaboration with the organization forged so that health foods, fruits, and vegetables, especially organic ones, and relevant nutritional information can be supplied to staff at affordable costs. Information is power as is commonly believed rightly. Empowered employees in all aspects of their wellness and growth will become an important boon to the organizations of the future.

Other strategies that are generally seen as capable of promoting wellness include promoting community agriculture, having a company dinner involving everyone every so often to promote healthy eating, establishing a company kitchen to provide healthy snacks, and provision of occasional talks on food and healthy living. Some companies every so often carry out checks on weight gains and healthy checks of employees. These are likely to become more prominent in the near future.

Perhaps some healthy living practices such as we find in some far east countries such as Japan and Thailand, of bicycling to work or to the supermarket, encouraging the use of the staircase, break time walks or even evening walks after work, may need to be adopted with increasing speed during the post COVID-19 era.

It is advisable for companies to continue promoting the internationally established smoke-free policies, non-discrimination policies, career services policies, counseling services policies, employee-initiated grievances policies, sexual harassment policies, and services for employees who have challenges, whether physical or mental. All these require concerted company support whether in a remote working or non-remote working workspaces. They are all very important aspects of employee wellness.

Employee growth means increase and change over time. A grown-up person is the one who is fully developed and mature. In the context of employees, growing into a job means learning to do the job skillfully. This growth means change in character and attitude. In human resources management, the all-encompassing term is human resource development or simply human resources training. It involves gaining new attitudes, learning new skills, and gaining new knowledge necessary for the future needs of the organization. It involves learning that which goes beyond today's job needs and has a more long-term focus. Gaining new Attitudes (A), Skills (S) and Knowledge (K) is meant to prepare employees to keep pace with the organization as it changes and grows (Mondy & Noe, 2005). As rapid change occurs in organizations today the ASK elements become more important. Today employees have become more conscious or more aware of their need for self-development and growth. This is generally because in the past societies almost everywhere were more communal and supportive especially in Africa and Asia. These support mechanisms have died out. Human beings have become more individualistic as earlier observed. Personal growth at work and even in society has become fundamental as one consequence of change. In addition, because of changes and modernization trends today, people have become more self-focused. Organizations have thus to be supportive of employee self-development and growth.

Strategies for improving employee growth and development are anchored mostly on training for skills development. They are commonly taken to include:

1. Fostering employee learning at work or away from work in a remote working environment.
2. Encouragement of Peer-to-Peer learning, and experience sharing.
3. Setting up a career development office to advise employees.
4. Supporting employees to attend relevant conferences.
5. Having clear policies for employee mentorship and apprenticeship.
6. Carrying out employee forecasting with a view to retaining and managing talent.

Hannon Schuyler (June 2016), Chief Purpose and Inclusion Officer, PwC, US, in an interview in June 2016 suggested several strategies for fostering employee welfare and growth. These appear to have wide support in practice and literature. It suffices to outline them at this point.

   a. **Make space for employees to create meaning:** to unlock insights through tools such as digital assessments and personal exploration exercises that encourage reflection.

b. **Provide structure—but not too much:** to make work more meaningful for employees while still supporting the collective goals of their team and organization.
c. **Create a culture that shows purpose:** can provide ongoing reinforcement and support for employees seeking greater meaning in their work.
d. **Get intentional with team building:** to get employees to come together for ongoing, shared experiences.

On the side of Human Resource Management (HRM) old policies may not work in the face of change. It is widely realized that organizations must think of new HR policies to address the issues brought about by change. The change being witnessed today engenders consideration of the following factors outlined below among other related ones.

1. New productivity models are called for along with measures of performance.
2. The traditional workspace is becoming less and less today. Leasing of buildings will be done in order to give away extra space that will not be needed anymore because of remote working. Some organizations may close their physical offices and some may sell them.
3. Business operations are expanding in diverse ways and leading more and more to the adoption of e-commerce.
4. Work-life balance considerations have risen to the fore and cannot be ignored.
5. Figuring out new social networks because of travel restrictions is a new challenge to confront.
6. Enhanced employee insurance schemes have to be considered.
7. Adaptive leadership is gaining prominence. This involves looking from the "balcony" of the company (management) to the wider context outside the organization.
8. The learning organization is making a firm imprint in operations. Organizational learning is becoming the "in thing" in the face of rapid change.
9. Sourcing for supplies from different places is going to become more important in the face of diminishing resources.
10. Human resource development geared toward its traditional role of preparing for the future has assumed a more significant meaning and role.

The starting point is to renew the mind set of management especially if the leadership styles existing and used in the organization are traditional in a sense. To change effectively managers must be transformed by the renewing of their minds. This calls for new leadership models that encourage engagement, inclusion, and freedom of employees to choose. Such leadership models need to be futuristic and thus strategic in nature as the future of work needs to be managed today not tomorrow. The TMT needs what Marques describes as design thinking and wakefulness.

> "Design thinking requires an open mind, and an open mind requires wakefulness: alertness to think further than the eye sees and think deeper than what is considered the common way" (Marques & Dhiman, 2018: 3)

The new leadership styles have a common feature known as inclusion which is about making sure everyone is involved and on board in participating in decision-making in the organization for the common good. Sturm (2006: 249) defines inclusion as "identifying the barriers to full participation and the pivot points for removing those barriers and increasing participation". There are many perspectives of looking at Inclusion. Some contributors to the discourse focus on a psychological approach to inclusion, defining it as "the degree to which an employee is accepted and treated as an insider by others" (Pelled et al., 1999). Other definitions focus on a sense of belonging, having voices heard, and feeling as though the organization values their perspectives and seeks their engagement (Wasserman et al., 2008).

What is commonly known in leadership literature is that all the theories and practices of leadership have some common shared themes. However, they all center on human relationships and the value of personal differences at work and in other places of interaction. In other words, everyone is important as a human being and also in the workspace in spite of his/her position in the organization, and also in spite of differences in mental, physical, religious, sexual, and other orientations.

One type of leadership known as servant leadership, first brought out by Robert K. Greenleaf (1977, 2002), provides many of the concepts of inclusion. Transformational leadership contains many of the basic concepts of inclusion. Since toward the end of 1990s, this leadership style has been researched heavily and is today seen as containing many of the concepts of the other leadership models. It provides some insights into what inclusion requires in several of its aspects. It has been established that this type of leadership style is ideal especially in the private and public sectors undergoing change. It activates followers to work closely with the leader to achieve results. It is ideal today where change is rapid and intense.

The concepts in transformational leadership put the individual human being at the center of the organization's aspirations and moves (Bass, 1990). The leaders must appreciate diversity, must accept that others too have worthwhile contributions to make, should be open to suggestions and constructive criticism, must avoid personal blind spots as well as flaws in the system, and work hard to ensure meritocracy. Transformational leaders empower their followers to perform beyond normal expectations. The many good aspects of this form of leadership cloud its dysfunctions that occur under certain contexts.

The above are some of the critical factors to observe in leadership in the twenty-first century (Rost, 1991).

Conclusion

The coronavirus crisis has impacted the world of work in fundamental ways. Workers' well-being has become an urgent agenda issue at work due to the changes engendered by the pandemic and other factors. Issues of employee engagement, wellness, and growth have assumed significance today in the wake of the COVID-19 pandemic. While the current global crisis itself might end soon, its impact on the global world of work may well endure. Due to the impact of the crisis, it is possible that some workers may begin to look for jobs that are more meaningful and that have strong social support networks, while others may begin to prioritize earnings and job security. In the short term, the most noticeable change brought on by the pandemic has been remote working with many employees working from home. Issues of decline in productivity and how to monitor workers in the remote work environment during the adjustment periods have risen to the fore but it is generally reported, mostly in social media that, the new modus operandi of work has brought about immediate benefits such as greater autonomy and cutting down of transportation costs and the inconveniences brought about by commuting to work.

Keeping expensive rental space has become an issue of concern with some companies said to have sold off their office space. Due to increased ICT developments and internet spread almost everywhere, the office today has become the laptop, the tablet, the mobile phone, and printing services in remote work environments or in the home space literally speaking. Of course, issues of shared experiences and the need to broaden one's horizons, through face to face interactions still have space in the work environment. It is not an issue of argument that social and intellectual capital is built by shared experiences with co-workers and by unplanned social interactions that broaden one's thinking. Moving forward, it will be important to maintain the benefits of working from home while still enabling employees and companies to build and sustain their social and intellectual capital. Monitoring and evaluating the workers under such circumstances are challenges that require intervention strategies.

References

Ansoff, H. I., & McDonnell, E. (1990). *Implanting strategic management*. Prentice-Hall. New York, NY

Bass, B. M. (1990). From transactional to transformational leadership: Learning to share the vision. *Organizational Dynamics, 18*(4), 19–31.

Beckhard, R., & Harris, R. T. (1987). *Organizational transitions: Managing complex change* (2nd ed.). Addison-Wesley.

Bennis, W., Benne, K., & Chin, R. (1969). *The planning of change* (2nd Ed.). Holt, Rinehart and Winston.

Collins COBUILD Dictionary. (1987). University of Birmingham (UK) and Collins Publishers, 660.

Ehlers, T., & Lazenby, K. (2010). *Strategic management: Southern African concepts and cases*. (3rd Ed.). Van Schaik Publishers.

Greenleaf, R. K. (1977). *Servant leadership: A journey into the nature of legitimate power and greatness*. Paulist Press.

Greenleaf, R. K. (2002). Essentials of servant-leadership. In L. C. Spears & M. Lawrence (Eds.), *Focus of leadership: Servant leadership for the 21st century* (pp. 19–25). Wiley.

Holt, S. (2018). Engaging generation Y: The millennial challenge in marques Joan and Dhiman Satinder (2018). *Engaged leadership: Transforming through future-oriented design thinking*. Springer International Publishing AG, part of Springer Nature.

Kotter, J. P. (1996). *Leading change*. Harvard Business School Press.

Lewin, K. (1958). Group decisions and social change. In E. E. Maccobby & T. M. Newcomb, & E. L. Hartley (Eds.), *Readings in social psychology* (pp. 330–344). Holt, Rinehart & Winston.

Marques, J., & Dhiman, S. (2018). *Engaged leadership: Transforming through future-oriented design thinking*. Springer International Publishing AG, part of Springer Nature.

Metcalfe, B., Metcalfe, J., Bradley, M., Mariathasan, J., & Samele, C. (2008). The impact of engaging leadership on performance, attitudes at work and wellbeing at work: A longitudinal study. *Journal of Health Organization and Management, 22*(6), 586–598.

Mondy, W. R.. & Noe M. R. (2005). *Human resource management*. (9th Ed.). Pearson: Prentice Hall.

Mutuku, S. M., & Mutuku, M. M. (2005). MBA term paper, "Managing Strategic Change" Alliant International University, Scripts Ranch, San Diego, California, USA

Naisbitt, J. (1984, February). *Megatrends: Ten new directions transforming our lives*. Warner Books.

Nickols Fred (2012). Change Management 101: A Primer. Distance Consulting. (http://www.nickols.us/change.htm)

Pelled, L., Ledford, G. E., Jr., & Mohrman, S. (1999). Demographic dissimilarity and workplace inclusion. *Journal of Management Studies, 36*(7), 1013–1031.

PwC. (2016). *Putting purpose to work: A study of purpose in the workplace*. https://www.pwc.com/us/en/purpose-workplace-study.html

Rao, M. S. (2018). Soft leadership and engaged leadership in Marques Joan and Dhiman Satinder (2018). *Engaged leadership: Transforming through future-oriented design thinking*. Springer International Publishing AG, part of Springer Nature.

Rosie Report, (2020). https://www.hbr:org/2021/09/who-is-driving-the-great-resignations?

Rost, J. C. (1991). *Leadership for the twenty-first century*. Praeger.

Senge, P. (1990). *The fifth discipline- the art and practice of the learning organization*. Currency Doubleday.

Schuyler, H. (June 2016). *Chief purpose and inclusion officer*, PWC, US. https://www.pwc.com/us/en/purpose-workplace-study.html

Society for Human Resource Management (SHRM). (2017). *Employee job satisfaction and engagement: The Doors are open.* https://www.shrm.org/resourcesandtools/tools-and-samples/toolkits/pages/sustainingemployeeengagement.aspx

Sturm, S. (2006). Architecture of inclusion: Advancing workplace equity in higher education. *The Harvard Journal of Law & Gender, 29,* 247.

Schuler, A. J. (2003). *Overcoming resistance to change: Top ten reasons for change resistance.* Retrieved on 1st April 2022, from http://www.schulersolutions.com/resistance_to_change.html

US Bureau of Labor and Statistics. (2021). https://www.bls.gov/news.release/jolts.nr0.htm

Wasserman, I. C., Gallegos, P. V., & Ferdman, B. M. (2008). Dancing with resistance: Leadership challenges in fostering a culture of inclusion. In *Diversity resistance in organizations* (pp. 175–200). Taylor & Francis Group/Lawrence Erlbaum Associates.

PART III

Personal Growth

CHAPTER 24

Conscious Practices Toward Personal and Collective Growth

Joan Marques

STRESS FACTORS OF THE CONTEMPORARY WORKER: AN OVERVIEW

With the accelerated pace of life, and the many unforeseen developments that keep changing the course we planned for ourselves, it is easy to become disheartened, even depressed, and left with a sense of confusion or even hopelessness. "Globalization and the new realities in the workplace have continued to redefine jobs and the management of human resources" (Matika & Muromo, 2021, p. 75). The recent COVID-19 pandemic presented us a vivid reminder that unexpected shifts can occur within a short time, causing after-effects that we could not have fathomed. First and foremost, the novel coronavirus pandemic and the resulting anti-COVID-19 government regulations and restrictions have tremendously affected human mobility behavior (Czech et al., 2021). In education, but also in corporate settings, the phenomenon of working from home became a significant and valid performance factor, whereas in the past it was considered unacceptable or insufficient in light of perceived quality standards.

With the mandatory isolation the pandemic brought upon humanity, institutions, and corporations that used to refute the legitimacy and efficiency of online performance, were left no choice but to reframe their paradigms, and rethink future practices and policies. The COVID-19 pandemic changed

---

J. Marques (✉)
School of Business, Woodbury University, Burbank, CA, USA
e-mail: joan.marques@woodbury.edu

© The Author(s), under exclusive license to Springer Nature Switzerland AG 2023
J. Marques (ed.), *The Palgrave Handbook of Fulfillment, Wellness, and Personal Growth at Work*,
https://doi.org/10.1007/978-3-031-35494-6_24

our collective interpretation of remote work, resulting in an increased elimination of the need for work-related travel (Grzelczak, 2021). While there was already a growing trend toward flexible use of office space in the past decades (Barath & Schmidt, 2022), the pandemic made it clear that large office spaces are ceasing to serve as a foundational requirement for organizations to perform, and with that, one may wonder what the future of many formerly busy downtown structures will become, as the purpose of shopping malls, multi-level office buildings, large brick and mortar service centers, and in-person education centers, has pivoted to the new reality of professional performance from the comfort of home. Whether or not the situation will continue to move toward a full-fledged remote realm or return to a brick and mortar work priority is left to be seen. Business leaders have a tendency to benchmark against their competitors, and follow suit based on what the leaders in their industry are doing. And while some corporate leaders state that they strive toward having their entire workforce back in the cubicles by 2025, there is also a vivid awareness that change is here to stay (Muraski, 2022).

Remote Work

While the trend of working from home definitely has its advantages, it has also brought its own set of concerns for workforce members. For starters, there is an increase in job-insecurity, because the option of remote performance has also enlarged the competition pool. Suddenly, the "local workforce" is no longer the one based in our hometown. Our colleagues can be anywhere in the state, nation, or even world, and deliver work at light speed, inexpensively, and on a continuous basis, due to time zone differences. This challenge, which had already been the status quo for several globally performing entities in the past, has now become a reality in sectors that had never dealt with it. While in the not so far past the challenge of jobs being outsourced was mainly manifested in the blue-collar work category, it has now made a rapid shift to the knowledge work echelons, and it has caused these workers to feel more vulnerable than ever before as they fear to be replaced by those who can do the job at a cheaper rate from an environment where the living standard is much lower (van Dam, 2022).

In addition, working from home in itself has, for many, caused an imbalance between workload, time pressure, and life satisfaction. Complaints about not being able to meet family obligations due to increased workload at home are on the rise, as many remote workers are being confronted with increased work–family conflicts that affect their life satisfaction (Demirbağ & Demirbağ, 2022). Palumbo (2020) supports this stance by adding that working at home often brings an intensification of work, along with an increased digital control of managers over remote workers, adding to workers' stress and anxiety due to the contamination that emerges between private life and work. Seen from the perspective of supervisors: these are also more concerned about the remote work situation, because they question their employees' productivity when they cannot see them behind their desks (Muraski, 2022).

Emotional Disconnect

Another challenge related to the trend of increased remote performance is of an emotional nature. While circumstances may demand different performance guidelines, humans are still emotional beings, dependent on connectivity, sensitive to unspoken vibes, and in need of informal bonding. "[C]onducting work within the home environment, inadequate workspace, childcare and social isolation represent stressors that have impacted employees' overall performance" (Barath & Schmidt, 2022, p. 1). With increased distance performance, trends such as "Do you have a sec to discuss this"? or "How'bout chatting further over lunch about that"? are no longer a given. Many workforce members may develop a sense of alienation and less connectedness as a result of the "new normal". Carey and Charbonneau (2022) cite a Canadian public opinion survey, which found that 40% of remote workers experience greater stress levels and nearly 50% feel less engaged with their work since the shift. Carey and Charbonneau (2022) conducted their own study on employee alienation based on remote working requirements, and found that "teleworkers who fit the 'conscientious' personality profile were less alienated in their new teleworker status, and by contrast 'extroverts' were more alienated than before the pandemic" (p. 491).

Another factor to consider is that, while working from home may be nice and could increase one's comfort level, it also has its downsides. Not every home is a peaceful place, and sometimes the absence of being at work serves as a welcome distraction or breather for those who may otherwise feel trapped in the same environment with the same people all the time. Working from home can cause frictions between home mates, and potentially lead to an impoverishment of social connections and conversational topics among the home mates. It can also lead to alienation from stakeholders, as the spontaneous connection is no longer part of the work scene. Nadiv (2022) presents another reason why some people have a harder time with working from home than others: the paradox-mindset, which entails that people have varying levels of ability to cope high levels of strain and tension. Those with a high paradox mindset simply deal better with the home-work tension than those who have a low level of paradox mindset.

Speed of Change

Yet another reason for workforce members to be concerned is the speed of change itself. New products, services, and trends are developed on a continuous basis, often at the expense of previous processes. This may explain why in our lifetime we have seen more businesses and services disappear than in any other generation before us. The way we do our shopping, planning, traveling, and even communicating today is rather different than how we did so two or three decades ago. There is so much we see disappearing and so much new emerging, that the pace becomes harder to keep up with as we grow older. The number of social media outlets we have to maintain to keep a steady profile in society is a good example. It seems as if every year introduces us to several new "must have" social media presences, each demanding regular posting and responding to stay current. Especially for those who need to maintain social connections in their professional performance, the rapid expansion of online communication modalities can be time- and energy-consuming.

Halkos and Bousinakis (2012) also underscore that change leads to elevated stress levels, which causes job satisfaction to decline. They add that when the change turns out to be fruitful, productivity increases, and stress gets reduced again. However, as the pace of changes continues to accelerate, it is easy to deduce that the upsurges of stress and job dissatisfaction occur more frequently. This, then, can lead to a disrupted sense of stability and overall inner peace for workforce members.

Lack of Stability

The increased pace of change also affects our sense of stability regarding our employment. Stress derives from perceptions of harm, threat, or challenge in a person's environment (Lazarus, 1993). With everything being prone to change, there is a continuous concern that our current job may not exist next year. This may not only be due to less expensive replacement from new colleagues oversees, but also to our current livelihood becoming obsolete. With the introduction of new ideas, many businesses find themselves no longer needed in the new reality. Video stores have been there, and so have travel agencies, and some major department stores. The internet has brought—and is still bringing—a transformation in how we think and act, and not everyone is equally pleased with that.

Smollan (2015) presents a correct reminder that not every change adds to increased stress. Some changes may also reduce stress, depending on one's position and what the change entails. Smollan also points out that most stress arises in the transition stage, which is in line with Bridges' Transition Model, which focuses on transition, not change, and explains the subtle difference of change being something that happens to people, even if they do not agree with it, and transition being the internal experience in people's minds as they go through change. Bridges (2010), who wrote important literature on change over the decades, reminds leaders to thoroughly contemplate the following three questions in any change situation: (1) What is changing? (2) What will be different because of the change? (3) Who's going to lose what? Considering the answers to these questions will force the leader to observe the many layers and angles to the pending change, and will enable them to clarify matters and guide the transition toward the change in a more responsible and compassionate way.

Mega Exposure

The internet has brought us a quantum leap in many areas of development, but has, at the same time, caused unforeseen disruptions in behavioral patterns. The increasing ease of spending substantial time online, has also brought about an increased exposure of what happens in every part of the world. We are continuously confronted with myriad developments, movements, criminal acts, and instances of immense suffering, near and far away. Although the argument can be made that learning about all these facts expands our horizons, it is also true that exposure at such a pace causes massive inner turmoil for those who are sensitive to the many troubles in the world. The internet has not merely brought us the ease of purchasing, banking, working, and learning from home, but is also exposing us to numerous shattering occurrences, which humans from even a half century ago were spared to see. The average person in a Western city today is very likely exposed to as much data as someone in the fifteenth century would encounter in their entire life (Vince, 2013). The demand this places on our psyche is immense, and it should therefore not come as a surprise that mental health conditions have increased worldwide according to the World Health Organization (WHO) (Williams, 2021).

Increased Diversity

Diversity is rightfully praised as a major advantage in workplaces overall: if managed well, a diverse workplace can cultivate broader mindsets and invoke greater creativity, leading to unprecedented innovation, hence, a competitive advantage. If members of a diverse workplace learn to work together well, they can learn a lot from each other, which also benefits them on an individual level, because people who know how to perform well in such work environments are an asset to almost any work environment.

Yet, if diversity is not managed well, it can lead to conflict situations, and require extended periods of trying to reach compromises among quarreling workers in order to get things done. Unguided diversity may also lead to heightened stress in a workplace, because humans, by nature, are homophilic, which means that they gravitate toward those they consider most similar to them. If one has always performed in diverse settings, working with folks from a variety of backgrounds is a welcome and eye-opening experience. However, for those who have been raised in homogeneous communities, it can be an immense challenge.

There are many more stress factors for contemporary workers, and upcoming developments and trends will not exactly protect us from those. Fortunately, there are also highly fulfilling practices to help us cope with today's challenges, and even convert seeming setbacks to wins.

Inspirational Practices for the Contemporary Worker: An Overview

There is no challenge so big that it cannot be overcome. Sometimes this happens at the individual level, and sometimes it can be accomplished as a team. In the next section, we will review some strategies workforce members can utilize to convert their workplace challenges into sheer fulfillment.

Individual Practices

There are numerous practices we can consider to restore our inner peace when we feel it has been disturbed. Some may gravitate to long walks in silence, others may engage in prayer, or read poetry. The practices described below are therefore merely a sample series that could be expanded at the reader's own leisure.

Meditation. Meditation has gained much traction in recent years, as more people became aware that it is a secular practice that is not necessarily coupled to any religion or philosophy. There are various kinds of meditation, and they all have great advantages, but insight meditation deserves a special mention due to its self-explanatory name: insight meditation. Formally, it is named "Vipassana", and it is aimed at regaining control over our mind without stressing over its wanderings. Goenka (2001), who reintroduced Vipassana on a massive scale to the contemporary world, stresses that practicing Vipassana contributes to becoming a better human being, and generating a peaceful and harmonious atmosphere around oneself and others. Goenka (2006) describes Vipassana as a useful instrument toward higher consciousness of people from all religions, cultures, and backgrounds.

One of the most powerful insights in the practice of Vipassana is the practice of focusing on our breath. Our breath represents a move from inhaling and exhaling and can be likened to every aspect of our life. We take our breath for granted and do not think about it until we get trouble breathing. But when we focus on it, we can see that our breath teaches us a number of important things. First of all, it varies: sometimes the left nostril works more prominently than the right nostril, and then the air can be felt more clearly to the dominant side. Overarchingly, our breath teaches us that nothing is permanent. Everything arises and passes, just like every breath we take. When we realize that nothing lasts, and that successes and failures, wins and losses, positions and possessions, relationships, and even our life ultimately expires, we may become more at ease with the ever-changing nature of work. We may also feel less disturbed about offensive behavior of others, and even develop compassion for those whom we initially felt repulsed by.

Marques et al. (2014) found that members of a workplace tend to agree on the value of developing greater focus at work when engaging in Vipassana meditation on a regular basis. The main advantages they recorded are, (a) greater emotional intelligence and less negative emotions, such as stress and other psychosomatic symptoms, and (b) enhanced awareness, which may lead to ceasing negative behavioral patterns due to greater compassion for stakeholders. As points of caution, Marques et al. (2014) mentioned that (a) practitioners of Vipassana meditation may become more sensitive, which may increase their discomfort in an indifferent workplace, and (b) practitioners may cease the meditation sessions if they consider them too time-consuming.

Identifying a Mentor. Mentors do not have to be part of our work environment. We can find mentors in every walk of life, and once we gravitate to a person whom we feel drawn to due to their wisdom, insights, and kindness, we may acquire great insights, which we did not entertain before. A good mentor is not sugarcoating reality, but rather helps us see reality through different lenses. These lenses can help us understand others' stances better, and relieve us from bottled up grief and anger that only made us feel miserable.

Organizations that set up mentorship programs also see greater successes among their workforce members, as this facility increases job satisfaction, organizational commitment, job performance, and career success for both, managers and mentees (Anderson, 2019). When there is so mentorship opportunity, future business leaders do not get the chance to learn and grow as they move on their career path (Anderson, 2019). In a study where employees were divided in two groups, one going through a mentoring program and the other through a traditional training program, it was found that the mentored group demonstrated greater leadership effectiveness than the one subjected to the traditional training program (Bjursell & Sädbom, 2018). Concurring that mentorship programs benefit both mentors and mentees, Bjursell and Sädbom (2018) emphasize that the individual and situational nature of mentorship forms a major advantage over any other form of learning and reflecting. They also add that mentorship is very focused on circumstances and adds meaning to the exchange between mentor and mentee. It has also been proven that mentoring helps enhance critical thinking skills, social competence, and specific knowledge that is otherwise not available.

The value of mentorship should not be underestimated when we consider the advancement of women and other minority groups in the workplace. Barkhuizen et al. (2022) point to mentorship as a crucial enabler of women's career advancement in work settings. When there is gender-based guidance and support in a professional environment, success is a natural consequence. Having a mentor can help advance careers, pull people out of disadvantaged positions, enhance workplace progress, and assist in establishing better work and home life balance (Barkhuizen et al., 2022).

Fanning (2020) stresses that, especially in challenging careers such as those related to finance, accounting, and STEM fields, it is important that members get exposed to mentors in all stages of their career, so that this type of guidance can help get them up to speed and propel them toward reaching their fullest potential.

Applying a Mindshift. Not everyone wants to look for a mentor. The good news is, that we already walk around with one all the time: our own self.

If we struggle with work-related tension, we can always take some time in seclusion to ask ourselves how we could shift the way we look at matters. It is not easy to do, because we often get hung up on our mindsets, and do not like to release our initial standpoint. But practice makes perfect, and once this has worked for us, the second time will be easier, and consecutive times even more. The first thought in applying a mind shift is the realization that you are currently suffering from the situation, and you need clarity. Secondly, you can contemplate on the reason for your suffering. Sometimes you cannot exactly lay the finger on the exact statement or circumstance that made you feel this way. Review them in your mind, until you can narrow down the moments that were most unpleasant. Then, you can try to place yourself in the shoes of those responsible for the unpleasant moments. What could their driving motive have been? Most of the time, people do not willfully hurt others' feelings, and if they do, there is often a deep-rooted fear at the foundation. This understanding can help us become more compassionate toward the other party, and start seeing the entire matter in a different light.

The practice above has much in common with mindfulness practice. Practicing mindfulness sounds as something that should come natural to us, humans, but how often do not we catch ourselves acting on "auto-pilot" and not even recalling how we got where we are? There has been much research done during the past decades on the impact that mindfulness can have on our behavior and the way we perceive matters. And because it affects our own perspectives, it also affects those we interact with. There are assessment exercises that can be used to improve mindfulness, such as the Kentucky Inventory of Mindfulness Skills (Baer et al., 2004) and the Mindful Attention and Awareness Scale—MAAS (Brown & Ryan, 2003).

Another effective way to get an understanding of mindfulness practice is through reflective journaling, as it can provide a sense of meaning to our actions. Taylor and Bishop (2019) describe how they used reflective journaling in business classes, where they invited students to write about their feelings before and after an activity. The deep personal analysis stemming from intense reflection sharpened their focus, enhanced their sense of calmness, and provided them a greater sense of emotional control.

Team Practices

While individual practices can get us a long way, we should not underestimate the value of team efforts toward personal and collective growth. Organizational researchers and coaches have developed and explored myriad practices in this regard. In the next section, we will briefly discuss some of these team practices.

Informal Gatherings. In organizational settings there are many ways in which people can interact outside of the regular work-related meetings. Randel and Ranft (2007) conducted a study that confirmed that job facilitation motivation relates to interorganizational information exchange, and Karl et al. (2005) posited, based on their research, that fun at work is essential for enhancing employee motivation and productivity, while reducing stress. Furthering their research on the above findings, Young et al. (2013) added that workplace fun does not just improve the team spirit in a work setting, but could also positively affect organizational performance. To confirm the above, Lyu and Zhu (2019) found that workplace ostracism and its socially exclusionary nature can have a negative effect on employees' job embeddedness, as it may weaken their affective commitment and enlarge their intention to exit the workplace.

Referring to a spiritual movement, Marques (2010) emphasizes the importance of exposing workforce members to senses of interconnection and mutuality. She adds that it has become increasingly understood that we should place safety and intrinsic rewards such as relationships and personal growth ahead of profit, and that we should embrace family and community with an emphasis on helping one another rather than just ourselves. Indeed, enhancing the sense of appreciation through informal connectivity, including, but not limited to, lunch, a retreat, happy hours, or other leisurely gatherings could have a profound effect on.

Sharing Peaks and Valleys. Not all members in a workplace share the same enthusiasm about openness, and perhaps they are rightfully cautious. In today's rapidly changing work settings, an appropriate degree of caution is recommended. However, sometimes the caution barriers are pulled up so high that it affects the spontaneity and trust levels in a department. It may be a good idea for team leaders to consider that openness starts with them.

Fosslien and Duffy (2019) point out that today's workforce members usually know more about each other than ever before, given the widely available social media outlets that are available at our collective fingertips. This may enhance a sense of personal connection, especially when kindness is being displayed. While Fosslien and Duffy (2019) advocate for the trend of shared vulnerability, they also warn against overdoing it: showing too much emotion all the time may come across as weakness. They suggest displaying honesty about feelings, but still providing clear guidance. More precisely, they recommend: (a) Pausing when inner emotions rise, and analyzing internally what the foundations are for these mounting emotions. Usually, a moment of pausing can restore emotional balance; (b) Explain briefly if moods soar, and do so without going into too much detail. It is often taken in the right spirit when at least some brief comment is made, alluding to the current state of mind; (c) Communicate the path ahead, as this usually resets the sense of balance, and demonstrates that things are under control; (d) Avoid oversharing, and this can easily be done by trying to envision how subordinates might assess your statements; and (e) Keep assessing the general spirit, so you can make behavioral and strategic adjustments where needed.

Notes of Appreciation. A very effective way of getting people to open up to one another is the application of "lollipop moments", as suggested by Drew Dudley in his 2010 Ted-X talk. Dudley encourages his audience to share positive impressions of how others have helped you with them. This open acknowledgment usually has a very positive effect, as people realize that their actions have been appreciated and not taken for granted. Depending on the size of a work team, the notes of appreciation could be implemented as a monthly, quarterly, or semi-annually. Granting people the chance to express their gratitude to others also nudges them in the direction of paying better attention about the contributions of others to the team. Patil et al. (2018) found that expressing gratitude toward one another has a positive impact on motivation, happiness, and contentment and respondents feel that there is still scope for further improvement in the culture of gratitude. White and George (2022) do remind us that different folks appreciate different strokes. "When appreciation is shown in the ways most meaningful to the recipient, many positive results occur: improvement in relationships with colleagues and supervisors, decrease in absenteeism, increase in employee engagement rises, as do customer satisfaction ratings" (White, 2017, p. 197). White and George (2022) found that older employees value appreciation primarily through words of appreciation and, second, quality time, with low priority for receiving tangible gifts. Younger employees, such as Gen Z's and Gen X'ers seem to have more interest in quality time as an expression of appreciation. Fortunately, White and George (2022) also add that the discrepancies in appreciation preferences are not immense, so the general intention is always appreciated.

Endnote

There is a wide range of conscious practices available toward personal and collective growth, and this chapter attempted to highlight first and foremost the many reasons why it is critical to be aware of the need for applying these practices. Three individual practices were highlighted, including Vipassana (insight) meditation, mentor identification to have a much-needed sounding board, and the application of a mind shift as a means to expand perspectives on experiences, and consider multiple viewpoints to learn to take matters in a positive spirit. There were also three team approaches presented, including informal gatherings, in order to enhance the sense of connectivity among team members; sharing peaks and valleys to enhance a sense of trust and openness, but with a mindful eye on keeping things authentic and not overdoing them; and notes of appreciation, which underscore to co-workers that their efforts have not gone unnoticed, but are appreciated. Figure 24.1 depicts the keynotes made in this chapter.

There is no rating scale to grade the impact or quality of each of these practices. It is, however, always good if the individual and collective efforts complement one another and contribute, each for themselves, to the desired outcome of a greater sense of connection, and an increased level of success for the collective work environment.

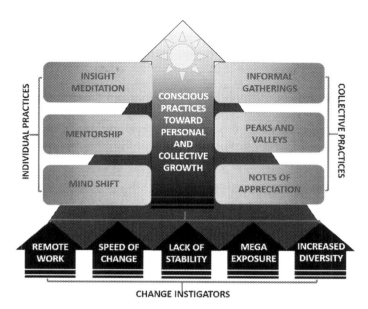

Fig. 24.1 Conscious practices toward personal and collective growth

REFERENCES

Anderson, T. (2019). Supporting career everests. *Leadership Excellence, 36*(11), 35–36.
Baer, R. A., Smith, G. T., & Allen, K. B. (2004). Assessment of mindfulness by self-report: The Kentucky Inventory of Mindfulness Skills. *Assessment, 11*, 191–206.
Barath, M., & Schmidt, D. A. (2022). Offices after the COVID-19 pandemic and changes in perception of flexible office space. *Sustainability, 14*(18), 11158.
Barkhuizen, E. N., Masakane, G., & van der Sluis, L. (2022). In search of factors that hinder the career advancement of women to senior leadership positions. *SA Journal of Industrial Psychology, 48*.
Bjursell, C., & Sädbom, R. F. (2018). Mentorship programs in the manufacturing industry. *European Journal of Training and Development, 42*(7), 455–469.
Bridges, W. (2010). Three questions. *Leadership Excellence, 27*(2), 15.
Brown, K. W., & Ryan, R. M. (2003). The benefits of being present: Mindfulness and its role in psychological well-being. *Journal of Personality and Social Psychology, 84*, 822–848.
Carey, D., & Charbonneau, É. (2022). Alienation in pandemic-induced telework in the public sector. *Public Personnel Management, 51*(4), 491–515.
Czech, K., Davy, A., & Wielechowski, M. (2021). Does the COVID-19 pandemic change human mobility equally worldwide? Cross-country cluster analysis. *Economies, 9*(4), 182.
Demirbağ, K. S., & Demirbağ, O. (2022). Who said there is no place like home? Extending the link between quantitative job demands and life satisfaction: A moderated mediation model. *Personnel Review, 51*(8), 1922–1947.
Dudley, D. (2010). Everyday leadership. *TEDx-Toronto*. www.ted.com/talks/drew_dudley_everyday_leadership

Fanning, L., CPA. (2020). The ethics of inclusion. *Strategic Finance, 102*(2), 15–16.

Fosslien, L., & Duffy, M. (2019, February 8). How leaders can open up to their teams without oversharing. *Harvard Business Review*. https://hbr.org/2019/02/how-leaders-can-open-up-to-their-teams-without-oversharing

Goenka, S. N. (2001). *Was the Buddha a Pessimist?* Vipassana Research Institute.

Goenka, S. N. (2006). *Peace within oneself for peace in the world*. Vipassana Research Institute.

Grzelczak, A. (2021). Remote work and its consequences for the employee in the time of the covid-19 pandemic. *European Research Studies, 24*, 399–411.

Halkos, G. E., & Bousinakis, D. (2012). Importance and influence of organizational changes on companies and their employees. *Journal of Advanced Research in Management, 3*(2), 90–103.

Karl, K., Peluchette, J., Hall, L., & Harland, L. (2005). Attitudes toward workplace fun: A three sector comparison. *Journal of Leadership & Organizational Studies, 12*(2), 1–17.

Lazarus, R. S. (1993). From psychological stress to the emotions: A history of changing outlooks. *Annual Review of Psychology, 4*, 1–21.

Lyu, Y., & Zhu, H. (2019). The predictive effects of workplace ostracism on employee attitudes: A job embeddedness perspective. *Journal of Business Ethics, 158*(4), 1083–1095.

Marques, J. (2010). Spiritual considerations for managers: What matters most to workforce members in challenging times. *Journal of Business Ethics, 97*(3), 381–390.

Marques, J., Dhiman, S. K., & Biberman, J. (2014). Teaching the un-teachable: Storytelling and meditation in workplace spirituality courses. *The Journal of Management Development, 33*(3), 196–217.

Matika, M., & Muromo, T. (2021). Work stress and its nexus with somatization and life satisfaction: The mediating role of coping on mental health. *Review of Human Factor Studies, 27*(1), 75–97.

Muraski, G. (2022, October 19). Labor market competition plays a huge role in remote work. *SMITH BRAIN TRUST*. Retrieved from Labor Market Competition Plays A Huge Role in Remote Work | Maryland Smith (umd.edu)

Nadiv, R. (2022). Home, work or both? The role of paradox mindset in a remote work environment during the COVID-19 pandemic. *International Journal of Manpower, 43*(5), 1182–1203.

Palumbo, R. (2020). Let me go to the office! An investigation into the side effects of working from home on work-life balance [Side effects of working from home]. *The International Journal of Public Sector Management, 33*(6), 771–790.

Patil, M., Biswas, S., & Kaur, R. (2018). Does gratitude impact employee morale in the workplace. *Journal of Applied Management—Jidnyasa, 10*(2), 21–36.

Randel, A. E., & Ranft, A. L. (2007). Motivations to maintain social ties with coworkers: The moderating role of turnover intentions on information exchange. *Group & Organization Management, 32*(2), 208–232.

Smollan, R. K. (2015). Causes of stress before, during and after organizational change: A qualitative study. *Journal of Organizational Change Management, 28*(2), 301–314.

Taylor, V. F., & Bishop, K. (2019). Bringing mindfulness practice to leadership and business education. *Journal of Leadership, Accountability and Ethics, 16*(5), 103–115.

van Dam, A. (2022, August 26). The remote revolution could lead to offshoring Armageddon. *The Washington Post*. https://www.washingtonpost.com/business/2022/08/26/remote-work-outsourcing-globalization/

Vince, G. (2013, May 16). Cities: How crowded life is changing us. *BBC Future*. https://www.bbc.com/future/article/20130516-how-city-life-is-changing-us

White, P. (2017). How do employees want to be shown appreciation? Results from 100,000 employees. *Strategic HR Review, 16*(4), 197–199.

White, P., & George, G. (2022). How preferences for types of appreciation differ across employee age groups. *Strategic HR Review, 21*(1), 25–30.

Williams, N. (2021, December 1). Are mental health issues increasing? *News-Medical.net*. https://www.news-medical.net/health/Are-Mental-Health-Issues-Increasing.aspx

Young, G. C., Kwon, J., & Kim, W. (2013). Effects of attitudes vs experience of workplace fun on employee behaviors. *International Journal of Contemporary Hospitality Management, 25*(3), 410–427.

Individual Resilience in a Volatile Work Environment

Isabel Ong and Chia-Yu Kou

INTRODUCTION

In light of the turbulent economic, political, and technological environment that organizations are currently operating in, the ability of employees to recover and even excel in the face of adversity has important consequences for contemporary workplaces.

Fisk and Dionisi (2010, p. 168)

The speed at which business environments are becoming increasing turbulent puts significant pressures on both organizations and the individuals within. For organizations, pressures on growth and operating margin drive them to changes such as focusing on cost reductions (Howell, 2016) or strategic decisions to enter new markets and develop new skillsets (Gulati et al., 2010). For individuals, those organizational changes are often associated with ambiguity and increased workload, and as a result, individuals may experience stress and burnout (Cartwright & Cooper, 1997), as well as a variety of perceived resource losses including threats to self-esteem, job losses (Nadler, 1982), loss of power or rank (Callan, 1993), or change in company culture (Mirvis, 1985).

I. Ong
Willis Towers Watson, London, UK

C.-Y. Kou (✉)
Cranfield School of Management, Cranfield University, Cranfield, UK
e-mail: chia-yu.kou-barrett@cranfield.ac.uk

With stress being associated with decreased productivity, increased turnover, and sickness absence (Baltzer et al., 2011; Williams, 2003), it can clearly have a highly undesirable impact on the revenue-generation of a company (Conner & Douglas, 2005). This has resulted in an increased interest in individual resilience as a vital factor of change success and how organizations can develop and maintain individuals' levels of resilience during turbulent times (Bardoel et al., 2014; Lengnick-Hall et al., 2011). Resilience is the capacity to rebound or bounce back during adversity (Luthans, 2002) and the "*most important positive resource to navigating a turbulent and stressful workplace*" (Avey et al., 2009, p. 682). Studies have found that resilient individuals can leverage their psychological resources to protect themselves from the negative effects of stress (Robertson et al., 2015), proactively prepare for hardships (Fredrickson et al., 2008), and increase their capacity to learn from adversity and take these learnings into their next challenge (Taylor et al., 2000; Waugh et al., 2008). Resilient individuals are more likely to welcome new experiences, be more adaptable and more emotionally stable during time of constant change (Avey et al., 2009). Resilient individuals also reduce the negative impacts of stress on organizational productivity brought about by organizational change. As such, resilient individuals have long-term benefits both to themselves as individuals and to their organizations (Rice & Liu, 2016).

While individuals may have the capacity to reframe or recover from stressful events, they may not always have access to the practices they leverage to assist in mitigating adversity. For example, individuals may not always be able to socialize with others or exercise to reduce their stress due to their physical fitness. An extreme case of this situation was exemplified during COVID-19 when social interactions were restricted. Likewise, when individuals faced sustained and compounding challenges, they could feel further drained and exhausted (Halbesleben & Buckley, 2004). In addition, resilience is context-dependent and can varyingly correspond to multiple aspects of life (Pietrzak & Southwick, 2011; Southwick et al., 2014). Assuming that resilient individuals will always have the capacity to maintain their resilience level seemed to be an erroneous assumption. It is therefore important to know what individuals do to maintain their resilience when their pathway to resilience is blocked.

To investigate this question, we conducted a qualitative study, looking at individuals' practices to maintain their resilience when the studied company was under major business change during the time where individuals' usual pathways to resilience were limited due to COVID-19 restrictions. This served as an extreme case, but provided good context to gain insight about what individuals do when they are less resourceful in maintaining their resilience (Siggelkow, 2007). The structure of the chapter is as follows: first, we will review the literature in enhancing individual resilience. After presenting the methodology and findings, we conclude with practical implications. We summarized practices that paved individuals' way to resilience and the managerial interventions that could assist individuals to combat their stress during turbulent times.

Enhancing Individual Resilience

How do individuals build their psychological resilience and thereby increase their ability to bounce back in turbulent environments? While there are debates on the development of resilience—whether resilience is trait-like (Connor & Davidson, 2003; Luthans et al., 2006; Luthar & Cicchetti, 2000; Masten & Obradovic, 2006) or could be developed (Bonanno, 2004; Masten & Reed, 2002; Youssef & Luthans, 2005), more recent research suggests that resilience depends on individuals' capacity to effectively utilize their internal and external assets and resources (Fletcher & Sarkar, 2013; Windle, 2011). Organizational interventions such as professional development opportunities, open communication with management, opportunities to contribute toward organizational decision-making, performance feedback, compensation, and benefits are useful not only at the point of stress but before a stressful event by priming a workforce's ability to better cope with the stressors emanating from change (Britt et al., 2016; Shin et al., 2012). However, these interventions are costly (Meyers et al., 2013).

Proactive and Reactive Pathways to Individual Resilience

At the individual level, the development of psychological resilience has been found to take both proactive and reactive forms (Everly, 2017; Luthans et al., 2006). A proactive approach centers around anticipating a requirement for resilient behavior to enable individuals to "*remain psychologically healthy despite being exposed to an adverse life event*" (Bonanno, 2004) whereas reactive forms of resilience development enable individuals to find pathways to resiliency as a reaction to a stressful event (Luthans et al., 2006) enabling them to recover quickly from the psychological impact of an adverse life event (Bonanno et al., 2010).

The development of proactive psychological resilience encompasses three approaches; process, risk, and asset strategies (Masten, 2001; Masten & Reed, 2002). Process strategies rely on the cognitive abilities of the individual to influence the ways in which they interpret events and experiences (Masten & Reed, 2002). These involve increasing their psychological capital through the development of hope, self-efficacy, and optimism. Risk strategies involve individuals proactively avoiding a circumstance in order to reduce its negative impact. At the time when it is difficult to predict when the stress may be unsurfaced, individuals may try to minimize the negative influence from adversity. This is most commonly manifested through the development of strong social networks which can be drawn upon during adverse life events (Luthans et al., 2006). Asset strategies involve individuals enhancing their personal resources and capabilities through the development of knowledge, skills, and/or abilities (Youssef & Luthans, 2005). In the context of organizational change, this can involve upskilling to improve their ability to complete their current role as well as enhancing their employability. In practice, these strategies can be

Table 25.1 Developing proactive resilience

Development of proactive resilience	Risk strategy (Luthans et al., 2006)	Process strategy (Masten & Reed, 2002)		Asset strategy (Youssef & Luthans, 2005)
	Building connections	Fostering wellness	Embracing healthy thoughts	Finding purpose
Building your resilience	• Prioritizing relationships • Joining a group	• Take care of your body • Practice mindfulness • Avoid negative outlets	• Keep things in perspective • Accept change • Maintain a hopeful outlook • Learn from your past	• Help others • Be proactive • Move toward your goals • Look for opportunities for self-discovery

aligned with the ten-point roadmap to resilience (Alvord et al., 2012) which is summarized in Table 25.1.

Individuals can also work to develop their reactive resilience as adversity happens. According to Bonanno (2004), there are four strategies to reactive resilience. These include psychological hardiness, repressive coping, positive emotion and laughter, and self-enhancement. Psychological hardiness refers to individuals' personality traits which assist them in coping with exposure to extreme stress based on their perceptions of their control over events, their perception of challenge (whether change is an opportunity to learn or change is a threat), and their commitment to involvement as opposed to withdrawing from the event (Bartone, 2000; Kobasa, 1979). Psychological hardiness thereby encourages transformational coping and can be developed through meaning-making processes and be influenced by the behaviors demonstrated by an authentic leader within the organization (Luthans et al., 2006).

Repressive coping refers to individuals avoiding unpleasant thoughts, emotions, and memories associated with an adverse life event (Weinberger, 1990). Self-enhancement refers a biased belief that they will almost always find a way to overcome and succeed in an adverse life event (Bonanno et al., 2005; Luthans et al., 2006; Taylor & Brown, 1988). Positive emotion and laughter assist individuals in reframing an adverse life event (Folkman, 2007; Folkman & Moskowitz, 2007). Self-enhancement and repressive coping strategies are regarded as a more short-term strategy because individuals may be unable to move beyond the source (Maddi et al., 2006).

While much has been said about the different pathways to resilience, less research has been conducted into how individuals develop their resilience when certain pathways to relieve their stress are restricted. For example, individuals might not always be available to visit their supporting circles when they want to. Where studies have been conducted, they have been within the context of extreme environments such as space travel, polar expeditions, and submariners (Brasher et al., 2010; Bartone et al., 2018) where challenges, starting point of challenges, and duration of the events were expected. However, in volatile work environments, challenges are often unexpected. Furthermore, previous studies were mainly based on quantitative data and therefore lack the detailed practices which individuals leverage during stressful events (Folkman & Moskowitz, 2000). The question of precisely how individuals maintain their resilience level when their capacity to relieve the stress is restricted therefore lacked empirical exploration. The present study directly addresses the absence in the literature by conducting a qualitative study in a financial company in the UK where the company was undergoing business changes during the COVID-19 pandemic. This coincided with a period of time when individuals were restricted in their ability to socialize and had limited access to outdoor exercise.

Research Context and Method

The setting for the study is within an S&P 500 financial services company in the UK. During our study year (May 2021), the company was experiencing major business change. The business change, which was focused on leveraging data and technology to accelerate innovation and growth, was planned before COVID-19 and announced to employees in March 2020. Although employees were aware of the prospect of a change in the business, they were not yet fully informed of the impact on the individual when we conducted interviews. At the point of the interview, announcements had been made regarding regional and team divestments as well as books of business which were being purchased by a competitor. In addition, there was a lack of clarity around the future structure, capability requirements and leadership of the business, as well as the extent to which redundancies would be made. In addition, participants had 14 months of working from home due to COVID-19 restrictions. Restrictions also included a reduction in access to face-to-face socialization, hospitality, hotels, gyms, entertainment, traveling, and holiday which encompassed a large part of individuals' usual pathways to resilience. This was, therefore, an ideal setting to gain greater insight into individuals' use of both proactive and reactive pathways to resilience while individuals faced restrictions.

Three types of data were collected: (1) semi-structured interviews were conducted. Senior managers nominated interviewees to enable a representative sample across gender, seniority within the organization as well as the level of involvement in the change program. An initial 22 possible individuals were contacted by email to see if they were interested in participating. A total of 13 interviews were conducted. Due to the social distancing restrictions, interviews were conducted virtually through Microsoft Teams, and participants kept their cameras on throughout the interview. Interviews focused on the individual's role in the company, their thoughts about the business change, and their approaches to maintaining their resilience. Interviews lasted between 30 and 45 minutes. We interviewed informants until interviews failed to reveal new insights (Strauss & Corbin, 1990). The interviews were recorded and transcribed verbatim which yielded 126 pages of single-spaced text. (2) on-site observations were carried out. The first author was able to attend meetings and have informal conversations with informants regarding the planning, execution, and integration of the business change which assisted in understanding the changes occurring within the company as well as employee reactions to the change. The first author was also able to have informal conversations with the participants to ensure the understanding was in line with the participants'. (3) Archival material including internal and external communications around the progress of the change such as town hall attendance, internet and intranet announcements as well as insights in industry publications were also gathered during fieldwork. These documents informed us about the business change.

The interview transcripts were analyzed using a thematic analysis (Braun & Clarke, 2006, 2020) approach to understand what strategies were employed by individuals dealing with a volatile environment. The analysis commenced with a close reading of the transcripts to increase familiarity with the data. The next step involved coding the data with a description that summarized the meaning of each extract, codes were then grouped based on similarity, and similar items were combined to form overarching themes. These emergent themes were examined to draw conceptual links with existing research, creating clusters which formed the key themes for discussion. A log was maintained throughout the phases of data collection and analysis, and a clear account of the research process was recorded to ensure the method of research can be understood (Smith, 2011) (Table 25.2).

FINDINGS

The key question that guided this study was: how do individuals maintain their resilience in the time where the work environment faced was constantly changing? Similar to previous research which found that individuals may use proactive (Luthans et al., 2006; Masten, 2001; Masten & Reed, 2002; Youssef & Luthans, 2005) or reactive resilience practices (Bonanno, 2004) to maintain one's resilience level, data analysis also showed that individuals used both proactive and reactive practices. We found that participants referred to proactive resilience pathways (70% of the total coding) more often than the reactive resilience pathways (30% of the total coding). Within each pathway, however, not all strategies were weighted equally. Specifically, given the strict social restriction during COVID-19, when employing proactive pathways, data showed that individuals predominately used process strategies, followed by risk strategies and then asset strategies. When using reactive pathways to individual resilience, the data showed that reactive resilience was developed predominantly through practices associated with hardiness, followed by repressive coping, methods of self-enhancement, and finally positive emotion. The

Table 25.2 Data structure

Emergent Theme: Proactive Resilience Pathway		Emergent Theme: Reactive Resilience Pathway	
Sub-theme	Summary of codes	Sub-theme	Summary of codes
Process strategy	Enablers for process strategy • Diet and exercising • Able to rest (e.g., taking breaks, taking time off for the self) • Flexibility at work • Foster wellnesswellness (e.g., maintaining a perspective, engaging wellness activity) • Environment, nature, and outdoors (e.g., appreciation for local community and environment, spending time outdoors) Inhibitor for process strategy • Increase work demand and inability to take rest (e.g., increase in working hours, lack of work/life boundaries, no time to take rest) • Increase personal pressure and decrease in self-confidence	Hardiness	Enabler for hardiness • New opportunities (e.g., developing new skills, increased responsibility, knowing new colleagues) • Belief in ability to influence outcomes • Accepting change Inhibitor for hardiness • Incongruence between individual and company change (e.g., unable to align one's purpose to the business change, unclear around the reasons for change)
Risk strategy	Enablers for risk strategy • Socializing with family, work colleagues, and friends Inhibitor for risk strategy • Increased isolation and alienation	Repressive Coping	Enabler for repressive coping • Compartmentalizing the situation • Seeking stability (e.g., leave the company) Inhibitor to repressive coping • Lack of control and stability (e.g., uncertainty around their existing role, management, team structure, uncertainty around career progression)
Asset strategy	Enabler for asset strategy • Self-awareness through reflection • Work role variation and challenge Inhibitor for asset strategy • Unable to perform their job	Positive Emotion Self-Enhancement	Enabler for positive emotion • Maintaining a positive mindset Enabler for self-enhancement • Confidence in own abilities

following section explicates the strategies of proactive and reactive practices to maintain individual resilience level.

Proactive Resilience Pathways

Interestingly, while prior research suggested that strategies leveraged may differ depending on seniority and change involvement (Olson & Tetrick, 1988), this study found that strategies leveraged were vastly consistent across gender, seniority level, and individual's involvement within the company change. Data showed that when individuals faced restricted pathways to maintain their psychological resilience, the ability to leverage process strategies (63%) becomes the most important pathway to proactive resilience, followed by risk strategies (21%) and then asset strategies (16%). In addition, while participants highlighted the impact of social distancing restrictions on their ability to leverage risk and asset strategies, a key finding was that a decrease in available time to rest significantly impacted their ability to maintain resilience.

Process Strategies: Enablers. Process strategies refer to ways that can influence individuals' interpretation of events and experiences (Masten & Reed, 2002). Data showed that process strategies were the most utilized strategy during the organizational change in the COVID-19 pandemic. Our analysis showed that participants could reframe the changing work environment through the following practices. Firstly, all the participants mentioned that exercise helped them to keep things in perspective: as well as helping them to "*not only… forget what has been troubling you, but [that they're] more likely to see it as insignificant…and you also just feel generally better about yourself*" (Participant 322, specialist). Other practices which were used by all participants were taking breaks. In particular, working from home seemed to empower individuals to take breaks throughout the day and working in a flexible manner was another way in which participants maintained their ability to positively interpret their external environment to maintain their psychological well-being. Participants across all levels have highlighted that

> [they] really like [their] lunch break and [that they have] been really disciplined and protective around [their] time around that…… I have really enjoyed the freedom to be more flexible in terms of planning my day. (Participant 122, specialist)

> …having the freedom to just pick and choose what you want to do…… the fact that you don't have to think, oh my god are we allowed to do that so that you can go and do things. (Participant 212, senior management)

This enabled them to feel more empowered and in control of the uncertain, external circumstances which enabled them to find the silver lining in their challenging circumstances.

Secondly, the data also showed that during times of constant change, participants found it helpful to reflect on their habits to gain a better understanding of themselves. In particular, a participant commented on how the restrictions during the pandemic helped them to reflect on their past behavior: "*There are a lot of working habits* before *the pandemic which were just not healthy, and at different points in the pandemic they've not been healthy either*" (Participant 322, specialist). Reflection during a period of constant change also helped individuals to gain a better idea of their personal boundaries:

> I've got a better idea of like rationally what my boundaries are, and what I need……I've certainly got a better idea of what makes me happy and not. (Participant 721, middle management)

and understand the importance of gaining perspective

> …it is all about keeping things in perspective, I certainly work hard but no one is going to die if I can't get all my work done. (Participant 521, senior management)

For participants who engaged in mindfulness practices such as meditation prior to the change and pandemic commented on how helpful they found it throughout this stressful event.

Finally, appreciation for one's surroundings and spending time outdoors also helped them to reframe the situation by allowing them to "*switch off a little.*" Participants fed back that

> …it makes you feel so much better, and even if you don't want to because it's raining you always come back feeling better. (Participant 212, senior management)

We noticed that this practice is predominately employed by participants from senior and middle management positions.

Process Strategies: Inhibitors. As for the inhibitors to individuals' capacity to reframe events, participants mentioned the increased working hours meant that they were not able to take time for themselves and to rest. A participant reported that

> The first quarter [of 2021] had been so busy for everyone at different points, everyone's been online really late. The weeks where I've felt the worst have been the ones where I have been working really late, staying until 9 or 9:30 [pm] and then felt that I hadn't any time for myself. I found that once I got into that mood, I started to really resent work. I started to resent myself and starting thinking 'Why am I even doing this?'. (Participant 322, specialist)

> Staring at the computer screen all day every day, and also when you're on camera…I feel like a really need to emphasize my movements and my facial

expressions so that people understand what I'm saying. You don't get those natural cues that you would in person. So it's really draining to be honest with you. And when you do it all day. (Participant 812, middle management)

Working from home also had implications for participants' abilities to maintain work/life boundaries, with some having to work, relax, and sometimes sleep in one room. For example:

...the biggest thing is that mentally you don't get that stop as much as when you used to when you left the office. When you left the office you could also leave work behind in the office, whereas now you bring it with you, and it's with you even on the weekends and when you sleep. (Participant 122, specialist)

The removal of the commute to and from the office has resulted in a lack of definition around the working day and week which has resulted in work being absorbed into every area of life. As a participant in middle management mentioned: "*my kitchen, and my living room is all one big room. Yeah, so no matter what I'm doing my laptop is the center of the room.*"
Participants also acknowledged an internal inhibitor to their psychological well-being which was the increased sense of pressure they placed on themselves. This was particularly prevalent in middle management and specialist levels. Interestingly, managerial interventions to help participants to deal with increased workload could result in a negative impact on work/life balance. For instance, managers assisting with the prioritization of work or suggesting that one finish the day can put more stress on participants. For example,

...a lot of the stress that I feel is me putting it on me. Nobody else is telling me that there's a strict deadline. It's just I have high standards and I want to meet deadlines or be quicker than the average person but to be honest it's not great, but it's something that I've had to deal with. (Participant 812, middle management)

This increased pressure meant that participants were not able to take rest, be it throughout or after the working day with participants finding that as a result their

...hours are a lot longer, way longer in fact, [so that they] rarely take lunch breaks...... it got to the point where [they] really really struggled to sleep. (Participant 211, specialist)

Risk Strategies: Enablers. Risk strategies refer to individuals' efforts to minimize the impact of an adverse event, and this was the second most leveraged set of activities used by participants to develop their proactive resilience. Similar to the previous research (Luthans et al., 2006), our analysis showed that socializing was a way of invoking a risk strategy as it enabled individuals to create a sense of shared experience and therefore, reduced the negative impact of a stressful event. Participants reported that

> ...it [was] nice to hear other people's stories...and if you are having a bad time, that shared experience makes it better. (Participant 211, specialist)

The types of socialization predominantly fell into three categories: socializing with family, colleagues, and friends. Prior to the pandemic, participants recalled that

> ...it was really social engagements [that helped them remain psychologically well]. If [they were] stressed, [they] would meet up with people in the evening after work. (Participant 655, specialist)

However, due to COVID-19 restrictions, the primary source of socialization mentioned in the data was mainly with family and colleagues. Participants described their social interactions with family and colleagues and said that they had

> ...become closer with [their] family and noticed that [they] were a bit more open with each other... they had spent a lot of time together over the past year as they became [their] social bubble. (Participant 812, middle management)

Participants of all levels found it beneficial to draw on social support in varying combinations, which demonstrated the adaptability of this strategy in the way participants shifted the primary source of support depending on what was available at the time.

Risk Strategies: Inhibitors. Unsurprisingly, the inhibitor to deploying risk strategies was increased isolation due to the restrictions in place. This was evident from the data in instances where participants who used to meet up with friends had become closer to family and colleagues. In addition, there were some variances when discussing the impact of risk strategies being restricted, which appeared to more keenly affect specialists and to a certain extent middle management. Participants cited an increased sense of isolation and alienation from friends as the main way in which this strategy was restricted. For example,

> Teams is very good for getting something done for like a specific amount of time and having no frills but often people don't take the time to catch up and get to know the other person. (Participant 322, specialist)

When senior managers faced the same socializing restriction, they appeared to be more proactive in developing new networks of social support. This proactivity resulted in both a widening and strengthening of their social support as they now feel they

> ... know [their] team members, personally now more than ever before. In those early days we didn't speak that much about our personal lives, but that has evolved, we've got really good at doing that now. (Participant 412, senior management)

Asset Strategies: Enablers and Inhibitors. Asset strategies refer to ways which increase individuals' capacity through acquiring new knowledge and skill, and this strategy (Youssef & Luthans, 2005) was mentioned the least by the participants (16% of the coding). Participants' practices in leveraging asset strategies fell into two categories. Firstly, participants reported an increased sense of self-awareness through their self-reflection during the volatile time. They felt that the pandemic benefitted them, as participant described:

> ... [it was] good to have a period of reflection. There are a lot of working habits before the pandemic which were just not healthy, and at different points in the pandemic they've not been healthy either. (Participant 322, specialist)

Periods of reflection enabled participants to be more aware of the habits which were not benefitting them which enabled them to change their behavior and increase their proactive resilience. In addition, although organizational change meant job losses for some, it also meant variation and opportunity around their existing role. For example, participants felt that:

> ...there have been some really quite exciting RFPs and opportunities...the challenges have been different, different things to get your head around so from that perspective, it does keep things fresh. (Participant 321, senior management)

The inhibitors which prevented individuals from building their asset reserves, unsurprisingly, were related to the increased workload. Participants were very conscious of this and mentioned their tiredness as an inhibitor to exploring the opportunities provided by the change to engage in self-reflection or development. For instance,

> When the kids would go to bed at eight, I'd come downstairs and just look at my emails for a couple of hours, because I've had sort of six, seven hours of emails during most people's working day. And frankly, not many people are accepting, phone calls at five, six in the morning, so my ability to kind of do those kinds of things was compressed really into a morning. Yeah, it was, it was tough. (Participant 121, senior management)

I feel just really really tired and you know there is a lot going on and you don't get the separation anymore, like I said I'm checking emails in all hours that I'm awake to be honest. (Participant 612, middle management)

Reactive Resilience Pathways

Analysis of interview data found that reactive strategies were achieved through activities associated with hardiness (44%), followed by repressive coping (28%), methods of self-enhancement (18%), and finally positive emotion (10%). When considering the differences in strategies leveraged across gender, level of seniority, and change involvement, data showed that employed strategies were similar across seniority and individual's involvement within the company change. When it came to the inhibitors of reactive resilience, data showed that the most mentioned inhibitors for reactive resilience pathways were associated with a sense of lack of control and stability (80% of the coding) and the inability to see the purpose of the change (20% of the coding). These two inhibitors were associated with hardiness and repressive coping respectively.

Hardiness Strategies: Enablers. Hardiness refers to individuals' innate ability to reframe adversity. Interestingly, participants across gender, seniority, and involvement with the change program demonstrated elements of hardiness as a key way of maintaining reactive resilience despite the constant changing work landscape. All participants mentioned their optimism around the potential for development and new opportunities. For example, they were

> excited about [the] sorts of opportunities that [the business change] might bring. If [they] play [their] cards right in terms of identifying things [they] might want to work on…… there might be an opportunity to forge a new role and try something new. (Participant 322, specialist)

> For me personally I feel I'm in a quite a good position to have hopefully a quite an exciting role [that would emerge after the business change]. (Participant 544, middle management)

Participants also showed excitement at the prospect of an increased scope of responsibilities, for example:

> the change will bring with it the biggest scope and scale of work, and new projects [they] never would have been able to work on before, and the opportunity to work with a new brand is incredibly exciting. (Participant 721, middle management)

Others looked forward to the opportunity to create new connections and learn from others, for example:

> meeting new people, having conversations and having a different perspective coming in. I know there isn't quite the same team at [the acquiring company] but there is something similar, and they might have a completely different skill set that I don't have and that would be really interesting. (Participant 211, specialist)

In addition to viewing changes as new opportunities which were adopted by all participants, the data further showed that senior management used hardiness strategies by accepting change, leveraging their social resources and creating a sense of control. To quickly recover from the impact of the potential business change, they responded that:

> ... be having conversations with people to say 'remember me' and 'think of me when you've got a new job'... just keeping in the line of sight as much as you can. (Participant 121, senior management)

> ...the other strategies [include thinking about your network]. How is your network? Are you maximizing your net worth by you talking to head-hunters? I'm certainly doing all of that. (Participant 212, senior management)

Hardiness Strategies: Inhibitors. While it is possible to view the new opportunities brought about by change, a lack of understanding around the purpose of the change could impact individuals' abilities to accept and embrace the opportunities:

> ...honestly don't understand what the business case for the change is. No one has explained that in a way I would understand. (Participant 521, senior manager)

Participants have also highlighted an incongruence felt between their values and those they perceive are that of the new business which has led to an inability to embrace the potential opportunities resulting from the change. For example, a participant described the impact of this incongruence:

> ...the human-interest stuff is just swept under the carpet, so it's quite difficult to kind of get excited by [the potential business change]. I also find it quite difficult to get excited by the management team when they seem to just treat people in the way that they do. (Participant 121, senior management)

> Whether rightly or wrongly, we always seemed like the nicer company, the more friendly employer of the two....I'm sad to see that go. (Participant 544, middle management)

The mix-match between personal values and the change significantly impacts on participants' ability to see the opportunity from change and inhibits them from moving forward from this challenging situation.

Repressive Coping: Enablers and Inhibitors. Repressive coping involves individuals finding ways to avoid unpleasant negativities when facing changes. This primarily takes the form of participants focusing on their work, saying that

> ...it has just been so bloody busy, that I have not had much of a chance to think too much about all of the ramifications. So there's a certain amount of the old ostrich syndrome, you know, head in the sand, try not to think about it, finger in the ears. (Participant 121, senior management)

Interestingly, among the participants, there were also those who were opting to leave the company to avoid the uncertainty and negative emotions associated with change. For example,

> ...have more of a reason to move because of the combination as it has created a lot of uncertainty......[it has meant that they] feel a lot safer and are less worried about being put in some random role where [they] don't know who the team is or where [they] might not even be based in London. (Participant 122, specialist)

By leaving the company, these participants seek stability externally and are therefore actively avoiding the negative emotions associated with the potential business change and have therefore regained a perceived level of control.

As for the inhibitor of repressive coping, a perceived lack of stability was highlighted as an inhibitor to individuals' abilities to bounce back quickly from the impact of the potential business change. This was found to be due to a lingering sense of uncertainty around the future of their role, team and management structure, career progression, and a perceived lack of communication around the change process. For example, a participant described the uncertain situation brought about by the business change, saying that "...*[there are] a lot of people who don't really know what new team, new job is going to look like. That creates a lot of uncertainty and anxiety.*"

When asked about what inhibits their ability to maintain psychologically well in the face of the potential business change, many mentioned stability, for example:

> I'm someone that really values stability. And maybe because we've had such a period of instability with Covid. It feels like another thing that is putting me on an uneven footing. (Participant 721, middle management)

A specialist further noted the impact of instability on career progression during change:

> there is always a bit of fear around where you'll be as a team, you know what position will I be in, how's this going to impact my career progression, and so on. I think that's the personal side of it, and I think at this point in time I don't know how that is going to play out. (Participant 211, specialist)

This was mirrored by a senior manager who said that

> ...at the moment is pretty difficult to get excited about [the potential business change], when all you see are people leaving and a lack of comms. (Participant 121, senior management)

Positive Emotion and Self-Enhancement. Positive emotion was mentioned across all levels of seniority and participants as a way of maintaining a positive mindset. For example, participants were aware of the importance and impact of maintaining an optimistic mindset in the face of change:

> ... if you go in with a negative mindset, then you might portray things, read things and understand things differently than if you go in with a slightly more positive mindset. Then you can think about it and take the opportunities that do come up. (Participant 211, specialist)

Self-enhancement refers to a positive bias toward oneself. We found that this strategy was mainly adopted by those within senior management. This manifested itself in a confidence in their own abilities which they believed would stand them in good stead in the changing landscape following the potential business change.

> ... been around long enough not to really be too worried. Whatever the situation I think I'm excited for what I could get involved in leading up to it and afterwards. Worst comes to the worst, I can go and do something else. I feel like I've got a lot of business skills that I've learned over the years that I wouldn't have to necessarily stick to the industry. (Participant 544, middle management)

Discussion

This study set out to understand how individuals build resilience when their habitual pathways to resilience were restricted. It aimed to do this by identifying the enablers and inhibitors of proactive and reactive resilience during changing work environment—at the time when a significant business change was announced during a global pandemic within an S&P company. This study detailed the practices individuals leveraged to maintain their resilience. For proactive resilience pathways, our participants tended to use process strategies. This included leveraging a combination of different practices, ranging from diet and exercise, rest, flexibility at work, fostering wellness through maintaining a perspective, engaging with wellness activities, and cultivating an appreciation of the outdoors. For reactive resilience pathways, our participants used hardiness through identifying the new opportunities that came with change, cultivating a belief in their ability to influence the outcome, and accepting change; and repressive coping strategies through compartmentalizing the situation and seeking stability. Our findings also highlighted the individuals' capacity to use and recombine their pre-existing resources when they were unable to use their usual practices to maintain individual resilience.

Interestingly, our data showed the possibility for individuals to exercise proactive and reactive pathways to enhance individual resilience despite their gender, level of seniority, level of involvement in the company change program. Prior research suggested that the way in which an employee responds to change can vary depending on their level of seniority within an organization. Olson and Tetrick (1988) argued that those who are of a lower level have little perceived control when circumstances change and are, therefore, more likely to leverage repressive coping techniques as a response, whereas those who are more senior tend to be more proactive and engaged with the change and thereby demonstrate elements of psychological hardiness. Kılınç (2014) also suggested that longer tenure in an organization leads to an individual demonstrating higher levels of psychological hardiness. It was therefore interesting to note that the data in this study found that participants of all levels demonstrated displays of hardiness, and that this was the predominant strategy leveraged across all levels of seniority. When considering an individuals' proximity to change, the primary strategy leveraged also remained unchanged. What was found was that individuals demonstrated a sense of optimism around the potential for new challenges and the resulting learning opportunities, as well as a general acceptance and openness to change, which aligns more closely with Masten's (2001) conclusion in her study into resilience that "*what began as a quest to understand the extraordinary has revealed the power of the ordinary.*"

Our findings also have managerial implications. While individuals can exercise proactive and reactive pathways, findings highlighted that an individual's ability to rest has a significant impact on their ability to build resilience. Not only do we have to consider the impact of an individuals' inability to rest on their physical capabilities to maintain their resilience, i.e., taking exercise, going outdoors etc., but a further and perhaps a more pressing issue is the impact of personal pressure on individuals exert on themselves and how that is leading to an inability for them to maintain or build their proactive resilience. Data showed that the increased sense of personal pressure led to an increase in presenteeism, which in turn saw participants working longer hours and not leaving their desks during the day, therefore not taking breaks. An increase in working hours meant that participants were not able to take breaks throughout the day, and a lack of work/life balance left participants unable to disconnect from work during the evening and weekends. This is consistent with the literature regarding the phenomenon of burn out which highlights the positive impact of rest on well-being (Dababneh et al., 2001; Finkbeiner et al., 2016; Tucker et al., 1999), and that exhaustion is the central driver for burnout (Cropanzano et al., 2003; Wigert, 2020).

Organizational interventions that can be considered include ensuring appropriate levels of resourcing to prevent overwork and encouraging employees to take long (annual leave, weekends) as well as short (during the working day) breaks, the key consideration here is how organizations are assisting employees who are exhibiting overly conscientious tendencies. An example could be to introduce mindfulness practices across the organization to increase self-awareness. According to mindfulness research, this can assist conscientious individuals in improving self-regulation (Masicampo & Baumeister, 2007; Shapiro et al., 2006). Future research could investigate how this could be done when organizations embrace virtual and hybrid working arrangements.

In addition, given the incongruence between individual and company values were inhibitors for hardiness, findings highlighted the impact that direct managers and senior managers can have in shaping individuals' meaning-making processes, and how their narratives could encourage subordinates to demonstrate optimism around the challenge. Organizations should consider how they factor this into their change management programs from a reactive resilience perspective, and their learning and development strategies from a proactive resilience perspective. Organizations could, for example, weave a narrative of opportunity in messaging before and during a change to facilitate employees in realizing their anticipation of new challenges, and development after the change has occurred to reinforce ideas of psychological hardiness. On a more continual basis, organizations could foster a culture that encourages and incentivizes healthy habits around diet and exercise, spending time outdoors and implementing more flexible working practices. Further research could analyze how managerial interventions may affect individuals' sense-making of the change, and the actual meaning of the change experienced by individuals.

Conclusion

As an exploratory qualitative study, this study identified individuals' practices to maintain their level of resilience during a turbulent working environment. Findings indicated that individuals could flex their ways to maintain resilience level yet overwork and being unable to rest served as the main reason to prevent individuals bouncing back to adversity.

References

Alvord, M., Comas-Diaz, L., Dorlen, R., Luthar, S., Maddi, S., Palmiter, D., O'Neill, H., Saakvitne, K., & Tedeschi, R. (2012). *Building your resilience*. https://www.apa.org/topics/resilience. Accessed 4 March 2022.

Avey, J. B., Luthans, F., & Jensen, S. J. (2009). Psychological capital: A positive resource for combating employee stress and turnover. *Human Resource Management, 48*, 677–693.

Baltzer, M., Westerlund, H., Backhans, M., & Melinder, K. (2011). Involvement and structure: A qualitative study of organizational change and sickness absence among women in the public sector in Sweden. *BMC Public Health, 11*, 318–334.

Bardoel, E. A., Pettit, T. M., De Cieri, H., & McMillan, L. (2014). Employee resilience: An emerging challenge for HRM. *Asia Pacific Journal of Human Resources, 52*, 279–297.

Bartone, P. T. (2000). Hardiness as a resiliency factor for United States Forces in the Gulf War. In J. M. Violanti, D. Paton, & C. Dunning (Ed.), *Posttraumatic stress intervention: Challenges, issues and perspectives* (pp. 115–133). Charles C Thomas.

Bartone, P. T., Krueger, G., & Bartone, J. (2018). Individual differences in adaptability to isolated, confined, and extreme environments. *Aerospace Medicine and Human Performance, 89*, 536–546.

Bonanno, G. A. (2004). Loss, trauma, and human resilience: Have we underestimated the human capacity to thrive after extremely aversive events? *American Psychologist, 59*, 20–28.

Bonanno, G. A., Brewin, C. R., Kaniasty, K., & La Greca, A. M. (2010). Weighing the costs of disaster: Consequences, risks, and resilience in individuals, families, and communities. *Psychological Science in the Public Interest, 11*, 1–49.

Bonanno, G., Rennicke, C., & Dekel, S. (2005). Self-enhancement among high-exposure survivors of the September 11th terrorist attack: Resilience or social maladjustment? *Journal of Personality and Social Psychology, 88*, 984–998.

Brasher, K., Dew, A., Kilminster, S., & Bridger, R. (2010). Occupational stress in submariners: The impact of isolated and confined work on psychological well-being. *Ergonomics, 53*, 305–313.

Braun, V., & Clarke, V. (2006). Using thematic analysis in psychology. *Qualitative Research in Psychology, 3*, 77–101.

Braun, V., & Clarke, V. (2020). One size fits all? What counts as quality practice in (reflexive) thematic analysis? *Qualitative Research Psychology, 18*, 328–352.

Britt, T. W., Shen, W., Sinclair, R. R., Grossman, M., & Klieger, D. (2016). How much do we really know about employee resilience? *Industrial and Organizational Psychology, 9*, 378–404.

Callan, V. J. (1993). Individual and organizational strategies for coping with organizational change. *Work and Stress, 7*, 63–75.

Cartwright, S., & Cooper, C. L. (1997). *Managing workplace stress*. Sage.

Conner, D. S., & Douglas, S. C. (2005). Organizationally-induced work stress: The role of employee bureaucratic orientation. *Personnel Review, 34*, 210–224.

Connor, K. M., & Davidson, R. T. (2003). Development of a new resilience scale: The Connor-Davidson resilience scale (CD-RISC). *Depression and Anxiety, 18*(2), 76–82. https://doi.org/10.1002/da.10113

Cropanzano, R., Rupp, D. E., & Byrne, Z. S. (2003). The relationship of emotional exhaustion to work attitudes, job performance, and organizational citizenship behaviors. *Journal of Applied Psychology, 88*, 160–169.

Dababneh, A., Swanson, N., & Shell, R. (2001). Impact of added rest breaks on the productivity and wellbeing of workers. *Ergonomics, 44*, 164–174.

Everly, G. S. (2017). *Psychological body armor: Lessons from neuroscience that can save your career, your marriage*. Crisis Intervention & CISM Resources, LLC.

Finkbeiner, K., Russell, P., & Helton, W. (2016). Rest improves performance, nature improves happiness: Assessment of break periods on the abbreviated vigilance task. *Consciousness and Cognition, 42*, 277–285.

Fisk, G. M., & Dionisi, A. M. (2010). Building and sustaining resilience in organizational settings: The critical role of emotion regulation. *Research on Emotion in Organizations, 6*, 167–188.

Fletcher, D., & Sarkar, M. (2013). Psychological resilience: A review and critique of definitions, concepts, and theory. *European Psychologist, 18*, 12–23.

Folkman, S. (2007). The case for positive emotions in the stress process. *Anxiety, Stress, and Coping, 21*, 3–14.

Folkman, S., & Moskowitz, J. T. (2000). Positive affect and the other side of coping. *American Psychologist, 55*(6), 647–654. https://doi.org/10.1037/0003-066X.55.6.647

Folkman, S., & Moskowitz, J. T. (2007). Positive affect and meaning-focused coping during significant psychological stress. In M. Hewstone, H. Schut, J. d. Wit, K. v. d. Bos, & M. Stroebe (Eds.), *The scope of social psychology: Theory and applications* (pp. 193–208). Psychology Press.

Fredrickson, B. L., Cohn, M. A., Coffey, K. A., Pek, J., & Finkel, S. M. (2008). Open hearts build lives: Positive emotions, induced through loving-kindness meditation, build consequential personal resources. *Journal of Personality and Social Psychology, 95*, 1045–1062.

Gulati, R., Nohria, N., & Wohlgezogen, F. (2010). Roaring out of recession. *Harvard Business Review, 88*(3), 62–69.

Halbesleben, R. B., & Buckley, M. R. (2004). Burnout in organizational life. *Journal of Management*. https://doi.org/10.1016/j.jm.2004.06.004

Howell, R. (2016). How to turn your cost-cutting strategy into a growth strategy. [online] Forbes. Available at: https://www.forbes.com/sites/strategyand/2016/08/11/how-to-turn-your-cost-cutting-strategy-into-a-growthstrategy/?sh=6696a49e7fc6. [Accessed 13 March 2021].

Kılınç, A. Ç. (2014). Examining psychological hardiness levels of primary school teachers according to demographic variables. *Turkish Journal of Education, 3*, 70–79.

Kobasa, S. C. (1979). Stressful life events, personality, and health: An inquiry into hardiness. *Journal of Personality and Social Psychology, 37*(1), 1–11.

Lengnick-Hall, C. A., Beck, T. E., & Lengnick-Hall, M. L. (2011). Developing a capacity for organizational resilience through strategic human resource management. *Human Resource Management Review, 21*, 243–255.

Luthans, F. (2002). The need for and meaning of positive organizational behavior. *Journal of Organizational Behavior, 23*(6), 695–706. https://doi.org/10.1002/job.165

Luthans, F., Vogelgesang, G., & Lester, P. (2006). Developing the psychological capital of resiliency. *Human Resource Development Review, 5*, 25–44.

Luthar, S. S., & Cicchetti, D. (2000). The construct of resilience: Implications for interventions and social policies. *Development and Psychopathology, 12*, 857–885.

Maddi, S., Harvey, R., Khoshaba, D., Lu, J., Persico, M., & Brow, M. (2006). The personality construct of hardiness, III: Relationships with repression, innovativeness, authoritarianism, and Pperformance. *Journal of Personality, 74*, 575–598.

Masicampo, E., & Baumeister, R. (2007). Relating mindfulness and self-regulatory processes. *Psychological Inquiry, 18*, 255–258.

Masten, A. S. (2001). Ordinary magic: Resilience processes in development. *American Psychologist, 56*, 227–238.

Masten, A. S., & Obradovic, J. (2006). Competence and resilience in development. *Annals of the New York Academy of Sciences, 1094*, 13–27.

Masten, A. S., & Reed, M.-G.J. (2002). Resilience in development. In C. R. Snyder & S. Lopez (Eds.), *Handbook of positive psychology* (pp. 74–88). Oxford University Press.

Meyers, M. C., Woerkom, M. V., & Bakker, A. (2013). The added value of the positive: A literature review of positive psychology interventions in organizations. *European Journal of Work and Organizational Psychology, 22*, 618–632.

Mirvis, P. H. (1985). Negotiations after the sale: The roots and ramifications of conflict in an acquisition. *Journal of Occupational Behavior, 6*, 65–84.

Nadler, D. A. (1982). Managing transitions to uncertain future states. *Organizational Dynamics, 11*, 37–45.

Olson, D. A., & Tetrick, L. E. (1988). Organizational restructuring: The impact on role perceptions, work relationships and satisfaction. *Group and Organizational Studies, 13*, 374–388.

Pietrzak, R. H., & Southwick, S. M. (2011). Psychological resilience in OEF–OIF veterans: Application of a novel classification approach and examination of demographic and psychosocial correlates. *Journal of Affective Disorders, 133*, 560–568.

Rice, V., & Liu, B. (2016). Personal resilience and coping with implications for work Part I: A Review. *Work, 54*, 325–333.

Robertson, I., Cooper, C., Sarkar, M., & Curran, T. (2015). Resilience training in the workplace from 2003 to 2014: A systematic review. *Journal of Occupational and Organizational Psychology, 88*, 533–562.

Shapiro, S., Carlson, L., Astin, J., & Freedman, B. (2006). Mechanisms of mindfulness. *Journal of Clinical Psychology, 62*, 373–386.

Shin, J., Taylor, M. S., & Seo, M.-G. (2012). Resources for change: The relationships of organizational inducements and psychological resilience to employees' attitudes and behaviors toward organizational change. *Academy of Management Journal, 55*(3), 727–748. https://doi.org/10.5465/amj.2010.0325

Siggelkow, N. (2007). Persuasion with case studies. *Academy of Management Journal, 50*, 20–24.

Smith, J. A. (2011). Evaluating the contribution of interpretative phenomenological analysis. *Health Psychology Review, 5*, 9–27.

Strauss, A., & Corbin, J. M. (1990). *Basics of qualitative research: Grounded theory procedures and techniques*. SAGE Publications.

Southwick, S. M., Bonanno, G. A., Masten, A. S., Panter-Brick, C., & Yehuda, R. (2014). Resilience definitions, theory, and challenges: Interdisciplinary perspectives. *European Journal of Psychotraumatology, 5*, 1–14.

Taylor, S. E., & Brown, J. D. (1988). Illusion and well-being: A social psychological perspective on mental health. *Psychological Bulletin, 103*, 193–210.

Taylor, S. E., Kemeny, M. E., Reed, G. M., Bower, J. E., & Gruenewald, T. L. (2000). Psychological resources, positive illusions, and health. *American Psychologist, 55*, 99–109.

Tucker, P., Smith, L., Macdonald, I., & Folkard, S. (1999). Distribution of rest days in 12 hour shift systems: Impacts on health, wellbeing, and on shift alertness. *Occupational and Environmental Medicine, 56*, 206–214.

Waugh, C. E., Fredrickson, B. L., & Taylor, S. F. (2008). Adapting to life's slings and arrows: Individual differences in resilience when recovering from an anticipated threat. *Journal of Research in Personality, 42*, 1031–1046.

Weinberger, D. A. (1990). The construct validity of the repressive coping style. In J. L. Singer (Ed.), *Repression and dissociation: Implications for personality theory, psychopathology and health* (pp. 337–386). University of Chicago Press.

Wigert, B. (2020). *Employee Burnout: The Biggest Myth*. [online] Gallup. https://www.gallup.com/workplace/288539/employee-burnout-biggest-myth.aspx. Accessed 12 June 2021.

Williams, C. (2003, June). Sources of workplace stress. *Perspectives*.

Windle, G. (2011). What is resilience? A review and concept analysis. *Reviews in Clinical Gerontology, 21*, 152–169.

Youssef, C. M., & Luthans, F. (2005). Resiliency development of organizations, leaders and employees: Multi-level theory building for sustained performance. In W. Gardner, B. J. Avolio, & F. O. Walumbwa (Eds.), *Authentic leadership theory and practice. Origins, effects, and development*. Elsevier.

CHAPTER 26

ReVisioning the Way We Work: Organizational Creative Capacity and Expanded Cultures of Care

Ginger Grant

INTRODUCTION

The COVID-19 pandemic devastated millions of lives and disrupted the world of work. This business disruption presents an opportunity for innovation to transform and improve organizations, leaders, employees, and stakeholders. To address a complex environment and global talent shortage, it is crucial that organizations "revision" the way we lead, work, adapt to change, and collaborate creatively in ways that leverage and grow available talent, moving from innovation control to a more dynamic, design-driven innovation delivery. In this new world of work, characterized by different ways of organizing and working, alternative leadership styles, new benchmarks, and caring work cultures are also required. A leadership growth mindset is essential to balance the elements of strategy, process, and culture essential for long-term success in a complex environment. The five generations now in the workforce add to the complexity challenge, with different value systems, aspirations, and goals. Ultimately, the pandemic may serve as a catalyst for revising legacy beliefs, structures, and the associated behaviors in business.

G. Grant (✉)
Humber College, Toronto, ON, Canada
e-mail: ginger.grant@humber.ca

© The Author(s), under exclusive license to Springer Nature Switzerland AG 2023
J. Marques (ed.), *The Palgrave Handbook of Fulfillment, Wellness, and Personal Growth at Work*,
https://doi.org/10.1007/978-3-031-35494-6_26

OUR NEW WORLD OF WORK

This new world refers to workers' changing landscape on a global stage. Advancements in technology and globalization combined with shifting demographic and socio-economic trends are rapidly evolving the working environment. Some key aspects to keep in mind in creating a new workforce:

Remote work. One thing we did learn (hopefully!) from the pandemic is that much can be done from home or other remote locations. Because of the increasing availability of technologies and internet connectivity, remote work is now a desired accommodation for many people. A remote or hybrid work program provides for great flexibility and creates a work-life balance that was not possible for most of us before the pandemic. Many employers simply would not consider such a move, thinking that employees must be physically present at the office in order to be productive. It took a pandemic to break that fixed way of thinking.

Flexible schedules. Along with remote work, more flexible working arrangements are now considered desirable if not mandatory. Aside from the obvious benefit of reducing traffic jams on freeways, flexible schedules provide employees with the freedom to attend to personal and/or family needs as those situations arise. During the pandemic, I had a member of my team who had to return to India for family reasons. During his absence, Canada shut down flights to and from India. He now truly was working from home (we did not inform HR). Because of the time difference, our team had 24/7 coverage and productivity increased. Eventually, he was able to return to Canada, but it did give me some food for thought and changed my perspective on flexible schedules and what working from "home" could mean.

Collaborative Work. The nature of the work we do is also changing and becoming more collaborative and project based. Many employees are working in teams, both within and across an organization, whether locally, nationally, or internationally. This requires employees to be more agile and adaptable as well as being fast learners. Our organizations must also be able to adjust to new ways of organizing work. In order to both retain and attract new talent, firms must be able to create flexible work environments that foster collaboration. Many organizations are creating cross-functional project teams which work together to solve complex problems.

Focus on Skills and Learning. Continuous learning and skill development, or upskilling, are becoming increasingly important. Investing in training and professional development programs to help employees keep up with changing technologies and job requirements can become a benefit that helps talent management.

Emphasis on EDI. An emphasis on equity, diversity, and inclusion is now a mandatory component of any organization. Making the effort to create a more inclusive work environment that embrace diverse perspectives and backgrounds will increase creative capacity across the organization. Healthy dissent is necessary to avoid groupthink that can keep an organization stagnant. Having a more inclusive and diverse workplace provides an environment where everyone feels valued and respected.

Gig Economy. The rapid increase in the gig economy has many implications for employees. It does offer more flexibility and autonomy, as workers can choose when and where to work. The downside is that workers may not have access to health insurance, sick leave, or retirement benefits. Job security may also become an issue both for employee and employer.

The Downside. The increasing use of automation and AI has the potential to transform many occupations and industries. However, it could also lead to job displacement and loss of traditional work. Automation has already been used to replace workers in banking, retail, customer service, and manufacturing. New AI platforms are making an impact on creative and education industries. This can lead to economic inequality, unemployment, and social unrest.

These considerations can lead to what has been called a "LEGO block workforce" that is made up of individuals with a variety of skills and backgrounds that can be easily assembled and reassembled to meet the needs of a variety of projects. In such a workforce, individuals are flexible, adaptable, and able to work collaboratively with others. They are also able to work independently and take initiative when needed. This requires a different style of leadership.

Leadership

The new world of work is also characterized by new ways of organizing work, new ways of working and, accordingly, new styles of leadership are required. To meet the demands of this new world of work, a number of principles are essential in forming a foundation of leadership skills needed not just to survive, but to thrive (adapted from Grant, 2017):

1. It is no secret that effective leaders must inspire as opposed to motivate. This ability to inspire is determined by integrity of character (who we are, what we stand for, and how we act), our alignment of purpose and our ability to create a culture of care. While motivation and inspiration may be used interchangeably in our conversations, they are not the same thing. Motivation is a drive to take action. Inspiration is the spark that ignites that drive. Effective leaders use their vision and passion to inspire their teams and communities.
2. Effective leaders develop self-awareness through ongoing self-reflection together with an ability to pay attention to others. We set an example through both words and purposeful action—we walk our talk. We show vulnerability-based trust first to set the example for those who follow.

Effective leaders recognize their strengths and weaknesses, manage their emotions, and adapt their behaviors to be context dependent. This will create a culture of accountability and responsibility in order to drive performance across the organization.
3. We need tools to help us become more reflective and attentive. In order to map a strategy moving forward, we need to first know where we stand. Getting a baseline allows us to measure our own effectiveness as well as identify organizational and cultural norms. It provides a starting point for understanding the current state of the culture. Corporate culture is the shared values, beliefs, behaviors, and attitudes that shape the way people work together. If left unconscious, culture can become a constraint on strategy. Culture by its very nature is invisible and is the accumulated learning of a group of people—the ways of thinking, feeling, and perceiving the world that have made them successful. That world has been permanently changed by the pandemic. A baseline is mandatory in order to set the path forward.
4. Many view organizational transformation as a top-down process that is driven by senior leaders, but the reality is that it takes place one person at a time. Organizational transformation is a complex process that involves changes to an organization's structure, strategy, culture, and systems. Culture is not something that can be changed overnight by the leadership team or a special group in human resources. Instead, we must focus on nourishing our human assets. By engaging with individual employees and addressing their concerns, effective leaders can help to overcome resistance to change and build support for the transformational process. We need to journey into our own hearts to discover our core beliefs and perceptual filters to better understand and then use the shared stories that align and inspire an organization. When individuals are engaged in the transformational process, they feel a sense of ownership and accountability for the success of the initiative. This can lead to greater commitment and dedication to making the necessary changes and can ultimately drive better outcomes.
5. While senior leaders play an important role in supporting change, it is the engagement and support of individual employees that ultimately determine success of the transformation process. One person at a time, leaders can create a culture of change that supports sustainable and impactful transformation. Our organizations will not achieve the results we desire unless our practices (and all policies and procedures) reflect our clearly communicated purpose. A culture audit enables organizations to be proactive rather than reactive in managing a cultural change and ultimately will drive success and improve performance.

In addition to these five principles of leadership, perhaps the most important characteristic that leaders need to have is the ability to shift from a fixed to a growth mindset. Popularized by Carol Dweck at Stanford, it is an essential

Table 26.1 Shifting from a fixed mindset to a growth mindset

Fixed Mindset—leads to a desire to look smart and therefore a tendency to	Growth Mindset—leads to a desire to learn and therefore a tendency to
Give up easily	Persist in the face of setbacks
See failure as fruitless or worse	See failures as essential to mastery
Ignore useful negative feedback	Learn from criticism
Feel threatened by the success of others	Find lessons and inspiration I the success of others
Avoids challenges	Embrace challenges with agility

Adopted from Oakes (2021, p. 33)

capability to successfully navigate and manage change. People with a growth mindset see failure as an opportunity to learn. They believe their ability can be developed through hard work and dedication and are willing to take risks and try new things in order to improve. One of my favorite sayings is "there are no mistakes, only research" (Table 26.1).

The Balance Between Strategy, Process, and Culture in the Face of Complexity

A growth mindset is able to balance the elements of strategy, process, and culture that are essential for the long-term success of any organization. Each element plays a critical role in shaping the organization's overall direction, effectiveness, and sustainability and they must be integrated and aligned in order to achieve the desired results.

In the past, our complicated world was adequately described by the term VUCA. VUCA was coined almost 30 years ago by management scholars and military strategists to describe the post-cold war world. The term was quickly adopted by organizations to describe the challenges they were facing.

Volatility (V) related to the unpredictable extent of change. Facing frequent challenges impacted the progress of daily activities. Uncertainty (U) was the result of these volatile environments as no one could accurate predict what tomorrow would bring. Complexity (C) was characterized by an environment where information was missing, incomplete or difficult to process. Ambiguity (A) was characterized by multiple messages, confusion, conflicts of interest and the difficulty of fully understanding a situation. The concept of VUCA worked for a long time and acted as a filter to create meaning in the face of uncertainty. Leaders needed to equip themselves with skills to navigate a VUCA world. However, the COVID-19 pandemic created such disruption that VUCA has become insufficient to describe our new complex reality.

One of the many painful lessons from the pandemic is our realization of what we did not know and could not anticipate. Prior to 2019, we were confident that simple problems could be solved by known solutions—we

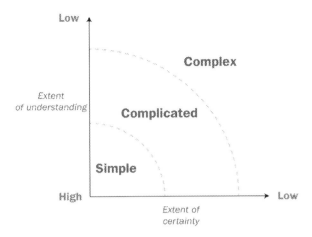

Fig. 26.1 Complexity vs understanding

understood what needed to be done and were certain we had the means to do so. As situations become more complicated, our understanding is less. We attempt to rely on our education and/or our lived experience and perhaps "best practices" we can find from experts in the field. The pandemic produced a complexity that we did not understand. We experienced the "low understanding and low certainty" of a highly complex situation. No rules to rely on. No experts to consult. We were on our own (Fig. 26.1).

In the face of this complexity, to now effect an organizational balance between strategy, process and culture, a realignment is necessary. However, the importance of obtaining a baseline cannot be underestimated. You will know where you stand before attempting a realignment.

Strategy

Taking stock of your old strategic plan, how must it now be adapted to reflect this new complexity in the new world of work? Review the organization's overall vision, mission, and goals, as well as the plans and tactics to be used to achieve these objectives. The baseline from a culture audit will provide a deeper understanding of the organization's strengths and weaknesses. Known opportunities and threats must also be identified—it may be traditional MBA language but still useful! Going through this classic exercise will provide a clearer sense of the shifting environment as well as the state of mind of employees and other stakeholders.

Process Mapping

Review your key processes—the systems and procedures that are used to execute the organization's strategy and achieve its goals. Effective processes are designed to be efficient, effective, and flexible so that the organization can respond quickly and effectively to changes in the external and internal environments. Do your processes support remote work, flexible schedules that promote collaboration? Do not make the mistake of having a blanket process to cover all employees. They are not the same! Remember, transformation takes place one person at a time.

Culture

Culture refers to the values, beliefs, norms, and practices that have shaped your identity as an organization. How have your values and beliefs changed as a result of the pandemic? What did you learn about your people? Make new norms and practices that reflect the talent you wish to retain and the talent you wish to attract—one person at a time.

Our new complex world requires new language. According to Jamais Cascio, an anthropologist and futurist, "In situations in which conditions aren't simply unstable, they're chaotic. In which outcomes aren't simply hard to foresee, they're completely unpredictable. Or, to use the particular language of these frameworks, situations where what happens isn't simply ambiguous, it's incomprehensible" (quoted in Sridharan, 2023). The acronym BANI was born. I think it perfectly describes our situation as we navigate this new world of work (Fig. 26.2).

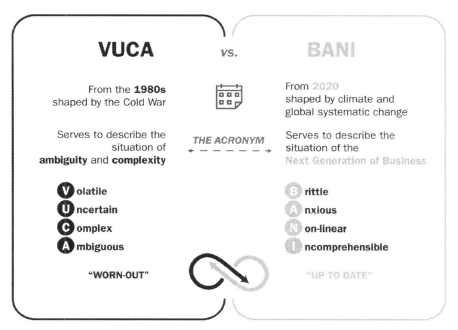

Fig. 26.2 VUCA vs BANI (Adapted from infographic by Stephan Grabmeier)

B—Brittle means fragile, breakable, something not as strong as it seems. I think the pandemic scared us—it reminded us of our vulnerability, our helplessness in the face of something we could not see but could be, and was in many cases, deadly.

A—Anxious refers to a feeling of helplessness, the false illusion of control. Change can produce feelings of anxiety in people, but I think we reached a new level of uncertainty. Anxiety can be temporary and subside as we adjust to the new circumstances, but it can also persist and require support or treatment to manage.

N—Non-Linear refers to the understanding that there is no straight line from A to B. While unpredictability occurs frequently in normal life, it usually is not sustainable especially over a long, continuous period of time, at least in Canada. We went into lockdown March 2020, and I started to return to work in the summer of 2022. In a non-linear situation, small changes or disturbances can have disproportionate effects on the overall system. They can arise in a wide range of contexts, from complex social or economic systems to natural systems like weather patterns. We could know such circumstances as the "butterfly effect."

I—Incomprehensible refers to our experience of not understanding what is happening, can't grasp it, can't interpret it, and therefore, can't find the answers to solve the problem. Incomprehensible situations can be particularly challenging, as they may leave us feeling helpless or overwhelmed. It can be hard to tell what to do and where to start when faced with such a situation.

Leadership in a Time of BANI

BANI circumstances evoke an emotional response that is difficult to handle for anyone. For leaders it requires extra effort, as we may be dealing with our own emotions as well as those of our team, employees, and stakeholders. The following suggestions discuss key leadership capabilities for the near future:

Brittleness needs capacity and resilience. Both capacity and resilience are two important concepts that are closely related to our ability to manage change and uncertainty. In an organizational context, capacity refers to the ability to effectively allocate resources and mobilize people and processes in place to meet current demands. To build capacity, organizations need to invest in their people. That may involve recruiting and retaining top talent, remaining flexible and attentive to individual needs as well as investing in professional development. Resilience refers to our ability to adapt and recover from unexpected events. In an organizational context, resilience can be enhanced by developing robust risk management frameworks, investing in continuity and scenario planning, and fostering a culture of adaptability.

Anxiety needs empathy and mindfulness. Empathy and mindfulness are two important skills that can help individuals and organizations to get though big changes. Empathy refers to the ability to understand and share the feelings of others and to see things from their perspective. By cultivating empathy, individuals can build stronger relationships with their colleagues, as not everyone will respond to anxiety in the same way. Mindfulness refers to the simple practice of being present. By giving your full attention to a person or situation, you can develop a greater sense of clarity and perspective which will create a more positive and productive work environment.

Nonlinearity needs context and adaptability. Context refers to an environment's specific circumstances; it involves understanding and adjusting to the challenges and opportunities being presented. To manage context effectively, organizations must cultivate a deep understanding of their internal and external environments. Using competitive intelligence to gather emerging market insights may produce unusual opportunities. Adaptability refers to the ability to quickly respond to changing circumstances. Organizations will need to adopt a proactive approach to change management.

Incomprehensibility demands transparency and intuition. Transparency refers to the practice of openly and honestly sharing information and communicating with others. By cultivating transparency, people and organizations can build trust and foster collaboration. Intuition is something we are all born with and then I think (unfortunately) traditional education systems force it out of our awareness. Intuition refers to the ability to understand or perceive something without conscious reasoning or evidence. The older I get, the more I cultivate and trust my intuition. It has served me well and provided me a deeper understanding of myself and how I respond and react, as well as greater insights into the behavior of others.

Organizations, leaders, teams, employees, and stakeholders will all face uncertainty and complexity in the future. Adopting these new resilient frameworks, mindsets, and practices will help to ensure they can innovate to make it through the storm (Table 26.2).

Multigenerational Workforce Realities

To add to our complexity challenge, we now have five generations in the workforce, with five different value systems, different aspirations, and goals. Each generation brings unique skills, experiences, and perspectives. By embracing these differences, organizations can create a culture that values diversity and inclusion and recognizes the different priorities of each generation. Actively seek out candidates from underrepresented groups. When you have a team that includes people from diverse backgrounds and experiences, they bring different perspectives and ideas to the table. That wider range of experiences can lead to better problem solving as well as consideration for different viewpoints. When your team can incorporate a wider range of factors and perspectives, you reduce bias, and the quality of decision-making improves. Top talent of all ages value diversity. A diverse workforce can help better understand and serve a diverse customer base. And by implementing such

Table 26.2 Old vs new way of work in uncertainty

When facing uncertainty	Old way of work	New way of work	When facing uncertainty
Slower, less innovative	Authority	Co-elevation	More and better ideas
Limited by structure	Hierarchy	Agility	Pivots and sprints forward
Team overwhelmed	Personal resilience	Team Resilience	Peer-to-Peer support
Caught off guard	Reacts to change	Foresees change	Ready to act
Risk averse to change	Prioritizes core business	Seeks constant reinvention	Discards old assumptions
Limited flexibility	Talent management	LEGO block workforce	Versatile and fluid
Doesn't inspire action	Mission focused	Purpose driven	Drives every decision
	Battles waves and trudges through to the finish line	Floats above turbulent waves and wins the race	

Adapted from Ferrazzi (2022, p. 10)

strategies, you can create an attractive environment that will help to attract top talent in the first place. Promoting diversity and inclusion is simply the right thing to do.

Aligning Employee and Leadership Perspectives on Culture

In a study conducted by HR research leader, i4cp (Institute for Corporate Productivity), ten common organizational culture types were identified, along with related leader and employee traits. The percentage represents how the company self-labeled their culture. Obviously, there are many more cultural types, but this table may provide food for thought for your own organization. How would you label your organization's culture? How would employees? And most importantly, how well would the leader and employee labels match? (Table 26.3)

How to Measure Your Organization's Workforce Baseline

My favorite saying is "assets now have feet" and, particularly in complex situations, it is no secret that any organization is only as good as the people in its workforce. Dr. Ron McKinley, chair of the ISO technical committee

Table 26.3 Aligning employee and leadership perspectives on culture

Culture	Leader traits	Employee traits	Example
Customer-focused 66.0%	Consultative, trustworthy	Relationship driven, proactive	T-Mobile
Performance 62.5%	Goal-oriented, relentless	Merit-based, competitive	Netflix
Innovative 52.1%	Entrepreneurial, resourceful	Creative, persistent	3M
Inclusive 47.9%	Sincere, cooperative	Diverse, relationship-focused	Accenture
Collaborative 47.9%	Facilitator, transparent	Open-minded, team-oriented	Twitter
Agile 47.2%	Boundaryless, visionary	Flexible, multi-talented	Amazon
Purpose Driven 45.1%	Altruistic, philanthropical	Compassionate, unselfish	Patagonia
Learning 36.1%	Intellectually curious, open-minded	Aspirational, ambitious	Microsoft
Quality 29.2%	Systems-oriented, objective	Accountability, caring	Disney
Safety 26.4%	Procedural, structured	Compliant, risk averse	Shell

Adapted from Oakes (2021, p. 78)

who developed the ISO standard baseline measurement criteria for human resources (HR) stated, "Workforce reporting is about rethinking how organizational value should be understood and evaluated and allowing for more data-driven decision making across workforce management" (quoted in Naden, 2019).

In establishing your baseline metrics, consider the ISO standards for HR criteria quality that cover the following areas.

Compliance

- Number and type of grievances filed
- Training hours on compliance and ethics
- External dispute resolutions
- Number, type, and source of external audit
- Finding and actions arising from these.

Costs

- Total workforce costs
- External workforce costs
- Ratio of the basic salary and remuneration for each workforce category
- Total costs of employment
- Cost per hire
- recruitment costs
- Turnover costs.

Diversity

- Workforce diversity with respect to age, gender, nationality, disability, job family, job level/hierarchy, qualification, and diversity of leadership team.

Leadership

- Leadership trust
- Span of control
- Leadership development
- Percentage of leaders/talents who have formal mentors and/or coaches
- Percentage of leaders who have the formal function of mentors or coaches.

Occupational Health and Safety

- Lost time for injury
- Number of occupational accidents
- Number of people killed during work (fatality, death, or mortality rate)
- Training hours on health and safety at work versus total amount of training hours
- Number of employees who participated in the training/total number of employees.

Organizational Culture

- Engagement, satisfaction, commitment
- Retention rate
- Productivity, including revenue, turnover, profit per employee
- Human capital return on investment.

Recruitment, Mobility, and Turnover

- Number of qualified candidates per position
- Quality per hire
- Average time to fill vacant positions; time to fill vacant critical business positions, internal/external recruitment
- Transition and future workforce capabilities assessment
- Percentage of positions filled internally
- Percentage of critical business positions filled internally
- Percentage of vacant critical business positions in relation to all vacant positions.

Employee Bench Strength

- Turnover rate
- Involuntary turnover rater
- Voluntary turnover rate (without retirement)
- Exit/turnover reasons/leaving employment by reason.

Skills and Capabilities

- Total developing and training costs
- Earning and development; percentage of employees who participate in training compared with total number of employees per year; average training hours per employee; number of training participants differentiated in training categories
- Internal mobility rate
- Workforce competency rate
- Succession planning.

Workforce Availability

- Absenteeism rate
- Full-time equivalents
- Number of employees
- Contingent workforce; independent contractors; temporary workforce
- Number of full-time and part-time employees.

(Adopted from http://www.iso/org.news/ref2357.html)

With new ISO reporting requirements, there is an increased attention on organizational culture and the means by which we measure it.

MOVING FORWARD—WHAT NEXT?

The pandemic caused a disruption that, if willingly examined, could lead to a process of significant change. The disruption interrupted our comfortable status quo and created new opportunities for innovation. When traditional ways of doing things are disrupted, it creates an opportunity to start redesign some things from scratch, a blank slate. Could this be a time where new ideas are explored, and approaches considered that would not have been acceptable in the past? Disruption can stimulate creativity and innovation. We have been forced to think "outside the box," challenge old assumptions and made to come up with new solutions to old problems. This can lead to innovative ideas that transform industries and create new markets. Entrepreneurs and innovators who can identify gaps in the marketplace and create solutions to fill them can capitalize on these opportunities and create new businesses. We have the opportunity to review our organizational processes and procedures and cast out the ones that block organizational agility. The pandemic forced many organizations to act quickly and decisively which created a sense of urgency and momentum for change.

Perhaps, in retrospect, the pandemic will be recognized as a catalyst for organizational and workforce changes to many legacy beliefs, structures, and behaviors that have lingered with us since the Industrial Revolution. With the rise of remote work and the gig economy, more employees are no longer tied to a physical location or a traditional employment contract. Instead, they are able to work from anywhere, at any time, and on a project-by-project basis. For organizations, the new world of work allows them to access a global talent pool and tap into new markets. It also requires them to rethink their traditional employment models and find new ways to manage and motivate a mobile workforce. Those who can embrace disruption and capitalize on its opportunities can drive innovation and shape the future. By doing so, they can harness the power of "assets with feet" and build a more resilient, innovative organization.

REFERENCES

Ferrazzi, K. (2022). *Competing in the new world of work*. HBR Press.

Grant, G. (2017). The untapped power of imagination in the workplace. In J. Neal (Ed.), *Handbook of personal and organizational transformation*. SpringerMeteor AG.

Naden, C. (2019, January 15). *New ISO Standard for human capital reporting*. http://www.iso/org.news/ref2357.html

Oakes, K. (2021). *Culture Renovation: 18 leadership actions to build an unshakeable company*. McGraw Hill.

2023 Priorities and Predictions. Institute for Corporate Productivity (i4cp).

Sridharan, M. (2023, February 21). *BANI—How to make sense of a chaotic world?* Think Insights. https://thinkinsights.net/leadership/bani/

CHAPTER 27

Conceptualizing Passion as an Entrepreneurial Pathway

Charlie Wall-Andrews and Reima Shakeir

INTRODUCTION

The entrepreneurial journey is a highly uncertain endeavour with unpredictable dynamics, and individuals who seek to be self-employed and succeed in their new venture must adapt to this reality (Anderson, 2008). The ongoing COVID-19 crisis severely restricted the operations of many businesses and caused a significant decline in trading and provides an excellent example of the difficulties entrepreneurs must contend with. Although the path of entrepreneurship may be characterized by anticipated and unforeseen challenges that could lead to failure, the attractive upsides include personal autonomy, financial success, and meaningful work. According to Lackéus (2017), there are two distinct types of entrepreneurs. The first type is primarily

---

The authors of this submission contributed equally.

C. Wall-Andrews (✉)
The Creative School, Toronto Metropolitan University, Toronto, ON, Canada
e-mail: charlie.wallandrews@torontomu.ca

R. Shakeir
Leonard N. Stern School of Business, New York University, New York, NY, USA
e-mail: rys217@stern.nyu.edu

focused on competition and seeks power, freedom, and money while discovering and exploiting new opportunities (Gonçalves, 2018). The second type is also involved in discovering and exploiting new opportunities, but they prioritize the values of the community and strive to undertake actions that benefit society as a whole. Chew et al. (2016, p. 716) state that entrepreneurship involves making changes to achieve benefits, which could be financial or the satisfaction of improving something for the greater good.

Most entrepreneurs must overcome not only momentary hardships but also continual struggles in the course of building their new business. Some research suggests that being passionate about a venture is one main reason why some entrepreneurs continue in the face of setbacks. Entrepreneurship scholars have compared entrepreneurial passion to a kind of motivating *"fire of desire"*. The general consensus is that passion is a central and strong motivation behind many entrepreneurial efforts.

Etymologically, 'passion' origins can be traced back to the Latin word 'passio' which means suffering (Åstebro, 2017). Psychologists have described the concept of passion using various related terms such as: goals with emotionally significant outcomes that are given high priority, dependency and addiction to activities that individuals enjoy, 'involvement', 'workaholism', and 'commitment'.

Numerous researchers and professionals have provided more specific definitions for the concept of passion, such as enthusiasm, joy, and even fervour that arises from the persistent and unwavering pursuit of a meaningful, demanding, and inspiring goal, and a lasting love.

Because passion appears to have such an important influence on entrepreneurial behaviour and business performance, an increasing number of conceptual studies are exploring this concept and its potential impact on the entrepreneurial domain. More empirical work is needed to confirm the nature and various effects of entrepreneurial passion, but preliminary evidence suggests that passion can be influenced by external factors and can fluctuate over time (Cardon & Kirk, 2015). Furthermore, passion on its own may not be enough for organizational success: state of mind plays a critical role in the success of an entrepreneurial venture. (Chemin, 2010) found that how entrepreneurs feel about their entrepreneurial activities directly correlates to their creativity, which in turn affects innovative organizational outcomes. Social psychologists have already established that positive emotions such as happiness influence task performance and entrepreneurial well-being. Overall, the happier entrepreneurs are with their endeavour, the more likely they will persist and perform better.

Kahneman and Deaton (2010) found that objective happiness, in particular, contributes to individual entrepreneurial enthusiasm. Su et al. (2020) reported that people who are enthusiastic and optimistic about their venture are better able to identify viable opportunities and make productive use of opportunities. Sen (1993) first proposed that happiness unlocks capabilities and freedom of choices, which led to a flurry of research into how emotions are linked to different aspects of human life. With regard to entrepreneurs in particular, Boehm et al. (2008) found that emotion is a prominent variable in all phases of the entrepreneurial process, and Foo (2011) reported that feeling angry or happy influences how an entrepreneur perceives risk. In essence, Vallerand's definition of passion is a powerful attraction or eagerness towards an activity that is personally significant, enjoyable, and receives a considerable investment of time and energy, according to Vallerand et al. (2003). Other scholars have reported that when entrepreneurs are happy; their feeling of well-being creates an atmosphere of trust and creativity in the workplace.

Recent research has gone a step further, exploring how happiness interplays with factors such as resilience, cognition, and the overall well-being of the entrepreneur. The findings of these studies suggest that being happy with a chosen entrepreneurial venture makes work feel more meaningful. Happiness also promotes more work autonomy, which contributes to an entrepreneur's well-being. In contrast, a negative mood lowers individual entrepreneurial well-being, leading to a lack of motivation. For example, an entrepreneur with less drive to perform is more likely to ignore or put off tedious or complicated tasks that may be essential to the survival of a business. Over time, this action will have a cumulative negative effect on the business. Overall, emotions including anger and happiness appear to affect the identification and evaluation of business opportunities, and to have a strong influence on entrepreneurial behaviour and determine how an entrepreneur reacts to circumstances in business.

More specifically, passion appears to be a central force propelling entrepreneurs to seek out specific ventures. Researchers have described passion in the context of entrepreneurship in different ways. Baum and Locke (2004) defined it as a "love for work," while Shane et al. (2003) referred to it as a "selfish love of work." Smilor (1997) described it as an enthusiastic pursuit of a challenging and uplifting purpose that brings joy and zeal. Chen et al. (2009) added that in entrepreneurship; passion is a highly valued emotional state that manifests through cognitive and behavioural expressions. They referred to it as "entrepreneurial passion." Passion makes an entrepreneur look forward to the daily grind and helps prevent depression related to the many hurdles involved in running a business. This point becomes particularly poignant among female entrepreneurs that face many challenges such as unequal access to funding from VC's and gender-based discrimination. Passion also contributes to organizational success, but many current and potential entrepreneurs want more: recent findings indicate increasing numbers of self-employed individuals are giving more priority to their well-being as they pursue the entrepreneurial path. Economic reasons for starting a business are still important, but the newest wave of entrepreneurs also want to enjoy the entrepreneurial process and feel good while performing their tasks (Gielnik et al., 2015). On a deeper level, the importance of passion cannot be denied as it relates to the desire for personal growth, which in turn influences the competitiveness and development of firms.

On the basis of the theoretical and practical background provided above, this study explored two non-economic motivational factors—happiness and personal growth—that spur people to change careers or follow their dreams through new venture creation. The following discussion provides an overview of the extant literature on entrepreneurial passion, motivation, and happiness. It adds to this body of work by conceptualizing how business owners can achieve personal growth and find happiness by working with passion. It also identifies the opportunities and challenges faced by entrepreneurs. It focuses on two main research questions:

1. *How can entrepreneurs attain personal growth and be happy while working with passion?*
2. *What challenges are these entrepreneurs likely to encounter as they pursue their goals?*

The insights from this research offer crucial practical implications. First, they reveal fundamental ways entrepreneurs can preserve and improve their physical, mental, and emotional well-being. Second, they will help individuals seeking a career in entrepreneurship by clarifying the role that emotions play in the entrepreneurial process. They also reveal how positive emotions such as happiness drive motivation and interact with factors such as entrepreneurial ability, entrepreneurial willingness, and the ability of entrepreneurs to acquire resources for their business.

Conceptual Foundations

Before beginning to conceptualize the two key constructs of this study, it is necessary to clarify five relevant concepts and how they tie together.

Entrepreneurial Passion

The past two decades have witnessed a substantial rise in the number of studies examining the significance of passion across a diverse range of activities. The most popular and commonly used definition of passion is the one proposed by Vallerand et al. (2003): a *"strong inclination or an intense feeling of positive emotions towards an activity that people like, that they find important, and in which they invest time and energy."* Cardon et al. (2009) built on this tripartite definition to define entrepreneurial passion as *"consciously accessible intense positive feelings experienced by engagement in entrepreneurial activities associated with roles that are meaningful and salient to the self-identity of the entrepreneur."* For the present study, entrepreneurial passion is defined as strong positive emotions about entrepreneurial-related activities. The study of entrepreneurial passion has greatly enhanced our comprehension of entrepreneurial activities, but it tends to overlook those entrepreneurs who are motivated to engage in such activities not because they are passionate about the process itself, but because they have a passion for the domain of their venture and the product or service it provides. This type of passion is referred to as "domain passion," which involves a strong interest in a particular domain related to the product or service of a venture, such as robotics, cycling, computer programming, fashion, or any other domain.

While some aspects of domain passion are included in entrepreneurship research, such as user entrepreneurship, lifestyle entrepreneurship, and the distinction between artisan/craftsman and growth-oriented entrepreneurs, they are relatively ignored in the literature on passion in entrepreneurship (Shah & Tripsas, 2007). Moreover, entrepreneurs with domain passion may be users of the product or service of their venture, but not all user-entrepreneurs possess domain passion, as they innovate to solve a problem.

Entrepreneurs with domain passion are not necessarily limited in their aspirations for growth of the venture, as is often assumed, and many high-growth ventures have begun with entrepreneurs who exhibit a great deal of domain passion. For instance, successful entrepreneurs like Steve Jobs, Steve Wozniak, Bill Gates, Mark Zuckerberg, Walt Disney, Coco Chanel, and Frank Lloyd Wright all possessed a passion for the domains related to their ventures, which contributed to their success. Entrepreneurs may possess entrepreneurial passion, domain passion, both, or neither, depending on their motivations and identities related to their ventures.

ENTREPRENEURIAL PASSION AND VENTURE CREATION

Research on entrepreneurial passion consistently suggests that it increases motivation. Pioneering work in the field revealed that entrepreneurial passion motivates stronger intentions to launch a new business and can stimulate productive use of available resources. Entrepreneurial passion appears to fuel persistence and creativity in entrepreneurial endeavours. Importantly, investors tend to view more passion in an entrepreneur as a positive signal of their motivation and that investors are particularly drawn to entrepreneurs who are passionate about their venture and demonstrate this by delivering logical and coherent presentations. Blanchflower and Oswald (1998) suggest that many entrepreneurs are enthusiastic about their business ideas but struggle with financial limitations in starting or developing their ventures. To overcome these constraints, they often seek financial support from investors such as angel investors and venture capitalists. Obtaining financial capital is crucial for the establishment, expansion, and sustainability of new ventures, which can help entrepreneurs pursue their passion. While previous research highlights the significance of passion to venture investors (Mitteness et al., 2012), it remains unclear what specifically investors expect founders to be passionate about. In other words, while we know that investors desire passionate founders, the object of that passion has yet to be explored.

Startup investors consider both the business opportunity and the founder's characteristics when making investment decisions, but the founder is typically viewed as the most significant factor. When information about a venture's viability is limited or unknown, investors rely on their "gut feeling" about the founder's qualities, which can lead to high returns. Passion is one such quality that researchers have studied to understand its impact on startup investors' funding decisions (Mitteness et al., 2012). Passion is a strong inclination towards an activity or object that one loves and invests time and energy in (Vallerand et al., 2003), and it has been shown to be significant in startup investors' funding decisions. However, while passion requires a target (an activity or object) to which it is directed, research has yet to specify the target of founder passion that is important to investors. Although it is generally accepted that passion is crucial to investors, particularly to angel investors, it is unclear which targets of founder passion investors value the most. Do investors prefer founders who are passionate about creating and developing new ventures or those who are passionate about the venture's field, such as software or biotechnology? With research on passion in entrepreneurship expanding, it is time to explore the various targets of founder passion in startup investment.

Entrepreneurial passion is an important aspect of entrepreneurship, and it refers to the intense positive feelings experienced by engaging in venture-related activities that are meaningful and salient to the self-identity of the entrepreneur. This passion encompasses various roles and activities central to the entrepreneurial process, including identifying new venture opportunities, founding new ventures, and developing new ventures. While some scholars have defined passion more generally as a love of one's work or enthusiasm, others have focused specifically on its connection to entrepreneurship (Gielnik et al., 2015). Murnieks et al. (2014) define passion in entrepreneurship as a strong and positive inclination towards activities related to starting and running a business. However, other scholars have adopted a more general view of entrepreneurial passion, studying it as a love of one's work, enthusiasm, and excitement when presenting one's business. Baum and Locke (2004) and Shane et al. (2003) fall into this category, as does Smilor (1997) who studied enthusiasm in entrepreneurship. Chen et al. (2009) and Mitteness et al. (2012) also examined the role of enthusiasm in the context of presenting one's business idea.

However, investors do not base their investment decisions solely on one criterion but rather consider a combination of factors. For startup investors, criteria related to experience are highly valued, such as demonstrated leadership, market familiarity, and a relevant track record. These factors provide an indication of the founder's expertise and ability to develop the business in a way that will generate a high return on investment. While a founder's passion for entrepreneurship and domain may signal future actions and commitment, experience provides investors with insight into knowledge, capability, social capital, and previous dedication, which are highly relevant in their investment decisions. Several studies (Carpentier, et al., 2012) have shown that experience is a critical factor in determining whether investors will invest in a given venture.

Entrepreneurial Motivation: Economic and Non-economic Motivation Behind Venture Creation

Entrepreneurial literature also suggests that motivation develops at a rate similar to that of passion. Motivation is generally defined as a form of driving force that activates or energizes someone to do something. Entrepreneurial motivation has been described as *"the set of energetic forces that originate within as well as beyond individuals to initiate behaviour and determine its form, direction, intensity, and duration"*. With regard to the mechanisms that trigger motivation in an entrepreneur, scholars have proposed two distinct types of motivation: economic motives and non-economic/intrinsic motives.

Economic motivation, which is based on classical economic theory, is based on the idea that maximizing wealth is the predominant force driving entrepreneurial behaviour. According to this theory, insufficient income and the pursuit of high economic returns is what attract people to start a business. However, this theory cannot explain certain critical areas of entrepreneurship, and the other end of the spectrum includes non-economic/intrinsic motivation, which can stems from a wide range of personal desires and external influences: the need for independence and the pursuit of happiness, self-realization, and personal growth, as well as government influences and prosocial concerns such as the desire to identify and leverage available resources to resolve social challenges and benefit society. Entrepreneurship is a dynamic and multifaceted phenomenon driven by a variety of motivations. The decision to embark on an entrepreneurial journey is influenced by a complex interplay of economic and non-economic factors. While economic motives, such as financial gains, play a significant role, non-economic motivations, including personal fulfilment and social impact, also contribute to the creation of ventures. In this section, we delve into the economic and non-economic motivations that underpin entrepreneurial endeavours.

Economic Motivation

1. *Financial Independence* One of the primary economic motivations for starting a venture is the desire for financial independence. Entrepreneurs seek to create their own wealth and escape the constraints of traditional employment. The potential for higher earnings, wealth accumulation, and the ability to control one's financial destiny can serve as powerful incentives.
2. *Wealth Creation* Entrepreneurs are often driven by the prospect of creating significant wealth. They aim to capitalize on innovative ideas

or identify market gaps, with the goal of generating substantial financial returns. The promise of financial rewards, including profits, equity stakes, and the possibility of an eventual exit through mergers or acquisitions, motivates individuals to take the risks associated with entrepreneurship.

3 *Job Creation and Economic Impact* Entrepreneurs contribute to job creation, thereby boosting economic growth. The desire to make a tangible impact on the economy by creating employment opportunities, stimulating innovation, and fostering economic development is a compelling motivation for many entrepreneurs. They recognize that their ventures can not only benefit themselves but also positively influence the lives of others.

Non-economic Motivations

1 *Autonomy and Independence* The pursuit of autonomy and independence is a non-economic motivation that drives individuals to start their own ventures. Entrepreneurs often crave the freedom to make their own decisions, define their own work culture, and chart their own course. They seek to escape the confines of hierarchical organizational structures and embrace the flexibility and control that entrepreneurship offers.

2 *Personal Fulfilment and Passion* Many entrepreneurs are motivated by a deep desire for personal fulfilment. They are driven by their passion for a particular idea, product, or industry. The ability to work on something they genuinely care about, find meaning in their work, and align their ventures with their personal values can be a powerful source of motivation.

3 *Impact and Legacy* Entrepreneurs aspire to create a lasting impact on society, leaving behind a meaningful legacy. They are motivated by the opportunity to solve significant problems, address social or environmental issues, and effect positive change. The desire to make a difference in the world and leave a mark beyond financial success drives entrepreneurs to take risks and persist in the face of challenges. Entrepreneurial motivation is a complex blend of economic and non-economic factors. While economic incentives such as financial independence and wealth creation are prominent drivers, non-economic motivations, including autonomy, personal fulfilment, and the desire to make a positive impact, also play crucial roles. Understanding the multifaceted nature of entrepreneurial motivation can help aspiring entrepreneurs cultivate a sense of purpose, align their ventures with their values, and sustain their drive throughout their entrepreneurial journeys.

The following discussion is intended to conceptualize how entrepreneurs can generate positive emotions and develop themselves, so the primary focus is on a single intrinsic motivation: passion.

Link Between Positive Emotions and Quality of Life

Scholars have recently begun to show more interest in how positive emotions can affect the quality of life or life satisfaction. Psychological outcomes and antecedents are of critical importance because positive emotions are known to be associated with positive benefits on health, longevity, social relationships, and personal income. Life satisfaction can affect all elements of human life, but the following discussion is limited to how emotional state influences how an individual processes information and how they respond to situations—and ultimately how emotional state affects quality of life. Research has confirmed that emotions alter perception and evaluation, and scholars have proposed different theoretical models to explain this phenomenon.

Two prominent theories are the emotion-as-information (or feeling-as-information theory) and the emotion-maintenance hypothesis. The emotion-as-information theory theorizes that emotions provide heuristic cues to people: positive emotions such as happiness signal an unproblematic or well-managed state of affairs, leading to looser, more expansive, less systematic, divergent thinking; in contrast, negative emotions suggest a problematic environment. The emotion-maintenance hypothesis builds on the emotional-as-information theory, incorporating the idea that people in positive emotional states are more likely to tackle a problem or situation in less problematic ways (Ali, 2014, p. 3). Overall, both positive and negative states of mind clearly affect how individuals interpret and relate with the world, and a happy mood helps one make better decisions and interact more positively with the world. Positive emotions have long been recognized as a vital aspect of human well-being. Beyond their immediate subjective experience, positive emotions play a significant role in shaping an individual's overall quality of life. Research consistently highlights the profound impact that positive emotions can have on various dimensions of well-being. Enhanced Psychological Well-being: Positive emotions are closely associated with enhanced psychological well-being. Experiencing feelings such as joy, happiness, gratitude, and contentment can contribute to a greater sense of life satisfaction, overall happiness, and fulfilment. Positive emotions help to counterbalance negative emotions, reduce stress, and improve mental health outcomes. By fostering positive emotions, individuals are more likely to have a positive outlook, greater resilience, and higher levels of self-esteem. Improved Physical Health: The impact of positive emotions extends beyond mental well-being and can have tangible effects on physical health. Research suggests that positive emotions are associated with lower levels of stress hormones, reduced inflammation, and a strengthened immune system. People who experience positive emotions more frequently tend to have better cardiovascular health, lower rates of chronic illnesses, and faster recovery from illness or injury. The connection between positive emotions and physical health underscores the holistic nature of well-being. Enhanced Social Relationships: Positive emotions play a crucial role in fostering meaningful social connections and nurturing supportive relationships. When individuals experience positive emotions, they are more likely to engage in prosocial behaviours, such as empathy, kindness, and generosity, which in turn strengthens social bonds. Positive emotions contribute to better communication, conflict resolution, and overall relationship satisfaction. Building positive emotions within oneself can have a ripple effect, spreading positivity to interpersonal interactions, and enhancing the quality of social relationships. Increased Resilience: Positive emotions act as a buffer against adversity and promote resilience in the face of challenges. Individuals who cultivate positive emotions are better equipped to cope with stress, setbacks, and life transitions. Positive emotions broaden one's perspective, enhance problem-solving abilities, and facilitate creative thinking, allowing individuals to approach difficulties with a more adaptive mindset. The ability to experience positive emotions amidst adversity contributes to psychological and emotional resilience, ultimately enhancing overall quality of life. Promoting Personal Growth and Flourishing: Positive emotions are closely intertwined with personal growth and flourishing. When individuals experience positive emotions, they are more open to new experiences, exhibit a growth-oriented mindset, and actively seek personal development opportunities. Positive emotions provide individuals with the motivation, energy, and optimism necessary to set and pursue meaningful goals. As a result, individuals who frequently experience positive emotions are more likely to engage in self-improvement, engage in lifelong learning, and strive for personal fulfilment. Positive emotions are powerful contributors to overall quality of life. They impact psychological well-being, physical health, social relationships, resilience, and personal growth. Cultivating positive emotions through practices such as gratitude, mindfulness, and nurturing supportive relationships can have profound effects on an individual's well-being. Recognizing the link between positive emotions and quality of life enables individuals to prioritize their emotional well-being, leading to a more fulfilling and flourishing existence.

INTERACTIONS BETWEEN PERSONAL GROWTH AND PASSION

Personal growth is a process of improving one's mental, physical, and emotional health and using this capability to act with awareness and in greater accord with one's values and potential (Levine et al., 2006). Personal growth is an essential component of a person's psychological well-being, and those with higher levels of this attribute tend to exhibit higher satisfaction in their work and personal lives (Wright et al., 2006). Many people prioritize mental and physical health, especially in the context of COVID-19 and its effects, and personal growth and development have an important life goal. Entrepreneurs do not wish to sacrifice their personal growth, even as they may zealously pursue venture creation.

Starting and running a business is known to be emotional and physically draining, especially when one is passion about the business. Our literature review revealed that the entrepreneurial process includes several experiences that act as catalysts or triggers for personal growth: these experiences are often intense and evoke strong emotions in entrepreneurs, even causing them to challenge their values (Chemin, 2010) or sense of self (Örtqvist et al., 2007). Specific experiences may include dealing with lack of or insufficient capital, difficulty in securing loans, managing cash flow, managing and assembling the right talent, dealing with competition, finding profitable customers, time management, and delegating authority.

Entrepreneurial passion can be a facilitator or barrier to personal growth during venture creation. The next sections will show that passion for work can be sub-divided into two main types, which can lead to very different results. Harmonious passion facilitates personal growth: it promotes reflection, emotional support, and prioritization of core values, in turn fostering greater mindfulness and personal development. In contrast, obsessive passion is synonymous with workaholism and is a barrier to self-growth: it invariably leads to fatigue, feelings of being overwhelmed, lack of personal time, and total burnout.

Methodology

We began by following the procedures outlined by Xiao and Watson (2019) and Shepherd et al. (2015) to conduct a systematic search for articles. Some previous literature has highlighted the need for more research on specific areas of happiness as they relate to entrepreneurship, but to date no comprehensive study has explored how individuals can find happiness and achieve personal growth in their entrepreneurial endeavours. Therefore, we searched three extensive databases: Google Scholar, Scopus, and Web of Science. We searched the titles, abstracts, and keywords of articles for the following terms: *entrepreneurial passion, happiness in entrepreneurship, entrepreneurial motivation, emotions in entrepreneurship, and happiness and subjective well-being of entrepreneurs*. Our initial search yielded a list of 420 articles. To ensure articles were specific and relevant to our review, we excluded all papers that did not focus specifically on our key search terms as these were central to our study. This second screening trimmed down our final sample to 40 relevant articles. We then conducted document analysis. Document analysis is a form of qualitative research in which documents are interpreted by the researcher to give voice and meaning around an assessment topic (Bowen, 2009). Articles can offer a foundation of knowledge and extensive data coverage, making them advantageous in situating one's investigation within its particular subject or domain.

Limitations

Although documents can be useful in providing a background and extensive coverage of data for research, they may not necessarily contain all the essential information required to address research questions. Some documents may offer limited or no valuable information, and others may be incomplete, contain inaccurate or inconsistent data, or have gaps in information, leading to a more extensive search for additional documents (Bowen, 2009). Additionally, some documents may not be accessible or readily available, and therefore, it is crucial to evaluate their quality and anticipate encountering difficulties or gaps when using document analysis.

Before conducting document analysis, it is essential to acknowledge and consider the potential presence of biases in the documents themselves and from the researcher's perspective. Both Bowen and O'Leary recommend a thorough assessment of the subjectivity of documents and one's understanding of their data to maintain the research's credibility (2009, 2014).

Conceptual Framework

Our conceptual framework draws heavily from the dualistic model of passion of Vallerand and Houlfort (2003). Briefly, venture owners can experience passion for work in two ways: (1) harmonious passion—where individuals internalize their activities in an autonomous way and keep their passion under control; or (2) obsessive passion—where individuals are emotionally dependent on work activities to the extent they become negatively controlled by their passion. In essence, harmonious passion gives an individual the drive to choose whether or not to do their passionate activity, while obsessive passion compels an individual to continue to engage with such activity even to personal detriment (Fisher et al., 2018).

We hypothesize that entrepreneurs working more with harmonious passion in their business will feel more positively about their work, and in turn lead to improved well-being (Carpentier et al., 2012). Several independent studies and reviews have reported that high levels of passion tend to be associated with better physical health, psychological functioning, self-growth, positive emotions, and overall well-being (Carpentier et al., 2012). Higher well-being has been linked to improved performances at work and a broad range of other settings including academics (Forest et al., 2012; Philippe et al., 2009).

We further theorize that the two types of passion involve different emotional experiences and consequences for an entrepreneur. Research evidence has consistently revealed strong positive correlations between harmonious passion and subjective well-being, and negative relationship between obsessive passion and subjective well-being, at work (Gorgievski & Bakker, 2010; Vallerand et al., 2007). Theoretically, these two passion variables also produce different outcomes of business performance. Harmonious passion facilitates flow and positive emotions when engaging in work activities. Obsessive passion results in rigid pursuit of an entrepreneurial activity that may produce positive outcomes despite the risk of incurring significant negative outcomes in one's personal life.

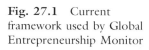

Fig. 27.1 Current framework used by Global Entrepreneurship Monitor

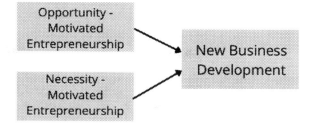

Fig. 27.2 Proposed conceptual framework that includes passion as a motivator

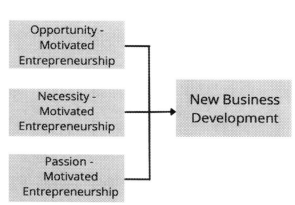

As shown in Fig. 27.1, most scholars have framed entrepreneurship as motivated by opportunity and necessity. However, the COVID-19 pandemic and associated changes in society have opened new doors for individuals to pursue entrepreneurship and follow their passion. The next sections build on our review of academic literature to develop a conceptual framework according to which passion is an independent motivational variable that can enable an entrepreneur to find happiness and achieve self-growth when working with passion. Figure 27.2 presents our proposed framework for conceptualizing passion as a motivator for entrepreneurship.

Conceptualizing How Entrepreneurs Can Achieve Personal Growth and Find Happiness by Working with Passion

Ever since the topic of entrepreneurship began to gain widespread attention in society, scholars have investigated what drives people to go into venture creation. They initially identified several motives, including a need to achieve financial independence or a desire to follow a passion, work from anywhere, seize an opportunity, personal circumstances, fulfil an unmet need in the market, set one's own deadline, and to have more spare time. More recently, and especially since the COVID-19 pandemic, scholars are discovering that individuals are choosing entrepreneurship mainly for non-economic gains such as personal growth happiness and happiness. For entrepreneurs, the journey of building and growing a business goes beyond financial success. It becomes a deeply personal endeavour that intertwines their identity, values, and aspirations. To thrive in this entrepreneurial pursuit, it is essential for individuals to work with passion—a driving force that not only fuels their motivation but also leads to personal growth and happiness. Aligning Values and Purpose: Working with passion involves aligning personal values and purpose with entrepreneurial endeavours. When entrepreneurs embark on ventures that resonate with their core values, they feel a strong sense of purpose and fulfilment. By identifying a mission that goes beyond monetary gains and contributes to a greater cause, entrepreneurs can tap into a deeper sense of meaning in their work. This alignment empowers them to overcome challenges, stay committed, and find happiness through the knowledge that their work is making a positive impact. Continuous Learning and Development: Passionate entrepreneurs view their work as a journey of continuous learning and development. They actively seek opportunities to acquire new skills, expand their knowledge base, and refine their expertise. By embracing a growth mindset, entrepreneurs not only enhance their professional capabilities but also experience personal growth. The pursuit of knowledge and mastery fuels their passion, allowing them to remain engaged, adaptable, and open to innovation. This commitment to lifelong learning contributes to their personal growth and overall happiness. Embracing Challenges and Resilience: Entrepreneurial ventures are accompanied by numerous challenges and setbacks. However, entrepreneurs driven by passion are more inclined to embrace these obstacles as opportunities for growth. By approaching challenges with a resilient mindset, entrepreneurs can develop the skills necessary to overcome adversity. Resilience strengthens their ability to bounce back from failures, adapt to changing circumstances, and find alternative paths to success. This ability to face challenges head-on and persevere leads to personal growth, enhanced self-confidence, and a greater sense of happiness in their entrepreneurial journey. Nurturing Well-being and Work-Life Balance: Passion-driven entrepreneurs recognize the importance of maintaining well-being and achieving work-life balance. They understand that sustainable success requires taking care of their physical, mental, and emotional health. By prioritizing self-care, setting boundaries, and nurturing healthy relationships, entrepreneurs can prevent burnout and create a supportive environment for personal growth. Achieving work-life balance allows entrepreneurs to find happiness not only in their professional achievements but also in their personal lives, fostering a sense of fulfilment and overall well-being. Cultivating Meaningful Connections and Collaboration: Passionate entrepreneurs understand the value of building meaningful connections and collaborating with like-minded individuals. They actively seek out networks, mentors, and partnerships that provide support, guidance, and inspiration. By surrounding themselves with a diverse community, entrepreneurs can exchange ideas, learn from others' experiences, and cultivate a sense of belonging. Meaningful connections and collaborations not only contribute to personal growth but also foster happiness by creating a sense of shared purpose and mutual support. Working with passion as an entrepreneur opens up pathways to personal growth and happiness. By aligning values and purpose, embracing continuous learning, cultivating resilience, nurturing wellbeing, and fostering meaningful connections, entrepreneurs can unlock their full potential. When entrepreneurs find joy and fulfilment in their work, they embark on a transformative journey that not only leads to professional success but also enhances their personal growth and overall happiness.

With this new development, some scholars have begun to propose constructs relating to how a person can achieve personal happiness and growth while being driven by passion. The next sections explore five interrelated elements that appear to foster this process, and then discuss ways to leverage these three elements.

Genetic Set Point for Happiness

Numerous descriptions of happiness exist, and the majority of them highlight a favourable mental state characterized by a sense of contentment and enjoyment (Ali, 2014; Coelho do Vale, 2016; Lackéus, 2017; Naudé et al., 2014). Numerous research studies (Marques, 2017; Pryce-Jones & Lindsay, 2014; Rodríguez-Muñoz & Sanz-Vergel, 2013) have confirmed the correlation between happiness, well-being, and employment (Gonçalves, 2018).

Similar to research findings about happiness in broader life, scholarly evidence has shown that happiness at work can be linked to personal and environmental factors. Some empirical findings suggest that genes and personality may determine a person's satisfaction with their work. Moreover, some evidence supports the idea that a person's disposition to happiness with their business is independent of the attributes or situations related to the work context. In general, an individual with a high disposition to core self-evaluations and positive affectivity—i.e., someone with high self-esteem, internal locus of control, emotional stability, and generalized self-efficacy— tend to be happier at work and in broader life (Cardon, et al., 2015).

It is commonly accepted that everyone has a predetermined or natural personal perspective or genetic set point (also called the 'top-down' models of well-being). From this perspective, individuals with stable disposition are naturally in a more or less positive state of mind, which directly affects their well-being and also colours their perceptions and how they evaluate circumstances and events that may influence their well-being.

From all indications, an entrepreneur's genes and inherent personality play a significant role in their happiness: research suggests that some individuals have are more natural predisposition to be happier compared to others. Studies involving twins have reported that as much as 50% variance of subjective well-being is determined genetically (Inglehart & Klingemann, 2000). Proponents of the set point theory argue that a person is predisposed to 'contain' a specific level of happiness and that they normally revert to that set point fairly fast after short-term disturbances caused by pleasant or unpleasant external events.

People who are naturally predisposed to be happy tend to routinely interpret events or situations differently from people who are naturally predisposed to unhappiness. They tend to be more cautious about engaging in social comparisons that might put them at a disadvantage, and to concentrate more on their achievements rather than dwelling on past failures and mishaps. They are tenaciously optimistic, and tend to have better coping techniques than less happier people. Dispositionally happy people also selectively place themselves in relationships and environments that promote subsequent happiness.

Some scholars have explored the mechanisms by which a person's disposition contributes to their happiness level at work. Building on the work of Bowling and Gilhooly (2005), Fisher (2010) identified three mechanisms that may affect disposition to happiness: the individual's ability to adapt and find an equilibrium level of satisfaction with their job; the level of sensitivity to events at work; and how fast the individual's job satisfaction reverts to equilibrium after exposure to positive or negative events at work. Moreover, evidence indicates that the influence of trait affectivity on an entrepreneur's level of satisfaction and happiness is moderated by state affect. Finally, research suggests that individuals scoring highly on self-evaluations are more likely to pursue self-concordant, intrinsic goals that would bring them happiness.

Choose a Business That Is the Right Fit

A second element related to happiness in entrepreneurship involves finding a business with the right fit. Many scholars have attempted to define and assess this kind of fit in various ways: at the personal level and also at the organizational level. Briefly, fit in business refers to a worker having the same qualities as the organization. Fit is usually conceptualized as personality fit or value fit with the company's culture or other employees; it is usually framed as needs—supplies fit or demands—abilities fit. Needs-supplies fit refers to a situation when a worker's individual needs are supplied by their organization, while demands—abilities fit refers to a situation in which a worker's skills and abilities match what the organization requires. Needs—supplies fit appears to be particularly important: a large body of evidence has shown that this form of fit is linked to organizational commitment and job satisfaction.

Overall, people tend to be much happier when placed in a work setting that fits their preferences in terms of needs, goals, values, and aspirations. The key is to find a business or field that fits one's personal skills, talents, and resources.

CREATE A FAIR, JUST, AND HEALTHY ORGANIZATIONAL CULTURE

The third element involved in achieving personal growth and finding happiness in entrepreneurship is a toxic-free workplace; i.e., building a good organization. Scholars focusing on organizational behaviour are aware that the primary causes of stress, happiness, or unhappiness in organizations are related to the characteristics of the job, the organization, and the manager.

Workplace happiness requires avoiding a culture of blame, disrespect, and control, and instead cultivating principles of justice, fairness, and respect. Within an organization, effective HR practices and a fair business culture can foster happiness among employees. Scholars have proposed a theory of organizational culture and effectiveness according to which happiness in a workplace increases when employees enjoy those they work with, trust one another, and are proud of what they do (Inglehart et al., 2008). When a business is built on trust, respect, fairness, and credibility, the result is a win-win for everyone involved: the employer, the employees, and the whole organization. Fisher (2010) identified three critical factors related to creating an engaged and enthusiastic work environment: equity (fairness, security, and dignified and respectful treatment), camaraderie with other employees; and achievement (job challenge, feedback, empowerment, and pride in the organization).

Another way to develop a healthy work culture is using the so-called high performance work approach (also known as the high commitment or high involvement approach). It involves being extremely selective in hiring, offering extensive training to workers, restructuring organizational teams to work autonomously, giving rewards based on organizational performance, adopting flat corporate structures, and providing job security. This approach tends to minimize employee turnover, contribute to financial performance, and boost quality and motivation. High performance work approaches also tend to improve affective commitment, satisfaction, and engagement, and these approaches are mediated by their effects on worker happiness. High performance work approaches may improve happiness by providing opportunities for employees to feel autonomous, competent, and connected to others.

These findings are supported by studies on perceived psychological climate within an organization: how individuals perceive cognitive, affective, and instrumental aspects of an organizational climate is strongly associated with happiness, as reflected by organizational commitment and job satisfaction. A meta-analysis revealed that certain dimensions of workplace climate (role, job, leader, organization, and workgroup) were consistently associated with satisfaction, personal development, and other organizational attitudes (Inglehart et al., 2008). Another issue is how fair the organization is perceived as being, which also contributes to the commitment and job satisfaction of the business owner (Douglas et al., 2018). Overall, specific organizational qualities and practices, as well as how they are viewed by employees, are consistent predictors of happiness—and these can cultivated by the founder of a venture.

BE INTENTIONAL ABOUT IMPROVING INDIVIDUAL HAPPINESS

As discussed above, happiness is partially determined by genetics, but it is also possible to be intentional about improving one's happiness in the workplace. Momentary happiness has been linked with effective performance as well as perceived progress towards a goal. Therefore, setting and pursuing small-scale intentional activities, or challenging but attainable short-term objectives, may improve feelings of happiness and boost personal growth.

To begin embracing happiness and working towards personal growth, an entrepreneur could first seek both person—organization and person—job fit when deciding on their business field of choice. Next, they could adjust their expectations to align with reality. If they discover they are not satisfied with their business of choice, they could leave it and choose another with a better fit. Very few studies have examined this phenomenon of switching careers by following entrepreneurs across various sectors. Boswell et al. (2005) conducted a related study but with a focus on executives switching careers between organizations, not on entrepreneurs. Still, their findings provide some valuable insights that could be applied to entrepreneurs. They found that executives who were not happy with their present job were more likely to change jobs within the next year and to have greater satisfaction with the new job. They referred to this phenomenon as the "honeymoon effect," but also found that this effect was short-lived and that satisfaction tended to revert to baseline levels in the second year.

One of many other ways an entrepreneur can improve their own happiness is by choosing a business with which they feel a connection. Some scholars have suggested that individuals are generally authentically happy when they feel connected or 'called' to a business, i.e., when they feel there is an important value or higher purpose attached to their venture (Feki & Mnif 2016). Employees may also 'craft' jobs in a way that will make the task enjoyable to them. Job crafting involves more than by modifying tasks; it entails psychological reframing of the meaning of tasks, as well as changing or building relationships with clients and co-workers. The idea is that people can craft tasks to build a positive self-image within the workplace, assert control, and to satisfy the human need to connect with others. Fisher (2010) explored this issue in the context of nursing and found that nurses may redraw the traditional image of their work—performing menial tasks ordered by a doctor—by redefining their tasks as rendering help to patients and helping them heal. This type of reframing can be successful in fostering both needs—supplies and demands—abilities, and can enhance happiness and personal growth in a business.

Another way for individuals to enhance their demands—abilities fit is by identifying their own personal strengths. Each employee or entrepreneur possesses a unique collection of personal talents, preferences, and strengths. The idea is to discover one's own unique attributes and then redesign activities that draw from and build on these strengths. Individuals should dedicate much of their daily effort to tasks that utilize their strengths; conversely, they should minimize effort on tasks that do not make use of their strengths. Following this advice is likely to yield greater self-actualization and competence and help individuals improve their level of happiness.

Finally, aspiring entrepreneurs can be intentional about improving their individual happiness by soliciting feedback about critical areas in their entrepreneurial endeavours that need to be revamped. Morecroft (1985) stressed that feedback should be sought not only for areas in which in the individual is lacking, but also for areas in which the individual has been praised: seeking feedback from both sides will provide a more reliable picture of the individual's reflected self. The Gallup research firm currently uses the Clifton Strength themes—a proprietary assessment questionnaire containing 34 questions—to measure a person's actual strength versus perceived strength. Other online surveys are available for collecting feedback about an individual's strengths, e.g., the VIA Inventory of Strengths (VIA-IS), previously known as the Values in Action Inventory. Similar to the Gallup survey, the VIA-IS is proprietary and is designed to identify the character strengths of an individual.

DESIGN AN ORGANIZATION WITH DESIRED VALUES

It is difficult to be happy or experience any positive personal growth within a toxic work environment. One way to ensure positive experiences within a business is to foster a positive work climate right throughout the entire organization, from management to the ground floor. Proudfoot et al. (2009) developed an effective intervention measure to improve organizational well-being: they designed an extensive cognitive behavioural therapy programme lasting 13 weeks: seven weeks for the actual training programme and an additional follow-up programme lasting six weeks. The programme teaches stressed sales agents how to eliminate dysfunctional thinking patterns and embrace a happier attributional style. The findings after three months revealed improvements in participants' well-being and job satisfaction; after two years, employee turnover was still reduced and job performance was still improved.

This discussion has explored how an entrepreneur might build an organization that is conducive to the happiness and personal growth of all employees. Specific steps could include: (1) creating a respectful, supportive, and healthy organizational culture; (2) designing jobs to be autonomous, interesting, and challenging; (3) supplying skilled leadership at all levels; (4) hiring based on person–job and person–organization fit; (5) minimizing minor hassles and increasing positive experiences; (6) encouraging workers to reframe less desirable tasks or work environment into a more acceptable narrative; (7) adopting high performance work strategies; and (8) offering recognition for good performance, security, and fair treatment (Binder & Coad 2013).

Conclusion

The results of this study are consistent with previous findings that passion is a powerful driver of happiness and personal growth in entrepreneurship. However, research also reveals that passion can be a two-edged sword: on the one hand, an individual who is passionate about their work is more likely to have the drive, energy, and motivation to keep going, and passion can lead to enormous satisfaction with work. On the other hand, passion can be a predictor of negative consequences like depression and burnout when an individual neglects other areas of their life without benefitting from their sacrifice. Overall, this work has yielded three crucial conclusions:

- Passion can be a pathway to positive emotions and personal growth for entrepreneurs, just as it can trigger negative results such as negative emotions and conflict.
- There are two main types of passion for work: harmonious passion and obsessive passion.
- Harmonious passion is significantly and positively related to happiness and personal growth among entrepreneurs, whereas obsessive passion poses a major hindrance to happiness and work satisfaction.

Passion is undeniably a powerful driver of happiness and personal growth in the realm of entrepreneurship. It fuels the drive, energy, and motivation that keep individuals going, and it can lead to tremendous satisfaction with their work. However, research also reveals that passion can be a double-edged sword. While passion can be a pathway to positive emotions and personal growth, it can also trigger negative consequences such as depression and burnout when individuals neglect other areas of their life without reaping the benefits of their sacrifices. As a result, it is crucial to understand the nuances of passion in entrepreneurship. The distinction between harmonious passion and obsessive passion is paramount. Harmonious passion, where individuals engage in their work willingly and with a sense of autonomy, is significantly and positively related to happiness and personal growth among entrepreneurs. This type of passion aligns with their values, fosters work-life balance, and contributes to overall well-being. On the other hand, obsessive passion, characterized by an uncontrollable urge and excessive preoccupation with work, poses a significant hindrance to happiness and work satisfaction. This intense drive can lead to negative emotions, conflict, and ultimately impede personal growth. To harness the positive power of passion, entrepreneurs must cultivate harmonious passion by finding alignment between their personal values and their entrepreneurial pursuits. This entails maintaining a healthy work-life balance, nurturing well-being, seeking support and collaboration, and recognizing the importance of personal growth beyond professional achievements. By developing a balanced and sustainable approach to their passion, entrepreneurs can create a fulfilling and purpose-driven entrepreneurial journey that enhances happiness, fosters personal growth, and avoids the pitfalls of burnout and negative consequences. In conclusion, passion is a formidable force that can propel entrepreneurs towards happiness and personal growth. It can ignite their entrepreneurial spirit, infuse their work with meaning, and contribute to their overall well-being. However, entrepreneurs must navigate the fine line between harmonious passion and obsessive passion, ensuring that their passion remains a source of inspiration and fulfilment rather than a path towards negative outcomes. By nurturing a healthy relationship with passion, entrepreneurs can unlock their true potential, experience personal growth, and find lasting happiness along their entrepreneurial path. In sum, most entrepreneurs will experience both types of passion intermittently during their business lifespan. Each type of passion contributes differently to entrepreneurial outcomes and the entrepreneur's life goals. This analysis has highlighted the importance of working with passion as a pathway to finding happiness and self-growth in entrepreneurship—but also demonstrates the need for harmonious passion. These findings contribute to the existing body of literature about entrepreneurship by clarifying the variables that can promote harmonious passion and consequently lead to happiness and personal development among entrepreneurs. More work is needed to identify practical techniques to harness the benefits of working with passion while simultaneously circumventing the pitfalls. Another pathway for research is to examine how passion manifests in the lived experience of female entrepreneurs with a focus on women of color.

References

Ali, A. J. (2014). Innovation, happiness, and growth. *Competitiveness Review, 24*(1), 2–4. https://doi.org/10.1108/CR-09-2013-0075

Anderson, P. (2008). Happiness and health: Well-being among the self-employed. *Journal of Socio-Economics, 37*(1), 213–236. https://doi.org/10.1016/j.socec.2007.03.003

Angulo-Guerrero, M. J., Pérez-Moreno, S., & Abad-Guerrero, I. M. (2017). How economic freedom affects opportunity and necessity entrepreneurship in the OECD countries. *Journal of Business Research, 73*, 30–37. https://doi.org/10.1016/j.jbusres.2016.11.017

Åstebro, T. (2017). The private financial gains to entrepreneurship: Is it a good use of public money to encourage individuals to become entrepreneurs? *Small Business Economics, 48*(2), 323–329. https://doi.org/10.1007/s11187-016-9777-y

Beugelsdijk, S., & Maseland, R. (2010). *Culture in economics: History, methodological reflections, and contemporary applications* (pp. 1–388). New York Cambridge University Press.

Binder, M., & Coad, A. (2013). Life satisfaction and self-employment: A matching approach. *Small Business Economics, 40*(4), 1009–1033. https://doi.org/10.1007/s11187-011-9413-9

Bowen, G. A. (2009). Document analysis as a qualitative research method. *Qualitative Research Journal, 9*(2), 27–40. https://doi.org/10.3316/QRJ0902027

Cardon, M. S., & Kirk, C. P. (2015). Entrepreneurial passion as mediator of the self-efficacy to persistence relationship. *Entrepreneurship Theory and Practice, 39*(5), 1027–1050.

Carpentier, J., Mageau, G. A., & Vallerand, R. J. (2012). Ruminations and flow: Why do people with a more harmonious passion experience higher well-being? *Journal of Happiness Studies, 13*(3), 501–518.

Chemin, M. (2010). Entrepreneurship in Pakistan: Government policy on SMEs, environment for entrepreneurship, internationalisation of entrepreneurs and SMEs. *International Journal of Business and Globalisation, 5*(3), 238–247.

Chew, L. M., Hoe, L. S., Kim, T. C., & Kiaw, L. W. Y. (2016). Self-perceived entrepreneurship skills for undergraduates of private university in Malaysia. *American Journal of Applied Sciences, 13*(6), 715–725. https://doi.org/10.3844/ajassp.2016.715.725

Coelho do Vale, R. M. I. (2016). *Felicidade, satisfação e qualidade de vida, solidão e percepção de saúde*. Retrieved from Observatório da Sociedade Portuguesa - Católica-Lisbon.

Davidsson, P. (2005). Methodological approaches to entrepreneurship: Past and suggestions for the future. *Small Enterprise Research, 13*, 1–21.

Dijkhuizen, J., Gorgievski, M., van Veldhoven, M., & Schalk, R. (2017). Well-being, personal success and business performance among entrepreneurs: A two-wave study. *Journal of Happiness Studies, 15*, 1–18. https://doi.org/10.1007/s10902-017-9914-6

Dijkhuizen, J., Veldhoven, M. V., & Schalk, R. (2016). Four types of well-being among entrepreneurs and their relationships with business performance. *Journal of Entrepreneurship, 25*(2), 184–210. https://doi.org/10.1177/0971355716650369

Douglas, E. J., & Shepherd, D. A. (2014). Self-employment as a career choice: Attitudes, entrepreneurial intentions, and utility maximization. In D. A. Shepherd (Ed.), *A psychological approach to entrepreneurship: Selected Essays of Dean A. Shepherd* (pp. 307–316). Edward Elgar Publishing Ltd.

Feki, C., & Mnif, S. (2016). Entrepreneurship, technological innovation, and economic growth: Empirical analysis of panel data. *Journal of the Knowledge Economy, 7*(4), 984–999. https://doi.org/10.1007/s13132-016-0413-5

Figueroa-Armijos, M., & Johnson, T. G. (2016). Entrepreneurship policy and economic growth: Solution or delusion? Evidence from a state initiative. *Small Business Economics, 47*(4), 1033–1047. https://doi.org/10.1007/s11187-016-9750-9

Fisher, R., Merlot, E., & Johnson, L. W. (2018). The obsessive and harmonious nature of entrepreneurial passion. *International Journal of Entrepreneurial Behavior & Research, 24*(1), 22–40. https://doi.org/10.1108/ijebr-01-2017-0011

Forbes. (2015). *Criaçao de Empregos na África Subsaariana*. http://www.djembe communications.com/wp-content/uploads/2016/07/Djembe-Insights_Forbes_Report_PT.pdf. Accessed on May 2018.

Forest, J., Mageau, G. A., Crevier-Braud, L., Bergeron, É., Dubreuil, P., & Lavigne, G. L. (2012). Harmonious passion as an explanation of the relation between signature strengths' use and well-being at work: Test of an intervention program. *Human Relations, 65*(9), 1233–1252.

Fox, S. (2016). Open prosperity: How latent realities arising from virtual-social-physical convergence (VSP) increase opportunities for global prosperity. *Technology in Society, 44*, 92–103. https://doi.org/10.1016/j.techsoc.2016.01.001

Freitas, C. P. P., Cankaya, E. M., Damásio, B. F., Haddad, E. J., Kamei, H. H., Tobo, P. R., & Koller, S. H. (2018). Personal growth initiative and subjective well-being: The mediation role of meaning in life. *Acción Psicológica, 15*(2), 39–50. https://doi.org/10.5944/ap.15.2.22002,M

Fuentelsaz, L., González, C., Maícas, J. P., & Montero, J. (2015). How different formal institutions affect opportunity and necessity entrepreneurship. *BRQ Business Research Quarterly, 18*(4), 246–258. https://doi.org/10.1016/j.brq.2015.02.001

GEM. (2017). *Global entrepreneurship monitor.* http://www.gemconsortium.org/report. Accessed on October 2017.

Gielnik, M., Spitzmuller, M., Schmitt, A., Klemann, D., & Frese, M. (2015). I put in effort, therefore I am passionate: Investigating the path from effort to passion in entrepreneurship. *Academy of Management Journal, 58*(4): 1012–1031.

GLOBE. (2014). *Global Leadership & Organizational Behavior Effectiveness.* http://globeproject.com/results/clusters/eastern-europe?menu=list. Accessed on February 2018.

Gonçalves, R. V. (2018). *Does entrepreneurship convey higher levels of happiness?* An analysis by type of entrepreneurship and national cultures.

Gorgievski, M. J., & Bakker, A. B. (2010). *Passion for work: Work engagement versus workaholism.* Edward Elgar Publishing.

Hofstede. (2006). What did GLOBE really measure? Researchers' minds versus respondents' minds. *Journal of International Business Studies, 37*(6), 882–896.

Hofstede. (2016). *Comparison between countries—Cultural dimensions.* http://geerthofstede.com. Accessed on November 2017.

House, R. J. (2004). *Culture, leadership, and organizations: The globe study of 62 societies.* Sage.

House, R. J., Quigley, N. R., & Luque, M. S. (2010). Insights from project globe: Extending global advertising research through a contemporary framework. *International Journal of Advertising, 29*(1).

Huggins, R., & Thompson, P. (2014). Culture, entrepreneurship and uneven development: A spatial analysis. *Entrepreneurship and Regional Development, 26*(9–10), 726–752. https://doi.org/10.1080/08985626.2014.985740

Inglehart, R., Foa, R., Peterson, C., & Welzel, C. (2008). Development, freedom, and rising happiness: A global perspective (1981–2007). *Perspectives on Psychological Science, 3*(4), 264–285. https://doi.org/10.1111/j.1745-6924.2008.00078.x

Inglehart, R., & Klingemann, H.-D. (2000). Genes, culture, democracy, and happiness. In E. Diener & E. M. Suh (Eds.), *Culture and subjective well-being* (pp. 165–183). The MIT Press.

Lackéus, M. (2017). Does entrepreneurial education trigger more or less neoliberalism in education? *Education and Training, 59*(6), 635–650. https://doi.org/10.1108/ET-09-2016-0151

Levine, R. B., Haidet, P., Kern, D. E., Beasley, B. W., Bensinger, L., Brady, D. W., Gress, T., Hughes, J., Marwaha, A., Nelson, J., & Wright, S. M. (2006). Personal growth during internship. *Journal of general internal medicine, 21*(6), 564–569.

Liu, D., Chen, X.-P., & Yao, X. (2010). From autonomy to creativity: A multilevel investigation of the mediating role of harmonious passion. *Journal of Applied Psychology*. Advance online publication. https://doi.org/10.1037/a0021294

Lunt, A. (2004). The implications for the clinician of adopting a recovery model: The role of choice in assertive treatment. *Psychiatric Rehabilitation Journal, 28*(1), 93–97. https://doi.org/10.2975/28.2004.93.97

Mahadea, D., & Ramroop, S. (2015). Influences on happiness and subjective well-being of entrepreneurs and labour: Kwazulu-natal case study. *South African Journal of Economic and Management Sciences, 18*(2), 245–259. https://doi.org/10.17159/2222-3436/2015/v18n2a8

Marques, J. F. (2017). Oh, what happiness! Finding joy and purpose through work. *Development and Learning in Organizations, 31*(3), 1–3. https://doi.org/10.1108/DLO-11-2016-0108

Martínez, S. H., & Pardo, C. A. (2013). Desire to undertake and Happiness: An exploratory study of the Global Entrepreneurship Monitor in Chile. *Journal of Technology Management and Innovation, 8*(1), 76–89.

Molina-Azorín, J. F., López-Gamero, M. D., Pereira-Moliner, J., & Pertusa-Ortega, E. M. (2012). Mixed methods studies in entrepreneurship research. *Applications and Contributions Entrepreneurship & Regional Development, 24*, 425–456. https://doi.org/10.1080/08985626.2011.603363

Morris, M. H., Pryor, C. G., Schindehutte, M., & Kuratko, D. F. (2012). *Entrepreneurship as experience: How events create ventures and ventures create entrepreneurs*. Edward Elgar Publishing Ltd.

Morrison, M., Tay, L., & Diener, E. (2011). Subjective well-being and national satisfaction: Findings from a worldwide survey. *Psychological Science, 22*(2), 166–171. https://doi.org/10.1177/0956797610396224

Mueller, S. L., & Thomas, A. S. (2001). Culture and entrepreneurial potential: A nine country study of locus of control and innovativeness. *Journal of Business Venturing, 16*(1), 51–75. https://doi.org/10.1016/S0883-9026(99)00039-7

Nataraajan, R., & Angur, M. G. (2014). Innovative ability and entrepreneurial activity: Two factors to enhance "quality of life." *Journal of Business and Industrial Marketing, 29*(6), 469–475. https://doi.org/10.1108/JBIM-09-2013-0205

Naudé, W., Amorós, J. E., & Cristi, O. (2014). "Surfeiting, the appetite may sicken": Entrepreneurship and happiness. *Small Business Economics, 42*(3), 523–540. https://doi.org/10.1007/s11187-013-9492-x

Oishi, S., Graham, J., Kesebir, S., & Galinha, I. C. (2013). Concepts of happiness across time and cultures. *Personality and Social Psychology Bulletin, 39*(5), 559–577. https://doi.org/10.1177/0146167213480042

O'Leary, Z. (2014). *The essential guide to doing your research project* (2nd ed.). SAGE Publications Inc.

Örtqvist, D., Drnovsek, M., & Wincent, J. (2007). Entrepreneurs' coping with challenging role expectations. *Baltic Journal of Management, 2*(3), 288–304.

Philippe, F. L., Vallerand, R. J., & Lavigne, G. L. (2009). Passion does make a difference in people's lives: A look at well-being in passionate and non-passionate individuals. *Applied Psychology: Health and Well-Being, 1*(1), 3–22.

Pirinsky, C. (2013). Confidence and economic attitudes. *Journal of Economic Behavior and Organization, 91,* 139–158. https://doi.org/10.1016/j.jebo.2013.04.013

Pryce-Jones, J., & Lindsay, J. (2014). What happiness at work is and how to use it. *Industrial and Commercial Training, 46*(3), 130–134. https://doi.org/10.1108/ICT-10-2013-0072

Rodríguez-Muñoz, A., & Sanz-Vergel, A. I. (2013). Happiness and well-being at work: A special issue introduction. *Revista de Psicologia del Trabajo y de las Organizaciones, 29*(3), 95–97. https://doi.org/10.5093/tr2013a14

Schumpeter, J. A. (2008). *Capitalism, socialism and democracy* (4th ed.). Harper Perennial.

Shah, S. K., & Tripsas, M. (2007). The accidental entrepreneur: The emergent and collective process of user entrepreneurship. *Strategic Entrepreneurship Journal, 1*(1–2), 123–140.

Sihombing, S. O., Pramono, R., Zulganef, Z., & Ismanto, I. (2016). Instrumental and terminal values of Indonesian micro-finance entrepreneurs: A preliminary report. *International Journal of Economic Research, 13*(3), 841–853.

Uchida, Y., Norasakkunkit, V., & Kitayama, S. (2004). Cultural constructions of happiness: Theory and emprical evidence. *Journal of Happiness Studies, 5,* 223–239.

Vallerand, R. J., Houlfort, N., & Fores, J. (2003). Passion at work. *Emerging Perspectives on Values in Organizations, 6*(8), 175–204.

Vallerand, R. J., Salvy, S. J., Mageau, G. A., Elliot, A. J., Denis, P. L., Grouzet, F. M., & Blanchard, C. (2007). On the role of passion in performance. *Journal of Personality, 75*(3), 505–534.

Wright, S. M., Levine, R. B., Beasley, B., Haidet, P., Gress, T. W., Caccamese, S., Brady, D., Marwaha, A., & Kern, D. E. (2006). Personal growth and its correlates during residency training. *Medical education, 40*(8), 737–745.

Xu, E. M., & Xiao, J. Q. (2014, August 17–19). *Government subsidy and institutional entrepreneur's risk taking.* Paper presented at the International Conference on Management Science and Engineering—Annual Conference Proceedings, Finland.

Yang, C., & Srinivasan, P. (2016). Life satisfaction and the pursuit of happiness on Twitter. *PLoS ONE, 11*(3), e0150881.

Zampetakis, L. A., Kafetsios, K., Lerakis, M., & Moustakis, V. S. (2017). An emotional experience of entrepreneurship: Self-Construal, emotion regulation, and expressions to anticipatory emotions. *Journal of Career Development, 44*(2), 144–158. https://doi.org/10.1177/0894845316640898

Zhang, H. Y., & Yang, N. D. (2010). *RETRACTED ARTICLE: Entrepreneurial orientation: An innovative construct in stimulating effective corporate entrepreneurship.* Paper presented at the Proceedings of the International Conference on E-Business and E-Government, ICEE 2010.

CHAPTER 28

Adding the "J" for Justice: How Executive Education Can Center Social Justice in Diversity, Equity, Inclusion (DEI) Training for Corporate Leaders

Mateo Cruz, Yaromil Fong-Olivares, Wiley C. Davi, and María Jose Taveras

We write this chapter amidst much social, political, and organizational strife in the US and worldwide. Only six months into the year, we see an ever-widening split between factions on sociopolitical issues including LGBTQ+ rights, reproductive rights, religious freedom, gun control, and race-based voting restrictions. Such divisions play out against the backdrop of the COVID-19 pandemic, mass shootings, record-high inflation rates, the January 6th hearings, and an escalation of the war in Ukraine. Neutrality is obsolete and corporations and their leaders face increasing pressure to take a public stand on issues of social inequality and human rights (Amis et al., 2021), two core tenets of social justice (Toubiana, 2014).

Unfortunately, business leaders receive little guidance on how to address or advance social justice through their organization's internal or external actions. Until only recently, the Association to Advance Collegiate Schools of Business (AACSB) did not require business education provide coursework on social impact or diversity and inclusion—two new areas added to the 2020 business accreditation standards (Berry et al., 2021). To fill the gap, business leaders attend Executive Education programs focused on diversity, equity, and inclusion (DEI) housed in top business schools. However, based on a search for "social justice" on Executive Courses, a web-based service that provides

M. Cruz (✉) · Y. Fong-Olivares · W. C. Davi · M. J. Taveras
Bentley University, Waltham, MA, USA
e-mail: mcruz@bentley.edu

© The Author(s), under exclusive license to Springer Nature Switzerland AG 2023
J. Marques (ed.), *The Palgrave Handbook of Fulfillment, Wellness, and Personal Growth at Work*,
https://doi.org/10.1007/978-3-031-35494-6_28

program details about executive course offerings in business schools worldwide, zero programs include "social justice" or related terms (e.g., justice, intersectionality, and anti-racism) in their descriptions. By comparison, 39 programs appear in a search for "diversity." Thus, although there is growing pressure for executive leaders to address social justice issues in the external environment, there are few executive learning resources leaders can access to develop the competencies to deliver.

For that reason, the purpose of this chapter is twofold. First, our goal is to survey the management literature to identify the competencies Executive Education programs target in DEI training to determine if any address social justice. Additionally, we evaluate learning objectives from DEI programs situated in the top 50 business schools in the US to better understand competencies in practice. Second, we describe the creation and design of a DEI certificate program for executives that centers on anti-racism and intersectionality to inform what a social justice approach may look like in Executive Education. Our aim is to provide insight to business school faculty and staff seeking to redesign their DEI offerings for executives to include competencies related to the advancement of social justice.

Studies indicate a direct link between diversity practices and employee engagement (McKinsey & Company, 2021), an important facet of employee well-being (Downey et al., 2015). We believe DEI work that centers on social justice can also increase organizational and societal well-being. Our goal in this chapter is to provide direction on how to collectively achieve this goal.

What is Diversity, Equity, and Inclusion (DEI) and Justice?

Before we review the competencies and learning objectives Executive Education programs target in DEI training, we first define DEI. "DEI" is currently the go-to acronym used to describe the various diversity, equity, and inclusion strategies organizations and their leaders engage in to effectively leverage differences among employees. "Diversity" refers to the attributes (visible and nonvisible) that differentiate group members. "Equity," as defined by Harvard Business Publishing Corporate Learning (2020, July 23), is: "Fair treatment for all while striving to identify and eliminate inequities and barriers." And "Inclusion" is "the degree to which an employee perceives that he or she is an esteemed member of the work group through experiencing treatment that satisfies his or her needs for belongingness and uniqueness" (Shore et al., 2011, p. 1265). In a way, DEI reflects work at different levels of analysis in the organization—diversity is about *individual differences* between social group members, inclusion is about *interpersonal and workgroup* experiences, and equity is about *institutional* policies or procedures. Thus, DEI training aims to equip leaders with the multilevel competencies needed to create a healthy and just organizational culture that allows for the "full integration of members of minority social categories into the social, structural, and power relationships of an organization or institution" (Brewer et al., 1999, p. 337, as cited in Devine & Ash, 2022, p. 1.5).

More recently, after the murder of George Floyd and subsequent rise of the Black Lives Matter movement, many DEI experts added the letter "J," for "justice," to their DEI programming in schools and organizations (i.e., JEDI). In an explanation of why they shifted their program focus from DEI to JEDI, Martinez and Truong (2021, April 9) write:

> ...racism plays a major role in how our institutions function and operate. Our job should be to examine these systems and structures and reimagine policies and practices that would seek to produce equitable outcomes. Leading with justice is reflected in the frameworks and scholarship that ground our office's work. Critical Race Theory and Anti-Oppressive pedagogy are central to our training and pedagogy.

Other DEI programs in businesses, science, medicine, and higher education followed suit, adding the "J" for justice (Hammond et al., 2021, September 23).

In parallel, the concept of Corporate Social Justice (CSJ) appeared as one of the Top 5 Workplace Trends in 2021 according to the Society for Industrial and Organizational Psychology (SIOP, Inc.) (Stark, 2021, January 20). Zheng (2020, June 15) describes CSJ as a modernized version of Corporate Social Responsibility (CSR), a business's commitment to social welfare (Carroll & Brown, 2018). Given emerging skepticism from consumers that CSR has become more of a marketing tactic than a real effort toward change, the updated version, CSJ, is defined as: "a framework regulated by the trust between a company and its employees, customers, shareholders, and the broader community it touches, with the goal of explicitly doing good by all of them." Zheng writes, "Consumers and other stakeholders want companies that see social good as a necessity, not just a marketing strategy. It's up to companies to respond to this new challenge" (2020, June 15).

Historically, DEI training for business leaders focused on developing competencies, described as knowledge, skills, and awareness (KSAs), at the individual and interpersonal levels of behavior in an effort to foster a healthy and inclusive workplace (Devine & Ash, 2022). A social justice focus, however, addresses the system dynamics, within and beyond the organization, that perpetuate oppression between and among organizational group members (Martinez & Truong, 2021, April 9). Though a newer area of focus, consumers and employees—particularly those from Gen Z—are demanding more from their leaders in response to social justice issues unfolding in the external environment that effect the organizational environment as well (Schroth, 2019). The question is: *Are Executive Education DEI programs designed to teach the KSAs (i.e., competencies) required to advance social justice?* We turn our attention next to the examination of DEI competencies that appear in Executive Education research and practice.

Which DEI Competencies Do Executive Education Programs Target?

To better understand which DEI competencies Executive Education programs target in DEI-specific training, we conducted a systematic literature review going back to 2005. For the purpose of this chapter, we focused on top management and psychology journals that publish research about adult learning and leadership (i.e., Executive Education), DEI, social justice, and change. Drawing from three designated topic areas in the *2021 Academic Journal Guide (AJG)* (Management Development & Education, MDEV&EDU; Organization Studies, ORG STUD; and Psychology, WOP-OB), we selected 20 journals to search (for a complete list of journals searched, see Appendix). To conduct the review, we used the keywords: "Executive Education," "diversity," "competency," "social justice," and "leader(ship) development." We accessed articles through appropriate databases (i.e., Business Source Complete, ProQuest One Academic, and ProQuest One Business) and reviewed abstracts within each journal.

Our search revealed the following findings. First, out of the 570 cites across all 20 journals using the search term "Executive Education" (2005–2022), *zero* articles focused on ways Executive Education programs develop leader competencies related to DEI *or* social justice—areas we believe are critical for personal and organizational growth and well-being. Four articles identified focus on women's leadership development programs (WLDPs) (e.g., Debebe et al., 2016; Ely et al., 2011; Hopkins et al., 2008; Sugiyama et al., 2016), and one on global leadership competencies (Brownell & Goldsmith, 2006). More recent work like Shore and Chung's (2021) description of leader orientations identifies leader behaviors for inclusion; however, to our knowledge, no paper yet examines how Executive Education programs develop leader orientations to advance DEI or social justice in organizations.

Outside of the context of Executive Education, 18 articles described or examined DEI competencies in the context of general leadership development (i.e., not executive education) and classroom learning. Of those 18, most focus on the skills or approaches educators and consultants can use to effectively teach or train DEI. For example, Bierema (2010) highlights the importance of "recognizing positionality, experience with marginalization, viewing diversity education as a developmental process, knowledge of the subject, and ability to facilitate diversity pedagogy" as competencies of those "best qualified to teach D, E, & I curricula" (p. 312). Edmondson et al. (2020) suggest management faculty create consciousness-raising experiences (CREs) in the classroom, described as an effective way to help students "wake up, and help organizations achieve their DEI goals" (p. 249). And, Cooper et al. (2008) review the challenges external consultants and trainers face when conducting DEI initiatives with clients. Each article offers clear direction for effective DEI teaching, training, and consulting; however, the articles focus more on the trainer than the learner.

Other articles identified in our search offer valuable insight on how to create effective learning environments for DEI work (Fujimoto & Härtel, 2017), or aim to examine barriers to effective diversity training for managers and leaders (Hayes et al., 2020; Nadiv & Kuna, 2020). Some evaluate or review the effectiveness of various diversity interventions themselves (Devine & Ash, 2022; Kim & Roberson, 2021; Kulik & Roberson, 2008; Pendry et al., 2007), although this focal area is out of scope for this chapter. Yet, notably few publications identify or discuss the specific DEI competencies leaders need to facilitate change in their organizations. The two articles we found that do included Ramsey and Latting's (2005) typology of 14 intergroup competencies organizational members need to effectively work across social group differences and Foldy and Buckley's (2017) reframing of cultural competence through a group relations lens to emphasize the importance of emotions in DEI work.

In sum, although there is no question that business leaders need DEI competencies to advance social justice, there appears to be little guidance in the management literature about how Executive Education programs currently target and train these areas.

How Do Executive Education Programs Approach DEI Training in Practice?

Though not much is published about how Executive Education programs develop DEI competencies, there are several programs that offer DEI training for corporate leaders. In order to examine the DEI competencies these programs develop, we evaluated websites and brochures from the top 50 business schools in the US designated by the 2022 Financial Times Business School Rankings (https://rankings.ft.com/rankings/2866/mba-2022). From this list, we visited each university website specific to Executive Education. We found that although all 50 schools offer a form of executive learning (i.e., workshops, certificates, and degree-granting programs), only 25 offer formal programming related to DEI or identity-based leadership (i.e., women in leadership, people of color in management, etc.). Of those 25, 20 take place entirely online, two are hybrid, and three take place in person. Understandably, how programs are offered is likely a function of COVID-19 and associated shifts in modalities. Most DEI programs are new, and 2022 will be the first time they take place. Some programs are self-paced and asynchronous, while others are cohort-based. Most take place within the span of one week (or 4–6 sessions).

Because our goal in this search was to better understand which DEI competencies are targeted in Executive Education, we compiled a repository of brochures from the 25 programs identified. When brochures were not available, we obtained information about the program from the website. Specifically, we evaluated the learning objectives named in each program write-up. Across 24 programs (one program did not have learning objectives) and

100+ learning objectives, we identified 11 overlapping themes or areas of focus in DEI training offered for executives: (1) Purpose or Personal Motivation for DEI Work (i.e., business case, moral case, and personal "why"); (2) Foundational Knowledge; (3) Diagnostic Skills; (4) Evidence-based Interventions; (5) Evaluation and Assessment; (6) Team Performance and Enhancement; (7) Inclusive Organizational Culture and Climate; (8) Unconscious Biases, Stereotypes, and Microaggressions; (9) Identity Work; (10) Change Leadership; and (11) Shared Learning (i.e., cohort-based learning). However, in a keyword search of the 100+ learning objectives, none listed social justice, justice, intersectionality, or anti-racism as focal learning areas. Four schools, however, did list "systemic racism" as a central content area.

SUMMARY OF FINDINGS

In sum, DEI training via Executive Education is on the rise. Half of the Top 50 business schools in the US offer some form of DEI training, although limited research exists about the DEI competencies targeted in these programs. Most programs are new. Yet, few at the time of this publication identify "social justice" or related terms in their offerings. This reflects a disconnect between demands from consumers and employees who expect corporate leaders address social justice issues including, but not limited to, systemic racism, anti-LGBT state laws, the overturning of Roe vs. Wade, and climate justice.

To address this gap, we next describe one Executive Education program that centers anti-racism and intersectionality in its design as two drivers of social justice. The purpose of showcasing this program is to provide insight and ideas to other faculty and staff in Executive Education about how we can collectively center social justice in our work with corporate leaders.

BENTLEY UNIVERSITY'S DIVERSITY, EQUITY, AND INCLUSION CHAMPION PROGRAM

Bentley University is a private, nonprofit business university located in the Greater Boston area known for its award-winning career services center and long-term return on investment (ROI)—ranked No. 8 of 4,500 US colleges and universities in 2022 (Georgetown University, 2022, February 18). Bentley's mission is arguably social justice focused, described as, "A place for successful leaders who set out to create positive change in our communities, organizations and the world" (About Bentley, 2022). As such, its degree programs and Executive Education offerings deliver business education that aligns.

One such program is the Diversity, Equity, and Inclusion Certificate for corporate leaders described as, "Experiential programming that prepares participants to be advocates of inclusion, who understand the importance of diversity, equity & inclusion (DE&I), and how to lead organizational change that will foster an inclusive workplace culture" (Executive Education:

Engaging Business Leaders to Meet the Challenges of Tomorrow, 2022). Referred to as the "DEI Champion Program," participants can opt-in to Level I and/or Level II offerings which span multiple levers for change (i.e., Level I focuses on individual and interpersonal KSAs and Level II focuses on team and organizational KSAs). Although current learning objectives also do not directly name "social justice," related terms "justice" and "intersectionality" are listed as key principles that inform program design and delivery (Diversity & Inclusion Certificate: Take Ownership of Your Organization's Diversity & Inclusion Journey, 2022).

Program History and Background

The development of the DEI Champion Program came about in the summer of 2019. In the year prior, Bentley's Executive Education team designed and delivered a series of "Undoing Unconscious Bias" sessions for a multinational corporation. The sessions were designed to balance the development of intrapersonal social identity awareness, one's own understanding and awareness of their multiple social group identities, with evidence-based principles that guide corporate culture change. The reason for striking this balance in the orginal design was based on the following assumption: *Without intrapersonal social identity consciousness development to uproot oppressive ideas about DEI, a leader cannot successfully lead organization change.* A key area of leader development in the DEI Champions Program is thus one that values and leverages *intersectional* diversity or "the way unique traits and identities interact with each other to impact access or barriers to opportunities, in both the workplace and society at large" (The Center for Women and Business, 2019, Winter). Moreover, culture change work toward inclusion touches all aspects of the organization—from the informal interactions between employees to the formal practices and procedures that guide equity and justice.

Bentley launched the DEI Champion Program in the spring of 2020. The program was designed prior to the onset of the COVID-19 pandemic and the murder of George Floyd. However, both events disrupted design and delivery. First, the program had to be redesigned for a virtual environment, and second, attendees who were not the initial target audience enrolled. Initially, the program was designed for an audience with basic working knowledge of DEI and social justice. Instead, program participants entered from various stages of social and racial identity development, eager to find a place to process the collective trauma of recent events. As a result, facilitators redesigned the program to begin with foundational work that addressed racial identity development, allowing participants—including Black, Indigenous, and People of Color (BIPOC) learners—to process feelings of rage, grief, and other emotions related to racialized experiences and racial trauma. In doing so, facilitators had to carefully navigate and encourage emotionally charged conversations and learning experiences. Otherwise, the class, like much of the US, risked dividing between those who "got it" and those who "did not." Though challenging, this unexpected focus on race led to a more purposeful intention on the part of the program team to create a multiracial and multicultural community centered on mutual learning (Schwarz, 2016). To do so effectively, the team leveraged Schwarz's (2016) approach to learning design, described next.

Mutual Learning Design Approach

Schwarz (2016) differentiates between a unilateral, one-directional teacher-to-learner approach and a mutual learning approach. The mutual learning approach is one where every participant is assumed to have valuable information to expand shared learning. When a program is designed using the mutual learning approach, inputs are in place to ensure all participants learn from one another and offer information from their unique perspectives. This approach framed the DEI Champion Program redesign.

To build the "container" for a mutual learning approach to occur, the DEI Champion Program team drew from Schwarz's (2016) facilitation model of mutual learning which demonstrates how mindsets drive behavior, behavior drives results, and results, in turn, mutually inform mindsets and behaviors via a double-loop learning (see Fig. 28.1).

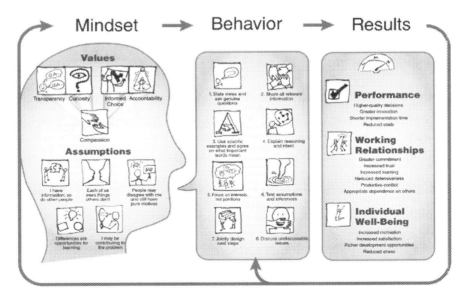

Fig. 28.1 The Schwarz model of mutual learning (*Source* Schwarz, R. M. (2016). *The Skilled Facilitator: A Comprehensive Resource for Consultants, Facilitators, Coaches, and Trainers*. John Wiley & Sons, Incorporated)

Mindset: Establishing Values and Assumptions

In the Schwarz model, the mindset input consists of values and assumptions the group adheres to throughout the program in an effort to establish trust and psychological safety. Although Schwarz (2016) identifies five core values in his model—transparency, curiosity, informed choice, accountability, and compassion—the DEI Champion Program uses Bentley University's core values which overlap: caring, collaboration, diversity, honesty, impact, learning, and respect (for a description of each value, please visit https://www.bentley.edu/about/mission-and-values). These core values provide a shared language about the beliefs that will guide mutual learning.

For example, Schwarz's model identifies "compassion" as "the emotional glue that holds all the core values together" (p. 71) because it requires the demonstration of empathy toward self and others when mistakes are made. Likewise, Bentley's core value of "caring" is described as follows: "We practice understanding, compassion and kindness. We recognize the whole person and their well-being, and we think beyond ourselves and our immediate goals to consider the impact our actions have on other people" (About Bentley, 2022). In the DEI Champion Program, this value is called upon when the facilitators describe the difference between intent and impact. For instance, when a participant unintentionally used the wrong pronoun for another participant during a program session—referred to as "misgendering"—the facilitation team leveraged the moment to demonstrate compassion for both parties. Rather than scolding or shaming the misgendering party, the facilitators engaged the group in a brave dialogue (Cruz et al., 2022) so that everyone could learn that naming the incident without blame could lead to a positive outcome. Going "live" in this way allowed facilitators to demonstrate how a caring learning climate can help participants work through "mistakes" that in most work situations result in breakdowns, human resources complaints, or other negative outcomes that ultimately cost the business money and morale. Thus, adopting core values in the program design helps create a psychologically safe learning environment.

The second part of the "mindset" input in Schwarz's model is assumptions. Assumptions are accepted, agreed-upon beliefs that contribute to a learning environment that enables nuance and complexity (2016). Schwarz's approach to mutual learning rests on five central assumptions:

1. I have information, so do others.
2. Each of us sees things others do not.
3. Differences are opportunities for learning.
4. People may disagree with me and still have pure motives.
5. I may be contributing to the problem.

These five assumptions are described and upheld in the DEI Champion Program in combination with Bentley's core values. For example, it is assumed that the self, regardless of role in the program (i.e., participant or facilitator), may unconsciously and unintentionally contribute to the "DEI problem" that most corporate leaders struggle with (e.g., Assumption #5). In the DEI Champion Program, the "DEI problem" is described as follows: *How do we learn to lead DEI change work with organizational citizens who possess varying beliefs and values, yet are aligned on the importance of DEI as a business and moral imperative*? (Roberts & Mayo, 2019).

One example of how Assumption #5 manifested in the programs was when a White facilitator used the word "minorities" to refer to people of color. At the time, the program's language was in transition from using "minorities" to "historically excluded" to highlight the systemic nature of exclusion more accurately. However, when the facilitator used the older term, a Black participant took offense and raised this to the group. The facilitators then led a discussion about how their use of outdated language may contribute to the "DEI problem." By naming the assumption and taking accountability for their role in the dynamic, the facilitators were able to engage the entire class on how to respond when an assumption is surfaced.

Behavior: Putting Concepts into Practice

Next, in the Schwarz model for mutual learning, mindsets drive behaviors. "Behaviors" are the enactment of values and assumptions and inform how we challenge one another, including facilitators, to engage in more complex learning that honors all experiences in the class. Specifically, Schwarz lists eight core behaviors enacted in a mutual learning environment:

1. State views and ask genuine questions.
2. Share all relevant information.
3. Use specific examples and agree on what important words mean.
4. Explain reasoning and intent.
5. Focus on interests, not positions.
6. Test assumptions and inferences.
7. Jointly design next steps.
8. Discuss undiscussable issues.

One effective behavior practiced in the DEI Champion Program is *discuss the undiscussables* (e.g., Behavior #8). This is an important practice for DEI(J) work, especially in conversations about bias, because it can help relieve the discomfort of raising difficult issues and normalize that while some topics may feel undiscussable they are critical to surface.

For example, during the program a *discuss the undiscussables* behavior occurred when a White male facilitator shared his observation that a Black male participant was quite active in the discussion and could therefore be perceived as dominating the conversation. This was a risky observation to raise given the racial identities of the two men. However, the White male facilitator named the dynamic because he had already established a good rapport with the Black male participant. By openly *discussing* what may feel like an *undiscussable* observation, the group was able to engage in a conversation about the pressure more vocal participants of color felt to speak up and the need from other (White) participants for more time to think before responding. The incident also surfaced racial dynamics in the group about the desire to hear from Black participants without acknowledging how that pressure adds stress—a familiar dynamic for people of color in the workplace. Additionally, a few women in the group acknowledged that they also wanted to share but were waiting for the right time, which led to a nuanced discussion about the intersection of gender and race and the combined effect on voice.

Thus, the combination of explicit and intentional norms for mindsets and behaviors in the learning design created a mutual learning environment in which the group could achieve better results together. Moreover, participants felt valued for their contributions and left with a greater sense of well-being because they felt proud for learning difficult lessons while unlearning painful biases.

Results: Performance, Relationships, Well-Being

The results of the DEI Champion Program align with the Schwarz model, in that, by the end of the program the cohort developed relationships that enabled honest and vulnerable unpacking of previously hidden memories, values, and assumptions about "the other." Because the mutual learning design first establishes trust, participants can examine their unconscious biases with less shame and more self-compassion. Additionally, participants recognize the lifelong nature of DEI work, including how much of a leader's personal life experiences influence their leadership approach to DEI and change.

Ultimately, the program ends up serving as a microcosm of the kind of workplace culture DEI Champions create—one where there is a psychologically safe relationship among employees who may commit unintentional acts of bias but learn from them. By creating such an environment, leaders and their employees can restore and deepen trust rather than damage relationships which increases stress and decreases productivity. Moreover, the mutual learning design sets the stage for participants to explore sensitive but necessary content specific to the "race and…" intersectionality approach to social justice, described next.

THE "RACE AND…" INTERSECTIONALITY APPROACH TO SOCIAL JUSTICE

Once a mutual learning environment is established, content in the DEI Champion Program centers on two areas that differentiate DEI from social justice work (see Fig. 28.2).

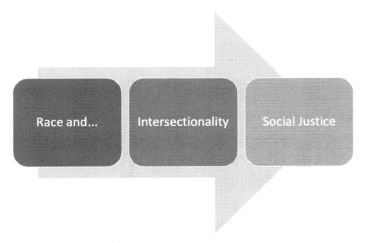

Fig. 28.2 The "Race and..." intersectionality approach to social justice

Race and...: Centering Identity Work on Race

Drawing from the work of Hardy (2016), DEIJ content focuses on personal experiences related to oppression and superiority in the context of race. In his work on anti-racism, Hardy (2016) differentiates between "tasks" of the subjugated and the "tasks" of the privileged and how privileged and oppressed "parts" of oneself engage in those tasks during conversations about social identity and race. From this perspective, everyone has multiple social identities that are "subjugated" and "privileged," and individuals adopt specific "tasks" in relation to those identities. Hardy explains that to engage in effective cross-race dialogue, individuals must manage the tasks that emerge from social identities that are historically excluded or those that confer unearned benefits. Additionally, he explains that individuals often speak first from their subjugated parts not their privileged parts.

For example, a Black man holding male privilege and facing racism may see himself as Black first and be unwilling to grapple with male privilege because it challenges a self-perception of oppression related to Blackness. Likewise, a White woman might see herself as a woman first and not as someone holding White privilege and may struggle to recognize the privileges that being White confers in today's workplace even when she is perhaps the only woman on a team of men. Hardy does not encourage a hierarchy of identities, nor does he aim to simplify the complexity of being excluded and included. Instead, he encourages integration of all our parts. This framing helps participants share and own their racialized experiences and creates opportunities to explore other social identities with minimal risk of shame, blame, or individualization.

Thus, the DEI Champion Program uses Hardy's work to frame conversations about race and intersectionality. In doing so, participants and facilitators are invited to challenge automatic responses coming from each individual's oppressed and oppressor parts. In other words, each group member has parts that are "oppressed" and parts that are "oppressor," and must manage those parts, examine them, and ultimately integrate them toward a whole sense of self in an effort to move beyond internalized beliefs. To advance these concepts, facilitators lead learning activities that prompt participants to work in small and large groups to answer questions specifically about experiences of their own race and racism.

In doing so, the DEI Champion Program intentionally centers race in service of intersectionality discussions that connect participants' earliest memories, education, family dynamics, and community experiences to their work as a change leader. To make Hardy's work more digestible for business leaders, the DEI Champion Program emphasizes that curiosity, a learning orientation, and comfort with noticing and being with what is emergent—good, bad, or just different—are core competencies individuals need to lead racially conscious conversations at work.

Intersectionality: Framing Identities in the Context of Race

"Intersectionality" is a term coined by Kimberlé Crenshaw to refer to the ways in which individuals, specifically Black women, face systemic barriers due to their embodiment of multiple historically excluded identities (Crenshaw, 2017). Other scholars have added to intersectionality scholarship by noting how intersectionality may pose barriers to opportunities and confer unearned privileges simultaneously (Holvino, 2010). The DEI Champion Program builds on the tradition of intersectional thinking with a "race and..." approach to intersectionality.

For example, on the first program day, participants engage in an exploration of "the story of self" (Ganz, 2007). They reflect on 3–5 racial life events that by their definition changed who they are. They then explore and share how those events connect to their commitment to DEIJ work. In one session, a participant shared a story about having a nanny from a different race. This story became a rich entry point for the group to examine unconscious assumptions that DEIJ is charity work or something "good" to do for those who have "less." This discussion also enabled the group's vulnerability to explore the systemic and historical inequities that drive migration, low-wage jobs, and lack of access to wealth-building opportunities for immigrants. By centering on early memories of race and racism, this activity allows participants to see each other's humanity with more empathy and explore how their early racial experiences shape their commitment to DEIJ.

After sharing the story of self and the personal "why" behind their commitment to DEIJ, the program moves participants to explore their race and intersectionality. Placing race at the forefront of social identity work allows participants to acknowledge how systemic racism and the history of the US influence DEIJ-related experiences within their organizations. The "race and..." intersectionality approach does not negate the importance of other social identity experiences, rather, it re-emphasizes that we exist in a social system that drives perceptions of self and others and therefore all humans, by definition, hold bias. The exploration of race as it relates to other social identities then helps participants face their own unconscious racism, make connections to external influences like media, school, and church, and ultimately leads to healing and integration of internalized biases that drive unconscious behavior.

A "race and..." intersectionality approach also prompts participants to self-identify and "own" their racialized identities first, which then opens an exploration of how racialized intersectionality influences employees' workplace experiences. Participants of all racial and ethnic backgrounds examine how racial bias is embedded in organizational life and how they benefit from their proximity to accepted norms that can extend privileges to some and create disadvantages for others. The result is increased awareness about racialized intersectional experiences of both privilege and oppression that affects all employees. The "race and..." intersectionality approach also prevents the pull to think of individuals only as their most visible social identities and as either oppressed or privileged. Additionally, rather than centering the experiences of participants from historically excluded groups and expecting them to educate dominant group members, the "race and..." intersectionality approach creates the space to question racialized experiences of intersectionality. This includes privileges for those who often think only about their marginalization and therefore minimize their experiences of privilege.

Finally, the "race and..." intersectionality approach prepares participants to model speaking about race at work, while honoring the diversity that workplaces hold. The program's key takeaway is that to lead DEIJ change in organizations, participants must develop confidence and comfort disclosing their own racialized experiences of intersectionality at work and in life.

A growing body of DEI research and practitioner insights based on years of DEI facilitation confirm that unacknowledged, unconscious ideas about social identities hinder a leader's work in advancing DEI and social justice in the workplace. Research points to the insufficiency of DEI training to create inclusive and equitable environments for employees. The literature, while discouraging, also provides evidence that education without opportunities for reflection and experimentation is not enough. The DEI Champion Program's mutual learning design and race-centered content highlight the importance of consciousness-raising and ultimately, connections to how systems inside and outside the organization inform culture and change (Ladson-Billings & Donnor, 2005).

How Does DEI(J) Work Advance Individual and Organizational Well-Being?

Change leaders know that DEI work cannot advance with an individualistic approach. The work of a change leader is to build a base of committed employees which snowballs into holistic organizational transformation. In doing so, DEI(J) work can lead to change at individual *and* organizational levels thereby enhancing the overall health and well-being of both.

At the individual level, employees develop the resilience and curiosity to be able to understand and address the microaggressions they may experience or witness at work in a way that depersonalizes them. Thus, a DEIJ approach to change can improve employee well-being and lead to a greater commitment to the organization. A DEIJ approach also increases inclusion which leads to a psychologically safe environment, allowing individuals to bring their entire selves to the organization thereby fostering innovation and enhancing productivity.

At the organizational level, a DEIJ approach advances change by boosting cultural resilience allowing employees to address issues at the systems level inside *and* outside the organization. By doing so, organizational healing is enacted. According to Hormann and Vivian (2005), organizations, like individuals, can endure trauma. These experiences can become embedded in the organization's culture, transmitted through stories and artifacts, and embodied by the members of the organization. With that in mind, no doubt the events related to the COVID-19 pandemic, the subsequent violence against Asian Americans, Black Americans, and the continued attacks on the rights of women and gender-variant people have and will continue to traumatize organizations. A DEIJ approach allows organizations to interrupt the trauma cycle by linking DEI competencies to the advancement of social justice.

Hormann and Vivian (2005) point to the ability to contain the organization's anxiety as a key aspect of intervening in traumatized organizations. By creating space for discomfort and bravery in conversations, developing skills related to facilitating such conversations, and employing a diagnostic model that embraces different levels of engagement, DEIJ helps leaders learn how to hold their own and others' anxiety through the process of change. Building a community of practice that transcends the time and space of the learning experience is another way that a DEIJ program equips change leaders with a diversity of perspectives, an external community of thought partners, and a place to process emotions that may be inappropriate for the workplace, yet, traumatic to the change agent. Thus, executive DEIJ training builds balance and community within the context of the external environment to and enable sustainability.

Key Takeaways

In assessing current executive offerings, DEI program designers and facilitators should take stock of the ways in which their programs may or may not address social justice. By incorporating social justice, programs that foster diversity, equity, and inclusion provide opportunities for change leaders to develop multilevel competencies to address the system dynamics that affect DEI within and beyond their organization. In addition, leveraging a mutual learning approach in program design allows all participants to explore their social identities through a "race and…" intersectionality frame. In doing so, each participant, regardless of racial or ethnic identity, receives an opportunity to explore the intersectional nature of their identities, privileges, and oppressions. Finally, we recognize the challenges and rewards of having racially conscious conversations in organizations and recommend opportunities for brave dialogues that depend on participants coming to them with curiosity, humility, and a learning orientation.

Conclusion

As business leaders recognize the need to create organizations where employees can thrive, Executive Education programs must help leaders develop DEI competencies that advance social justice. More specifically, a social justice approach helps address system dynamics within and outside the organization. More importantly, a DEIJ approach to executive learning can make an impact at the societal level, where change is desperately needed. In an era when demand for corporate social justice is only bound to increase, Executive Education programs can foster transformational learning when they design for justice.

References

About Bentley. (2022, July 10). *Mission and values.* https://www.bentley.edu/about/mission-and-values

Amis, J., Brickson, S., Haack, P., & Hernandez, M. (2021). Taking inequality seriously. *Academy of Management Review, 46*(3), 431–439.

Berry, L. L., Reibstein, D. J., Wijen, F., Van Wassenhove, L., Voss, C., Gustafsson, A., Vereecke, A., & Bolton, R. (2021). Encouraging business scholars to address societal impact. *AACSB.*

Bierema, L. L. (2010). Diversity education: Competencies and strategies for educators *Advances in Developing Human Resources, 12*(3), 312–331.

Brewer M. B., von Hippel W., & Gooden M. P. (1999). Diversity and organizational identity: The problem of entrée after entry. In D. A. Prentice, & D. T. Miller's (Eds.), *Cultural divides: Understanding and overcoming group conflict* (pp. 337–363). Russell Sage Found.

Brownell, J., & Goldsmith, M. (2006). Meeting the competency needs of global leaders: A partnership approach. Commentary on meeting the competency needs of global leaders: An executive coach's perspective. *Human Resource Management, 45*(3), 309–336.

Business School Rankings. FT.com. (n.d.). Retrieved from https://rankings.ft.com/rankings/2866/mba-2022

Carroll, A. B., & Brown, J. A. (2018). Corporate social responsibility: A review of current concepts, research, and issues. *Corporate Social Responsibility, 39*–69.

Cooper, S., Wilson-Stark, K., Peterson, D. B., O'Roark, A. M., & Pennington, G. (2008). Consulting competently in multicultural contexts. *Consulting Psychology Journal: Practice and Research, 60*(2), 186–202.

Crenshaw, K. W. (2017). *On intersectionality: Essential writings*. The New Press.

Cruz, M., Fong-Olivares, Y., & Davi, W. C. (2022). Brave dialogues: An essential leadership practice to foster diversity, equity, and inclusion in organizations. In *Leading with diversity, equity and inclusion* (pp. 123–135). Springer.

Debebe, G., Anderson, D., Bilimoria, D., & Vinnicombe, S. M. (2016). Women's leadership development programs: Lessons learned and new frontiers. *Journal of Management Education, 40*(3), 231–252.

Devine, P. G., & Ash, T. L. (2022). Diversity training goals, limitations, and promise: A review of the multidisciplinary literature. *Annual Review of Psychology, 73*, 403–429.

Diversity & Inclusion Certificate: Take Ownership of Your Organization's Diversity & Inclusion Journey (2022, July 10). Retrieved from https://www.bentley.edu/centers/executive-education/diversity-inclusion-champion-certificate

Downey, S. N., van der Werff, L., Thomas, K. M., & Plaut, V. C. (2015). The role of diversity practices and inclusion in promoting trust and employee engagement. *Journal of Applied Social Psychology, 45*(1), 35–44.

Edmondson, B. S., Edmondson, V. C., Adams, J., & Barnes, J. (2020). We challenge you to join the movement: From discourse to critical voice. *Journal of Management Education, 44*(2), 247–266.

Ely, R. J., Ibarra, H., & Kolb, D. M. (2011). Taking gender into account: Theory and design for women's leadership development programs. *Academy of Management Learning & Education, 10*(3), 474–493.

Executive Education: Engaging Business Leaders to Meet the Challenges of Tomorrow (2022, July 10). Retrieved from https://www.bentley.edu/centers/executive-education

Foldy, E. G., & Buckley, T. R. (2017). Reimagining cultural competence: Bringing buried dynamics into the light. *The Journal of Applied Behavioral Science, 53*(2), 264–289.

Fujimoto, Y., & Härtel, C. E. (2017). Organizational diversity learning framework: Going beyond diversity training programs. *Personnel Review*, 1120–1141.

Ganz, M. (2007). *Telling your public story: Self, us, now*. Cambridge.

Georgetown University|Center on Education and the Workforce. (2022, July 10). *Ranking 4,500 Colleges by ROI* (2022). Retrieved from https://cew.georgetown.edu/cew-reports/roi2022/

Hammond, J. W., Brownell, S. E., Kedharnath, N. A., Cheng, S. J., & Byrd, W. C. (2021, September 23). Why the term 'JEDI' is problematic for describing programs that promote justice, equity, diversity and inclusion. *Scientific American*. Retrieved from https://www.scientificamerican.com/article/why-the-term-jedi-is-problematic-for-describing-programs-that-promote-justice-equity-diversity-and-inclusion/

Hardy, K. V. (2016). Toward the development of a multicultural relational perspective in training and supervision. *Culturally Sensitive Supervision and Training: Diverse Perspectives and Practical Applications*, 3–10.

Harvard Human Resources (2022, July 10). *Diversity, inclusion, and belonging glossary of terms*. https://edib.harvard.edu/files/dib/files/dib_glossary.pdf

Hayes, T. L., Oltman, K. A., Kaylor, L. E., & Belgudri, A. (2020). How leaders can become more committed to diversity management. *Consulting Psychology Journal: Practice and Research, 72*(4), 247–262.

Holvino, E. (2010). Intersections: The simultaneity of race, gender and class in organization studies. *Gender, Work & Organization, 17*(3), 248–277.

Hopkins, M. M., O'Neil, D. A., Passarelli, A., & Bilimoria, D. (2008). Women's leadership development strategic practices for women and organizations. *Consulting Psychology Journal: Practice and Research, 60*(4), 348–365.

Hormann, S., & Vivian, P. (2005). Toward an understanding of traumatized organizations and how to intervene in them. *Traumatology, 11*(3), 159–169.

Kim, J. Y., & Roberson, L. (2021). I'm biased and so are you. What should organizations do? A review of organizational implicit-bias training programs. *Consulting Psychology Journal: Practice and Research, 74*(1), 19–39.

Kulik, C. T., & Roberson, L. (2008). Common goals and golden opportunities: Evaluations of diversity education in academic and organizational settings. *Academy of Management Learning & Education, 7*(3), 309–331.

Ladson-Billings, G., & Donnor, J. (2005), The moral activist's role of Critical Race Theory scholarship. In N. Denzin, & Y. Lincoln (Eds.), *The Sage handbook of qualitative research* (3rd ed.). Sage Publications.

Martinez, K., & Truong, K. A. (2021). From DEI to JEDI. *Diverse: Issues in higher education*. https://diverseeducation.com/article/211514

McKinsey & Company (2021). *Women in the Workplace 2021*. https://www.mckinsey.com/featured-insights/diversity-and-inclusion/women-in-the-workplace

Nadiv, R., & Kuna, S. (2020). Diversity management as navigation through organizational paradoxes. *Equality, Diversity and Inclusion: An International Journal, 39*(4), 355–377.

Pendry, L. F., Driscoll, D. M., & Field, S. C. (2007). Diversity training: Putting theory into practice. *Journal of Occupational and Organizational Psychology, 80*(1), 27–50.

Ramsey, V. J., & Latting, J. K. (2005). A typology of intergroup competencies. *The Journal of Applied Behavioral Science, 41*(3), 265–284.

Roberts, L. M., & Mayo, A. J. (2019). Toward a racially just workplace. *Harvard Business Review*.

Schroth, H. (2019). Are you ready for Gen Z in the workplace? *California Management Review, 61*(3), 5–18.

Schwarz, R. M. (2016). *The skilled facilitator: A comprehensive resource for consultants, facilitators, managers, trainers, and coaches*. John Wiley & Sons.

Shore, L. M., & Chung, B. G. (2021). Inclusive leadership: How leaders sustain or discourage work group inclusion. *Group & Organization Management*, 1059601121999580.

Shore, L. M., Randel, A. E., Chung, B. G., Dean, M. A., Holcombe Ehrhart, K., & Singh, G. (2011). Inclusion and diversity in work groups: A review and model for future research. *Journal of Management, 37*(4), 1262–1289.

Stark, A. (2021, January 20). *Top 10 Work Trends for 2021.* SIOP. https://www.siop.org/Research-Publications/Items-of-Interest/ArtMID/19366/ArticleID/4914/Top-10-Work-Trends-for-2021?MessageRunDetailID=4183262381&PostID=24564630

Sugiyama, K., Cavanagh, K. V., van Esch, C., Bilimoria, D., & Brown, C. (2016). Inclusive leadership development: Drawing from pedagogies of women's and general leadership development programs. *Journal of Management Education, 40*(3), 253–292.

The Center for Women and Business. (2019, Winter). *Workplace Inclusion—Nurturing a Culture of Care and Belonging.*

Toubiana, M. (2014). Business pedagogy for social justice? An exploratory investigation of business faculty perspectives of social justice in business education. *Management Learning, 45*(1), 81–102.

Zheng, L. (2021, August 27). We're entering the age of Corporate Social Justice. *Harvard Business Review.* https://hbr.org/2020/06/were-entering-the-age-of-corporate-social-justice

CHAPTER 29

Workforce Members with Disabilities: An Underutilized Talent Pool for Mutual Growth

Cara W. Jacocks and R.G. Bell

INTRODUCTION

Disability and Labor Force Trends

Persons with Disability in the US Labor Force

Since 2008, the United States Bureau of Labor Statistics has relied on monthly data collected by the US Census Bureau known as the Current Population Statistics report (CPS) to accurately identify members of the disabled workforce in the US. According to the February 2022 Economic New Release, the CPS is "a monthly survey of about 60,000 eligible households that provides information on the labor force status, demographics, and other characteristics of the nation's civilian noninstitutional population age 16 and over (Bureau of Labor Statistics, 2022a, b). This survey adheres to 90% confidence interval standards and identifies a person with a disability, as a member of the US labor force household who replies "Yes" to any of the following items:

- Is anyone deaf or does anyone have serious difficulty hearing?
- Is anyone blind or does anyone have serious difficulty seeing even when wearing glasses?

C. W. Jacocks (✉) · R.G. Bell
Satish and Yasmin Gupta College of Business, The University of Dallas, Irving, TX, USA
e-mail: cjacocks@udallas.edu

© The Author(s), under exclusive license to Springer Nature Switzerland AG 2023
J. Marques (ed.), *The Palgrave Handbook of Fulfillment, Wellness, and Personal Growth at Work*,
https://doi.org/10.1007/978-3-031-35494-6_29

- Because of a physical, mental, or emotional condition, does anyone have serious difficulty concentrating, remembering, or making decisions?
- Does anyone have serious difficulty walking or climbing stairs?
- Does anyone have difficulty dressing or bathing?
- Because of a physical, mental, or emotional condition, does anyone have difficulty doing errands alone such as visiting a doctor's office or shopping? (Bureau of Labor Statistics, 2022a, b).

Members of a US household who fall in line with the definition above, and are over the age of 16 years old, are then identified as a member of the US disabled labor force, and additional demographic information is obtained such as employment status (employed/unemployed), self-employment status, hours generally worked (full-time/part-time), industry placement, and employment/unemployment rates specific to the US disabled workforce (Bureau of Labor Statistics, 2022a, b).

Based on CPS data, the BLS has compiled a report entitled "Persons with a Disability: Labor Force Characteristics" with the latest report being released in February, 2022 that highlights 2021 data (Bureau of Labor Statistics, 2022a, b). Positive momentum occurred for persons with disabilities in the US labor force from 2020 to 2021, as the employment rate increased from 17.9% in 2020 to 21% in 2022. This was also true for the nondisabled workforce, as employment increased 1.9 percent from 2020 to 2021. And the unemployment rate "declined from 2020 to 2021, to 10.1 percent and 5.1 percent, respectively" for both disabled and nondisabled members of the US workforce (Bureau of Labor Statistics, 2022a, b). Authors noted these labor force growth trends are due to the impact the COVID-19 pandemic had on labor force trends for the past two years. This was especially apparent as the employment rate for the disabled workforce reached the same ratio reported in 2019 (the pre-pandemic employment growth rate (Bureau of Labor Statistics, 2022a, b). Undoubtedly, statistical trends related to the disabled workforce will shift from year-to-year, pending world events and global market trends, and should be consulted frequently by persons of interest.

The Bureau of Labor Statistics also noted some labor force highlights related to the disabled workforce. These highlights appear to be relatively consistent as they have remained "highlights" for a several years now, and include:

- Half of all persons with a disability were aged 65 and over, nearly three times larger than the share for those with no disability.
- Across all age groups, persons with disabilities were much less likely to be employed than those with no disabilities.
- Across all educational attainment groups, unemployment rates for persons with a disability were higher than those for persons without a disability.

- In 2021, 29 percent of workers with a disability were employed part time, compared with 16 percent for those with no disability.
- Employed persons with a disability were more likely to be self-employed than those with no disability.
- In 2021, persons with a disability accounted for 11.9 percent of the civilian noninstitutional population.
- Overall, women were somewhat more likely to -2- have a disability than men, partly reflecting the greater life expectancy of women.
- In 2021, the prevalence of disability continued to be higher for Blacks and Whites than for Hispanics and Asians (Bureau of Labor Statistics, 2022a, b).

Some cumulative highlights touch on education level, part-time vs. full-time occupational status, self-employment rates, industry placement, and barriers to employment access for disabled workers. Simply put, members of the disabled workforce were less likely to have earned degrees or certifications from institutions of higher education and/or vocational programs. Similarly, disabled workers "across all levels of education" were much less likely to be employed compared to their nondisabled peers (Bureau of Labor Statistics, 2022a, b). Workers with disabilities were much more likely to obtain part-time work, rather than meaningful full-time employment. Whereas nondisabled workers were more likely to work in full-time occupations (Bureau of Labor Statistics, 2022a, b). Members of the disabled workforce were also more likely to work in service industry vocations and/or be self-employed as well (Bureau of Labor Statistics, 2022a, b). This is likely due to post-secondary vocational preparedness programs that direct many graduates to the service industry, as well as systemic and organizational barriers to access traditional, full-time occupations (Jacocks & Bell, 2020; National Council on Disability, 2020). Barriers to access meaningful, full-time employment for persons with disabilities are not an issue specific to the US, however. Similar systemic and organizational barriers exist across the global labor force for persons with disabilities.

Persons with Disability and the Global Labor Force
The United Nations attempted to collect data on the persons with disabilities global workforce and arrived at three conclusions, compiled into a factsheet report (United Nations, n.d.). First, concrete data on workers with disabilities was difficult to access across nearly every nation surveyed. Regardless, the UN was able to identify several barriers to meaningful and gainful employment for persons with disabilities that seem to exist uniformly across many countries (United Nations, n.d.).

Secondly, one prevalent, pervasive, and somewhat predictable barrier is tied to perceptions of members of the disabled workforce. Simply put, "Myths abound, including that persons with disabilities are unable to work and that accommodating a person with a disability in the workplace is expensive" (United Nations, n.d.). Contrary to these outdated fears about employing members of the disabled workforce, many companies have learned there is great benefit to hiring disabled employees including improved production, redacted turnover, and positive workplace culture (to name a few) (Lindsay et al., 2018). In other words, members of the disabled workforce are, in fact, capable of contributing a great deal to their respective workplaces and communities (Lindsay et al., 2018; United Nations, n.d.). A quote from a former US congressperson who was also a member of the disabled workforce is very telling:

> "Few employers are willing to hire workers with disabilities. Fear is the biggest barrier," said former Congressman Tony Coelho, an epilepsy sufferer himself and one of the authors of the Americans with Disabilities Act. "It's really fear of the unknown." The best way to eliminate such fears, he argues, is to hire persons with disabilities. "You'll find out that a lot of those things that you're fearful of are not true." (United Nations, n.d.)

The third fact compiled in the UN fact sheet addresses a common desire for meaningful, gainful employment shared by a large majority of members of the disabled workforce, across all nations represented in the United Nations' research. Their review led to uncovering several benefits of hiring persons with disabilities that they argue should be widely dispersed, on a global level. They include:

- Just like others, the majority of persons with disabilities want a dignified and productive life.
- Employment provides not only income but also opportunities for social participation. This is especially important for persons with disabilities.
- Spending on systems and facilities for persons with disabilities is not for the privilege of a small minority, but an investment for everyone.
- Diverse work groups develop better solutions to business challenges.
- Many companies have found that by employing persons with disabilities, they have been better able to understand and serve their customers with disabilities. Adapting services to meet the diverse needs of persons with disabilities allows business to develop greater flexibility, builds reputation, and reaches out to a [sizable] market (United Nations, n.d.).

Authors of the factsheet then go on to list several quotes from corporate and political leaders across several nations that depict the vast benefits of hiring workers with disabilities. One such corporate example, developed by Accenture, describes in detail the many positive aspects of employing individuals with disabilities, regarding both disabled and nondisabled employees. In other words, in this particular corporate scenario, inclusive hiring and work practices benefited everyone. It is a common misconception that promoting inclusivity in social and work realms primarily benefits those with disabilities, when there is ample evidence that nondisabled individuals and organizations at large benefit greatly from inclusive systems as well.

GETTING TO EQUAL: THE DISABILITY INCLUSION ADVANTAGE|ACCENTURE

Accenture, "a leading global professional services company" that "provides a broad range of services and solutions in strategy, consulting, digital technology, and operations," frequently partners with nonprofit think tanks and/or research consortiums to conduct innovative research that "shapes trends and creates data-driven insights about the most pressing issues global organizations face" (Accenture, 2018). Accenture employs 738,000 workers in over approximately 120 countries, and greatly prioritizes "thought-provoking research" (Accenture, 2018, 2023). One particular study, *Getting to Equal: The Disability Inclusion Advantage*, conducted by Accenture and the American Association of People with Disabilities (AAPD) and Disability:IN (two research-driven nonprofit organizations that strive to improve life and work for people with disabilities) found that it is very advantageous for global organizations to create inclusive workspaces for a variety of reasons (Accenture, 2018).

The *Getting to Equal* study "assessed 140 leading disability-inclusive companies with select data from a four-year sample of the DEI" (Accenture, 2018). Furthermore, "The assessment revealed key differentiating factors, activities and best practices in 45 of the 140 companies (32 percent). All companies that [participated] in the DEI [were] already advancing disability inclusion" (p.16). Through this rigorous partnered research, Accenture identified 45 "champion" organizations ("Disability Inclusion Champions") as organizations that were "providing leading-edge disability programs and initiatives that can be potentially implemented by others." (Accenture, 2018, p. 16). "Improvers" also emerged in the *Getting to Equal* study where the main purpose was to analyze the benefits of hiring workers with disabilities, primarily, financial performance (Accenture, 2018). "Improvers" were defined as "those companies that ranked in the top 25 percent of our own improvement score metric" (Accenture, 2018). In assessing both "Champions" and "Improvers," this partnered research determined that there are many benefits to hiring members of the disabled workforce that extend beyond increased profit margins (Accenture, 2018). One such benefit is higher levels of innovation demonstrated by disabled workers.

Innovation

A large body of research has determined that workers with disabilities in particular bring a great deal of innovation to their respective workspaces (Accenture, 2018; Friedner, 2015; Kalargyrou & Volis, 2014; Scott et al., 2017). Disabled workers are often required to get creative when innovating accommodations for themselves in order to "adapt to the world around them" (e.g., innovating a doable solution for workplace transportation, augmented communication devices, etc.), and this heightened level of ingenuity benefits colleagues and organizational systems (Accenture, 2018). Accenture describes this innovation advantage as:

> Persons with disabilities have to be creative to adapt to the world around them. As such, they develop strengths such as problem-solving skills, agility, persistence, forethought and a willingness to experiment—all of which are essential for innovation. Having employees with disabilities across departments helps ensure that the products and services that go to market are truly inclusive. And making things more accessible for persons with disabilities can translate into products and services from which everyone benefits— for instance, home devices using natural voice recognition, driving sales and growth. (Accenture, 2018, p. 12; Girma, 2017)

Scholarship surrounding innovation and disability has identified specific instances where hearing-impaired and autistic employees demonstrated high levels of creativity (Friedner, 2015; Scott et al., 2017). And additional research in the hospitality industry examined inclusive initiatives in the hospitality sector. In a particular case scenario, subjects described creative benefits in the hospitality sector as "[creating] innovative services and improve[ing] problem-solving ability," "[creating] new business opportunities" and improving overall organizational innovation (Kalargyrou & Volis, 2014, pp. 442–444).

Productivity, Retention, and Turnover

The *Getting to Equal* study also determined succinctly that everyone benefits from an inclusive workspace and that "working alongside employees with disabilities makes non-disabled individuals more aware of how to make the workplace more inclusive and better for everyone" (Accenture, 2018, p. 13). Results from this study as well as other peer-reviewed research articles demonstrate that productivity increases in organizations that promote inclusive hiring and work practices (Bengisu & Balta, 2011; Bitencourt & Guimaraes, 2012; Friedner, 2015; Graffam et al., 2002; Hartnett et al., 2011; Kalargyrou, 2014; & Schartz et al., 2006) as well as employee retention, and turnover decreases (Accenture, 2018; Buciuniene et al., 2010; Chi & Qu, 2003; Harnett et al., 2011; Hernandez & McDonald, 2010; Kalargyrou, 2014; Kuo & Kalargyrou, 2014; Zivolich & Weiner-Zivolich, 1997). The *Getting to Yes* study states that "Staff turnover is also lower—by up to 30 percent—when a well-run disability community outreach program is in place" (Accenture, 2018, p. 13). Many of these studies cited additional benefits to inclusive workspaces and contend that inclusive hiring and retaining employees with disabilities are not as challenging or costly as once believed.

Inclusive Sourcing, Enhanced Reputation, and Diverse Consumer Base

Organizational leaders have deduced over the years that a diverse supply base provides organizations with a very competitive advantage. Creating an inclusive workspace has directly impacted many businesses' ability to source goods and supplies from diverse arenas. Diverse and inclusive sourcing comes with many competitive benefits including (according to Accenture, 2018, p. 13):

- Access to new suppliers, innovative solutions, and cost savings through increased competition;
- Awareness of diverse customer needs, increased market share, and shareholder value; and
- Brand enhancement and recruitment/retention of employees who want meaningful work.

As previously stated, increased inclusive sourcing can lead to overall enhanced organizational and/or brand reputation by building and promoting a caring more inclusive image (Buciuniene et al., 2010; Hartnett et al., 2011). Inclusive workspaces have also been proven to lead to a more diverse consumer base as organizations that employ members of the disability community are generally more aware of the diverse needs of a nuanced customer base, and are therefore more capable of accessing and meeting the needs of the "third-largest market segment in the U.S., after Hispanics and African-Americans" (Accenture, 2018, p. 14). This market expands tremendously when extended to caregivers of individuals with disabilities, and others who prioritize inclusive brands and organizational systems. Additional peer-reviewed research supports this finding of an expanded market share advantage (Kalargyrou, 2014; Kalargyrou & Volis, 2014).

A Systematic Review of Disability and the Workplace

Abundant research demonstrates that inclusive workspaces undoubtedly come with higher revenue margins. However, the advantages of inclusive organizational systems to both disabled and nondisabled workers are enormous, and an extensive amount of scholarship (beyond the *Getting to Equal* study) has identified many of these benefits. Lindsay, et al. published a meta-analysis in the Journal of Occupational Rehabilitation titled, "A Systematic Review of the Benefits of Hiring People with Disabilities" in which the authors identified salient research that examined the many benefits of employing persons with disabilities (Lindsay, et al., 2018). Many of the identified research studies have been cited in previous sections as supportive evidence for the larger *Getting to Equal* study. There are many benefits this particular study neglected to address, however.

Primary Benefits to People with Disabilities

There is a great deal of scholarship, for example, that highlights the many benefits of meaningful, gainful employment that directly impact members of the disabled workforce. Decades old research demonstrates that workers with disabilities who maintain consistent employment have an overall improved quality of life (Eggleton et al., 1999). Relatedly, workers within the disabled workforce also demonstrated enhanced levels of self-esteem when meaningfully and gainfully employed (Buciuniene et al., 2010; Blessing and Jamieson, 2009; Irvine & Lupart, 2008; Owen et al., 2015) and maintain a heightened sense of independence (Clark et al., 1998; Kuiper et al., 2016). Employed workers with disabilities also generally experience an expanded social network and sense of community that they frequently rely on (and their communities) when attempting to access employment opportunities (Kuiper et al., 2016). Simply put, workers with disabilities experience many of the same positive effects of attaining and maintaining meaningful, and gainful employment echoing a common statement frequently resounded throughout the disability community, which is—disability rights are HUMAN rights. Additional benefits to customers, coworkers, and organizations were published in the Lindsay et al. study (2018).

Profit and Cost Effectiveness and Customer Loyalty/Satisfaction

Findings from several streams of scholarship emerged in the form of increased earnings for organizations who employed workers with disabilities (Buciuniene et al., 2010; Hartnett et al., 2011; Kalargyrou & Volis, 2014; Schartz et al., 2006, Wolffe & Candela, 2002; Zivolich & Weiner-Zivolich, 1997). Worker disabilities ranged from the hearing impaired to employees with cognitive impairments, and across several organizational types across varying sectors, sales revenue increased. And several studies found that perceptions of an inclusive workspace led to earnings in the form of cost savings (hiring, training, and retraining). Through one particular study, authors noted that one specific organization under analysis "reported over $19 million in financial benefits, mainly in the form of tax credits, over a 6-year period, and an additional savings of $8.4 million on recruitment and training due to improved retention" (Lindsay et al., 2018, p. 648; Zivolich & Weiner-Zivolich, 1997). Sales profits are not the only tangible factor positively related to the increased hiring of workers from the disabled workforce.

Customer Loyalty/Satisfaction

Across several businesses including the hospitality, telecommunications, and other various sectors, businesses that maintained an employee base of disabled workers experienced significantly increased customer loyalty and satisfaction (Bengisu & Balta, 2011; Graffam et al., 2002; Kalargyrou & Volis, 2014; Kalef et al., 2014; Kuo & Kalargyrou, 2014; Rosenbaum et al., 2017; Siperstein et al., 2006; Zivolich & Weiner-Zivolich, 1997). Workers identified documented disabilities that included vision impairments, intellectual disability, and other various types of disabilities. Siperstein and colleagues specifically noted that all participants in their research "responded positively towards companies that are socially responsible, including 92% of consumers who felt more favorable toward those that hire individuals with disabilities" (2006, p. 3). They further noted that "participants also had strong positive beliefs about the value and benefits of hiring people with disabilities, with 87% specifically agreeing that they would prefer to give their business to companies that hire individuals with disabilities" (Siperstein et al., 2006, p. 3). A diverse consumer base benefits the bottom line; however, a diverse and inclusive culture benefits everyone.

Inclusive/Diverse Work Culture

The bulk of the research addressed in the systematic review of the benefits of hiring workers with disabilities (Lindsay et al., 2018) focuses on overwhelming positive advantages related to building and sustaining an inclusive workplace culture (Bitencourt & Guimaraes, 2012, Buciuniene et al., 2010; Hartnett et al., 2011; Henry et al., 2014; Hernandez et al., 2008; Kalargyrou & Volis, 2014; Kalef et al., 2014; Morgan & Alexander, 2005, Owen et al., 2015; Schartz et al., 2006; Scott et al., 2017; Solovieva et al., 2009; Wolffe & Candela, 2002; Zivolich & Weiner-Zivolich, 1997). Workplaces that integrated disability training awareness initiatives reported an enhanced, inclusive workplace culture. Additional positive effects noted in studies that assessed inclusive workplace culture were: strengthened workforce, an overall more positive working environment, and enhanced workplace relationships across all workers both disabled and nondisabled. These are just a summary of the benefits that stem from inclusive workplace culture across several research endeavors; undoubtedly, there are additional benefits worth examination.

Despite the abundant evidence of benefits related to hiring workers with disabilities, significant barriers to workplace access still exist for the disabled workforce in the US. The US Bureau of Labor Statistics describes primary barriers as: lack of access to transportation, lack of education or training, lack of workplace accommodations, lack of social and governmental support, coworker stigma toward disability and disabled workers, and lack of overall job search assistance such as job counseling (BLS, 2020). Many institutions of higher education in the US have become cognizant of the benefits of hiring members of the disability community for decades as well as access barriers, and have implemented programs at the post-secondary level to accommodate students with the specific barriers of: *lack of education and training and lack of job counseling resources.*

Overcoming Barriers Through Inclusive Higher Education

There are currently 316 post-secondary programs that offer an immersive and inclusive higher education learning experience for adults with disabilities (Think College, *College Search* n.d.). These programs range from 2 to 4 years and offer a variety of forms of assistance, but the primary goal of each of these higher education programs is to equip and prepare graduates with disabilities for independent living and employment. Think College, an institute for community inclusion at the University of Massachusetts (Boston), is a research consortium that has created and published a wealth of information to guide individuals with intellectual disability (and their caregivers) as they navigate higher education opportunities. In the "about" section of the Think College website, the organizational mission and vision is clearly articulated as:

> Think College provides resources, technical assistance and training related to college options for students with intellectual disability, and manages the only national listing of college programs for students with intellectual disability in the United States.
>
> We are a national technical assistance, research, and evaluation center dedicated to developing, expanding, and improving higher education options for students with intellectual disability.
>
> With a commitment to equity and excellence, Think College supports evidence-based and student-centered research and practice by generating and sharing knowledge, guiding institutional change, informing public policy, and engaging with students, professionals and families. (Think College, About, 2023)

Think College is dedicated to creating opportunities that lead to meaningful community inclusion for persons with disabilities, ID (Intellectual Disability) specifically, by researching and creating awareness about the post-secondary opportunities neurodivergent workers have to assist in overcoming organizational access barriers that still exist. Inclusive higher learning programs recognized by Think College are considered TPSID programs (Transitional Post-Secondary Programs for Students with Intellectual Disabilities) and are hosted by community colleges, private universities, and public universities across the US. Some of these inclusive post-secondary programs receive federal funding from the US Department of Education. Generally, federal grants are extended to these programs as they have demonstrated a significant effort to expand reach and create advanced learning/training opportunities for students with intellectual disabilities.

Aggie ACHIEVE: An Exemplar Post-Secondary Inclusive Program

One particular federally funded TPSID program hosted by Texas A&M University (College Station, TX), is the Aggie Achieve Program. Aggie Achieve is described as:

> [A] comprehensive transition program (CTP) for young adults with intellectual and developmental disabilities (IDD) who have exited high school. Aggie ACHIEVE provides an inclusive and immersive college education and equips students for employment in the community. Aggie ACHIEVE aligns coursework, internship opportunities, and extracurricular activities with each student's academic interests and employment goals. (Aggie ACHIEVE, 2023)

Aggie Achieve is designed to offer neurodivergent students and students with ID an immersive and inclusive higher education experience through classroom instruction. Students have access to a variety of courses through Texas A&M University's standard core curriculum as well as specialized courses that offer lessons on independent living, vocational training, internships, career services and job counseling, and social skills. Moreover, students enrolled in the Aggie ACHIEVE program are exposed to a typical college experience as they are fully included in many of the traditions and social activities their typically developing peers are involved in. Graduates of the Aggie ACHIEVE program earn a Certificate of Interdisciplinary Studies from Texas A&M, and Aggie ACHIEVE is one of a few federally funded, 4-year TPSID programs that offers financial aid and on-campus housing. Appendix A features Aggie ACHIEVE as well as 19 other US programs that meet these four criteria (federally funded, 4-year institution, financial aid, and on-campus housing).

Post-secondary higher education opportunities are a monumental step forward for persons with intellectual disability or disabilities. In a study conducted by Think College, results determined that many graduates of TPSID programs "either had a paid job (at exit or within 90 days)" or "were participating in unpaid career development activities" (Grigal et al., 2020, p. 20). Furthermore, this study found that 2 years after graduation, 66% of graduates maintained paid employment (p. 24), and authors ultimately concluded, "By creating viable paths to and through higher education and coupling these experiences with a continued focus on employment, the TPSID programs support increased independence as well as personal and professional growth for students with intellectual disability" (p. 28). This employment statistic (66%) is significantly higher than the general employment rate for persons with disabilities, previously stated as 21% (BLS, 2022a, b). Despite these significant advancements in opportunities for higher learning, training, job counseling, and job placement, employees with disabilities continue to face hurdles in gaining access to meaningful, gainful employment. Studies have found that social and community supports that assist people with disabilities in attaining and maintaining employment, and independent living, shift from state to state in the US. The following section will focus on the need for appropriate support services in the US and in particular, states ranked as offering minimal support for people with intellectual disability.

Addressing Persistent Systemic Barriers

As previously noted by data published by the Bureau of Labor Statistics, barriers in gaining access to employment still exist for the many members of the disabled workforce and include lack of transportation, lack of workplace accommodations, coworker stigma toward disability, etc., (BLS, 2020). Many states in the US offer support services that assist disabled workers in overcoming these barriers, such as public transportation, comprehensive health care coverage (Medicaid), general social and community services the promote independent living, or living with direct family members (for added support), and direct workforce supports (UCP & ANCOR, 2019). Research conducted by United Cerebral Palsy and the ANCOR Foundation ranked participating states across the US by assessing a variety of areas that directly impact support members of the disabled workforce receive (or lack thereof) that included: the promotion of independence, keeping families together, direct services to those in need, and health, safety, and overall quality of life (UCP & ANCOR, 2019). UCP has historically collected data and published research findings in what is referred to as *The Case for Inclusion Report* for years. In 2019, UCP partnered with ANCOR "through its Included. Supported. Empowered. Campaign" and published "comprehensive set of data for our nation, plus all 50 states and the District of Columbia, to protect the gains we've made and identify areas in which more progress is needed" (UCP & ANCOR, 2019, p. 3). These published findings continue to guide persons with disabilities (and their respective caregivers) as they seek assistance and employment opportunities in the US.

The Case for Inclusion Report 2019

As previously stated, *The Case for Inclusion Report* assessed several key areas in determining an overall state ranking system. Promoting independence was one key area and assessed by the 80/80 Home and Community Standard which is defined as "80 percent of all individuals with I/DD are served in the community and 80 percent of all resources spent on those with I/DD are for home (less than 7 residents per setting) and community support" (UCP & ANCOR, 2019, p. 12). This area was also assessed by the number of state institutions that exist in a particular state or region, as these institutions promote isolation rather than independence and inclusion. The Home-Like Setting Standard was also assessed in ranking states on the promotion of overall independence which the report defines as "at least 80 percent of all individuals with I/ DD are served in settings such as their own home, a family home, in a shared living /host home setting or small group settings with fewer than four residents"

(p. 12). And finally, promoting independence was measured by the availability of self-directed services offered by a particular state, where individuals with disabilities can best select and access the services they need based on their unique disability and related needs and accommodations (UCP & ANCOR, 2019).

"Promoting productivity" was very clearly measured by job placement rates, average number of hours worked per disabled employee, and job placement within 1 year. "Keeping families together" was measured by the percentage of support services available to families to remain an intact family (rather than separating family members into foster care services or institutional settings). Authors of *The Case for Inclusion* provide further context by stating, "These support services help families that are caring for children with disabilities at home, which helps keep families together, and people with disabilities living in a community setting" (UCP & ANCOR, 2019, p. 13). Simply put, some states offer more family-focused programs and related support services than others. Lastly, "Health, Safety, and Quality of Life" was measured by "the National Core Indicators (NCI) survey, a comprehensive quality-assurance program that includes standard measurements to assess outcomes of services" (UCP & ANCOR, p. 13).

Again, many families in the disability community rely on the results from this report to assist in navigating various state systems and support services. Appendix B offers the comprehensive list of state rankings published by *The Case for Inclusion Report 2019*. The top three ranking states were Arizona (#1), Oregon (#2), and Vermont (#3), and the bottom three ranking states were Texas (#49), Arkansas (#50), and Mississippi (#51). It is especially notable that the state of Texas ranked near the bottom of this list, as Texas is an affluent state with an abundance of business resources and a flourishing state economy. Furthermore, the state of Texas offers a large number of post-secondary education programs, including the previously noted Aggie ACHIEVE program, and the current governor of the state (Governor Greg Abbott) is himself a member of the disabled workforce. It is salient that future research examines the relationship between TPSID programs and state-supported services for members of the disability workforce, beyond graduating from these programs. Think College states that an accreditation process is in development to assess TPSID higher education programs. The current model proposes "student services standard 6" which will assess job placement (Think College, 2021, p.18). How these results vary by state should be very telling.

Social Entrepreneurship

Keeping the aforementioned barriers in mind coupled with the lack of social and community support offered by many US states, many members of the disabled workforce in the US are creating their own business ventures where they can bypass many of these hurdles and tailor an entrepreneurial position to their specific disability-related needs. According to the US Census Bureau, individuals with disabilities are twice as likely to innovate and execute their own business ventures, compared to their nondisabled counterparts. Many speculate this can be tied to the innovation-related benefit related to hiring disabled workers, described in a previous section. Members of the disabled workforce are consistently required to adapt to environments that lack appropriate and necessary accommodations. Thus, many workers with disabilities are well-equipped to improvise, which is a necessary trait for successful business venturing. Additionally, because of the obstacles they face as members of the disabled workforce, many entrepreneurs with disabilities innovate business enterprises with a social entrepreneurship angle that directly benefits the disabled workforce (Jacocks & Bell, 2020).

Social entrepreneurship research endeavors are beginning to recognize this trend as contextually bounded and localized (Jacocks & Bell, 2020). In other words, many social entrepreneurial ventures initiated by workers with disabilities emerge as a direct response to discriminatory governmental and institutional structures that drastically limit the employment opportunities of persons with disabilities (Jacocks & Bell, 2020). There are many such ventures across the US. Jacocks and Bell (2020) analyze three cases: Austin's Underdawgs, Dreamers' Coffee Merchants, and Collettey's Cookies. Each case represents a unique form of business ownership. Austin's Underdawgs is a Food Truck business owned by an adult with Down syndrome (Austin), offers event catering services, an online storefront with merchandise and Austin's famous "dawgsauce," as well as franchising opportunities. A portion of Underdawg's proceeds indirectly supports The Mingus Job Accelerator through The Each and Everyone Foundation. The Mingus Job Accelerator is a vocational training program for workers with intellectual disabilities (Jacocks & Bell, 2020). Dreamers Coffee Merchants is an organization with an MLM (multilevel marketing) compensation structure that offers affordable start-up business opportunities and ample support resources for individuals with disabilities. Dreamers' also supports training opportunities and externships for members of the disabled workforce through the TigerLIFE program, another post-secondary higher education program offered through the University of Memphis. Collettey's Cookies is a traditional bakery owned by an adult with Down syndrome (Collettey) with a physical storefront and online sales platform. A portion of funds earned by Collettey's Cookies is directly donated to her 501c3, Collettey's Leadership Program, where aspiring entrepreneurs with disabilities receive training, mentoring, and coursework as they refine their skills as burgeoning business owners (Jacocks & Bell, 2020). There are many more cases of entrepreneurs with disabilities engaging in social entrepreneurship ventures that benefit the disabled workforce. Again, cases noted in this section represent different forms of business ownership (traditional, MLM, and franchising).

Conclusion

In conclusion, employers on a global level need to be more aware of the benefits to hiring and sustaining a labor base of workers with disabilities. Hiring more workers with disabilities is just the beginning; however, employers need to start focusing on creating more inclusive workspaces overall. Again, the benefits are vast and based on the evidence presented in this chapter, drastically offset the resources it requires to create and implement inclusive/diversity training, inclusive work culture, and the provision of physical and/or work-related accommodations.

Furthermore, post-secondary higher learning programs need to continue developing relationships with local agencies, but simultaneously reach out to external educational programs at the secondary, intermediate, and elementary school levels. Neurotypical students at the secondary level are generally aware of the post-secondary options through "college colors" day through many public school systems, information gained from friends, family members, school counselors, teachers, etc. However, very few public school officials are even aware that post-secondary higher education is an option for their disabled students, while over **300** of these programs exist around the US. And very much like neurotypical students preparing for higher education opportunities, students with disabilities and their educational teams need more information to assist with decisions about vocational programs vs. 2-year community college programs vs. 4-year university programs, etc. Additionally, it would be beneficial to disabled workers and their caregivers if post-secondary higher learning programs worked to compare accreditation data with state resources/support data. Perhaps a research alliance between programs, think tanks, and corporations would assist with this (similar to the UCP and ANCOR research alliance). This would also assist at the secondary level where key decisions are made about higher education opportunities and options.

Lastly, while this chapter primarily addresses the disabled workforce from a US perspective, there are global ramifications. For example, *The Case for Inclusion* clearly outlines states that offer more social, communication, and government support for workers with disabilities (UCP & ANCOR, 2019). Governments and business leaders in regions beyond the US can learn from the varying state models (and relative state success rates and rankings) and begin to integrate workers with disabilities into their local economies via appropriate and reasonable support measures given various regional cultures and resources. While there are many obstacles US workers with disabilities face in gaining access to employment, the outlook is much bleaker in many other countries around the globe.

Appendix A
List of Inclusive Post-Secondary Education Programs in the US

Program	College/university	State	Private/public	Length of program
Access ETSU	East Tennessee State University	Tennessee	Public	2 years
Aggie ACHIEVE	Texas A&M University	Texas	Public	4 years
Aggies Elevated-Eastern	Utah State University Eastern	Utah	Public	Missing
Blackburn and Beyond	Blackburn College	Illinois	Private	4 years
CarolinaLIFE	University of South Carolina	South Carolina	Public	4 years
CrossingPoints Certificate in Occupational Studies	The University of Alabama	Alabama	Public	3 years
Eileen Hoffman Hafer UMatter Program	University of South Florida St. Petersburg campus	Florida	Public	3 years
Elmhurst Learning and Success Academy (ELSA)	Elmhurst University	Illinois	Private	4 years
Inclusive Education Services	University of Central Florida	Florida	Public	2 years
Integrated Studies	Gwynedd Mercy University	Pennsylvania	Private	4 years
Integrated Studies (Millersville)	Millersville University	Pennsylvania	Pubic	4 years
Leadership and Integrative Studies	Lock Haven University	Pennsylvania	Public	4 years
Ready for Life (Calvin)	Calvin University	Michigan	Private	4 years
The Career and Community Studies (TCNJ)	The College of New Jersey	New Jersey	Public	4 years
Transition and Career Studies	Georgian Court University	New Jersey	Private	4 years
Transition University for Career Advancement and Successful Adulthood	Texas A&M University San Antonio	Texas	Public	2 years
UMSL Succeed	University of Missouri-St. Louis	Missouri	Public	2 years
UNT ELEVAR	University of North Texas	Texas	Public	4 years

(continued)

(continued)

Program	College/university	State	Private/public	Length of program
Wayfinders—California State University, Fresno	California State University, Fresno	California	Public	2 years
WSU ROAR	Washington State University	Washington	Public	2 years

*Table data generated from www.thinkcollege.net search option. Criteria used for search were as follows: • Offers financial aid (CTP); • Offers housing; • 4-year university or college; • Federally funded TPISD program

APPENDIX B
CASE FOR INCLUSION STATE RANKINGS TABLE

State	Promoting independence		Tracking health, safety + quality of life		Keeping families together		Promoting productivity		Reaching those in need		Overall score + ranking
	50% of total ranking		15% of total ranking		8% of total ranking		12% of total ranking		15% of total ranking		
Arizona	44.4	6	12.7	22	7.6	1	6.4	29	15	12	86 1
Oregon	44.7	5	13.1	19	4.5	12	7.8	6	15	1	85.1 2
Vermont	45.3	3	13.2	16	4.1	15	8.6	2	12	41	83.3 3
Missouri	41.3	18	13.9	4	4.6	10	6.9	20	15	13	81.7 4
Kentucky	43.8	7	13.9	5	3.7	18	5.6	46	14.2	23	81.2 5
Hawaii	43.6	8	12.5	24	5.1	8	4.8	49	15	1	81 6
New Hampshire	46.1	2	8.2	36	3.7	17	7.1	13	15	14	80 7
Ohio	40.8	25	13.5	13	6.8	2	6.2	35	12.1	40	79.4 8
California	42.7	13	7.7	42	6.7	3	6.9	17	15	1	79.1 9
South Dakota	37	41	13.7	7	5.4	6	7.8	5	15	1	79 10
Maryland	43	11	12.6	23	1.2	49	7.9	3	14	29	78.7 11
South Carolina	38.9	35	13.2	18	6.3	5	6.8	22	13.3	35	78.5 12
Michigan	44.7	4	7.9	38	3.6	20	7	15	15	1	78.3 13
Wisconsin	47.8	1	8.8	37	4.4	13	5.8	42	11.9	43	78.2 14
Dist. of Columbia	39.7	30	13.6	10	2.2	37	7.4	9	15	1	77.9 15
Indiana	39.2	34	13.7	8	3.2	27	6.5	25	14.8	16	77.5 16
Utah	40	28	13	20	3.4	25	6.9	19	14	28	77.3 17
New York	38.5	36	13.2	17	4.2	14	6.4	28	15	1	77.3 18
Pennsylvania	41.8	15	13.8	6	3.7	16	6.1	39	11.4	47	76.9 19

(continued)

(continued)

State	Promoting independence		Tracking health, safety + quality of life		Keeping families together		Promoting productivity		Reaching those in need		Overall score + ranking
	50% of total ranking		15% of total ranking		8% of total ranking		12% of total ranking		15% of total ranking		
Delaware	41.1	21	8.4	31	4.6	11	7.6	7	15	1	76.8 20
Minnesota	39.6	31	13.6	11	5	9	6.5	26	11.8	45	76.4 21
Georgia	41.5	16	14	2	2	39	5.5	48	12.8	37	75.7 22
Nebraska	39.8	29	12.9	21	1.8	42	7.1	14	14	27	75.5 23
Maine	41.1	20	13.2	15	0.4	51	6.2	34	14.5	18	75.5 24
Nevada	43.3	9	7.6	44	3	29	7.1	12	14.2	24	75.2 25
Tennessee	41.5	17	14.2	1	2.3	36	6.5	24	10.4	48	74.9 26
Colorado	43.1	10	7.9	40	1.2	50	7.9	4	14.4	21	74.4 27
Idaho	41.2	19	8.4	32	3.3	26	6.2	33	15	1	74.2 28
Alabama	39.3	33	14	3	1.6	46	4.5	50	13.7	31	73 29
Washington	42.4	14	0	46	5.4	7	10.1	1	14.9	15	72.7 30
Connecticut	36.6	43	13.5	12	3.5	23	7.1	11	11.7	46	72.5 31
Rhode Island	40.4	27	8.7	27	2.4	34	5.5	47	15	1	72 32
Wyoming	40.8	24	8.3	34	3.5	22	6.8	21	11.8	44	71.3 33
Florida	40.9	23	8.8	26	3	30	3.2	51	13.6	34	69.5 34
Massachusetts	39.4	32	7.8	41	2.5	33	7.3	10	12	41	69 35
Louisiana	35.4	45	8.4	33	6.4	4	6.2	36	12.1	39	68.5 36
Kansas	37.4	39	8.5	30	1.9	40	6.4	27	14.1	26	68.4 37
New Jersey	36.9	42	8.8	25	2.4	35	5.8	43	14.3	22	68.3 38
Virginia	38.2	38	7.7	43	3.1	28	6.9	18	10.2	49	66.1 39
Alaska	42.8	12	0	46	1.6	45	7	16	14.4	19	65.9 40
North Carolina	33.5	48	8.6	28	3.7	19	6.3	31	13.6	33	65.8 41
West Virginia	41	22	0	46	1.9	41	7.5	8	14.4	20	64.9 42
New Mexico	40.5	26	1.6	45	2.7	32	6.7	23	12.7	38	64.2 43
Illinois	28.5	49	13.5	14	1.8	44	5.7	45	14.1	25	63.6 44
Iowa	38.2	37	0	46	1.5	47	6.3	30	14.6	17	60.7 45
North Dakota	37.2	40	0	46	2	38	5.9	40	15	1	60.2 46
Oklahoma	34	47	8.3	35	1.8	43	6.1	38	9.1	50	59.3 47
Montana	35.3	46	0	46	3.5	21	6.2	32	14	30	59.1 48
Texas	36	44	13.6	9	3.5	24	5.9	41	0	51	59 49
Arkansas	26.1	50	8.5	29	1.3	48	6.1	37	13.3	36	55.3 50
Mississippi	21.9	51	7.9	39	2.9	31	5.7	44	13.7	32	52.1 51

*Adapted from the Case for Inclusion Report 2019

REFERENCES

Accenture. (2018). *Getting to equal: The disability inclusion advantage*. https://www.accenture.com/t20181108T081959Z__w__/us-en/_acnmedia/PDF-89/Accenture-Disability-Inclusion-Research-Report.pdf#zoom=50

Accenture. (2023). *Accenture fact sheet Q2 FY23*. https://newsroom.accenture.com//content/1101/files/Accenture_Factsheet_Q2_FY23.pdf

Aggie ACHIEVE. (2023). *About*. https://aggieachieve.tamu.edu/about/

Bengisu, M. & Balta, S. (2011). Employment of the workforce with disabilities in the hospitality industry. *Journal of Sustainable Tourism, 19*(1), 35–57.

Bitencourt, R. S., & Guimaraes, L. B. (2012). Inclusion of people with disabilities in the production system of a footwear industry. *Work, 41*(Suppl 1), 4767–4774.

Blessing, L. A., & Jamieson, J. (1999). Employing persons with a developmental disability: Effects of previous experience. *Canadian Journal of Rehabilitation, 12*, 211–221.

Buciuniene, I., Bleijenbergh, I., & Kazlauskaite, R. (2010). Integrating people with disability into the workforce: The case of a retail chain. *Equality, Diversity and Inclusion: An International Journal, 29*(5), 534–538.

Bureau of Labor Statistics. (2020). Barriers to employment for people with disabilities. *TED: The Economics Daily*. https://www.bls.gov/opub/ted/2020/barriers-to-employment-for-people-with-a-disability.htm

Bureau of Labor Statistics. (2022a). *TED: The Economics Daily*. https://www.bls.gov/opub/ted/2022a/19-1-percent-of-people-with-a-disability-were-employed-in-2021.htm

Bureau of Labor Statistics. (2022b). *Persons with a disability: Labor Force Characteristics*. https://www.bls.gov/news.release/pdf/disabl.pdf

Centers for Disease Control and Prevention. (2023, January 5). *Disability impacts all of us infographic*. https://www.cdc.gov/ncbddd/disabilityandhealth/infographic-disability-impacts-all.html

Chi, C.G.-Q., & Qu, H. (2003). Integrating persons with disabilities into the workforce. *International Journal of Hospitality & Tourism Administration, 4*(4), 59–83.

Clark, R. E., Xie, H., Becker, D. R., & Drake, R. E. (1998). Benefits and costs of supported employment from three perspectives. *The Journal of Behavioral Health Services Research, 25*(1), 22–34, 78.

Eggleton, I., Robertson, S., Ryan, J., & Kober, R. (1999). The impact of employment on the quality of life of people with an intellectual disability. *Journal of Vocational Rehabilitation, 13*(2), 95–107.

Friedner, M. (2015). Deaf bodies and corporate bodies: New regimes of value in Bangalore's business process outsourcing sector. *The Journal of the Royal Anthropological Institute, 21*(2), 313–329.

Girma, H. (2017, September 13). Break down disability barriers to spur growth and Innovation. *Financial Times*. https://www.ft.com/content/d8997604-97ab-11e7-8c5c-c8d8fa6961bb

Graffam, J., Smith, K., Shinkfield, A., & Polzin, U. (2002). Employer benefits and costs of employing a person with a disability. *Journal of Vocational Rehabilitation, 17*(4), 251–263.

Grigal, M., Hart, D., Papay, C., Wu, X., Lazo, R., Smith, F., & Domin, D. (2020). Annual report of the Cohort 2 TPSID model demonstration projects (Year 5, 2019–2020). *Think College National Coordinating Center.* https://thinkcollege.net/sites/default/files/files/TCReports_Year5_TPSID.pdf

Hartnett, H. P., Stuart, H., Thurman, H., Loy, B., & Batiste, L. C. (2011). Employers' perceptions of the benefits of workplace accommodations: Reasons to hire, retain and promote people with disabilities. *Journal of Vocational Rehabilitation, 34*(1), 17–23.

Henry, A. D., Petkauskos, K., Stanislawzyk, J., & Vogt, J. (2014). Employer-recommended strategies to increase opportunities for people with disabilities. *Journal of Vocational Rehabilitation, 41*(3), 237–248.

Hernandez, B., McDonald, K., Divilbiss, M., Horin, E., Velcoff, J., & Donoso, O. (2008). Reflections from employers on the disabled workforce: Focus groups with healthcare, hospitality and retail administrators. *Employee Responsibility & Rights Journal, 20*(3), 157–164.

Hernandez, B., & McDonald, K. (2010). Exploring the costs and benefits of workers with disabilities. *Journal of Rehabilitation, 76*(3), 15–23.

Irvine, A., & Lupart, J. (2008). Into the workforce: Employers' perspectives of inclusion. *Developmental Disabilities Bulletin, 36*, 225–250.

Jacocks, C., & Bell, G. (2020). Entrepreneurs with disabilities: Making a difference in society through social entrepreneurship. In J. Marques, & S. Dhiman (Eds.), *Social entrepreneurship and corporate social responsibility: Management for professionals.* Springer.

Kalargyrou, V. (2014). Gaining a competitive advantage with disability inclusion initiatives. *Journal of Human Resources in Hospitality & Tourism, 13*(2), 120–145.

Kalargyrou, V., & Volis, A. A. (2014). Disability inclusion initiatives in the hospitality industry: An exploratory study of industry leaders. *Journal of Human Resources in Hospitality & Tourism, 13*(4), 430–454.

Kalef, L., Barrera, M., & Heymann, J. (2014). Developing inclusive employment: Lessons from telenor open mind. *Work, 48*(3), 423–434.

Kuiper, L., Bakker, M., & Van der Klink, J. (2016). The role of human values and relations in the employment of people with work-relevant disabilities. *Social Inclusion, 4*(4), 176.

Kuo, P.-J., & Kalargyrou, V. (2014). Consumers' perspectives on service staff with disabilities in the hospitality industry. *International Journal of Contemporary Hospitality Management, 26*(2), 164–182.

Lindsay, S., Kagliostro, E., Albarico, M., Mortaji, N., & Karon, L. (2018). A systematic review of the benefits of hiring people with disabilities. *Journal of Occupational Rehabilitation, 28*, 634–655.

Morgan, R. L., & Alexander, M. (2005). The employer's perception: Employment of individuals with developmental disabilities. *Journal of Vocational Rehabilitation, 23*(1), 39–49.

National Council on Disability. (2020). 2020 Progress report on national disability policy: Increasing disability employment. https://ncd.gov/sites/default/files/NCD_Progress_Report_508_0.pdf

Owen, F., Li, J., Whittingham, L., Hope, J., Bishop, C., Readhead, A., & Mook, Ll. (2015). Social return on investment of an innovative employment option for persons with developmental disabilities. *Nonprofit Management Leadership, 26*(2), 209–228.

Rosenbaum, M. S., Baniya, R., & Seger-Guttmann, T. (2017). Customer responses towards disabled frontline employees. *International Journal of Retail & Distribution Management, 45*(4), 385–403.

Schartz, H. A., Hendricks, D., & Blanck, P. (2006). Workplace accommodations: Evidence based outcomes. *Work, 27*(4), 345–354.

Scott, M., Jacob, A., Hendrie, D., Parsons, R., Girdler, S., Falkmer, T., & Falkmer, M. (2017). Employers' perception of the costs and the benefits of hiring individuals with autism spectrum disorder in open employment in Australia. *PLoS ONE, 12*(5), e0177607. https://doi.org/10.1371/journal.pone.0177607

Siperstein, G. N., Romano, N., Mohler, A., & Parker, R. (2006). A national survey of consumer attitudes towards companies that hire people with disabilities. *Journal of Vocational Rehabilitation, 24*(1), 3–9.

Solovieva, T. I., Walls, R. T., Hendricks, D. J., & Dowler, D. L. (2009). Cost of workplace accommodations for individuals with disabilities: With or without personal assistance services. *Disability and Health Journal, 2*(4), 196–205.

Think College. (n.d.), *College search*. Think College. (n.d.). https://thinkcollege.net/college-search

Think College. (2021). *Report on model accreditation standards for higher education programs for students with intellectual disability: Progress on the path to education, employment, and community living: Models, standards, guidance, and review requirements.* https://thinkcollege.net/sites/default/files/files/TCreport_accred_modelstandards_2021.pdf

Think College. (2023). *About: What is think college?* https://thinkcollege.net/about/what-is-think-college

United Cerebral Palsy & ANCOR Foundation. (2019). *The case for inclusion report 2019.* https://caseforinclusion.org/application/files/5715/5534/1836/UCP_Case_for_Inclusion_Report_2019_Final_Single_Page_041519.pdf

United Nations. (n.d.). *Disability and employment: Fact sheet 1.* https://www.un.org/development/desa/disabilities/resources/factsheet-on-persons-with-disabilities/disability-and-employment.html

Wolffe, K., & Candela, A. (2002). A qualitative analysis of employers' experiences with visually impaired workers. *Journal of Visual Impairment & Blindness, 96*(9), 1200–1204.

World Health Organization. (n.d.). https://www.who.int/news-room/fact-sheets/detail/disability-and-health

Zivolich, S., & Weiner-Zivolich, J. S. (1997). A national corporate employment initiative for persons with severe disabilities: A 10-year perspective. *Journal of Vocational Rehabilitation, 8*(1), 75–87.

CHAPTER 30

Servant Leadership: An Inextricable Technique and Persuasive Criterion for Emerging Leaders

Nidhi Kaushal

INTRODUCTION

Servant leadership is often culturally applauded for its potentially ethical and spiritual influence on organizational life and perpetuates a theology of leadership (Eicher-Catt, 2005), and this process reflects a cultural shift toward positive leadership behaviors and includes value for ethics and relationships (Lemoine & Blum, 2019). This approach demands a leader with a character that encourages confidence because he has the knowledge and moral conviction to define actual life's purpose to the followers (Hammargren, 2007), and acts as a centrifugal force that directs followers' perspective from a self-serving toward other-serving orientation and empowers them to be productive and pro-social catalysts (Eva et al., 2019). Leaders who understand and serve the needs of all fellows are more respected and valued by organizations or society and exhibit the dignity that they aim to serve with working (Ambali et al., 2011). They should exhibit persuasive mapping and altruistic leadership qualities to make their employees feel empowered and stimulate their innovative behavior, commitment, and trust (Krog & Govender, 2015). Success requires cooperation, and the servant leader identifies it through the value of joint effort of employees and the leader (Hannay, 2008), and servant leaders,

N. Kaushal (✉)
Leadership Practitioner/Researcher, Yamunanagar, India
e-mail: nidhi.k3333@gmail.com

© The Author(s), under exclusive license to Springer Nature Switzerland AG 2023
J. Marques (ed.), *The Palgrave Handbook of Fulfillment, Wellness, and Personal Growth at Work*,
https://doi.org/10.1007/978-3-031-35494-6_30

either men or women, often show altruistic motives, and their effective persuasion offers compelling reasons to get followers to engage because they reflect agentic servant leadership behaviors (Barbuto & Gifford, 2010).

Servant leadership is a value-based style of leadership for introducing transformation in modern organizations through morality and values (Minnis & Callahan, 2010). It involves employee commitment and organizational citizenship behavior through the values of empowerment, humility, and empathy to create a positive organizational culture (Setyaningrum, 2017). Ethics emphasize the interrelatedness of human beings, and in leadership practice, followers judge their leaders by standards of morality and scrutinize their behavior (Gabriel, 2015), and the ethical approach of servant leadership lies as a holistic system for the entire organization, a defining method of practicing leadership that focuses on character and virtue (McMahone, 2012). A servant leader acts as a motivating factor for followers' development and inspiration as an example, enhances independence and opportunity, and helps in the pursuance of their interests (Bass & Steidlmeier, 1999), because of his sacrifice for the care and interest of others on the basis of self-stability (Reynolds, 2011).

Self-efficacy is the characteristic trait of leaders for servant leadership, which shows their devotedness and loyalty, while the service indicates the pure emotion and absolute personality of a servant. Although the responsibility of a leader is very dynamic under the organizational framework and he has to make continuous efforts to improve his working style and behavior, which required an analysis of different strategies and their influence. In this approach, there is a requirement of several innovative procedures with wisdom and insight, and Indian scriptures, tales, and lucid concepts based on rationality have a significant role in providing new perspectives and act as guiding principles of classical philosophies. The instances of folks from the common life also have a valuable and influential aspect in learning the art of selfless service, which are implicit for getting an enriched reference of servant leadership. They have represented the value of character strength, sacrifice, and devoutness in their deeds and selfless approach of serving humanity to get supreme bliss, while the *Vedic* texts have described the service of beings as the first religion of a person by giving a poignant reference to dharma. This chapter has implicitly mentioned the related and beneficial aspects of service for modern leaders to embrace the servant leadership approach for thriving execution of tasks and improving their demeanor. It has been categorized into five important sections: (1) Servant Leadership as an Inherent Approach and Perspective of Women Leaders; (2) The Essential Trait of Humility for a Leader's Efficacious Functioning; (3) The Implication of *ŚrīMad Bhagavad GīTā* in Servant Leadership and its Spiritual Orientation; (4) Conscientiousness, Devoutness, and Sensibility in the Context of Serviceability.

Literature Review

Servant leadership theory is an ideal approach for women leaders to manage and operate through serving others, whose implications have been presented for others as examples in literary works (Minnis & Callahan, 2010). This style is helpful and an ideal for women to change the associated cognitive dissonance of man leaders, along with holistic management and enhancing the performance of the organizational members (Lemoine & Blum, 2019). It is an extension of leadership models and focuses on reaching others through moral development and serving with full potential (Hammargren, 2007). Servant leaders are engaged in effective communication and relationship-building processes in the organization to develop interest and passion in the team and provide means to succeed, which act as a guide of the people to aspire for serving their family and friends (Raju, 2019). They aspire to bring out the best in the associated people, and build a sense of community, and make a shift in the metaphors of autocratic or power-oriented leaders (Ambali et al., 2011), and give preference to others above themselves (Newman, 2018). They always look for feedback on their strengths and weaknesses by making employees feel comfortable and assuring that it has based on valid sources (Hannay, 2008). In today's business environment, servant leadership emphasizes the active involvement of employees and organizationally committed attitudes and behaviors to achieve goals (Setyaningrum et al., 2020). For a gender-integrative perspective of leadership, it has required to envision leadership behaviors and attitudes equally, which can be achieved through servant leadership and perceived as a blend of feminine and masculine qualities of leadership and asserts genuinely building up people's spirits and abilities (Reynolds, 2016).

In the active management process, leaders monitor followers' performance and correct them, and they also act as an enhancer of their self-determination and effective processor of their greatest happiness (Bass & Steidlmeier, 1999). The relationship of leaders and members prospers knowledge exchange to leadership educators and gives an understanding of the complex dynamics operating between them (Barbuto & Hayden, 2011). Real teamwork requires cooperative behavior among the members, mutual trust, and a committed perspective toward the goal (Lencioni, 2016). Value-based leaders are motivated, interested, and committed to making a difference through the influence of their Value-based leadership, which includes a philosophy of multifaceted life approach (Kraemer, 2011). They are outstanding because of their concentrated approach and similar characteristics of humility, and this fact has directed the importance of humility in leadership (Chiu et al., 2012). Efficient and influential leaders have humbly approached the problem and discern their character strengths (Kerr, 2017). They are kind and thoughtful and always accessible and noticeable during times of stress and crisis (Gabriel, 2015), and they often emulate the self-sacrificing nature of spiritual or religious leaders, which they have admired (Eicher-Catt, 2005).

There is a significant aspect of wisdom to make people aware and break all barriers because it enlightens people about the equality and respect of women, who adhere to fulfill their duty (Marina & Fonteneau, 2012). Women are more skilled than others at conflict handling in their leadership roles, autocratic style, and evaluation of performance (Eagty et al., 1992). They are no less effective and committed at leading than men and exceed them in the use of democratic or participative style (Hoyt & Simon, 2017). Specific perspectives of history, the biases about gender and leadership have constantly influenced opportunities for women to demonstrate their unique abilities, while the significant leadership style and accomplishments of the legendary social activist Mother Teresa (1910–1997) as an outstanding female leader have best suited in this aspect (Cao & Anderson, 2020). The rising standards and positions of women at the leadership levels in the organization provide leadership educators a new perspective to highlight their value and significance as utmost competent leaders (Reynolds, 2011). An understanding of role expectations by men or women affects the perception of their leadership (Lewis, 2000). Despite changes in the leadership framework, there are still challenging conditions that appear in the organization for women to encounter in attaining roles that yield substantial power and authority (Koenig et al., 2011). The Indian concept of giving or philanthropically assisting is a mix of traditional considerations of family, kinship, castes, clan, community, and religious factors, whereas corporate giving is a strategic act of social responsibility to assist with altruistic motives (Niumai, 2011).

Humility is a significant virtue related to the servant, authentic and spiritual leadership for the humane orientation by the leader (Huizinga, 2016). It is the core competency of leadership and business, which acts as a behavioral supplement for leaders (Owens & Hekman, 2012). It is the core aspect of servant leadership and is unique due to its focus on leaders' transparency about their developmental processes (Fei & Wu, 2018), which has reflected through actions rather than emotions (Prince, 2016). It is a relationship-oriented quality that enhances the social interactions among the employees (Ali et al., 2020), and its practice reflects the servant leader's behavior and functioning and acts as a potential motivational factor in servant leadership (Morris et al., 2005). Humble means holistically oriented toward sacred acts rather than self-oriented activities (Standish, 2007), and humble leadership is an intrinsically relational, efficient, and requisite manner of a leader in a group (Schein & Schein, 2018). Humble leaders reflect respect and consider every perspective of employees toward serving and improving the organization for outstanding outcomes and enhance their personalities to make them more humane (Cable, 2018).

Śrīmad Bhagavad Gītā signifies the Indian context of leadership with effective lessons of selfless behavior and also develops mindfulness and strengthens the character of a leader, which paves the way to humanity (Muniapan, 2010). It encapsulates the philosophy of *Vedas* (Nandagopal & Sankar, 2011), and has universally accepted by scholars as a book containing all the principles and philosophies (Khan, 1992). This scripture teaches the mechanism of achieving bliss and harmony through doing good to humanity and also idealizes the format of the servant leadership approach to develop equanimity and harmony among people of all categories. It describes the strength of human virtues of compassion, modesty, self-discipline through selfless service to attain complacence and transcendence in life (Dhiman, 2018). Good works always lead to spiritual salvation and are considered and expected to be performed by people of all religious categories (Luddy, 2001).

Gopal Krishna Gokhale was the leader of eminent personality (Nanda, 1995), and he was a devoted person and maintained his faith and devotion toward his ideals (Kumari, 2020). As a servant leader, he realized the requirement of education policy and more equalitarian and progressive modernization of social organizations for the country's growth (Bharathi & Sharma, 1998). He identified that the people of India have the strength to elevate the heritage of their culture and civilization to the world, and they abhor revolution and preferred self-leadership as the constitutional method. They should have lived with cooperation and not in isolation for their growth and utilized their own resources and activities (Banerjea, 1925). The era of moderate leaders has phases, many social and political transformations which have a historical perspective as well. These leaders were humble persons and naive enough to practice the politics of protest and petition (Nanda, 1995), and he was a nationalist along with a moderate and worked with the conflux of true zeal, faith, and dutifulness (Kumari, 2018). Along with Mahatma Gandhi, he had pointed his concepts based on ancient heritage (Jayapalan, 2000), and he had tried to glorify the great old Indian civilization to revitalize the dormant spirit of people (Khimta, 2021).

Servant Leadership as an Inherent Approach and Perspective of Women Leaders

Servant leadership successfully combines the feminine perspective as women's leadership experience has been recognized for its potential to transform the androcentric systems of organizations because the concept of courageous women has the aspect of challenging authority as a leader as well as a follower (Reynolds, 2020). Female communal stereotype refers to an interpersonally sensitive orientation because they are assumed to be helpful, kind, and sympathetic and get motivated by affiliation and assistance (Scott & Brown, 2006). Woman's qualities of cooperation, mentoring, and collaboration are vital to leadership and help leave past practices and initialize innovative and progressive change (Eagly et al., 2003). Kindness from the religious perspective is an attribute, a behavioral activity, and a cognitive emotion (Haskins & Thomas, 2018), and thoughtful and kind women are always aware, sensible, and concerned for communal development (Budworth & Mann, 2010).

Women leaders have identified and acknowledged the sense of responsibility to their community holistically and recognized accountability and participation of everyone in leadership (Sylvia et al., 2010). They adopt collaborative and empowering leadership styles needed to emphasize the participative and open communication needed for success (Paustian-Underdahl et al., 2014). They are enlightened, enthusiastic, ambitious, responsible, hardworking, motivated, organized, and holds positive personality traits of empathy, competence, and aptitude (Schneider & Bos, 2014). The leadership of women leaders has based on perceived intelligence (Blaker et al., 2013), and as leaders, they prefer to operate with a cooperative leadership style that includes an implicit collaboration of all employees in the organizational framework (Eagly & Johnson, 1990). They are oriented toward reciprocity, responsibility, and participation of the organizational members, which have also focused on maintaining relationships and empowerment (Wibbeke & McArthur, 2013).

Even in the *Vedic* period, women have high intellectual standards and equality, which depict their prestige and respect for observance in the present era (Rout, 2016). They are advanced by their demeanor and excellent style of leadership because an understanding of the emotional aspects makes them proficient in everything (Eagty et al., 1992). Their behavior in leadership has demonstrated a more empowered objective style and enlightenment (Latu et al., 2013), and the commitment of women leadership to honor duties and obligations generates more reliability of the employees (Cao & Anderson, 2020). Women may be prejudice from stereotypic beliefs, but they can navigate a complex maze of challenges in their leadership and often proved to be more efficient during the crisis (Hoyt & Simon, 2017), and the elimination of prejudices that prevent the access of women to leadership positions in the organization is necessary, which required the adoption of structural measures (Rincón et al., 2017). There is a congruence between the characteristics of women and their leadership tasks because they are inherent occupants of the roles required to succeed as a leader (Eagly & Karau, 2002), and the lifestyle of women at home and within the community empowers them to operate as servant leaders within the parameters of everyday life (Marina & Fonteneau, 2012).

The role of women at high levels in the organization is always challenging and generates a paradox for the leadership educators or male leaders to accept this change (Reynolds, 2011). Despite the socio-economic status, they have made significant contributions to social progress apart from power and profit because they hold the wisdom to understand the gap between need and provision without any expectation (Sundar, 1996). The concept of philanthropy and its practices by entrepreneurs or merchants has a significant place in ancient Indian society, which includes distribution of apportion of surplus wealth for the good of society and considered to be a noble act, and it has an impact on the corporate actions of social responsibility (Aswathappa, 2008). Philanthropy acts are altruistic movements for enhancing human lives and include benevolence and compassion to support the needy (Niumai, 2011). The role of religion and culture has a significant influence in determining the contours of women's philanthropic activities (Luddy, 2001). The virtues of women, like effective relationship-building, communication, and non-hierarchical attitudes, have made them valuable servant leader for organizational positions (Hammargren, 2007). In the related aspects and implications of sacrifice and selflessness of women leaders in servant leadership, and to show the importance and the strength of the feministic attributes, a story has been given below:

Once at a place in north India, there lived a well-known Seth (ancient name of businessman), and he had a variety of businesses. He had two married boys, and both were young, educated, cultured, civilized, and were engaged in his business with his father. Both his daughters-in-law were also well-mannered, cultured, and belong to very decent and wealthy families. Out of all of them, his younger daughter-in-law, Kamala, was very soft-spoken, friendly, courteous, and service-lover, and she was skilled as well as responsible in household chores, and with her virtues, she had impressed everybody at home.

But time does not always go the same, and there are always ups and downs in business work. So, once, there was a terrible recession in that Seth's business, and he had a loss of fifty lakh rupees due to his high stock of goods. A large amount of money had drowned in other traders and brokers, and he also had to sell his land and property to pay everyone's money, but still, about ten lakh rupees was left as a loan amount.

Everything was at stake to pay off the loan, and he was deeply worried because there was no hope of getting money further. His younger daughter-in-law was a very thoughtful and prudent woman and she was observing the critical circumstances of her home. She decided to help her father-in-law to get rid of trouble. She had precious jewels given to her by her parents, and to overcome the paucity of funds, she thought of selling her jewelry and told her husband that if she didn't help now, then the respect of the ancestors would be lost, and father-in-law has to suffer mental troubles, and that wouldn't be right.

She argued that the most valuable jewel for a woman is her husband, and her happiness lies in the satisfaction of him and his parents. Her husband's heart was filled with joy, and he got overwhelmed with her words. After her husband's consent, she gave all the jewels to her mother-in-law and pleaded her to accept this. She had requested them so politely that they could not deny her, even though they had not had any desire to accept the items. Their heart swelled, and they blessed her from the core of their heart.

In this way, the respect and credibility of Seth saved, and he started his business operations. Consequently, with the grace of God, his hardwork, and the collective efforts of his family members, all the losses were recovered in the third executive year of the business. His condition became better than the previous state because the land and property had increased, and all women had more jewels than before. There was more happiness in the house, and true relation of affection, love, and respect had established among all the members.

Thus, the servant leadership approach of the daughter-in-law has manifested her efficiency in overcoming the crisis because her self-sacrificing character, thoughtfulness, and concern for others have presented her as a sincere servant leader and set an example for the prospective leaders. This story provides a great lesson in learning dynamic leadership practice and understanding the concept of patience and sacrifice (Goyal, 2005).

Every woman is idealized as the symbol of Shakti (Goddess Durga) in Indian culture, who is able to analyze the urgency of every critical situation through her intrinsic virtue of wisdom and sensitivity. Women empowerment and leadership doesn't mean to become intense or commanding, but it means to develop courage and self-confidence psychologically among women because their generous and kind attitude is beneficial to deal with adversity in a cordial and peaceful manner that also makes them aware of their hidden aptitude of leadership to execute patiently and selflessly while considering the well-being of all. A servant leader should be self-sacrificing and benevolent and not self-centered or conceited, and he should realize the utmost duty or dharma of assisting others or fulfilling their interests and observe philanthropy because an initiative of altruism through dedication, compassion, and mindfulness by taking into account the prevailing circumstances of the group or organization's members is always beneficial.

This story implies the wisdom, strength, thoughtfulness, modesty, prudence, and spirit of sacrifice of a woman and unveils that feministic traits are not her weakness but her strength, which demonstrate her power of selfless service. It contains a great lesson that reinforces the spirit of sacrifice of the servant leader and gives an introduction to the novel perspective of servant leadership. Thus, sacrifice renders courage and self-confidence in a person and connects him with selflessness, which enhances his personality as a human being. It also breaks the myth of advantage in a materialistic perspective and leads to divinity, which paves the way to human welfare and develops harmony and compatibility in life.

The Essential Trait of Humility for a Leader's Efficacious Functioning

Humility is the most obstinate among all virtues because it empowers a person to behave gladly and humbly helpful (Standish, 2007), and it involves altruistic motivation related to one's values and behavior (Davis et al., 2016). A person with the quality of humility is always interested and understand others, which empowers him to accept the odd circumstances contrary to his expectations (Chiu et al., 2012). The observance of humility is the potential function of the leader to enhance other's performance with the perspective of making them competent and reliable, and regarding their efforts (Morris et al., 2005). His practice of humility in his leadership helps raise the other's performance and realize their significance to the organization because he is always self-aware, confident, and focused on maintaining sustainability (Žiaran et al., 2015). The humility of the leader in genuine terms recognizes everyone equally and reflects his respect for the team members to value their contribution (Kraemer,

2011), and its practice enhances his power of patience and determination, which makes leadership effective (Dickson, 2011).

Servant leaders demonstrate a prudent character which has a positive influence on others (Newman, 2018), and in the representation of their disposition, humility has a significant aspect and an absolute requirement of the present leaders to follow servant leadership (Prince, 2016). They have never looked for any reward and worked with full enthusiasm and standards for organizational growth and development because they are self-reflective and follow the mechanism of servant leadership by effacing their ego, power, and authority (Raju, 2019). Humility refers to a similar situational perspective, while modesty refers to a circumscribed personal situation (Davis et al., 2016), because modesty is an external behavior, while humility is an internal quality (Liu & Liu, 2019), and it is the quality or state of being unassuming (Kerr, 2017). The trait of humility is the combination of dignity, sincerity, equitableness, and generosity-like attributes that make it a significant leadership skill (Žiaran et al., 2015). It includes calmness and mindfulness, which generates a harmonious leadership skill to overcome problematic situations (Huizinga, 2016).

There is a connection between religious orientation and the personality functioning of the leaders, which serves as an influencing factor to assess and discern themselves (Richards, 1991). The self-effacing effort has required enough courage, confidence, potential, and vision to overcome the pride (Raju, 2019). Being humble means identify oneself, openness and honesty, commitment, spirituality, and devotion (Lomenick, 2015). Humble leaders have realized, assessed, and admitted their strengths, weaknesses, and mistakes, and they have learned from others and encourage authentic humility to be followed by people in the organization (OC et al., 2019). They recognize the employees' potential and modify the virtues, which are valuable for organizational teamwork (Lencioni, 2016). Humble leadership is concerned with developing a culture of purposeful sustainable movements (Schein & Schein, 2018), because it facilitates leader-follower psychological freedom and support (Ali et al., 2020). Humble leaders have a strong impact on team effectiveness because they develop a significant positive link between members with balanced processing of information and humility (Rego et al., 2018), and they have the courage to tolerate the flaws of subordinates, diminish stress, and appreciate their efforts to instill self-confidence and motivation for innovation (Liu & Liu, 2019). Humility is above ego and pride and is compatible with esteem and confidence (Žiaran et al., 2015). It is a rare personality trait to adhere, for favorable results because humble leaders instill values among followers, teams, or organizations (Owens & Hekman, 2012). Modest or humble people always appreciate and regard others rather than themselves (Budworth & Mann, 2010). The survival of an organization is in the interaction of human beings and their relationships with each other, which requires humble leadership that enables them to maintain a congenial environment (Schein & Schein, 2018), and supportive leadership behavior of humble leaders develops an inclusive organizational learning climate within the organization through openness, empowerment, and innovation (Fei & Wu, 2018).

Stories connect individuals with their traditions and reinforce a sense of community, and enthrall them. They provide a mechanism of laws, values, religions, and knowledge, which provide a map of success through wisdom for the group (Andersen, 2012). Folk experience and innovation have gathered through tales and expressed through storytelling, where narrative and thematic are retained throughout the composition (Kociatkiewicz & Kostera, 2016). Learning through narratives is not an obligatory discourse, but this approach is beneficial in influencing employees to define a leader's moral intentions and role of duties in leadership. It identifies classical qualities of leadership and virtue, which are different from commands, and includes a relatively open influential process (Auvinen et al., 2013). The necessity of humility for servant leaders in servant leadership approach to enhance performance and maintain character strength has been recognized here through a story:

In a village, a man had worked as a peon in the village office. He was a noble, kind, enthusiastic, and modest person and used to serve water to passers-by, at the village bus stand, in his free time after his job. One day in the scorching Sun, a bus full of passengers came into the village and stopped under the cool shade of the Neem tree. After seeing that the bus has arrived, he stood with clear shining cups and cold water for the passengers. After seeing that the bus had arrived, he stood with clear shining cups and cold water, and as soon as the bus stopped, all passengers distraught with thirst and heat started demanding water. He was already familiar with this situation and giving water with quickness and readiness. He was running so intensely that no one should be left without drinking cold water on the bus.

As per the usual custom, after drinking water, some travelers started giving some coins to him, but he politely refused to take anything, and after seeing his modesty, everyone got stunned and impressed because, in today's time of inflation, there is no dearth of people hoping to get a lot in return by doing a little work. Thus, the behavior of this person who refused to take the labor in such a situation deserved a reward, and everyone started advising him to take it. But he argued that there he has only three members in the family, and from his salary, all three of them get sustenance, so why should he be tempted to get more now?

In the meantime, the slackness of the bus had also gone away. And that gentleman was standing with folded hands as if he was giving farewell to the passengers. He was very hardworking, and surely present when the bus came in the afternoon, and serving water for the last few years without any salary and only for self-satisfaction. He was a rural, cultured man, servitor, confident person who served altruistically, and a true servant leader of humanity (Solanki, 2016).

A leader's reputation is analyzed and associated with his particular profession, status, and authority, which shows the influence of his position on his personality. While the dedication and performance of an ordinary person to his duty indicate his personality as a leader, but often his work or service doesn't get any recognition due to his less approachability and popularity in the common world, rather leadership is expected and exemplified from a great person as a leader, and his personality comes to the fore in the society or organization. Servant leadership is idealized from the characteristics of an individual, who is humble, self-respecting, self-effacing, generous, and self-confident and is always helpful, and under this framework of traits, the reference or perspective of this leadership style has been observed in various instances of common life, where he performs the role of a servant leader by his conscientiousness and modest behavior. He has lived a very independent, courageous, honorable and blissful, and satisfying life and makes the service of humanity and its well-being the real goal of his life. The sincerity of his character is not recognized by his status, but his pure emotions, simplicity, and integrity generate respect for him.

It is an exemplary and relevant context of servant leadership and summarized in this story and asserts that an individual who has a pure heart and is full of faith, follows his dharma, and adheres to his duty with devotedness, signifies to be a servant leader. A peon is a humble person and the main character of this story, who gets self-satisfaction in serving others by giving water only, treats everybody with humility, and does not want anything in return but experiences contentment and pleasure in their service. His qualities of modesty, self-efficacy, and devotedness have reflected his servant leadership approach because he leads with his instincts of ethics and principles and considers serving humans with a sense of spirituality as honoring divinity. This narrative has a great lesson for a modern leader, which exhibits the significance of modesty and humbleness. He should be well-mannered, thoughtful, and practice humility in his behavior to enrich his personality, which develops mindfulness toward the well-being of his employees and followers, and he should regard the act of service as a task of endurance, courage, and reverence of humanity.

THE IMPLICATION OF ŚRĪMAD BHAGAVAD GĪTĀ IN SERVANT LEADERSHIP AND ITS SPIRITUAL ORIENTATION

Spirituality unfolds a more comprehensive aspect of leadership by integrating the character, behavior, and traits of the followers, and its practice represents the care and concern by all means for the individuals (Reave, 2005). From the perspective of spiritual integrity, the servant leader has considered all creatures, from the ant to the universe, related to God, and if everybody helps each other selflessly, then they have served the almighty indeed. With an emotional outlook, he strives to provide comfort to all beings indulged in their work, including maintaining their interests and well-being through integrity and reliability (Goyandka, 2017). He is always attentive and careful, and does not do any work that may cause some loss or grief to the benefactor in the end, and does not allow his subordinate, employee, or laborer to become lazy, dull, foolish, doodle, or scandalous, and to make them virtuous, committed, dutiful, intelligent, and obedient, he toils with his perfect, loving, and ideal behavior. With a giving away gratitude, he never shows off and holds an impression to encourage others to serve, and he neither sees the power of service in himself nor does he know his ownership over any means worthy of service. Accordingly, adherence to the moral values of humanity in organizations can be done through the concept of working selflessly.

Śrīmad Bhagavad Gītā is the most significant scripture and has the essence of all spiritual philosophies, which presents the strategy of self-realization through selfless actions and the art of forming a link with the divine while performing everyday life chores (Dhiman, 2018). In this scripture, Lord Shree Krishna has manifested the unity inherent in the diversity of Indian philosophy and the approach to attain supreme bliss through benevolence and selfless service to humanity (Nandagopal & Sankar, 2011). It confers being continuously active even after the performer has achieved the highest bliss by Jnana yoga (knowledge or bhakti (devotedness)), and this perspective makes the world active and alive through morality (Khan, 1992). This *Vedic* text has given importance to the self-leadership approach by a leader's ability including, his personality traits like self-esteem, control, and self-efficacy along with psychological attributes such as values, motivation, and attitudes, and it also signifies the obligation of duty for developing harmony in the work environment (Muniapan, 2010).

This book reveals the principles of a leader, and his kind of service and personality as a servant has been stated in its verse 4 of chapter 12.

> sanniyamyendriya-grāmaṁ sarvatra sama-buddhayaḥ
> te prāpnuvanti mām eva sarva-bhūta-hite ratāḥ [12:4]

Meaning—Mastering their senses, acting at all times with equanimity, rejoicing in the welfare of all beings, they too will reach me at last (Mitchell, 2010). It refers to an individual who is rationally aware and concerned, dedicatedly help others, and has infinite faith and reverence in God, can attain divinity through serving selflessly.

This *Shloka* manifests the attitude and prospect of a servant leader because, as a devotee, he does consider the presence of the almighty in every person and maintains that no one is separated from his grace. So in the task of his serving, he does not expect or ask for anything, and he revels in the well-being of all, and nothing destabilizes his passion, mind, or intellect (Marballi, 2015). This verse also demonstrates the concept of *Sama Buddhi* (evenness and equality for everyone) in every sense, and every means, in every being. He has a sincere perspective of the good of humanity, and his ultimate goal is to keep striving for its improvement, and he molds his life accordingly. It also highlights the characteristics, nature, qualities, and actions of the servant leader and proposes his aspect in servant leadership that he conducts his activities by controlling his senses and effectively with the help of his spiritual power, which makes his deeds divine, and inspirational for others.

The dharma or obligation of Humans has been elaborately explained in Indian scriptures like *Vedas, Upanishads, Puranas,* and *Smritis*. The main relevant and required characteristics have been recognized as ten principles by scholars, which are common and beneficial to every individual, irrespective of his caste, religion, and belief system, and their implication and effectiveness for the servant leader is given below:

1. The leader of humanity should have patience, satisfaction, and tolerance, and he should not be deterred from objections. Being a wise person, he does not give up in the face of difficulty and unfavorable conditions and always does welfare for others because endurance is the foundation of humanity.
2. He provides the opportunity to his opponent and forgives his actions because he has employed all his efforts and strength for success to come forward with inspiration on the path of progress with the truth.
3. Suppression for a leader means the grace of mind, restraining or keeping the mind in constant auspicious thoughts and spiritual behavior.
4. *Asteya* means not stealing while various kinds of cheatings, bribing, black marketing, applying tricks to exploit others, looting, taking the cover of religion and escaping from the law, and committing small or big thefts implies the degradation of humanity. So, the greed to get more than what a human required, enjoyment, and arbitrary expenditure should be prohibited.
5. The leader should have a pure heart and be free from pompousness, pretense, and fond gratitude. He should get rid of anger, greed, fascination, jealousy, pride, rage, malice, hatred, treachery, and arrogance through Intrinsic purification, and this process requires soul inspection, deliberation, introspection, etiquette which are extremely necessary.
6. Humans have ears, skin, eyes, tongue, and nose as five Knowledge senses, and the power to obtain, motion, eloquence, renunciation, and bliss and enjoyment are called senses of karma or deeds, and with their restraint, a servant leader deserves to be called a true human being.
7. There should be the highest development of moral intelligence in human beings because humanity can be saved only through adherence to principles and ethics.
8. Intelligent and wise leaders pave the way for success and progress to others, while ignorant, ill-considered, or superstitious people trapped in stereotypes cannot be entitled to be called civilized people. So, self-knowledge is superior among all disciplines, which generates the light of wisdom in the heart.

9. A person's true religion is his sincerity and truth, and remaining identical in behavior and speech, staying away from the show-off, using words of clear intentions and meaning, and not hurting and troubling others signifies the humanitarian approach of the leader.
10. To be free from anger, calmness of the mind, tolerance, goodwill, affection, empathy, kindness, compassion, humility represents the servant leader's character in his deeds.
11. A sincere servant leader should be calm, soft, tolerant, and humble, and the growth of these virtues develops true humanity. He is the spirit of the society and holds the maturity of dharma, karma, opulence, glory, affluence, prosperity, and quietness, and has cosmic and divine qualities to create heaven on earth (Mahendra, 2014).

A true servant leader serves without being selfless and without pride and does not assume any right over others whom he serves. Neither does he do any favor, nor does he show any need to thank or receive gratitude from them. Being humble and spiritual, he believes that God is graceful and has made me an instrument in the happiness of others, and gratefully considers the act of serving humanity to be divine inspiration and power. He does service through the perspective of spiritual psychology and never holds that he has served because true service is for his own pleasure. He does not differentiate and consider it his duty/dharma to serve the living beings because he has a pure vision and understands the meaning and significance of service (Poddar, 2014).

Conscientiousness, Devoutness, and Sensibility in the Context of Serviceability

Servant leadership specifies a motivation for selfless serving and emphasizes the effect of followers' growth that has correlated with organizational functioning for a significant outcome (Dierendonck, 2011), and envisions the future reality, and is an important antecedent of trust and confidence psychologically through its diverse structures (Kumar, 2018). A selfless servant leader has the strength of humility, courage, insight, and expertise to inspire followers in realizing their responsibility, control, autonomy, and formulate their ideas (Cable, 2018). He always analyzes the prospective outcome and influence of his efforts on the group members, which reflect his more comprehensive approach as a thoughtful person to examine the impact of every decision on the eminence of the organization. Swindoll (1998) observes that a servant leader has the ability to understand the points of criticism and listen with discernment and analyze its source and the motive. He is accountable to the people, whom he leads with allegiance, and performs effectively with his quality of loyalty (Prosser, 2007), and acts freely with a motivation to provide comfort or assist others, and does not wish to get recognized.

Social leaders of any nation reflect the image or status of their communities and are responsible for the growth or decline of the people. They have a significant role in remarkably identifying, addressing, and representing the framework of servant leadership because they hold a lovable emotion for the people, including a helpful impression on them. There have been many such legendary leaders who dedicated their lives to the service of humanity and exemplified themselves as devoted servants because they have taken a vow to improve the condition of others and being helpful always. Service is not done by selfishness but by the spirit of sacrifice, and with this mechanism, the anecdote of Gopal Krishna Gokhale as a servant leader is presented here in the context of servant leadership.

Gopal Krishna Gokhale (1866–1915) was a politician, economist, philosopher, writer, and revolutionary. He was born in the epoch of Indian history, which made him and which he lived to develop (Deogirika, 1969). He was an indomitable optimist and a great man of society (Bharathi & Sharma, 1998), and has the strength and character of selfless devotion as a virtue (Deogirikar, 1964). He held the contemporary point of view to the life of a civilized person, along with maintaining a nationalist ideology of traditional Indian values and culture (Kumari, 2020). He had always examined his conduct in the light of morals, principles, and ideals, and castigated herself for any wrong deeds, and considered his right works as high opportunities of service (Sastri, 1937). He was sensible toward public responsibility and encouraged the creed of *Swadeshi* as a policy of voluntary protectionism (Bharathi & Sharma, 1998). He believed that individuals should have to make their contribution to humanity, which they get in return with interest in the form of a rich treasure of wisdom and insight (Banerjea, 1925). His mentor/Guru Mahadev Govind Ranade (1842–1901) was the most influential personality and a scholar, social reformer, judge, and author (Khan, 1992) who had taught him sincerity, dedication, and tolerance, and he attributed the success of his work to him, which signified his humility (Nair, 1989). He was great in the very sense of the word and had unrivaled leadership qualities developing youth insights for public welfare and encouraging them to become servant leaders (Sastri, 1937).

Zeal of Serving—He had established 'Servants of India' (an organization for nation-building) in 1905, which included young, enthusiastic, and selfless workers who had taken a vow to lead a simple life of dedication for social work and become pioneers in the service to fulfil the need and grievances of people (Nair, 1989). It trained them as kindred spirits to help people (Agrawal, 2008). He initiated the first short-term training in the organization for its members and assigned the duty of performing welfare activities and serving others. He adhered to Jesuit principles of sacrifice for the common good (Bharathi & Sharma, 1998), and the protection of the rights of all communities and creeds (Khimta, 2021).

Sense of Sacrifice and Rationality—He was certainly a prudent servant leader and vitally realized the sacrifice that his family had made for his education, and remained grateful through life, and had taken care of them as well

(Sastri, 1937), and learned the value of self-sacrifice from the strength of his brother's compassion and respect for him (Agrawal, 2008). He was brilliant in his studies and had an exceptional memory and retention ability, and as a teacher, he trained his pupils to become rich in self-respect, devotedness, and knowledge (Bharathi & Sharma, 1998), and he also had the knowledge of Sanskrit and had memorized *Vikramorvasiyam* (a Sanskrit play written by ancient Indian poet Kālidāsa of fifth century CE) (Sastri, 1937). He was an intellectual mathematician and co-authored a book on arithmetic with his fellow N. J. Bapat for primary students (Gupta & Gupta, 2006). Due to his comprehensiveness of judgment and mental clarity, he never fell into the academic fallacy of contempt (Deogirikar, 1964). He believed in self-reliance, *Swadeshi*, and the advancement of education and used religious concepts and historical examples to educate people (Jayapalan, 2000). As an enthusiastic reformer and writer, he conducted a daily newspaper, *Jnanaprakash* (Nair, 1989), and also worked as an editor of the English side of an Anglo Marathi weekly journal called *Sudharak*. He was an eminent speaker, and his speeches had an influencing power and credibility (Bharathi & Sharma, 1998).

Commitment for Well-being and Responsibility—Being a servant leader and reformer, he struggled to purify the public administration service and introduced racial equality, which was indigenously necessary from the political and cultural perspectives (Bharathi & Sharma, 1998). He had played a significant role in representing the Indian people to the British administration during the independence movement because he had the remarkable knack of saying the hardest thing in the gentlest language and obeyed the severest of discipline in his life (Brown, 1970). He had represented himself as an outstanding spokesman in England for India's cause (Nair, 1989), and as a political leader, he had drafted his own memorandum of his evidence of intellectuality, courage, clarity, and eloquence, which was also its skill presentation and lucid exposition. It was his oral examination that had given his performance the quality of a triumph (Nanda, 2015). He was a true servant and Karmayogi and never deflected from his ideals by the vicissitudes of a political career (Deogirika, 1969), and his political ideology had revolved around the prevailing socio-political issues rather than the fundamental political nation of state or sovereignty (Kumari, 2020). Cast in a heroic mold, he was a humble person, and his life's significant deeds and intellectual efforts have reflected him as an astute and assiduous politician (Tikekar, 2015). He preferred the virtue of gradualism to expand the sphere of service and felt it significant from an autocratic to a democratic lifestyle (Bharathi & Sharma, 1998), and believed in self-leadership. He received equal respect from his fellows and counterparts because of his high abilities, massive and well-cultivated intellect, and keen power of analysis and criticism (Khan, 1992). His opponent leaders even admired and respected him and recognized him as a good orator, debater, statesman, and friend rather than a member of the council (Deogirikar, 1964).

Respect for Dharma and Humanity—He was the political guru of Mahatma Gandhi (1869–1948), who had learned the amicable, systematic, and constitutional method of achieving *Swarāj* from him (Nair, 1989), and admired him as a man of religion (dharma), truth, and humanity (Khimta, 2021), and called him a saint with a heroic heart (Aiyer, 1973). Gandhiji had shown his reverence to him in the following words: He was chaste in thought, word, and deed, a master of lucid exposition, a speaker who inspired without inflaming, never afraid of strife but loved amity, a worker who obeyed as well as commanded. His love and reverence for country people were genuine, and for serving them, he completely eschewed all happiness and self-interest (Nair, 1989). Despite various conflicts, he had determined to the patriotism because his religion and ideal were pure, and he empowered people for their splendor of humanity (Sastri, 1937). He educated the people in nationalism and for national unity through presenting the concept of a progressive society, modern state, and civil liberty and addressed them for their cooperation to welfare (Jayapalan, 2000).

Being the leader of the society, he used to observe his every work and activity, and his selfless approach, sacrifice, commitment, devoutness, and self-effacement had presented his profile of a capable, effective, and altruistic personality. His humility was the strength of his character, and his wisdom of reformation was his treasure, and he had been blissful to get opportunities to serve human beings for their growth and prosperity. He had dedicated his life to the service of others and was always ready to help the needy because he realized the people's emotional perspective of agony or distress. Therefore, his unique abilities of honesty and conscientiousness have determined him as a successful servant leader under the modern framework of servant leadership, which also have the significant aspect and relevance in learning classical approaches and tactics. His life's work of service exhibits him as a noble person and sets the example of an enthusiastic leader.

The deeds of a person of character become principles and ideals for others, and this kind of harmony in his conduct is called character strength. Strength of character, conscience, and truth develops firm belief in an individual, and he behaves accordingly to get the desired results. No fear and temptation can deter a prudent man from his duty because sustaining the purity of the character through enduring hardships increases its strength, and tenacity resides in the strength of character, which increases endurance, and also sacrifice develops through conscience and faith rises through commitment. So a servant leader should keep on protecting and fulfilling the rights and resolutions of others through every tendency and analyzed his efficiency with his wisdom (Poddar, 2015).

Where the thing is needed, it is to be given joyfully without any desire to retaliate and referred to as the sincere service of humanity because a true servant works with a noble and kind perspective. He gets such a wonderful satisfaction and great pleasure in doing service and does not want anything other than it, and even his desire is far away, he does not accept any gain even after getting it unwillingly. He considers adversity as an opportunity of service and a challenge and tackles it with patience, courage, dedication, and sincerity. Accordingly, it requires a holistic perspective, a courageous approach, and the mindfulness of a leader.

Conclusion

Service is not the only service, but it is the spirit and a way to express oneself with affinity, which addressees a high degree of spiritual practice and austerity. Its context is imperative and relevant in servant leadership because it enriches a leader's mindfulness through the development of an emotional perspective and refines his leadership potential. It enables a leader to restrain aspirations and desires by means of selflessness and spirituality, which is a mechanism to obtain sacredness with cooperation for the well-being of humanity. This chapter has integrated all associated dimensions of servant leadership and highlights the primacy of the virtues like modesty, kindness, devoutness, and sacrifice and their impression on the act of service. A leader's work has primarily included a blend of power and responsibility and exemplary for his followers, which can be transformed into an ideal of the highest order through practicing these qualities and working with a spirit of service. The reflection of servant leadership has also been embodied in tales, which is exemplary and effective in analyzing the obligation of the leader, and the ancient texts like Śrīmad Bhagavad Gītā has the ideological and visionary lessons as the guiding principles of the leader. Consequently, the wisdom-related aspects of service play an influential role in creating an ideal personality of the leader through superiority of character strength, guides his humanitarian conceptions in servant leadership.

Reflection Questions
1. How does the practice of humility, modesty, or self-efficacy magnify the personality and potential of a leader?
2. Why women's tendency of kindness and sacrifice is significant, and what is the role of these qualities in servant leadership?
3. What is selflessness, and how it leads to making the act of service excellent?
4. How the Indian scripture Śrīmad Bhagavad Gītā is valuable in learning leadership behavior through the spiritual perspective of dharma.
5. Why the servant leadership has an integral aspect of serving humanity?

Relevant Lessons
1. The modesty of the servant leader depicts his high ideals and values and his respect for others.
2. During serving others, the spirit of sacrifice and kind behavior shows the strength of the character and the affinity of a leader.

3. Selflessness has a significant role in changing the perspective of people from materialistic to sacredness and attaining happiness.
4. Adherence to the lessons of Śrīmad Bhagavad Gītā purifies the deeds and character of a servant leader through spirituality and provides an introduction to the true meaning of service.
5. The development of devoutness in work and sincere serving with altruism maintain the leader's respect for humanity and exhibit his competency and insight.

References

Agrawal, L. M. (2008). *Freedom fighters of India*. Isha Books.
Aiyer, S. (1973). *Gopal Krishna Gokhale, 107 birthday address*. Bombay University.
Ali, M., Zhang, L., Shah, S. J., Khan, S., & Shah, A. M. (2020). Impact of humble leadership on project success: The mediating role of psychological empowerment and innovative work behavior. *Leadership and Organization Development Journal, 41*(3), 349–367.
Ambali, A. R., Suleiman, G. E., Bakar, A. N., Hashim, R., & Tariq, Z. (2011). Servant leadership's values and staff's commitment: Policy implementation focus. *American Journal of Scientific Research, 13*, 18–40.
Andersen, E. (2012). *Leading so people will follow*. Wiley.
Aswathappa, K. (2008). *International Business* (3rd ed.). McGraw-Hill Education (India) Pvt Limited.
Auvinen, T. P., Lämsä, A.-M., Sintonen, T., & Takala, T. (2013). Leadership manipulation and ethics in storytelling. *Journal of Business Ethics, 116*, 415–431. https://doi.org/10.1007/S10551-012-1454-8
Banerjea, S. S. (1925). *A nation in making: Being the reminiscences of fifty years of public life*. Oxford University Press.
Barbuto, J. E., & Gifford, G. T. (2010). Examining gender differences of servant leadership: An analysis of the agentic and communal properties of the servant leadership questionnaire. *Journal of Leadership Education, 9*(2), 4–22.
Barbuto, J. E., & Hayden, R. W. (2011). Testing relationships between servant leadership dimensions and Leader Member Exchange (LMX). *Journal of Leadership Education, 10*(2), 22–37.
Bass, B. M., & Steidlmeier, P. (1999). Ethics, character, and authentic transformational leadership behavior. *Leadership Quarterly, 10*(2), 181–217. https://doi.org/10.1016/S1048-9843(99)00016-8
Bharathi, K. S., & Sharma, J. N. (1998). *Encyclopaedia of eminent thinkers: The political thought of Gopal Krishna Gokhale* (Vol. 27). Concept Publishing Company.
Blaker, N. M., Rompa, I., Dessing, I. H., Vriend, A. F., Herschberg, C., & Vugt, M. (2013). The height leadership advantage in men and women: Testing evolutionary psychology predictions about the perceptions of tall leaders. *Group Processes and Intergroup Relations, 16*(1), 17–27. https://doi.org/10.1177/1368430212437211
Brown, D. M. (1970). *The nationalist movement: Indian political thought from Ranade to Bhave*. University of California Press.

Budworth, M.-H., & Mann, S. L. (2010). Becoming a leader: The challenge of modesty for women. *Journal of Management Development, 29*, 177–186.

Cable, D. (2018). How humble leadership really works. *Harvard Business Review*, 1–6.

Cao, Z., & Anderson, V. (2020). Management and economic strengths of feminine leadership-five insights frame. *Advances in Economics, Business and Management Research, 159*, 612–614.

Chiu, T.-C. S., Huang, H. S., & Hung, Y. (2012). The influence of humility on leadership: A Chinese and western review. *International Conference on Economics, Business and Marketing Management, IPEDR, 29*, 129–133.

Davis, D. E., McElroy, S. E., Rice, K. G., Choe, E., Westbrook, C., Hook, J. N., Tongeren, D. R. V., DeBlaere, C., Hill, P., Placares, V., & Worthington, E. L. (2016). Is modesty a subdomain of humility? *The Journal of Positive Psychology, 11*(4), 439–446. https://doi.org/10.1080/17439760.2015.1117130

Deogirika, T. R. (1969). *Gopal Krishna Gokhale*. Publications Division, Ministry of Information and Broadcasting, Government of India.

Deogirikar, T. R. (1964). *Builders of modern India: Gopal Krishna Gokhale*. Publications Division, Ministry of Information and Broadcasting, Government of India.

Dhiman, S. (2018). *Bhagavad Gītā and leadership: A catalyst for organizational transformation*. Springer International Publishing.

Dickson, J. (2011). *Humilitas: A lost key to life, love, and leadership*. Zondervan.

Dierendonck, D. (2011). Servant leadership: A review and synthesis. *Journal of Management, 37*(4), 1228–1261. https://doi.org/10.1177/0149206310380462

Eagly, A. H., & Johnson, B. T. (1990). Gender and leadership style: A meta-analysis. *Psychological Bulletin, 108*(2), 233–256.

Eagly, A. H., & Karau, S. J. (2002). Role Congruity theory of prejudice toward female leaders. *Psychological Review, 109*(3), 573–598. https://doi.org/10.1037//0033-295X.109.3.573

Eagly, A. H., & Carli, L. L. (2003). The female leadership advantage: An evaluation of the evidence. *The Leadership Quarterly, 14*, 807–834. https://doi.org/10.1016/j.leaqua.2003.09.004

Eagty, A. H., Makhijani, M. G., & Klonsky, B. G. (1992). Gender and the evaluation of leaders: A meta-analysis. *Psychological Bulletin, 111*(1), 3–22.

Eicher-Catt, D. (2005). The myth of servant-leadership: A feminist perspective. *Women and Language, 28*(1), 17–25.

Eva, N., Robinb, M., Sendjayac, S., Dierendonckd, D. V., & Liden, R. C. (2019). Servant leadership: A systematic review and call for future research. *The Leadership Quarterly, 30*, 111–132.

Fei, Z., & Wu, Y. J. (2018). How humble leadership fosters employee innovation behavior—A two-way perspective on the leader-employee interaction. *Leadership and Organization Development Journal, 39*(3), 375–387. https://doi.org/10.1108/LODJ-07-2017-0181

Gabriel, Y. (2015). The caring leader—What followers expect of their leaders and why? *Leadership, 11*(3), 316–334. https://doi.org/10.1177/1742715014532482

Goyal, G. (2005). *Aadarsh Manav Hridaya*. Gita Press.

Goyandka, J. (2017). *Prem Ke Vash Me Bhagwan*. Gita Press.

Gupta, K. R., & Gupta, A. (2006). Gopal Krishna Gokhale. In K. R. Gupta & A. Gupta (Eds.), *Concise encyclopaedia of India* (pp. 1023–1025). Atlantic Publishers & Distributors.

Hammargren, L. R. (2007). Comment, servant leadership and women in the law: A new nexus of women, leadership and the legal profession. *University of St. Thomas Law Journal, 4*(3), 624–642.

Hannay, M. (2008). The cross-cultural leader: The application of servant leadership theory in the international context. *Journal of International Business and Cultural Studies, 1,* 1–12.

Haskins, G., & Thomas, M. (2018). Kindness and its many manifestations. In G. Haskins, L. Johri, & M. Thomas (Eds.), *Kindness in Leadership* (pp. 8–25). Routledge.

Hoyt, C. L., & Simon, S. (2017). Social psychological approaches to women and leadership theory. In S. R. Madsen (Ed.), *Handbook of research on gender and leadership* (pp. 85–99). Edward Elgar Publishing.

Huizinga, R. B. (2016). An understanding of humility-based leadership impacting organizational climate. *Emerging Leadership Journeys, 9*(1), 34–44.

Jayapalan, N. (2000). *Indian political thinkers: Modern Indian political thought.* Atlantic Publishers and Distributors.

Kerr, A. (2017). *The humility imperative: Why the humble leader wins in an age of ego.* Lulu Publishing Services.

Khan, M. S. (1992). *Tilak and Gokhale: A comparative study of their socio-politico-economic programmes of reconstruction.* Ashish Publishing House.

Khimta, A. C. (2021). *Gopal Krishna Gokhale. Revisiting modern Indian thought: Themes and perspectives.* Taylor & Francis.

Kociatkiewicz, J., & Kostera, M. (2016). Grand Plots of management bestsellers: Learning from narrative and thematic coherence. *Management Learning, 47*(3), 324–342. https://doi.org/10.1177/1350507615592114

Koenig, A. M., Eagly, A. H., Mitchell, A. A., & Ristikari, T. (2011). Are leader stereotypes masculine? A meta-analysis of three research paradigms. *Psychological Bulletin, 137*(4), 616–642.

Kraemer, H. M. (2011). *From values to action: The four principles of values-based leadership.* Wiley.

Krog, C. L., & Govender, K. (2015). The relationship between servant leadership and employee empowerment, commitment, trust and innovative behavior: A project management perspective. *SA Journal of Human Resource Management, 13*(1), 1–12. https://doi.org/10.4102/sajhrm.v13i1.712

Kumari, M. (2018). *The life and times of Gopal Kirshna Gokhale.* Prabhat Prakashan.

Kumari, M. (2020). *Biography of Gopal Krishna Gokhale.* Prabhat Prakashan.

Latu, I. M., Mast, M. S., Lammers, J., & Bombari, D. (2013). Successful female leaders empower women's behavior in leadership tasks. *Journal of Experimental Social Psychology, 49,* 444–448.

Lemoine, G. J., & Blum, T. C. (2019). Servant leadership, leader gender, and team gender role: Testing a female advantage in a cascading model of performance. *Personnel Psychology, 74,* 3–28. https://doi.org/10.1111/peps.12379

Lencioni, P. (2016). *The ideal team player: How to recognize and cultivate the three essential virtues.* Wiley.

Lewis, K. M. (2000). When leaders display emotion: How followers respond to negative emotional expression of male and female leaders. *Journal of Organizational Behavior, 21,* 221–234.

Liu, Z., & Liu, W. (2019). Humble leadership and employee creativity: The mediating role of knowledge hiding. *Journal of Business Management and Economic Research (JOBMER)*, 3(5), 29–45.

Lomenick, B. (2015). *H3 leadership: Be humble. Stay hungry. Always hustle.* Harper Collins Leadership.

Luddy, M. (2001). Women and philanthropy in nineteenth-century Ireland. In K. D. McCarthy (Ed.), *Women, philanthropy, and civil society* (pp. 9–28). Indiana University Press.

Mahendra, R. (2014). *Anandmay Jeevan.* Gita Press.

Marballi, G. K. (2015). *Journey through the Bhagavad Gita—A modern commentary ebook.* Lulu.com.

Marina, B. L. H., & Fonteneau, D. Y. (2012). Servant leaders who picked up the broken glass. *The Journal of Pan African Studies*, 5(2), 67–83.

McMahone, M. (2012). Servant leadership as a teachable ethical concept. *American Journal of Business Education*, 5(3), 339–346.

Minnis, S. E., & Callahan, J. L. (2010). Servant leadership in question: A critical review of power within servant leadership. *Educational Human Resource Development Program*, Texas A&M University, June Conference, 1–20.

Mitchell, S. (2010). *The Bhagavad Gita.* Ebury Publishing.

Morris, J. A., Brotheridge, C. M., & Urbanski, J. C. (2005). Bringing humility to leadership: Antecedents and consequences of leader humility. *Human Relations*, 58(10), 1323–1350. https://doi.org/10.1177/0018726705059929

Muniapan, B. (2010). Perplexity, management and business in India. In S. Lowe (Ed.), *Managing in changing times: A guide for the perplexed manager* (pp. 317–346). SAGE Publications.

Nair, B. (1989). *Remembering our leaders* (Vol. 5). Children's Book Trust.

Nanda, B. (1995). *The moderate era in Indian Politics.* Oxford University Press, India.

Nanda, B. R. (2015). *Gokhale: The Indian moderates and the British Raj.* Princeton University Press.

Nandagopal, R., & Sankar A. R. N. (2011). *Indian ethos and values in management.* McGraw-Hill Education (India) Pvt Limited.

Newman, A. (2018). *Building leadership character.* SAGE Publications.

Niumai, A. (2011). Indian Diaspora philanthropy: A sociological perspective. *Man in India*, 91(1), 93–114.

Oc, B., Daniels, M. A., Diefendorff, J. M., Bashshur, M. R., & Greguras, G. J. (2019). Humility breeds authenticity: How authentic leader humility shapes follower vulnerability and felt authenticity. *Organizational Behavior and Human Decision Processes*, 158, 112–125. https://doi.org/10.1016/j.obhdp.2019.04.008

Owens, B. P., & Hekman, D. R. (2012). Modeling how to grow: An inductive examination of humble leader behaviors contingencies, and outcomes. *Academy of Management Journal*, 55(4), 787–818. https://doi.org/10.5465/amj.2010.0441

Paustian-Underdahl, S. C., Walker, L. S., & Woehr, D. J. (2014). Gender and perceptions of leadership effectiveness: A meta-analysis of contextual moderators. *Journal of Applied Psychology*, 99(6), 1129–1145. https://doi.org/10.1037/a0036751

Poddar, H. P. (2014). *Bhavrog ki Rambaan Dawa.* Gita Press.

Poddar, H. P. (2015). *Ek Mahatma Ka Prasad.* Gita Press.

Prince, D. (2016). *Pride versus humility.* Whitaker House.

Prosser, S. (2007). *To be a servant-leader.* Paulist Press.

Raju, A. (2019, December 14). *Be a self-effacing leader*. Retrieved December 14, 2019 from Thehindu: https://www.thehindu.com/education/be-a-self-effacing-leader/article30305415.ece

Reave, L. (2005). Spiritual values and practices related to leadership effectiveness. *The Leadership Quarterly, 16*, 655–687.

Rego, A., Cunha, M. P., & Simpson, A. V. (2018). The perceived impact of humility on team effectiveness: An empirical study. *Journal of Business Ethics, Springer, 148*(1), 205–218.

Reynolds, K. (2011). Servant-leadership as gender-integrative leadership: Paving a path for more gender-integrative organizations through leadership education. *Journal of Leadership Education, 10*(2), 155–171.

Reynolds, K. (2016). Servant-leadership a feminist perspective. *International Journal of Servant Leadership, 10*(1), 35–63.

Reynolds, K. (2020). Do women stand back to move forward? Gender differences on top US business leaders' messages of servant leadership. *The International Journal of Servant-Leadership, 14*(1), 487–523.

Richards, P. S. (1991). Religious devoutness in college students: Relations with emotional support adjustment and psychological separation from parents. *Journal of Counselling Psychology, 38*(2), 189–196.

Rincón, V., González, M., & Barrero, K. (2017). Women and leadership: Gender barriers to senior management position. *Intangible Capital, 13*(2), 319–352.

Rout, N. (2016). Role of women in ancient India. *Odisha Review*, 42–47.

Sastri, V. S. (1937). *Life of Gopal Krishna Gokhale*. Bangalore Printing and Publishing Company.

Schein, E. H., & Schein, P. A. (2018). *Humble leadership: The power of relationships, openness, and trust*. Berrett-Koehler Publishers.

Schneider, M. C., & Bos, A. L. (2014). Measuring stereotypes of female politicians. *Political Psychology, 35*(2), 245–266. https://doi.org/10.1111/pops.12040

Scott, K. A., & Brown, D. J. (2006). Female first, leader second? Gender bias in the encoding of leadership behavior. *Organizational Behavior and Human Decision Processes, 101*, 230–242.

Setyaningrum, R. P. (2017). Relationship between servant leadership in organizational culture, organizational commitment, organizational citizenship behaviour and customer satisfaction. *European Research Studies Journal, XX*, 3A, 554–569.

Setyaningrum, R. P., Setiawan, M., & Surachman, & Irawanto, D. W. (2020). Servant leadership characteristics, organisational commitment, followers' trust, employees' performance outcomes: A literature review. *European Research Studies Journal, XXIII, 4*, 902–911.

Solanki, M. R. (2016). *Hriday Ki Aadarsh Vishalata*. Gita Press.

Standish, N. G. (2007). *Humble leadership: Being radically open to god's guidance and grace*. Rowman & Littlefield Publishers.

Sundar, P. (1996). Women and philanthropy in India. Voluntas: *International Journal of Voluntary and Nonprofit Organizations*, 412–427.

Swindoll, C. R. (1998). *Hand me another brick: Timeless lessons on leadership*. Thomas Nelson.

Sylvia, E., Grund, C., Kimminau, K. S., Ahmed, A., Marr, J. M., & Cooper, T. (2010). Rural women leaders. *Journal of Leadership Studies, 4*(3), 23–31. https://doi.org/10.1002/jls.20174

Tikekar, A. (2015). The legacy of Gopal Krishna Gokhale. *Freedom First, 572*, 1–36.

Wibbeke, E., & McArthur, S. (2013). *Global Business Leadership* (2nd ed.). Routledge.
Żiaran, P., Renata, K., Katarína, M., & Hana, P. (2015). Humility and modesty in leadership—A bibliometric perspective. *Acta Universitatis Agriculturae ET Silviculturae Mendelianae Brunensis, 63*(6), 2221–2228.

CHAPTER 31

Leader Growth and Development: Authenticity Enablers and Stumbling Blocks

Kurt April

INTRODUCTION

The origins of the concept of 'authenticity' can be found in ancient Greek philosophy ('know thyself') (Parke & Wormell, 1956). The English word 'authentic' gets its etymology from the Greek word *authento*, which means to have complete power (Trilling, 2009). Individuals who are masters of their own realm are said to be functioning authentically (Kernis & Goldman, 2006). In their work, Algera and Lips-Wiersma (2012) utilize the psychological definition of authenticity as referring to a person living their life according to the needs of their inner being, rather than submitting to the conventions of society, their early conditioning, or conforming to an authoritarian system. The concept of authenticity has also evolved in modern times through influences from positive psychology literature (Cameron & Dutton, 2003) and leadership literature (April et al., 2000). This has given rise to a positive construct of authenticity, and particularly authentic leadership, characterized by descriptors such as genuine, dependable, honest, trustworthy, real, and true (Dharani et al., 2021; Luthans & Avolio, 2003). Owning one's personal experiences and acting in agreement with one's true self are now considered characteristics of authenticity, and behaving in line with one's actual self involves expressing and acting on one's true feelings (Harter, 2002). Thus, it comprises self-awareness

K. April (✉)
University of Cape Town, Cape Town, South Africa
e-mail: kurt.april@uct.ac.za

and behaving in accordance with one's real self by stating one's honest opinions and values (Luthans & Avolio, 2003) and putting boundaries in place to secure those (Cloud, 2013).

In its most basic form, authenticity can be defined as the extent to which a leader acts as their true self. This can be related subjectively from their own feelings (Beddoes-Jones & Swailes, 2015) or objectively by the assessment of others (Impett et al., 2013). Lenton et al. (2013) considered authenticity to be a state or disposition of being, and stated that practical authenticity was not a stable entity but more of a situational phenomenon in which an individual's mood and emotions can alter the sense of genuineness that they feel and display. Mood is thereby the controlling factor to change the structure of a leader's accessible self—positive moods increase the accessibility of favorable self-relevant information, while negative moods increase the accessibility of unfavorable self-relevant information, known as a mood self-congruence effect. While a leader's core self would therefore be unaltered, their outer perception would become incongruent with their authentic self—thereby setting them up for psychological cognitive dissonance. This incongruence can be described in relation to external forces, influences, and pressures, as work (in various disciplines) and everyday life require interaction and connection with others (Algera & Lips-Wiersma, 2012, p. 119). At work, individuals may find themselves slowly integrating with, or distancing themselves from, the dominant norms, behaviors, and workplace cultures, in relation to their fundamental identities, levels of connectedness, core sense of belonging, and comfortability with personal disclosure and willingness to reveal their true intentions and selves. In fact, when conforming to or assimilating to dominant workplace norms and behaviors that breach a person's authentic self, people experience cognitive dissonance and 'feelings of twoness', akin to Du Bois' double consciousness concept (Foner, 1970)—a salient framework for conceptualizing the existential reality of the marginal person and perceptions of the dominant culture. Employees, in general, require: (a) *significance*, (b) *competence* and *self-confidence*, and (c) *authenticity* and *likability* in their workplaces (April et al., 2023). They fear loss of these, and when these are either under threat or not allowed for, their alienation triggers psychological defensiveness and, sometimes, dysfunctional behavioral responses. The costs of this alienation are negatively associated with psychological well-being, physical well-being, engagement, creativity, affective commitment, job satisfaction, career motivation, work effort, and work-to-family enrichment (Chiaburu et al., 2013; Hartel et al., 2005; Hirschfeld et al., 2000; Tummers & Den Dulk, 2013; Zhang et al., 2016).

In psychology and relating to authenticity, Fromm (2001) refers to free human existence without conforming to conventions of society or a political system. In work on radical authentic leadership, though, emphasis is given to the importance of individual freedom and personal responsibility in being authentic, while at the same time highlights the fact that authenticity requires interaction and connection with others (Algera & Lips-Wiersma, 2012). Effective leadership, it is argued, is navigating the tension along that continuum (April et al., 2013). In law, Aristotle believed that ethics concerned with one's pursuit of a greater good through self-realization is associated with virtue to create a full life (Hutchinson, 1995). In arts, Kivy (1995) signified the self-expression of an artist without submitting to historical tradition or current trends. The high importance of authenticity is underscored in almost all cases, even stated to be an indicator of the extent to which a person is fully functioning or fulfilling their potential (van den Bosch & Taris, 2014). Goffee and Jones (2005) noticed that authenticity is not to be declared on one's own, but it is all about others' perceptions of the individual. According to April et al. (2023), visibility at work, being seen fully, authentically, and accurately by others, are important for individual self-determination and authenticity, and for organizational outcomes such as commitment, engagement, motivation, and sense of belonging. Acts of discrimination, stereotyping, and relentless suspicion leave marginalized individuals and groups feeling like they are invisible and when they are 'seen' they feel monitored, heightening their fears, anxieties, and behavioral adjustments based on the different aspects that separate them from the dominant group (p. 146). Interestingly, some scholars argue that people cannot be "entirely authentic or inauthentic [but that] they can more accurately be described as achieving levels of authenticity" (Avolio & Gardner, 2005, p. 320). On the other hand, Harter (2002) is of the opinion that "authenticity implies that one acts in accord with the true self, expressing oneself in ways that are consistent with inner thoughts and feelings" (p. 382). Such self-awareness, of one's beliefs, values, motivations, personal power, action and its accompanying consequences, is linked to one's happiness, or 'eudemonia', which occurs from successfully completing activities that are in alignment with one's true calling/*voca*/purpose (Kernis & Goldman, 2006).

Ultimately, authenticity is the enactment of important beliefs, values, principles, and identities (Conger et al., 2018) or "the unobstructed operation of one's true—or core—self in one's daily enterprise" (Kernis & Goldman, 2006, p. 294). Authenticity narratives, particularly narratives used in the workplace, are used by leaders to show others who they really are (O'Neil et al., 2022). Rees et al. (2021) build on existing work in authenticity, self and identity, and communications, to propose that individuals simultaneously have an 'unfiltered self' (based on a lack of restraints), a 'normative self' (based on sensible categories), and an 'aspirational self' (based on ideals) that serve to meet competing intrapersonal needs for self-verification, self-regulation, and self-enhancement, respectively. Further, the authors posit that: individuals rely on different logics to communicate with others about these referent selves in order to enact authenticity. In turn, behavioral (mis)alignment with one's intended message about the self, shapes felt (in)authenticity, which informs self-conscious emotions (pride, shame, guilt) reflecting individuals' self-evaluations that, over time, influence individuals' identification with the organization (p. 1). Overall, their theoretical framework offers a more dynamic, alternative conceptualization of authenticity as opposed to the simple (and more general) understanding that it is the straightforward alignment between an individual's inner self and outward behaviors—specifically, their research suggests that the particular path by which individuals feel (in)authentic in given episodes, rather than simply whether they feel authentic, may be more critical for both individual well-being and organizational relationships than currently believed. Authenticity and authenticity narratives therefore also affects a leader's relationships with acquaintances, supporters, and work colleagues, as honesty, intentions, clarity of personal values, and transparency are hallmarks of these relationships.

Enablers of Authenticity

Self-Awareness

Self-awareness serves as cornerstones of authentic leadership (Gardner et al., 2005) and, given the busy-ness and overwork of modern life, individuals do not always have the time or energy resources to regularly engage in conscious self-awareness practices and do not always create the space for reflective and contemplative practices to interrogate their own intrinsic beliefs, expectations, values, and motivations. Given an individual's psychological growth stage and maturity, through self-introspection and reflection (George et al., 2007), a person can achieve greater self-awareness by working to understand how she/he/they interpret their environment (Gardner et al., 2005), the various forces at work in their workplace and societal relationships (April et al., 2023), and their place in it (Dharani et al., 2021)—a dynamic working self-concept. Self-awareness requires a disciplined commitment to self-mastery and a willingness to learn. Self-mastery, therefore, allows a leader to discover herself/himself/their selves and master her/his/their focused choices, capabilities and be comfortable with the consequences of choice which, in turn, stimulates interpersonal synergies with, and trust in, others (as leaders begin to really know themselves, they often want to and do get to know others better). Such learning about personal motives, values, ethics, strengths, and weaknesses engenders an intrapersonal trust, necessary for overall well-being (April et al., 2013; Kernis, 2003). April et al. (2006) go further by adding that, in addition to learning, leaders have to also unlearn and ultimately relearn. Leaders should be encouraged to test the validity of their beliefs about the future, their own growth into roles within it, the scope of their work and interdisciplinary exposure, and how they 'show up' in the tension-filled space between the present and the future. This is an important element in overcoming the liability of (previous) success. According to April et al. (2013), the presumed correctness of past actions and interpretations thereof are reinforced by repeated success, creating heuristics, biases and ensuing complacency which ultimately breeds rejection of new information and experiences. Self-awareness work lays the groundwork for, and invites, new responses and worldviews/mental maps, mostly by allowing leaders to themselves 'discover' (a critical learning element) the inadequacies of their cognitive and emotional maps and to initiate new responses, as opposed to offering them solutions upfront. What is called for is not total abandonment of past certainties but a balance of past certainties and new possibilities, akin to Argyris and Schön's (1978) 'double-loop learning' or what Senge (1992) terms 'generative learning'.

Personal Vision

A personal vision is an embodiment of who a leader is and what she/he/they may perceive to be her/his/their purpose (*voca*), priorities, and focused perceptions, and influences and guides whom and what they get involved with, and how they 'show up' in that involvement. Arguably, such a personal vision is the most decisive factor in determining their personal growth and experiences. A leader's calling (*voca*) will find them if they continually do the right things—but they must be willing to do the hard, preparatory inner work. Additionally, there has to be a willingness or compulsion to articulate what has been 'heard' (internally) by the leader and clarity regarding the level at which it has been 'heard' and, therefore, 'responded from'. Part of the important work to be done by individuals is in holding themselves accountable for their own unlearning and reframing of mental models, thereby making it possible for change toward authentic behavior, in line with their personal vision, and sustained over time (being cognizant of 'who' and 'what' will sustain them over the long term). At its heart, this is an attempt to reorient individual values, core assumptions, and norms and behaviors through deconstructing cognitive and emotional supportive structures and addiction to past thoughts and emotions, as well as the very chemicals and bio-electrical pathways in the body that sustain them (April et al., 2013, p. 12). A personal vision enables the necessary and crucial shift from 'importance' to 'significance', from 'being out of balance' to 'wellness', and from 'drudgery' to 'fulfillment'. Perhaps most importantly, it engenders results for the common good. Often such vision is accompanied by a personal story/narrative, which creates new presence and voice within the leader and, when shared, initially grows within a certain polis/locality but, through relationships and awakened communities-of-interest, transcends locality. This personal growth can also be supported by personal/executive coaches, therapists, and psychiatrists—in fact, some leaders have found regular sessions with spiritual leaders to also be of immerse value in keeping on the path toward congruency between personal vision, values, and enacted behavior, resulting in overall wellness.

Ethics and Morals

Luthans and Avolio (2003) determined that authentic individuals draw on positive psychological characteristics such as confidence, hope, and resiliency, and claimed that ethics and morals were central to authentic leadership and its development. Some leaders report persisting with inauthentic acts and behavior, as they learnt to derive benefit from being able to blend into environments at low stakes, feeling that others would never really get to know who they truly were. Sparrowe (2005) asserted that the creation of narratives of their authentic selves, built upon the subjectivity of others, aids leaders in making a cognitive or less conscious decision to go along with the artifice to their advantage or in order to shield their true persona from discovery. Many leaders report on the internal conflict over whether it was more beneficial to consciously present an illusion, a strong element of transference, even while it did not create a true sense of belonging and connectedness or consideration for the feelings of others, or to carry on inauthentically since it gave them access and greater opportunities (moral motivation). A serious challenge arises, though, for those who continue such inauthentic behavior into romantic engagements. For both workplace and romantic engagements, social motivations that shape their own values and behaviors are called into question. May et al. (2003) argue that authentic leaders cultivate and make use of their moral reserves to authentically act with courage in the face of ethical dilemmas and to sustain ethical behavior. Identity formation, linked to individuals' ethical stances, brings a sense of agency (i.e., autonomy and self-directedness), responsibility, integrity, commitment, and psychological maturity (Côté & Levine, 2002). Thus, leaders who have made identity commitments (i.e., decided certain things are important to who they are), ideally through a process of exploration, tend to engage in less risky behaviors, have fewer mental health problems, and experience greater psychological well-being (Hardy et al., 2019). However, competing views from Cooper et al. (2005), Shamir and Eilam (2005), and Sparrowe (2005) question defining authenticity inclusive of these positive psychological characteristics when referring to workplace leadership. Their perspectives see the positive psychological resources and positive ethical perspective as consequences and not inherent characteristics of authentic leadership (Avolio & Gardner, 2005).

Openness and Deep Care

Handler's (1986) framework took authenticity to be a construct entirely derived from the culture and environment/context specific to an individual, and noted that environments which positively reaffirm an individual's true self create inclinations toward openness and love, thereby reinforcing the inclination to remain genuine (Adams, 2006). When leaders can express who they really are, and be honest and transparent with their emotions, intentions, and actions, it creates trust in relationships—such a critical element of high-performing teams in the workplace. According to Ford and Harding (2011), most work environments eventually make true authenticity impossible, requiring acceptance that everyone should align with one collective form for the greater good versus encouraging individualistic tendencies (true selves) that could lead to destructive dynamics in an organization. It is for this reason that Rapiya et al. (2023) challenge the global dominance of Western, individualistic work orientations and instead advocates different philosophical construction of work and workplace interactions, e.g., integrating the southern African concept of Ubuntu into the modern workplace, which emphasizes deep care and aligned action for others, openness to solidarity, social sensitivity, consciousness of community, behaving for the common good, and interconnectivity with others and the environment. When employees sense that they are deeply cared for, and that others (especially those in charge and with positional power) are invested in their well-being and happiness, they show up more engaged and willing to employ their discretionary effort (Dharani & April, 2022). In this way, a greater number of individuals will be able to show up more authentically in their work and workspaces, as well as feel higher levels of fulfillment in what they do and how they interact.

Intentions and Imperfection

Many leaders report great value in embracing all the experiences, challenges, and things that are unique to them. The Japanese philosophy of wabi-sabi has proven to be a great enabler of authenticity for many—leaders working with their flaws, not against them, and not denying their challenges and imperfections (Dharani et al., 2021). Focused attention and narrative inquiry into their life histories and lived experiences have given fresh insights for action toward fulfillment (using narrative identity reconstruction—Castelló et al., 2023). All people bear scars from adverse conditions in their lives and their relationships—and, metaphorically using the Japanese practice of kintsugi as a life lens, this could be *their very gifts* to the world later on in life (e.g., being involved in social justice issues, fighting for the marginalized, providing solutions for those in poverty or who are unemployed, etc.). When referring to entrepreneurial failure, Castelló et al. (2023) state: "In this discursive practice, entrepreneurs deal with the transition imposed by failure by presenting a change between their pre-failure and post-failure identity. In the narration of their past experiences, they often assign their past incompetence to their old, 'unlearned' selves, and depict themselves as more capable entrepreneurs after failure. Thus, the failure becomes integral to a positive journey through which they have grown as a person. Entrepreneurs describe themselves as more learned, often including in the narration of the experience of failure and how it transformed them into a better person—one who can handle extreme situations and is generally wiser" (p. 12). Also, being able to focus attention on present-moment growth ('learning and unlearning as they go') has been facilitative of 'authentic being' for many leaders, as opposed to having to keep a constant eye on goals that must be achieved. By remaining aware of their choices (and consequences of choices) and focusing on the process of daily self-improvement toward an intention(s) have enhanced leaders' feelings of in-the-moment well-being—noting that 'intentions' are things that align with people's spirit/*voca*/energy, whereas goals are hard lines in the sand. Some useful and enabling intention statements have been: 'I want to feel more comfortable in my clothes' (versus the goal of wanting to lose 20 kg in 3 months); 'I want to live with greater abundance' (versus the goal of wanting to be a millionaire by the time you are 35 yrs old); 'I want to feel good about standing in front of people when I speak to crowds' (versus the goal of wanting to be a globally recognized speaker who is regularly invited to speak around the world); 'I want to make a true connection with someone who will cherish me' (versus the goal of wanting to be married by the age of 30).

Self-Efficacy and Self-Confidence

An enabler of authenticity for leaders is self-confidence: the confidence to courageously express and persist in authentically putting out honest views and feedback, calmly and rationally, and the confidence to act and behave with efficacy in accordance to one's values, identity, and true character (Bandura, 1997; Dharani et al., 2021). As far as career decisions and personal development are concerned, Zhang et al. (2021) demonstrated in their study that authenticity positively relates to career decision self-efficacy over time, and vice versa, and Satici et al. (2013) could show that social self-efficacy was positively related to authentic living, and was negatively related to accepting external influence, and self-alienation. Bandura (1997, p. 3) defined self-efficacy as "people's beliefs about their capabilities to produce designated levels of performance that exercise influence over events that effect their lives"—the belief in an individual's capability to achieve specific goals or tasks. Self-efficacy has proven to be a useful construct in spheres ranging from phobias (Bandura et al., 1975), depression (Muris, 2002), career choice behavior (Betz, 2005), and managerial functioning (Gangloff & Mazilescu, 2017). Self-confidence and personal fulfillment are also closely related concepts. Self-confidence refers to the belief and trust that a leader has in their abilities, qualities, and judgments. It is a feeling of assurance and certainty that they can succeed and accomplish their goals. Personal fulfillment, on the other hand, is the sense of satisfaction and happiness that comes from achieving their goals, pursuing their passions, and living a meaningful life. Self-confidence plays a crucial role in personal fulfillment as it allows leaders to take risks, overcome challenges, and pursue their passions without fear or doubt (Bayat et al., 2019). When they have confidence in their abilities and decisions, leaders are more likely to set goals that align with their values and interests, work toward them with persistence and grit (Warner & April, 2012), and ultimately achieve a sense of fulfillment and satisfaction. In contrast, a lack of self-confidence can lead to self-doubt, indecisiveness, and avoidance of challenges or opportunities. It can also hinder personal growth and development, as leaders may shy away from taking risks or pursuing their passions for fear of failure or rejection. Therefore, building self-confidence is essential for authenticity and personal fulfillment. Some ways to build self-confidence include setting achievable goals and putting manageable steps in place to achieve those goals (Bloom, 2013; Sellars, 2004), focusing on strengths and accomplishments (Rath & Conchie, 2008), practicing self-compassion (Neff & Knox, 2020), seeking support and feedback from others (Hermanto et al., 2017), and learning new skills and knowledge (Stanley & Williamson, 2017).

Self-Regulation

Beddoes-Jones and Swailes (2015) constructed a three-pillar model of authenticity, stating that it is evolved from a person's self-awareness, ethics, and self-regulation. A critical enabler of authentic leadership is self-regulation (Gardner et al., 2005). Self-regulation includes methods whereby people apply self-control through: (i) self-determination—managing actions through internal monitoring processes, (ii) unbiased processing, (iii) relational transparency, (iv) establishment of personal principles, (v) evaluating inconsistencies between principles and actions, and (vi) determining activities for addressing discrepancies (April et al., 2013; Deci & Ryan, 2000; Gardner et al., 2005; Kernis, 2003; Stajkovic & Luthans, 1998). Workplace performance-related constructs can be conceptualized as part of the well-being concept, with 'burnout' being the prominent example of such an inclusion of performance-related constructs within the well-being concept. Without self-regulation capabilities, leaders, engaged in long hours and overwork, expose themselves to burnout (impairment of individual well-being) which often manifests as: emotional exhaustion, depersonalization, and lack of personal accomplishment. The subjective experience of not being able to realize one's performance potential refers to a psychological state in which individuals perceive that they are unable to reach their full capabilities or achieve their desired level of performance (Sonnentag, 2002, p. 407). Many emerging leaders report that, in order to climb the social and economic ladders, they have been reticent in establishing proper boundaries for themselves (ineffective self-gatekeepers): institutional boundaries, boundaries between diverse cultures and ethnicities, and interpersonal boundaries—resulting in compromised personal relationships, compromised health (including personal energy degradation and jeopardized mental health), and compromised resilience. Boundaries can be completely segmented (roles are separated), integrated flexibly (allowing for a boundary to accommodate the demands of other domains), or integrated permeably (extent to which aspects of another domain is allowed to enter)—the latter two does pose the risk of role blurring (Ashforth et al., 2000; Clark, 2000; Demerouti, 2015; Desrochers & Sargent, 2004; Dharani et al., 2022). Authentic leaders tend to manage the alignment of their values with their objectives and behaviors through self-regulation. Sparrowe (2005), though, criticizes self-regulatory behaviors as they are unable to appropriately manage the changing nature of the individual, which emerges from the narrative self-process (Avolio & Gardner, 2005). Therefore, being more purposeful about their intentionality and subsequent action in setting boundaries between work and private life, as well as between time with others and with themselves and not be completely 'pulled in' by the 'economic machine', is a core enabler for improving leaders' bandwidth for authentic compassion and improving their own mental health. According to Saunders (2015), "dispositions are formed by repeated intentionality and right actions" (p. 123). By opening themselves up to outside sources such as therapist and coaches, leaders can inject energy and intelligence into their own sense-making around their intentional dispositions and subsequent actions (Cloud, 2013).

STUMBLING BLOCKS OF AUTHENTICITY
Societal Expectations

Simmons (2009) highlights the psychological impact of gender stereotypes, particularly 'the good girl' on both the fulfillment and well-being of individuals: "The good girl walked a treacherous line, balancing mixed messages about how far she should go and how strong she should be; she was to be *enthusiastic* while being *quiet*; *smart* with *no opinions on things*; *intelligent* but a *follower*; *popular* but *quiet*. She would be something, but not too much". She further asserts that the 'curse of the good girl' cuts to the core of authentic selfhood, demanding that girls curb the strongest feelings and desires that form the patchwork of a person—even though girls outnumber boys in college and graduate school, graduate at higher rates, and in high school they pursue more leadership roles and extracurricular activities than boys do. Society urges leaders to be perfect, particularly women leaders: given them a troubled relationship with failure, with innovation, a dysfunctional orientation toward continued comparison ('there is always someone or something better or worse than me'), and a dysfunctional relationship with judgment ('as I am now, I am not good enough'); it expects women not to brag about achievements and also not speak up (diminishing their ability to advocate for pay rises, personal development, and promotions, and not to challenge and provide constructive criticism); it expects women to be selfless (limiting the expression of their own needs and wants); and, it demands modesty and reservedness (depriving them of permission to commit to strengths, goals, and operating outside of the box). In sum, girls and women are socialized to show up inauthentically and, unsurprisingly, it has severe effects on their selfhood, self-confidence, self-efficacy, and ultimately their fulfillment in work and life in general. When leaders chase perfection, they wear themselves down since the mindset of perfectionism engenders perpetual unease and is always moving (no point of arrival, and is circular), unyielding and is an overwhelming state.

Contingent Self-Esteem

Leaders with high contingent self-esteem are always striving for success, seek validation for their actions, avoid failure to reinforce their self-worth, and are more prone to being less considerate as they want to succeed at all costs, which might come at the expense of others (Crocker & Park, 2004). Kernis and Goldman (2006) found that contingent self-esteem is a stumbling block to authenticity and its components. They defined contingent self-esteem as the degree to which an individual's self-value is contingent on satisfying expectations, meeting standards or accomplishing specific objectives or evaluations. Furthermore, to avoid social disapproval they are more prone to social sanctions (Chekroun, 2008). Leaders with contingent self-esteem are compelled to meet social demands and value themselves based on specific results, and seek recurrent relational reassurance. Drawing on Eastern wisdom and self-determination theory (Deci & Ryan, 2000), Wang and Li's (2018) study conceptualized a new form of maladaptive self-esteem, the power contingent self-esteem, which is extremely contingent on an individual's sense of power, and posits that it is related to low subjective well-being by making people experience less authenticity. A number of leaders report that they carry an underlying concern relating to expectations of their Boards, as well as broader organizational stakeholders (behavioral expectations, achievement expectations, task expectations, financial expectations)—and those concerns are continuous and ever-present. They also claim to become fiercely protective of their time and energy as they get more busy trying to achieve results and meet, oftentimes, unrealistic demands (compromising their self-care, rejuvenation, and support systems). This is amplified when leaders idealize mentors and specific supervisory Board members, through transference, and wanting to please them and appear competent/credible for them—further eroding their authenticity. Kernis et al. (2008) argue that this is problematic in that contingent self-esteem requires ongoing social acceptance and affirmation by others. Such individuals are prone to having low self-esteem if they are unable to achieve specific goals (Toor & Ofori, 2009), and do not always exercise courage in speaking up for themselves and sharing their concerns and challenges (Dharani et al., 2021) therefore rendering them 'voice-conforming' and 'power-pleasing' with diminished authenticity and credibility with followers when witnessed.

Inability to Process Negative Feedback

One of the stumbling blocks of authenticity is individuals' inability to maturely process negative feedback, particularly in the workplace—when individuals get regular feedback from supervisors, managers, executive leaders, and Board members, when they have scheduled performance reviews, and when they are subjected to 360 feedback reviews. In general, feedback which addresses task accomplishment processes (Kluger & DeNisi, 1996) can be differentiated from feedback which is closely linked to meta-tasks and self-related issues (usually obtained through self-seeking by an individual) (Ashford & Cummings, 1983). Many leaders report the fact that they do not value or even enjoy criticism when receiving feedback (more so for meta-tasks and self-related issues, than for task accomplishment), even when constructive, and though many positive and constructive things are shared when receiving feedback (informally or formally), they only really remember and ruminate on the negative aspects of that feedback (impacting their overall well-being). They psychologically distance themselves from negative feedback by thinking through and offering external attributions, justifications, or rationalization for it (shielding narratives, in order to preserve their identity and self-concept), and often will 'normalize' their behavior/action that received the negative feedback as part and parcel of regular work (so as not to deal with the anxiety that emerges when 'standing out' from what is expected, and rather prefer to remember themselves as valued by colleagues and their workplace through other objective standards and workplace values—such as, qualifications, work experience, skillset, knowledge … a form of self-affirmation). This psychological distancing also withdraws individuals from empathic engagement with others, and in actioning compassionate acts on behalf of others. However, feedback-seeking behavior (as opposed to avoidance and distancing) has been shown to have positive effects on individual well-being, with one of the reasons being the reduction in uncertainty and role ambiguity (Sonnentag, 2002).

Mimicking and Acculturation

The workplace is a meeting space of diverse and contested social orientations, in which some have primacy and others are deemed less credible. This could be due to *common language and communication styles* (same language, direct or indirect communication styles, the need for high context when communicating or low context, being expressive when communicating or being instrumental, or being informal or formal when communicating), *sense of humor* (similar wittiness, a keen ear for satirical humor or not, when to use humor socially or in workplace settings), *religion* (formal religion or broader spirituality in expressing an acknowledgment for someone or something much larger than the individual, denominations of religion, particular faiths), *orientation toward power* (enjoyment of rank, hierarchy, or liking equality and workplace democracy a lot more), *competitiveness* (collaborative in approach or competitive in approach), *structure* (pedantic about structure or more flexible regarding structure), *thinking styles* (more deductive in thinking style or approaches, being linear or more systematic), *sexual orientation* (heterosexual, transgender, gay, lesbian, queer, asexual, bisexual, fluid, etc.), *workplace environments* (comfortable with certainty, control and predictability, or happy in chaos, uncertainty and unpredictability), *orientation to action or being* (being–presence–allowing–noticing vs. doing–action–problem-solving), *how time is viewed* (single-focus or multi-focus in relation to time, seeing time as fixed or fluid, thinking about time in the present, or the future, circular, or even believing in accessing time in the past, views on reincarnation, punctuality), *similar orientations to personal space* (enjoy people keeping their distance when communicating or engaging, or enjoy being close-up or touching someone when communicating or engaging), or a host of other differentiating aspects. As a result, some individuals embark on processes of acculturation in order to cope with the environment in which they find themselves and purposefully attempt behavioral shifts to adopt the culture of the most powerful and the most privileged in the workplace—for some, the outcome can range from very positive adaptations through to very negative ones; the latter relating to acculturative stress: which include social, psychological, and physical health consequences (Bouvy et al., 1994, p. 238). A number of people of color, and some in leader positions, reported about the uncomfortableness, felt shame and continuous anxiety for attempting to mimic behaviors, hobbies, music interests, movies, language and accents of (economically and socially powerful) white work colleagues, in order to be accepted in the workplace (April et al., 2023, p. 36). Doubly frustrating is when individuals present an inauthentic version and altered identity of themselves to try and conform and fit in, but then still cannot establish deep relationships and friendships—only to realize that aspects of their identities will forever taint them as out-groups. Many report that, ultimately, they personally feel guilty for not presenting their true selves. Fullel (2018) explores the motives and personal costs of mimicry and identity reconstruction. Ray's (2019) research attempted to bridge the subfields of organizational theory, as well as race and ethnicity, arguing that workplaces are racial structures—cognitive schemas connecting organizational rules to social and material resources, as well as being spaces of conflict relating to interactions, inauthentic engagements, exclusion, unequal treatment, resulting in cognitive and mental degradation. Similarly, and reported in the April et al. (2023) study, many individuals with atypical genders (LGBTQIA+) and women in the workplace reported the pressures they felt to conform under heteronormative environments and pervasive hegemonic masculinity. For the sake of well-being and fear of further marginalization, many chose not to disclose their gender identification or started behaving inauthentically as cisgender, prototype males in the workplace. Many report the effects of such long-term inauthenticity: anxiety, feeling unwell, depression, effects on their body weight, and mental health challenges.

Conclusion

In conclusion, leader development and authenticity are closely linked. Authenticity has centuries-old roots in various cultures around the globe, and has evolved to include the idea that an individual can live dynamically in accordance with their inner being, free from the constraints of irrelevant personal conditioning, biased mental models, dominant workplace norms and behaviors, and outdated workplace heuristics and societal constraints. The personal costs of inauthenticity and alienation are negatively associated with various aspects of well-being, engagement, and fulfillment. Authenticity therefore is a key aspect of effective leadership and is characterized by self-awareness, the ability and courage to express oneself in accordance with one's true beliefs and identity, and congruence between espoused and enacted values. Developing authenticity in leaders requires an awareness and recognition of the unique challenges and pressures that leaders face (as it can be quite lonely), particularly in the context of work, as well as regular focus on and time for self-reflection and introspection, acting on opportunities for learning and growth, and a commitment to personal mastery. Leaders who prioritize authenticity are better able to build trust and relationships with their teams, mentors, and stakeholders, and are more effective at responsibly creating workplace cultures of openness, integrity, transparency, and dignity. Ultimately, the development of authentic leaders, premised on values-based and responsible leader orientations, is critical to creating more effective, just, inclusive workplace cultures and societies.

References

Adams, W. W. (2006). Love, open awareness, and authenticity: A conversation with William Blake and D. W. Winnicott. *Journal of Humanistic Psychology, 46*(1), 9–35. https://doi.org/10.1177/0022167805281189

Algera, P. M., & Lips-Wiersma, M. (2012). Radical authentic leadership: Co-creating the conditions under which all members of the organization can be authentic. *Leadership Quarterly, 23*(1), 118–131. https://doi.org/10.1016/j.leaqua.2011.11.010

April, K., April, A., & Wabbels, H. (2006). Growth through unlearning. *Develop, 3*, 78–81.

April, K., Dharani, B., & April, A. (2023). *Lived experiences of exclusion in the workplace: Psychological and behavioural effects*. Emerald Publishing.

April, K., Kukard, J., & Peters, B. K. G. (2013). *Steward leadership: A maturational perspective*. University of Cape Town Press.

April, K., Macdonald, R., & Vriesendorp, S. (2000). *Rethinking leadership*. Juta Academic.

Argyris, C., & Schön, D. A. (1978). *Organizational learning: A theory of action perspective*. Addison-Wesley.

Ashford, S. J., & Cummings, L. L. (1983). Feedback as an individual resource: Personal strategies of creating information. *Organizational Behavior and Human Performance, 32*(3), 370–398. https://doi.org/10.1016/0030-5073(83)90156-3

Ashforth, B. E., Kreiner, G. E., & Fugate, M. (2000). All in a day's work: Boundaries and micro role transitions. *Academy of Management Review, 25*(3), 472–491. https://doi.org/10.5465/AMR.2000.3363315

Avolio, B. J., & Gardner, W. L. (2005). Authentic leadership development: Getting to the root of positive forms of leadership. *The Leadership Quarterly, 16*(3), 315–338. https://doi.org/10.1016/j.leaqua.2005.03.001

Bandura, A. (1997). *Self-efficacy: The exercise of control*. Freeman.

Bandura, A., Jeffery, R. W., & Gajdos, E. (1975). Generalizing change through participant modeling with self-directed mastery. *Behaviour Research and Therapy, 13*(2–3), 141–152. https://doi.org/10.1016/0005-7967(75)90008-X

Bayat, B., Akbarisomar, N., Tori, N. A., & Salehiniya, H. (2019). The relation between self-confidence and risk-taking among the students. *Journal of Education and Health Promotion, 8*, 27.

Beddoes-Jones, F., & Swailes, S. (2015). Authentic leadership: Development of a new three pillar model. *Strategic HR Review, 14*(3), 94–99. https://doi.org/10.1108/SHR-04-2015-0032

Betz, N. (2005). Career self-efficacy. In F. T. L. Leong, & A. Barak (Eds.), *Contemporary models in vocational psychology* (pp. 55–78). Lawrence Erlbaum Associates, Publishers.

Bloom, M. (2013). Self-regulated learning: Goal-setting and self-monitoring. *The Language Teacher, 37*(4), 46–50.

Bouvy, A., van de Vijver, F. J. R., Boski, P., & Schmitz, P. (Eds.). (1994). *Journeys into cross-cultural psychology*. Garland Science.

Cameron, K., & Dutton, J. (Eds.). (2003). *Positive organizational scholarship: Foundations of a new discipline*. Berrett-Koehler Publishers.

Cooper, C., Scandura, T. A., & Schriesheim, C. A. (2005). Looking forward but learning from our past: Potential challenges to developing authentic leadership theory and authentic leaders. *The Leadership Quarterly, 16*(3), 475–493. https://doi.org/10.1016/j.leaqua.2005.03.008

Castelló, I., Barbera-Tomás, D., & Vaara, E. (2023). Moving on: Narrative identity reconstruction after entrepreneurial failure. *Journal of Business Venturing, 38*(4), 106302. https://doi.org/10.1016/j.jbusvent.2023.106302

Chekroun, P. (2008). Social control behavior: The effects of social situations and personal implication on informal social sanctions. *Social and Personality Psychology Compass, 2*(6), 2141–2158. https://doi.org/10.1111/j.1751-9004.2008.00141.x

Chiaburu, D. S., Diaz, I., & De Vos, A. (2013). Employee alienation: Relationships with careerism and career satisfaction. *Journal of Managerial Psychology, 28*(1), 4–20. https://doi.org/10.1108/02683941311298832

Clark, S. (2000). Work/family border theory: A new theory of work/family balance. *Human Relations, 53*, 747–770. https://doi.org/10.1177/0018726700536001

Cloud, H. (2013). *Boundaries for leaders: Results, relationships and being ridiculously in charge*. HarperCollins Publishers.

Conger, M., McMullen, J. S., Bergman, B. J., Jr., & York, J. G. (2018). Category membership, identity control, and the reevaluation of prosocial opportunities. *Journal of Business Venturing, 33*(2), 179–206. https://doi.org/10.1016/j.jbusvent.2017.11.004

Côté, J. E., & Levine, C. G. (2002). *Identity formation, agency, and culture: A social psychological synthesis*. Lawrence Erlbaum Associates.

Crocker, J., & Park, L. E. (2004). The costly pursuit of self-esteem. *Psychological Bulletin, 130*(3), 392.

Deci, E. L., & Ryan, R. M. (2000). The "what" and "why" of goal pursuits: Human needs and the self-determination of behavior. *Psychological Inquiry, 11*(4), 227–268. https://doi.org/10.1207/S15327965PLI1104_01

Demerouti, E. (2015). Strategies used by individuals to prevent burnout. *European Journal of Clinical Investigation, 45*(10), 1106–1112. https://doi.org/10.1111/eci.12494

Desrochers, S., & Sargent, L. (2004). Boundary/border theory and work-family integration. *Organization Management Journal*, *1*(1), 40–48. https://scholarship.shu.edu/omj/vol1/iss1/11

Dharani, B., & April, K. (2022). Investigating happiness at work along the organizational life cycle: Moderating role of locus of control. *Problems and Perspectives in Management*, *20*(1), 216–228. https://doi.org/10.21511/ppm.20(1).2022.19.

Dharani, B., April, K., & Harvey, K. (2021). *The poetic journey of self-leadership: Leadership development along stages of psychological growth*. KR Publishing.

Dharani, B., Guntern, S., & April, K. (2022). Perception differences in burnout: A study of Swiss-German managers and subordinates. *Journal of Occupational and Environmental Medicine*, *64*(4), 320–330. https://doi.org/10.1097/JOM.0000000000002425

Foner, P. S. (Ed.). (1970). *W.E.B. Du Bois speaks: Speeches and addresses 1890–1919* Pathfinder Press.

Ford, J., & Harding, N. (2011). The impossibility of the "true self" of authentic leadership. *Leadership*, *7*(4), 463–479. https://doi.org/10.1177/1742715011416894

Fromm, E. (2001). *The fear of freedom* (2nd ed.). Routledge.

Fullel, T. (2018). *Motives of mimicry in Philip Roth's the human stain* (Unpublished Masters of Arts in English thesis). Central Department of English, Tribhuvan University

Gangloff, B., & Mazilescu, C.-A. (2017). Normative characteristics of perceived self-efficacy. *Social Sciences*, *6*(4), 139. https://doi.org/10.3390/socsci6040139

Gardner, W. L., Avolio, B. J., Luthans, F., May, D. R., & Walumbwa, F. O. (2005). "Can you see the real me?" A self-based model of authentic leader and follower development. *Leadership Quarterly*, *16*(3), 343–372. https://doi.org/10.1016/j.leaqua.2005.03.003

George, B., Sims, P., McLean, A. N., & Mayer, D. (2007). Discovering your authentic leadership. *Harvard Business Review*, *85*(2), 129–138.

Goffee, R., & Jones, G. (2005). Managing authenticity: The paradox of great leadership. *Harvard Business Review*, *83*(12), 86–94. https://hbr.org/2005/12/managing-authenticity-the-paradox-of-great-leadership

Handler, R. (1986). Authenticity. *Anthropology Today*, *2*(1), 2–4. https://doi.org/10.2307/3032899

Hardy, S. A., Francis, S. W., Zamboanga, B. L., Kim, S. Y., Anderson, S. G., & Forthun, L. F. (2019). *Journal of Clinical Psychology*, *69*(4), 364–382. https://doi.org/10.1002/jclp.21913

Hartel, C., Zerbe, W. J., & Ashkanasy, N. M. (2005). *Emotions in organisational behaviour*. Lawrence Erlbaum Associates, Inc., Publishers.

Harter, S. (2002). Authenticity. In C. R. Snyder & S. J. Lopez (Eds.), *Handbook of positive psychology* (pp. 382–394). Oxford University Press.

Hermanto, N., Zuroff, D. C., Kelly, A. C., & Leybman, M. J. (2017). Receiving support, giving support, and self-reassurance: A daily diary test of social mentality theory. *Personality and Individual Differences*, *107*, 37–42. https://doi.org/10.1016/j.paid.2016.11.013

Hirschfeld, R. R., Feild, H. S., & Bedeian, A. G. (2000). Work alienation as an individual-difference construct for predicting workplace adjustment: A test in two samples. *Journal of Applied Social Psychology*, *30*(9), 1880–1902. https://doi.org/10.1111/j.1559-1816.2000.tb02473.x

Hutchinson, D. S. (1995). Ethics. In J. A. Barnes (Ed.), *The Cambridge companion to Aristotle* (pp. 195–231). Cambridge University Press.

Impett, E. A., Javam, L., Le, B. M., Asyabi-Eshghi, B., & Kogan, A. (2013). The joys of genuine giving: Approach and avoidance sacrifice motivation and authenticity. *Personal Relationships, 20*(4), 740–754. https://doi.org/10.1111/pere.12012

Kernis, M. H. (2003). Toward a conceptualization of optimal self-esteem. *Psychological Inquiry, 14*(1), 1–26. https://doi.org/10.1207/S15327965PLI1401_01

Kernis, M. H., & Goldman, B. M. (2006). A multicomponent conceptualization of authenticity: Theory and research. In M. P. Zanna (Ed.), *Advances in experimental social psychology* (Vol. 38, pp. 283–357). Elsevier Academic Press. https://doi.org/10.1016/S0065-2601(06)38006-9

Kernis, M. H., Lakey, C. E., & Heppner, W. L. (2008). Secure versus fragile high self-esteem as a predictor of verbal defensiveness: Converging findings across three different markers. *Journal of Personality, 76*(3), 477–512. https://doi.org/10.1111/j.1467-6494.2008.00493.x

Kivy, P. (1995). *Authenticities: Philosophical reflections on musical performance*. Cornell University Press.

Kluger, A. N., & DeNisi, A. (1996). The effects of feedback interventions on performance: A historical review, a meta-analysis, and a preliminary feedback intervention theory. *Psychological Bulletin, 119*(2), 254–284. https://doi.org/10.1037/0033-2909.119.2.254

Lenton, A. P., Bruder, M., Slabu, L., & Sedikides, C. (2013). How does "being real" feel? The experience of state authenticity. *Journal of Personality, 81*(3), 276–289. https://doi.org/10.1111/j.1467-6494.2012.00805.x

Luthans, F., & Avolio, B. (2003). Authentic leadership development. In K. Cameron & J. Dutton (Eds.), *Positive organizational scholarship: Foundations of a new discipline* (pp. 241–258). Berrett-Koehler Publishers.

May, D. R., Chan, A. Y. L., Hodges, T. D., & Avolio, B. J. (2003). Developing the moral component of authentic leadership. *Organizational Dynamics, 32*(3), 247–260. https://doi.org/10.1016/S0090-2616(03)00032-9

Muris, P. (2002). Relationships between self-efficacy and symptoms of anxiety disorders and depression in a normal adolescent sample. *Personality and Individual Differences, 32*(2), 337–348. https://doi.org/10.1016/S0191-8869(01)00027-7

Neff, K. D., & Knox, M. C. (2020). Self-compassion. In V. Zeigler-Hill, & T. K. Shackelford (Eds.), *Encyclopedia of personality and individual differences*. Springer International Publishing. https://doi.org/10.1007/978-3-319-28099-8_1159-1

O'Neil, I., Ucbasaran, D., & York, J. G. (2022). The evolution of founder identity as an authenticity work process. *Journal of Business Venturing, 37*(1), 106031. https://doi.org/10.1016/j.jbusvent.2020.106031

Parke, H. W., & Wormell, D. (1956). *The Delphic oracle*. Blackwell.

Rapiya, A., April, K., & Daya, P. (2023 forthcoming). Leader identity dissonance: Spirituality challenges of black African professionals in the workplace. *Effective Executive, 26*(1), tba.

Rath, T., & Conchie, B. (2008). *Strengths based leadership*. Gallup Press.

Ray, V. (2019). A theory of racialized organizations. *American Sociological Review, 84*(1), 26–53. https://doi.org/10.1177/0003122418822335

Rees, L. L., Lehman, D., & Ramanujam, R. (2021). Me, me, and me: The process of felt (in)authenticity at work through multiple referent selves. *Academy of*

Management Proceedings, (1), 1. https://doi.org/10.5465/AMBPP.2021.15432abstract

Satici, S. A., Kayis, A. R., & Akin, A. (2013). Investigating the predictive role of social self-efficacy on authenticity in Turkish university students. *Europe's Journal of Psychology, 9*(3), 572–580. https://doi.org/10.5964/ejop.v9i3.579

Saunders J. (2015). Compassion. *Clinical Medicine, 15*(2), 121–124. https://doi.org/10.7861/clinmedicine.15-2-121

Sellars, C. (2004). *Building self-confidence*. The National Coaching Foundation.

Senge, P. M. (1992). Mental models. *Planning Review, 20*(2), 4–44. https://doi.org/10.1108/eb054349

Shamir, B., & Eilam, G. (2005). "What's your story?" A life-stories approach to authentic leadership development. *The Leadership Quarterly, 16*(3), 395–417. https://doi.org/10.1016/j.leaqua.2005.03.005

Simmons, R. (2009). *The curse of the good girl: Raising authentic girls with courage and confidence*. Penguin Press.

Sonnentag, S. (2002). Performance, well-being and self-regulation. In S. Sonnentag (Ed.), *Psychological management of individual performance* (pp. 406–424). Wiley.

Sparrowe, R. T. (2005). Authentic leadership and the narrative self. *The Leadership Quarterly, 16*(3), 419–439. https://doi.org/10.1016/j.leaqua.2005.03.004

Stajkovic, A. D., & Luthans, F. (1998). Social cognitive theory and self-efficacy: Going beyond traditional motivational and behavioral approaches. *Organizational Dynamics, 26*(4), 62–74. https://doi.org/10.1016/S0090-2616(98)90006-7

Stanley, J., & Williamson, T. (2017). Skill. *Noûs, 51*(4), 713–726. http://www.jstor.org/stable/26631463

Toor, S.-U.-R., & Ofori, G. (2009). Authenticity and its influence on psychological well-being and contingent self-esteem of leaders in Singapore construction sector. *Construction Management and Economics, 27*(3), 299–313. https://doi.org/10.1080/01446190902729721

Trilling, L. (2009). *Sincerity and authenticity*. Harvard University Press.

Tummers, L. G., & Den Dulk, L. (2013). The effects of work alienation on organisational commitment, work effort and work-to-family enrichment. *Journal of Nursing Management, 21*(6), 850–859. https://doi.org/10.1111/jonm.12159

van den Bosch, R., & Taris, T. W. (2014). Authenticity at work: Development and validation of an individual authenticity measure at work. *Journal of Happiness Studies, 15*(1), 1–18. https://doi.org/10.1007/s10902-013-9413-3

Warner, R., & April, K. (2012). Building personal resilience at work. *Effective Executive, 15*(4), 53–68.

Wang, Y., & Li, Z. (2018). Authenticity as a mediator of the relationship between power contingent self-esteem and subjective well-being. *Frontiers in Psychology, 9*, 1066. https://doi.org/10.3389/fpsyg.2018.01066

Zhang, G., Chan, A., Zhong, J., & Yu, X. (2016). Creativity and social alienation: The costs of being creative. *The International Journal of Human Resource Management, 27*(12), 1252–1276. https://doi.org/10.1080/09585192.2015.1072107

Zhang, C., Zhou, J., Dik, B. J., & You, X. (2021). Reciprocal relation between authenticity and career decision self-efficacy: A longitudinal study. *Journal of Career Development, 48*(5), 607–618. https://doi.org/10.1177/0894845319884641

CHAPTER 32

Reducing the Barriers to Flow Experience Through Development of Consciousness

Anil K. Maheshwari, Deeppa Ravindran, Mohan Gurubatham, and Nupur Maheshwari

INTRODUCTION

A VUCA (Volatile, Uncertain, Complex, and Ambiguous) era requires ways for improving well-being and effectiveness (Maheshwari et al., 2022; Nandram & Bindlish, 2017). The flow experience is a state of optimal performance with a balance of skill and challenge, that often leads to peak experience and a sense of great accomplishment (Csikszentmihalyi, 1991; Kotler, 2021). Flow experiences have prerequisites in terms of unambiguous task requirements, mastery of craft, and a basic equivalence between task challenge and skill level. Flow experiences are often experienced in autotelic activities, where the activity is highly practiced and is inspiring. Csikszentmihalyi (2020) associated flow with states of self-actualization, intrinsic motivation, and play. Flow has been related closely with other ways for human flourishing such as positive psychology (Seligman & Csikszentmihalyi, 2000), work engagement (De

---

A. K. Maheshwari (✉)
Maharishi International University, Fairfield, IA, USA
e-mail: akmaheshwari@miu.edu

D. Ravindran
Kuala Lumpur, Malaysia

M. Gurubatham
Department of Psychology, HELP University, Kuala Lumpur, Malaysia

N. Maheshwari
Fairfield, IA, USA

© The Author(s), under exclusive license to Springer Nature Switzerland AG 2023
J. Marques (ed.), *The Palgrave Handbook of Fulfillment, Wellness, and Personal Growth at Work*,
https://doi.org/10.1007/978-3-031-35494-6_32

Fraga & Moneta, 2016), synchronicity (Nelson-Isaacs, 2019), and well-being (Bryce & Haworth, 2002).

Higher states of consciousness (Maheshwari, 2021, 2023) are based on refinement of the nervous system to support inner silence, and associated with freedom from stress, heightened creativity, fluid thinking, and effortless action. Regular practice of Transcendence using a technique such as Transcendental Meditation can help in getting firmly established in higher states of consciousness, which lead to enlightenment, lower stress, greater health, and creating more frequent experiences of creativity and effortlessness (Goldstein et al., 2018; So & Orme-Johnson, 2001; Valosek et al., 2018). Could the experience of flow be facilitated by developing and operating from higher states of consciousness? We present an empirical study that shows that development of higher states of consciousness may lower the barriers to having frequent and deeper flow experiences. This may help leaders and managers to potentially experience more flow states through transcending toward higher states of consciousness.

THE FLOW EXPERIENCE

Flow is a state of immersion in the task at hand, with great progress and productivity (Csikszentmihalyi, 1991). It is often also known as being 'in the zone' of smooth and effortless performance. Csikszentmihalyi (1991, 2020) said that the choice of the word 'flow' implied being carried effortlessly by a river of inner energy or consciousness. One feels lucky, as in being in the right place at the right time. Csikszentmihalyi (2020) contended that the condition of flow is central to accomplishment of life goals, and that one wants to experience flow again and again. Desire for repeated experience of flow may thus be central to human motivation and achievement. Pearson (2016) reports on historical figures who have fathomed ineffable flow experiences including Laozi, the Buddha, Rumi, Meister Eckhart, and many others.

Characteristics of Flow

The flow experience is reported to be a state of optimal performance, where there can be sudden insight or remarkable efficacy in activity (Csikszentmihalyi, 1991). Flow has been described as an altered state of consciousness, where the sense of space and time dissolves, and self-awareness disappears (Zausner, 2022). Bakker and van Woerkom (2017) describe flow as a short-term peak experience that is characterized by absorption, work enjoyment, and intrinsic motivation, that is positively related to job performance. Those experiencing flow often report a high level of performance and a sense of perfection (Kotler, 2021). The flow experience is a joyful experience for the experiencer even as it tends to arise unpredictably. Flow experience (Csikszentmihalyi, 2020; Kotler, 2021; Nelson-Isaacs, 2019) has garnered enormous interest as a way of creating well-being and effortless productivity.

Csikszentmihalyi (1991, 2020) used an experience sampling approach to discover the experience of flow. He discovered that for a flow experience to arise, there were certain essential prerequisites. (1) The task requirements should be unambiguously specified, (2) the experiencer should have developed a mastery of craft, and (3) there should be a close balance between the task challenge and the skill level. Csikszentmihalyi (1991) lists many additional characteristics of flow experience. The performer should have intrinsic motivation, be completely concentrated on the task, and receive immediate unambiguous feedback. Flow also produces an experience of timelessness with ease and effortlessness in action. In flow, paradoxically, one may feel a sense of control by losing self-consciousness and any worries about success. Kotler (2021) recommended that the sweet spot for flow experience is 90–120 minutes of uninterrupted concentration activity. This should be followed by returning to the present moment with gratitude.

The choice of task is important for flow to occur. Flow is often seen to occur in well-defined tasks with defined boundaries, such as playing a musical instrument, competing in a sport, or leading a seminar. Such activities allow a world-class practitioner to perform and improvise without strain and struggle, thus providing the ingredients for flow to occur (Harung & Travis, 2018). There is a complete focus on the task at hand and leaving no room for irrelevant information. For example, Kang (2023) reports that music teachers' flow experiences present different characteristics in two related but different sets of tasks, one found in performance and the other in teaching. Music teachers cited topics pertaining to challenge, skills, absorption, enjoyment, and flow disruption, when describing flow in performance. In contrast, they cited topics pertaining to feedback, goal clarity, and group flow when describing flow in teaching.

Dietrich (2003) found that altered states of consciousness such as flow are associated with decreased activity in the prefrontal cortex, which is the CEO part of the brain responsible for higher-order cognitive functions such as self-reflection, memory, temporal integration, and working memory. In a state of flow, this area is believed to down-regulate which may trigger the feelings of loss of self-consciousness and the awareness of time. Dietrich (2004) posits that the flow state is a period during which a highly practiced skill that is based on the implicit knowledge base is implemented without interference from the active thinking system.

Conditions for Flow

Csikszentmihalyi (1988) credited Carl Jung with the idea that psychic energy is finite and thus there would be a limit to how long the flow states would last. Csikszentmihalyi (1991, 2020) described why there needs to be a clear alignment of skill and challenge. Too high a challenge creates stress, and too much skill vis-à-vis challenge tends to create boredom. Behavioral strategies that may facilitate flow fall into three main categories around the person, the task, and the skill level.

Personal Sense of Agency: Self-referral leadership implies self-direction at work, eliminating work that does not serve their purpose (Bakker & van Woerkom, 2017). It also implies a sense of agency in accomplishing the task. Autonomy or self-determination at work (Deci & Ryan, 1995) may facilitate flow experience. Salanova et al. (2006) found that personal resources (i.e., self-efficacy beliefs) and organizational resources (including social support climate and clear goals) facilitate work-related flow (work absorption, work enjoyment, and intrinsic work motivation). Being curious and having passion and purpose connects the doer with their activity and thus a high level of concentration is possible, without distractions.

Work Design: This involves amending job requirements and environment so that work is more rewarding and satisfying (Bakker & van Woerkom, 2017). Playful work design can foster amusement and even entertainment (Nachmanovitch, 1991). Kotler (2021) found that making a clear goals list and checking off all completed items on one's list tends to create a sense of progress and induces flow (Amabile & Kramer, 2011). Interruptions and disruptions, on the other hand, are attention-robbers, and a great hindrance to flow (Nakamura & Csikszentmihalyi, 2009). A pile of unfinished tasks also tends to obstruct flow (Peifer et al., 2020).

Skill level: The person should be aware of one's strengths and be playing to them (Bakker & van Woerkom, 2017). Koehn et al. (2013) demonstrated positive associations between the ability to visualize the task prior to its performance and the inducement of a flow state. Flowing together as a team can bring greater sense of total skill and be more enjoyable (Walker, 2010).

DEVELOPMENT OF CONSCIOUSNESS

Consciousness is primary and is the basis of all experience (Maharishi Mahesh Yogi, 1966). Throughout history, there have been sages and saints who have expounded upon the importance of this experience. In the *Bhagavad Gita* (2:48), Lord Krishna advises Arjuna to be 'Established in yoga, and then perform action' (Maharishi Mahesh Yogi, 1967). The *Bhagavad Gita* thus exhorts us to establish our awareness in the field of the Self, pure consciousness, and then act from that elevated state with coherence, balance, peace, and living harmoniously with nature.

Human beings can experience many states of consciousness. Waking state is the normal state of consciousness that one experiences when one is awake and engaged in daily activities. Sleeping state is the state of consciousness that one experiences when asleep. Dreaming is the state of consciousness that one experiences during REM sleep, when one has vivid dreams. There is a fourth and higher state of consciousness called Transcendental Consciousness (TC).

Maharishi Mahesh Yogi (1978, p. 383) claims that 'The transcendent (fourth state) is the absolute, non-changing, non-variable, eternal, infinite,

Table 32.1 States of consciousness

State of consciousness	Self-Awareness	Content of experience
Sleep state	None	None
Dream state	None	Illusory
Waking	Individual ego (lower self)	Perceptions, thoughts, feelings
Transcendental consciousness	Unbounded pure consciousness (higher self)	None
Cosmic consciousness	Unbounded pure consciousness (higher self)	Perceptions, thoughts, feelings
Refined cosmic consciousness	Unbounded pure consciousness (higher self)	Finest relative perceptions of infinite correlations in everything
Unity consciousness or Brahman consciousness	Unbounded pure consciousness (higher self)	Fluctuations within pure consciousness '…all things in terms of the Self'

Source Maheshwari (2021, 2023)

unboundedness of life—which is the inner core of everyone's life.' The experience of TC has been recognized in ancient Vedic literature, such as the *Bhagavad Gita*. When Consciousness is left free to experience itself, that is transcendence. The intellect becomes aware of itself through transcending itself. By direct unmediated experience one can realize the true self as beyond time and form, beyond thoughts and objects. TC has also been characterized by a state of restful alertness (Wallace, 1970, 1993), which is physiologically described by high EEG coherence in the Alpha 1 (8–10 hz) range, and by reduced respiration and oxygen consumption Travis et al. (2009). During TC, the mind becomes more peaceful, relaxed, efficient, and wakeful (Harung & Travis, 2018).

Beyond TC, the next higher state is cosmic consciousness (CC), when the absolute inner silence of TC is accessible even during waking state. Enhanced cosmic consciousness is a state of finest perception, where there is barely any distinction between the outer and inner reality. The highest state of Unity Consciousness is a state of unified perception, where everything is perceived as a reverberation of one's own Self. This is the state that is reported by seers and sages as the ultimate state of oneness (Maharishi Mahesh Yogi, 1978). The seven states are described in terms of awareness of Self and the world in Table 32.1.

V-theory of Transcendence

Maheshwari (2021, 2023) presents V-theory as a simple and flexible framework for how one could transcend surface reality and develop their consciousness to higher levels of pure consciousness or TC. V-theory shows that the

Fig. 32.1 V-theory: A 2-step model of transcendence

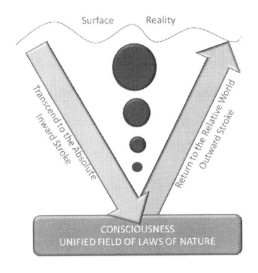

universe can be alternately experienced at two different levels: in its dynamic diversity of impulses of the ego at the top of the V, and its silent transcendental unity at the bottom of the V (Fig. 32.1).

The upper level is the level of diverse dynamic action. The bottom level is the level of the transcendent, the source of pure potential. The path to understanding and participating in the continuous transformation of the world at the top of the V is through experiencing the silent unity at the bottom of the V. The first step is to choose a path or practice to transcend surface reality and connect with the pure consciousness at the bottom of the V. It is called the inward stroke. Staying for a certain period at the bottom of the V helps in bringing deep rest and energy to the mind. The second step of the V is to return to the dynamic surface reality. This is called the outward stroke. One recognizes that multiple transcending practices may be considered in the context of a simple 2-step V-model of an inward and outward stroke. Transcendence can be achieved effectively through Transcendental Meditation (TM) (Travis & Shear, 2010). Other approaches from other traditions of transcendence too could be conceived through V-theory with the premise that the Consciousness at the bottom of the V is primary, self-referral, and independent of matter.

Almost all spiritual traditions prescribe their own means of transcending (Wilber, 2000). Some suggest prayer and devotion as a way of reaching God. Others suggest sacred practices to cleanse oneself and reach the transcendent state. There are many meditation techniques from Eastern traditions including Vedic, Buddhist, Chinese, Zen, and others. Some meditations are premised on there being an ultimate reality, for example Vedic meditations. Regular practice of TM technique by college students has been shown to lead to higher brain integration score, which is indicative of lower stress and higher creativity

(Travis et al., 2009). Once the student develops higher creative capacity, they can naturally grow their knowledge organically and holistically, with the least amount of effort and a great sense of accomplishment and fulfillment (Travis, 1979). The way to enhance integrative learning is thus to enliven the student's own consciousness.

Transcendental Meditation (TM) is a standardized and well-researched practice to experience consciousness in its pure form (Maharishi Mahesh Yogi, 1966). It is a simple mental technique practiced twice a day for twenty-minute sessions. The experience involves exploring finer states of thought until the mind transcends, and is left in its simplest state of pure consciousness itself. Regular practice of TM enables the inner experience of silence to be enjoyed and integrated into activity eventually becoming established as an all-time higher state of consciousness (Wallace, 1993). Regular practice of Transcendence using a technique such as TM can help in getting firmly established in higher states of consciousness, enlightenment, and more frequent experiences of creativity and effortlessness (Alexander et al., 1993; So & Orme-Johnson, 2001). In a recent study of eighty-one women in Uganda, Goldstein et al. (2018) found that practice of TM led to significant improvement in self-efficacy, perceived stress, and quality of life. Valosek et al. (2018) similarly found that the benefits of TM for ninety-six central office staff at the San Francisco Unified School District included significant improvement in emotional intelligence and decrease in perceived stress. With continued regular practice of TM and more advanced practices, a further higher state may be gained, which is called Cosmic Consciousness (CC). This can be a permanent state, which could be akin to being in flow all the time. This is the state of Nirvana described by Lord Buddha (Pearson, 2016). One can reach an even higher state of unity consciousness where everything is perceived as impulses in one's own unbounded awareness. This is full enlightenment or life in ultimate fulfillment (Maharishi Mahesh Yogi, 1966).

Comparing Flow Experience and Higher States of Consciousness

We model flow and higher states of consciousness at three different levels—of task/action, body/mind/ego, and fundamental reality—to map their commonalities and differences. Figure 32.2 shows a three-level model comparing Flow and Consciousness.

At the level of task and action, Flow requires an appropriate level of skill-challenge balance. Flow experience normally occurs on highly practiced tasks that are autotelic in nature. Higher states of consciousness open the awareness to the wider canvas and can support the entire range of tasks including those that require broader comprehension and challenges. This may be a key difference that will be tested empirically.

At the level of the body/mind/ego, both approaches may lead to loss of awareness of one's own self and time. The reason for loss in case of flow is the

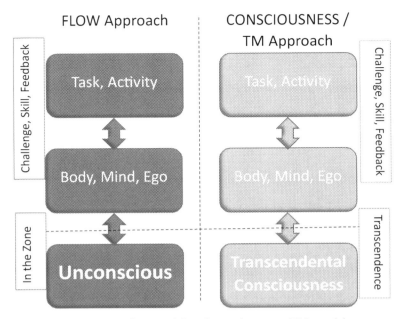

Fig. 32.2 Comparing the flow model and consciousness/TM models

functioning from the implicit mind without any interruptions or distractions. In higher states of consciousness, the loss of awareness and time arises because of the experience of unity or oneness with the whole universe.

At the level of ultimate reality, the flow experience relies on the Jungian notion of the unconscious as the source of psychic energy that feeds the flow experience and helps in creating the effortless experience. The Consciousness approach considers Unity Consciousness as the ultimate reality which can be achieved by systematic regular practice of techniques of transcendence, such as TM. Table 32.2 discusses the similarities between Flow and Higher States of Consciousness in greater detail.

However, there are some key differences and they are shown in Table 32.3.

Higher States of Consciousness Facilitating Flow Experience

Csikszentmihalyi (2020) identified three additional states for flow to occur: self-actualization, intrinsic motivation, and play. In higher states of consciousness, Maslow's (1943) theory of self-realization is achieved, motivation is self-referential (Deci & Ryan, 1995), and everything can become play (Nachmanovitch, 1991). Developing a higher state of consciousness thus may potentially help with fulfilling all three strategies for a frequent flow experience.

Table 32.2 Similarities between flow and higher states of consciousness

	Dimension	Flow	Higher states of consciousness
1	Challenge and skill	The task should not be too easy for a person to feel bored, but at the same time, it should not be difficult	There is a feeling of effortlessness where one is not feeling bored or stressful. In higher states of consciousness, the Self witnesses activity and non-activity
2	Activity and awareness merge	When a person's activity and awareness merge, a person feels as if action is automatic; they do not have to think about it	In cosmic consciousness, activity springs forth naturally (Ho & Heaton, 2023). In unity consciousness, oneness permeates one's entire being
3	Timelessness	A person loses track of time	The experience of the Self is beyond time and space (Droit-Volet & Dambrun, 2019)
4	Loss of self-consciousness	There is a sense of immenseness during activity where the object and the self is one and cannot be distinguished	In higher states of consciousness, the nervous system always has self-awareness
5	Effortlessness	One experiences a sense of effortlessness and spontaneity	Higher states produce conditions of inner silence, bliss, and 'effortless effort'
6	Sense of control	The person feels a sense of control. They are not stressed about the outcome of the situation, nor are they worried about failure	Self is beyond worry, and awareness is beyond duality, in a state of undivided continuum beyond time and space
7	An autotelic experience	There is a feeling of pleasure while doing something that one truly enjoys	In higher states, inner bliss is a continuum, even when one needs to plan and consider outcomes

Maharishi Mahesh Yogi (1975, 1995) described five fundamentals of progress in life as: Stability, Adaptability, Integration, Purification, and Growth. Table 32.4 shows how fundamentals of progress can be achieved through Flow state and higher states of consciousness.

Harung and Travis (2018) reported that top athletes, top managers, and world-class musicians all scored high on Brain Integration Scale (Travis et al. 2009), which indicates that the brain is more coherent, is wakeful, and is efficient. Top managers scored high on moral reasoning. Challenges and turbulence abound in businesses, however. In higher states of consciousness, one can maintain field independence and an internal state of unbounded awareness regardless of the external circumstances in life (Gurubatham, 2023).

Table 32.3 Differences between flow and higher states of consciousness

	Dimension	Flow	Higher states of consciousness
1	Clarity of goals	The person would have clear goals and know exactly what they would like to achieve	In inner silence, there is spontaneity in terms of selecting goals; ambiguity is not a problem as one has cultivated the acceptance of coexistence of opposites
2	Unambiguous feedback	Feedback that is received during the activity should be unambiguous, that lets the person in flow know how well they are doing	While experiencing inner silence, the self does not pass judgments on the experience itself. The nervous system is cultured to maintain inner silence amid any circumstance or feedback
3	Duration of the experience	Flow is experienced sporadically and temporarily (in periods of approximately 90–120 minutes), as psychic energy is depleted	Silence in action is independent of external conditions or stimuli. The experience of higher states is permanent, when fully developed
4	Physiological response	The prefrontal cortex is shut down. There are higher skin galvanic responses in the flow, which is an indication of arousal	In CC and higher, brain is highly integrated with alpha-1 waveforms showing coherent brain functioning at all times
5	Psychic response	Focus and concentration requires the use of psychic energy to elicit flow. The self has a limited amount of psychic energy, as an individual cannot focus for long	Once higher states become permanent, that inner silence in action can be a living reality
6	Nature of self	The self is described in terms of thoughts, feelings, and emotions. There is resemblance to the experience of spontaneity, naturalness, effortlessness, and joy	The Self is described as a witness that is the blissful, peaceful, unmanifest, non-dual source of thought, and the field of pure consciousness

Empirical Study of Effect of Higher States of Consciousness on Flow Experiences

This study was conducted by one of the authors, Deeppa Ravindran, to compare flow experience and development of higher states of consciousness. Flow experience was compared among non-TM practitioners and TM practitioners, during the performance of their favorite (autotelic) activity or hobby. It is a qualitative study that employs semi-structured interviews to allow flexibility to probe into participants' own subjective flow experience as they are the experts of their own experience.

Participants were selected based on having an autotelic activity. Autotelic means an activity or any creative work or play that is enjoyed for its own

Table 32.4 Fundamentals of progress related to flow experience and higher states of consciousness

Fundamentals of progress	Flow experience	Transcendence to higher states of consciousness
Stability	Mastery of craft, sport, vocation, or avocation, stable knowledge and/or muscle memory is a pre-requisite for the flow experience. There must be an equivalence of challenge to skill. World-class musicians, athletes, and top managers score high on Brain Integration scale (Harung & Travis, 2018)	In higher states the individual experiences unbounded awareness, beyond time and space. The nervous system is more stable (field independence) and one's consciousness is more self-referential. One grows in internal stability during change. Harung and Travis (2018) reported on high levels of Brain Integration scale where the brain is more relaxed, wakeful, and efficient
Adaptability	Within a stable framework, one can play and adapt to changing circumstances. One feels invincible	Higher states develop creativity, fluid intelligence, field independence, mental efficiency, practical intelligence, and emotional intelligence
Integration	The flow experience is an expression of an integrated body/mind condition. Top managers, athletes, and musicians score high on Travis' Brain Integration Scale	Higher states infuse and integrate unbounded awareness of pure consciousness into waking, dreaming, and sleep states of consciousness
Purification	To have the flow experience, one needs to be one-pointed and not distracted. Top athletes, musicians, artists, actors, and leaders all know this and value time	Higher states dissolve deeply rooted stress, thereby enabling a fuller expression of one's full potential
Growth	The flow experience challenges one to grow and accelerates growth, self-efficacy, and enjoyment	Growth to higher states of consciousness leads to ego development and maturity

sake. None of the respondents practiced TM at that time. In all, 75 college student subjects were invited to fill out a structured questionnaire about their hobbies or favorite activities. 31 of them filled in the survey, and reported on their various hobbies which included running, playing music, public speaking, practicing yoga, designing software, creating artwork, writing, baking, and dancing. All of them reported to be engaged in their hobbies because they truly enjoyed them regardless of monetary rewards. From this pool of 31, 16 participants were selected for the interview process. Eight of them had learned and practiced TM while the other eight did not practice TM (but may have practiced other techniques or nothing at all). The final interview sample included twelve females and four males between the ages of 22 and

Table 32.5 Flow dimensions coded for all interviews (8 TMers and 8 non-TMers)

Sl No	Flow themes	# of participants reporting the theme	
		Non-TMers	TMers
1	Balance of challenge and skills	8	8
2	Clarity of goals	6	4
3	Unambiguous feedback	8	4
4	Activity and awareness merge	8	8
5	Timelessness	8	8
6	Loss of self-consciousness	6	6
7	Sense of control	8	8
8	Effortlessness	8	8
9	Autotelic experience	8	8
10	Experience of inner silence	3	8
11	Glimpsing cosmic consciousness	1	4
12	Glimpsing unity consciousness	3	4

50 years. The interviews were semi-structured based on about 20 questions, and lasted about 40 minutes each. In addition, the researcher was open to any other themes beyond the conceptualized theoretical framework that may be experienced by the participants.

The interview scripts were transcribed and coded by the researcher. General themes and codes were based on the characteristics of flow described by Csikszentmihalyi (1991), combined with components from characteristics of higher states of consciousness (Maheshwari, 2021). The overall themes and codes are shown in Table 32.5. Each interview was coded to show whether a flow theme was reported in the interview or not. Table 32.5 shows the number of people that reported experiencing that particular theme in the flow state, by TMers and non-TMers.

Data Interpretation

There were similarities and differences on approximately an equal number of theme by those that practiced TM and those that did not. In 7 of out of 12 dimensions of flow and higher states of consciousness, there was no difference between TMers and non-TMers. All the subjects reported challenge-skill balance, merging of self and activity, loss of awareness of time, loss of awareness of self, effortlessness, sense of control, and autotelic experience.

In 2 of the 9 dimensions of flow—having clear goals, and unambiguous feedback (shaded in Table 32.5)—more non-TMers reported these experiences than TMers. Csikszentmihalyi (2020) emphasized having clear goals and unambiguous feedback as two of the most important requirements for flow experience to occur. Higher states of consciousness may thus facilitate a flow state even in the absence of those two strong prerequisites.

In the 3 dimensions of glimpses of higher states of consciousness (shaded in Table 32.5), fewer non-TMers reported such states than TMers. Most notably, the experience of inner silence was described by all TM practicing participants, but by only 3 of the non-TMers. This may be a direct result of the regular practice of TM (Alexander et al., 1993). Similarly, glimpses of higher states of consciousness were also reported by more TMers than non-TMers.

Here below are some excerpts from the interview scripts.

1. *Clarity of Goals*: A non-TMer yoga practitioner had flexibility as the main goal, and reported: 'While I am in the [yoga position] I want to be flexible and be able to do the pose well and my other goal is to reduce the pain in my shoulders.' One TMer was without a specific goal and said: 'I do not think about what I want to paint. My artwork is spontaneous, what I want to paint at that moment comes automatically. I do not have to do anything; it's automatic.'
2. *Unambiguous Feedback*: A non-TMer experiencing Flow said: 'While playing the piano I know if I have made a mistake. I quickly play a new set of notes so that the song would be more melodious.'
3. *No awareness and concern about their level of performance*: A TMer stated that: 'During the course of writing, I had no concern about my writing. Only after I have finished, I would excitedly read what I have written and then I would find pleasure.'
4. *Merging of action and awareness*: A non-TMer artist said: 'I can't force my inspiration; if I force it I will lose it [inspiration]. The inspiration is from the outside, like the universe or God. Something just pops into my head, and I do it. There is a lot of spontaneity while painting. The task requires *effort* in holding the brush sometimes, but it is not difficult.' A TMer shared his experience while playing computer games: 'I feel that when I am playing the game, it is Silence... While playing there is no stress, I do not worry about a single thing... Silence does not require effort. I can go into silence easily while playing the game.'
5. *No Awareness of the Self*: A non-TMer artist mentioned that: 'I feel like I am a vessel channeling inspiration and ideas from the universe. It is something from the universe... it feels like pleasure... sometimes joy ...I feel that my persona is merged with the painting... the painting is really me...it is my image.'
6. *No Awareness of time*: The TMer pianist stated that after TM she feels: 'refreshed and clear in my mind. I feel light as if all my pressure and stress is released.'
7. *Inner silence* or restful alertness: One non-TMer said that: 'I find silence in prayer, while I am talking to God. I also experience silence when I am thinking and reflective about events of the day, the meaning of life and who I am.' Another non-TMer reported feeling of inner

silence while playing video games: 'I feel a sense of detachment from the world. While playing my game, I do not worry about anything as there is silence...no stress... this is a place for me. The silence [the Self] helps me to concentrate.' A TMer described: 'I feel silence and a sense of peace. Inside my heart is peaceful, while there I have no thoughts...there are soft images, but it doesn't not affect me...after I get deeper into the meditation I have experienced no thought.' One practitioner of a non-TM, stated that: 'As I am meditating...I go deeper within myself...I feel as if there is a tunnel... where I go deeper into myself. I experience no thoughts...this lasts a few minutes.'

8. *Glimpsing Cosmic Consciousness during sleep*: all participants reported being aware that they were as if in a dream. A representative example was: 'When I have a bad dream, I feel like I am in a television shows, I would feel really sad ...I would tell myself that I am in a bad dream.' A TMer described witnessing during sleeping (being aware of the Self): 'While I am sleeping, I am witnessing the Self. I witnessed...I know that this is a dream... I also experience "silence" during sleep.'

9. *Glimpsing Cosmic Consciousness during activity*: One TMer experienced silence while painting and doing other daily activities: 'In my daily life, when I am doing my cooking, painting and any repeated activity I experience witnessing silence. I feel a sense of actually witnessing that I am painting, picking the color... I feel coherent within me...I am experiencing witnessing the process of painting.'

10. *Glimpsing Refined Cosmic Consciousness*: One non-TMer experienced oneness while painting and another found that musical notes came from a source outside her while composing music. Another said: 'When I am walking (in a park) and I see a lot of trees, I know that I am organic...I am part of nature...at the organic level I know that.... I am the same as them [the trees].'

11. *Glimpsing Unity Consciousness*: A TMer said: 'When I was in silence... I was detached from my thoughts... I am part of the system [everything that exists]. I am not important as I am part of everything.' Another TMer stated that: 'When you get silence...you and the entire environment, the stone, the bird... Are all part of the environment.'

12. *Reduction of Stress Levels*: A mother of two said: 'I used to get so angry when my son is naughty and behaves badly...but after TM, I do not get as angry as before, now I am calmer.'

Discussion and Future Directions

In a VUCA (Volatile, Uncertain, Complex, and Ambiguous) world where pandemics, wars, climate change, and other grand challenges stress the mind, there is great interest in creating well-being for a stressed workforce through expansion of consciousness of the workforce (Maheshwari et al., 2022). In our study, significantly fewer TM practitioners than non-TMers reported the need for clarity of task. This helps manage *Uncertainty* in the VUCA environment where the goals and tasks are not always clear. Fewer TM practitioners than non-TMers reported the need for unambiguous feedback. This helps manage the *Ambiguity* in situations where the interpretations are not always clear. This suggests that development of higher states of consciousness may help with lowering the requirements for achieving flow state by mitigating the impact of *Uncertainty* and *Ambiguity* aspects in the VUCA environment. Our study elicited experiences of flow with a variety of practitioners in different environments to generate new insights. However, this was an exploratory study that suggests avenues that merit further research. It could lead to further studies that examine the relationships with larger sample sizes. This encourages further research to understand how development into higher states of consciousness can help increase flow frequency and intensity.

More organizations should study these benefits and consider adopting the practices of transcendence (such as TM) for creating a favorable work environment where everyone can experience flow while performing a wide variety of tasks such as creative activities. Research questions could include what kind of flow experiences would happen in the organization if an entire management team were experiencing deep purposefulness because of higher states of consciousness (Nader & Maheshwari, 2023). Perhaps life would flow in enjoyment, creativity, and purpose. One can imagine an entire organization flowing together in harmony and effectiveness. The five fundamentals of progress would be so well developed that the leaders would be both stable and highly adaptable to environmental changes and integrate new ideas to grow their business in a healthy way.

REFERENCES

Alexander, C. N., Swanson, G. C., Rainforth, M. V., Carlisle, T. W., Todd, C. C., & Oates, R. (1993). Effects of the Transcendental Meditation program on stress-reduction, health, and employee development: A prospective study in two occupational settings. *Anxiety, Stress, and Coping, 6*, 245–262.

Amabile, T., & Kramer, S. (2011). *The progress principle: Using small wins to ignite joy, engagement, and creativity at work.* Harvard Business Press.

Bakker, A. B., & van Woerkom, M. (2017). Flow at work: A self-determination perspective. *Occupational Health Science, 1*(1), 47–65.

Bryce, J., & Haworth, J. (2002). Wellbeing and flow in sample of male and female office workers. *Leisure Studies, 21*(3–4), 249–263.

Csikszentmihalyi, M. (1988). Motivation and creativity: Toward a synthesis of structural and energistic approaches to cognition. *New Ideas in Psychology, 6*(2), 159–176.

Csikszentmihalyi, M. (1991). *Flow: The psychology of optimal experience.* Harper Perennial.

Csikszentmihalyi, M. (2020). *Finding flow: The psychology of engagement with everyday life.* Hachette UK.

Deci, E. L., & Ryan, R. M. (1995). Human autonomy. In *Efficacy, agency, and self-esteem* (pp. 31–49). Springer.

De Fraga, D., & Moneta, G. B. (2016). Flow at work as a moderator of the self-determination model of work engagement. In *Flow experience: Empirical research and applications* (pp. 105–123).

Dietrich, A. (2003). Functional neuroanatomy of altered states of consciousness: The transient hypofrontality hypothesis. *Consciousness and Cognition, 12*(2), 231–256.

Dietrich, A. (2004). Neurocognitive mechanisms underlying the experience of flow. *Consciousness and Cognition, 13*(4), 746–761.

Droit-Volet, S., & Dambrun, M. (2019). Awareness of the passage of time and self-consciousness: What do meditators report? *PsyCh Journal, 8*(1), 51–65.

Goldstein, L., Nidich, S., Goodman, R., & Goodman, D. (2018). The effect of Transcendental Meditation on self-efficacy, perceived stress, and quality of life in mothers in Uganda. *Health Care for Women International, 39*(5), 1–24.

Gurubatham, M. R. (2023). Fluid intelligence for higher order thinking: Balancing the subjective and objective for sustaining impactful wisdom in this era of disruption. In A. K. Maheshwari (Eds.), *Consciousness-based leadership and management, Volume 2: Organizational and cultural approaches to oneness and flourishing*. Palgrave-Macmillan.

Harung, H. S., & Travis, F. (2018). *World-class brain*. Brain Integration Systems, LLV.

Ho, J., & Heaton, D. (2023). Dao and management: A consciousness-based understanding. In A. K. Maheshwari (Ed.), *Consciousness-Based Leadership and Management: Vedic and Other Philosophical Approaches to Oneness and Flourishing (Vol. 1)*. Palgrave-Macmillan.

Kang, S. (2023). An exploratory study of music teachers' flow experiences between performing and teaching music. *Journal of Research in Music Education, [s. l.], 70*(4), 407–424.

Koehn, S., Morris, T., & Watt, A. P. (2013). Flow state in self-paced and externally-paced performance contexts: An examination of the flow model. *Psychology of Sport & Exercise, 14*(6), 787–795.

Kotler, S. K. (2021). *The art of impossible: A peak performance primer*. HarperCollins.

Maharishi Mahesh Yogi. (1966). *The science of being and art of living*. MIU Press.

Maharishi Mahesh Yogi. (1967). *Maharishi Mahesh Yogi on the Bhagavad-Gita: A new translation and commentary, Chapters 1–6*. International SRM Publications.

Maharishi Mahesh Yogi and World Plan Executive Council. (1975). *Fundamentals of progress, scientific research on the Transcendental Meditation Program to develop the full potential of the individual*. World Plan Executive Council.

Maharishi Mahesh Yogi. (1978). *Enlightenment to every individual: Invincibility to every nation*. MIU Press.

Maharishi Mahesh Yogi. (1995). *Maharishi university of management: Wholeness on the move*. Maharishi Prakshan.

Maslow, A. (1943). A theory of human motivation. *Psychological Review, 50*(4), 370–396.

Maheshwari, A. K. (2021). Higher consciousness management: Transcendence for spontaneous right action. *Journal of Management, Spirituality & Religion, 18*(6), 77–91.

Maheshwari, A. K. (2023). Introduction to consciousness-based leadership and management. In A. K. Maheshwari (Eds.), *Consciousness-based leadership and management, Volume 1: Vedic and other philosophical approaches to oneness and flourishing*. Palgrave-Macmillan.

Maheshwari, A. K., Werd, M. R. P., Travis, F., Rainforth, M., & Lipman, J. (2022). Workplace well-being: An experimental investigation into benefits of consciousness-based architecture. *Journal of Management, Spirituality & Religion, 19*(1), 73–92.

Nachmanovitch, S. (1991). *Free play: Improvisation in life and art*. Penguin.

Nader, T., & Maheshwari, A. K. (2023). Consciousness as the source of purposeful leadership. In A. K. Maheshwari (Eds.), *Consciousness-based leadership and management, Volume 1: Vedic and other philosophical approaches to oneness and flourishing*. Palgrave-Macmillan.

Nakamura, J., & Csikszentmihalyi, M. (2009). Flow theory and research. In C. R. Snyder & S. J. Lopez (Eds.), *Handbook of positive psychology* (pp. 195–206).

Nandram, S. S., & Bindlish, P. K. (2017). *Managing VUCA through integrative self-management* (p. 338). Springer.

Nelson-Isaacs, S. (2019). *Living in flow: The science of synchronicity and how your choices shape your world*. North Atlantic Books

Pearson, C. (2016). *The supreme awakening: Experiences of enlightenment throughout time and how you can cultivate them*. Maharishi University of Management Press.

Peifer, C., Syrek, C., Ostwald, V., Schuh, E., & Antoni, C. H. (2020). Thieves of flow: How unfinished tasks at work are related to flow experience and wellbeing. *Journal of Happiness Studies, 21*, 1641–1660.

Salanova, M., Bakker, A. B., & Llorens, S. (2006). Flow at work: Evidence for an upward spiral of personal and organizational resources. *Journal of Happiness Studies, 7*(1), 1–22.

So, K. T., & Orme-Johnson, D. (2001). Three randomized experiments on the longitudinal effects of the Transcendental Meditation technique on cognition. *Intelligence, 29*, 419–440.

Seligman, M. E., & Csikszentmihalyi, M. (2000). *Positive psychology: An introduction* (Vol. 55, No. 1, p. 5). American Psychological Association.

Travis, F. (1979). The Transcendental Meditation technique and creativity: A longitudinal study of Cornell University undergraduates. *The Journal of Creative Behavior*.

Travis, F., Haaga, D., Hagelin, J., Tanner, M., Arenander, A., Nidich, S., Gaylord-King, C., Grosswald, S., Rainforth, M., & Schneider, R. (2009). A self-referential default brain state: Patterns of coherence, power, and eLORETA sources during eyes-closed rest and Transcendental Meditation practice. *Cognitive Processing, 11*(1), 21–30.

Travis, F., & Shear, J. (2010). Focused attention, open monitoring and automatic self-transcending: Categories to organize meditations from Vedic, Buddhist and Chinese traditions. *Consciousness and Cognition, 19*(4), 1110–1118.

Valosek, L., Link, J., Mills, P., Konrad, A., Rainforth, M., & Nidich, S. (2018). Effect of meditation on emotional intelligence and perceived stress in the workplace: A randomized controlled study. *The Permanente Journal, 22*, 17–172.

Wallace, R. K. (1970). Physiological effects of transcendental meditation. *Science, 167*(3926), 1751–1754.

Wallace, R. K. (1993). *The physiology of consciousness*. Maharishi International University Press.

Walker, C. J. (2010). Experiencing flow: Is doing it together better than doing it alone? *The Journal of Positive Psychology, 5*(1), 5–11.

Wilber, K. (2000). *Integral psychology: Consciousness, spirit, psychology, therapy*. Shambhala Publications.
Zausner, T. (2022). *The creative trance: Altered states of consciousness and the creative process*. Cambridge University Press.

CHAPTER 33

Conscious Business Performance in a Global Village

Victor Senaji Anyanje and Thomas Anyanje Senaji

INTRODUCTION

Territorial boundaries are becoming murkier due to the increasingly interconnected world, new markets and preponderance of the information age. The oft seamless and borderless reach of the Internet continues to avail avenues for widespread and real-time reach of information which can be accessed by distinct audiences simultaneously for use and decision-making. This does not, however, preclude information overload, hence the need for recipients to sieve through and extract what is relevant for their needs. Notwithstanding the foregoing, organizations of all types have an imperative to perform satisfactorily in their chosen markets both domestically and across geographically dispersed global locations.

"Digital Economy" has gained traction over the last few decades thanks to the advancement in information and communication technologies with the internet as a catalyst. Electronic commerce, thanks to the Internet has for instance, also entrenched a platform for global conduct of business by stakeholders usually domiciled in different jurisdictions and who are diverse in their cultures, interests, persuasion or worldview but who must find common ground to effectively conduct business.

V. S. Anyanje · T. A. Senaji (✉)
The East African University, Nairobi, Kenya
e-mail: prof.thomas@teau.ac.ke

© The Author(s), under exclusive license to Springer Nature Switzerland AG 2023
J. Marques (ed.), *The Palgrave Handbook of Fulfillment, Wellness, and Personal Growth at Work*,
https://doi.org/10.1007/978-3-031-35494-6_33

Thus, globalization continues to obscure traditional territorial boundaries that once before delimited the scope of application of norms or normative principles across domestic territories.

The conduct of business in a global village is underpinned today by cross-boundary transactions whose common facets include the choice of law to apply in the event of a dispute between or among parties to a transaction. Yet, before formal dispute resolution channels can be invoked, best practice may favor that such parties attempt informal but effective mechanisms to resolve such disputes. To this end, businesses are presumed to have *efficient* mechanisms to address conflicts that arise, a responsibility that majorly lies with managers of these organizations whose conflict management or leadership should be up to the required standard. In terms of this efficiency, various principles come to fore as tenets of a conscious business. In this regard, transparency, impartiality, accountability, timeliness and cost efficiency feature prominently. It is therefore not in doubt that managerial competence, including their cognition, conscience, decision-making and social skills are crucial for satisfactory performance of businesses in a global environment—village. The concepts of global village, cognition and conscience are explored next as contextual variables of business followed by a discussion of conscious business performance in a global setting.

This chapter adverts that the concept of global business conscience is one necessarily subject of dynamic contextual definition characterized or influenced by prevailing societal persuasions as to what *universally acceptable* standards of business conduct command recognition and application within a global setting.

Global Village: Diversity Paradigm

The notion of "global village" implies the interconnectedness of people throughout the world partly made possible by advances in technologies including transport, telecommunications and related technologies. It also underpins the need to recognize diversity that exists across national, regional and continental boundaries and their implications for business strategy and performance of organizations in the global arena.

Business conduct today is increasingly subject to vast and varying degrees of existential norms that may or may not have the consistency or notoriety to achieve the universality sufficient to comprehensively or conclusively define *conscious* or *conscientious* business. Thus, the raw materials for conscious business performance in a global village can be thought of as including cognition, self-regulation and conscience which should essentially be enacted by all organizational members—managers and staffs of global organizations, as well as other stakeholders. However, the buck stops with managers who are charged with the responsibility of steering global businesses to prosperity.

Since the global village is underpinned by diversity and multi-level complexity, organizations need to build capability to muster this diversity and complexity to succeed. For instance, there are diverse cultures and complex political-legal systems that have important implications for the conduct of global business for which organizations should have commensurate strategy, plans, policies, tactics, as well as operational rules and procedures.

Organizations must therefore continually review or align their cultures to reflect the prevailing demands on conscious business within a borderless environment. One challenge however is to achieve universality of *standards* in an environment predominately defined by distinct and oftentimes conflicting attitudinal conviction on what yardsticks govern, among others, cross-boundary, cross-jurisdictional and cross-cultural behavior. This is a fundamental question that businesses must confront in their quest for conscious or conscientious global identity, co-existence and sustainability.

Cognition

In order to operate in a global environment, organizations need to adopt or adapt to the "global natives" disposition, which requires sensitivity to the global environment which presents diverse political, legal, economic, cultural, technological as well as concerns for the natural environment—mountains, lakes, rivers and "life on earth" comprising flora and fauna and other resources—the sustainability concerns. Since managers have the responsibility to navigate their organizations through these imperatives, their perception, interpretation, decision-making and the resulting action based on environmental cues are crucial because this determines success or failure in the global village. This is the essence of cognition—the ability to correctly sense environmental cues, process them, make sound decisions and act with the required speed according to the dynamism in the global business environment which is characterized by VUCA—Volatility, Uncertainty, Complexity and Ambiguity (Bennett & Lemoine, 2014). It is about distinguishing between important and urgent issues and acting effectively in order to achieve global business goals. The implication is that a high premium should be placed on cognitive complexity of global managers—the ability to effectively process multiple-level environmental cues and effectively manage the organizations. Further, the perception of salience by managers and employees of global businesses has important implications for success of global business operations. This is the ability to discern what is important for the success of the business and what is not. This requires a deep sense of discernment—managerial cognition (e.g., Kairu & Senaji, 2021; Stubbart, 1989)—and the accompanying cognitive complexity.

Conscience

Social Cognitive Theory, proposed by Bandura, and from which self-regulation theory derives, focuses on an individual's learning through dynamic, reciprocal and continuous interactions between the environment and themselves

(Bandura, 1998). Since strategy is about the relationship between an organization—managers and staff—and its environment on a continuous basis, this theory is suited from exampling how managers behave in the face of global business operating environment demands. According to Self-regulation Theories which "focus on the ways individuals direct the course of their development as they select and pursue goals and modify goal pursuit based on personal and environmental opportunities and constraints" (Newman & Newman, 2020, p. 213). The psychological system which informs decisions includes mental processes central to a person's ability to make meaning of experiences and take action and emotion, memory, perception, motivation, thinking and reasoning, language, symbolic abilities and one's orientation to the future are examples of psychological processes. When these processes are integrated, they provide the resources for managing information, solving problems and navigating reality (Newman & Newman, 2020). These processes contribute to individual differences in motivation, persistence, independence, ingenuity, personal goals and feelings of self-determination.

Consequently, in making decisions about their businesses, any manager or global business leader needs "to be aware". By this we mean, the capacity to anticipate the impact of decisions, actions and practices on society and exercise what may be referred to as "self-regulation" including by summoning their emotional intelligence reservoirs. More specifically, leaders of organizations need to discern the salient features in their operating environments as well as adopt appropriate regulatory focus with regard to global business imperatives comprising the macro-, micro- and organizational-level factors. This sounds easier said than it is the case in practice, where some global managers' decisions leave a sour taste in the mouths of beholders. Cases of consciously exporting unethical practices to areas of weak regulatory enforcement are not uncommon pointing to global operations devoid of conscience or rather with perverted conscience (Senaji et al., 2021).

Sustainable Performance

The era of predominantly focusing on shareholders' value consistent with Agency Theory (see Eisenhardt, 1989) though still important, has paved way for multi-stakeholder considerations of performance. Therefore, the assessment of performance becomes complex and even more so at global-level operations of businesses. This calls for a comprehensive stakeholder mapping and attention to the varying needs of the business ecosystem to avert an otherwise unconscious global business in the eyes of some key stakeholders such as environment conservation pressure groups. Hence, managerial competence in the management of stakeholder expectations depending on the value they appropriate for the business and the relative power that each stakeholder wields is paramount if not essential for a globally conscious business. Stakeholders can include customers, government, debtors, creditors, shareholders, management, employees, competitors and civil society. Consequently, the global operation should post satisfactory performance across all its stakeholders. In this regard, though the balanced score card which comprises four perspectives—financial, customer, internal processes and learning and growth (Kaplan & Norton, 2007)—is one of the frameworks that can be used to assess performance, the notion of Triple Bottom Line—Profits, People and Planet—is crucial for measuring performance of global operations; and the extent to which performance reflects these dimension is an indication of a "responsible" global business. While "profits" addresses shareholder value, "people" underpins care of the community in terms of provision of quality products and services and employment. Planet involves protection of the natural environment by reducing the use of natural resources and replenishing the environment as well as mitigating adverse climate change through reduction of greenhouse gas emissions. Indeed, there are targets for reduction of global warning to which a number of international airlines (see Air France-KLM Group, 2022) have committed in their strategies; similar initiatives are being implemented across other industries including the use of "clean energy". A further indicator of "people" dimension is diversity across culture, gender and other dimensions. This is consistent with the assertion:

> with an increasingly informed society, driven in part by the internet and the social media, sharp focus is now on how organizations are managed in terms of the critical value of soft skills, workplace diversity, change readiness, moral responsibility, and sustainability awareness. (Senaji et al., 2021, p. 250)

Conscious Business Performance

Conscious business performance implies the conduct of business in consideration of all environmental factors and related nuances necessary to realize the goals of the organization across all its stakeholders. It requires operating with "care". In our context, "care" means deliberate understanding of the needs and concerns of the society that the global business serves and acting to protect them from harm or exploitation such focusing on super profits, substandard products and degradation of the natural environment by embodying ethical conduct. A related notion is cultural awareness, cultural sensitivity and cultural competency which imply knowledge of and adaption to various cultures in the global arena while conducting business. Furthermore, cultural competency comprises both knowledge and behavior where managers act in a manner that recognizes, is sensitive to, and cares about the differences that exist among people and societies while conducting global business. Thus, though conceptually complex, conscious business performance can be viewed from the perspective of how well the disposition of business leaders in terms of their cognition and behavior is attuned to the demands of the business operating environment, leading to the formulation of strategy and execution in a manner that ensures value to stakeholders.

Moreover, at the core of business consciousness resides the *regard* for the most vulnerable segments of stakeholders that are likely to be most affected by otherwise unconscious business practices. Thus, business consciousness within the global village can or normatively should entail pursuit for or of profit that is consumer and environment cognizant. At the very basic thence, business endeavor should encompass value chains, operations and decisions that support consumer well-being and environmental sustainability. Beyond these, business decisions should also be diversity tolerant to support the wide-range inclusion of the diverse and distinct market compositions.

This behooves businesses to prioritize investment in deliberate conscientious initiatives that relax traditional profit-centric objectives such as through deliberate corporate social responsibility which, albeit voluntary, usually depict *regard*, *care* or *attention* beyond shareholder profit. Business culture should also underpin collective, participatory and tolerant discourse on the business ethos that defines internal business behavior. Oftentimes, organizational culture would determine the conduct of the business within the entire life cycle of operations until the product or service is available or utilized. Therefore, what the people within an organization perceive as the operational organizational culture will ultimately impact the end product of a given venture.

The quality of a business endeavor will as a result draw from explicit and implicit organizational culture that the members of the organization practice, infer or inculcate based on the business culture of the organization in question. Such active organizational culture can impact the business consciousness of an entity which may be dependent or independent of global business conscience that could take the form of an amalgam of accepted national business norms that attain universal or extra-territorial acclaim through consensus within the global amphitheater.

Managerial Capability for Conscience

Micro foundations of dynamic capabilities are increasingly important in the search for factors that support strategic change (Helfat & Peteraf, 2015). At the level of the individual manager, "managerial cognitive capability" is the capacity of an individual manager to perform one or more of the mental activities that comprise cognition. These mental activities should be those that are essential for the effective running of an organization in the framework of dynamics capability of a firm (Adna et al., 2020). In this regard, managerial cognitive capability:

> highlights the fact that capabilities involve the capacity to perform not only physical but also mental activities... cognitive capabilities are likely to underpin dynamic managerial capabilities for sensing, seizing, and reconfiguring, and explain their potential impact on strategic change of organizations. ... the heterogeneity of these cognitive capabilities may produce heterogeneity of

dynamic managerial capabilities among top executives, which may contribute to differential performance of organizations under conditions of change. (Helfat & Peteraf, 2015, p. 831)

The importance of managerial cognition in performance of global businesses is underscored by Maitland and Sammartino (2015) who found "substantial heterogeneity in the mental models these individuals used to make sense of the opportunity due to differences in individuals' experience along four dimensions: international breadth, depth, diversity and prior strategic decision-making" and argued,

> these cognitive processes – how individuals exercise judgment about information search parameters, assessment and decision integration, and how decision teams coalesce in their thinking – are crucial micro foundations for modeling heterogeneity in firm-level internationalization strategies and performance. (p. 733)

Elements of Conscious Business Performance

Thus, conscientious business performance goes beyond pursuit for profit to include auxiliary conduct within the value chain relating to *how* the business handles other usually human-related aspects of pre-production, production and post-transaction services such as customer support and protection of consumers against any harm that may be associated with the consumption of products and services transacted in the "global village". This extends to the interaction of the business activities with the natural environment including waste management and disposal, green economy and recovery and sustainability. Arguably, the measure of Conscious Business Performance can be said to encompass the conduct of the business within the regulatory gray areas. To wit, *how does the business operate in the unregulated space?*

If business ethics denote the morally sound options in situations of competing ethical alternatives, then business consciousness must derive from the alternative that outweighs the available options for the good of the greatest number, not just the shareholders. Hence, to pursue profit should only become a primary consideration once the business is minded that the output of their venture will not adversely affect their target end-users or consumers. From a consumer perspective therefore, Conscious Business Performance is determined by the extent to which consumer welfare prevails over pure pursuit of profit.

Primarily, business consciousness can be self-inculcated where the business *suo moto* adopts conduct deemed as conscientious or externally induced by market forces that exert pressure upon a business to conduct its affairs in a certain manner *especially* where existing regulations do not expressly govern the conduct of such businesses or business activities. An example would be an over-the-top (OTT) service where the market entrant deploys predatory tactics to capitalize on non-regulation by offering services without a license or providing services at grossly uncompetitive prices at the expense, and to the detriment of incumbents. Such practices, albeit immoral, may not necessarily be illegal more so where no law prohibits their methods as is the case in most emerging markets which are in the process of building their regulatory capacity in the digital economy. However, these practices have been fitting candidates for regulatory intervention to provide for fair market or trade practices since the temptation to exploit voids in existing legal and regulatory frameworks can be very compelling despite best intentions of business managers.

Invariably, where the notoriety of a business practice is so overtly adverse and unfair to other stakeholders within the market sufficient to instigate murmurs of resounding proportions, the regulators have in such instances been called upon to reign in and restore market sanctity as part of binding business conscious imperatives through regulations which inevitably impose involuntary consciousness applicable to all indiscriminately. This is an infusion of consciousness among otherwise unconscientious business operations.

From the foregoing, it is evident that conscientious managers are needed to lead businesses in the dynamic global business environment.

Sustainability: An Example of Conscious Global Business Conduct

Adopting a sustainability mindset is an example of conscious business operations because it is informed by the fact that any operation should have regard about the future, and not only of the organization, but of the planet as well. As part of its sustainability strategy, Air France-KLM commits to a 30% reduction per revenue ton kilometer of its well-to-wake jet fuel greenhouse gas emissions by 2030 compared to 2019, the benchmark year. These CO_2 emissions reduction targets for 2030 were approved by the Science Based Targets initiative (SBTi) which aim to ensure that Air France-KLM's decarbonization strategy is consistent with scientific objectives. The Group's strategy includes an ambitious plan to modernize and renew the fleets of Group airlines with latest generation aircraft, emitting 20–25% less carbon dioxide (CO_2) compared to their predecessors which is consistent with reduction of global warming hence mitigation of climate change and positive effort toward the sustainability of the planet for future generations (Air France-KLM Group, 2022).

The other sustainability initiatives in the area of clean transport and energy include electric vehicles, solar energy and hydropower generation installations accompanied by significant reduction in use of fossil fuels and hydrocarbons-based power generation and diesel/petrol propelled transportation vehicles. These requirements have important implications for manufactures of transportation vessels and other equipment that require various forms of energy to operate. They also call for improvement of efficiency in power consumption in the framework of sustainable production and consumption which is an important pillar of the United Nations sustainable development goals (SDGs) (SDG 12). It is noted that:

Humanity has a tendency to consume things without regard for consequences or global fairness. And this, in turn, puts a massive set of blinkers over countries and creates some jarring contrasts...basically, Goal 12 wants to create a lot more circular behavior—economies that reuse what they consume and cut down on overall production and people that think about the consequences of their daily actions. (McCarthy, 2015)

This calls for concerted effort to ensure that countries implement ultra-efficient waste management systems that do things like cutting food waste in half by 2030 and ensure that there is no pollution in waterways, air and soil. For instance, while Africa suffers great effects of climate change, it is least responsible for the emission of greenhouse gases which cause global warming hence the need for countries in the Global North to collaboratively support the continent's mitigation efforts. This inevitably includes planet conscious business operations from the Global North, and which have operations in the Global South. This sustainability consciousness is borne of managers' cognition of its salience and their managerial cognitive ability (see Helfat & Peteraf, 2015). The dimensions of salience include impact, sensitivity and interest and have been found to significantly influence competitiveness of an organization from the perspective of both efficiency, such as profit; and effectiveness as measured by innovation (see Kairu & Senaji, 2021).

In this regard, performance of organizations should be also assessed in the context of planet sustainability measures particularly in the framework of SDG 12—whether sustainable production and consumption is being implemented by measuring key performance indicators, and targets, as well as by examining how this performance is being reported by global business. In particular, the factors that managers of organizations consider as impactful, of interest and which they perceived as sensitive have implications for competitiveness of the organization (Kairu & Senaji, 2021).

Engendering Conscience—Leading from the Heart

Given the importance of conscience in the conduct of business in the global arena, the question *"Are global businesses sufficiently conscious?"* is pertinent. If the answer is not in the affirmative, then the need to engender consciousness becomes as imperative as it is urgent partly due to the fact that consumers of services and products as well as governments and civil society are increasingly discerning of how businesses operate and how they impact society.

In order to ensure conscious business performance, deliberate steps need to be taken including capacity building of businesses in cultural sensitivity, diversity, ethics, legal frameworks and tastes and preferences of communities within which operations are carried out. Further, enhancing the cognitive complexity and agility of managers and employees of global businesses is required. In other words, global competence skills are required if a global business has to perform satisfactorily. In particular, cultural sensitivity, including while operating across time zones and languages is crucial.

Pitfalls: Greed and Corruption

Challenges to conscious business performance can take various forms including cultural incompetence of, as well as greed and corruption by both managers and the global organizations they represent. Consequently, a global business operation should not fall into the trap of "one-size-fits-all" mindset particularly with regard to culture as well as other business success determinants including firm-, industry-, country-, regional- and even global-level factors. For example, failure to understand the political-legal complexities across global business destinations is a recipe for disaster. Similarly, culture differs across nations (see e.g., Hofstede, 2001) hence the need for managers posted across different nations to be trained ahead of such assignments lest they experience "culture shock" and failure in those markets.

Specifically, expatriates need this training. It is therefore necessary for global business operations to be "open to learning" in the host countries while not ignoring the businesses' objectives. This involves understanding of the policies, laws, regulations, culture—beliefs and norms as well as economic and technological factors such as levels of education and skills, demographics, etc., and incorporate this in decision-making and daily operations. This may sound obvious. However, the relative emphasis on each one of these factors determines success or failure. Furthermore, unethical and illegal behavior are areas of concern that require attention and action in the global setting.

It is also noted that reciprocity norm—a cultural disposition of "scratch my back and I scratch yours"—is related with ethical compromise (Tangpong et al., 2012) hence the need for managers to be aware and adopt appropriate behavior in destinations where reciprocity norm is prevalent. For example, overemphasis on the financial results at the expense of employee welfare or adherence to a certain minimum ethical standard, results in unsatisfactory performance or even sanctions from authorities in the host country.

State of Affairs, Reflections and Research Agenda

Performance of organizations are not sufficiently conscious going by some cases of breach of trust including corporate greed and corruption that continue to be reported in popular press. In this regard, corporate impropriety is still a problem including unethical practices in destinations with weak regulatory enforcement frameworks. Consequently, there is opportunity for the adoption of sound corporate governance, which can mitigate against some of the unconscientious global business practices.

Furthermore, there is an increasing realization of the need to engage in "conscious business" in the "global village" and that comprehensive performance management across profit, people and planet is required. Additionally, conscience and care in business is still an opportunity for global organizations to leverage for superior performance.

Based on the foregoing, some potential areas of further inquiry to generate knowledge required to enhance conscious business performance include an examination of the relationship between cognition and conscious business performance, as well as an inquiry into antecedents and consequences of conscious business performance on shareholder value or global trade.

REFERENCES

Adna, B. E., Sukoco, B. M., & Wright, L. T. (Reviewing editor). (2020). Managerial cognitive capabilities, organizational capacity for change, and performance: The moderating effect of social capital. *Cogent Business & Management, 7*, 1. https://doi.org/10.1080/23311975.2020.1843310

Air France-KLM Group. (2022, December 1). Air France-KLM CO_2 emissions reduction targets for 2030 approved by the Science Based Targets initiative (SBTi)*. *Destination Sustainability*. Retrieved April 9, 2023 from https://www.airfranceklm.com/en/newsroom/air-france-klm-co2-emissions-reduction-targets-2030-approved-science-based-targets-0

Bandura, A. (1998). Personal and collective efficacy in human adaptation and change. In J. G. Adair, D. Belanger & K. L. Dion (Eds.), *Advances in psychological science: Personal, social and cultural aspects* (Vol. 1, pp. 51–71). Psychology Press.

Bennett, N., & Lemoine, G. J. (2014, January–February). What VUCA really means for you. *Harvard Business Review*.

Eisenhardt, K. M. (1989). Agency theory: An assessment and review. *The Academy of Management Review, 14*(1), 57–74. https://doi.org/10.2307/258191

Helfat, C. E., & Peteraf, M. A. (2015). Managerial cognitive capabilities and the microfoundations of dynamic capabilities. *Strategic Management Journal, 36*(6), 831–850. http://www.jstor.org/stable/43897807

Hofstede, G. (2001). *Culture's consequences: Comparing values, behaviors, institutions and organizations across nations*. SAGE.

Kairu, J. K., & Senaji, T. A. (2021). Exploring salience as a strategic disposition in Kenya. *Advances in Social Sciences Research Journal, 8*(5). https://doi.org/10.14738/assrj.85.10159

Kaplan, R., & Norton, D. (2007). Using the balanced scorecard as a strategic management system [online]. *Harvard Business Review*. Retrieved April 9, 2023, from https://hbr.org/2007/07/using-the-balanced-scorecard-as-a-strategic-management-system

Maitland, E., & Sammartino, A. (2015). Managerial cognition and internationalization. *Journal of International Business Studies, 46*, 733–760. https://doi.org/10.1057/jibs.2015.9

McCarthy, J. (2015, September 9). *Global Goal 12: Sustainable consumption and production: Rethinking daily and global decisions*. Global Citizen. Retrieved April

11, 2023, from https://www.globalcitizen.org/en/content/global-12-sustainable-consumption-and-production/?gclid=CjwKCAjw586hBhBrEiwAQYEnHbuLp4pzwcRRlaHh17cphFFK6CqIy-uUyuK46sn4C6i41nmlXyn4AhoCr2EQAvD_BwE

Newman, B. M., & Newman, P. R. (2020). Introduction. In B. M. Newman & P. R. Newman (Eds.), *Theories of adolescent development* (pp. 113–116). Academic Press. https://doi.org/10.1016/B978-0-12-815450-2.09992-7

Senaji, T. A., Anyanje, V. S., & Anyango, J. R. (2021). Exploring business conscience. In J. Marques (Eds.), *Business with conscience: A research companion* (pp. 250–262). Routledge. https://doi.org/10.4324/9781003139461

Stubbart, C. I. (1989). Managerial cognition: A missing link in strategic management research. *Journal of Management Studies, 26*(4), 325–347.

Tangpong, C., Li, J., Hung, K.-T., & Senaji, T. (2012). The effect of reciprocity norm on ethical compromise: A cross-cultural investigation. *The 43rd Annual Meeting of the Decision Sciences Institute*, November 17–20, 2012, San Francisco, CA.

INDEX

A
absence of meaning at work, 38
adult learning, 526
anti-racism, 524, 528, 534
Arendt, H., 79–81, 87, 88
Attention Deficit Hyperactivity Disorder (ADHD), 326–328, 331
authenticity, xii, 104, 106, 185, 210, 213, 316, 589–592, 594–597, 599, 601, 602

B
BANI, 489, 490
boundaries, x, 16, 17, 130, 145, 146, 153, 154, 164, 166, 261, 294, 345, 401–415, 434, 467, 469, 470, 590, 597, 598, 609, 625–627
boundary management, x, 401, 403, 405–407, 410–416
burnout, ix, 70, 177, 221, 222, 267–269, 276, 290, 366, 377, 388, 391, 394, 395, 397, 398, 405, 409, 461, 477, 507, 516, 597

C
calling, vi, 29, 43, 47, 60, 61, 63–67, 69, 151, 185, 200, 593
caring culture, xi, 483
church, 24, 25, 27, 28, 30, 536

cognition, 499, 626, 627, 629–631, 633, 635
collaboration, v, 3, 30, 85, 104, 176, 211, 216–222, 238, 308, 346, 435, 437, 484, 489, 491, 531, 569, 570
collaborative leadership, 211, 212, 219, 222
collective growth, x, 454, 456
compassion, ix, xi, 147, 179, 210, 219, 235, 372–374, 377–379, 381, 452, 453, 531, 569, 570, 572, 578, 580, 598
compassion at work, 211, 372, 374
complexity, viii, 67, 132, 150, 187, 188, 198, 209, 212, 214, 233, 241, 242, 268, 270, 272–276, 344, 372, 380, 392, 393, 426, 487, 488, 491, 531, 534, 626, 627, 633, 634
conscience, 147, 304, 309, 310, 312, 316, 581, 626, 628, 630, 633, 635
consciousness, vii, xii, 164–167, 169, 170, 172, 177, 180, 193, 194, 196, 243, 305, 309–311, 452, 535, 536, 590, 595, 608–615, 617–621, 630–633
consciousness gap, 167, 168
corporate culture, 342, 343, 371, 381, 432, 486, 529
COVID-19, v, vii, x, 60, 84, 176, 183, 184, 198, 210, 212, 217–222, 242,

255–258, 267, 268, 270, 272–277, 324, 327, 328, 332, 388–390, 393–396, 398, 426–429, 437, 441, 447, 462, 465, 466, 468, 471, 483, 487, 497, 506, 509, 510, 523, 527, 529, 537, 544
creative-spiritual agency (CSA), vii, 184, 199, 201
creativity, 14, 21, 27, 45, 83, 85, 154, 171, 191–195, 197–200, 214, 220, 221, 327, 329, 331, 341, 346, 372, 429, 451, 495, 498, 499, 501, 548, 590, 608, 612, 613, 617, 621
cultural practices, ix, 91, 339, 345–348

D

devoutness, 566, 581, 582
digital job characteristics, ix
dignity, vi, ix, xii, 97–104, 107, 108, 216, 219, 221, 239, 295, 305, 306, 309, 310, 356–358, 360, 361, 364, 365, 565, 573, 602
dirty work, ix, 355, 356, 360
disability, xi, 162, 218, 325, 331, 494, 543–557
diversity, viii, x, 21, 116, 211, 213, 214, 217, 218, 305–308, 326, 380, 381, 390–392, 394, 440, 451, 484, 491, 492, 494, 524, 526, 527, 529, 531, 536, 537, 557, 576, 612, 626, 629–631, 633
diversity, equity, and inclusion (DEI), xi, 523–529, 531–533, 535, 536, 538, 547
domestic, 4–9, 13, 14, 80, 626

E

emotion, 11, 22, 98, 103, 104, 108, 126, 234, 324, 377, 402, 409–411, 455, 464, 466, 467, 473, 476, 499, 505, 566, 569, 579, 628
empathy, vii, 22, 101, 103, 215, 221, 231–244, 293, 294, 307, 349, 390, 490, 491, 531, 535, 566, 570, 578
employee engagement, vii, 29, 151–153, 162, 381, 387, 393, 427, 430, 433–435, 441, 456, 524

employees, vii–xii, 12, 19–21, 27–30, 34–36, 38, 40, 41, 43, 45–47, 59, 60, 63, 64, 69, 70, 86, 97, 99, 102, 105, 107, 108, 115–119, 121–125, 127, 128, 143–145, 147, 151–155, 161, 166, 170–172, 174–178, 183–186, 200, 212–217, 220, 221, 239, 243, 255, 258–262, 268, 275, 276, 285, 289, 306, 307, 309, 318, 325, 328, 332, 339–346, 348–351, 358, 360, 361, 364, 366, 371–376, 381, 382, 387, 393, 395–397, 401–412, 414, 415, 428–431, 433–441, 449, 453, 455, 456, 465, 477, 478, 483–486, 488–492, 494–496, 512–515, 524, 525, 528, 529, 533, 536–538, 546, 548–550, 553, 565, 567, 568, 570, 573–575, 595, 627, 628, 633
employee well-being, 39, 97, 100, 108, 275, 537
engagement, x, 16, 34, 45, 70, 80, 87, 102, 104, 116, 117, 120, 123, 124, 151–153, 162, 175, 177, 178, 194, 198, 215, 216, 222, 242, 340, 342, 343, 347, 350, 351, 359, 363, 377, 381, 387–390, 393, 395–398, 408, 409, 412, 415, 427–430, 433–436, 440, 441, 486, 494, 500, 513, 524, 537, 590, 591, 600, 602, 607
engineering, vii, 67, 144, 147–151, 153, 269
entrepreneurial passion, 498–502, 507
entrepreneurs, vi, viii, ix, xi, 70, 71, 113–117, 119–132, 323, 325, 327–333, 495, 497–504, 506–509, 511, 512, 514–517, 556, 570, 595
entrepreneurship, ix, 70, 93, 113–117, 120, 122–126, 130–132, 323–333, 346, 372, 497–503, 507, 509, 510, 512, 513, 516, 517, 556
equality, 217, 306, 314, 317, 568, 570, 576, 580, 600
eudaimonia, vi, 42, 79–81, 87, 91, 93
Executive Education, xi, 523–529, 538

F

flow, xii, 10, 177, 193, 198, 238, 308, 376, 378, 507, 508, 607–610, 613–619, 621
folklore, 314
fulfillment, v, vi, ix, xii, 6, 10–17, 63, 69, 70, 73, 93, 98, 99, 101, 102, 114, 115, 117–119, 124, 128, 131, 132, 177, 183, 221, 222, 325, 328, 331, 393, 428, 433, 434, 452, 595–597, 613

G

global village, 626, 627, 630, 631, 635
gratefulness, 304, 315, 316, 318
growth, v, viii, x–xii, 4, 11, 22, 35–37, 42, 47, 63, 69, 79, 84, 98, 101–104, 106–108, 115, 116, 119, 123, 124, 128, 142, 153, 155, 175, 178, 185, 189, 191, 192, 197, 210, 211, 304, 316, 318, 324, 325, 332, 333, 342, 346, 371, 372, 377, 380, 427, 428, 430, 433, 434, 436–438, 441, 454–456, 461, 465, 483, 486, 487, 499–501, 503, 506, 507, 509–511, 514–517, 526, 544, 548, 553, 569, 573, 578, 579, 581, 592, 593, 595, 596, 602, 617, 629

H

happiness, xi, 10, 12, 33, 37, 38, 42, 48, 80, 114, 176, 193, 303–305, 308, 310–312, 314, 316–318, 324, 351, 397, 428, 433, 456, 498–500, 503, 505, 507, 509–517, 567, 571, 578, 581, 591, 595, 596
happy, 11, 92, 150, 165, 263, 305, 314, 316, 317, 373, 391, 455, 499, 505, 512, 514, 515, 600
health, vii–x, 14, 41, 42, 65, 66, 70, 72, 98, 100, 103–105, 107, 108, 117, 120, 124, 128–131, 142, 148, 162, 164, 165, 170, 171, 176, 179, 180, 183, 186, 210–212, 215, 216, 218–222, 231, 232, 235, 238–242, 244, 253, 269, 287, 292, 294, 324, 328, 329, 340, 357, 360, 366, 374, 388–395, 397–399, 429, 437, 451, 485, 494, 505, 506, 508, 537, 554, 594, 597, 598, 601, 608
healthcare organizations, 210, 218, 222
humiliation, 99, 102, 104–107, 310

I

identity, viii, ix, 36, 39, 41, 44, 46, 47, 64, 72, 82, 83, 88, 89, 106, 127, 171, 187, 188, 196, 217, 218, 220, 239, 256, 257, 281–287, 289, 291–293, 295–298, 306, 310, 312, 316, 340, 356, 357, 361, 364, 379, 397, 403, 410, 432, 489, 502, 527, 529, 534, 536, 538, 591, 594–596, 600–602, 627
identity work, 81, 127, 281–285, 287, 291, 293, 295–298, 361, 535
identity workspaces, viii, 282–285, 296–298
ideology, 195, 304–306, 309–312, 318, 579, 580
immigrant entrepreneurs, vi, 114, 117, 124–127, 129, 131, 132
inclusion, viii, x, 21, 116, 175, 177, 209, 213, 214, 216–218, 222, 271, 283, 391, 399, 427, 429, 434, 436, 437, 440, 484, 491, 492, 523, 524, 526, 528, 529, 537, 552, 554, 597, 630
inclusive leadership, vii, 209–222, 390
individual practices, 454, 456
individual resilience, viii, 268–276, 462, 466, 477
industry, 85, 128, 129, 179, 185, 253, 259, 262, 267, 275, 276, 343, 357, 359–362, 365, 366, 430, 448, 466, 544, 545, 548, 634
innovation, viii, xi, 21, 113, 143, 192, 193, 209, 219, 260, 329, 333, 341, 372, 376, 381, 451, 465, 483, 495, 496, 537, 547, 548, 556, 573, 574, 598, 633
integral model, 179
intersectionality, 391, 392, 397, 524, 528, 529, 533–536, 538

L

labor, xi, 4–17, 21, 61, 62, 71, 81, 93, 97, 183, 238, 239, 252, 284, 295, 297, 358, 360, 362, 427, 543–545, 557, 574

Latin America, ix, 83, 340–342, 344–348, 351

leader, vii, xii, 27, 28, 44, 102, 105, 108, 142, 143, 147, 150, 152–154, 172, 174, 210, 212–222, 239–242, 262, 311, 315, 340, 343, 394, 396, 406, 407, 411, 412, 414, 440, 450, 464, 492, 513, 526, 533, 535–537, 565, 566, 568–582, 590, 592, 593, 596, 601, 602, 628

leadership, vi, vii, ix, xi, xii, 6, 9, 19–21, 23, 29, 44, 45, 65, 67, 100, 141–147, 151, 153–155, 171, 173, 178, 210–222, 232, 239–242, 269, 298, 303, 306, 310, 331, 340–344, 350, 371–373, 375, 381, 388–391, 393, 395–398, 426, 428, 430, 435, 439–441, 453, 465, 483, 485, 486, 490, 494, 502, 516, 526, 527, 533, 565–582, 589–592, 594, 597, 598, 602, 610, 626

leadership development, 212, 216, 221, 494, 526

leading, v, vii, ix, 30, 40, 62, 68, 100, 120, 123, 142–145, 147, 151, 152, 154, 155, 162, 172, 174, 183, 193, 195, 199, 200, 210, 242, 328, 331, 332, 341, 389, 394–399, 402, 405, 431, 432, 434, 439, 451, 477, 499, 505, 508, 525, 537, 547, 568, 609, 629

levels, 537

M

mattering, vi, 97, 102, 103, 107, 108

meaning, vi, vii, x, 3, 5–7, 10–17, 25, 33–48, 59–61, 63–65, 80, 82, 88, 89, 92, 98, 108, 115, 120, 183–188, 190, 193, 196–198, 200, 212, 213, 216, 217, 222, 233, 256, 260, 275, 295, 307, 308, 317, 333, 358, 360, 361, 364, 365, 388, 395, 426, 427, 430, 434, 438, 439, 453, 454, 464, 466, 478, 487, 507, 514, 576, 578, 619, 628

meaning at work, vi, 34–39, 43–45, 47, 48

meaningful work, 20, 34, 39, 47, 122, 184–189, 198–201, 295, 497, 549

mindset, vii, xi, 46, 71, 90, 126, 142, 147, 148, 150, 194, 209, 210, 217, 222, 397, 449, 451, 454, 476, 483, 486, 487, 491, 530–533, 598, 632, 634

modesty, 569, 572–575, 582, 598

motivation, x, 23, 39, 44, 45, 60, 64, 90, 91, 98, 117–119, 126, 127, 132, 152, 171, 196, 213, 222, 237, 306, 314, 329, 330, 332, 340, 343, 351, 372, 376, 378, 379, 403, 454–456, 485, 498–501, 503, 504, 507, 513, 516, 572, 573, 576, 578, 590, 591, 594, 607–609, 614, 628

mutuality of mattering, vi, 97, 102, 103, 107, 108

mythology, 190, 303, 310

N

new technologies, 8, 149, 256, 258, 262, 346

new world of work, xi, 173, 174, 483, 485, 488, 489, 496

O

oneness, 161, 162, 164, 165, 170, 175, 611, 614, 615, 620

online social networks (OSNs), x, 402, 406–409, 412, 414

organizational change, vii, 184, 213, 217, 382, 431, 461–463, 468, 472, 528

organizational culture, 63, 108, 175, 210, 216, 305, 307, 316, 318, 341, 342, 350, 357, 371–374, 492, 495, 513, 515, 524, 566, 630

organizational wellness, vii, 162, 169–172, 180

organizations, vi–ix, xi, xii, 4, 19, 24, 28, 34, 44, 46, 47, 60, 63, 66, 69, 98, 99, 103, 107, 143, 144, 146,

INDEX 641

148, 152–154, 161, 162, 169,
172–180, 185, 186, 188, 192, 210,
211, 215–219, 221, 222, 254, 258,
281, 283, 306, 307, 324, 341–343,
346–348, 351, 356, 357, 371–374,
376, 377, 379–382, 388, 391, 394,
395, 398, 412–415, 425–429, 431,
432, 434–439, 448, 453, 461, 462,
478, 483, 484, 486, 487, 490, 491,
496, 513, 514, 524–528, 535–538,
547–550, 565, 566, 569, 573, 576,
621, 625–631, 633–635

P

pandemic, v, vii, x, xi, 19, 27, 60, 84,
  183, 184, 200, 210, 212, 215,
  217–222, 242, 255–262, 267, 268,
  275, 324, 332, 372, 388, 390, 394,
  426, 427, 429, 432, 441, 447–449,
  465, 468, 469, 471, 472, 476, 483,
  484, 486, 487, 489, 490, 495, 496,
  509, 510, 523, 529, 537, 544
peace, 29, 30, 67, 73, 144, 303, 304,
  307, 309, 310, 316–318, 450, 452,
  610, 620
peak experiences, 147, 193, 196, 607,
  608
peer coaching groups (PCGs), ix, 372,
  373, 377–382
perceived stress, viii, 267–276, 613
performance, viii, xii, 34, 42, 45, 60, 79,
  118, 144, 149–153, 162, 172–174,
  177, 178, 192, 193, 210, 212, 214,
  217, 218, 220, 221, 239, 259, 260,
  269, 312, 325–327, 330, 331, 333,
  340–343, 345, 347, 349, 351, 372,
  373, 376, 404, 405, 407–409, 411,
  412, 414, 415, 431, 435, 436, 439,
  447–450, 453, 455, 463, 486, 498,
  508, 513–516, 547, 567, 568, 572,
  574, 575, 580, 596, 597, 599,
  607–610, 616, 626, 628, 629, 631,
  633–635
personal growth, vi, xi, 35–37, 42, 47,
  63, 69, 79, 115, 116, 128, 185,
  197, 211, 324, 332, 342, 371, 430,

433, 438, 455, 499, 500, 503, 506,
507, 510, 513–516, 593, 596
personal mastery, 602
personal vision, 593
planetary health, ix, x, 388–395,
  397–399
postindustrial society, 251–254, 262,
  263
postmodernism, 251, 252, 256, 257,
  263
precarious work, 281–287, 289, 296,
  297
presence of meaning at work, 37, 38
prosocial behavior, 234–237, 239
purpose, vi, 5, 10, 27, 29, 34–39, 41,
  42, 44–48, 59–62, 64, 66–73, 81,
  97–99, 116, 122, 127, 128, 132,
  149, 178, 185, 199, 200, 217, 221,
  222, 255, 314, 323, 332, 344, 371,
  378, 393, 434, 435, 439, 448, 467,
  473, 474, 485, 486, 499, 514, 524,
  526, 528, 547, 565, 591, 593, 610,
  621

Q

quiet quitting, viii, 183, 282, 285–287,
  289, 290, 295–298

R

racially conscious, 538
relational cultural theory (RCT), vi, 97,
  100–108
resilience, viii, x, 23, 40, 113, 217, 222,
  268–272, 274–276, 282, 296, 333,
  346, 391, 392, 397, 462–466, 468,
  470, 473, 476–478, 490, 492, 499,
  537, 597
resistance, 98, 103, 105–108, 289, 296,
  297, 431–433, 486
role theory, 131, 402

S

sacrifice, xii, 66, 73, 304, 312, 506,
  516, 566, 571, 572, 579, 581, 582
search for meaning at work, 34, 44

self-awareness, 21, 165, 169, 209, 216, 467, 472, 478, 485, 589, 591, 592, 597, 602, 608, 615
self-efficacy, 45, 70, 463, 566, 575, 576, 596, 598, 610, 613, 617
self-employment, vi, 114–119, 122–125, 128, 132, 329, 544, 545
selflessness, 571, 572, 582
self-presentation theory, 402, 403
self-regulation, 259, 411, 478, 591, 597, 626–628
Shepherd, D.A., 118, 145–147, 153, 154, 323, 325, 326, 330, 507
shepherding, vii, 144–147, 153
social affiliation, 234, 237
social justice, xi, 98, 216, 303, 305, 395, 523–529, 533, 538, 595
soft skills, v, 19–24, 26, 27, 29, 30, 346, 629
spiritual awareness, 63
spiritual gifts, 67
spirituality, 22, 29, 59, 63–65, 69, 191, 192, 195–200, 415, 573, 575, 582, 600
Śrīmad Bhagavad Gītā, 566, 568, 576, 582
stigma, ix, 117, 355–357, 360, 361, 364–366, 551, 554
strategic change, x, 426–428, 430, 431, 630
stress, v, viii–xi, 15, 23, 40, 66, 115, 120, 123, 124, 151, 162, 166, 168, 170, 177–179, 186, 193, 222, 234, 237, 242, 267–277, 282, 326, 330, 360, 366, 372, 388, 393–398, 404, 409, 415, 448–453, 455, 461–465, 470, 513, 533, 567, 573, 601, 608, 609, 612, 613, 617, 619, 620

T

task performance, ix, 269, 339–341, 343, 347, 351, 498
team consciousness, 166, 167
team practices, 454
technology family, 23, 27, 407
thrifting, vi, 79–83, 85–93
tolerance, 193, 252, 303–309, 312, 318, 341, 577–579
transcendence, 191, 198, 199, 308, 569, 608, 611–614, 617, 621
transformation, 8, 9, 64–66, 165, 190, 196–198, 211, 251, 253, 255, 263, 307, 372, 391, 428, 435, 450, 486, 489, 537, 566, 612
transformational leadership, ix, 45, 210, 339–343, 350, 390, 440

U

uncertainty, ix, 21, 27, 38, 40, 68, 120, 282, 283, 323, 325, 327, 328, 341, 348, 349, 393, 467, 475, 487, 490–492, 600
unpredictability, viii, 268–270, 272–276, 347, 490, 600

V

values & morals, 242, 253, 304, 307, 310, 576
venture creation, xi, 331, 500, 506, 507, 509
virtues, 10, 12, 28, 29, 42, 80, 81, 103, 219, 253, 303–307, 310, 312–316, 318, 566, 568–574, 578–580, 582, 591
virtuous actions, 79, 80, 88
Volatile, Uncertain, Complex, and Ambiguous (VUCA), xii, 252, 253, 487, 489, 607, 620, 621, 627

W

well-being, vi–x, 15, 34–37, 39–43, 48, 63, 66, 79–81, 88, 91, 97–103, 105–108, 113–132, 142, 164, 165, 176, 178, 179, 186, 210, 211, 214, 219, 220, 222, 231, 236, 238–240, 259, 268, 269, 275, 276, 281–284, 287, 295–298, 305, 306, 310–312, 318, 323–333, 357, 366, 371–373, 376–378, 380, 381, 387–395, 397–399, 409, 410, 412, 414, 415, 441, 468, 470, 477, 498–500, 506–508, 511, 512, 515, 524, 525, 531, 533, 572, 575, 576, 582, 590, 592, 594, 595, 597–602, 607, 608, 620, 630

INDEX   643

wellness, v–x, xii, 15, 17, 69, 114, 162, 164, 166, 169–180, 211, 220–222, 231–233, 235–244, 304, 310, 316, 318, 427–430, 433, 437, 441, 476, 537, 593

women entrepreneurs, vi, 114, 117, 121–124, 127, 129–131, 327

work, v–xi, 5–17, 19–22, 25–30, 33–48, 59–67, 69–73, 83, 92, 106, 113–115, 117–124, 126, 127, 129, 130, 132, 143, 144, 149–155, 162, 163, 165–167, 169, 170, 172–174, 176–178, 180, 183–188, 193, 198, 210–217, 220, 221, 232, 233, 238–240, 242, 252–263, 268–270, 272, 274–276, 281–285, 290–294, 296, 297, 308–310, 312, 315, 316, 318, 325, 326, 328, 330–333, 339–346, 348, 350, 351, 355–366, 371–377, 387–389, 392, 393, 395, 397–399, 401, 402, 404–415, 425, 426, 428–430, 434–441, 448, 449, 451–456, 464–468, 470, 473, 475–477, 483–492, 494, 496–502, 506–509, 511–517, 524–529, 531–537, 545–549, 557, 571, 574–576, 579, 581, 582, 589–596, 598, 600–602, 607, 610, 616, 621

work design, ix, 39, 41, 170, 173, 339, 344–346, 348, 350, 351, 610

work engagement, 66, 70, 210, 220, 242, 339–343, 347, 349, 350, 388, 408–410, 412, 415, 607

workforce, xi, 22, 40, 46, 86, 151, 173, 178, 220–222, 283, 341, 346, 428, 434, 448–450, 452, 453, 455, 463, 483–485, 491–496, 543–547, 550, 551, 554–557, 620

work fulfillment, v, 6, 10, 11, 13, 15, 17, 70, 114, 331, 428, 434, 595

work-life balance, ix, 13, 17, 63, 123–125, 129, 130, 132, 220, 261, 330, 394, 395, 398, 412, 414, 439, 484

work motivation, 341, 347, 351, 610

workplace dignity, ix, 97–100, 107, 108, 306, 356, 357, 364

workplace inclusion, 209

workplace(s), v–viii, 9, 13, 22, 28–30, 33–36, 38, 40–47, 66, 69, 80, 97–99, 101, 103, 105, 107, 108, 146, 151, 167, 170–173, 175, 176, 178, 179, 200, 209, 210, 215, 231, 235, 239–244, 258–260, 263, 269, 275, 281–285, 287, 289–297, 304, 306, 307, 310, 314, 316, 318, 325, 341–343, 348, 357, 358, 360, 372–375, 377, 378, 380, 381, 387, 388, 393–395, 397, 398, 401, 404–409, 411, 412, 415, 433, 447, 451–453, 455, 485, 499, 513, 514, 524, 525, 528, 529, 533, 534, 536, 537, 545, 546, 548, 551, 554, 590–592, 594, 595, 597, 599–602, 629

work tasks, viii, 41, 268, 270, 272, 274–277